P9-BJT-741

# SOMETHING ABOUT THE AUTHOR

# SOMETHING ABOUT THE AUTHOR

Facts and Pictures about Authors

and Illustrators of Books for Young People

Anne Commire

# VOLUME 17

GALE RESEARCH
BOOK TOWER
DETROIT, MICHIGAN
48226

Also Published by Gale

*CONTEMPORARY AUTHORS*

*A Bio-Bibliographical Guide to Current Writers in
Fiction, General Nonfiction, Poetry, Journalism,
Drama, Motion Pictures, Television,
and Other Fields*

(Now Covers Nearly 56,000 Authors)

*Associate Editors:* Agnes Garrett, Helga P. McCue

*Assistant Editor:* Linda Shedd

*Consultant:* Adele Sarkissian

*Sketchwriters:* Dianne H. Anderson, Rosemary DeAngelis Bridges,
Mark Eisman, D. Jayne Higo, Ross Parker, Susan L. Stetler

*Research Assistant:* Kathleen Betsko

*Editorial Assistants:* Lisa Bryon, Catherine Coray,
Susan Pfanner, Elisa Ann Sawchuk

Library of Congress Catalog Card Number 72-27107

Copyright © 1979 by Gale Research Company. All rights reserved.

ISBN 0-8103-0098-2

# Table of Contents

Introduction   vii        Illustrations Index   283

Acknowledgments   ix        Author Index   293

# Introduction

Beginning with Volume 15, the time span covered by *Something about the Author* was broadened to include major children's writers who died before 1961, which was the former cut-off point for writers covered in this series. This change will make *SATA* even more helpful to its many thousands of student and professional users.

Authors who did not come within the scope of *SATA* have formerly been included in *Yesterday's Authors of Books for Children,* of which Gale has published two volumes.

It has been pointed out by users, however, that it is inconvenient to have a body of related materials broken up by an arbitrary criterion such as the date of a person's death. Also, some libraries are not able to afford both series, and are therefore denied access to material on some of the most important writers in the juvenile field.

It has been decided, therefore, to discontinue the *YABC* series, and to include in *SATA* at least the most outstanding among the older writers who had been selected for listing in *YABC*. Volumes 1 and 2 of *YABC* will be kept in print, and the listings in those two volumes will be included in the cumulative *SATA* index.

# GRATEFUL ACKNOWLEDGMENT

is made to the following publishers, authors, and artists, for their kind permission to reproduce copyrighted material. ■ **ABELARD-SCHUMAN (London).** Illustrations by Uta Glauber from *How the Willow Wren Became King* by Uta Glauber. Copyright © 1970 by Aberlard-Schuman, Ltd. Illustrations © 1970 by Emme-Edizioui, Milano. Reprinted by permission of Abelard-Schuman. ■ **ABINGDON PRESS.** Illustration by Fritz Kredel from *The Silent Storm* by Marion Marsh Brown and Ruth Crone. Copyright © 1963 by Abingdon Press. Reprinted by permission of Abingdon Press. ■ **ADDISON-WESLEY PUBLISHING CO.** Illustration by Charlotte Hough from *Galapagos: The Enchanted Islands* by Richard Hough. Text © 1975 by Richard Hough. Illustrations © 1975 by J. M. Dent & Sons, Ltd. Reprinted by permission of Addison-Wesley Publishing Co. ■ **AMERICAN LIBRARY ASSOCIATION.** Sidelight excerpts from *British Children's Authors* by Cornelia Jones and Olivia R. Way. Reprinted by permission of American Library Association. ■ **ANDERSEN, LTD.** Illustration by Tony Ross from *Hugo and the Man Who Stole Colours* by Tony Ross. Reprinted by permission of Andersen, Ltd. ■ **ARCHON BOOKS.** Sidelight excerpts from *Charles Lamb and His Contemporaries* by Edmund Blunden. Copyright assigned to Cambridge University Press. Reprinted by permission of Archon Books. ■ **ARTIA PUBLISHERS (Czechoslovakia).** Illustration by Karel Svolinsky from *Tales from Shakespeare* by Charles and Mary Lamb. Illustrations copyright © 1962 by Karel Svolinsky. Reprinted by permission of Artia Publishers. ■ **ATHENEUM PUBLISHERS.** Illustration by Irene Haas from *The Maggie B.* by Irene Haas. Copyright © 1975 by Irene Haas./ Illustration by Mila Lazarevich from *Settle Your Fidgets* by Carol Farley. Copyright © 1977 by Carol Farley. Both reprinted by permission of Atheneum Publishers. ■ **G. BELL & SONS, LTD.** Illustration by Ernest H. Shepard from *Everybody's Lamb*, a collection of letters and essays of Charles Lamb. Edited by A.C. Ward. Reprinted by permission of G. Bell & Sons, Ltd. ■ **BELL & HYMAN, LTD.** Sidelight excerpts from *Everybody's Lamb* edited by A.C. Ward. Copyright 1933 Bell & Hyman, Ltd. Reprinted by permission of Bell & Hyman, Ltd. ■ **BILLBOARD PUBLISHERS, INC.** Sidelight excerpts from an article "The Sculpture of George Papashvily," in *American Artist*, October,1955. Reprinted by permission of Billboard Publishers, Inc. ■ **BLACKIE & SON, LTD.** Sidelight excerpts from *My Line of Life* by W. Heath Robinson. Reprinted by permission of Blackie & Son, Ltd. ■ **BOBBS-MERRILL CO.** Sidelight excerpts and illustration by Booth Tarkington from *Your Amiable Uncle* by Booth Tarkington. Copyright 1949 by John T. Jameson, Donald Jameson and Booth T. Jameson./ Illustration by John Wolcott Adams from *A Hoosier Romance* by James Whitcomb Riley. Copyright 1910 by the Century Co. Copyright 1912 by Bobbs-Merrill./ Photographs and illustrations by Howard Chandler Christy and Ethel Franklin Betts from *James Whitcomb Riley's Complete Works*. Copyright 1916 by James Whitcomb Riley./ Sidelight excerpts from *Letters of James Whitcomb Riley* edited by William Lyon Phelps. Copyright 1930 by the Bobbs-Merrill Co., renewed 1958./ Sidelight excerpts from *The Maturity of James Whitcomb Riley* by Marcus Dickey. Copyright 1922 by the Bobbs-Merrill Company, renewed 1950./ Sidelight excerpts from *The Youth of James Whitcomb Riley* by Marcus Dickey. Copyright 1916 by the Bobbs-Merrill Co., renewed 1947. All reprinted by permission of Bobbs-Merrill Co. ■ **THE BODLEY HEAD, LTD.** Illustration by W. Heath Robinson from *The Incredible Adventures of Professor Branestawm* by Norman Hunter. Reprinted by permission of The Bodley Head, Ltd. ■ **BONANZA BOOKS.** Illustration by Harrison Cady from *The Crooked Little Path* by Thornton W. Burgess. Copyright © MCMXLVI by Thornton W. Burgess./ Photograph from *N. C. Wyeth* by Douglas Allen and Douglas Allen, Jr. Copyright © 1972 by Douglas Allen and Douglas Allen, Jr. Both reprinted by permission of Bonanza Books, a division of Crown Publishers. ■ **BRADBURY PRESS.** Illustration by Donald Mackay from *The Stone-Faced Boy* by Paula Fox. Copyright © 1968 by Paula Fox. Copyright © 1968 by Donald A. Mackay./ Illustration by Susan Jeffers from *Three Jovial Huntsmen*, a Mother Goose Rhyme adapted by Susan Jeffers. Copyright © 1973 by Susan Jeffers. Both reprinted by permission of Bradbury Press. ■ **BRANDT & BRANDT.** Illustration by Gordon Grant from *Penrod Jashber* by Booth Tarkington. Copyright 1929 by Doubleday, Doran and Co. Reprinted by permission of Brandt & Brandt. ■ **A. S. BURACK.** Sidelight excerpts from an article, "The Practice of Playwriting," by Mary C. Chase, June 6, 1963 in *The Writer*. Reprinted by permission of A. S. Burack. ■ **CAMBRIDGE UNIVERSITY PRESS.** Sidelight excerpts from *Charles Lamb and His Contemporaries* by Edmund Blunden. Copyright assigned to Cambridge University Press. Reprinted by permission of Cambridge University Press. ■ **JONATHAN CAPE, LTD.** Illustration by William Stobbs from *The Sixpenny Runner* by Lois Lamplugh. Reprinted by permission of Jonathan Cape, Ltd. ■ **CHILDREN'S PRESS.** Illustration by Robert Ulm from *Battle for Quebec* by Susan and John Lee. Copyright © 1975 by Regensteiner Publishing Enterprises, Inc. Reprinted by permission of Children's Press. ■ **CITATION PRESS.** Sidelight excerpts from *Books Are By People* by Lee Bennet Hopkins. Reprinted by permission of Citation Press, a division of Scholastic Book Services. ■ **JONATHAN CLOWES, LTD.** Art concept of illustration by Simon Stern from *Dragonfall 5 and the Empty Planet* by Brian Earnshaw. Illustrations copyright © 1973 by Methuen Children's Books, Ltd. Reprinted by permission of Jonathan Clowes, Ltd. ■ **WILLIAM COLLINS SONS & CO., LTD.** Illustration by Irene Haas from *The Maggie B.* by Irene Haas. Copyright © 1975 by Irene Haas. Reprinted by permission of William Collins Sons & Co., Ltd. ■ **WILLIAM COLLINS & WORLD PUBLISHING CO.** Illustration by Alain Trez from *Le Petit Chien* by Denise and Alain Trez. Reprinted by permission of William Collins & World Publishing Co. ■ **CONSTABLE & CO.** Illustration by W. Heath Robinson from *Bill the Minder* by W. Heath Robinson. Reprinted by permission of Constable & Co. ■ **CORNELL UNIVERSITY PRESS.** Sidelight excerpts from *The Letters of Charles and Mary Anne Lamb* edited by Edwin W. Mars. Copyright © 1975 by Cornell University. Reprinted by permission of Cornell University Press. ■ **COSMOPOLITAN.** Sidelight excerpts from an article, "Mary Chase—Success Almost Ruined Her," by Eleanor Harris, February, 1954, in *Cosmopolitan*. Reprinted by permission of *Cosmopolitan*. ■ **COWARD, McCANN AND GEOGHEGAN, INC.** Illustration by John Schoenherr from *Black Lightning* by John Giegling. Text copyright © 1975 by John A. Giegling. Illustrations copyright © 1975 by John Schoenherr. Reprinted by permission of Coward, McCann and Geoghegan, Inc. ■ **THOMAS Y. CROWELL CO.** Illustration by Paul Galdone from *Paul Revere's Ride* by Henry Wadsworth Longfellow. Illustrations copyright © 1963 by Paul Galdone. Reprinted by permission of Thomas Y. Crowell Co. ■ **DELL PUBLISHING.** Illustration by Anson Lowitz from *Barefoot Abe* by Sadyebeth and Anson Lowitz. Copyright © 1967 by Sadyebeth and Anson Lowitz. Reprinted by permission of Dell Publishing. ■ **J. M. DENT & SONS, LTD.** Illustration by Charlotte Hough from *Galapagos: The Enchanted Islands* by Richard Hough. Text © 1975 by Richard Hough. Illustrations © 1975 by J. M. Dent and Sons, Ltd./ Illustration by Michael Godfrey from *The Little Duke* by Charlotte M. Yonge. Illustrations © 1963 by J. M. Dent and Sons, Ltd. Both reprinted by permission of J. M. Dent & Sons, Ltd. ■ **DOUBLEDAY AND CO.** Illustration by Paul Galdone from *Hans Brinker: Or The Silver Skates* by Mary Mapes Dodge. Illustrations copyright 1954 by Nelson Doubleday, Inc./ Illustration by T.H. Robinson from *The Swiss Family Robinson* by Johann David Wyss./ Illustration by W. Heath Robinson from *Bill the Minder* by W. Heath Robinson./ Sidelight excerpts from *The World Does Move* by Booth Tarkington./ Illustration by Gareth Floyd from *Flight to the Forest* by Barbara Willard. Copyright © 1967 by Barbara Willard./ Illustration by from *The Dove in the Eagles Nest* by Charlotte M. Yonge. All reprinted by permission of Doubleday and Co. ■ **DUCKWORTH, LTD.** Illustration by Charles Robinson from *The Happy Prince* by Oscar Wilde. Reprinted by permission of Duckworth, Ltd. ■ **E. P. DUTTON AND CO., INC.** Illustration by Michael Godfrey from *The Little Duke* by Charlotte M. Yonge. Illustrations © 1963 by J. M. Dent and Sons, Ltd. Reprinted by permission of E. P. Dutton and Co., Inc. ■ **FARRAR, STRAUS AND GIROUX.** Jacket illustration by Jennifer Tuckwell from *Corcoran's the Name* by Olaf Ruhen. Copyright © 1956, 1957, 1959, 1963, 1964, 1965, 1967 by Olaf Ruhen. Reprinted by permission of Farrar, Straus and Giroux. ■ **FOLLETT PUBLISHING CO.** Illustration by Tony Ross from *Hugo and the Man Who Stole Colours* by Tony Ross. Reprinted by permission of Follett Publishing Co. ■ **FOUR WINDS PRESS.** Illustration by George Solonevich from *Dinosaurs and More Dinosaurs* by M. Jean Craig. Copyright © 1965 by Jean Craig. Copyright © 1965 by Scholastic Magazines, Inc. Reprinted by permission of Four Winds Press, a division of Scholastic Book Services. ■ **GAGE PUBLISHING CO. (Toronto).** Illustration by Blair Drawson from *Arthur, Their Very Own Child* by Blair Drawson. Reprinted by permission of Gage Publishing Co. ■ **GAMBIT, INC.** Photographs from *The Wyeths: The Letters of N. C. Wyeth, 1901-1945* edited by Betsy James Wyeth. Copyright © 1971 by Betsy James Wyeth. Reprinted by permission of Gambit, Inc. ■ **GREENWILLOW BOOKS.** Illustration by Tom Huffman from *Alcohol—What It Is, What It Does* by Judith S. Seixas. Copyright © 1977 by Judith S. Seixas and Tom Huffman./ Illustration by Ruthven Tremain from *Fooling Around with Words* by Ruthven Tremain. Copyright © 1976 by Ruthven Tremain. Both reprinted by permission of Greenwillow Books, a division of William Morrow and Co. ■ **GROSSET AND DUNLAP, INC.** Illustration by Fritz Kredel from "The Six Servants" in *Grimms' Fairy Tales* by the Brothers Grimm. Copyright 1945 by Grosset & Dunlap, Inc./ Illustration by Fritz Kredel from *Pinocchio* by C. Collodi. Copyright 1946 by Grosset & Dunlap, Inc./ Illustration by Gordon

Grant from *Penrod* by Booth Tarkington. Copyright 1914 by Doubleday and Co. All reprinted by permission of Grosset and Dunlap, Inc. ■ **HARCOURT BRACE JOVANOVICH, INC.** Illustration by N.M. Bodecker from *Knight's Castle* by Edward Eager. Copyright 1956 by Harcourt, Brace and World and Macmillan & Co., Ltd. (London)./ Illustration by N.M. Bodecker from *Magic by the Lake* by Edward Eager. © 1957 by Harcourt, Brace and World./ Illustration by N.M. Bodecker from *Seven-Day Magic* by Edward Eager. © 1962 by Edward Eager./ Photograph from *Sweet Pea: A Girl Growing Up in the Rural South* by Jill Krementz./ Illustration by Nicolas from *Alphonse, That Bearded One* by Natalie Savage Carlson. Copyright 1954 by Harcourt Brace and World, Inc./ Illustration from *Finders Keepers* by Will and Nicolas. Copyright 1951 by William Lipkind and Nicolas Mordvinoff./ Illustration by Nicolas from *The Two Reds* by Will. Copyright © 1950 by William Lipkind and Nicolas Mordvinoff./ Illustration by Maud and Miska Petersham from *Rootabaga Stories*, part one, by Carl Sandburg. Copyright 1922, 1923 by Harcourt Brace Jovanovich, Inc. Copyright 1950, 1951 by Carl Sandburg./ Illustrations by Maud and Miska Petersham from *Rootabaga Stories*, part two, by Carl Sandburg. Copyright 1922, 1923 by Harcourt Brace Jovanovich, Inc. Copyright 1950, 1951 by Carl Sandburg. All reprinted by permission of Harcourt Brace Jovanovich, Inc. ■ **HARPER & ROW, PUBLISHERS.** Jacket illustration by Frank Schoonover from *Tales from Shakespeare* by Charles and Mary Lamb./ Sidelight excerpts from *Anything Can Happen* by George and Helen Papashvily./ Sidelight excerpts from *All the Happy Endings* by Helen Papashvily./ Sidelight excerpts from *Home and Home Again* by George and Helen Papashvily./ Illustration by Jack Wilson from *Thanks to Noah* by George and Helen Papashvily. Copyright 1946, 1950, 1951 by George and Helen Waite Papashvily./ Illustration by Simon Lissim from *Yes and No Stories* by George and Helen Papashvily. Copyright 1946 by George and Helen Papashvily./ Illustration by Fritz Siebel from *Amelia Bedelia* by Peggy Parish. Text Copyright © 1963 by Margaret Parish. Pictures copyright © 1963 by Fritz Siebel./ Illustration by Maurice Sendak from *Maggie Rose—Her Birthday Christmas* by Ruth Sawyer. Copyright 1952 by Ruth Sawyer Durand./ Illustration by C.E. Chambers from *The Turmoil* by Booth Tarkington. Copyright 1914, 1915 by Harper & Row, Publishers, Inc. Renewed 1943 by Booth Tarkington. All reprinted by permission of Harper & Row, Publishers, Inc. ■ **HAWTHORN BOOKS, INC.** Illustration by Jean Webster from *Dear Enemy* by Jean Webster. Copyright © 1915 by Jean Webster. Reprinted by permission of Hawthorn Books, Inc. ■ **HEINEMAN, LTD.** Illustration by Charles Robinson, R.I., from *The Secret Garden* by Frances Hodgson Burnett. Reprinted by permission of Heinemann, Ltd. ■ **HODDER & STOUGHTON, LTD.** Illustration by W. Heath Robinson from *Song of the English* by Rudyard Kipling. Reprinted by permission of Hodder & Stoughton, Ltd. ■ **HOLIDAY HOUSE.** Sidelight excerpts and illustration by Bob Kuhn from *Big Red* by Jim Kjelgaard. Copyright © 1945 by Jim Kjelgaard./ Illustration by Charles Banks Wilson from *Rebel Siege* by Jim Kjelgaard. Copyright 1943, 1953 by Jim Kjelgaard. Illustrations copyright 1953. All reprinted by permission of Holiday House. ■ **HOLT, RINEHART AND WINSTON, INC.** Sidelight excerpts and illustrations by Don Freeman from *Come One, Come All!* by Don Freeman. Copyright 1949 by Don Freeman./ Illustration from *The Story Book of Things We Wear* by Maud and Miska Petersham. Copyright 1939 by the John C. Winston Co./ Jacket design by Alan Cober from *Smudge of the Fells* by Joyce Gard. Copyright © 1965 by Joyce Gard. All reprinted by permission of Holt, Rinehart and Winston, Inc. ■ **HORN BOOK, INC.** Sidelight excerpts from an article, "Marjorie Hill Allee," by Amy Winslow in *Horn Book*, May, 1946. Copyright © 1946 by The Horn Book, Inc./ Sidelight excerpts from an article, "L. Leslie Brooke," By Anne Carroll Moore in *Horn Book*, May 1941./ Sidelight excerpts from an article, "Small Children and Books," by Alice Dalgliesh in *Horn Book*, August, 1933./ Sidelight excerpts from an article, "Alice Dalgliesh and Her Book," by Louise Seaman Bechtel in *Horn Book*, March, 1947./ Sidelight excerpts from *Horn Book Reflections*, selected by Elinor Whitney Field in *Horn Book*./ Sidelight excerpts from an article, "A Father's Minority Report," by Edward Eager in *Horn Book*, March, 1948./ Sidelight excerpts from an article by Paula Fox in *Horn Book*, August, 1974./ Sidelight excerpts from *Illustrators of Children's Books, 1946-1956* compiled by B.M. Miller and others./ Sidelight excerpts from *Illustrators of Children's Books: 1744-1945* compiled by Bertha E. Mahony and others./ Sidelight excerpts from the Caldecott Award acceptance speech by Nicolas Mordvinoff in *Horn Book*, August, 1952./ Sidelight excerpts from *Caldecott Medal Books: 1939-1957* edited by Bertha Mahoney Miller and Elinor Whitney Field./ Sidelight excerpts from *Newberry Medal Books: 1922-1955*, edited by Bertha Mahoney Miller and Elinor Whitney Field./ Sidelight excerpts from Ruth Sawyer's acceptance speech in *Horn Book*, October, 1965./ Sidelight excerpts from an article, "Our Fair Lady," by Margaret Durand McCloskey in *Horn Book*, October, 1966. All reprinted by permission of Horn Book, Inc. ■ **HOUGHTON MIFFLIN CO.** Sidelight excerpts from *Thomas Bailey Aldrich* by Ferris Greenslet. Copyright 1908 by Ferris Greenslet./ Illustration by Manning De V. Lee from *A House of Her Own* by Marjorie Hill Allee./ Illustration by Manning De V. Lee from *The Road to Carolina* by Marjorie Hill Allee./ Illustration by Hattie Longstreet Price from *Susanna and Tristram* by Marjorie Hill Allee. Copyright © 1957, by Barbara Allee Angell and Mary Allee Barth. Copyright 1929 by Marjorie H. Allee./ Illustrations by N.C. Wyeth from *The Long Roll* by Mary Johnston. Copyright 1911 by Mary Johnston./

Illustration by N.C. Wyeth from *The Pike County Ballads* by John Hay./ Illustration by N.C. Wyeth from *Susanna and Sue* by Kate Douglas Wiggin./ Illustration by Paul Galdone from *The Lady Who Saw the Good Side of Everything* by Pat Decker Tapio. Text copyright © 1975 by Pat Decker Tapio. Illustrations copyright © 1975 by Paul Galdone. All reprinted by permission of Houghton Mifflin Co. ■ **HUTCHINSON AND CO.** Illustration by Charles Robinson from *Margaret's Book* by H. Fielding-Hall. Reprinted by permission of Hutchinson and Co. ■ **HERBERT JOSEPH, LTD.** Sidelight excerpts from *The Life and Art of W. Heath Robinson* by Langston Day. Reprinted by permission of Herbert Joseph, Ltd. ■ **ALFRED A KNOPF.** Illustration by Kurt Wiese from *Freddy the Detective* by Walter R. Brooks. Copyright 1932 by Walter R. Brooks./ Illustration by Kurt Wiese from *Freddy Goes Camping* by Walter R. Brooks. Copyright 1948 by Walter R. Brooks./ Illustration by Don Bolognese from *The Wicked Pigeon Ladies in the Garden* by Mary Chase. Copyright © 1968 by Mary Chase. Illustrations copyright © 1968 by Don Bolognese. All reprinted by permission of Alfred A. Knopf. ■ **LADIES HOME JOURNAL.** Cover illustration from *Ladies Home Journal*, March, 1922. Reprinted by permission of *Ladies Home Journal*. ■ **LERNER PUBLICATIONS.** Illustration by H. Hechtkopf from *Jonah's Journey* by Danah Haiz. Copyright © 1973 by Massada Press, Ltd./ Illustration by R.L. Markham from *Help!* by Mary Lou Vandenburg. Copyright © 1975 by Lerner Publications Co. Both reprinted by permission of Lerner Publications. ■ **J. B. LIP-PINCOTT CO.** Sidelight excerpts and photographs from *Booth Tarkington: Gentleman from Indiana* by James Woodress. Copyright 1954, 1955 by James Woodress./ Illustration by Harold Berson from *Loretta Mason Potts* by Mary Chase. Copyright © 1958 by Mary Chase./ Sidelight excerpts from *A Sense of Story* by John Rowe Townsend./ Illustration by Paul Bransom from *The Wahoo Bobcat* by Joseph Wharton Lippincott. Copyright 1950 by Joseph Wharton Lippincott./ Decorations by Franz Geritz from *Lost Queen of Egypt* by Lucile Morrison. Copyright 1937 by J. B. Lippincott Co. Copyright renewed 1965 by Lucile Morrison./ Sidelight excerpts from *Dogs and People* by George and Helen Papashvily./ Illustration by Joel Schick from *The Gobble-Uns'll Git You Ef You Don't Watch Out*, based on James Whitcomb Riley's "Little Orphant Annie." Illustrations and illustrator's notes copyright © 1975 by Pongid Productions./ Illustration by W. Heath Robinson from *The Adventures of Uncle Lubin* by W. Heath Robinson. All reprinted by permission of J. B. Lippincott Co. ■ **LITTLE, BROWN AND CO.** Sidelight excerpts and photograph from *Now I Remember: Autobiography of an Amateur Naturalist* by Thornton Waldo Burgess. Copyright 1960 by Thornton Waldo Burgess. / Illustration by Harrison Cady from *The Adventures of Chatterer the Red Squirrel* by Thornton W. Burgess. Copyright 1915 by Little, Brown and Co./ Illustrations by Lemuel Palmer from *Tales from the Storyteller's House* by Thornton W. Burgess. Copyright 1937 by Thornton W. Burgess. Copyright © renewed 1956 by Louis Doherty and the Third National Bank, Hampden County, Executor of the Estate of Thornton W. Burgess./ Illustration by Fritz Kredel from *Moonfleet* by J. Meade Falkner./ Illustration by N.C. Wyeth from *The Bounty Trilogy* by Charles Nordhoff and James Norman Hall. Copyright 1932 by Charles Nordhoff and James Norman Hall. Illustration copyright 1940 by Little, Brown, and Co. All reprinted by permission of Little, Brown and Co. ■ **LOTHROP, LEE AND SHEPARD.** Art concept of illustrations by Simon Stern from *Dragonfall 5 and the Empty Planet* by Brian Earnshaw. Illustrations copyright © 1973 by Methuen Children's Books, Ltd./ Illustration by Loretta Holz from *Mobiles You Can Make* by Loretta Holz. Copyright © 1975 by Loretta Holz. Both reprinted by permission of Lothrop, Lee and Shepard, a division of William Morrow and Co. ■ **MACMILLAN AND CO., LTD. (London).** Illustration by N.M. Bodecker from *Seven-Day Magic* by Edward Eager. © 1962 by Edward Eager./ Illustration by N.M. Bodecker from *Knight's Castle* by Edward Eager. Copyright 1956 by Harcourt, Brace and World and Macmillan & Co., Ltd./ Illustration by J. Priestman Atkinson from *The Trial: More Links of the Daisy Chain* by Charlotte M. Yonge. All reprinted by permission of Macmillan and Co., Ltd. ■ **MACMILLAN PUBLISHING CO.** Illustration by Ingrid Fetz from *Maurice's Room* by Paula Fox. Copyright © Paula Fox 1966. Copyright © 1966 Macmillan Publishing Co./ Illustration by Maud and Miska Petersham from *The Box with Red Wheels* by Maud and Miska Petersham. Copyright 1949 by Maud and Miska Petersham./ Illustration by Maud and Miska Petersham from *In Clean Hay* by Eric P. Kelly. Copyright 1953 by Macmillan Publishing Co./ Illustration from *The Silver Mace* by Maud and Miska Petersham. Copyright © 1956 by Macmillan Publishing Co./ Illustrations by Maud and Miska Petersham from *Tales from Shakespeare* by Charles and Mary Lamb. Copyright 1923 by The Macmillan Co./ Jacket design by Roger Hane from *The Man Who Founded Georgia* by J. Gordon Vaeth. Copyright © 1968 by J. Gordon Vaeth. Copyright © 1968 by The Macmillan Co. All reprinted by permission of Macmillan Publishing Co. ■ **MASSADA PRESS, LTD. (Jerusalem).** Illustration by H. Hechtkopf from *Jonah's Journey* by Danah Haiz. Copyright © 1973 by Massada Press, Ltd. Reprinted by permission of Massada Press, Ltd. ■ **McGRAW-HILL BOOK CO.** Illustration by Paul Galdone from *Anatole and the Cat* by Eve Titus. Copyright © 1957 by Eve Titus and Paul Galdone. Reprinted by permission of McGraw-Hill Book Co. ■ **DAVID McKAY CO., INC.** Illustration by Jo Polseno from *This Hawk Belongs to Me* by Jo Polseno. Copyright © 1976 by Jo Polseno./ Illustration by N.C. Wyeth from *Robinson Crusoe* by Daniel

DeFoe. Copyright permission, courtesy of David McKay Co., Inc. Both reprinted by permission of David McKay Co., Inc. ■ **JULIAN MESSNER.** Illustration by Russell Hoover from *French Explorers of North America* by David J. Abodaher. Copyright © 1970 by David J. Abodaher. Reprinted by permission of Julian Messner. ■ **THE MINERVA PRESS, LTD.** Illustration by W. Heath Robinson from *A Midsummer Nights Dream* by William Shakespeare. Copyright © 1976 by The W. Heath Robinson Estate and The Minerva Press, Ltd. Reprinted by permission of The Minerva Press, Ltd. ■ **WILLIAM MORROW AND CO.** Illustration by Lee J. Ames from *TRACTORS* by Herbert S. Zim and James R. Skelly. Copyright © 1972 by Herbert S. Zim and James R. Skelly. Reprinted by permission of William Morrow and Co. ■ **J. MURRAY, LTD.** Illustration by Kathleen Hale from *Orlando the Judge* by Kathleen Hale. Reprinted by permission of J. Murray, Ltd. ■ **THOMAS NELSON, INC.** Photograph by J.H. Prince from *Languages of the Animal World* by J.H. Prince. Reprinted by permission of Thomas Nelson, Inc. ■ **ORESKO.** Sidelight excerpts from *Randolph Caldecott: Lord of the Nursery* by Rodney K. Engen. Reprinted by permissoin of Oresko. ■ **OXFORD UNIVERSITY PRESS.** Illustration by Jennifer Miles from *The Little Duke: Richard the Fearless* by Charlotte M. Yonge. Reprinted by permission of Oxford University Press. ■ **PANTHEON BOOKS.** Illustration by Reginald Marsh from *The Story of a Bad Boy* by Thomas Bailey Aldrich. Copyright 1951 by Pantheon Books./ Illustration by Uri Shulevitz from *The Carpet of Soloman* by Sulamith Ish-Kishor. Copyright © 1966 by Sulamith Ish-Kishor and Uri Shulevitz./ Illustration by Stan Mack from *Jethro's Difficult Dinosaur* by Arnold Sundgaard. Text copyright © 1977 by Arnold Sundgaard. Illustrations copyright © 1977 by Stan Mack./ Illustration by Ronni Solbert from *White Monkey King* retold by Sally Hovey Wriggins. Text copyright © 1977 by Sally Hovey Wriggins. Illustrations © 1977 by Ronni Solbert. All reprinted by permission of Pantheon Books, a division of Random House, Inc. ■ **PELHAM BOOKS.** Illustration by William Stobbs from *A Gaping Wide-Mouthed Waddling Frog* by William Stobbs. Copyright © 1977 William Stobbs. Reprinted by permission of Pelham Books. ■ **PENGUIN BOOKS, LTD.** Sidelight excerpts from an article in *The Thorny Paradise* by Barbara Willard, edited by Edward Blishen. Reprinted by permission of Penguin Books, Ltd. ■ **G. P. PUTNAM'S SONS.** Illustration by Don Almquist from *Spring Is Like the Morning* by M. Jean Craig. Illustrations © 1965 by Don Almquist. Reprinted by permission of G. P. Putnam's Sons. ■ **THE SAALFIELD PUBLISHING CO.** Illustration by George Lawson from *The Little Duke* by Charlotte M. Yonge. Copyright 1932 by The Saalfield Publishing Co. Reprinted by permission of The Saalfield Publishing Co. ■ **ST. MARTINS PRESS.** Sidelight excerpts from *Charles Robinson* by Leo de Freitas. Reprinted by permission of St. Martins Press. ■ **SATURDAY EVENING POST.** Sidelight excerpts from an article "She Didn't Write It For Money—She Says," by Wallis M. Reef, in *Saturday Evening Post*, September 1, 1945./ Sidelight excerpts from an article, "As I Seem to Me," by Booth Tarkington, in *Saturday Evening Post*, July 5, 1941, July 12, 1941, August 16, 1941, August 23, 1941. All reprinted by permission of *Saturday Evening Post*. ■ **CHARLES SCRIBNER'S SONS.** Illustration by Katherine Milhous from *A Book for Jennifer* by Alice Dalgliesh./ Illustrations by Flavia Gag from *The Davenports and Cherry Pie* by Alice Dalgliesh./ Photographs by Bill Sears, drawings by Ken Longtemps from *Sometimes I Dance Mountains* by Byrd Baylor. Copyright © 1973 by Byrd Baylor./ Illustration by Elisabeth MacIntyre from *Ambrose Kangaroo* by Elisabeth MacIntyre./ Illustration by Elisabeth MacIntyre from *Mr. Koala Bear* by Elisabeth MacIntyre./ Illustration by N.C. Wyeth from *The Black Arrow* by Robert Louis Stevenson. Copyright 1916 by Charles Scribner's Sons; renewal copyright 1944 by N.C. Wyeth./ Illustration by N.C. Wyeth from *The Little Shepherd of Kingdom Come* by John Fox, Jr. Copyright 1903, 1931 by Charles Scribner's Sons; renewal copyright © 1959./ Illustration by N.C. Wyeth from *Treasure Island* by Robert Louis Stevenson. Copyright 1911 by Charles Scribner's Sons./ Illustration by N.C. Wyeth from *The Mysterious Island* by Jules Verne. Copyright 1918 Charles Scribner's Sons; renewal copyright 1946 Carolyn B. Wyeth and Charles Scribner's Sons. All reprinted by permission of Charles Scribner's Sons. Illustration by N.C. Wyeth from *Treasure Island* by Robert Louis Stevenson, courtesy of Mrs. Andrew Wyeth. ■ **SIMON AND SCHUSTER, INC.** Illustrations by Laszlo Kubinyi from *The Cat and the Flying Machine* by Laszlo Kubinyi. Copyright © 1970 by Laszlo Kubinyi. Reprinted by permission of Simon and Schuster, Inc. ■ **TIME, INC.** Sidelight excerpts from an article, "Fifty Years in the Green Meadow," by Paul O'Neil in *Life*, November 14, 1960. Reprinted by permission of Time, Inc. ■ **VIKING PRESS.** Illustration by Don Freeman from *Dandelion* by Don Freeman. Copyright © 1964 by Don Freeman./ Illustration by Don Freeman from *Mike's House* by Julia L. Sauer. Copyright 1954 by Julia L. Sauer and Don Freeman./ Illustration by Kate Seredy from *The Christmas Anna Angel* by Ruth Sawyer. Copyright 1944 by Ruth Sawyer and Kate Seredy. Copyright © renewed 1972 by David Durand and Kate Seredy./ Illustration by Robert McCloskey from *Journey Cake, Ho!* by Ruth Sawyer. Copyright 1953 by Ruth Sawyer and Robert McCloskey. All reprinted by permission of Viking Press. ■ **FREDERICK WARNE & CO., LTD.** Illustration by L. Leslie Brooke from *The Golden Goose Book*, "The Golden Goose." Copyright © 1976 by Frederick Warne and Co./ Illustration by L. Leslie Brooke from *Little Bo Peep: A Nursery Rhyme Picture Book* by L. Leslie Brooke. Copyright © 1922 by Frederick Warne & Co., Ltd./ Sidelight excerpts and illustrations from

*Yours Pictorially: Illustrated Letters of Randolph Caldecott* edited by Michael Hutchins. Copyright © by Frederick Warne and Co., Ltd./ Illustration by Paul Galdone from *Dance of the Animals* by Pura Belpre. Copyright © 1972 by Pura Belpre. Illustrations copyright © by Paul Galdone./ Illustration by T.H. Robinson from *The Book of Robin Hood* by A.L. Haydon. All reprinted by permission of Frederick Warne & Co., Ltd. ■ **WATSON-GUPTILL PUBLICA—TIONS.** Portrait of Booth Tarkington by James Montgomery Flagg from *James Montgomery Flagg* by Susan Meyer. Copyright 1974 by Watson-Guptill. Reprinted by permission of Watson-Guptill Publications. ■ **FRANKLIN WATTS, INC.** Sidelight excerpts from *Tellers of Tales* by Roger Lancelyn Green. Reprinted by permission of Franklin Watts, Inc. ■ **WEATH-ERVANE BOOKS.** Illustration by Arthur Rackham from *Tales from Shakespeare* by Charles and Mary Lamb. Copyright © 1975 by Crown Publishers. Reprinted by permission of Weathervane Books. ■ **WEYBRIGHT AND TALLEY.** Illustration by Antony Maitland from *To London! To London!* by Barbara Willard. Text copyright © 1968 Barbara Willard. Illustrations copyright © 1968 by Antony Maitland. Reprinted by permission of Weybright and Talley. ■ **ALBERT WHITMAN AND CO.** Illustration by Meyer Seltzer from *Will You Carry Me?* by Edna Walker Chandler. Copyright © 1965 by Albert Whitman and Co. Reprinted by permission of Albert Whitman and Co. ■ **H. W. WILSON CO.** Sidelight excerpts from *Current Biography 1945.* Copyright © 1946 by the H. W. Wilson Co. Reprinted by permission of H. W. Wilson Co. ■ **THE JOHN C. WINSTON CO.** Illustration by Norman Guthrie Rudolph from *Last Voyages of the Mayflower: A Story of the Pilgrims' Ship* by Kenneth Allsop. Copyright 1955 by Kenneth Allsop. Reprinted by permission of the John C. Winston Co. ■ **WORLD'S WORK, LTD.** Illustration by Fritz Siebel from *Amelia Bedelia* by Peggy Parish. Text copyright © 1963 by Margaret Parish. Pictures copyright © 1963 by Fritz Siebel. Reprinted by permission of World's Work, Ltd.

Photographs of N.C. Wyeth reprinted by permission of the Delaware Art Museum./ Illustration from *The X Cars: Detroit's One-of-a-Kind Autos* by Henry B. Lent. Copyright © 1971 by Henry B. Lent. Reprinted with permission of the Excalibur Automobile Corp./ Illustration by N.C. Wyeth from *The Bounty Trilogy* by Charles Nordhoff and James Norman Hall. Copyright 1932 by Charles Nordhoff and James Norman Hall. Illustration copyright © 1940 by Little, Brown & Co. Reprinted by permission of The Free Library of Philadelphia./ Photograph of Booth Tarkington reprinted by permission of the Indianapolis Museum of Art, The Penrod Society and the Martha Delzell Memorial Fund./ Illustration by Aubrey Beardsley from *King Arthur in Fact and Legend* by Geoffrey Ashe. Copyright © 1969, 1971 by Geoffrey Ashe. Reprinted by permission of The National Library of Scotland./ Photograph of Wyeth's studio reprinted by permission of Pennsylvania Historical and Museum Commission./ Illustration by N.C. Wyeth from *Robin Hood* by Paul Creswick. Reprinted by permission of Estate of N.C. Wyeth, courtesy of the New York Public Library.

# SOMETHING ABOUT THE AUTHOR

**DAVID J. ABODAHER**

## ABODAHER, David J. (Naiph) 1919-

*PERSONAL:* Surname is pronounced Ab-o-dar; born February 1, 1919, in Streator, Ill.; son of Simon George (a grocer) and Rose (Ayoub) Abodaher; married Lynda Haddad, September 16, 1945 (divorced); children: Lynda Anne (Mrs. Robert Henderson), and adopted son, Mounir Consul. *Education:* Attended University of Notre Dame and University of Detroit. *Politics:* Independent (most often Democrat). *Religion:* Roman Catholic. *Home:* 20965 Lahser Rd., Southfield, Mich. *Office:* Kenyon & Eckhart Advertising, 1 Parklane Blvd., Dearborn, Mich.

*CAREER:* Program director or production manager of radio stations in Oklahoma City, Okla., 1938-40, Kalamazoo, Mich., 1940-41; radio director of advertising firms in Detroit, Mich., 1944-50; self-employed radio-television writer and producer, 1950-56; Jam Handy Organization, Detroit, Mich., writer, 1956-59; Ford Motor Co., Detroit, Mich., free-lance sales promotion writer, 1961-64, free-lance advertising and sales promotion writer, 1971-76; J. Walter Thompson Co., Detroit, Mich., senior writer, 1964-67; Kenyon & Eckhardt Advertising, Dearborn, Mich., senior writer, 1969-71, 1976—. Radio chairman of Michigan War Finance Committee, 1944-50, and Detroit Retailers Public Service Committee, 1944-50. *Military service:* U.S. Army, Signal Corps, 1942-44; became staff sergeant.

*WRITINGS*—Juveniles: *Under Three Flags: The Story of Gabriel Richard,* Hawthorn, 1965; *Daniel Duluth: Explorer of the Northlands,* Kenedy, 1966; *French Explorers of North America,* Messner, 1970.

After four days of hard paddling through the fast-flowing waters of the St. Laurence and around jagged rocks and tumbling rapids, he saw the stockaded walls of Montreal. ■ (From *French Explorers of North America* by David J. Abodaher. Illustrated by Russell Hoover.)

Young adult: *Warrior on Two Continents*, Messner, 1968; *Freedom Fighter*, Messner, 1969; *Rebel on Two Continents*, Messner, 1970; *Mag Wheels and Racing Strips*, Messner, 1974; *Compacts, Subs and Minis: Be Your Own Mechanic*, Messner, 1976; *The Fantastic Formula 1 Racing Cars*, Messner, 1979; *Speed Makers: The Cars and Their Drivers*, Messner, 1979; *The Sports Car Challenge*, Messner, 1980.

Contributor of short stories to magazines. Wrote, produced, and directed one half-hour color motion picture for Sisters of St. Joseph, Nazareth, Mich.; author of network radio features and documentaries, including "Famous Jury Trials" and "Smoke Dreams."

*WORK IN PROGRESS:* Biography of Pierre Radisson; an adult biography of Alphonse Marie Ratisbonne.

*SIDELIGHTS:* "Writing is, and I'm sure always has been, the ruling passion of my life. My father, with typical Lebanese leanings, wanted me to become a lawyer and I did begin my college years in pre-law. Sales of what I now consider pretty bad pulp stories pushed any serious thoughts of becoming a legal mind into my never-never land. Then, when WJR in Detroit offered me a staff writing job during my senior year in the university—one that would not wait for graduation—I jumped at the chance. I have never regretted that move.

"I've concentrated on books for young people because I have felt an increasing concern over the lack of reading on the part of so many of today's teenagers. However, there may be some hope for the future. The Children's Book Fair,

initiated in the early '70's by the Detroit Public Library and the Detroit *Free Press* is instilling renewed interest in books among the young. So, too, is the Book Fair in Port Huron, sponsored by that city's *Times-Herald*. In the six appearances I've made at these two annual programs interest seems to have grown year by year.

"The principal point I try to get across when I address a group at the Book Fairs, or an English class at a high school, is the importance of reading in developing a well-rounded personality, one that will pay dividends in the individual's future."

*HOBBIES AND OTHER INTERESTS:* Photography, sports and international travel.

## ALDRICH, Thomas Bailey    1836-1907

*PERSONAL:* Born November 11, 1836, in Portsmouth, New Hampshire; died March 19, 1907, in Boston, Massachusetts; son of Elias Taft and Sarah Abba (Bailey) Aldrich; married Lilian Woodman, 1865; children: Charles (died, 1904), Talbot. *Home:* Tenant's Harbor, Maine.

*CAREER:* Novelist, poet, and editor. Employed as a clerk in an uncle's counting house in New York, 1852-55. Held various journalistic jobs, including junior literary critic of the New York *Evening Mirror*, 1855, assistant editor of N. P. Willis' *Home Journal*, 1856, war correspondent during the Civil War for the New York *Tribune*, 1861, and managing editor of the *Illustrated News*, 1862-65. Editor of *Every Saturday*, 1865-74, and of *Atlantic Monthly*, 1881-90.

*WRITINGS*—Novels and short stories: *Daisy's Necklace, and What Came of It*, Derby & Jackson, 1857; *The Course of True Love Never Did Run Smooth*, Rudd & Carleton, 1858; (editor) *Out of His Head*, Carleton, 1862; *Pansy's Wish: A Christmas Fantasy with a Moral*, Marion, 1870; *The Story of a Bad Boy*, Fields, Osgood, 1870 [other editions illustrated by A. B. Frost, Houghton, 1895; Harold M. Brett, Houghton, 1923; Edwin J. Prittie, J. C. Winston, 1927; Henry C. Kiefer, J. H. Sears, 1928; Leslie Turner, Saalfield, 1936; Reginald Marsh, Pantheon Books, 1951; Roberta Moynihan, Junior Deluxe Editions, 1956]; *Marjorie Daw, and Other People*, J. R. Osgood, 1873, reissued, Mss Information, 1972 [another edition illustrated by John C. Clay, Houghton, 1908]; *Prudence Palfrey*, J. R. Osgood, 1874; *A Midnight Fantasy* [and] *The Little Violinist*, J. R. Osgood, 1877; *Miss Mehetabel's Son*, J. R. Osgood, 1877; *The Queen of Sheba*, J. R. Osgood, 1877; *A Rivermouth Romance*, J. R. Osgood, 1877.

*The Stillwater Tragedy*, Houghton, 1880, reprinted, Gregg Press, 1968; (with Margaret Oliphant and Wilson Oliphant) *The Second Son*, Houghton, 1888, reissued, 1974; *Wyndham Towers*, Houghton, 1890; *An Old Town by the Sea*, Houghton, 1893; *Two Bites at a Cherry, with Other Tales*, Houghton, 1894, reissued, Mss Information, 1972; *A Sea Turn and Other Matters*, Houghton, 1902, reprinted, Books for Libraries, 1969; *Ponkapog Papers*, Houghton, 1903, reprinted, Books for Libraries, 1969.

Poems: *The Bells: A Collection of Chimes*, J. C. Derby, 1855; *The Ballad of Babie Bell, and Other Poems*, Rudd & Carleton, 1859; *Pampinea, and Other Poems*, Rudd & Carleton, 1861; *Poems*, Carleton, 1863; *The Poems of Thomas Bailey Aldrich*, Ticknor & Fields, 1865; *Pere Antoine's Date Palm*, Welch, Bigelow, 1866; *Cloth of Gold, and Other Poems*, J. R. Osgood, 1874; *Flower and Thorn, Later Poems*, J. R. Osgood, 1877; *The Poems of Thomas Bailey Aldrich* (illustrated by the Paint and Clay Club), Houghton, 1882; *Mercedes, and Later Poems*, Houghton, 1884; *The Household Edition of the Poems of Thomas Bailey Aldrich*, Houghton, 1885; *The Sisters' Tragedy, with Other Poems, Lyric and Dramatic*, Houghton, 1891; *Unguarded Gates, and Other Poems*, Houghton, 1895; *Judith and Holofernes*, Houghton, 1896.

Other: *From Ponkapog to Pesth*, Houghton, 1883; *Mercedes* (two-act drama), Houghton, 1894; *The Large Paper Edition of the Writings of Thomas Bailey Aldrich*, eight volumes, Riverside Press, 1897; *Judith of Bethulia* (a play, based on the author's poem, *Judith and Holofernes;* first produced in Boston, Massachusetts at the Tremont Theatre, October 13, 1904), Houghton, 1904; *The Ponkapog Edition of the Writings of Thomas Bailey Aldrich*, nine volumes, Houghton, 1907, reprinted as *The Works of Thomas Bailey Aldrich*, AMS Press, 1970; *Pauline Pavlovna* (a dramatic, romantic play), E. S. Werner, 1914.

Also series editor of *Young Folks Library*, 10 volumes, reissued, Auxiliary Educational League (Chicago), 1953.

*ADAPTATIONS*—Movies: "Judith of Bethulia," Biograph, 1913, rereleased, Film Classic Exchange, 197?; "Her Condoned Sin," based on *Judith of Bethulia*, Biograph, 1917.

Plays: Sally Dixon Wiener, *Marjorie Daw* (one-act musical; produced in New York City at the Library and Museum of

**THOMAS BAILEY ALDRICH, 1866**

the Performing Arts, February 2, 1970), Studio Duplicating Service, 1970.

*SIDELIGHTS:* Born **November 11, 1836** in Portsmouth, New Hampshire, the only child of Elias Taft Aldrich and Sarah Abba (Bailey) Aldrich. "I could boast of a long line of ancestors, but won't. They are of no possible benefit to me, save it is pleasant to think that none of them were hanged for criminals or shot for traitors, but that many of them are sleeping somewhere near Bunker Hill. . . . My genealogical tree, you will observe, grew up some time after the Flood, with other vegetation. I will spare myself this warm day the exercise of climbing up its *dead* branches and come down to one of the lower 'sprigs,' but by no means 'the last leaf upon the tree.'" [Ferris Greenslet, *Thomas Bailey Aldrich*, Houghton, 1908.[1]]

"I may truthfully say I was an amiable, impulsive lad, blessed with fine digestive powers, and no hypocrite. I didn't want to be an angel and with the angels stand; I didn't think the missionary tracts presented to me by the Rev. Wibird Hawkins were half so nice as *Robinson Crusoe;* and I didn't send my little pocket-money to the natives of the Feejee Islands, but spent is royally in peppermint-drops and taffy candy. In short, I was a real human boy, such as you may meet anywhere in New England, and no more like the impossible boy in a story-book than a sound orange is like one that has been sucked dry. . . .

"Whenever a new scholar came to our school, I used to confront him at recess with the following words: "My name's Tom Bailey; what's your name?' If the name struck me favorably, I shook hands with the new pupil cordially; but if it didn't, I would turn on my heel, for I was particular on this point. Such names as Higgins, Wiggins, and Spriggins were deadly affronts to my ear; while Langdon, Wallace, Blake, and the like, were passwords to my confidence and esteem.

"I was born at [Portsmouth] but, before I had a chance to become very well acquainted with that pretty New England town, my parents removed to New Orleans, where my father invested his money so securely in the banking business that he was never able to get any of it out again. . . .

"I was only eighteen months old at the time of the removal, and it didn't make much difference to me where I was, because I was so small; but several years later, when my father proposed to take me North to be educated, I had my own peculiar views on the subject. . . .

"You see I was what is called 'a Northern man with Southern principles.' I had no recollection of New England: my earliest memories were connected with the South . . . my old negro nurse, and with the great ill-kept garden in the centre of which stood our house,—a whitewashed stone house it was, with wide verandas,—shut out from the street by lines of orange, fig, and magnolia trees. I knew I was born at the North, but hoped nobody would find it out. I looked upon the misfortune as something so shrouded by time and distance that maybe nobody remembered it. I never told my schoolmates I was a Yankee, because they talked about the Yankees in such a scornful way it made me feel that it was quite a disgrace not to be born in Louisiana, or at least in one of the Border States." [Thomas Bailey Aldrich, *The Story of a Bad Boy,* Houghton, 1869.[2]]

**Spring, 1849.** Brought back to Portsmouth to prepare to enter Harvard College. "As we drove through the quiet old town, I thought [Portsmouth] the prettiest place in the world; and I think so still. The streets are long and wide, shaded by gigantic American elms, whose drooping branches, interlacing here and there, span the avenues with arches graceful enough to be the handiwork of fairies. Many of the houses have small flower-gardens in front, gay in the season with china-asters, and are substantially built, with massive chimney-stacks and protruding eaves. A beautiful river goes rippling by the town, and, after turning and twisting among a lot of tiny islands, empties itself into the sea.

"'The Nutter House,'—all the more prominent dwellings in [Portsmouth] are named after somebody; for instance, there is the Walford House, the Venner House, the Trefethen House, etc., though it by no means follows that they are inhabited by the people whose names they bear,—the 'Nutter House,' to resume, has been in our family nearly a hundred years, and is an honor to the builder (an ancestor of ours, I believe), supposing durability to be a merit. If our ancestor *was* a carpenter, he knew his trade. I wish I knew mine as well. Such timber and such workmanship don't often come together in houses built nowadays.

"Imagine a low-studded structure, with a wide hall running through the middle. At your right hand, as you enter, stands a tall black mahogany clock, looking like an Egyptian mummy set up on end. On each side of the hall are doors (whose knobs, it must be confessed, do not turn very easily), opening into large rooms wainscoted and rich in wood-carvings about the mantel-pieces' and cornices. The walls are covered with pictured paper, representing landscapes and sea-views. In the parlor, for example, this enlivening figure is repeated all over the room: —A group of English peasants, wearing Italian hats, are dancing on a lawn that abruptly resolves itself into a sea-beach, upon which stands a flabby fisherman (nationality unknown), quietly hauling in what appears to be a small whale, and totally regardless of the dreadful naval combat going on just beyond the end of his fishing-rod. On the other side of the ships is the main-land again, with the same peasants dancing. Our ancestors were very worthy people, but their wall-papers were abominable.

"There are neither grates nor stoves in these quaint chambers, but splendid open chimney-places, with room enough for the corpulent back-log to turn over comfortably on the polished andirons. A wide staircase leads from the hall to the second story, which is arranged much like the first. Over this is the garret. I needn't tell a New England boy what a museum of curiosities is the garret of a well-regulated New England house of fifty or sixty years' standing. Here meet together, as if by some preconcerted arrangement, all the broken-down chairs of the household, all the spavined tables, all the seedy hats, all the intoxicated-looking boots, all the split walking-sticks that have retired from business, 'weary with the march of life.' The pots, the pans, the trunks, the bottles,—who may hope to make an inventory of the numberless odds and ends collected in this bewildering lumber-room? But what a place it is to sit of an afternoon with the rain pattering on the roof! what a place in which to read *Gulliver's Travels,* or the famous adventures of Rinaldo Rinaldini!

"My grandfather's house stood a little back from the main street, in the shadow of two handsome elms, whose overgrown boughs would dash themselves against the gables whenever the wind blew hard. In the rear was a pleasant garden, covering perhaps a quarter of an acre, full of plum-trees and gooseberry-bushes. These trees were old settlers, and are all dead now, excepting one, which bears a purple plum as big as an egg. This tree, as I remark, is still standing, and a more beautiful tree to tumble out of never grew anywhere. In the northwestern corner of the garden were the stables and carriage-house opening upon a narrow lane. You may imagine that I made an early visit to that locality to inspect [the pony]. Indeed, I paid her a visit every half-hour during the first day of my arrival. At the twenty-fourth visit she trod on my foot rather heavily, as a reminder, probably, that I was wearing out my welcome. She was a knowing little pony, that Gypsy. . . .

"[Her] quarters were all that could be wished, but nothing among my new surroundings gave me more satisfaction than the cosey sleeping apartment that had been prepared for myself. It was the hall room over the front door.

"I had never had a chamber all to myself before, and this one . . . was a marvel of neatness and comfort. Pretty chintz curtains hung at the window, and a patch quilt . . . covered the little truckle-bed. The pattern of the wall-paper left nothing to be desired in that line. On a gray background were small bunches of leaves, unlike any that ever grew in this world; and on every other bunch perched a yellow-bird, pitted with crimson spots, as if it had just recovered from a severe attack of the small-pox. That no such bird ever existed did not detract from my admiration of each one. There were two hundred and sixty-eight of these birds in all, not counting those split in two where the paper was badly joined. I counted them once when I was laid up with a fine black eye, and falling asleep immediately dreamed that the whole flock suddenly took wing and flew out of the window. From that time I was never able to regard them as merely inanimate objects.

"A wash-stand in the corner, a chest of carved mahogany drawers, a looking-glass in a filigreed frame, and a high-backed chair studded with brass nails like a coffin, constituted the furniture. Over the head of the bed were two oak shelves, holding perhaps a dozen books,—among which were *Theodore,* or *The Peruvians; Robinson Crusoe;* an odd volume of *Tristram Shandy;* Baxter's *Saints' Rest,* and a fine English edition of the *Arabian Nights,* with six hundred wood-cuts by Harvey.

"Shall I ever forget the hour when I first overhauled these books? I do not allude especially to Baxter's *Saints' Rest,* which is far from being a lively work for the young, but to the *Arabian Nights,* and particularly *Robinson Crusoe.* The thrill that ran into my fingers' ends then has not run out yet. Many a time did I steal up to this nest of a room, and, taking the dog's-eared volume from its shelf, glide off into an enchanted realm, where there were no lessons to get and no boys to smash my kite. In a lidless trunk in the garret I

**It was a dirty night, as the sailors say. The darkness was something that could be felt as well as seen—it pressed down upon one with a cold, clammy touch.** ■ (From *The Story of a Bad Boy* by Thomas Bailey Aldrich. Illustrated by Reginald Marsh.)

**Many a time did I steal up to this nest of a room, and, taking the dog's eared volume from its shelf, glide off into an enchanted realm, where there were no lessons to get and no boys to smash my kite. ■** (From *The Story of a Bad Boy* by Thomas Bailey Aldrich. Illustrated by A. B. Frost.)

subsequently unearthed another motley collection of novels and romances, embracing the adventures of Baron Trenck, Jack Sheppard, Don Quixote, Gil Blas, and Charlotte Temple,—all of which I fed upon like a bookworm.

"I never come across a copy of any of those works without feeling a certain tenderness for the yellow-haired little rascal who used to lean above the magic pages hour after hour, religiously believing every word he read, and no more doubting the reality of Sindbad the Sailor, or the Knight of the Sorrowful Countenance, than he did the existence of his own grandfather.

"Against the wall at the foot of the bed hung a single-barrel shot-gun,—placed there by [grandfather] who knew what a boy loved, if ever a grandfather did. As the trigger of the gun had been accidentally twisted off, it was not, perhaps, the most dangerous weapon that could be placed in the hands of youth.

"[Grandfather] was a hale, cheery old gentleman, as straight and as bald as an arrow. He had been a sailor in early life; that is to say, at the age of ten years he fled from the multiplication-table, and ran away to sea. A single voyage satisfied him. There never was but one of our family who *didn't* run away to sea, and this one died at his birth. My grandfather had also been a soldier,—a captain of militia in 1812. If I owe the British nation anything, I owe thanks to that particular British soldier who put a musket-ball into the fleshy part of Captain [Aldrich's] leg, causing

that noble warrior a slight permanent limp, but offsetting the injury by furnishing him with the material for a story which the old gentleman was never weary of telling and I never weary of listening to.

"At the time I came to [Portsmouth] my grandfather had retired from active pursuits, and was living at ease on his money, invested principally in shipping. He had been a widower many years; a maiden sister . . . manag[ed] his household. [She] also managed her brother, and her brother's servant, and the visitor at her brother's gate,—not in a tyrannical spirit, but from a philanthropic desire to be useful to everybody. In person she was tall and angular; she had a gray complexion, gray eyes, gray eyebrows, and generally wore a gray dress. Her strongest weak point was a belief in the efficacy of 'hot-drops' as a cure for all known diseases.

"The first shadow that fell upon me in my new home was caused by the return of my parents to New Orleans. Their visit was cut short by business which required my father's presence in Natchez, where he was establishing a branch of the banking-house. When they had gone, a sense of loneliness such as I had never dreamed of filled my young breast. I crept away to the stable, and, throwing my arms about Gypsy's neck, sobbed aloud. She too had come from the sunny South, and was now a stranger in a strange land.

"The little mare seemed to realize our situation, and gave me all the sympathy I could ask, repeatedly rubbing her soft nose over my face and lapping up my salt tears with evident relish.

"When night came, I felt still more lonesome. My grandfather sat in his arm-chair the greater part of the evening, reading . . . the local newspaper. There was no gas in those days, and the Captain read by the aid of a small block-tin lamp, which he held in one hand. I observed that he had a habit of dropping off into a doze every three or four minutes, and I forgot my homesickness at intervals in watching him. Two or three times, to my vast amusement, he scorched the edges of the newspaper with the wick of the lamp; and at about half past eight o'clock I had the satisfaction—I am sorry to confess it was a satisfaction—of seeing the [Portsmouth newspaper] in flames.

"My grandfather leisurely extinguished the fire with his hands, and [his sister] who sat near a low table, knitting by the light of an astral lamp, did not even look up. She was quite used to this catastrophe.

"There was little or no conversation during the evening. In fact, I do not remember that any one spoke at all, excepting once, when the Captain remarked, in a meditative manner, that my parents 'must have reached New York by this time'; at which supposition I nearly strangled myself in attempting to intercept a sob.

"I was glad when ten o'clock came, the bedtime for young folks, and old folks too. . . . Alone in the hall-chamber I had my cry out, once for all, moistening the pillow to such an extent that I was obliged to turn it over to find a dry spot to go to sleep on.

"My grandfather wisely concluded to put me to school at once. If I had been permitted to go mooning about the house and stables, I should have kept my discontent alive for months. The next morning, accordingly, he took me by the hand, and we set forth for the academy, which was located at the farther end of the town.

"[The school] was a two-story brick building, standing in the centre of a great square piece of land, surrounded by a high picket fence. There were three or four sickly trees, but no grass, in this enclosure, which had been worn smooth and hard by the tread of multitudinous feet. I noticed here and there small holes scooped in the ground, indicating that it was the season for marbles. A better playground for baseball couldn't have been devised.

"On reaching the school-house door, the Captain inquired for [Mr. DeMerritt]. The boy who answered our knock ushered us into a side-room, and in a few minutes—during which my eye took in forty-two caps hung on forty-two wooden pegs—[Mr. DeMerritt] made his appearance. He was a slender man, with white, fragile hands, and eyes that glanced half a dozen different ways at once,—a habit probably acquired from watching the boys.

"After a brief consultation, my grandfather patted me on the head and left me in charge of this gentleman, who seated himself in front of me and proceeded to sound the depth, or, more properly speaking, the shallowness, of my attainments. I suspect my historical information rather startled him. I recollect I gave him to understand that Richard III. was the last king of England.

"This ordeal over, [Mr. DeMerritt] rose and bade me follow him. A door opened, and I stood in the blaze of forty-two pairs of upturned eyes. I was a cool hand for my age, but I lacked the boldness to face this battery without wincing. In a sort of dazed way I stumbled after [Mr. De-Merritt] down a narrow aisle between two rows of desks, and shyly took the seat pointed out to me.

"The faint buzz that had floated over the school-room at our entrance died away, and the interrupted lessons were resumed. By degrees I recovered my coolness, and ventured to look around me.

"The owners of the forty-two caps were seated at small green desks like the one assigned to me. The desks were arranged in six rows, with spaces between just wide enough to prevent the boys' whispering. A blackboard set into the wall extended clear across the end of the room; on a raised platform near the door stood the master's table; and directly in front of this was a recitation-bench capable of seating fifteen or twenty pupils. A pair of globes, tattooed with dragons and winged horses, occupied a shelf between two windows, which were so high from the floor that nothing but a giraffe could have looked out of them.

"Having possessed myself of these details, I scrutinized my new acquaintances with unconcealed curiosity, instinctively selecting my friends and picking out my enemies,—and in only two cases did I mistake my man.

"Nothing else occurred that morning to interrupt the exercises, excepting that a boy in the reading class threw us all into convulsions by calling Absa'om *A-bol'-som,*—'Abolsom, O my son Abolsom!'

"My social relations with my new schoolfellows were the pleasantest possible. There was always some exciting excursion on foot,—a ramble through the pine woods, a visit to . . . a high cliff in the neighborhood,—or a surreptitious

**Holding one another by the hand, and chanting a low dirge, the Mystic Twelve revolved about me.** ■ (From *The Story of a Bad Boy* by Thomas Bailey Aldrich. Illustrated by A. B. Frost.)

row on the river, involving an exploration of a group of diminutive islands, upon one of which we pitched a tent and played we were the Spanish sailors who got wrecked there years ago. But the endless pine forest that skirted the town was our favorite haunt. There was a great green pond hidden somewhere in its depths, inhabited by a monstrous colony of turtles. [My schoolmate] who had an eccentric passion for carving his name on everything, never let a captured turtle slip through his fingers without leaving his mark engraved on its shell. He must have lettered about two thousand from first to last. . . .

"In August we had two weeks' vacation. It was about this time that I became a member of the [Portsmouth] Centipedes, a secret society composed of twelve of the . . . Grammar School boys. This was an honor to which I had long aspired, but, being a new boy, I was not admitted to the fraternity until my character had fully developed itself.

"It was a very select society, the object of which I never fathomed, though I was an active member of the body during the remainder of my residence at [Portsmouth], and at one time held the onerous position of F.C.,—First Centipede. Each of the elect wore a copper cent (some occult association being established between a cent apiece and a centipede!) suspended by a string round his neck. The medals were worn next the skin, and it was while bathing one day at . . . [the] Point, with [my classmates] that I had my curiosity roused to the highest pitch by a sight of these singular emblems. As soon as I ascertained the existence of a boys' club, of course I was ready to die to join it. And eventually I was allowed to join.

"The initiation ceremony took place in [my classmate's] barn, where I was submitted to a series of trials not calculated to soothe the nerves of a timorous boy. Before being led to . . . the loft over my friend's wood-house,—my hands were securely pinioned, and my eyes covered with a thick silk handkerchief. At the head of the stairs I was told in an unrecognizable, husky voice, that it was not yet too late to retreat if I felt myself physically too weak to undergo the necessary tortures. I replied that I was not too weak, in a tone which I intended to be resolute, but which, in spite of me, seemed to come from the pit of my stomach.

"'It is well!' said the husky voice.

"I did not feel so sure about that; but, having made up my mind to be a Centipede, a Centipede I was bound to be. Other boys had passed through the ordeal and lived, why should not I?

"A prolonged silence followed this preliminary examination, and I was wondering what would come next, when a pistol fired off close by my ear deafened me for a moment. The unknown voice then directed me to take ten steps forward and stop at the word halt. I took ten steps, and halted.

"'Stricken mortal,' said a second husky voice, more husky, if possible, than the first, 'if you had advanced another inch, you would have disappeared down an abyss three thousand feet deep!'

"I naturally shrunk back at this friendly piece of information. A prick from some two-pronged instrument, evidently a pitchfork, gently checked my retreat. I was then conducted to the brink of several other precipices, and ordered to step over many dangerous chasms, where the result would have been instant death if I had committed the least mistake. I have neglected to say that my movements were accompanied by dismal groans from different parts of the [loft].

"Finally, I was led up a steep plank to what appeared to me an incalculable height. Here I stood breathless while the by-laws were read aloud. A more extraordinary code of laws never came from the brain of man. The penalties attached to the abject being who should reveal any of the secrets of the society were enough to make the blood run cold. A second pistol-shot was heard, the something I stood on sunk with a crash beneath my feet, and I fell two miles, as nearly as I could compute it. At the same instant the handkerchief was whisked from my eyes, and I found myself standing in an empty hogshead surrounded by twelve masked figures fantastically dressed. One of the conspirators was really appalling with a tin sauce-pan on his head, and a tiger-skin sleigh-robe thrown over his shoulders. I scarcely need say that there were no vestiges to be seen of the fearful gulfs over which I had passed so cautiously. My ascent had been to the top of the hogshead, and my descent to the bottom thereof. Holding one another by the hand, and chanting a low dirge, the Mystic Twelve revolved about me. This concluded the ceremony. With a

merry shout the boys threw off their masks, and I was declared a regularly installed member of the [P.M.C.]

"A boy's life in a secluded New England town in winter does not afford many points for illustration. Of course he gets his ears or toes frost-bitten; of course he smashes his sled against another boy's; of course he bangs his head on the ice; and he's a lad of no enterprise whatever, if he doesn't manage to skate into an eel-hole, and be brought home half drowned. All these things happened to me. . . ."[2]

**October 6, 1849.** Father died of cholera on a Mississippi River Steamer at Memphis. ". . . [Grandfather and I] were alone together in the sitting-room, and he began slowly to unfold the letter, I understood it all. I caught a sight of my mother's handwriting in the superscription, and there was nothing left to tell me.

"My grandfather held the letter a few seconds irresolutely, and then commenced reading it aloud; but he could get no further than the date.

"'I can't read it, Tom,' said the old gentleman, breaking down. 'I thought I could.'

"He handed it to me. I took the letter mechanically, and hurried away with it to my little room, where I had passed so many happy hours.

"The week that followed the receipt of this letter is nearly a blank in my memory. I remember that the days appeared endless; that at times I could not realize the misfortune that had befallen us, and my heart upbraided me for not feeling a deeper grief; that a full sense of my loss would now and then sweep over me like an inspiration, and I would steal away to my chamber or wander forlornly about the gardens. I remember this, but little more.

"As the days went by my first grief subsided, and in its place grew up a want which I have experienced at every step in life from boyhood to manhood. Often, even now, after all these years, when I see a lad of twelve or fourteen walking by his father's side, and glancing merrily up at his face, I turn and look after them, and am conscious that I have missed companionship most sweet and sacred.

"One evening the Captain came smiling into the sitting-room with an open letter in his hand. My mother had arrived at New York, and would be with us the next day. For the first time in weeks—years, it seemed to me—something of the old cheerfulness mingled with our conversation round the evening lamp. I was to go to Boston with the Captain to meet her and bring her home. I need not describe that meeting. With my mother's hand in mine once more, all the long years we had been parted appeared like a dream. Very dear to me was the sight of that slender, pale woman passing from room to room, and lending a patient grace and beauty to the saddened life of the old house.

"Everything was changed with us now. There were consultations with lawyers, and signing of papers, and correspondence; for my father's affairs had been left in great confusion. And when these were settled, the evenings were not long enough for us to hear all my mother had to tell of the scenes she had passed through in the ill-fated city.

"The Captain wished to carry out his son's intention and send me to college, for which I was nearly fitted; but our means did not admit of this. The Captain, too, could ill afford to bear the expense, for his losses by the failure of the New Orleans business had been heavy. Yet he insisted on the plan, not seeing clearly what other disposal to make of me.

"In the midst of our discussions a letter came from my Uncle [Frost], a merchant in New York, generously offering me a place in his counting-house. The case resolved itself into this: If I went to college, I should have to be dependent on [the Captain] for several years, and at the end of the collegiate course would have no settled profession. If I accepted my uncle's offer, I might hope to work my way to independence without loss of time. It was hard to give up the long-cherished dream of being a Harvard boy; but I gave it up."[2]

**1852.** Accompanied by his mother, Aldrich moved to New York where he accepted a clerkship with his uncle, Charles Frost. "Under his shockingly bluff manner he had a heart as sensitive as a child's and as sympathetic as a woman's—for those he loved. He had faults and virtues enough to set up five or six conventional men. I shall never forget his goodness to me and mine. At his funeral (or rather at the slight services held at his house before the remains were taken to Portsmouth) a pathetic thing happened. A little group of mourners, totally unknown to the family, made its appearance—a shabby lot of old men and women and one or two striplings. These forlorn figures were persons whom Mr. Frost had helped in one way or another. Some of them he had boarded in hospitals, others he had established in the junk-business, and others again he had assisted with small weekly sums of money when they were out of work. I can picture how he bullied them and swore at them—and helped them. 'There goes the only friend I ever had,' muttered a shabby old man who looked as if he had been picked up at a bric-á-brac shop."[1]

Aldrich recalled later in life that he wrote "a lyric or two every day before going downtown."[1] He continued spending his summers in Portsmouth. "The beautiful old town in which we all passed our childhood! How her loveliness deepens and freshens year by year, as if the waters of the Piscataqua, sparkling at her lip, had their rise in those Fountains of Perpetual Youth which Ponce de Leon sought! How our purest memories have crystallized about her! What a strong sentiment it is that periodically impels us to flock back to her from every point of the compass—making her the Mecca of loving pilgrimages! We who are Portsmouth born and bred never get wholly away from the glamour of early association."[1]

**1855.** Published "The Bell: A Collection of Chimes by T.B.A." The volume was entitled *The Bells,*—

> "Because in bells there something is to me
> Of rhythms and the poets of gone years—
> A sad reverberation breeding tears,
> Touching the finer chords of Memory!"[1]

Developed an affection for Longfellow.

"I was not, in those days, fond of reading poetry, though I feasted on prose. By chance a volume of poems was in my hand. It was the *Voices of the Night.* I opened it at 'The Footsteps of Angels.' Never before did I feel such a gush of emotion. The poem spoke to me like a human voice; and from that time I loved Longfellow, and I wrote poetry—such as it is."[1]

As I leaned over the rail in this mood, a measly looking little boy with no shoes said that if I would come down on the wharf he'd lick me for two cents, —not an exorbitant price. But I didn't go down. I climbed into the rigging, and stared at him. ■ (From *The Story of a Bad Boy* by Thomas Bailey Aldrich.)

**1856.** Sub-editor of the *Home Journal.* "I had no idea of what *work* is till I became 'sub.' I have found that reading proof and writing articles on uninteresting subjects, 'at sight,' is no joke. The cry for 'more copy' rings through my ears in dreams, and hosts of little phantom printer's devils walk over my body all night and prick me with sharp-pointed types. Last evening I fell asleep in my armchair and dreamed that they were about to put me 'to press,' as I used to crush flies between the leaves of my speller, in schoolboy days.

"Do you remember Parsons' traveller, who, stopping at an inn, had

> 'Little to eat and very much to pay,'

or something of the sort? I occupy a similar position. The *Home Journal's* motto is:—

> 'Pretty good pay BUT very much to do!'

I have turned from a 'literary Bohemian' . . . to that mythical and underrated individual called 'a sub.'

"But alas for Poetry!

"Pegasus refuses to trot in editorial harness, point-blank. . . .'"[1]

**1858.** Abandoned *Home Journal* to become associate editor of the *Saturday Press.*

**1860.** *Saturday Press* expired. Aldrich returned briefly to a life of authorship.

**1861.** War correspondent during the Civil War. "I have just returned from a long ride into the enemy's country. I have been on horseback two days—and two nights, I was going to say, but I did get out of the saddle to sleep. What a strange time I had of it. House of the New York *Tribune* and myself started on a reconnoissance under the wing of General Stapel and staff. We had not ridden an hour through those wonderful Virginia woods when I got separated from the party, and haven't laid eyes on 'em since—excepting Ned House, who has just reached Washington, having given me up for lost. I don't quite know how it was, but suddenly I found myself alone in a tangle of dense forest and unknown roads. Close on the rebel lines, not knowing quite in what direction, without a guide, and nothing to eat—you may imagine that I wished myself on the harmless banks of the Piscataqua. Well, I did. To crown all, a moonless night was darkening down on the terrible stillness; and as the darkness grew I caught glimpses of lurid camp-fires here and there—a kind of goblin glare which lent an indescribable mystery and unpleasantness to the scene. Whether these were the camp-fires of friend or foe I had no means of telling. I put spurs to my horse and dashed on—now by the black ruins of a burnt farmhouse, now by some shadowy ford where a fight had evidently taken place, for I saw trees that had been barked by cannon-balls, and here and there significant mounds under which slept New England braves. I did not feel alone at such places; for my fancy beheld long lines of infantry, and parks of artillery, and squares of cavalry, moving among the shadows, in a noiseless conflict. I wish I'd time to tell you of the ride—how I stole by the sentinels, and at last feeling that I was going straight to Manassas, stopt and held a council of war with T.B.A. It dawned on me that Washington lay in the *east.* The sun was sinking directly before me in the *west,* so I sensibly turned my horse and rode back. Gracious heavens! how many miles I must have ridden! To make a long story short, I slept on my horse's neck in the woods, we two lying cosily together, and at sunrise, oh so hungry, I saw far off the dome of the Capitol and the Long Bridge. Here I am, a year older in looks. I have feasted, and . . . shall go to bed and sleep three days."[1]

**1865.** Married Lilian Woodman. In 1905 he wrote: "To-morrow Lillian and I shall have been married forty years! Forty happy years with only one great sorrow. How many married pairs in this sad world can say as much?"[1]

Moved from New York to Boston where he became editor of *Every Saturday.*

**1867.** "One morning in the spring of 1867 Mr. Longfellow came to the little home in Pinckney Street, where we had set up housekeeping in the light of our honeymoon. As we lingered a moment at the dining-room door, Mr. Longfellow turning to me said, 'Ah, Mr. Aldrich, your small round table will not always be closed. By and by you will find new young faces clustering about it; as years go on, leaf after leaf will be added until the time comes when the young guests will take flight, one by one, to build nests of their own elsewhere. Gradually the long table will shrink to a circle again, leaving two old people sitting there alone together. This is the story of life, the sweet and pathetic poem of the fireside. Make an idyl of it. I give the idea to you.'

Several months afterward I received a note from Mr. Longfellow in which he expressed a desire to use this *motif* in case I had done nothing in the matter. The theme was one peculiarly adapted to his sympathetic handling, and out of it grew 'The Hanging of the Crane.'"[1]

**1868.** Twin boys born, Charles and Talbot. "I have TWO fine boys, born yesterday morning! Everything seems to be well with my wife and with the little fellows. God bless the three of them! and I am exceedingly happy."[1]

**1870.** To accommodate a larger family, ". . . I have bought a young Palace on Charles Street—cellar frescoed, coalbin inlaid with mother-of-pearl and the skulls of tax-collectors, and joyous birds, in gilded cages, in every room, warbling promissory notes to the tune of seven per-cent! . . ."[1]

Moved to Ponkapog, Mass. ". . . you ought to see *my* Mansion at Ponkapog. It couldn't have cost less than $1500 to build. And then the land. Land at Ponkapog brings $25 per acre; but then real estate has gone up of itself, if you let it alone. They have to put manure on it to keep it down. The house is furnished in a style of Oriental splendor. Straw matting everywhere—even in the servants' rooms straw matting. It's as common with us as Turkey rugs and Wilton carpets in the houses of the poor. . . . I like to see a man living within his means—and content.

". . . I never was so comfortable. . . . I've one hundred and twenty-five chickens! I have butter that would cost you a dollar per pound in New York, and milk that you cannot get at any price. . . . With the rent of the house in Charles Street, and the dollars which literature brings me, I am more independent than the late A. T. Stewart ever was. . . ."[1]

**1881.** Editorial chair of *Atlantic Monthly.* "Between the *Atlantic Monthly* business and the storming of my Charles Street house, where an unpaying tenant has intrenched himself and refuses to surrender, I have had my hands full. . . . I have a very clear understanding of the responsibilities I have assumed in taking the editorship of the *Atlantic.* I accepted the post only after making a thorough examination of my nerve and backbone. I fancy I shall do very little writing in the magazine, at first. I intend to edit it. I am lost in admiration of [William Dean] Howells, who found time to be a novelist.

"I am nearly dead with the details of office-work, and have run off to the old Indian Farm to bind up some wounds in the mind. Leaving out Sundays, and my trip to New York, I have not had a day's vacation since the first of last March. No, I haven't a novel or anything in hand, except a lyric or two which I shall print in *Harper's* Magazine. I shall not print any of my verses in the *Atlantic.* No man shall say that I crowded him out and put myself in. I find it devilish difficult to get good poems for the Maga. Our old singers have pretty much lost their voices, and the new singers are so few! My ear has not caught any new note since 1860. By Jove! I wish there were a nest of young birds in full song now! . . . I am slowly making up my mind to publish none but incontestably fine poems in the *Atlantic*—which means only about four poems per year. . . . If you could see the piles of bosh sent to this office you'd be sick at heart."[1]

**1890.** Relinquished his editorship and became a man of letters and leisure. ". . . I am so happy these days that I

**THOMAS BAILEY ALDRICH**

sometimes half suspect some calamity lurking round the corner."[1]

**November 12, 1895.** "I was 59 yesterday. It is unpleasant to be 59; but it would be unpleasanter not to be, having got started." [Mary Silva Cosgrave, "The Life and Times of Thomas Bailey Aldrich," *Horn Book,* August, 1966.[3]]

**1900.** Elder of the twin sons, Charles, married, then was afflicted with a sudden hemorrhage of the lungs and Aldrich hastened to his side in the Adirondacks. "We are very pleasantly settled and like the quiet life here. We are on the edge of the village with the mountains for our immediate neighbors. Our house, a new and spacious villa which we were lucky to get, stands on a plateau overlooking Saranac River. Two or three hundred yards away at our feet is the cottage in which [Robert Lewis] Stevenson spent the winter of '87. He didn't like Saranac Lake, and I fancy was not very popular. It is a beautiful spot, nevertheless. The sunsets and the sunrises compensate one for the solitude, which moreover has a charm of its own.

"Of all places in the world this is the place in which to read. We've taken an overgrown cottage on the outskirts of the town, which at night looks like a cluster of stars dropped into the hollow. The young Aldriches have a cottage near by, and there are two or three other houses visible—when it doesn't snow. It snows nearly all the time in a sort of unconscious way. I never saw such contradicting, irresponsible weather. It isn't cold here, for human beings, when it is 20 degrees below zero. Everything else is of course frozen stiff. The solitude is something you can cut with a knife. Icicles are our popular household pets. I am cultivating one that is already four feet long—I am training it outside, you understand, on a north gable. I feel that all this is giving you a false idea of our surroundings, which are as beautiful as a dream. Every window frames a picture of bewildering and capricious loveliness. If our dear boy only

continues to gather stength we shall have a happy winter in this little pocket-Switzerland. He is very thin and white and feeble. At times I have to turn my eyes away, but my heart keeps looking at him."[1]

**1901.** "*Dec.* 24-25, [1901]. For the last few years I have had a suspicion that there is something not at all merry in Merry Christmas—that sinister flavor which one detects in one's birthdays after one has had fifty or sixty of them. . . . This morning our boy was able to come downstairs and watch the revealing of a pathetic little Christmas tree in his front parlor. When he was brought up here on the 1st of October he was not expected to live through the journey. And now we have seen him sitting in his armchair and smiling upon the children as the gifts were plucked for them from the magical branches."[1]

**1903.** The holidays came and went—"the hollow days," he called them,—and Charles' life flickered to its close. "If anything should happen to my boy I'd never again set pen to paper. If the task were begun it would be left unfinished."[1]

**March 6, 1904.** Charles died at thirty-six of tuberculosis. In his melancholy Aldrich wrote: ". . . I've no dramatic ambition, or ambition of any kind. If everything I have written should be absolutely obliterated I shouldn't cry."[1]

**March 19, 1907.** Died in Boston, Mass. Buried in Mount Auburn Cemetery besides his son, Charles. "For myself I regard death merely as the passing shadow on a flower."[1]

*FOR MORE INFORMATION SEE:* Francis Bartlett, *Catalogue of the Works of Thomas Bailey Aldrich,* 1898, reprinted, Scholarly Press, 1976; Ferris Greenslet, *The Life of Thomas Bailey Aldrich,* Riverside Press, 1908, reprinted, Kennikat, 1965; Elizabeth Rider Montgomery, *Story behind Great Books,* McBride, 1946; Samuel Sloan Duryee, *Thomas Bailey Aldrich, 1836-1907: Inspired Poet of the Piscataqua,* Newcomen Society in North America, 1951; Charles E. Samuels, *Thomas Bailey Aldrich,* Twayne, 1965; M. S. Cosgrave, "Life and Times of Thomas Bailey Aldrich," *Horn Book,* April-August, 1966.

# ALLEE, Marjorie Hill    1890-1945

*PERSONAL:* Born June 2, 1890, in Carthage, Indiana; died April 30, 1945, in Chicago, Illinois; daughter of William B. and Ann Mary (Elliott) Hill; married Warder Clyde Allee (a zoologist), September 4, 1912; children: Warder (died, 1923), Barbara, Mary. *Education:* Earlham College, student, 1906-08; University of Chicago, Ph.B., 1911. *Religion:* Society of Friends (Quaker). *Home:* Chicago, Illinois.

*CAREER:* Author of children's books. Taught in a one-room school house for a year, at the age of eighteen; became interested in writing around 1929; strongly supported numerous civic and social organizations, helping to set up the Chicago Summer Work Camps among other projects. *Member:* League of Women Voters, Chicago Children's Reading Round Table. *Awards, honors;* Newbery Medal, runner-up, 1932, for *Jane's Island;* Child Study Association of America/Wel-Met Children's Book Award, 1944, for *The House.*

**The late fall weather was just cold enough to make hard exercise a pleasure; he worked in a glow, with hardening muscles.** ■ (From *The Road to Carolina* by Marjorie Hill Allee. Illustrated by Manning De V. Lee.)

*WRITINGS*—All published by Houghton, except as noted: (With husband, Warder Clyde Allee) *Jungle Island,* Rand McNally, 1925; *Susanna and Tristram* (illustrated by Hattie Longstreet Price; Junior Literary Guild selection), 1929, reissued, 1957; *Judith Lankester* (illustrated by H. L. Price), 1930; *Jane's Island* (illustrated by Maitland De Gogorza; Junior Literary Guild selection), 1931; *The Road to Carolina* (illustrated by Manning De V. Lee), 1932; *Ann's Surprising Summer* (illustrated by M. De Gogorza), 1933; *A House of Her Own* (illustrated by M. De V. Lee), 1934; *Off to Philadelphia!* (illustrated by David Hendrickson), 1936; *The Great Tradition* (illustrated by Cyrus Le Roy Baldridge), 1937; *The Little American Girl* (illustrated by Paul Quinn; Junior Literary Guild selection), 1938; *Runaway Linda* (illustrated by D. Hendrickson; Junior Literary Guild selection), 1939; *The Camp at Westlands* (illustrated by Erick Berry, pseudonym of Allena Champlain Best), 1941; *Winter's Mischief* (illustrated by George Gillett Whitney), 1942; *The House* (illustrated by Helen Blair), 1944; *Smoke Jumper* (illustrated by M. De V. Lee), 1945.

*SIDELIGHTS:* **June 2, 1890.** Born near Carthage, Indiana. She spent her childhood on her grandfather's farm quite alone, but she loved to read and tramp around the farm. "I grew up on the farm my great-grandfather had bought in the

early days of the state, near Carthage, Indiana, in a community of self-respecting Quakers, most of whose ancestors, like mine, had migrated from the Carolinas." [Amy Winslow, "Marjorie Hill Allee," *Horn Book,* May 1946.[1]]

**1899.** Won her first award for writing, a prize from a farm magazine. Books and magazines were more essential than a new dress. "As a member of our family, I possessed those books and they possessed me."[1]

**1906-08.** Attended Earlham College.

**1911.** Received her Ph.B. from the University of Chicago.

**1912.** Married Warder Clyde Allee, a professor of zoology at the University of Chicago. The couple had three children.

**1923.** Son, Warder, died at the age of ten in a traffic accident.

**1925.** Second daughter, Molly, born two years after the tragic death of her son. Her oldest daughter was named Barbara.

**...A big boy was presuming to differ with the teacher. Old Benny would have roared and reached for the beech rods on the rack above Catherine's desk.** ■ (From *A House of Her Own* by Marjorie Hill Allee. Illustrated by Manning De V. Lee.)

**"I'm not ha-appy," said Tristram.**

**"What is it, brother? Tell me." Susanna knelt on the floor beside his bed and smoothed his tumbled hair.**
■ (From *Susanna and Tristram* by Marjorie Hill Allee. Illustrated by Hattie Longstreet Price.)

The family spent almost every summer at Woods Hole, Massachusetts. She saw in the Marine Biological Laboratory on Cape Cod "... the scientific spirit working in bare perfection."[1] Allee used the laboratory as background for one of her best-liked stories, *Jane's Island.*

**1929. Susanna and Tristram** published. The book marked the beginning of a sixteen-year association with Houghton Mifflin. Allee's method of working was always careful, and when it came time for the actual writing, she worked with great intensity, ruthlessly budgeting her time, and completely immersing herself in the story. In *Recipe for a Book* she described her method when these characters became headstrong. "From experience with this kind of block I have learned to lapse into passivity, to hunt for some different occupation, preferably monotonous and undemanding on the mind, and let the conflict settle itself without my conscious interference. In the case of a person like myself, whose real occupation is housekeeping, this can be arranged one way or another. . . . Ironing may be indicated. This is a soothing and monotonous occupation, in which I am not likely to be much interrupted. Susanna on her old white horse first came riding toward me beyond an ironing board."[1]

**1930.** Husband was stricken with a rare malady which left him completely dependent on a wheel chair. Although the

tragedy would have crushed a lesser spirit, Allee continued her civic and social activities and her writing.

**1941-45.** As an uncompromising pacifist, Allee considered World War II, with its shattering of good-will between nations, a tragedy. She resigned from the Hyde Park League of Women Voters when that organization pledged its support of the lend-lease bill. In a public letter of protest, she criticized their support of the bill as "naive and mischievous to represent this bill . . . as the 'substitute for war which has long been sought.'"[1]

**April 30, 1945,** Died in Chicago, Illinois. One friend wrote of her: "It is rare for a person to be both intelligent and kind."

*FOR MORE INFORMATION SEE:* Amy Winslow, "Marjorie Hill Allee," *Horn Book,* May, 1946; Stanley J. Kunitz, editor, *Junior Book of Authors,* 2nd edition, revised, H. W. Wilson, 1951; (obituary) *New York Times,* May 1, 1945.

## ALLSOP, Kenneth 1920-1973

*PERSONAL:* Born January 29, 1920, in Leeds, Yorkshire, England; son of John and Mary Ann (Halliday) Allsop; married Betty Creak, 1942; children: Tristan Andrew Lindley, Amanda Susan, Fabian Halliday. *Education:* Privately edu-

**When they were swung back on deck, they could utter hardly a sound from shock and cold.** ■ (From *Last Voyages of the Mayflower: A Story of the Pilgrims' Ship* by Kenneth Allsop. Illustrated by Norman Guthrie Rudolph.)

cated. *Home:* Gurneys, Holwell, Hitchin, Hertfordshire, England. *Agent:* Sterling Lord Agency, 75 East 55th St., New York, N.Y. 10022. *Office:* British Broadcasting Corporation, Broadcasting House, London, W.1, England.

*CAREER:* Press Association, reporter, 1948-50; *Picture Post,* feature writer, 1950-55; *Independent Television News,* reporter and commentator, 1955-57; *London Evening Standard,* feature writer and columnist, 1955-57; *London Daily Mail,* literary editor and book critic, 1957-64; British Broadcasting Corporation, London, "Twenty-four Hours" television program, resident interviewer, 1960—. *Military service:* Royal Air Force, 1940-43. *Awards, honors:* John Llewellyn Rhys Memorial Prize for his novel, *Adventure Lit Their Star,* 1950.

*WRITINGS: Adventure Lit Their Star,* Latimer House, 1949, revised edition, Macdonald, 1962, Crown, 1964; *The Sun Himself Must Die* (short stories), Latimer House, 1950; *The Daybreak Edition,* Percival Marshall, 1951; *Silver Flame,* Percival Marshall, 1951; *The Last Voyages of the Mayflower,* Winston, 1955; *The Angry Decade* (criticism), British Book Center, 1958; *Rare Bird,* Hutchinson, 1958; (with Robert Pitman) *A Question of Obscenity,* Scorpion Press, 1960; *The Bootleggers and Their Era,* Doubleday, 1961; *Scan* (collected journalism), Hodder & Stoughton, 1965. Records columnist for *Nova.* Regular contributor to *The Spectator, Encounter, Twentieth Century, New York Times,* and *Daily Telegraph.*

*WORK IN PROGRESS: Hard Travellin',* a study of the American migrant worker, for Hodder & Stoughton.

*HOBBIES AND OTHER INTERESTS:* Ornithology and jazz.

(Died May 25, 1973)

**GEOFFREY ASHE**

**Sir Belvedere casts away Excalibur.** ■ (From *King Arthur in Fact and Legend* by Geoffrey Ashe. Illustrated by Aubrey Beardsley.)

## ASHE, Geoffrey (Thomas) 1923-

*PERSONAL:* Born March 29, 1923, in London, England; son of Arthur William (a travel agency general manager) and Thelma (Hoodless) Ashe; married Dorothy Irene Train (now a teacher), May 3, 1946; children: Thomas, John, Michael, Sheila, Brendan. *Education:* St. Paul's School, Hammersmith, England; University of British Columbia, B.A. (first class honours), 1943; Trinity College, Cambridge University, B.A., first in English tripos, 1948. *Religion:* Catholic. *Home:* Chalice Orchard, Well House Lane, Glastonbury, Somerset, England. *Agent:* A. D. Peters, 10 Buckingham St., London W.C.2, England.

*CAREER:* Polish University College, London, England, lecturer in English, 1948-50; Newman Neame (publishers), London, industrial research assistant, 1949-51; Ford Motor Co. of Canada, Windsor, Ontario, Canada, administrative assistant, 1952-54; Post Office Department, Toronto, Ontario, Canada, technical officer, 1954-55; The Polytechnic, London, England, lecturer in management studies, 1956-68. *Member:* Royal Society of Literature (fellow), Camelot Research Committee (secretary), Glastonbury Assembly Rooms Trust (chairman).

*WRITINGS: The Tale of the Tub: A Survey of the Art of Bathing Through the Ages,* Newman Neame, 1950; *King Arthur's Avalon,* Collins, 1957; *From Caesar to Arthur,* Collins, 1960; *Land to the West,* Collins, 1962; *The Land and the Book,* Collins, 1965; *The Carmelite Order,* Carmelite Press, 1965; *Gandhi,* Stein & Day, 1968; *The Quest for Ar-*

*thur's Britain,* Pall Mall Press, 1968; *All About King Arthur,* W. H. Allen, 1969, published in the United States under the title *King Arthur in Fact and Legend,* Nelson, 1969; *Camelot and the Vision of Albion,* Heinemann, 1971; *The Art of Writing Made Simple,* W. H. Allen, 1972; *The Finger and the Moon,* Heinemann, 1973; *Do What You Will,* W. H. Allen, 1974; *The Virgin,* Routledge and Kegan Paul, 1976; *The Ancient Wisdom,* Macmillan, 1977. Author of play, "The Glass Island," 1964. Contributor to various periodicals; columnist in *Resurgence* magazine, 1973-78.

*WORK IN PROGRESS: Guidebook to Arthurian Britain.*

# BROOKE, L(eonard) Leslie    1862-1940

*PERSONAL:* Sometimes listed as Leslie Brooke; born September 24, 1862, in Birkenhead, Cheshire, England; died May 1, 1940; son of Leonard D. Brooke; married Sybil Diana Brooke (a cousin), 1894; children: Leonard (died, 1918), Henry. *Education:* Attended the Royal Academy Schools in London, England. *Home:* Hampstead, England.

*CAREER:* Professional painter; illustrator; author.

*WRITINGS*—All self-illustrated: *Johnny Crow's Garden: A Picture Book,* Warne, 1903, reprinted, 1961; *Johnny Crow's Party: Another Picture Book,* Warne, 1907, reprinted, 1967; *Johnny Crow's New Garden,* Warne, 1935, reprinted, 1956; *Leslie Brooke's Little Books,* Warne, 1950.

Illustrator: Mary Louisa Molesworth, *Nurse Heatherdale's Story,* Macmillan, 1891; Molesworth, *The Girls and I: A Veracious History,* Macmillan, 1892; Molesworth, *Stories*

**L. LESLIE BROOKE**

**"I have indeed emptied a cask of wine, but what is a drop like that to a thirsty man?"** ■ (From *The Golden Goose Book.* Illustrated by L. Leslie Brooke.)

*for Children* (illustrated with Walter Crane), Macmillan, 1893; Molesworth, *Mary,* Macmillan, 1893; Molesworth, *My New Home,* Macmillan, 1894; Molesworth, *The Carved Lions,* Macmillan, 1895; Molesworth, *The Oriel Window,* Macmillan, 1896; Molesworth, *Miss Mouse and Her Boys: A Story for Girls,* Macmillan, 1897; Andrew Lang, editor, *The Nursery Rhyme Book,* Warne, 1897, new edition, Dover, 1972; Robert Browning, *Pippa Passes* (poem), Duckworth, 1898; Thomas Nash, *A Spring Story,* Dent, 1898.

Edward Lear, *The Pelican Chorus and Other Nonsense Verses,* Warne, 1900, reprinted, 1954 [also see below]; Lear, *The Jumblies and Other Nonsense Verses,* Warne, 1900, reprinted, 196? [also see below]; Lear, *Nonsense Songs,* Warne, 1900, reprinted, circa 1969 (contains *The Pelican Chorus* and *The Jumblies*); Eleanor G. Hayden, *Travels Round Our Village: A Berkshire Book,* Constable, 1901; Sir George Francis Hill, *The Truth about Old King Cole, and Other Very Natural Histories,* Warne, 1910, reprinted, 1931; Lawrence P. Jacks, *Mad Shepherds, and Other Human Studies,* Williams & Norgate, 1923; Anthony Trollope, *Barchester Towers,* Gresham, 1924; Robert H. Charles, *A Roundabout Turn* (poems), Warne, 1930; Jakob L. K. Grimm and Wilhelm K. Grimm, *The House in the Wood, and Other Old Fairy Stories,* Warne, 1909, reprinted, 1947.

Traditional rhymes and fairy tales; all published by Warne: *The Story of the Three Little Pigs,* 1904; *Tom Thumb,* 1904; *The Story of the Three Bears,* 1904; *The Golden Goose Book,* 1904, reprinted, circa 1964; *The Tailor and the Crow: An Old Rhyme with New Drawings,* 1911, reprinted, circa, 1956; *A Nursery Rhyme Picture Book,* 1913, reprinted, circa 1959; *The Man in the Moon: A Nursery Rhyme Picture Book,* 1913, reprinted, circa 1964; *Oranges and Lemons: A Nursery Rhyme Picture Book,* 1913, reprinted, circa 1964; *Ring o' Roses,* 1922, reprinted, circa 1958; *Little Bo-Peep: A Nursery Rhyme Picture Book,* circa 1964. Also illustrator of the following books published by Warne: *Art Fairy Stories;*

**Wee Willie Winkie runs through the town,**
**Upstairs and downstairs in his nightgown,**
**Rapping at the window, crying through the lock,**
**"Are the children in their beds, for now it's eight o'clock?"**

■ (From *Little Bo Peep: A Nursery Rhyme Picture Book* by L. Leslie Brooke. Illustrated by the author.)

*Warne's Colored Fairy Tales* (illustrated with Henry M. Brock); and *This Little Pig Went to Market: A Nursery Rhyme Picture Book*.

ADAPTATIONS—Filmstrips: "Johnny Crow's Garden" (sound filmstrip, record or cassette, text booklet), Weston Woods; "The Three Little Pigs" (one filmstrip of a four filmstrip set, average number of frames: 76, average running time: 10 min., records or cassettes; also one captioned filmstrip of a four filmstrip set, average frames: 61), Walt Disney, (one filmstrip of a four filmstrip set, sound color, 69 frames each), Encyclopaedia Britannica.

Recordings: "The Three Little Pigs" (record and cassette, ten storybooks, teacher's guide), Walt Disney; "The Three Little Pigs" (rehearsal and performance record, teacher's guide, twenty reading scripts), Doubleday Multimedia; "The Three Little Pigs and Other Fairy Tales," read by Boris Karloff (six cassettes, teacher's guide), Caedmon.

SIDELIGHTS: **September 24, 1862.** Born in Birkenhead, Cheshire, England. "I was born at Birkenhead and received most of my art training at the Schools of the Royal Academy in London. My brother and I were always drawing—like any other children—and I went on drawing; there is my whole story." [Anne Carroll Moore, "L. Leslie Brooke," *Horn Book*, May, 1941.[1]]

**1894.** Married Sybil Brooke, his cousin.

**1901.** Illustrated *Travels Round Our Village: A Birkshire Book*, an adult book. "As to the drawings which were mostly done at the turn of the century, . . . I think that they have caught something of the hard roughness of surface of the Berkshire village life that is unconscious of its own underlying humanity. 'The Village' was West Hundred, but the book, both in text and illustrations, is an amalgam of three neighbouring villages—West and East Hundred and Harwell (where we ourselves lived) and there are few figures in my share that were not drawn directly from, or from memory of,

They **sailed away for a year and a day.... ■** (From *Nonsense Songs* by Edward Lear. Illustrated by L. Leslie Brooke.)

**Well, the little Pig woke at four the next morning, and bustled up, and went off for the apples, hoping to get back before the Wolf came; but he had farther to go, and had to climb the tree, so that just as he was coming down from it, he saw the Wolf coming, which, as you may suppose, frightened him very much. ■** (From *The Three Little Pigs* by L. Leslie Brooke. Illustrated by the author.)

individual inhabitants, if not always from the same person that the author had in mind. Possibly had the illustrations been done with less respect for fact they might have been more amusing."[1]

**1903.** Brooke, who became known for his gentle humor and detailed animal sketches, had his first major success, *Johnny Crow's Garden: A Picture Book*. "There never was a time when the name of Johnny Crow was not familiar to me, yet I had never thought of making a picutre book of his garden until Mrs. Brooke suggested it."[1]

**1918.** Son, Leonard, killed in World War I. Felt out of touch with children, unable to complete illustrations for the book he was working on.

**May 1, 1940.** Died.

FOR MORE INFORMATION SEE: *Horn Book,* special issue, May, 1941; Stanley J. Kunitz and Howard Haycraft, editors, *Junior Book of Authors,* Wilson, 2nd edition, 1951; A. C. Moore, "Leslie Brooke: Pied Piper of English Picture Books," and L. H. Smith, "A Canadian Tribute to Leslie Brooke," both reprinted in *A Horn Book Sampler on Children's Books and Reading,* edited by Norma R. Fryatt, Horn Book, 1959.

## BROOKS, Walter R(ollin)   1886-1958

PERSONAL: Born January 9, 1886, in Rome, New York; died August 17, 1958; son of William Walter and Fannie (Stevens) Brooks; married Anne Shepard, January 22, 1909 (deceased); married Dorothy Carman Collins, January 6,

"Nevertheless, their crimes and offenses have nothing to do with the case which we are now considering, and I wish you, in listening to their evidence, to make up your opinion without reference to any prejudice you may have against them on that score. It is Jinx who is being tried now, not the rats. Do I make myself clear?" ▪ (From *Freddy the Detective* by Walter R. Brooks. Illustrated by Kurt Wiese.)

1953. *Education:* University of Rochester, student, 1904-06; Homeopathic Medical College, New York City, student, 1906-08. *Home:* Roxbury, New York.

*CAREER:* Writer. Began writing as a child; became associate editor of *Outlook,* 1928-32; worked on the editorial staff of several magazines, including *New Yorker,* 1933, and *Fiction Parade,* 1933-37; employed for a time in the field of publicity and advertising. *Member:* Delta Kappa Epsilon.

*WRITINGS*—Fiction except as noted: *New York: An Intimate Guide* (nonfiction), Knopf, 1931; *Ernestine Takes Over: A Novel* (illustrated by Herbert Roese), Morrow, 1935; *The Story of Freginald* (illustrated by Kurt Wiese), Knopf, 1936; *The Clockwork Twin* (illustrated by K. Wiese), Knopf, 1937; *Jenny and the King of Smithia* (illustrated by Decie Merwin), Grosset, 1947; *Henry's Dog Henry* (illustrated by Aldren A. Watson), Knopf, 1965; *Jimmy Takes Vanishing Lessons* (illustrated by Don Bolognese; first published in *Story Parade Magazine*), Knopf, 1965.

"Freddy" series; published by Knopf; illustrated by Kurt Wiese, except as noted: *To and Again* (illustrated by Adolfo Best-Maugard), 1927, new edition published as *Freddy Goes to Florida,* 1964; *More To and Again,* 1930, reissued as *Freddy Goes to the North Pole,* 1959; *Freddy the Detective,* 1932; *Wiggins for President,* 1939, reissued as *Freddy the Politician,* 1948; *Freddy's Cousin Weedly,* 1940; *Freddy and the Ignormus,* 1941; . . . *and the Perilous Adventure,* 1942; . . . *and the Bean Home News,* 1943; . . . *and Mr. Camphor,* 1944; . . . *and the Popinjay,* 1945; . . . *the Pied Pier,* 1946; . . . *the Magician,* 1947; . . . *Goes Camping,* 1948; . . . *Plays Football,* 1949; . . . *the Cowboy,* 1950; . . . *Rides Again,*

1951; . . . *the Pilot,* 1952; *The Collected Poems of Freddy the Pig,* 1953; *Freddy and the Space Ship,* 1953; . . . *and the Men from Mars,* 1954; . . . *and the Baseball Team from Mars,* 1955; . . . *and Simon the Dictator,* 1956; . . . *and the Flying Saucer Plans,* 1957; . . . *and the Dragon,* 1958.

Also contributor of fiction to various magazines.

*SIDELIGHTS:* Born and raised in Rome, New York, Brooks began writing as a child when he and his friends would create and produce their own neighborhood plays. During his teenage years he attended a military school near Peekskill, the University of Rochester for two years, and then left for New York City to study medicine.

After two years at Homeopathic Medical College in New York City, he abandoned medicine to marry Anne Shepard.

Brooks' first children's book was published in 1927. From that time until his death in 1958, he continued to write well over thirty books for children. Besides children's books, Brooks worked on the editorial staff of several magazines and was also employed in the publicity and advertising fields. His home before his death was in Roxbury, New York. ". . . No one ever Tells All. He merely Tells All He Knows." [Walter R. Brooks, *New York: An Intimate Guide,* Knopf, 1931.[1]]

*FOR MORE INFORMATION SEE:* Stanley J. Kunitz, editor, *Junior Book of Authors,* revised edition, H. W. Wilson, 1951; Obituaries—*New York Times,* August 19, 1958; *Publishers Weekly,* September 8, 1958; *Wilson Library Bulletin,* October, 1958.

**He wore a dress with big roses all over it which he had pulled right on over Mr. Camphor's suit.** ■ (From *Freddy Goes Camping* by Walter R. Brooks. Illustrated by Kurt Wiese.)

# BURGESS, Thornton W(aldo)    1874-1965 (W. B. Thornton)

*PERSONAL:* Born January 14, 1874, in Sandwich, Massachusetts; died June 5, 1965; son of Thornton Waldo and Caroline F. (Hayward) Burgess; married Nina E. Osborne, June 30, 1905 (died, 1906); married Fannie P. Johnson, April 30, 1911; children: (first marriage) Thornton Waldo. *Education:* Graduated from high school in 1891; attended business college in Boston for one year. *Residence:* Hampden, Massachusetts.

*CAREER:* Editor and author of books for children. Held early jobs as a cashier and assistant bookkeeper in a shoe store. Began working for the Phelps Publishing Company, as an office boy, 1895, becoming a reporter for one of the firm's weekly magazines, 1895-1911, and literary and household editor for Orange Judd weeklies, 1901-11. Burgess was an associate editor of *Good Housekeeping*, 1904-11, and founded and directed the Burgess Radio Nature League, where for six years he gave weekly talks. *Awards, honors:* Litt. D., from Northwestern University, 1938.

*WRITINGS*—"Old Mother West Wind" series, published by Little, Brown: *Old Mother West Wind* (illustrated by George Kerr), 1910, reissued, 1960; *Mother West Wind's Children* (illustrated by George Kerr), 1911 [another edition illustrated by Harrison Cady, 1962]; *Mother West Wind's Animal Friends* (illustrated by Kerr), 1912; *Mother West Wind's Neighbors* (illustrated by George Kerr), 1913 [another edition illustrated by H. Cady, 1968]; *Mother West Wind "Why" Stories* (illustrated by Harrison Cady), 1915; *Mother West Wind "How" Stories* (illustrated by Cady), 1916; *Mother West Wind "When" Stories* (illustrated by Harrison Cady), 1917; *Mother West Wind "Where" Stories* (illustrated by Harrison Cady), 1918.

"Boy Scouts" series, published by Penn Publishing: *The Boy Scouts of Woodcraft Camp* (illustrated by C. S. Corson), 1912; *The Boy Scouts on Swift River* (illustrated by C. S. Corson), 1913; *The Boy Scouts on Lost Trail* (illustrated by C. S. Corson), 1914; *The Boy Scouts in a Trapper's Camp* (illustrated by F. A. Anderson), 1915.

"Bedtime Story-Books" series, all original editions published by Little, Brown and illustrated by Harrison Cady, except as noted: *The Adventures of Johnny Chuck*, 1913; . . . *of Reddy Fox*, 1913; . . . *of Unc' Billy Possum*, 1914; . . . *of Mr. Mocker*, 1914; . . . *of Jerry Muskrat*, 1914, reissued, Grosset & Dunlap, 1962; . . . *of Peter Cottontail*, 1914, reissued, Grosset & Dunlap, 1970 [an abridged edition illustrated by Phoebe Erickson, Grosset & Dunlap, 1967]; . . . *of Grandfather Frog*, 1915; . . . *of Chatterer, the Red Squirrel*, 1915; . . . *of Danny Meadow Mouse*, 1915; . . . *of Sammy Jay*, 1915, reissued, Grosset & Dunlap, 1962; . . . *of Old Mr. Toad*, 1916; . . . *of Old Man Coyote*, 1916, reissued, Grosset & Dunlap, 1962; . . . *of Buster Bear*, 1916; . . . *of Prickly Porky*, 1916; . . . *of Poor Mrs. Quack*, 1917, reissued, Grosset & Dunlap, 1962; . . . *of Paddy the Beaver*, 1917; . . . *of Jimmy Skunk*, 1918; . . . *of Bobby Coon*, 1918; . . . *of Ol' Mistah Buzzard*, 1919; . . . *of Bob White*, 1919.

"Wishing Stone" series—all illustrated by Harrison Cady: *Tommy and the Wishing Stone*, Century, 1915, reissued, Grosset & Dunlap, 1959; *Tommy's Change of Heart*, Little, Brown, 1921, reissued, Grosset & Dunlap, 1959; *Tommy's Wishes Come True*, Little, Brown, 1921, reissued, Grosset & Dunlap, 1959; "Green Meadow" series—published by Little, Brown; all illustrated by Harrison Cady: *Happy Jack*, 1918; *Mrs. Peter Rabbit*, 1919; *Old Granny Fox*, 1920; *Bowser the Hound*, 1920; "Green Forest" series—published by Little, Brown, except as noted; all illustrated by Harrison Cady: *Lightfoot the Deer*, 1921; *Whitefoot, the Wood Mouse*, 1922, reissued, Grosset & Dunlap, 1962; *Blacky the Crow*, 1922; *Buster Bear's Twins*, 1923, reissued, Grosset & Dunlap, 1970.

"Smiling Pool" series—published by Little, Brown, except as noted; all illustrated by Harrison Cady: *Billy Mink*, 1924; *Little Joe Otter*, 1925; *Jerry Muskrat at Home*, 1926, reissued, Grosset & Dunlap, 1962; *Longlegs the Heron*, 1927; "Little Color Classics" series—published by McLoughlin; all illustrated by Harrison Cady: *Little Pete's Adventure*, 1941; *Little Red's Adventure*, 1942; *Little Chuck's Adventure*, 1942.

Animal stories—all illustrated by Harrison Cady, except as noted: *The Burgess Animal Book for Children* (illustrated by Louis Agassiz Fuertes), Little, Brown, 1920, reissued, Grosset & Dunlap, 1965; *The Christmas Reindeer* (illustrated by Rhoda Chase), Macmillan, 1926; *Happy Jack Squirrel Helps Unc' Billy*, Stoll & Edwards, 1928; *Grandfather Frog Gets a Ride*, Stoll & Edwards, 1928; *A Great Joke in Jimmy Skunk*, Stoll & Edwards, 1928; *The Neatness of Bobby Coon*, Stoll & Edwards, 1928; *Baby Possum's*

*Queer Voyage,* Stoll & Edwards, 1928; *Digger the Badger Decides to Stay,* Stoll & Edwards, 1928.

*Tales from the Storyteller's House* (illustrated by Lemuel Palmer), Little, Brown, 1937; *While the Story-Log Burns* (illustrated by Palmer), Little, Brown, 1938; *The Three Little Bears,* Platt & Munk, 1940; *Reddy Fox's Sudden Engagement,* Platt & Munk, 1940; *Peter Rabbit Proves a Friend,* Platt & Munk, 1940; *Paddy's Surprise Visitor,* Platt & Munk, 1940; *Bobby Coon's Mistake,* Platt & Munk, 1940; *Young Flash, the Deer,* Platt & Munk, 1940; *Animal Stories* (illustrated by Harrison Cady), Platt & Munk, 1942, reissued as *The Animal World of Thornton Burgess,* 1961; *Baby Animal Stories* (illustrated by P. Erickson), Grosset & Dunlap, 1949; *Peter Rabbit and Reddy Fox* (illustrated by Mary and Carl Hauge), Wonder Books, 1954.

Nature stories: *The Burgess Bird Book for Children* (illustrated by L. A. Fuertes), Little, Brown, 1919, reissued, Grosset & Dunlap, 1965; *The Burgess Flower Book for Children,* Little, Brown, 1923; *The Burgess Seashore Book for Children* (illustrated by W. H. Southwick and George Sutton), Little, Brown, 1929; *Wild Flowers We Know,* Whitman, 1929; *On the Green Meadows: A Book of Nature Stories* (illustrated by Harrison Cady), Little, Brown, 1944; *At the Smiling Pool: A Book of Nature Stories* (illustrated by Harrison Cady), Little, Brown, 1945; *The Crooked Little Path: A Book of Nature Stories* (illustrated by Harrison Cady), Little, Brown, 1946; *The Dear Old Briar Patch: A Book of Nature Stories* (illustrated by Harrison Cady), Little, Brown, 1947; *Along Laughing Brook: A Book of Nature Stories* (illustrated by Harrison Cady), Little, Brown, 1949; *Nature Almanac* (illustrated by P. Erickson), Grosset & Dunlap, 1949; *At Paddy Beaver's Pond: A Book of Nature Stories* (illustrated by Harrison Cady), Little, Brown, 1950; *The Littlest Christmas Tree* (illustrated by M. and C. Hauge), Wonder Books, 1954; *The Burgess Book of Nature Lore: Adventures of Tommy, Sue, and Sammy with Their Friends of Meadow, Pool, and Forest* (illustrated by Robert Candy), Little, Brown, 1965.

Other: (Author of text with others) *The Bride's Primer: Being a Series of Quaint Parodies on the Ways of Brides and Their Misadventures Interlarded with Useful Hints for Their Advantage* (illustrated by F. Strothmann), Phelps Publishing, 1905; *The Burgess Big Book of Green Meadow Stories* (illustrated by Harrison Cady), Little, Brown, 1932; *The Wishing-Stone Stories* (illustrated by Harrison Cady), Little, Brown, 1935; *A Robber Meets His Match,* Platt & Munk, 1940; *A Thornton Burgess Picture Book* (illustrated by Nino Carbe), Garden City Publishing, 1950; *Aunt Sally's Friends in Fur; or, The Woodhouse Night Club* (with photographs by the author), Little, Brown, 1955; *Stories around the Year* (illustrated by P. Erickson), Grosset & Dunlap, 1955; *50 Favorite Burgess Stories: On the Green Meadows* [and] *The Crooked Little Path* (illustrated by Harrison Cady), Grosset & Dunlap, 1956; *Bedtime Stories* (illustrated by C. and M. Hauge), Grosset & Dunlap, 1959; *Now I Remember: Autobiography of an Amateur Naturalist,* Little, Brown, 1960; *The Million Little Sunbeams* (illustrated by Harrison Cady), Six Oaks Press, 1963.

Contributor to magazines, including *Country Life in America* (under pseudonym W. B. Thornton), and *Good Housekeeping.*

*ADAPTATIONS*—Recording: "The Adventures of Jimmy Skunk" (phonotape; 90 minutes), Taped Books Project, 1973.

*SIDELIGHTS:* **January 14, 1874.** Born in Sandwich, Massachusetts. "I was born on old Cape Cod. . . . To a certain extent man is a reflection of his environment. It exerts an influence on his character and development that he cannot escape. He may not be aware of it. He may scoff at the idea of it. But it is there, working through his subconsciousness all through life. Especially is this true of the environment of his youth. If this has been spent in a fixed locality, say the land of his birth, he is for better or worse as much a product of his native soil as other living things that spring from it. The atmosphere of his surroundings is an intangible but powerful factor in his growth and development.

"I am a Cape Codder by birth and by inheritance through a long unbroken line of ancestors back to Thomas Burgess, one of the founders of the oldest town on the Cape, Sandwich. . . . It has been said that Cape Codders by birth rather than by adoption have salt in their hair, sand between their toes, and herring blood in their veins. Of these they never wholly rid themselves, nor do they want to.

". . . It is true that those who have spent the greater part of their lives far from the Cape return to it at intervals. They must. It is the homing urge of the herring that brooks no denial. They are subject to fits of nostalgia for which there is no known cure. It may be brought on by the high whine of wind around a corner of buildings; by the fierce spate of rain against a window; by the honking of wild geese in the airways above the city. Others may boast of their ancestry but the pride of the born Cape Codder is the land of his birth.

"In this there is something elementary, something of pounding surf, of shifting sands, the taste of salt on the lips, the flash of sun on distant dunes, the mingled smells of marsh muck, salt hay, and stranded fish, the mewing of gulls, the whistling of shore birds, the restless rise and fall of the tides, the silvery gleam of fresh waters in emerald settings, the resinous odor of scrub pines. I am sure that no man who was born and grew up on the Cape ever doubts that having created the rest of the world, God made Cape Cod and called it blessed.

"It is a land where the wind-whipped sand of the shore bites and stings, the beach grass cuts, and the facts of life are hard; but where the sky is blue, the air is soft, and the harshness of life is tempered by faith—it is where the real and the unreal meet, and the impossible becomes probable. One can believe anything on the Cape, a blessed relief from the doubts and uncertainties of the present-day turmoil of the outer world. If in truth there is a sea serpent, sooner or later it will be cast up on the shores of Cape Cod. If there are mermaids—when I am on the Cape I believe in them devotedly—it is there they will be found. I myself have seen there a red-and-white whale, striped like a barber's pole. And if a striped whale, why not a sea serpent and mermaids? Why not indeed?

"In this atmosphere I was born and spent my boyhood. From it I have never wholly escaped. I can still close my eyes and see sea serpents and mermaids and striped whales. Though in my writing I strive not to deviate from the prosaic facts as Mother Nature presents them, I cannot avoid seeing them myself in the enchanted atmosphere in which I made my first field observation and whales became red-and-white for all time. Looking back through the years, I wonder if it was not then that the pattern of my life was set.

"It was my very good fortune to be born minus the proverbial silver spoon and to spend my formative years in a

**THE CROOKED LITTLE PATH** begins at the edge of the woods and winds among the trees far into the Green Forest to the Great Mountain. It makes sudden bends this way and that way. It twists and turns around stumps and big rocks. It climbs little hills and runs down the other sides....It wouldn't do to go to bed on a full stomach so Old Mother Nature had taken away his appetite. He may not have known this but it was so. Had he been hungry he would have had an excuse, a good excuse, for not going to bed. And he was sleepy although he wouldn't admit it even to himself. It was bedtime but he didn't want to go to bed, and he didn't intend to go to bed—yet. That is what he told himself anyway. ■ (From *The Crooked Little Path* by Thornton W. Burgess. Illustrated by Harrison Cady.)

lovely small village before the era of too much and too fast. For this I have long been thankful. In those days a penny was regarded with respect, to the unskilled a dime represented a full hour of honest work, and a quarter of a dollar was, to me, a small fortune.

"My father died when I was nine months old. Mother and I spent the first few years in the home where she had lived from the time when she was left an orphan at four years of age until she married. An aunt and uncle had taken her in as a daughter, and they were, and in my memory still are, 'Grandfather and Grandmother.' He was Charles C. P. Waterman. He had come to Sandwich as clerk of the Boston and Sandwich Glass Company soon after the factory was started by Deming Jarvis." [Thornton Waldo Burgess, *Now I Remember: Autobiography of an Amateur Naturalist*, Little, Brown, 1960.[1]]

**1891.** ". . . In a class of nine I graduated from the Sandwich high school. I did not know then, for I had dreams of college, that it was to be my alma mater. . . . I find it of interest that of the six boys and three girls in that graduating class, two boys were to become authors of books, one a successful newspaperman, in time dean of the political reporters at the State House, one a local news reporter, and one of the girls a successful teacher in the local schools. Of these only one had the benefit of a college education.

"Mother was unable to attend the graduation exercises, a bitter disappointment to both of us. In the years ahead she was to have a very large and vital part in such success as I attained. It was her faith, her never-failing encouragement, her constant self-denial that made possible our independence on a very meager income. Alas, she was not to live to share in the honors that ultimately came to me. Much as these have meant to me . . . they would have meant infinitely more could I have shared them with Mother.

"The summer and winter following graduation I worked in a village grocery store, taking my turn on the delivery wagon far out in the country in all sorts of weather. The following summer I tried a business venture of my own. With rented horse and wagon I peddled fresh fruit obtained from a wholesale house in Boston. I just about broke even. But I had dividends of a sort. There was a lot of leftover fruit to eat, and I always was fond of fruit. Meanwhile Mother kept on with her candy business insofar as health permitted.

"After long and prayerful consideration we agreed that our mutual dream of a college education for me must be given up. There were no visible opportunities for a business career in the home town. We had to face the hard fact that I must find a place for myself out in the world at large. The mere thought made us both homesick. I was of a somewhat bashful and retiring disposition, definitely not a go-getter.

"Grandfather offered to finance a term at a commercial school in Boston. A retired successful country merchant, the dear old man could see little if any practical value in higher education. A school of business training was a wholly different matter. He was glad to help with that. Sometimes I wonder what he would have done had he had the prescience in those early days to foresee my inborn distaste for practical business and inability to grasp its fundamental principles.

"Be that as it may, our household goods were shipped to Somerville, a suburb of Boston, where Mother and I started housekeeping in a small apartment. That winter I commuted to Boston by horsecar, the electric trolley not having

reached Somerville. Enrolled in a well-known business school, I spent the winter trying to master bookkeeping and learning to hate figures, of which I never was overly fond. Nor did my handwriting grow appreciably more like the beautiful penmanship I desperately but vainly endeavored to copy.

"The net result was that at the end of the term I became the unhappy cashier and more unhappy assistant bookkeeper in a well-known Boston shoe store. The salary paid for my carfare and lunches and required no bookkeeping to keep track of.

"A hectic summer followed. There were three partners in the business, all baseball fans. When home games were scheduled it was an almost daily occurrence for one or another of the partners to grab a five-dollar or larger bill from the till and rush off to the game, forgetting to leave a memorandum if I happened to be elsewhere. I would go home to fret and worry over the shortage in the day's account until the next day discreet and diplomatic inquiries would straighten the matter out. At the end of each month the books must be balanced and this meant an evening or two of extra work without overtime pay. There was, however, an allowance of fifty cents for supper. I learned at that time how much can be squeezed out of half a dollar. It was worth learning.

"Sometimes when there was a shortage of salesmen I helped out on the floor. There I made another discovery—I disliked selling as much as I did trying to get the same answer twice to a column of figures. In short, the unpleasant fact that I was a misfit in the business world was rubbed into me rather painfully every day, and there seemed to be nothing I could do about it. I knew of no other activity that might permit me to make a happier living. I knew beyond any doubt what I didn't want to do, but got no glimmer at all of what I might like to do. . . .

"Mother was not well enough to continue housekeeping. We were obliged to give up the apartment and she went to Springfield to live with her sister. For the first time we were parted. It was difficult and saddening for both. I secured a small hall bedroom in a private home in Somerville and of course continued to work in Boston. Those were lean days, lonesome days, to a considerable degree dark days. The period of distrustful seeking to find the as yet undiscovered self usually is a time of darkness."[1]

**May 27, 1894.** He wrote his mother:

"My precious Mother:

"Well, everything is over now and we must make the best of it. I've gotten quite nicely settled now and think I shall like it very well, but of course it is not a home. I told you I could get all my clothes in that washstand and I was right. It is exceedingly quiet here which I thoroughly appreciate. As small as the room is I don't know as I would care for a much larger one.

"June 3—Yes, it is but very little more than a week since you left but it seems a long, long time ago we were breaking up the home that meant so much to both of us and where we were planning this and that for the future. However, you must keep bright as you can, dear, knowing that I am well cared for at present and that the future is in God's keeping only. . . .

"That Christmas I did get to spend with Mother. . . . Then comes a gap in the letters to the following summer. That found me job-seeking. To complete the situation I suffered a serious attack of malaria. Under date of July 9, 1895, I wrote [to mother]:

"I received a very nice letter from Grandma and with it $10. It was a godsend, for I never was so hard up in my life. Uncle Charlie also made me a present of $5 and would take no refusal. It hurts me to take it all. I must not be discouraged but must keep a good heart and will come out right, says Grandmother. She is very glad I am well and oh, remarkable, says that health is more to be desired than riches. I have had a haircut and shampoo. Oh luxury! Couldn't afford it before. Have no work as yet but am watching every chance. Am living on faith, hope and doughnuts. The first two are not very satisfying. The third fills space. Well dear, am trying not to be discouraged and am staving off the blues, though last week I was in a very tight hole. Keep a brave heart and all will be well.

"About this time I began writing bits of verse, rhymes . . . for my own amusement. From early years I had been a great reader and fond of poetry, but I do not recall that in school days I was much given to producing the doggerel that so often is a phase of adolescence. I do recall that in those early days I did some alleged humorous verses that were published in a house organ of a Boston concern that employed a cousin of mine, my first appearance in print.

"Now in these days of floundering uncertainty I found a form of relief in turning rhymester, in seeking self-expression in verse. *Forest and Stream,* a well-known sporting periodical, published some verses of mine to a four-pound trout that I had yet to catch. Then *Recreation,* at that time in its early struggling days, gave an illustrated two-page spread to my 'When the Scoters Fly.' In each case the honorarium was a complimentary copy of the magazine. But that was compensation enough—it was recognition; I saw my name in type as an accredited author.

"Business depression resulting in curtailment of help cost me my job. For weeks I lived on little, daily scanned the wanted columns in the papers, and made the rounds of the employment agencies. Somehow a copy of a small paper called *Brains,* devoted to advertising, fell in my hands. On impulse I bought a couple of inches of space in its columns and therein advertised in verse my services as a writer of advertising copy in verse:

> "SAVE TIME, LABOR
> AND TROUBLE
>
> " Get a good man
> That can wield a good pen:
> Let him advertise for you,
> Tho' it cost you a ten!
>
> "And in that way you will
> save all three. Try my work,
> and if not satisfactory, just
> return it. Ads in rhyme a
> specialty.
>
> T. W. BURGESS
> 12 GRAND VIEW AVE.,
> SOMERVILLE, MASS.

**"What's that?" Sammy asked sharply. "I always knew you to be a coward, but this is the first time I have ever known you to admit it. Whom are you running away from?"** ■ (From *The Adventures of Chatterer the Red Squirrel* by Thornton W. Burgess. Illustrated by Harrison Cady.)

"It was preposterous. It was absurd. Of course. It was, and still is, inconceivable that that little investment drawn from my meager capital should pay off in hard cash, but it did. Moreover, it paid a tremendous extra dividend in that it definitely settled for all time the question of what I wanted to do. I wanted to write. From that time on I knew that I must somehow make my living with my pen. There was not even a shadow of doubt.

". . . There is a great degree of satisfaction for one to be able to say it was here, or there, that he made his start. I suspect that more often than not it is impossible to pinpoint this very beginning, the factual planting of the seed of success. In my case it can be done. It was that little advertising rhyme in *Brains.*

"As soon as that issue of *Brains* was off the press, I received a request to call at once at an advertising agency in Boston. As requested, my response was prompt. In fact, I may say it was in some haste. Those were hungry days. As a stimulant to prompt reaction and endeavor I know of nothing equal to an empty stomach.

"The agency was doing some advertising for the Miles Standish Spring Water Company. A booklet was wanted, a booklet in verse. Could I paraphrase Longfellow's epic of Miles Standish, reduce it to twenty short verses, and incidentally introduce the discovery of a spring, *the* spring, by Miles Standish? Oh crass temerity of youth! I could and I would. Many times I have blushed at the memory of my audacity.

"At that time my boyhood chum was studying at the Massachusetts Institute of Technology. He came to my room to spend the evening on the day I wrote the epic. He listened critically while I read it aloud. He nodded approval, then brought me back to earth with a practical question. 'How much are you going to ask for it?' he wanted to know.

"'I think I ought to get five dollars for it,' said I.

"'Man, you're crazy!' he cried. 'Don't ask a cent less than fifteen.'

"'You're the one who is crazy,' I retorted. 'No one would pay fifteen dollars for this. I did it in about three hours. No one will pay any such sum for three hours' work.'

"Ernest was the better businessman. He argued so convincingly that the next morning when I started for the agency I was uncertain. Perhaps he was right and I had underrated myself.

"At the office I found the president of the Spring Water Company had come in. My modest emulation of Mr. Longfellow . . . was given him to read. He liked it. It met with his instant approval. The manager of the agency turned to me. 'What do we owe you?' he asked.

"The dreaded crucial moment had come. 'What will you pay me?' I stammered.

"'You're selling; we're buying; how much?' he replied.

"This was business. I hated business. This sounded like bargaining and I never could haggle. I can't to this day. I thought of Ernest. 'Fifteen dollars,' I mumbled and half caught my breath at my brashness. Then I really did catch it at the celerity with which those three five-dollar bills appeared. How right my chum was! And how innocent we both were as to what that agency probably had expected to pay.

"That was the first money I ever earned with my pen. It was a heady stimulant. . . ."[1]

**1895.** Began working for the Phelps Publishing Company in the capacity of office boy, then graduated to reporter, literary household editor and finally to associate editor. "That first winter I eked out my five dollar week salary by taking care of the furnace at the editor's home at night, taking up the ashes and so on. For this work I received a small but welcome sum. I was paying a dollar and a half a week for my room in a private home in that same neighborhood. This made the care of the furnace a comparatively easy matter. My meals I had downtown at a lunchroom, where I could get an egg sandwich and a cup of coffee for breakfast for fifteen cents, and other meals in proportion. I walked the two miles each way between my rooming house and office. So I kept wholly within my income, but of course I was not buying any new clothes and few luxuries.

"The *Homestead*'s photographer made use of the office boy to carry his big camera and equipment on various assignments. I began to do some of the stories to go with the photographs. So while still office boy, I became part-time reporter and was given a desk in the city room. That desk was a throne to me.

"I began contributing verse and short articles to the household departments of the farm papers. Now and then a story for boys or for little children was accepted by the literary editor. It all went in on my office boy's salary. That was all right. The pleasure of seeing my stuff in print was sufficient recompense. Then, too, it was recognition. Time went fast. There was a new office boy and I was getting ten dollars a week. I was up a rung on the ladder and on my way.

"Meanwhile, my good grandfather was disappointed. The dear old man could see no financial future for me in my chosen line of work. I strongly suspect he felt that his help in giving me a term at the commercial school had been money wasted. As to probable financial returns in the future, I was under no illusions myself. However, I was confident I could earn enough to make a living for Mother and myself. And God he praised, I was doing what I wanted to do. Even in the prospect of hard work and long hours for small pay I had substituted happiness for unhappiness.

"There were other considerations and compensations. No longer was I blindly groping for the ladder. My feet were on the lower rungs, to be sure, but they were firmly planted there. I might not be able to climb very high, probably wouldn't be, but the opportunity was there. What I could make of it was up to me. That in itself was compensation beyond price. For the first time I was finding happiness in my work. It was not that there was no drudgery in it. There was. Is there any work whatever entirely free from the disagreeable? I didn't enjoy doing boy's work when I was on the edge of manhood's estate. But I found the happiness that results from having an objective to strive for.

"Those were the days when the bicycle was the forerunner of the automobile. Everyone rode. Bicycle racing, amateur and professional, was a popular and major sport. Springfield had a famous half-mile track where each fall the final championship meet of the year was held. All through the summer men were in training there. I became sports editor of the *Homestead,* covering bicycle racing, the Eastern League ball games and other sports. I made weekly trips across the Connecticut River to gather news in the Boston & Albany railroad shops. A weekly column of news of the fraternal orders became my responsibility. When well-known local citizens died it fell to me to visit the house of mourning to solicit a photography of the deceased and gather the facts for an obituary write-up. I didn't like this. Especially I disliked being invited in to view the body of the departed one, and this was of frequent occurrence. But it was all part of the work.

"Assignments for special articles and write-ups began to come my way. In short, I was a full-fledged reporter. I was even allowed from time to time a special column of my own. All this was on the weekly *Springfield Homestead.* At the same time I had become editor of the correspondence departments of the agricultural papers and a regular contributor of verse and stories to the household departments of these papers.

"The first automobile in America, the Duryea, was being tested on Springfield streets. I interviewed one of the two Duryea brothers, the inventors. In time I had in the *Homestead* what I think was the first automobile column in a

HE OPENED ANOTHER CLAM AND WASHED IT AND ATE IT

(From *Tales From the Storyteller's House* by Thornton W. Burgess. Illustrated by Lemuel Palmer.)

newspaper. The Phelps Company took over the then defunct *Good Housekeeping* magazine. My field broadened. I became a sort of editorial utility man on that magazine. My uncredited contributions were many and varied—serious verse and nonsense verse, special articles on all sorts of subjects, original short puzzle-stories for use amid the advertising pages. It was all wonderful training. The salary was still low, but in due course I had the title of managing editor, a recompense that was no strain on the treasury but was aimed to make me feel good. Of course it did.

"... My weekly salary was raised to the munificent sum of fifteen dollars per week, the head of the company for which I worked stipulated that for the first year I should do no outside writing. All the long years since I have wondered why he made that stipulation, for up to that time I had done no outside writing, nor had I considered doing any. . . . Shortly, after the expiration of the stipulated year a wire from a friend connected with our New York office called me to the big city. He told me that a new magazine had recently been started there. The editors, with one or two of whom he was acquainted, had been looking for a writer to do a special line of work they had in mind but had failed to find one who could do it just the way they wanted it done. He had told them he knew someone who could do it, had made an appointment, then wired me to come down. The magazine was *Country Life in America,* the most beautiful pictorial magazine of its day.

"It was a somewhat awed young man who was admitted to the inner sanctum of the editorial rooms and introduced to the editor in chief. Briefly, but clearly, he outlined to me an outdoor calendar to be run monthly. It was to cover all outdoor interests and activities—bird life with approximate nesting and migrating dates based on the latitude of New York; wild flowers, when and where to look for them; gardening activities month by month; outdoor sports of all kinds in their given seasons. It was breath-taking, a bit overwhelming. I was neither naturalist, botanist, agricultural expert, nor sports authority; merely an unknown writer with feet as yet on the lower rungs of the ladder.

"'Can you do it?' The question was direct and blunt. It called for an equally direct and blunt reply.

"Common sense, with complete comprehension of the enormity of the task and my utter lack of authoritative and technical qualifications for it, whispered 'No.' But opportunity was holding open the door. Without hesitation I said 'Yes.' Many, many times since I have wondered at my temerity.

"'Good,' said the ruling power. 'Now, what about price?' It was all as simple as that.

"At the mention of price I really did hesitate. My ignorance of prevailing rates for literary work of any kind was on a par with my ignorance of the subjects I was undertaking to write about. Save for the advertising verses I have before mentioned, no writing of mine had ever been paid for directly. All that I had ever written for the publication with which I was connected—verse, stories, special articles—had come within the compass of my meager salary.

"My hesitation was noticed. 'How will a cent and a half a word do?' I was asked.

"Had I been asked, 'How will a million dollars do?' I doubt if I would have been more flabbergasted. In my inexperience

I had never dreamed that writing was ever paid for by the word. I had a momentary vision of receiving a cent and a half every time I used even the shortest preposition. Selling words! It was a completely new idea to me.

"Perhaps my hesitancy was misconstrued. Anyway, the suggestion was made that I go home and do the first installment. If it was satisfactory and the work seemed to warrant an upward adjustment of the suggested price, this undoubtedly could be arranged.

"I returned home in something of a daze, a dreamlike mental fog. Truly the impossible had happened. It was incredible. Then I began to take stock of the situation, of what I had committed myself to do. I began to realize the enormity of my presumption. The work must be done outside of business hours. Evenings, Sundays and holidays afforded the only available time. Although the year for which I had agreed to do no outside writing had expired several months previously, it seemed best that the powers controlling my weekly stipend should not know for the present of my outside efforts, always supposing said efforts were a success. So I wrote under my own name reversed, W. B. Thornton.

"The work ahead involved in that little three-letter word 'yes,' spoken so easily in New York, was tremendous, to say nothing of its impact on my future career. It meant seemingly endless hours of research, of checking and rechecking. In its field *Country Life* was authoritative. There could be no slips. All my bird work would pass under the critical eyes of Dr. Frank Chapman, world-famous ornithologist of the American Museum of Natural History. All my botanical and horticultural work would have to survive the scrutiny of Dr. Liberty Bailey of Cornell University. No, there could be no slips. In selection of material and presentation I was given a free hand.

"In due course, with inward quaking and trepidation, the first installment was entrusted to Uncle Sam for safe delivery. Then suspense, dragging intolerable suspense, was broken by the return of the installment. It was the same, yet it wasn't the same at all. It was wholly and completely changed. It had gone out as the two-fingered hunt and punch product of the typewriter. It had come back in four full page proofs of the printer's art, beautifully illustrated. But the context was unchanged, practically word for word as I had written it. When later the check in payment arrived, my first check for bona fide literary work, the cent and a half had increased to two cents a word.

"From the start the calendar was a success. It was widely quoted. I had arrived. Rather, W. B. Thornton had arrived. His reputation as a nature writer grew. Other magazines began asking for articles. Meanwhile *Country Life* was taking more material than the calendar. I recall that in one issue there were, besides the calendar, three articles under three different names and all from my typewriter. Then came a letter from *World's Work,* at that time a magazine of note devoted to world affairs and problems of the day. Could W. B. Thornton write for it an article on the part agricultural machinery had had in world development by the increase of food supplies through its use? Presumably the editors knew that I was connected with a house publishing several leading farm papers, so probably was well posted on the subject. The fact was, my editorial work was in the literary and household departments of the various publications.

"I did know a plow, a mowing machine, a hayrake, a toothed harrow and a disk harrow when I saw them. Never had I seen a reaper, binder, threshing outfit or other modern farm machinery save in pictures. Here was a subject of which I literally knew almost nothing. What should I say? Common sense said 'No.' Opportunity said 'Yes.' I said 'Yes.'

"Again nights, Sundays and holidays were devoted to research. The magazine spent a year getting photographs from various parts of the world to illustrate the article. Following its publication I received an inquiry from the Department of Agriculture in Washington asking if I could suggest anyone to head a department on agricultural machinery about to be established."[1]

**1904.** Became associate editor of *Good Housekeeping*. "Meanwhile, the powers that ruled at home had discovered the identity of W. B. Thornton. I was then on the editorial staff of *Good Housekeeping* and had done much writing for it, all of which had appeared without credit. Now the name W. B. Thornton began to appear. It was pleasing. It was a form of recognition. It gave a certain sense of satisfaction even though it added nothing to salary checks.

"Often in the years since I have wondered just what the result would have been in my life and career had I said 'No' instead of 'Yes' on those two momentous occasions. 'No' is a word of finality. It is conclusive. It is the end. On the other hand, 'yes' is inconclusive. It guarantees nothing, but it holds the door of opportunity ajar. Nothing is lost. Much may be gained. It is up to the individual. All too often 'no' is the word of the coward, the quitter. 'Yes' may well be a dare to attainment and success. Life has taught me that he who dares nought wins nought.

". . . In my time with *Good Housekeeping* I had written a few lines of humorous text illustrated by F. Strothman that had appeared on facing pages as a monthly feature of the magazine for a full year. It had been well enough received for the publishers to put it between covers with credit to me as the author. Until then I had been just a writer."[1]

**Summer, 1905.** ". . . I was married to Nina E. Osborne of West Springfield, Massachusetts. Her belief in my abilities and faith in my future success were a never-failing source of inspiration when I most needed it. In her love and faith, which in full measure she shared with my mother, I found such stimulation and encouragement that the added responsibilities I had assumed were a joy, in no sense a burden. Together we planned and schemed to stretch the small salary to cover increased costs of daily living and still leave enough for simple pleasures that would require small outlay.

"She had grown up in a New England environment and atmosphere similar to my own. From early training she had convictions and attitudes toward debt and social obligations like those that had brought Mother and myself thus far free of debt and independent. Freely and fully we talked over each new situation and problem as it appeared. She knew exactly my financial situation and was aware that my prospects along those lines, while not discouraging, were hardly likely to ever put her in the mink stole social stratum.

"To her, as to me, money was to be desired but was the least part of the success we dreamed of. A forty-dollar-a-week salary on which to support three people involved real problems. We talked them over together. We agreed we would go without rather than run in debt for anything not absolutely necessary. We worked out a code for happy living . . .

"The integrity of a man is the measure of his character.
A man's honor is a possession without price.
A bad reputation travels too fast and too far to be caught up with.
He who cheats another cheats himself more.
A liar is too yellow to face the truth.
The worth of a man's honor cannot be evaluated.
A man without honor is a social outcast.
Contracting bad debts is the coward's way of stealing.
Though in the present it is difficult to live up to high standards, it will be more difficult in the future to live down a bad reputation.
A good reputation built slowly deed by deed may be destroyed by a single act.
The integrity of today will not be lost tomorrow, for tomorrow never is.

"We had been married a little less than a year when our son was born and his mother gave her life for his. It was a crushing blow. However, I still had my mother and my baby son to work for. In my work I found refuge, and through God's mercy sustaining strength.

"*Good Housekeeping* was growing and in proportion demands on my small talents increased. I had become what might be called general utility man, pinch hitter if you please, in both editorial and advertising departments. I supplied fillers in verse, special articles, short stories, bits of humor. I may not have realized it, probably did not, but these varied demands were giving me priceless opportunities to develop such abilities as I might possess, together with experience in versatile writing that would be of inestimable value in years to come.

"With this work on *Good Housekeeping* I was also literary and household editor of the Orange Judd Weeklies, all for the munificent salary of forty dollars per week. It meant many evenings in the office and no overtime pay."[1]

**1910.** *Old Mother West Wind* published. ". . . I have always felt that I really became an author with the publication of *Old Mother West Wind*. . . . This was the first of my numerous books about Peter Rabbit and his friends of the Green Meadows and the Green Forest. The stories in the first volume were not written for publication but for my motherless small son, who with one of his grandmothers was visiting in Chicago for a month. Every night after dinner I wrote a story or some verses and mailed them to him. Later two or three of these stories were published in *Good Housekeeping*.

"One day an editorial representative of one of the oldest publishing houses in America—Little, Brown and Company of Boston—visited our editorial rooms to call on my superior, the editor in chief. In course of conversation the latter said, nodding in my direction, 'Burgess over there has some interesting stories for children.'

"The visitor came over to my desk, introduced himself, and asked to see the stories. He read one or two, asked how many I had, then urged me to get them together and send them to Little, Brown for consideration as a possible book. This I agreed to do, but with no enthusiasm. I was under the all too general impression that to obtain favorable consideration of a manuscript an unknown writer must have friends in court, or some personal influence. I could not have been more wrong.

"I sent the stories, fourteen of them, all I had. Somewhat to my astonishment, within a week or two the unbelievable had happened—I had signed a contract that would make me a bona fide author. It was for *Old Mother West Wind*. Two more stories were needed to fatten the small volume. On two successive nights I went back to the office and put a story on the dictaphone to be transcribed the next day. When these were mailed, a total of sixteen stories, I told my home folks that I had written every last animal story I knew, that I was written out. It was true—then.

"In its first year *Old Mother West Wind* sold over two thousand copies and I was congratulated on having a successful book for children. My royalty was two hundred and ten dollars. It was an eye opener for me. The road to fortune via children's books dwindled to the narrowest of paths, hardly worth following. Anyway, I was an author.

"How well I recall the thrill of seeing and handling . . . *Old Mother West Wind*. I leafed my first copy through from cover to cover; put it down only to pick it up again and do it all over. How eagerly I looked for the illustrations! I looked that little volume through the first thing in the morning and the last thing at night. That book was mine, my very own, every line of it. It was the child of my brain. I was an author, accepted as such. Not only had I written a book, it had been published by one of the most famous publishing houses in America. It was a small volume, but there it was in my hands, visible, tangible evidence of a dream come true. How I gloated over the title page! How eagerly I read the book reviews! How I tingled all over when I saw window displays of *my* book, and *my* name in big type! Over and over I would say to myself, 'That is mine. I wrote it. I wrote it.' It was my first really great thrill. I have had several since but none greater.

"When the publishers asked for another book the following year, I realized this was proof that despite the small sales for the first year I had written a modestly successful book. Meanwhile the spring had been refilling. So *Mother West Winds's Children* came from the press. . . . Then I felt that beyond all question I was an author, especially when in numerous reviews I saw that magic word coupled with my name."[1]

**1911.** ". . . I married Fannie P. Johnson of Ithaca, New York, who was to be for thirty-nine years my best critic, constant adviser and help. I now had my wife, two stepchildren in their teens, my small son and my mother for whom to assume responsibility.

"A few months later came an unexpected blow. Of a Friday night I learned that *Good Housekeeping* had been sold and was to be published in New York. The following Monday morning I found a memorandum on my desk: 'T.W.B. —Two weeks from date your services will be dispensed with.' It was signed with the initials of the president of the company, the man who had given me the job of office boy in the editorial rooms a little over fifteen years before. There was no word of regret that the long association was to be severed, no sentiment whatever. It was all straight cold-blooded business. I never have liked business.

"Almost at once I had the temporary good fortune to connect with a local advertising agency. For a few months I drew a salary as a copy writer, in free time writing children's stories and verse and learning at first hand how limited was the magazine market for such material, and how little was paid for it when it was accepted.

"The advertising connection lasted for several months. The period that followed was difficult, a struggle with uncertainty through which the loyalty and encouragement of my wife never failed me. The going was rough. One week there might be twenty-five dollars from the sale of a story and the next week nothing.

"With ever-increasing regard for a fixed regular income I assailed the market for stories, verse, special features and advertising copy. I found said market completely materialistic, unsympathetic, and with no consideration whatever for an author's desire to eat regularly. It also was prodigal in the use of rejection slips.

"One thing I learned at this time was that an author writing to sell should never regard his work as a brain child. He should look on it strictly as a piece of merchandise. When the work is regarded in this way, rejection slips no longer affect the heart with stabs at the ego, but become a challenge to salesmanship. I discovered that it was futile to offer cotton to one who wanted silk, or silk to one in quest of cotton. The market should be studied before the sales approach.

"It was during that momentous year of struggle and uncertainty that Mother died. She had lived to see the publication of my first two books and recognition of her son as an accepted writer for children, but she did not live to see the broader field which was soon to open for me and which would have meant so much to her.

". . . A publisher approached me to ask if I could and would write a book for Boy Scouts and other boys in the Scout age. Up to that time I had done only short stories, my books being collections of these. Such a book as suggested would be in the nature of a juvenile novel. Under the prick of the aforementioned spur I became bold. What was there to lose? I said I could and I would. I did. *The Boy Scouts of Woodcraft Camp* was an immediate success. A companion volume was wanted for the following year.

"So by 1913 I was devoting all my time to the daily stories and books. Much research was necessary, so I was kept fully occupied. That year brought out another volume in the West Wind series, the first two in the Bedtime Storybook series, which was destined to run to twenty volumes, and the second Boy Scout book in a series of four."[1]

**1916.** ". . . It was suggested that I write a bird book for children. I hesitated. At that time there were bird books and bird books, as there have been ever since in increasing numbers. It seemed to me doubtful if there was place for another, even though written specially for young readers. Finally I agreed to undertake the work. It involved much research to select the birds most likely to be seen by the greatest number of children throughout this broad land of ours, then to portray these accurately in appearance and habits and to arouse and stimulate the interest of young readers and the small folk who were still being read to. It required a new approach to the subject matter and a new presentation.

"Children everywhere knew and loved Peter Rabbit. The more familiar birds were Peter's neighbors. Who could be better able to find out and tell about them? I enlisted Peter's help.

"The book, beautifully illustrated by America's great and beloved naturalist-artist, the late Louis Agassiz Fuertes, was published the next year. Almost at once it became a best seller. . . . I cherish the review of it by Dr. William T. Horn-

A SHARP GRINNING FACE WATCHED THEM OUT OF SIGHT

(From *Tales From the Storyteller's House* by Thornton W. Burgess. Illustrated by Lemuel Palmer.)

aday. It is to me a priceless tribute. He wrote: 'It rings true and is by far the best bird book for children that we have ever seen. In fact it is the very book that anxious mothers, the children, and the booksellers have all been waiting for for twenty years.'

"*The Bird Book* was followed by the *Animal Book, Flower Book* and *Seashore Book,* all following the same pattern, presenting accurate natural history in entertaining story form.

"From the start my stories were as popular in Canada as in the States. I was no longer at the foot of the ladder, but well on my way up. I was proving that I could make good on my own. It was a wonderful feeling. . . ."[1]

**1922.** ". . . By request I wrote for *Natural History,* Vol. XXII, No. 2, the official magazine of the American Museum of Natural History in New York City, an article entitled 'Nature as the Universal Teacher.' . . .

"Nature was the first teacher of the human race. With this statement no one can take issue. It was not until our prehistoric ancestors began to observe the workings of nature and tried to discover the laws governing the manifestations which they observed, that they began to rise above the animals surrounding them. Every upward step since is traceable directly to increased knowledge of the laws governing life, and these laws are the laws of Nature and have existed from the beginning. Nature was the first teacher and still is the universal teacher.

"This being true, it seems to me a fatal defect in our present educational systems that nature study is given so small a part. In the curriculum of the average public school nature study has such a minor place that it becomes almost negligible. Yet it should be the foundation on which the educational system is based.

"This statement is broad and I am aware that it is likely to be vigorously challenged. Nevertheless, in my own mind there is not a shadow of doubt that it is true. I make the statement out of an extended experience which is constantly driving home to me the fact that in the study of Nature lies the key to the most successful mental, moral, and spiritual development of the child.

"When I began writing animal stories for children, it was with the sole purpose of teaching the facts about the forms of animal life most familiar to American children. I endeavored to do this by stimulating the imagination, which is the birthright of every child, at the same time holding absolutely to the truth so far as the facts concerning the subject of each story were concerned. As the stories grew in number, surprising discoveries were made.

"The first of these was the universal interest in animals and birds. It is not confined to children. I question if there is another subject which can even approach animal life in universal appeal to young and old. Whether the child be of the country or the city, he or she is at once interested by animals. This interest is instinctive. It goes back to the day of the 'dawn man.' By force of circumstances his sole interest in life must have been in the animals and other creatures surrounding him. His very existence depended on constant observation of them. Such intelligence as he had was constantly concerned with them. The larger forms were an ever-present menace to his existence and the lesser forms were

his chief source of food supply. This interest has persisted ever since, and probably always will persist.

"The second discovery was that nature study is unequaled as a vehicle for conveying information of all kinds. The driest of facts if embedded in a nature story written so as to appeal to the imagination will not only be unhesitatingly accepted but will be permanently retained. Intuitively the smallest child is conscious that he is superior to any animal. He knows that he is a higher being. No child will admit that any animal knows more than he does, and this is especially true in regard to the small animals. Much as the adult looks down to the level of the child, the child in turn looks down to the level of the squirrel and the rabbit.

". . . I do have a recipe for children's stories which I follow more or less closely. It is my own special recipe worked out and proved through the years. It is as follows:

"INGREDIENTS—One fact, a liberal amount of imagination with truth, a moral lesson, plenty of good action, adventure or lively dialogue, humor or pathos as desired, sometimes both, and a reasonable amount of simple English."[1]

**January, 1924.** ". . . The Radio Nature League was born and with it began a labor of love that was to continue for nearly a decade. The purpose of the League was to preserve and conserve American wild life, including birds, animals, flowers, trees and other living things, and also the natural beauty spots and scenic wonders of all America.

"Whoever would make a simple but comprehensive conservation pledge was invited to send me name, age and address and would be enrolled as a member of the Radio Nature League. As the names rolled in they were card indexed. By this simple method I was able to form a mental picture of my unseen audience. In announcing the birth of the League I stated that the first to enroll from each state would become a charter member. The program had hardly ended when by phone the first charter member was enrolled from another state. Before I left the studio three states were represented. By noon the next day there were fourteen charter members.

"Applications came in floods. Whole families were enrolled from baby to grandpa. All walks in life were represented. The popularity of the program increased week by week. Now when I look back I marvel that I should have been listened to for a full half hour week after week. But radio was new then."[1]

**Winter, 1950.** Suffered a cerebral thrombosis while shoveling his eighty foot long driveway of his house in Springfield. "I've always felt a man ought to do his own snow shoveling. Didn't seem right to hire a boy to do it although they were always ringing the bell. It took me a couple of hours, but I did a good, neat job. But the next day I started falling down. My wife wanted to call the doctor but I said no. I didn't feel sick. But the next morning I started to get the mail and I fell down again. This time I hit a table and knocked a lot of glass on the floor, and it made a terrible crash. Well, Mrs. Burgess insisted then, and I told her I'd go up and lie down. I had some birdseed in a little bag and it spilled on the way up the stairs and I thought I'd better gather it up. Do you know, I was still on my hands and knees trying to pick up that seed when the doctor got there. My fingers were numb. Doctor told me I had a cerebral thrombosis and took me off to the hospital in an ambulance." [Paul O'Neil, "Fifty Years in the Green Meadow," *Life,* November 14, 1960.[2]]

**THORNTON W. BURGESS**

A few days later his wife also suffered a massive cerebral hemorrhage which claimed her life five months later.

Burgess sold his Springfield house in the year after his wife's death and moved into a pre-Revolutionary farmhouse in Hampden. He continued writing his daily bedtime tales and remarked in 1956 that he had written "a story a day, except Sundays, since February 17, 1912. That's forty-three years." [Arthur S. Harris, Jr., "The Bedtime Story Man," *Nature,* January, 1956.[3]]

**June 5, 1965.** Died of lung cancer in Hampden, Massachusetts at the age of ninety-one. "The child of today with plastic mind is the citizen of tomorrow with fixed ideas. The time to make sure that the ideas are right is before they become fixed. World peace and the future of the human race are in the children of today. The story is the most acceptable and effective way of conveying knowledge and guidance to the child mind and establishing them therein. The animal story, because of the psychological factor involved, the intuitive feeling of superiority on the part of the child, is the most effective form of story. Thus I much, much prefer to write for children. In so doing I feel a greater sense of real power than could ever be mine were I a writer for adults or in high political office.

"Peter Rabbit's oft repeated advice to the children the world over who know and love him is:

> "'With open mind go on your way,
> And add to knowledge every day.'"[1]

*FOR MORE INFORMATION SEE:* H. C. Kenney, "Neighbor Burgess," *Christian Science Monitor Magazine,* January 10, 1948; Stanley J. Kunitz and Howard Haycraft, editors, *Junior Book of Authors,* second edition revised, H. W. Wilson, 1951; A. S. Harris, "The Bedtime Story Man," *Nature,* January, 1956; J. Bryan, "Mother Nature's Brother," in *Saturday Review Gallery,* Simon & Schuster, 1959; Thornton Waldo Burgess, *Now I Remember: Autobiography of an Amateur Naturalist,* Little, Brown, 1960; P. O'Neil, "Fifty Years in the Green Meadow," *Life,* November 14, 1960; D. M. Fox, "Thornton W. Burgess Recalls a 90-Year Romance with Nature," *Audubon Magazine,* September, 1964; L. Levine, "Unforgettable Thornton W. Burgess," *Readers Digest,* October, 1967; Brian Doyle, editor, *Who's Who of Children's Literature,* Schocken Books, 1968.

Obituaries: *New York Times,* June 6, 1965, June 7, 1965; *Publishers Weekly,* June 14, 1965; *Time,* June 18, 1965; *Newsweek,* June 21, 1965; *Library Journal,* September 15, 1965.

(Died June 5, 1965)

## CALDECOTT, Randolph (J.) 1846-1886

*PERSONAL:* Born March 22, 1846, in Chester, Cheshire, England; died February 12, 1886, in St. Augustine, Florida; son of an accountant; married Marion H. Brind, 1880. *Education:* Attended the Manchester School of Art. *Home:* London, England.

*CAREER:* Employed in a bank in Whitchurch, Shropshire, 1861-67, and later in a bank in Manchester, 1867-72; freelance artist and illustrator in London, 1872-86. *Member:* Brasenose Club. *Awards, honors:* Since 1938 the Caldecott

**RANDOLPH CALDECOTT**

(From *Yours Pictorially,* the illustrated letters of Randolph Caldecott, edited by Michael Hutchins.)

Medal has been awarded annually to the illustrator of the most distinguished picture book for children published in the United States during the preceding year.

*ILLUSTRATOR*—"Picture Books"; all published by Routledge: *The House That Jack Built,* 1878; William Cowper, *The Diverting History of John Gilpin,* 1878; Oliver Goldsmith, *Elegy on the Death of a Mad Dog,* 1879; *The Babes in the Wood,* 1879; *Three Jovial Huntsmen,* 1880; *Sing a Song of Sixpence,* 1880; *The Queen of Hearts,* 1881; *The Farmer's Boy,* 1881; *The Milkmaid,* 1882; *Hey Diddle Diddle, the Cat and the Fiddle* [and] *Baby Bunting,* 1882; *The Fox Jumps over the Parson's Gate,* 1883; *A Frog He Would A-Wooing Go,* 1883; *Come, Lasses and Lads,* 1884; *Ride a Cock-Horse to Banbury Cross* [and] *A Farmer Went Trotting upon His Grey Mare,* 1884; Goldsmith, *Mrs. Mary Blaize,* 1885; *The Great Panjandrum Himself,* 1885. All of the above titles are currently in print, published by Warne.

"Picture Book" collections: *Picture Book, No. 1,* Warne, 1879; *Picture Book, No. 2,* Warne, 1879; *Picture Book, No. 3,* Warne, 1883; *Picture Book, No. 4,* Warne, circa 1907; *Hey Diddle Diddle Picture Book,* Routledge, 1883; *Panjandrum Picture Book,* Warne, 1885; *The Complete Collection of Pictures and Songs* (preface by Austin Dobson), Routledge, 1887; *Randolph Caldecott's Second Collection of Pictures and Songs,* Warne, 1895.

Other illustrated works: Henry G. Blackburn, *The Harz Mountains: A Tour in the Toy Country,* S. Low, 1872; Louisa Morgan, *Baron Bruno; or, The Unbelieving Philosopher, and Other Fairy Stories,* [London], 1875; Washington Irving, *Old Christmas,* 1875; Irving, *Bracebridge Hall,* Macmillan, 1876; Irving, *The Sketch Book,* Macmillan, 1876; Alice Carr, *North Italian Folk: Sketches of Town and Country Life,* Chatto & Windus, 1878; H. G. Blackburn, *Breton Folk: An Artistic Tour in Brittany,* S. Low, 1880; Juliana H. Gatty Ewing, *Daddy Darwin's Dovecot,* Christian Knowledge Society, 1881; Aesop, *Some of Aesop's Fables,* Macmillan, 1883; Ewing, *Lob Lie-by-the-Fire,* Christian Knowledge Society, 1883; Ewing, *Jackanapes,* Christian Knowledge Society, 1884; A.Y.D., *The Owls of Olynn Belfry,* Scribner & Welford, 1885; Jean de La Fontaine, *Fables de La Fontaine: A Selection,* Macmillan, 1885; Hallam Tennyson, *Jack and the Beanstalk: English Hexameters,* Macmillan, 1886.

Collections: *Randolph Caldecott's "Graphic" Pictures,* Routledge, 1883; *A Sketch-Book of Randolph Caldecott's,* Routledge, 1883; *More "Graphic" Pictures,* Routledge, 1887; *Randolph Caldecott's Last "Graphic" Pictures,* Routledge, 1888; *The Complete Collection of Randolph Caldecott's Contributions to the "Graphic,"* Routledge, 1888; *Gleanings from the "Graphic,"* Routledge, 1889; *Randolph Caldecott's Sketches* (introduction by Henry Blackburn), Low, Marston, 1890; *"Graphic" Pictures,* four volumes in one, Routledge, 1891; *Randolph Caldecott's Painting Book,* S.P.C.K. (Society for the Promotion of Christian Knowledge), 1895.

Contributor of drawings and illustrations to various periodicals, including *Will o' the Wisp, The Sphinx, London Graphic, London Society, Punch, Pictorial World, Harper's Magazine,* and *New York Daily Graphic.*

*SIDELIGHTS:* **March 22, 1846.** Born in Chester, England. Son of an accountant.

**1852.** From the age of six, he wandered through the local countryside sketching from nature, carving wooden animals, modelling in clay and painting. These artistic endeavours were discouraged by his father.

**1861.** Took a position as a bank clerk in Whitechurch, Shropshire.

**1867.** Transferred to a bank in Manchester. "Caldecott used to wander about the bustling, murky streets of Manchester, sometimes finding himself in queer out-of-the-way quarters often coming across an odd character, curious bits of antiquity and the like. Whenever the chance came, he made short excursions into the adjacent country, and long walks which were never purposeless. Then he joined an artists' club and made innumerable pen and ink sketches. Whilst in this city so close was his application to the art that he loved that on several occasions he spent the whole night in drawing."

**The Stage Coachman** ■ (From *Old Christmas* by Washington Irving. Illustrated by Randolph Caldecott.)

"**Four and Twenty Blackbirds.**" ■ (From *Sing a Song of Sixpence*. Illustrated by Randolph Caldecott.)

[Henry Blackburn, *Randolph Caldecott: A Personal Memoir of His Early Art Career,* Simpson, Low Marston, Searle and Rinington, 1887.[1]]

Became evening student at Manchester School of Art.

**July 3, 1868.** First drawings published in *Will o' the Wisp,* a humorous weekly. "I suppose you will receive a *Will o' the*

*Wisp* this week. As I know at present, there will only be one sketch by me—the rest of the space being this month devoted to a new artist, who I dare say will eclipse me." [*Yours Pictorially: Illustrated Letters of Randolph Caldecott,* edited by Michael Hutchins, Warne, 1976.[2]]

**February, 1871.** Work appeared in *London Society.*

**1872.** Quit Manchester, moved to London to earn his way as a free-lance illustrator. "I had the money in my pocket sufficient to keep me for a year or so, and was hopeful that during that time my powers would be developed and my style improved so much that I should find plenty of work." [Rodney K. Engen, *Randolph Caldecott: Lord of the Nursery,* Oresko, 1976.[3]]

"London is of course the proper place for a young man, for seeing the manners and customs of society, and for getting a living in some of the less frequented grooves of human labour, but for a residence give me a rural or marine retreat. I sigh for some 'cool sequestered spot, the world forgetting, by the world forgot.' "[1]

"You know how devoted I was to business when I was a quill-driver; well, now I am still more devoted, and hope by a strict attention to business and by still supplying the best article at the lowest price to merit a continuance of the favours which the nobility, clergy, &c.

"I have just got into a new workshop next door at the back, and there I light my stove and carry on my business. Do you want a sign-board? or an equestrian statue? or an elegant wallpaper?"[2]

**March 28, 1873.** "About the middle of February I went down into the country to make some studies and sketches, and remained for more than a month. Had several smart attacks on the heart, a little wounded once, causing that machine to go up and down like a lamb's tail when its owner is partaking of the nourishment provided by bounteous Nature."[3]

**January 17, 1875.** "I stick pretty close to business, pretty much in that admirable and attentive manner which was the delight, the pride, the exultation of the great chiefs who strode it through the Manchester banking halls. Yes, I have not forsaken those gay—though perhaps, to the heart yearning to be fetterless, irksome—scenes without finding that the world ever requires toil from those sons of labour who would be successful.

"However, during the last year I managed to do a lot of work away from town, and enjoyed it. Sometimes it was expensive, because when at the cottage in Bucks, we of course mixed with the county families and had to 'keep a carriage' to return calls, return from dinner, and so forth."[1]

Here is "a meditation for the New Year"—"You will excuse me talking of myself when I tell you that amongst the resolutions for the New Year was one only to talk of matters about which there was a reasonable probability that I knew something. Now human beings are a mystery to me, and taking them all round I think we may consider them a failure. If I do not understand anything that belongs to myself, how can I understand what belongeth to another? This . . . with your clear intellect, you will see is sound.

"I often think of the scenes and faces and jokes of banking days, and have amongst them many pleasant reminiscences. Perhaps we shall all meet again in that land which lies round the corner!"[1]

**October, 1875.** *Old Christmas* published to unanimous acclaim. "Surely it has seldom happened in the history of illus-

**"The Cottage," Farnham Royal** ■ (From *Randolph Caldecott: His Early Art Career* by Henry Blackburn.)

**Three Pelicans and Tortoise (Oil Painting)** ■ (From *Randolph Caldecott: His Early Art Career* by Henry Blackburn.)

tration that an author should be so very closely followed—if not overtaken—by his illustrator!''[3]

With his success the work and pressure increased: ''I wish I had had a severe training for my present profession. Eating my dinners, so to speak. I have now got a workshop, and I sometimes wish that I was a workman. Art is long: life isn't.

''I feel I owe somebody an apology for staying in the country too long, but don't quite see to whom it is due, so I shall stay two or three days longer, and then I shall indeed hang my harp on a willow tree. It is difficult to screw up the proper amount of courage for leaving the lambkins, the piglets, the foals, the goslings, the calves, and the puppies.''[3]

**1876.** Exhibited first painting at the Royal Academy.

**December, 1877.** Journeyed to the Riviera, France and Northern Italy for his health.

**1878.** Wrote to a fledgling artist: ''Your packet reached me safely, and as I call to mind very readily my feelings in times gone by, after I had posted a piece of literary or artistic composition to some friend acquainted with the dread editor of some magazine, or even to the dread editor himself, I think it only your due that I should write to you without delay about

the sketches of country life which you have kindly allowed me to read, and my opinion of which you flatter me by desiring to know. You ask me for my candid opinion; in these cases I always try to be candid. Editors of magazines, I know, are smothered by the quantity of literary matter poured in upon them, and as a rule they only read those papers which bear a name already favourably known to them. If a friend of an editor hints that he has in his pocket a manuscript which he would like him to read, the editor seizes his hat and rushes away to keep some vague appointment which he has suddenly remembered. To persuade an editor to read the work of a new author is a feat which can only be done by a person having great influence over him, or by a man in whose judgment the editor trusts, vowing that the said work is very excellent. Now I have not the necessary influence over any present editor to persuade him to read your MSS. to oblige me. And as to the editors with whom I am acquainted, I cannot say that I would care to trouble them with them, because after carefully reading them myself I have come to the conclusion that they are not quite up to the standard required.

''I think it right to tell you this in a plain and earnest way, so as to save you any suspense which might end in disappointment. To go more particularly into the matter, which I hope you will allow me to do, I think that your papers are, as they

The orchestra was in a small gallery, and presented a most whimsical grouping of heads. ▪ (From *Old Christmas* by Washington Irving. Illustrated by Randolph Caldecott.)

stand, hardly interesting enough for the mass of readers, though to me they draw out pictures which please, and also revive old associations. Their fault, however, if I may speak of faults, is not so much in subject as in style. You have chosen simple subjects, in which is no harm, of course; but simple subjects in all branches of art require a masterly hand to delineate them. The slightest awkwardness of execution is noticed, and mars the simplicity of the whole. When a thrilling story is told, or a very interesting and novel operation described, faults of style are overlooked during the excitement of hearing or reading. Is it not so? Now it is very curious how similar and strange events happen in different places, and how an account of what happened in one place gets told far away and the name of another spot substituted. I send you by book-post a story similar to yours about the church, written years ago by my friend Edwin Waugh, who lives not far from you. His previous narration of the tale utterly takes away from you, unfortunately, any chance of telling it in print. These things do occur sometimes in periodicals—I mean repetitions—and nobody is to blame.

"Oh! these magazines, of how many efforts have they been the graves, I wonder? I have buried cherished morsels of literature and many drawings in their gloomy depths. But I am glad of it now.

"I have by me a very good comedy in MS. written by a gentleman in your neighbourhood, and I have much difficulty in getting it read by people who might help it forward in the world. They often keep such things a year or two, and then return them unread, if inquired about. But I am hoping to get it looked at in influential quarters; looked at, if nothing more. The author has already printed and published one comedy. Then on my table here lie two pieces of poetry written by the tutor of a young gentleman whom I met on the Riviera last spring. He trusted these to me at Genoa, and I have not yet been able to get them off my hands. Believe me, there are many authors and authoresses trying to push their works forward to be seen or read by the world, and but few are heard, and fewer remembered. Another friend of mine two or three years ago sent me a MS. which he had read amidst the applause of a gathered circle of chums. They were delighted! They praised and cheered! I read the MS. and was obliged to write a melancholy letter, giving an unfavourable opinion on many important points—an opinion agreed in by two or three others whom I had consulted. My friend was not pleased, and showed it; but a little while after he wrote to thank me for opening his eyes. Do not think that I fancy myself a lofty critic. And do not consider me a final court of appeal; but believe that I have tried to give honestly, what you frankly asked me for, my opinion of your MSS. which I herewith return, and thank you for giving me the pleasure of reading them."[2]

Travelled to Brittany. "On this journey I have seen more pleasing types of Bretons (and Bretonnes, especially) than in my former rambles in the Côtes du Nord; but there is generally something wrong about each hotel. This particular inn is comfortable. Seven Americans, two or three of them ladies, and about four French people dined with us, mostly of the artist persuasion.

"Dignity and Impudence" ▪ (From *Randolph Caldecott: His Early Art Career* by Henry Blackburn. Sketch by Randolph Caldecott.)

**Returning from labour—Pont Aven, 1878.** ■ (From *Randolph Caldecott: His Early Art Career* by Henry Blackburn.)

"The village and the river sides, the meadows and the valleys reek with artists. A large gang pensions at another inn here.

"On approaching Pont Aven the traveller notices a curious noise rising from the ground and from the woods around him. It is the flicking of the paint brushes on the canvasses of the hardworking painters who come into view seated in leafy nooks and shady corners. These artists go not far from the town where is cider, billiards and tobacco."[1]

**1879.** Bought his first country home at Wybournes, Kemsing near Sevenoaks, Kent.

Elected member of Manchester Academy of Fine Arts.

**March 18, 1880.** Married Marion Brind.

During the early 1880's he was occupied with commissions from *Punch* and *Graphic*.

**1883.** Illustrated *Aesop's Fables*.

He had many admirers including fellow artists—

Kate Greenaway: "I've been to call on the Caldecotts today with Mrs. Evans. My brother showed some of his new drawings yesterday at Racquet Court. They are uncommonly clever. The Dish running away with the spoon—you can't imagine how much he has made of it. I wish I had such a

mind. I'm feeling very low about my own powers just now. . . ."[3]

Henry Blackburn: "He drew with greater freedom, as he expressed it, preferring, as so many illustrators do, to put in tints with a brush, to be rendered in line by skilful engravers. But at the same time he delighted in showing the power of line in drawing, studying 'the art of leaving out as a science,' doing nothing hastily but thinking long and seriously before putting pen to paper, remembering as he always said, 'the fewer the lines, the less error committed.'"[3]

Austin Dobson: "The open-air life of England, with all its freshness and breeziness, its pastoral seduction and its picturesque environment, is everywhere present in his work. He has the art, too, of being elegant without being effeminate, and of being tender without being mawkish. . . . No taint clings to them of morbid affection or sickly sentiment: they are the general pictorial utterances of a manly, happy nature delighting in innocent pleasure, and dowered as few English artists have been with gifts of refinement and grace."[3]

William Clough: "If the art, tender and true as it is, be not of the highest, yet the artist is expressed in his work as perhaps few others have been. Nothing to be regretted—all of the clearest—an open-air pure life—a clean soul. Wholesome as the England he loved so well. Manly, tolerant, and patient under suffering. None of the friends he made did he let go. No envy, malice, or uncharitableness spoiled him; no social

(From "Baby Bunting." Illustrated by Randolph Caldecott.)

flattery or fashionable success, made him forget those he had known in his early years."[3]

**February 12, 1886.** Died in St. Augustine, Florida, age forty, with his career as an artist spanning a mere ten years.

The *Caldecott Medal,* a contemporary tribute, is awarded annually for "most distinguished American picture book for children in the United States during the preceding year." Recipients are selected by the Children's Service Division of the American Library Association.

His joy and life-giving intention is simply stated: "Please say that my line is to make smile the lunatic who has shown no sign of mirth for many months."[3]

*FOR MORE INFORMATION SEE:* Henry G. Blackburn, *Randolph Caldecott: A Personal Memoir of His Early Art Career,* S. Low, 1886, reprinted, Singing Tree Press, 1969; Mary Gould Davis, *Randolph Caldecott, 1846-1886: An Appreciation,* Lippincott, 1946; Bertha E. Mahony, "Kate Greenaway and Randolph Caldecott: Their First Hundred Years," *Horn Book,* March, 1946; Anne Carroll Moore, "The Three Owls' Notebook," *Horn Book,* March, 1946; Hilda Van Stockum, "Caldecott's Pictures in Motion," *Horn Book,* March, 1946; Jacqueline Overton, "Illustrators of the Nineteenth Century in England," in *Illustrators of Children's Books, 1744-1945,* edited by Bertha E. Mahony and others, Horn Book, 1947.

Stanley J. Kunitz and Howard Haycraft, editors, *Junior Book of Authors,* Wilson, 2nd edition, 1951; F. Laws, "Randolph Caldecott," in *Saturday Book,* edited by John Hadfield, Macmillan, 1956; Bertha Mahony Miller, "Randolph Caldecott, for Whom the Award Is Named," in *Caldecott Medal Books: 1938-1957,* edited by B. M. Miller and Elinor Whitney Field, Horn Book, 1957; J. H. Bodger, "Caldecott Country," *Horn Book,* June, 1961; Brian Doyle, editor, *The Who's Who of Children's Literature,* Schocken Books, 1968; Michael Hutchins (editor), *Yours Pictorially: Illustrated Letters of Randolph Caldecott,* Warne, 1976; Rodney K. Engen, *Randolph Caldecott: Lord of the Nursery,* Oresko, 1976.

(From *A Frog He Would A-Wooing Go.* Illustrated by Randolph Caldecott.)

## CHASE, Mary (Coyle) 1907-

*PERSONAL:* Born February 25, 1907, in Denver, Colo.; daughter of Frank Bernard (a salesman) and Mary (McDonough) Coyle; married Robert Lamont Chase (a newspaper reporter), June 7, 1928; children: Michael Lamont, Colin Robert, Barry Jerome. *Education:* Attended Denver University, 1921-23, University of Colorado, 1923-24. *Agent:* Samuel French, Inc., 25 West 45th St., N.Y., N.Y. 10036. *Address:* 505 Circle Dr., Denver, Colo. 80206.

*CAREER: Rocky Mountain News,* Denver, Colo., reporter, 1928-31; freelance correspondent, International News Service and United Press, 1932-36; publicity director, National Youth Administration, Denver, Colo., 1941-42, Teamsters Union, 1942-44; playwright and author of books for children. *Member:* Dramatists' Guild. *Awards, honors:* William MacLeod Raine award from the Colorado Authors League, 1944; Pulitzer Prize, 1945, for *Harvey;* Litt. D., University of Denver, 1947.

*WRITINGS*—Plays: "Me Third," first produced in Denver, Colo. at the Federal Theater, 1936, first produced in New York as "Now You've Done It," 1937; *Sorority House* (three-act; first produced in Denver, 1939), Samuel French, 1939; *Too Much Business* (one-act), Samuel French, 1940; "A Slip of a Girl," first produced in Camp Hall, Colo., 1941; *Harvey* (three-act; first produced on Broadway at the Forty-Eighth Street Theatre, November 1, 1944), Dramatists Play Service, 1950, reissued, 1971; "The Next Half Hour," first produced in New York, 1945; *Mrs. McThing* (two-act; first produced on Broadway, February, 1952), Oxford University Press, 1952, revised edition, Dramatists Play Service, 1954; *Bernardine* (two-act; first produced on Broadway, 1952), Oxford University Press, 1953, revised edition, Dramatists Play Service, 1954; "Lolita," first produced in Abington, Va., 1954; *The Prize Play,* Dramatists

Play Service, 1961; *Midgie Purvis* (two-act; first produced on Broadway, 1961), Dramatists Play Service, 1963; *The Dog Sitters* (three-act), Dramatists Play Service, 1963; *Mickey* (two-act; based on her novel, *Loretta Mason Potts*), Dramatists Play Service, 1969; *Cocktails with Mimi,* Dramatists Play Service, 1974.

For children: *Loretta Mason Potts* (novel; illustrated by Harold Berson), Lippincott, 1958; *The Wicked Pigeon Ladies in the Garden* (illustrated by Don Bolognese), Knopf, 1968.

*ADAPTATIONS*—Films: "Sorority House" was filmed by RKO-Radio, 1939; "Harvey," starring James Stewart, was filmed by Universal Pictures, 1950; "Bernadine," was filmed by Twentieth Century-Fox, 1957.

*SIDELIGHTS:* **February 25, 1907.** Born in West Denver, Colorado; Chase's mother, Mary (McDonough) Coyle, had come from Ulster County, Ireland at the age of sixteen. Frank Coyle, her father, had drifted to Colorado after an unsuccessful attempt to reap a fortune in the Oklahoma land rush. After their marriage, he became a salesman for a flour mill. Mary Coyle was the last of the four Coyle children. She received gay and reverent attention from her father, her mother, her four uncles, her sister and her two brothers. She remembered an incident where her mother chased away several boys for throwing snowballs at an old woman. "'Never be unkind or indifferent to a person others say is crazy,' Mary McDonough Coyle said to her daughter. 'Often they have a deep wisdom. We pay them a great respect in the old country, and we call them fairy people, and, it could be, they are sometimes.'" [From an article entitled "She Didn't Write It For Money—She Says," by Wallis M. Reef, *The Saturday Evening Post,* September 1, 1945.[1]]

(From the movie "Bernardine," starring Pat Boone and Dick Sargent. Copyright 1957 by Twentieth Century-Fox.)

**1915.** At the age of eight, read *A Tale of Two Cities,* in which was scrawled on the fly leaf: "My name is Mary Coyle. I am eight years old. I have just read this book. Don't you think that I am smart?"[1]

She never lost this particular confidence, and retained, throughout her childhood, an advanced reading taste. "I got the highest grades for studies and the lowest for deportment. I had a reputation for physical daring and some notoriety for getting other children into mischief. Mother tried to hide the gamin qualities of her child with bonnets of feathers and ribbons, but they didn't hide anything at all; just made the combination confusing, although certainly arresting."[1]

At ten, Chase was reading Thomas De Quincy and at fifteen began Xenophon's *Anabais* in Greek.

**1922.** Graduated from the West Denver High School and entered the University of Denver, where she remained two and a half years before she went to Boulder to attend the University of Colorado.

At the end of a year at Colorado the future playwright, who had completed a major in the classics in two years, joined the staff of the *Rocky Mountain News* as a reporter. John P. Lewis, the city editor of the *News* recalled her work there: "Mary, like all girls on smaller papers around the country, did society and club notes and things like that, and finally

was taken over on the city staff to be a sob sister. . . . In the sob sister's life, by the rules of this tradition, were the more infantile and more unpleasant chores in journalism . . . never being sane and normal but always writing highly artificial tragedy or forced humor. . . . Mary didn't take things very seriously on the surface, and we used to wonder if she would ever grow up. More recently some of us who knew her then have begun to suspect that maybe she grew up sooner than the rest of us."

She was an aggressive city reporter. Once Chase was in the middle of a personal telephone conversation just as a verdict was to be read in a murder trial. She cut the conversation short, returned to the courtroom and got the verdict. As she was going into her office, another reporter asked about the call. "Oh, that was dad," she said. "Our house is on fire." She turned in her copy, then went home and wrote a story about the fire. The paper bought her a new dress to replace one that was burned up.[1]

**June 7, 1928.** Married Robert L. Chase, a tall, serious reporter who was also employed by the *News.* For three more years she worked on the *News* with him, until an irresistible idea for a practical joke on the city editor overtook her. Telephoning him, she posed as a needy woman who had received an unsatisfactory Christmas basket from the Good Fellows club. "Them apples you handed me got worms in them," she said, as soon as [the editor] picked up the phone.

(From the movie "Harvey," starring James Stewart. Copyright 1950 Universal Pictures Co., Inc.)

"That's a fine Christmas present. Did you keep all the good apples yourself?"

"I'm sorry," [the editor] said. "We buy them wholesale, and they are supposed to be the best—"

"Don't give me that. These'd turn your stomach. Do you want my kids to eat them and all get worms?"

"I'm very busy, lady. If you'll give me your name—"

"My name's O'Hanrahan. Mrs. Beatrice Lillian Gwendolyn O'Hanrahan. What's yours?"

[The editor] told her his name, and asked for Mrs. O'-Hanrahan's address.

"I live at Fourteen-forty Blake. Where do you live? And I got seven children. How many you got?"

"That doesn't matter!" [the editor] screamed. "I'll have somebody check on your basket!"

"I want to know how many kids you got. You know how many I got. You ashamed? You trying to hide something?"

It went on and on, [the editor] screaming, Mrs. O'Hanrahan relentlessly talking. Finally, she said, "Oh, so you won't talk, won't even talk about them lousy apples. Well, let me tell you—let me tell you what I think: You're a cheap, lying, apple-stealing, penny-pinching rat. Now what do you think?"[1]

When the practical joke was exposed and the city editor discovered the true identity of the irate caller, Chase was fired.

**1931.** At home, Chase involved herself with bearing children, reading plays, writing and fighting for popular causes.

**1936.** First play, "Me Third," produced in Denver, Colorado about the same time that her third son was born. "... What are the most important techniques for the beginning playwright to master? Well! Well! Well! First of all, is the beginner a playwright?

"If so, he was born a playwright, with an instinct for the theater. If not, he cannot learn playwriting, as he could not learn to sing without a voice or to dance without an innate sense of rhythm.

"He may have a desire and talent to spin stories and a need to communicate to others his sense of the wonder and beauty and terror of life; he may have understanding of character, a feel for narrative and style. He may have all of these qualities and yet not be a playwright. He may be a great artist, a superb intellect, a Titan of literature. He may be much,

much more talented than a playwright and yet not be a playwright.

"What then is a playwright? First, he is one who has a heightened awareness of the living presence of other human beings in the same room—a room seating five people or a theater seating five hundred. He has an awareness of creatures, animal creatures, a love and a fear of them; a knowledge of the banked fires of conflict between them and an almost guilty excitement in the desire to stir these fires into blaze; above all, he has a need to attract these animals, to please them, to entertain them, satisfy them and even uplift them. It is a social act, theater. And the playwright is closer to the actor than he is to the novelist; closer to the clown than to the professor; closer to the evangelist and the minister in the pulpit than he is to the scholar in the library." [From an article entitled "The Practice of Playwriting," by Mary C. Chase, *The Writer*, June, 1963.[2]]

**1937.** "Me Third" produced in New York. The play lasted only seven weeks. "The theater is a mysterious, mystical place. And just as each play, no matter how much craft you learn, has within it a special secret which you alone must solve (perhaps in outright defiance of one of the rules of the craft you've learned) so each play has its own vitality and its own fate and will find its way somehow to the stage. Play your hunches about your work.

"The theater is like war. The audience is your enemy to be overcome. At first it is illnatured and skeptical and 'show me.' Your play is your plan of attack. You must meet your audience at the point where they are at this moment in time, interest them, hold them and try to lift them.

"If your play fails and the audience wins, leaving the theater intact—unmoved, unamused—pay no attention to the notices explaining why. And don't pore over Sunday newspaper articles about your work or any other playwright's, measuring yourself and your plays against the weighty edicts handed down by journalists. These are the armchair generals leaning back to give opinions after the battle. They are around the theater but not 'of' it. Nobody really understands the theater until he has risked everything for it. Until he himself has known 'flop sweat.'"[2]

**1939.** "Sorority House," a play based on her personal rejection by a sorority when she was in college, was produced. The play was sold to the movies for a few thousand dollars. "We bought a Ford with the money and paid all our bills." [From an article entitled "Mary Chase—Success Almost Ruined Her," by Eleanor Harris, *Cosmopolitan*, 1954.[3]]

**Summer, 1944.** Finished writing "Harvey" (originally titled "The White Rabbit"). The play took Chase two years to write, working after her three children had gone to bed and her husband had gone to his evening job. "I rewrote it fifty times. My pooka [spirit in animal form] was represented at first by a canary; when I changed it to a rabbit of man's size, although the change had its advantages, the situations required more delicate handling."

Before sending the play to producer Brock Pemberton in New York City, she tried it out relentlessly on friends. "When the playwright has a draft of his play which pleases him, he should not put it into an envelope and mail it to a producer—yet. He should try it out, reading it aloud to a group of three or more people in his home. He doesn't need to invite experts to these readings—just people. He should notice when, during the reading, the chairs scrape, the

bracelets rattle, and the bodies shift positions; when there is a blessed stillness or wholehearted laughter. But he should never, never, never listen to the friends who expound to him afterward on where the play went off and why. The friends don't know. The critics won't know. He must know. His audience has reacted or not reacted. The playwright watches, suffers, and learns why."[2]

"I even tried ["Harvey"] on a cleaning woman one day. She listened to the play instead of cleaning the house."[3]

**Fall, 1944.** "Harvey" opened in Boston and Chase was sure that she had a success. "Just before we left New York for Boston, a member of the cast gave me a two-dollar bill. He got it in change someplace and asked me to keep it for good luck. Then, a short time later, Josephine Hull gave me a four-leaf clover. Then, as I was walking to the theater on opening night in Boston, a huge truck drove slowly next to the curb. The driver turned his head and said casually, 'Hello, Love.' It wasn't an attempted pickup; he didn't even smile. I noticed he wore a dirty leather jacket and his face was solemn and well shaped under the grime, and his eyes were dark and thoughtful. He didn't stop, but drove on without another glance. Somehow, it seemed like benediction, and it was the third sign."[1]

**November, 1944.** "Harvey" opened on Broadway, where it ran for four and a half years. However, none of this success was apparent to Chase who, on the morning after the opening, returned to her home and family in Denver and began energetically housecleaning. "Dust was everywhere, because the place had been shut up for weeks, with the boys farmed out with friends. After I'd attacked the dust, I went down to the basement and threw an armful of clothes into the washing machine. Then I heard the telephone ring. It was the first of thousands of calls from strangers. This was a Hollywood agent, asking if he could fly to Denver at once to sign me up to write movies. I said no, but I had a hard time finishing the laundry. From then on, the telephone never stopped ringing."[3]

For several years after the financial success of "Harvey," the playwright found it difficult to cope with notoriety. "Any precipitous change is a terrible shock in itself, whether you lose all your money or make a fortune. But nobody seems to realize this. If you lose everything overnight, everyone gives you sympathy. But if you make a great deal of money, no one sympathizes or even seems to understand what a shattering thing has happened to you. I became deeply unhappy, and suspicious of everyone. A poison took possession of me, a kind of soul sickness."[3]

**1947.** Three years after "Harvey," Chase began to work on another play. "Work is the solution; it stays with you when all else is gone."[3]

Chase began work on a play for children. The idea for the play ("Mrs. McThing") came from a childhood memory. Chase recalled a friend of her mother's who said, "Last week we buried that whining, querulous old harridan we called our mother, but we all knew she wasn't *really* our mother. Mother was a happy, pretty woman who was taken away twelve years ago. They left this stick in her place, and it was the stick we buried."[3]

The play was a mixture of whimsy with fake gangsters and fairy tale witchcraft.

**A chilly wind blew over the garden. The stars seemed to stand still.** ■ (From *The Wicked Pigeon Ladies in the Garden* by Mary Chase. Illustrated by Don Bolognese.)

(From the stage production of "Harvey," starring Frank Fay. Photo courtesy of New York Public Library at Lincoln Center.)

**1952.** "Mrs. McThing" successfully opened on Broadway with Helen Hayes in the lead role.

**Fall, 1952.** While "Mrs. McThing" was still on Broadway, another play opened in a nearby theater. "Bernadine," a play about the world of teenage boys was also enthusiastically received by the New York audience. "I got the idea from watching my sons and their friends around the house, and I wrote the play about them and for them."[3]

**1957.** Twentieth Century-Fox produced "Bernadine."

Most of Chase's writing has been done in a tiny unheated room where she stoically imprisoned herself for five hours daily. Huddled over her typewriter, she drank coffee and chain smoked while she worked on a play or a new idea. "People ask me if I don't find those five hours lonely. Not at all. It is only when I am writing that I feel really complete. When I am in one of my writing trances, I am cushioned against the sadnesses and griefs of the world."[3]

Mary Coyle Chase's work is characterized by human comedy, intensified by a delicate fantasy applied to the most unlikely situations and people. Tales of Irish folklore told to her by an uncle introduced her to the Celtic pookas and banshees which appear in her writings.

The original production starred Frank Fay and Josephine Hull and was a smash hit on Broadway, with 1775 performances. James Stewart starred in the motion picture version produced by Universal Pictures in 1950, and also in the television version presented by the Hallmark Hall of Fame, March 22, 1972, on NBC. The printed version of the play has been translated into nearly every foreign language.

Helen Hayes and Brandon de Wilde appeared in the 1952 production of *Mrs. McThing,* a mixture of whimsy with fake gangsters and fairy-tale witchcraft. *Saturday Review*'s comments on the printed version included, "It is exciting to find how the charm and originality of *Mrs. McThing* come out in the printed play almost as vividly as they do on the stage with the expert playing a fantasy that is, too, convincing realism." *Horn Book* added, "Of course nothing can take the place of seeing Helen Hayes and the children on the stage, but even in the reading one feels the magic spell cast by Mrs. McThing. . . . And the book provides one thing the theater does not give the audience—the completely delightful stage directions."

Mrs. Chase has also written books for children. The *Chicago Tribune*'s description of *Loretta Mason Potts* included, "How right and natural that the creator of *Harvey* and *Mrs. McThing* should now write a magical tale for boys and girls. Surely, Loretta Mason Potts will take her place among the memorable characters of children's literature and her story should be a favorite for a long time to come." *Kirkus* added, "Much of the poignancy of Peter Pan lingers over this fantasy and though it appears to lack the dimensions of *Alice in Wonderland,* it sings with its own special charm of unabashed fancy and resounding good sense, which made the author's *Harvey* a favorite of adult audiences. . . ." Her latest book, *The Wicked Pigeon Ladies in the Garden* was described by *Library Journal* as, "An unusually good contemporary gothic story . . . [that] conveys without preaching that the power of love can triumph over evil and that the power of imagination is limitless."

Colin Mason was ten years old before he learned he had an older sister. And he never forgot this day— because things were never the same again. ■ (From *Loretta Mason Potts* by Mary Chase. Illustrated by Harold Berson.)

*FOR MORE INFORMATION SEE:* W. M. Reef, "She Didn't Write It for Money, She Says," in *More Post Biographies,* edited by John E. Drewry, University of Georgia Press, 1947; E. Harris, "Mary Chase: Success Almost Ruined Her," *Cosmopolitan,* February, 1954; Stanley J. Kunitz, editor, *Twentieth Century Authors,* first supplement, H. W. Wilson, 1955.

# CRAIG, M. Jean

*PERSONAL:* Children: two daughters, one son.

*CAREER:* Author of books for children. *Awards, honors: Where Do I Belong?* was a selection of the American Institute of Graphic Arts Children's Book Show, 1971-72.

*WRITINGS—For children: The Dragon in the Clock Box* (illustrated by Kelly Oechsli), W. W. Norton, 1962; *Boxes* (illustrated by Joe Lasker), W. W. Norton, 1964; *What Did You Dream?* (illustrated by Margery Gill; Junior Literary Guild selection), Abelard-Schuman, 1964; *Spring Is Like the Morning* (illustrated by Don Almquist), Putnam, 1965; *Dinosaurs and More Dinosaurs* (illustrated by George Solonevich), Four Winds Press, 1965, reissued, Scholastic Book Services, 1973; *The Long and Dangerous Journey* (illustrated by Ib Ohlsson), W. W. Norton, 1965; *The New Boy on*

(From *Spring Is Like the Morning* by M. Jean Craig. Illustrated by Don Almquist.)

*the Sidewalk* (illustrated by Sheila Greenwald), W. W. Norton, 1967; *Summer Is a Very Busy Day* (illustrated by D. Almquist), Putnam, 1967; *Not Very Much of a House* (illustrated by Almquist), W. W. Norton, 1967; *Questions and Answers about Weather* (illustrated by Judith Craig), Four Winds Press, 1969; *Pomando* (illustrated by Enrico Arno), W. W. Norton, 1969.

*Puss in Boots* (a revised edition of the fairy tale), Scholastic Book Services, 1970; *Where Do I Belong?* (illustrated by Ray Cruz), Four Winds Press, 1971; *The Three Wishes,* Scholastic Book Services, 1971; (compiler) *The Sand, the Sea, and Me* (poems; illustrated by Audrey Newell), Walker, 1972; *The Adventures of Tom Thumb* (illustrated by Haig and Regina Shekerjian), Scholastic Book Services, 1972; (with William C. Grimm) *The Wondrous World of Seedless Plants,* Bobbs-Merrill, 1973; *Little Monsters* (Junior Literary Guild selection), Dial, 1977; *The Donkey Prince* (revised edition from Grimm's fairy tale; illustrated by Barbara Cooney), Doubleday, 1977; *The Man Whose Name was not Thomas* (illustrated by Diane Stanley Zuromskis), Doubleday, 1979. Also translated from French, *Babar Comes to America,* Random House.

*SIDELIGHTS:* M. Jean Craig has been fascinated by nature and science from her earliest years, when with her father's encouragement she collected flowers and leaves and developed an interest in birdwatching. Born in New York City, she grew up in New Brunswick, New Jersey, "a just-right-sized town surrounding Rutgers." She got out of high school during the Depression but managed one year of college before having to look for work. "I got my first job at seventeen, wrapping packages in a Newark department store basement for $7.50 a week—a 48-hour week! In the years following I worked in, or on the edge of, the fields of biological research, public opinion analysis, publishing, and so on, having picked up enough knowledge of shorthand and typing to call myself a secretary. I didn't really like secretarial work but I somehow always managed to find perfectly fascinating bosses, so I spent most of my work time maneuvering them into long, interesting, time-consuming talk sessions. I al-ways felt most of the work didn't really *need* to be done, anyway.

"As a child, I always wrote things very easily and without thinking about it—letters and school compositions and camp skits—and I couldn't understand why other people had trouble doing so. As I got older, I sometimes used to write things down for myself to read, but I never thought of being a writer. I think I still write things down for myself to read—that is, I start a story by writing a sentence, or thinking of a person, or an idea, and then keep on going to see how it will turn out. I don't know anything that's more fun and more exciting than that."

About the creatures shown in the photographs in *Little Monsters,* she says: "They *are* little. Each one is so little that you could hold it in your hand. And they do have strange shapes and colors and faces, like monsters. But a monster is not a real animal. It is something that someone has made up purposely to be frightening. The animals in this book are all real animals. Nothing that is natural and real is monstrous. So of course these animals are not monsters at all."

A *New York Times* critic wrote of *Spring is Like the Morning* that "All the wonderment of unfolding buds and of animals emerging from hibernation with their young is described in terms a child will understand, and pictures in illustrations sure to please...." *Library Journal* termed it "artistic in appearance and accurate in text."

Of *What Did You Dream?,* the *Christian Science Monitor* said that "Margery Gill's colored drawings with their fine craftsmanship exactly echo the mood of the text to make a book for a very special, sensitive child." The *New York Times,* however, commented that the book "reaches high but only partially succeeds, for though the text is successfully poetic, it strains to make its point. Margery Gill's sensitive illustrations alternate dreamlike, blue-and-white pages with others of vivid colors to heighten an early morning mood."

He was a little dinosaur, only 6 feet long. His head was nearly as big as the rest of his body, and his shield went away back over his shoulders. ∎ (From *Dinosaurs and More Dinosaurs* by M. Jean Craig. Illustrated by George Solonevich.)

*Dinosaurs and More Dinosaurs* was described by the *Christian Science Monitor* as written in "pellucid, kindly prose.... Solonevich's dramatic pictures in greenish monochrome are probably as realistic as most ... some of the illustrations may seem terrifying to very sensitive children; some have a certain reptilian charm."

M. Craig's book, *The Dragon in the Clock Box* has been printed in twelve countries.

*FOR MORE INFORMATION SEE: Horn Book,* August, 1969, June, 1974.

## DALGLIESH, Alice    1893-

*PERSONAL:* Surname is pronounced *dal*-gleesh; born October 7, 1893, in Trinidad, British West Indies; naturalized a U.S. citizen; daughter of John and Alice (Haynes) Dalgliesh. *Education:* Attended Pratt Institute; Teachers College, Columbia University, B.A.; Columbia University, M.A. *Home:* P.O. Box 283, Woodbury, Conn.

*CAREER:* Editor and author of children's books. Taught in elementary schools for several years before accepting a position in Horace Mann Kindergarten; also taught courses in children's literature at Teachers College. Was children's book editor for Charles Scribner's Sons; was also in charge of reviews of children's books for *Parents Magazine.* *Awards, honors:* Runner-up for the Newbery Medal, 1945, for *The Silver Pencil,* 1953, for *The Bears on Hemlock Mountain,* and, 1955, for *The Courage of Sarah Noble;* runner-up for the Caldecott Medal, 1955, for *The Thanksgiving Story.*

*WRITINGS*—For children: *A Happy School Year* (illustrated by Mary Spoor Brand), Rand, McNally, 1924; *West Indian Play Days* (illustrated by Margaret Evans Price), Rand, McNally, 1926; *The Little Wooden Farmer [and] The Story of the Jungle Pool* (illustrated by Theodora Baumeister), Macmillan, 1930, reissued as *The Little Wooden Farmer,* Collier Books, 1971; *The Blue Teapot: Sandy Cove Stories* (illustrated by Hildegard Woodward), Macmillan, 1931; *First Experiences with Literature,* Scribner, 1932; *The Choosing Book* (illustrated by Eloise Burns Wilkin), Mac-

millan, 1932; *Relief's Rocker: A Story of Sandy Cove and the Sea* (illustrated by H. Woodward), Macmillan, 1932; *America Travels: The Story of a Hundred Years of Travel in America* (illustrated by H. Woodward), Macmillan, 1933, reissued, 1961; (compiler) *Christmas: A Book of Stories Old and New* (illustrated by Woodward), Scribner, 1934; *Roundabout: Another Sandy Cove Story* (illustrated by Woodward), Macmillan, 1934.

*Sailor Sam* (self-illustrated), Scribner, 1935; *The Smiths and Rusty* (illustrated by Berta and Elmer Hader), Scribner, 1936; *Long Live the King!* (illustrated by Lois Maloy), Scribner, 1937; *Wings for the Smiths* (illustrated by B. and E. Hader), Scribner, 1937; *America Builds Homes: The Story of the First Colonies* (illustrated by L. Maloy), Scribner, 1938; *America Begins: The Story of the Finding of the New World* (illustrated by Maloy), Scribner, 1938; (compiler) *Once on a Time* (illustrated by Katherine Milhous), Scribner, 1938; *The Young Aunts* (illustrated by Charlotte Becker), Scribner, 1939; (compiler) *Happily Ever After* (selected fairy tales; illustrated by K. Milhous), Scribner, 1939; *The Hollyberrys* (based on characters originated by Cleo Bennett; illustrated by Pru Herric), Scribner, 1939.

*Wooden Shoes in America* (illustrated by Lois Maloy), Scribner, 1940; *A Book for Jennifer* (illustrated by K. Milhous), Scribner, 1940; *Wings around South America* (illustrated by Milhous), Scribner, 1941; *Three from Greenaways* (illustrated by Gertrude Howe), Scribner, 1941; *They Live in South America* (illustrated by K. Milhous), Scribner, 1942; *Gulliver Joins the Army* (illustrated by Ellen Segner), Scribner, 1942; *The Little Angel: A Story of Old Rio* (illustrated by K. Milhous), Scribner, 1943; *The Silver Pencil* (illustrated by Milhous), Scribner, 1944; *Along Janet's Road* (illustrated by

**ALICE DALGLIESH**

Milhous), Scribner, 1946; *Reuben and His Red Wheelbarrow* (illustrated by Ilse Bischoff), Grosset & Dunlap, 1946; (compiler) *The Enchanted Book* (illustrated by Concetta Cacciola), Scribner, 1947; *The Davenports Are at Dinner* (illustrated by Flavia Gág), Scribner, 1948; *The Davenports and Cherry Pie* (illustrated by F. Gág), Scribner, 1949.

*The Bears on Hemlock Mountain* (ALA Notable Book; illustrated by Helen Sewell), Scribner, 1952; *The Thanksgiving Story* (ALA Notable Book; illustrated by H. Sewell), Scribner, 1954; *The Courage of Sarah Noble* (ALA Notable Book; illustrated by Leonard Weisgard), Scribner, 1954; *The Columbus Story* (ALA Notable Book; illustrated by Leo Politi), Scribner, 1955; *Ride on the Wind* (adapted from *The Spirit of St. Louis* by Charles A. Lindbergh; illustrated by Georges Schreiber), Scribner, 1956; *The Fourth of July Story* (illustrated by Marie Nonnast), Scribner, 1956; *Adam and the Golden Cock* (illustrated by L. Weisgard), Scribner, 1959.

SIDELIGHTS: **October 7, 1893.** Born in Trinidad, British West Indies; the daughter of John and Alice (Haynes) Dalgliesh. Her father was a Scottish businessman and her mother was the daughter of an English sugar-planter.

Dalgliesh's early childhood was spent on the tropical island in a close family structure. "It was wonderful to be isolated as we were in Trinidad because one read what was in the house over and over. I can visualize now every book and exactly where it stood, and the rows of Dickens, Scott and Thackeray. My family let me choose things quite by myself, and how well I remember the thrill of finding *The Rose and the Ring.* Then at the one-room school, I could listen to the older classes' English lessons. We often did needlework while the teacher read aloud. My father read aloud to me too. How well I remember his Scottish voice telling me about Wee MacGregor." [Louise Seaman Bechtel, "Alice Dalgliesh and Her Books," *Horn Book,* March, 1947.[1]]

**1903.** At the age of ten Dalgliesh's father died and she went to England with her mother for further education. They later returned to Trinidad.

**1912.** Determined to become a teacher, Dalgliesh set out for New York City. After graduation from Columbia University with degrees in both education and English, Dalgliesh taught kindergarten and elementary education for seventeen years. Her first books, published while still a college student, were *A Happy School Year* and *West Indian Playdays.*

**1931.***The Blue Teapot* published. "One book of mine which I would like to have keep on living is *The Blue Teapot.*"[1]

**1933.** Besides teaching in elementary schools, Dalgliesh taught courses in children's literature at Teachers College, Columbia University. The course began with twenty students and ended with eighty before she went into publishing. Dalgliesh was very concerned with children and their experiences with books. Her classroom experience was a valuable sounding board. "Every day of the school week I share books with four and five-year-old children. Every day they make their own choices and come to me with favorite books tucked under their arms. So violent are the arguments over what is to be read that sometimes we have to make a 'waiting list' or 'count out.' Naturally, the children have taught me a good deal about their likes and dislikes. Under such circumstances one loses most (not all!) prejudices and learns to put aside even the most cherished notions about books. I was brought up on Kate Greenaway, but it doesn't hurt in the

least to find that her books are never among the *request* readings. Four and five-year-olds are very contemporary-minded. Recognizing this, many of our 'young' booklists might well be taken out of camphor and thoroughly renovated. We should really have two types of booklist, one for the average child and one for the child with unusual appreciations.

"What are the books that my children choose again and again? *Peter Rabbit, Little Black Sambo, Karl's Wooden Horse, Millions of Cats, Herbert the Lion, The Little Wooden Farmer* (probably my influence!), the *Snipp Snapp Snurr* books, the *Angus* books, *The Greedy Goat, Clever Bill,* and others equally simple and child-like. It is no use saying that a book is 'artistic' or 'unusual'; if it hasn't a well-written childlike story *it won't live.* Many of our most elaborate picture books pass quietly on for this very reason. Good pictures do not carry a poor story very far. If there is one outstanding thing that our picture books need it is improvement in *text.*

"If a book is to be a favorite with small children it must pass some severe tests. First of all, the content must be childlike and must concern itself with things in which children are really interested. Children like familiar things. A picture book which strains to be bizarre or 'different,' which wraps its story in too thick a fog of 'atmosphere' is not for little children. I can see why five-year-olds should be vitally concerned with the doings of Angus, with the adventures of Peter Rabbit, with the naughtiness of the Greedy Goat, but I certainly can't see why they should be much concerned with the love affairs of a Spanish cockroach. And they are not!

"Then, if a book is to be a favorite, it must also pass the test of being read aloud over and over. All those who make books for small children should read them aloud to a number of children to see if they have that clarity and smoothness that make for good reading aloud. When a book becomes a favorite, children make it their own by memorizing it partly or entirely, so picture-story books should be simple and clear enough to make this possible. This does not mean that colorful words should be omitted; children love to try the flavor of a new word. There is, however, a certain way of writing, a certain clear simplicity of phrase, a rhythm that makes books easy to read aloud and easy to remember. We find this easy, smooth-flowing writing in *Millions of Cats* and in *Little Black Sambo.* Almost any day I am likely to find four-year-old Georgiana, who cannot really read a word, with a group gathered around her while she 'reads' fluently and with confidence.

"'If we only had a cat,' sighed the very old woman.

"'A cat?' asked the very old man.

"'Yes, a sweet little fluffy cat,' said the very old woman.

"'I will get you a cat, my dear,' said the very old man.

"It slips along so easily! There are not so very many books that do this. Too many of our picture-story books have carelessly written, wandering texts. Many foreign picture books suffer in translation. Elsa Beskow's books are examples of this, with *Pelle's New Suit* as an exception.

"Our picture books also need to be more interesting, to make better use of surprise and suspense. *Peter Rabbit* and *Little Black Sambo* have lived through the years because they are real adventure stories. Will Little Black Sambo lose

Upstairs and down, downstairs and up, from one room to another, packing, unpacking, straining to close suitcases only to open them again for some object that had been forgotten.
■ (From *The Davenports and Cherry Pie* by Alice Dalgliesh. Illustrated by Flavia Gag.)

*all* his fine clothes? Will Peter ever get out of Mr. McGregor's garden? It is hard for us to realize that the suspense *holds* even in the twentieth reading. A supersensitive little girl asked me not to read *Angus Lost* 'because he may not get home.' 'But you *know* he gets home,' I said unintelligently. 'I've read it to you several times.' 'Well,' she said, 'you never can tell. *Some day he might not get home!*' Some time Little Black Sambo might be eaten by a tiger. Who can tell? Most children enjoy the uncertainty. We do not need 'nursery mysteries,' but we do need a little wholesome excitement once in a while.

"Another great need is for more books of real childlike humor. Books that children consider 'funny' are few and far between. Their humor is so crude and so physical that it is hard for us to approximate it. It takes real courage to read Hugh Lofting's *Story of Mrs. Tubbs* aloud to a group of six-year-old children, so great is the hilarity over 'Beefsteak-and-Onions!' And some teachers are afraid of hilarity, or of any mob enthusiasm. One teacher told me that she had put *Angus and the Ducks* away in a cupboard because she was afraid to read it to her group of forty children. What was her fear? Why, the chorus of 'Quacks' and 'Woofs' that followed when the story became familiar, the laughter that came each time the ducks nipped Angus' tail!

"Perhaps the weakest of our younger children's books are those that are intended to convey information. Most of them suffer from being deadly dull. It seems to me that someone is always pointing out to me some particularly ineffectual book of information with the caustic remark, 'I suppose *you* like that because you are a teacher.' As a matter of fact, being a teacher and using the book with children probably helps me to realize its failings. There is no reason why informative books should not be as attractive and as lively as other books. Some of those written for older children are far superior to the younger ones. I wonder why we have no American books that are like *Pelle's New Suit,* a charming book so full of pleasant gardens and flowery meadows that one scarcely suspects it of being 'the story of wool.' Little children are most eager to hear about trains and boats and airplanes and all the exciting events of this modern world. But it is very sad when stories are stuffed so full of information that they bulge obviously. Four and five-year-olds prefer the thrill of an imaginary ride on an engine, with maybe a *little* information tucked in deftly here and there, to being told in cold print that an engine has so many wheels on each side. There is a great deal of room for experimentation in this field; at present there are no informative books for young children that are entirely satisfactory.

"We are finding out a good deal about the interests of younger children. The next few years will probably bring a number of experimental books. The best thing that could happen to our picture-story books is that none of them should be reviewed until they have been tried with children. No sincere experiment should be condemned without trial simply because the book does not seem to measure up to certain preconceived adult standards. Some of our most popular children's books have had a slow and difficult start, but have found their way into the booklists because the children themselves have forced this recognition. Some of the books that have been on the booklists for many years might well make way for newcomers that are more childlike and more readable. There should be nothing static about books for the youngest children." [Alice Dalgliesh, "Small Children and Books," *Horn Book,* August, 1933.[2]]

**1934.** Joined the staff of Scribner's as Editor of Books for Young Readers. Dalgliesh lived for many years in her beloved home in Brookfield, Connecticut. She considered Connecticut her adopted state. "In the winter I live in New York—I am Children's Book Editor for Charles Scribner's Sons. Summers I spend in my two-hundred-year-old house in Connecticut."[1]

**1944.** *The Silver Pencil* published. She said that she liked ". . . to write about places where I have lived."[1] Her Connecticut home was in *The Silver Pencil*. Indeed, much of the book was firmly based on her personal experiences. The book is based on her childhood in Trinidad, her school days in England, and her early years of teaching. Her own father had given her a silver pencil, a challenge to the young girl who was already finding satisfaction in writing.

**1945.** *The Silver Pencil* was the runner-up for the Newbery Medal.

**1953.** Runner-up for the Newbery Medal for *The Bears on Hemlock Mountain.* "One of the books that has given me the most writing fun is *The Bears on Hemlock Mountain.* An author of books for boys and girls is always on the lookout for stories or for ideas that can be made into stories. The story for this book came to me in a rather interesting way.

"One spring, some years ago, Katherine Milhous and I went to Harrisburg in Pennsylvania. She was looking for more material for a book she was writing, *Herodia the Lovely Puppet,* and I was her editor on the book. We went to see Colonel Henry Shoemaker, who is state archivist. That means he keeps records for the state of Pennsylvania. It is his hobby, as he travels around the state, to pick up bits of stories and folklore and piece them together for his newspaper column. He let us go through his files.

"In those files I found the outline—just the outline—of this story about the boy and the bears. Colonel Shoemaker did not know where he had picked it up. But there it was—the story, handed down by word of mouth, of how a boy was sent to bring home a big iron pot and how he hid under it when two bears came along. It was, of course, a 'tall tale,' but it seemed to me quite charming. It had in it something of Red Riding Hood and something of the little pig that hid in the churn when the wolf came along. Perhaps that's how the story started, but no one seems to know.

"First, I wrote it as a magazine story called 'The Christmas Bears.' It was quite different then and did not please me. [Later] . . . at my house in Connecticut, I wrote it again. This time it came easily. I could see the boy—his name was, I decided, Jonathan—making big footprints in the snow when he went over Hemlock Mountain. I looked out into the garden. There on the well was a perky red squirrel. Birds were hopping on the lawn. A young rabbit came out and sat up, washing his face with his paws. Why, of course, that was it! Jonathan was a boy who liked creatures—birds and squirrels and rabbits. And when the bears came, it was the birds and squirrels and rabbits who kept up his courage. Yes, that was how it was. As I sat writing by my big fireplace, there was a large iron pot hanging on the crane—not large enough for Jonathan to hide under, to be sure, but it, too, helped with the story.

"When the writing was finished, I asked Helen Sewell to illustrate it. Somehow she seemed to know just how Jonathan felt about the bears on Hemlock Mountain and how his many aunts and uncles and little cousins looked. Moreover

"It must have wreaths," he said and placed the wreaths from Mama's dress at each side of the headstone. Jennifer was somewhat taken aback by this. ■ (From *A Book for Jennifer* by Alice Dalgliesh. Illustrated by Katherine Milhous.)

she has a little nephew named Jonathan. If you look in the front of the book, you'll see it is dedicated to him—Jonathan Noon.'' [Alice Dalgliesh, ''How I Found My Story,'' *Young Wings*, July, 1952.[3]]

**1955.** Runner-up for the Newbery Medal for *The Courage of Sarah Noble*.

**1960.** Retired from Scribner's. Under her skillful editorship, the children's book department gained a distinguished list of writers and artists. Her discoveries include such famous talents as: Leo Politi, Katherine Milhous, Marcia Brown and Genevieve Foster. After her retirement from Scribner's, Dalgliesh became the editor of children's book reviews for the *Saturday Review of Literature*. Throughout her life Dalgliesh was inspired by a very deep love and understanding of real children. ''Children are my major interest; they come first; and second, books in relation to children; never *just books*. . . . I write different kinds of stories for different kinds of children.''[1]

*FOR MORE INFORMATION SEE:* Alice Dalgliesh, ''Small Children and Books,'' *Horn Book*, August, 1933; Louise Seaman Bechtel, ''Alice Dalgliesh and Her Books,'' *Horn Book*, March, 1947; Stanley J. Kunitz and Howard Haycraft, editors, *Junior Book of Authors*, second revised edition, H. W. Wilson, 1951; Alice Dalgliesh, ''How I Found My Story,'' *Young Wings*, July, 1952; *Horn Book*, August, 1976.

It was quite a process, the combing out of Cherry's tight coat, with only an occasional slight whine when the comb caught in a snarl, or as her nails were trimmed. ■ (From *The Davenports and Cherry Pie* by Alice Dalgliesh. Illustrated by Flavia Gag.)

**Alice Dalgliesh, with her godchild, Linda.**

# DRAWSON, Blair 1943-

*PERSONAL:* Born October 16, 1943 in Winnipeg, Manitoba, Canada; son of Richard Robert and Florence Carter Drawson; married Noel Saville (divorced, 1973); married Bibi Caspari (a mime and dancer), October 19, 1974. *Education:* Attended Ontario College of Art, 1963-66. *Politics:* ''Anti-political.'' *Religion:* ''Religious, but no church affiliation.'' *Home and office:* 69 Westmoreland Ave., Toronto, Ontario M6H 2Z8, Canada. *Agent:* John Locke, 15 East 76th St., New York, N.Y. 10021.

*CAREER:* Illustrator in Toronto, Ontario, 1966-70, 1975—, in St. Helena, Calif., 1970-73, and in Norwalk, Conn., 1974-75. Illustrator for various magazines throughout the United States and Canada. Exhibition at Vintage 1864 in Yountville, Calif. in 1972.

*WRITINGS*—Author and illustrator: *The Bug and Her Friends*, Harcourt, 1976; *I Like Hats!*, Gage, 1977; *Do Something Special on Your Birthday*, Gage, 1977; *Flying Dimitri*, Groundwood Books, 1978; *Arthur, Their Very Own Child*, Gage, 1979; *Mary Margaret's Tree*, Groundwood Books, 1980.

Illustrator: Barbara Brenner, *Mystery of the Plumed Serpent*, Houghton, 1972; Eleanor Kay, *Read About the School Nurse*, F. Watts, 1972; Addie, *The Silly Book of Animals*, Golden Press, 1973; Jerry Lane, *In the Zoo*, Ginn, 1974; Patty Wolcott, *I'm Going to New York to Visit the Queen*, Addison-Wesley, 1974; Wolcott, *Pickle Pickle Pickle Juice*, Addison-Wesley, 1975.

*SIDELIGHTS:* "It seems that the work of the artist is to provide a gentle reminder of what we may have lost in 'growing up'. When we were children, the world looked, felt, smelled, and tasted in ways which are more or less only faintly recalled in adult life. The impressions we received then—terrifying as they were at times—were fueled and made exquisite by our great innocent sense of possibility. This was the possibility of finding things and finding things out.

"Until I was about nine, I thought myself to be the only person in the world named Blair. It seemed to me that there was perhaps a magical property to my name. On several occasions a curious thing happened to demonstrate this. While washing my face or brushing my teeth at the bathroom sink, I would find myself staring at my reflection in the mirror. I would then begin to whisper, over and over, the incantation, 'Blair, Blair, your name is *Blair*.' This released a mechanism whereby I would seem to float up in the air, and sort of hover there in the vicinity of the light fixture. From there I could look down at the back of my head and see my own face gazing at its image in the glass. It was altogether an awesome sensation, and one which I came to write about in a book entitled *Flying Dimitri*."

"My earliest awareness of pictures was in the realm of cartoons and movie posters. Whenever I drew a picture, I put in a special effort to make it funny. I enjoyed the reactions of my classmates when they perceived some *bon mot* of mine depicted on school drawing paper, or in the margins of texts and notebooks. Indeed, some drawings were done on the blackboard itself, encouraged by the teacher.

"Years later, upon leaving art school in my third year, I found myself living hand to mouth in an abandoned mansion. It occurred to me that it might be fun to do some water color paintings of comical animals. I showed the results to a publisher in Toronto and was asked to illustrate a story for their school series. I knew absolutely nothing about illustration then, having devoted my time at school to fine art drawing and painting only. Therefore, it soon became plain that learning the technical side of illustration was going to be a process of painful trial and error. Eventually I decided to try my hand at writing manuscripts. That too was a matter of trial and error. Lately I have begun to do easel paintings again, to supplement my illustration in water color."

When asked about his traveling experiences, Drawson commented, "I spent several months in Mexico and Central

"We'll name him *Arthur*," they agreed,
    "*Or Marigold*, **if a she.**
**And Marigold will dance and sing**
    **While Arthur plays happily."**
**And so they dreamed of their very own child,**
    **But nothing came to be.**
■ (From *Arthur, Their Very Own Child* by Blair Drawson. Illustrated by the author.)

**BLAIR DRAWSON**

America, poking about in ruins, and bumbling along in Spanish. (I also bumble along in French.)

Drawson's influences are "widespread and never-ending; they come from all of history and the entire world of phenomena. In terms of writers of children's books, I have the deepest respect for William Steig, and in a broader context, for C. G. Jung."

*HOBBIES AND OTHER INTERESTS:* Jazz (he is an amateur jazz musician), playing tenor saxophone and flute.

## EAGER, Edward (McMaken)   1911-1964

*PERSONAL:* Born in 1911, in Toledo, Ohio; died October 23, 1964, in Connecticut; children: Fritz. *Education:* Attended Harvard University.

*CAREER:* Playwright, lyricist, and author of children's books. Mainly associated with plays produced on Broadway, he first began writing children's books in 1951 to entertain his young son. *Awards, honors:* Ohioana Book Award, 1957, for *Knight's Castle,* and 1963, for *Seven-Day Magic.*

*WRITINGS*—All illustrated by Nils Mogens Bodecker and published by Harcourt, except as noted: *Red Head* (illustrated by Louis Slobodkin), Houghton, 1951, reissued, E. M. Hale, 1961; *Mouse Manor* (illustrated by Beryl Bailey-Jones), Ariel Books, 1952; *Half Magic* (ALA Notable Book), 1954, reissued, 1970; *Playing Possum: Story* (illustrated by Paul Galdone), Putnam, 1955; *Knight's Castle,* 1956, reissued, 1965; *Magic by the Lake,* 1957; *The Time Garden,* 1958; *Magic or Not?,* 1959; *The Well-Wishers,* 1960; *Seven Day Magic,* 1962.

Plays: "Two Misers," 1943; (lyricist) "Dream with Music," 1944; (lyricist) "Sing out Sweet Land," 1944; (lyricist) *Adventures of Marco Polo: A Musical Fantasy* (book by William Friedberg and Neil Simon; music by Clay Warnick and Mel Paul; first produced as a television special, 1956), Samuel French, 1959; (with Alfred Drake) "Dr. Willy Nilly," 1959; "The Happy Hypocrite," 1968.

*ADAPTATIONS*—Plays: (With Alfred Drake) Carlo Goldoni, "The Liar," 1950; (with A. Drake) Ugo Betti, "The Gambler," 1952; Luigi Pirandello, "Call It Virtue" (based on the play, "The Pleasure of Respectability"), 1963; (with A. Drake) "Ruganntino," 1964.

Also adapted numerous operas and operettas including Jacques Offenbach's "Orpheus in the Underworld" and Wolfgang Amadeus Mozart's "Marriage of Figaro," produced by NBC-TV, 1954.

*SIDELIGHTS:* Born in 1911 in Toledo, Ohio, Eager was raised there. He went to school in Maryland and Massachusetts, where he attended Harvard University. As a child he was always reading and especially loved L. Frank Baum's "Oz" books.

After college, Eager lived in New York City for fourteen years until he moved to a house on a river in Connecticut where, as he said, he hoped "to stay put." It wasn't until 1951 that he began to write children's stories. Before that he worked primarily as a playwright and lyricist, writing plays and songs for the theater, radio and television.

**EDWARD EAGER**

...Since you can always find more drinking glasses and glass ashtrays and perfume bottles than you can anything else when you're building a magic city, the whole area sparkled with transparent domes and pinnacles. ■ (From *Knight's Castle* by Edward Eager. Illustrated by N. M. Bodecker.)

Eager enjoyed reading books to his young son, Fritz, and it was this pastime that started him writing books for children. "In most families I know the father doesn't do the reading-aloud; the mother does. In our house it's different. My wife Jane doesn't like children's books, apparently never did. Except for a burning interest in the doings of one Flaxie Frizzle (unknown to the lists of Miss Moore and Miss Eaton) her formative years seem to have been spent absorbing the complete works of Shaw, Sheridan and Thackeray.

"On the other hand I like children's books, remember all those I knew, and still have most of them. So when our son Fritz was three and had outgrown linen picture books, I took over. At first it was easy, because I owned all the Beatrix Potters, and these, with a few side excursions into Lear and Laura E. Richards and the well-known fairy tales, took up the next year. Then I found that too many of the other books in my own collection, while their pictures might still hold a nostalgic charm for me, were disillusioningly empty as to text. Unaided and unadvised, I started fighting my way through the accumulated nursery literature of the past twenty-five years (also dipping into some older books that had somehow never come my way).

"... I've found out about *The Horn Book, Treasure for the Taking* and *The Three Owls* volumes, and I feel competent to take on the field. But in the meantime we've made a few dis-

coveries that, inexplicably to me, are passed by in the recommended lists. In some other cases we disagree with the learned ladies. . . .

"Two major discoveries Fritz and I made are, unaccountably, overlooked by all the best authorities. One is Enid Bagnold's classic *Alice and Thomas and Jane,* the best 'realistic' story for young children I know of. The irresistibly comic illustrations—some by the author, some by her young daughter, Laurian Jones,—the refreshing informality of the style, the charming relationship between the children and their parents combine to make this a must for every family. . . .

"Then there is M. D. Hillyard's *The Exciting Family,* an almost perfect nonsense story written to provide a text for a group of pictures painted by two young Russian children. Here is a book which speaks directly to a child in a child's own language. E. M. Delafield, in one of the *Provincial Lady* books, pronounced it 'enchanting,' which is how we found out about it, but I've run across no mention of it by American authorities. It was Fritz's first 'long book,' and two years' rereading hasn't dimmed its charm for him—or for me.

"I believe these last two books are both out of print at the moment [1948], but that shouldn't discourage an ingenious parent. Both turn up frequently if one will look

**The dragon sneezed and sputtered and coughed. Otherwise, it was not physically hurt. Its hurt went deeper. To be salted and ammoniaed by a domestic housewife is humiliating to a dragon and makes it feel small.** ■ (From *Seven-Day Magic* by Edward Eager. Illustrated by N. M. Bodecker.)

about—unlike the magnificent works of E. Nesbit which I am now vainly chasing through New York's thrift shops and secondhand bookstores. A copy of *Alice and Thomas and Jane* has been sitting unsold on the children's shelf of one New York bookshop (on East Forty-ninth Street, if anyone wants a clue) for the past year, and I have myself bought two copies of *The Exciting Family* since last summer,—one at a fire sale in Toledo, Ohio. This lent it added charm for Fritz, as he can still smell the smoke in the slightly singed binding.

"I'm well aware that the best authorities on children's reading turn the other way when an Oz book goes by. But these were so much the favorites of my youth that I couldn't forbear trying them again on Fritz. I found the earliest volumes—*The Wizard of Oz, The Land of Oz, Ozma of Oz*—to have a certain homely American charm which in a way compensates for their lack of literary distinction. As L. Frank Baum continued to expand the series, his writing deteriorated, and some of his later books really typify all one doesn't like about the America of the World War One period. When Ruth Plumly Thompson took over the series, a startling change took place. If Mr. Baum's writing was labored, Miss Thompson's was obviously a labor of pure love. All too soon

the law of diminishing returns set in for her, too, but in her earlier books, she shows a fine ear for a pun, a real feeling for nonsense and, in lieu of style, a contagious zest and pace that sweep the reader beyond criticism. I still maintain that *Kabumpo in Oz,* her best effort, is a fine book, and Fritz thinks so, too. . . .

"I've learned one important thing in three years. It's possible to read to a young child without boring either child or parent. I think the parent's boredom is just as important as the child's. I'd like to take all the empty, pedestrian picture books away from all the beginning fathers and mothers in the world, give them copies of *The Enchanted Castle* or *Peter Churchmouse* or *Timothy Turtle* instead, and watch the difference—to the parents now, to their children eventually. A mother yawning over *Cunning Cunning and His Feathered Comrades* (and I'm not sure I made that one up) isn't going to 'bring up' her child half so well as a mother laughing with *Mr. Popper's Penguins* or *Kersti and Saint Nicholas.*" [From an article entitled, "A Father's Minority Report," by Edward Eager, *Horn Book,* March, 1948.[1]]

Through his son, Eager discovered E. Nesbit and it wasn't coincidence that his own magic books bear a striking resemblance to those of Nesbit's, since he considered her the best children's writer of all time. "My childhood occurred too late for the original Nesbit era, and too soon for the revival sponsored in this country by William Rose Benét, Christopher Morley, May Lamberton Becker, Earle Walbridge and others (not to mention the firm of Coward-McCann, which earned everlasting honor by beginning to reissue her books in 1929, and has continued to do so ever since).

"I was dimly aware of the renewal of interest in Nesbit in the early thirties, but since I was then entering my own early twenties, with no thought of ever again having anything to do with the world of children's books, it all seemed very remote.

"It was not till 1947 that I became a second-generation Nesbitian when I discovered a second-hand copy of *Wet Magic,* while casting about for books to read to my son. I have not got over the effects of that discovery yet, nor, I hope, will I ever.

"Probably the sincerest compliment I could pay her is already paid in the fact that my own books for children could not even have existed if it were not for her influence. And I am always careful to acknowledge this indebtedness in each of my stories; so that any child who likes my books and doesn't know hers may be led back to the master of us all.

"For just as Beatrix Potter is the genius of the picture book, so I believe E. Nesbit to be the one truly 'great' writer for the ten-, eleven- and twelve-year-old. (I don't count Lewis Carroll, as in my experience the age when one stops being terrified by, and begins loving, *Alice* is about thirteen and half. And Kenneth Grahame, whose *The Golden Age* had an undoubted influence on the Nesbit style, is an author to wait for, too, I think. . . .)

"How to describe the Nesbit charm for those who don't yet know? Better for them to stop reading this . . . and read the books themselves. I have read all I could find of those that matter (she wrote countless potboilers that are not worth searching for). And I have read the excellent biography by Doris Langley Moore, never published in this country but still obtainable, I believe, from England.

**As for Martha, she knew no bounds. "Pinch them, fairies, black and blue!" she cried. And running among the pirates, she suited the action to the words.**
■ (From *Magic by the Lake* by Edward Eager. Illustrated by N. M. Bodecker.)

"I do not mean to equate genius with arrested mental or emotional development. But there are lucky people who never lose the gift of seeing the world as a child sees it, a magic place where anything can happen next minute, and delightful and unexpected things constantly do. Of such, among those of us who try to write for children, is the kingdom of Heaven. And in that kingdom E. Nesbit stands with the archangels." [Edward Eager, "Daily Magic," *Horn Book Reflections*, selected by Elinor Whitney Field, Horn Book, 1969.[2]]

Beginning in 1951, Eager wrote several children's books. *Red Head*, his first book, is about his son Fritz who, as he said, ". . . hated his red hair when he was in kindergarten in New York and strangers would stop him on the street and say, 'Hi, Red.'"

In 1954 Eager began writing his magic books. "When I was eight-to-twelve, I lived across from a family of three girls who are, to a certain extent, the prototypes for Jane and Katharine and Martha of *Half Magic* and *Magic by the Lake*. *Knight's Castle* was inspired by my son's model collection of knights and by his games with them after he saw the movie 'Ivanhoe.'"

In 1962 his last children's book, *Seven-Day Magic* won the Ohioana Book Award. In 1964 he worked with Alfred Drake on the English lyrics to *Ruggantino*, the Italian musical show which was produced on Broadway.

On October 23, 1964 he died in Connecticut at the age of fifty-three.

*FOR MORE INFORMATION SEE:* Edward Eager, "A Father's Minority Report," *Horn Book,* March, 1948; Muriel Fuller, editor, *More Junior Authors*, H. W. Wilson, 1963. Obituaries—*New York Times,* October 24, 1964; *Publishers Weekly,* November 9, 1964; Brian Doyle, editor, *Who's Who of Children's Literature,* Schocken Books, 1968; Edward Eager, "Daily Magic," *Horn Book Reflections,* Elinor Whitney Field, editor, Horn Book, 1969.

## EARNSHAW, Brian    1929-

*PERSONAL:* Born December 26, 1929, in Wrexham, Wales; son of Eric and Annie (Barker) Earnshaw. *Education:* Cambridge University, B.A., 1952, M.A., 1955; University of Bristol, Certificate in Education, 1957; University of London, Diploma of Education, 1970. *Politics:* "Varying." *Religion:* Church of England. *Home:* Marchmont, Parabola Rd., Cheltenham, England. *Office:* St. Paul's College, Cheltenham, Gloucestershire, England. *Agent:* Jonathan Clowes Ltd., 19 Jeffery's Place, London NW1 9PP, England.

*CAREER:* "Taught English at a poor public school, a good grammar school, and a charming comprehensive school," 1952-65; currently teacher of creative writing at St. Paul's College, Cheltenham, England. Warden, Pembrokeshire National Park, 1963-65.

**BRIAN EARNSHAW**

**Sometimes the Minims creaked and rustled back, as if they were clearing up a point, but never for long. The boys almost went to sleep with all these lulling tree sounds. ■** (From *Dragonfall 5 and the Empty Planet* by Brian Earnshaw. Art concept of illustrations by Simon Stern.)

*WRITINGS: And Mistress Pursuing,* Hodder & Stoughton, 1966; *At St. David's a Year* (poems), Hodder & Stoughton, 1968; *Planet in the Eye of Time* (science fiction), Hodder & Stoughton, 1968.

"Dragonfall Five" series: *Dragonfall Five and the Space Cowboys,* Methuen Children's Books, 1972, Lothrop, 1975; *. . . and the Royal Beast,* Lothrop, 1972; *. . . and the Empty Planet,* Lothrop, 1973; *. . . and the Hijackers,* Methuen Children's Books, 1974; *. . . and the Master Mind,* Methuen Children's Books, 1975; *. . . and the Super Horse,* Methuen Children's Books, 1977; *. . . and the Haunted World,* Methuen Children's Books, in press.

*WORK IN PROGRESS:* A novel and collection of thirty poems, entitled *Living with Men.*

*SIDELIGHTS:* "When I write my children's science fiction I have got Jonathan Swift at the back of my mind. Children seem to me to be dangerously sentimental and soft centered.

They are certainly exposed to a tidal wave of loose thinking on T.V. and in the press, so I consciously try in my books to make them think on other planets about the humbug which surrounds us on this [one]. For instance *Dragonfall 5 and the Hijackers* is about Womens Lib, *Dragonfall 5 and the Master Mind* is about democracy, the Super Powers, and the third world. In England no one worried about this but America seems much more alert to authors who are trying to get at children's minds. American publishers have the view, which I honestly believe may be correct, that if you don't discuss a problem it will go away.

"Technically my books are shallow. . . . What I enjoy about science fiction is the way you can create poetic new environments that half exist on earth but need extending on another planet. I enjoy 18th century Gothic novels and my latest *Dragonfall 5 and the Haunted World* is an extension of Horace Walpole with a few of my friends in starring roles. I can never write a character in a book unless I identify it with someone real whom I know, to give me the speech patterns and keep me enjoying the writing.

"I have always invented stories as long as I can remember. When I was eight at school the teachers used to ask me round to their class rooms to tell a story if the teacher wanted some time off to mark. I tried my hand at adult writing first but I didn't enjoy it because I was always getting trapped in violence and moral angles which didn't suit me. So I am an escapist towards the ideal hankering after a life scheme that is all one enjoyable game.

"It would be unfair not to mention my mother because I suspect I only began writing because she kept on reminding me how good I was when I was in the primary grades."

*FOR MORE INFORMATION SEE: Punch,* March 27, 1968.

**PAULA FOX**

**He looked at the bear in its penguin costume. "I wonder if I could spray you with perfume," he said.** ■ (From *Maurice's Room* by Paula Fox. Illustrated by Ingrid Fetz.)

## FOX, Paula 1923-

*PERSONAL:* Born April 22, 1923, in New York City; daughter of Paul Hervey (a writer) and Elsie (de Sola) Fox; married Richard Sigerson (divorced, 1954); married Martin Greenberg, June 9, 1962; children: (first marriage) Adam, Gabriel. *Education:* Attended Columbia University. *Home:* Brooklyn, New York.

*CAREER:* Author. Worked in Europe for a year as a reporter for a news agency. State University of New York, professor, beginning 1963. University of Pennsylvania, visiting professor, 1977. *Member:* P.E.N., Author's League. *Awards, honors:* Finalist in the National Book Award Children's Book Category, 1971, for *Blowfish Live in the Sea;* National Institute of Arts and Letters Award, 1972; Guggenheim fellow, 1972; Newbery Medal, 1974, for *The Slave Dancer;* Hans Christian Andersen Medal for all children's books, 1978.

*WRITINGS: Maurice's Room* (illustrated by Ingrid Fetz), Macmillan, 1966, reissued, 1972; *A Likely Place* (illustrated by Edward Ardizzone), Macmillan, 1967; *How Many Miles to Babylon?* (illustrated by Paul Giovanopoulos), D. White, 1967, reissued, Washington Square Press, 1970; *Poor George,* Harcourt, 1967; *The Stone-Faced Boy* (ALA Notable Book; illustrated by Donald A. Mackay), Bradbury Press, 1968; *Dear Prosper* (illustrated by Steve McLachlin), D. White, 1968; *Portrait of Ivan* (illustrated by Saul Lambert), Bradbury Press, 1969; *The King's Falcon* (*Horn Book* Honor List; illustrated by Eros Keith), Bradbury Press, 1969; *Hungry Fred* (illustrated by Rosemary Wells), Bradbury Press, 1969; *Blowfish Live in the Sea,* Bradbury Press, 1970; *Desperate Characters* (adult), Harcourt, 1970; *The Western Coast,* Harcourt, 1972; *Good Ethan* (Junior Literary Guild selection; illustrated by Arnold Lobel), Bradbury Press, 1973; *The Slave Dancer* (ALA Notable Book; illustrated by E. Keith), Bradbury Press, 1973; *The Widow's Children,* Dutton, 1976; *The Little Swineherd And Other Tales* (illustrated by Leonard Lubin), E. P. Dutton, 1978.

*SIDELIGHTS:* Paula Fox was born in New York City in 1923 and received her education in three countries. She went to elementary schools in New York and in Cuba and to high schools in New Hampshire and Montreal. She described herself as "a traveling child" who seldom lived any place longer than a year or two and seldom saw either of her parents. Her father was a writer and she felt that her career was influenced by him. "I attended nine schools before I was twelve, by which time I had discovered that freedom, solace, and truth were public libraries." [Augusta Baker, "Paula Fox," *Horn Book,* August, 1974.[1]]

Fox studied at Columbia University but left before she received a degree, studied piano at the Juilliard School in New York, and began working at the age of seventeen. "My career sounds like flap copy of the 1930s. The strangest, but not the worst, job I ever had was punctuating Italian madrigals of the fifteenth century. I assume my employer thought my guess was as good as his. I worked in Europe for a year, for Victor Gollancz, then as a string reporter for a news agency. I've taught school for seven years, sold two television plays, written two novels for grown-ups. I started writing late by most standards, I guess. Now I can't seem to stop." [John Rowe Townsend, *A Sense of Story,* Lippincott, 1971.[2]]

In 1963 she began writing her novels. In 1971 she received a National Institute of Arts and Letters Award for recognition of her work, a Guggenheim Grant in 1971-72 and the Newbery Medal for *The Slave Dancer* in 1974. "Writing is immodest although the experience of it is full of chagrin, even of mortification. A writer dares to claim that he or she will tell you a story about people and circumstances you know the writer could not have known. Because writers have sovereignty over their own inventions, they appear to make an outrageous claim: They will tell you everything about the characters in their stories. This is a world, they say; and every stick of its furnishings—every gesture and grimace of the people who live among these furnishings—is true and revealed. But this is not what happens in life. In real life, we stammer, we dissimulate, we hide. In stories, we are privy to the secrets, the evasions, the visions of characters in a fashion which real life only permits us during periods of extraordinary sensibility, before habit has made us forget that the cries behind the locked doors are our own.

**Gus pressed his nose against the chilled window pane. It was light out now. From the eastern sky, an extraordinary radiance emanated from three red lines that stretched along the sky as far as he could see.** ■ (From *The Stone-Faced Boy* by Paula Fox. Illustrated by Donald Mackay.)

"The effort of writing is to approximate being, but our books can only have a degree of success. As we all know, when we put away the book we have been reading and return to the consciousness of the moment, art is not life. Our own individual lives are not finished inventions, but questions we can only partly answer.

"No writer can truly answer the question, 'Why did you write that book about those people?' Because, though the story between the book's covers is finished, the impulse that generated the story has been a question all along. I write to find out. I write to discover, over and over again, my connections with myself, with others. Each book deepens the question. It does not answer it.

"The ultimate experience of abandonment is to be abandoned; the ultimate experience of injustice is to feel its outrage in every part of one's life; of hunger, to be hungry; of violation, to be violated. And so the immodesty and claims of a novelist are appalling. Yet, lying just behind that immodesty is a nearly overpowering sense of how little one knows, of how one must labor with the stuff of one's own life and struggle against the narrowness of one's own experience of life. It *is* an appalling claim. Without that claim and without those stations along the way that fall far short of ultimate experiences but from which one can sense what it might be like to go the whole journey, no book can be written." [Paula Fox, "Newbery Award Acceptance," *Horn Book,* August, 1974.[3]]

"I never think I'm writing for children, when I work. A story does not start *for* anyone, nor an idea, nor a feeling of an idea; but starts more for oneself . . . I think any story is a metaphor. It is not life. There is no way out but to pick a glove that conforms most to the hand. But the glove is never the hand, only a shape. And a child's hand is not an adult's. So, of course, I do write for children, *or* for adults. But the connection between them, the differences even, don't seem to me to be really relevant, only talking-points. What applies to good writing is, I think, absolute, whether for children or grown-ups, or the blind or the deaf or the thin or the fat . . . I am just starting another children's book and another novel—and I hope I shall remember which is which."[2]

". . . A recurrent theme of Paula Fox's [books for children]," John Rowe Townsend wrote in *A Sense of Story,* "is that of noncommunication and lack of understanding between young and old. It is not the generation gap, exactly, but Miss Fox lives in the world we know at our nerve-ends, in which the old comfortable certainties can no longer be relied on. . . ."

The *New York Times* said of *How Many Miles to Babylon?* that, "There is a dual sense of isolation here; both the isolation of a lonely childhood and the further isolation of an impoverished urban existence. . . . What is rare and valuable . . . is its unblunted vision of the way things are, and its capacity to evoke the sense of what it is to live as so many people do live in this city, in this time." The *Times* also reviewed *The Stone-Faced Boy,* and commented that, "The surrealistic quality of Paula Fox's writing, so ably demonstrated in *How Many Miles to Babylon?* is also present in this work. [Her] books are for discerning readers who are able to take joy in getting below the surface, readers who can take a simply-stated thought and recognize the complexities it conveys."

A motion picture entitled "Desperate Characters" and based on Paula Fox's novel was released by Paramount Pictures in 1970, and starred Shirley MacLaine.

*FOR MORE INFORMATION SEE: Horn Book,* August, 1969, April and December, 1970, April and August, 1974; John Rowe Townsend, *A Sense of Story,* Longman, 1971; Margery Fisher, *Who's Who in Children's Books,* Holt, 1975; Lee Kingman, editor, *Newbery & Caldecott Medal Books: 1966-1975,* Horn Book, 1975; *Children's Literature Review,* Volume I, Gale, 1976.

# FREEMAN, Don   1908-1978

*PERSONAL:* Born August 11, 1908, in San Diego, Calif.; son of Mortimer Roy (a salesman) and Hazel (Currier) Freeman; married Lydia Cooley (an artist), June 30, 1931; children: Roy Warren. *Education:* Attended Art Students League of New York for two years. *Address:* 1932 Cleveland Ave., Santa Barbara, Calif. 93103.

*CAREER:* Began as a trumpet player in a jazz band; free lance artist, painter, and print-maker; graphic artist with the *New York Times* and *New York Herald Tribune* for more than 20 years; author and illustrator of books for children. *Awards, honors:* Book World Children's Spring Book Festival Award, 1953, for *Pet of the Met;* runner-up for the Caldecott Medal, 1958, for *Fly High, Fly Low;* Southern California Council on Literature for Children and Young People Award, 1962, for *Come Again, Pelican,* 1976, for *Will's*

*Quill;* Commonwealth Club of California Award, 1974, for *The Paper Party.*

*WRITINGS*—All for children and all self-illustrated, except as noted: *It Shouldn't Happen* (American wit and humor), Harcourt, 1945; *Come One, Come All!* (autobiography), Rinehart, 1949; (with wife, Lydia Freeman) *Chuggy and the Blue Caboose,* Viking, 1951; (with L. Freeman) *Pet of the Met,* Viking, 1953; *Beady Bear,* Viking, 1954, reissued, 1971; *Mop Top,* Viking, 1955, reissued, 1970; *Fly High, Fly Low* (ALA Notable Book), Viking, 1957, reissued, 1972; *The Night the Lights Went Out,* Viking, 1958; *Norman the Doorman,* Viking, 1959; *Space Witch,* Viking, 1959; *Cyrano the Crow,* Viking, 1960; *Come Again, Pelican,* Viking, 1961; *Ski Pup,* Viking, 1963; *Botts, the Naughty Otter,* Golden Gate Junior Books, 1963; *The Turtle and the Dove,* Viking, 1964; *Dandelion,* Viking, 1964.

*A Rainbow of My Own,* Viking, 1966; *The Guard Mouse,* Viking, 1967; *Add-a-Line Alphabet,* Golden Gate Junior Books, 1968; *Corduroy,* Viking, 1968; *Tilly Witch,* Viking, 1969; *Quiet! There's a Canary in the Library,* Golden Gate Junior Books, 1969; *Forever Laughter,* Golden Gate Junior Books, 1970; *Hattie the Backstage Bat,* Viking, 1970; *Penguins of All People!,* Viking, 1971; *Inspector Peckit,* Viking, 1972; *Flash the Dash* (Junior Literary Guild selection), Childrens Press, 1973; *The Paper Party,* Viking, 1974, Penguin, 1977; *The Seal and the Slick,* Viking, 1974; *Will's Quill,* Viking, 1975; *The Chalk Box Story,* Lippincott, 1976; *Bearymore,* Viking, 1976; *A Pocket for Corduroy,* Viking, 1978.

Illustrator: William Saroyan, *The Human Comedy,* Harcourt, 1943, revised edition, 1971; James Thurber, *White Deer,* Harcourt, 1945; Justin B. Atkinson, *Once around the Sun,* Harcourt, 1951; Julia L. Sauer, *Mike's House,* Viking, 1954, reissued, 1970; Jane Randolph, *Circus in Peter's Closet,* Crowell, 1955; Ann N. Clark, *Third Monkey,* Viking, 1956; Anne H. White, *The Uninvited Donkey,* Viking, 1957; Clyde R. Bulla, *Ghost Town Treasure,* Crowell, 1958; Dorothy Koch, *Monkeys are Funny that Way,* Holiday, 1962; W. Saroyan, *My Name Is Aram,* Harcourt, 1963; A. N. Clark, *This for That,* Golden Gate Junior Books, 1965; Astrid Lindgren, *Bill Bergson and the White Rose Rescue,* Viking, 1965; Myra B. Brown, *Best Friends,* Golden Gate Junior Books, 1967; Elizabeth Hall, *Voltaire's Micromegas,* Golden Gate Junior Books, 1967; Ruth A. Sonneborn, *Seven in a Bed,* Viking, 1968; Helen Bauer, *California Indian Days,* Doubleday, 1968; M. B. Brown, *Best of Luck,* Golden Gate Junior Books, 1969; Robert Burch, *Joey's Cat,* Viking, 1969; Julia Cunningham, *Burnish Me Bright,* Pantheon, 1970; Jacklyn M. Matthews, *Edward and the Night Horses,* Golden Gate Junior Books, 1971; Elizabeth K. Cooper, *The Wild Cats of Rome,* Golden Gate Junior Books, 1972; J. Cunningham, *Far in the Day,* Pantheon, 1972; Marjorie Thayer, *The Christmas Strangers,* Childrens Press, 1976; Richard Peck, *Monster Night at Grandma's House,* Viking, 1977.

*ADAPTATIONS*—Filmstrips: "Norman The Doorman," Weston Woods.

*SIDELIGHTS:* **August 11, 1908.** Born in San Diego, California. Freeman and brother, Warren, were placed with a guardian, Mrs. Blass, when they were quite young. Their father visited them on Sundays. "My story begins when the world was a town named Chula Vista in a place especially designed for kids to stub their toes on. Here in Chula Vista, California, a few miles above the border of Mexico, I re-

**DON FREEMAN**

member discovering that I was alive and free—to a certain extent.

"Life in those days seemed to consist solely of freckles, pepper trees, and a woman named Mrs. Blass. More than anything else her presence became the inevitable obstacle standing in the way of complete freedom. Through certain arrangements which were not made entirely clear to me at the time, Mrs. Blass had become the guardian over my brother Warren, myself, and a boy named Botsford Beverforden. She was extremely strict and appropriately plump, endowments which would have been perfectly acceptable to us had she not also possessed a zealous urge to remake the rest of the world in her own image and likeness.

"Botsford's parents were both living at the time; however, they were living apart from each other. His father, I remember hearing, was in the consular service attached to some country as distant as Siam, while his mother shivered in Alaska. Mrs. Blass had come into the picture opportunely by contracting to care for Botsford until his far-flung family could pull itself together.

"My brother Warren, having four more years to his credit than both Bots and myself, was allowed a comparatively free rein while we two were held in firm check. Any failure on our part to toe the line brought forth cool beads of perspiration on Mrs. Blass's brow like the early morning dew on a pumpkin—a condition we gradually learned to recognize as the first sign of an impending storm.

"Without a doubt the brightest and most anticipated event of the week came on Sunday—the day my father traveled out to see us. It was his only chance to shower us with affection, as he worked hard the full week in a clothing store in San Diego eleven miles away. I believe he lived for this day just as much as we lived for the few hours we could be with him.

"Each Sunday he would bring us presents—always three of a kind; although Botsford was not his boy, he was included in everything. Sometimes he brought clothes, sometimes games, but always he remembered to bring me drawing materials.

"We longed for the day when we could live in San Diego and see my father more often. Happily, sooner than we dared hope, this move was unexpectedly precipitated." [Don Freeman, *Come One, Come All!*, Rinehart, 1949.[1]]

When floods threatened their home in Chula Vista, the Freeman boys moved with Mrs. Blass and their father to San Diego into a small house owned by their guardian. "San Diego in those days purred along like a contented cat. Not that the inhabitants were in the least bit lazy; they just seemed to surge ahead but in one place—and a more beautiful place for such placid movement could not possibly be found. From nearly every window in the entire town the view of the bay was almost inescapable. However, our house on Kalmia Street had many windows but none of them exposed the bay, which was perfectly all right because we had other things—kids next door. I wanted neighbors more than I wanted a view. I had had all the scenic wonders I needed. The floodwaters would hold me for a long time.

"I daresay that Kalmia Street held more life and energy than any other thoroughfare in town, most of which to be sure was expended by one family in particular, the Bartletts. Mrs. Bartlett had several children, with another always in process. Some of their names are implanted in my memory like a sailor's tattoo: the girls' names were Delight, Joanna and Rosemary and my special pals were Squeek and Legler.

"The houses themselves were two- or three-story affairs, ours being by far the funniest: a two-story square stuccoed contraption with a windowed topknot called the solarium. In this solarium Mrs. Blass kept all her precious keepsakes, such as a pair of crutches that once belonged to her deceased husband, several charcoal portraits of relatives and one of a very small boy in a lace collar, wearing long black stockings (we were never told who he was).

"It got to be a full house, especially when my father came and lived with us. He had the room next to mine and it did begin to feel more like home. Although we rarely saw him during the week, since he rose early and worked late, just knowing he was close by helped a lot. Ever so faintly I could recall having felt this sensation of home before. That was

*The circus tent as seen from my window*

(From *Come One, Come All!* by Don Freeman. Illustrated by the author.)

(From *Come One, Come All!* by Don Freeman. Illustrated by the author.)

during the brief period when my father and mother and Warren and myself lived together on A Street, farther downtown. Of my mother I remember only her frailty and strong devotion.

"Having my father in the same house—well, it was like having somebody on your side, though he never interfered in any way with our appointed guardian's sense of direction. Mrs. Blass had been recommended by a close friend of my mother's, and in her last long illness she had asked her to help care for us. Though circumstances prevented my father from being with us as often as he would have liked, his move to Kalmia Street was a reminder of a dim and pleasanter past and it brightened up the somewhat disjointed present.

"The greatest adjustment for living in the town of San Diego came with learning to wear shoes. After this quaint custom was accepted, there was nothing else to do but live abundantly within the limits of Mrs. Blass's eagle eye.

"Our living in San Diego really gave me the hoped-for chance to see my father more often. Saturday afternoons were usually spent with him in the clothing store where he worked for a gruff boss named Mr. McCusick. For a while Mr. McCusick had me convinced that he was a bear in human disguise, as he succeeded in scaring me whenever I arrived at the store asking for my father.

"When I wasn't busy sketching the customers [in the clothing store] I wandered around the block inspecting the penny arcades and ten-cent movies that showed hair-raising serials, the story content of which I stored up for our own back-yard after-school productions. Saturday nights I had the privilege of eating dinner with my father, and whenever he didn't work in the evening he would take me to see the local stock company's stage shows. These were rare and memorable moments for me. My father loved the theater and rarely missed a production if he could help it. Together we saw such plays as 'Checkers' and 'Seven Keys to Baldpate.' We would sit in the balcony and take turns looking through a small pair of opera glasses which he greatly prized."[1]

**Christmas, 1918.** "It was like my father to know exactly what I wanted without my ever having to hint. For my tenth Christmas he gave me a present of a shiny brass trumpet.

"No directions went along with the gift of the trumpet because my father knew the problem of learning how to play the instrument would have to be my own worry. But there was no worry to it. Whenever Mrs. Blass went out of the house I turned on the records and sat next to the Victrola and blew myself red in the face. Eventually I got wind of how to play scales and a few other essentials, and after several months I played along with the best recorded orchestras in the nation."[1]

**Late 1920's.** Graduated from high school. "My attributes as a student can best be passed over, saving untold embarrassment all around. It is enough to say that I did graduate, though hardly with honors. It is a pleasure to recall that commencement day, since I know I will never have to relive it.

"As the solemn exercises began, terror seized me. From out of nowhere a telegram appeared. It was handed down the long row of frigid classmates and I knew it was addressed to me. I imagined its contents: STEP OUT OF LINE CALCULATIONS SHOW DISCREPANCY IN GRADE MARKING MAKING IT IMPOSSIBLE FOR YOU TO GRADUATE.

"But I was wrong! the telegram contained an invitation from my grandmother to come to San Diego and take a summer course in art—her graduation gift to me!

"It had been an unquestioned intention to make for New York immediately, but my grandmother's gift offering disarmed me and the enticement was irresistible.

"Studying art in the San Diego School of Fine Arts, situated in the midst of beautiful Balboa Park, had its value, although at first staying in San Diego seemed like a retrogressive step and it bothered my conscience. But soon I found that drawing from the nude model and studying anatomy were important activities and I became increasingly grateful to my grandmother for her present. . . .

"I found a room on the other side of town, on Hermosa Street, and spent several mornings in the public library, where the sanctity of these walls became a refuge for reflection. I read Dickens, Dana, and Robert Henri's *Art Spirit,* and looked through all the popular magazines studying the illustrations. But all this was evading the issue. I knew I could no longer put off the idea of having to start earning a living. Art and illustration and the cool library were all right, indulgences certainly to be desired, and yet they were luxuries that had temporarily to take a back seat.

"The trumpet my father had given me for a Christmas present many years before still came in handy, and once in a while I found myself torn between a life playing the horn and a life using the pencil. Whenever I heard Bix Beiderbecke play cornet solos on the latest recordings I would have put my soul in hock to have been able to blow hot licks like his.

". . . To pay my New York train fare plenty of musical notes had to be blown from my trumpet, and eventually I had no trouble securing small-time engagements for nearly every night.

"I played my first job in a tough boxing arena on the sailor side of San Diego, in a five-piece band. Our job was to strike up tunes immediately after a fighter hit the canvas for a K.O. The leader of the band knew more about boxing than he knew about music. He could tell to the punch how long the boxers would last, and before they went down for the count we had our instruments poised ready to rip into a chorus of 'If You Knew Susie Like I Know Susie.'"[1]

**Fall, 1929.** Hitch-hiked from California to New York, playing his trumpet on one night stands across the country. "One state after another rolled out its vast earth-green rug under me. I was well on my way at last.

"But making a beeline across the map of America took slightly longer than calculated. I had to make a stopover in Indianapolis in order to do a little financial refueling. Picking up a few one-night orchestra engagements gave the needed pecuniary push and then I was ready to hitch a ride the rest of the distance.

"Standing on the highway just outside the city limits, I waved a battered trumpet case relentlessly at every moving object to come over the hill heading east. After a good hour of this exercise and with both my thumbs going numb I still had no luck.

"During this quiet spell by the roadside I could almost hear myself thinking, it was so peaceful—and if there was anything to be avoided at this stage, it was an examination of my own thoughts.

"True, I was now free and on my own for the first time, and yet having so much freedom all at once rather overwhelmed me. I hoped that no one would ask me what I intended doing and exactly what I wanted out of life because I realized one thing while waiting there—I had no clear answer.

"My mind was a menagerie of desires: I wanted to be an artist, certainly, but I wanted just as much to see New York and find out how everybody lived and how they looked and acted. I wanted to play a horn, too—this was probably the only thing I had a grain of confidence in doing—and along with this I wanted to find out whether or not it was possible to earn a living, at anything. What it came right down to, I suppose, was that I only wanted to live and look around."[1]

Finally arrived in New York City. "Dazed at finding myself unexpectedly without a job and yet more than a little dazzled at having landed at last in New York, I stood on the corner of 47th Street and Broadway holding my horn in one hand and my suitcase in the other. From the open windows above came sounds of saxophones, pianos and trombones. This, I knew instinctively, was Tin-Pan Alley!

"By seven o'clock, dirty and dog-tired, I decided to call it quits and I checked into a small hotel off Broadway. After cleaning up and attempting a quick snooze I went out again for a bit to eat and to take in the Great White Way at night.

"The following day I reluctantly decided to have one last fling at picking up a steady job off the sidewalks. . . . But no luck. As a last resort I wandered into the Gaiety Building on Broadway, five floors packed with small-time sad theatrical agents. Each floor had nothing to offer but discouragement—except the fifth. Here the door of one of the offices was wide open. Taking this as a sign of cordiality, I walked in.

"Inside the stuffy and active office a singing sister act was giving a tryout. The walls were plastered with photographs of faintly famous entertainers; all had autographed their smiling faces to their agent, who at this moment sat talking into a pay phone planted on top of his desk. This must be Al Romero if the name on the door meant anything.

"In the middle of his conversation he suddenly stopped and looked up at—not at me, exactly, but at the trumpet case I was carrying. We eyed each other for a few seconds.

"Then, as he held his hand over the phone receiver, he shouted,'Hey a trumpet! I just now got a call for a trumpet job. Want to work?'

(From *Mike's House* by Julia L. Sauer. Illustrated by Don Freeman.)

"'What's in it?' I asked him, fortifying myself against any further trickery.

"'It's a wedding reception at Hennington Hall down on the East Side. Eleven bucks. So I ask you, do you take it or don't you?'

"'Sure, but I gotta be guaranteed the eleven,' I said."[1]

**1929-1930.** Supported himself by playing trumpet. Studied with John Sloan and Harry Wickey at the Art Students League. He also travelled around New York with his sketchbook and by drawing, came to know New York. "New York and I were rapidly becoming good friends; in fact, instead of feeling like a stranger I began to feel as if we had known each other all our lives. Everyone was accepted on equal terms, and made you wonder where you'd been keeping yourself. But along with all this felicity went an inescapable obligation. I knew I had to do something in return for the privilege of being a part of such a family. Everything demanded to be recorded, and my great worry was that the dimestore supply of sketchbooks might run out. They seemed to have only a limited stock and I was practically buying them in carloads. They were small, inconspicuous, leather-bound books which looked like textbooks. I liked them for that reason. Sketch pads sold in art stores are obviously arty and a menace. Eyes always start bulging, heads twist around, crowds gather, and an artist usually has to give up sketching. It's a natural reaction; even sign painters are bothered by gawkers. I know that if ever I happened to come across an artist sketching I would break my neck to get a look at what he was doing. But curiosity not only kills cats, it kills creation.

"That is why these dime-store books gave me the protection I needed. Whenever I started sketching, I pretended to be making out a laundry list or adding up a column of figures, mumbling aloud. This worked fairly well as a distraction, though I knew I couldn't go on mumbling such stuff as 'three socks, six shorts, four shirts' forever. Yet I had to keep drawing so as to let the world know what wonderful people I had come across—not only the way they looked, but the way they invented lives for themselves out of nothing: carrying signs, fishing for change through sidewalk gratings, shining shoes, peddling gardenias, selling corsets, plugging song hits, washing windows, sharpening knives. They made the streets a feast for artists.

"... From the instant I stepped into John Sloan's painting class, his forceful flow of wisdom made being there seem the rarest privilege anyone could ever have.

"The very appearance of the man sang out his greatness: his sharp eyes, jutting chin, his brushed-forward sheaf of steel-gray hair helped keynote his character. Even his brilliant emerald-green tie exposed the fact that his ancestors were Irish. But what he had to say let us know even more convincingly that he came from high-voltage stock. Never in my life had I seen or heard anything to beat him. His words were like sparks and his ideas charged me with a live current of inspiration. Interspersed among his serious remarks was a sharp, deep, and devastating wit.

"His criticisms were given in an impersonal manner, never addressed directly to the student whose work he happened to be commenting upon but spoken so that all could hear. Art instruction to him apparently, was no private affair, it was as public as breathing, and he used our individual efforts merely as a springboard for discoursing on more vital matters. Philosophically, whatever Mr. Sloan had to say on art tied up directly with everything else in the world from nature to politicians. I gathered readily that he was just as vehemently opposed to seeing a student slave away meticulously copying the shadows on a figure as he was opposed to seeing the citizens of the nation complacently putting up with corruption; and he flayed both approaches with his blowtorch honesty. According to him, shadows were merely the absence of light, and if as students we were there to study how to create substance with color, then shadows hardly mattered. Form came first.

"His forthright observations of the work upon which he based his remarks made me quite nervous. I dreaded his seeing what I had awkwardly commenced painting. . . . Anything that reeked of the slick made him sick, and he said so in no uncertain terms.

"My work certainly came under the heading of clumsiness, but something of the slick also crept in—a mistaken notion of trying to give the impression of competence. All this had to go and a personal expression put in its place.

"Mr. Sloan encouraged us to feel as free as possible in interpreting the figure as long as we were not influenced by the 'photographic.' The 'camera eye' he called anything that looked flat. 'The camera can't think!' he said. 'It only photographs lies. If you would believe the camera's statements about nature, you would have to believe that the hand that is nearest you is always larger than the hand farther back. But this isn't so, both hands are the same size—that is, they were before the camera was invented. The artists in the past were never bothered by this sort of distortion—look at Rembrandt, Leech, Van Gogh—they actually resisted perspective!'

"The smoke-filled cafeteria at the League rated more adherents to varying schools of thought than any other department of the institution and fiercely enthusiastic discussions were always going on. All the students, however, agreed on one subject wholeheartedly—the importance of food.

"Early one noontime while sitting in the lunchroom finishing a bowl of soup, I felt vibrations from several powerful voices emanating from the classroom adjoining. Not a single booming word penetrated the wall distinctly, but rarely had I felt such compelling ardor, especially over art and, if I knew my vibrations, these were certainly most sincere.

"Printed on the door of the classroom was *Subjects: Etching and Lithography.* Lithography is a medium for drawing on stone with a greased pencil and it had always interested me, but since I hadn't yet learned how to draw on paper I judiciously put off getting involved with this fascinating process. Now the sounds from inside the class made me think I was missing something.

"Next day I signed up for instruction in this class and not long afterwards I too was shouting explosively. I found that the lithographic medium fitted my temperament to a T-square. The sensitive surface of the flat stone was so rewarding that it set me to work translating into prints all the random sketches I had gathered about town.

"Now my weekly calendar read something like this: Lithographing in the morning, painting in the afternoon and Broadwaying at night."[1]

**Early 1930's.** His trumpet playing ended quite abruptly when he lost his trumpet on the subway. "One night I was coming home on the subway and was so busy sketching I didn't realize it was my stop until it was almost too late. I lurched out of the train, the doors closed behind me, and I realized I had left my trumpet inside. I know it sounds melodramatic, but there I was pounding on the door. Losing my horn made me face the fact that I would have to make my living by drawing. I started submitting work to Arthur Folwell, the editor of the *Herald Tribune* Sunday section. My work kept piling up on his desk as Mr. Folwell found it quite resistible. Then one Saturday night when I was walking up Eighth Avenue, I bought a Sunday paper, and there was one of my drawings printed on the front page of the drama section!"

"Had the drama editor known what a weekly pest I was to become after that, he probably would have reconsidered before using this first drawing. Every Monday afternoon at four, for the next several years, I appeared at his desk loaded with material gathered from my adventures through the stage doors of all the current productions. Having ecstatically crashed into the theater with this one drawing, it was almost unbelievable to me that such a privilege could also be a way of earning a living—seeing the plays and being paid for it at the same time!

"However, not *all* the drawings I showered on the drama department were used, far from it. Two long months went by before another drawing of mine appeared. It seems other artists had to live also. I became used to the routine of wildly opening the Sunday paper to find my drawing had been left out. The editor possessed a special gift for encouraging artists. He did it with such verbose versatility that it was almost worth going to see him every Monday just to hear how he would paraphrase his eloquent rejection.

"These drawings as they appeared were paid for by the column; in other words, if a drawing stretched across three columns I would be paid thirty dollars, ten a column. No matter how deep the drawing, it was the width that counted, a fact which may account somewhat for the tendency of my compositions to take on a rather wide rectangular shape!

"The appearance in print of this first drawing established necessary proof for the press agents of the various shows that I had legitimate business backstage.

"After having once passed through the stage door, I was a goner, given over completely to the fantastic backstage world of scene shifters, electricians, seamstresses, chorus girls and stars. . . .

"After several of my drawings had appeared in the newspapers, including the now defunct New York *World* and the going concern called the New York *Times,* the desire to see something of mine printed on the glossy pages of a magazine prompted me to gather up enough courage to see the editor of *Theatre* Magazine. The art editor must have had a heart of gold, for right off she sent me out on an assignment to cover a rehearsal of Ziegfeld's 'Show Girl.'

"I had the opportunity of meeting most of the famous Broadway actors and actresses. At first meeting the stars in their dressing rooms made me nervous, but later I found that they were nothing but people with a coating of greasepaint. Most of them put up with my snooping, probably because their publicity agents told them it might mean getting their faces in the Sunday paper."[1]

**It all began the day Mrs. Blass suddenly fell victim to an urge to make soldiers out of us. ■** (From *Come One, Come All!* by Don Freeman. Illustrated by the author.)

Freeman's drawings appeared in the *Herald Tribune* for many years. His impressions of New York became a regular feature of the New York *Times* drama section and his work also appeared in *Christian Science Monitor, Theatre* Magazine and several other magazines and newspapers.

**June, 1931.** Married Lydia Cooley, an artist whom he had met while enrolled for the summer at San Diego School of Fine Arts. The couple made New York their home. Theater life continued to be lucrative—Freeman did a series of posters and a series of sketches for the famous New York restaurant, Sardi's. ''Came spring and came the girl from California and I could not help being extremely delighted and personally proud of the show my city put on for her welcome. New York emerged from the long winter with all the eagerness of a young bear romping out of hibernation. The population flocked into the sunshine seeking every opportunity to get out from under the cold gray shadows. Central Park flourished with enraptured couples. 'Keep off the grass' signs lost all authority—everyone broke the law and nature ruled supreme.

''Perhaps I was biased, but spring in the country could be no match for spring in the city! Seasonal signs of the earth's awakening were everywhere. In the windows of the drab tenements mattresses bloomed, pillows popped out on fire escapes with all the profusion of an orchard of blooming apple trees.

''Yes, the city in all its grimy glory helped me win over my girl Lydia to my way of life. Her name now became synonymous with spring. It was love at first sight between her and the city and soon afterward we were married in a little church around the corner from the Little Church Around the Corner.

''Word reached California about our matrimonial amalgamation. Not having heard from my old guardian Mrs. Blass for such a great while, it came more or less as a shock when a letter finally did arrive. She seemed not to be quite her buoyant self, probably because she learned that the girl was of my own choosing and not hers.

''Our honeymoon was spent revisiting all the places I had written Lydia about. She had to see Mulberry Street, Orchard Street, and the Bowery, and of course Broadway. We took our time wandering around. Sometimes we got caught in sudden spring showers, but nothing stopped us from sketching almost everything we saw. I hadn't dared hope she would feel as I did about the city but there she was, driven to make water colors and drawings of the city with the same elation as I had first felt. She found subjects I had blindly passed by. It seemed incredible to me that I could have skipped so much.

''Eventually she met all my friends, who accepted her unanimously as I knew they would.''[1]

**1943.** While Freeman and his wife lived on 14th Street in Greenwich Village he was asked by Saroyan to illustrate his books, *My Name is Aaron* (1940) and *The Human Comedy.* ''Mr. Saroyan looked at my drawings and said, 'I want you to illustrate my new book!' I thought I'd never hear from him again, but I was wrong. I did, and later, I did the illustrations for his *My Name is Aaron* and *The Human Comedy.*'' [''Don Freeman,'' *Books are by People,* Lee Bennett Hopkins, Citation Press, 1969.[2]]

**1945.** Illustrated James Thurber's novel, *White Deer. It Shouldn't Happen,* a book of cartoons based on Freeman's experiences in the Army during World War II, was published.

**Dandelion decided to sit on Jennifer Giraffe's front steps until his mane was dry. ■** (From *Dandelion* by Don Freeman. Illustrated by the author.)

**1949.** Only son, Roy, was born in Santa Barbara, California where Freeman and his wife had returned to live.

**1951.** With his wife, Lydia, wrote and illustrated his first book for children, *Chuggy and the Blue Caboose*. It was a California librarian, Marge Raskin, who encouraged Freeman to publish his book. "Marge encouraged me to send in a book I did for my son. 'Send it to a publisher,' she said. It was published, and since then I've been hooked. Illustrating children's books is an expression of the theatre for me. I can create my own theatre in picture books. I love the flow of turning the pages, the suspense of what's next. Ideas just come at me and after me. It's all so natural. I work all the time, long into the night, and it's such a pleasure. I don't know when time ends. I've never been happier in my life!"[2]

**1953.** Won the Book World Children's Spring Book Festival Award for his second book, *Pet of the Met*.

**1958.** Runner-up for the Caldecott Medal for *Fly High, Fly Low*.

**1964.** *Dandelion* was published. A Freeman idiosyncrasy was the habit of checking into a hotel as a book deadline approached so that he wouldn't be distracted. "I've finished books in hotels in San Francisco, Los Angeles, New York City, and a host of other big cities. *Dandelion*, a funny account of a lion who decides to live up to his name, was done in a gloomy hotel room in Washington, D.C."[2]

**1968.** *Corduroy,* a story about a stuffed bear in green corduroy overalls was published. The Freemans made Santa Barbara their home although the artist still was in love with city living. "If I had a map of the world and someone gave me a thumbtack to place where I would *not* want to live, I'd put it on Santa Barbara. We live in a wooden house, sort of a mountain cabin. When someone asks me about it, I just say, 'It's beautiful—but I don't mind it!' I'm a city guy. I love big cities. I love to be involved with big cities. I only need one bush or one tree—out there I have too many. People keep me going. My hobby is living."[2]

**1973.** *Flash the Dash,* his twenty-fifth children's book was published. "As best I can recall, the idea for *Flash the Dash* began creeping up on me a few years ago, right after meeting two lively dachshunds who belonged to a friend of mine. These two dogs wanted to play games with me and they wouldn't take 'No, not now' for an answer. I remember innocently throwing some sort of rubber object as far as possible, only to have them dash after it and bring it back and lay it in my lap. I suppose they took turns. Anyway, this so-called game went on and on until my arm and patience grew weak to the point of exhaustion.

"Little did I know that these two perpetual-motion pets would continue chasing me in my mind for months afterwards. Finally one day I sat down and started putting together a story about a dachshund who delivered telegrams. The name Flash came naturally but the name for his mate took a bit of headscratching. Yes, she had to be Sashay."

**February 1, 1978.** Died at the age of sixty-nine. His latest book, *A Pocket for Corduroy,* was in press at the time of his death. Many of Freeman's books have been translated into foreign languages. In all editions, hardcover and paperback, there are more than one million copies of his books in print today. "Creating picture books for children fulfills all my enthusiasms and interests and love of life."

*FOR MORE INFORMATION SEE: Kirkus,* September 15, 1949; *Christian Science Monitor,* November 10, 1949, May 7, 1964; *New York Times,* November 13, 1949, April 12, 1953, October 6, 1957; *New York Herald Tribune Book Review,* December 11, 1949, May 17, 1953, November 17, 1957; *Chicago Sunday Tribune,* June 7, 1953; Bertha M. Miller and others, compilers, *Illustrators of Children's Books, 1946-1956,* Horn Book, 1958; *Horn Book,* June, 1963, June, 1966, April, 1977; Muriel Fuller, editor, *More Junior Authors,* H. W. Wilson, 1963; Lee Kingman and others, compilers, *Illustrators of Children's Books, 1957-1966,* Horn Book, 1968; Lee B. Hopkins, *Books Are by People,* Citation Press, 1969; *Contemporary American Illustrators of Children's Book,* Rutgers University Art Gallery, 1974.

(Died February 1, 1978)

## GALDONE, Paul 1914-

*PERSONAL:* Born in Budapest, Hungary; emigrated to the United States in 1928; married wife, Jannelise; children: Joanna, Paul Ferencz. *Education:* Studied art at the Art Student's League and New York School for Industrial Design. *Home:* New City, New York.

*CAREER:* Author and illustrator of books for children. Early jobs included bus boy, electrician's helper, and fur dryer. Worked for four years in the art department at Doubleday. *Military service:* United States Army Engineers, World War II. *Awards, honors:* Runner-up for the Caldecott Medal, 1957, for *Anatole,* and 1958, for *Anatole and the Cat* (both written by Eve Titus).

*WRITINGS*—All self-illustrated: (With Eve Titus) *Basil of Baker Street,* McGraw-Hill, 1958; *Paddy the Penguin,* Crowell, 1959; (with E. Titus) *Anatole over Paris,* McGraw-Hill, 1961; *Hare and the Tortoise,* McGraw-Hill, 1962; (with Feenie Ziner) *Counting Carnival,* Coward-McCann, 1962; *The First Seven Days,* Crowell, 1962; *Little Tuppen,* Seabury, 1967; *The Horse, the Fox, and the Lion,* Seabury, 1968; *Life of Jack Sprat, His Wife, and Cat,* McGraw-Hill, 1969; *The Monkey and the Crocodile,* Seabury, 1969; (with Richard W. Armour) *All Sizes and Shapes of Monkeys and Apes,* McGraw-Hill, 1970; (with daughter, Joanna Galdone) *Honeybee's Party,* F. Watts, 1972; *The Moving Adventures of Old Dame Trot and Her Comical Cat,* McGraw-Hill, 1973; (with J. Galdone) *Gertrude, the Goose Who Forgot,* F. Watts, 1975; *The Magic Porridge Pot,* Seabury, 1976.

Illustrator and reteller: *Old Woman and Her Pig,* Whittlesey House, 1960; *The House That Jack Built,* Whittlesey House, 1961; *The Three Wishes,* Whittlesey House, 1961; Mother Goose, *Tom, Tom, the Piper's Son,* McGraw-Hill, 1964; Francois Rabelais, *The Wise Fool,* Random House, 1968; *Henny Penny,* Seabury, 1968; *Androcles and the Lion,* McGraw-Hill, 1970; *Three Little Pigs,* Seabury, 1970; *History of Little Tom Tucker,* McGraw-Hill, 1970; *Obedient*

**PAUL GALDONE**

"I have a trouble, mynheer," answered Hans, casting down his eyes. Then lifting them again with almost a happy expression, he added, "but it is Hans who can help mynheer van Holp this time." ■ (From *Hans Brinker: Or The Silver Skates* by Mary Mapes Dodge. Illustrated by Paul Galdone.)

*Jack*, F. Watts, 1971; *The Town Mouse and the Country Mouse*, McGraw-Hill, 1971; Aesop, *Three Aesop Fox Fables*, Seabury, 1971; *The Three Bears*, Seabury, 1972; Peter C. Asbjornsen, *The Three Billy Goats Gruff*, Seabury, 1973; Joseph Jacobs, *Hereafterthis*, McGraw-Hill, 1973; *The Little Red Hen* (ALA Notable Book), Seabury, 1973; Grimm Brothers, *Little Red Riding Hood*, McGraw-Hill, 1974; Grimm Brothers, *The Frog Prince*, McGraw-Hill, 1974; *The Gingerbread Boy*, Seabury, 1975; Charles Perrault, *Puss in Boots*, Seabury, 1976.

Illustrator: Ellen MacGregor, *Miss Pickerell Goes to Mars*, Whittlesey House, 1951; Edward Fenton, *Nine Lives*, Pantheon, 1951; Ruthven Todd, *Space Cat*, Scribner, 1952, reissued, 1971; E. MacGregor, *Miss Pickerell and the Geiger Counter*, McGraw-Hill, 1953; Doris T. Plenn, *Green Song*, McKay, 1954; E. MacGregor, *Miss Pickerell Goes to the Arctic*, McGraw-Hill, 1954, reissued, 1967; Mary Mapes Dodge, *Hans Brinker*, Doubleday, 1954; Miriam Schlein, *How Do You Travel*, Abingdon, 1954; William O. Steele, *Winter Danger* (ALA Notable Book), Harcourt, 1954; E. MacGregor, *Theodore Turtle*, Whittlesey House, 1955; W.

O. Steele, *Tomahawks and Trouble*, Harcourt, 1955; Edward M. Eager, *Playing Possum*, Putnam, 1955; E. MacGregor, *Mr. Ferguson and the Fire Department*, Whittlesey House, 1956; W. O. Steele, *Lone Hunt*, Harcourt, 1956; Eve Titus, *Anatole*, Whittlesey House, 1956; Margaret T. Burroughs, *Did You Feed My Cow?*, Crowell, 1956; Amy Hogeboom, *Audubon and His Sons*, Lothrop, 1956; Clyde T. Bulla, *Sword in the Tree*, Crowell, 1956; R. Todd. *Space Cat Meets Mars*, Scribner, 1957; F. Mowat, *The Dog Who Wouldn't Be*, Little, 1952; E. Titus, *Anatole and the Cat*, McGraw-Hill, 1957; M. Franklin and Eleanor K. Vaughan, *Rusty Rings a Bell*, Crowell, 1957; W. O. Steele, *Flaming Arrows* (ALA Notable Book), Harcourt, 1957; C. R. Bulla, *Old Charlie*, F. Watts, 1957; W. O. Steele, *Perilous Road* (ALA Notable Book), Harcourt, 1958; M. Franklin and E. K. Vaughan, *Timmy and the Tin-Can Telephone*, Crowell, 1959; Nathaniel Hawthorne, *The Golden Touch*, McGraw-Hill, 1959; W. O. Steele, *Far Frontier*, Harcourt, 1959.

Mother Goose, *Old Mother Hubbard and Her Dog*, McGraw-Hill, 1960; Scott Corbett, *The Lemonade Trick*, Little, Brown, 1960; Eve Merriam, *A Gaggle of Geese*, Knopf, 1960; Alfred Steinburg, *Woodrow Wilson*, Putnam, 1961; S. Corbett, *The Mailbox Trick*, Little, Brown, 1961; William Wise, *The Cowboy Surprise*, Putnam, 1961; Helen E. Buckley, *Grandmother and I*, Lothrop, 1961; Cora Cheney and Ben Partridge, *Rendezvous in Singapore*, Knopf, 1961; Karin Anckarsvard, *Robber Ghost*, translated from the Swedish by Annabelle Macmillan, Harcourt, 1961; Helen E. Buckley, *Grandfather and I*, Lothrop, 1961; Esther M. Meeks, *Jeff and Mr. James' Pond*, Lothrop, 1962; Edward Lear, *The Two Old Bachelors*, McGraw-Hill, 1962; K. Anckarsvard, *Madcap Mystery*, translated from the Swedish by A. Macmillan, Harcourt, 1962; Alice E. Goudey, *Sunnyvale Fair*, Scribner, 1962; John G. Saxe, *The Blind Men and the Elephant*, McGraw-Hill, 1963; Henry Wadsworth Longfellow, *Paul Revere's Ride*, Crowell, 1963; S. Corbett, *The Disappearing Dog Trick*, Little, Brown, 1963; Wilson Gage, pseudonym of Mary Q. Steele, *Miss Osborne-the-Mop*, World Publishing, 1963; Robert Barry, *Mister Willowby's Christmas Tree*, McGraw-Hill, 1963.

Rhoda Bacmeister, *People Downstairs, and Other City Stories*, Coward-McCann, 1964; Vitali Bianki, *Peek the Piper*, Braziller, 1964; Johanna Johnston, *Edie Changes Her Mind*, Putnam, 1964; S. Corbett, *The Limerick Trick*, Little, Brown, 1964; Francis Hopkinson, *The Battle of the Kegs*, Crowell, 1964; Mary O'Neill, *People I'd Like to Keep*, Doubleday, 1964; E. Titus, *Anatole and the Poodle*, Whittlesey House, 1965; John Greenleaf Whittier, *Barbara Frietchie*, Crowell, 1965; Richard W. Armour, *The Adventures of Egbert the Easter Egg*, McGraw-Hill, 1965; Oliver Wendell Holmes, *The Deacon's Masterpiece*, McGraw-Hill, 1965; Bible, *Shadrach, Meshach, and Abednego*, Whittlesey House, 1965; Helen E. Buckley, *The Little Boy and the Birthdays*, Lothrop, 1965; S. Corbett, *The Baseball Trick*, Little, Brown, 1965; K. Anckarsvard, *Mysterious Schoolmaster*, translated from the Swedish by A. Macmillan, Harcourt, 1965; Hans Peterson, *Brownie*, Lothrop, 1965; Dale Fife, *Who's in Charge of Lincoln*, Coward-McCann, 1965.

E. Titus, *Anatole and the Piano*, McGraw-Hill, 1966; J. Johnston, *That's Right, Edie*, Putnam, 1966; *The History of Simple Simon*, McGraw-Hill, 1966; Francis Scott Key, *The Star-Spangled Banner*, Crowell, 1966; Ivan Kusan, *Koko and the Ghosts*, Harcourt, 1966; E. Lear, *Two Laughable Lyrics*, Putnam, 1966; R. W. Armour, *Animals on the Ceiling*, McGraw-Hill, 1966; Wilson Gage, *The Ghost of Five Owl Farm*, World Publishing, 1966; Lee G. Goetz, *A Camel*

**That night millions of cats marched through Anatole's dreams, shouting "Down with Anatole! Down with Anatole!"** ■ (From *Anatole and the Cat* by Eve Titus. Illustrated by Paul Galdone.)

*in the Sea,* McGraw-Hill, 1966; Sidney Offit, *The Adventures of Homer Fink,* St. Martin, 1966; Edgar Allan Poe, *Three Poems of Edgar Allan Poe,* McGraw-Hill, 1966; Wylly Folk St. John, *The Secrets of Hidden Creek,* Viking, 1966; R. W. Armour, *A Dozen Dinosaurs,* McGraw-Hill, 1967; Guy Daniels, *The Tear's Riddles,* McGraw-Hill, 1967; S. Corbett, *The Turnabout Trick,* Little, Brown, 1967; Barbara Rinkoff, *Elbert, the Mind Reader,* Lothrop, 1967; N. Hawthorne, *Pandora's Box: The Paradise of Children,* McGraw-Hill, 1967; Patricia M. Martin, *Woody's Big Trouble,* Putnam, 1967; Letta Schatz, *Whiskers, My Cat,* McGraw-Hill, 1967; Judy Van der Veer, *Wallace the Wandering Pig,* Harcourt, 1967; R. W. Armour, *Who's in Holes,* McGraw-Hill, 1967; Paul Showers, *Your Skin and Mine,* Black, 1967; Franklyn M. Branley, *High Sounds, Low Sounds,* Crowell, 1967.

R. W. Armour, *Odd Old Mammals,* McGraw-Hill, 1968; W. O. Steele, *The Buffalo Knife,* Harcourt, 1968; Richard Shaw, *Budd's Noisy Wagon,* F. Warne, 1968; Augusta R. Goldin, *Sunlit Sea,* Crowell, 1968; Grimm Brothers, *The Bremen Town Musicians,* McGraw-Hill, 1968; Clement C. Moore, *A Visit from St. Nicholas,* McGraw-Hill, 1968; Peggy Mann, *The Boy with a Billion Pets,* Coward-McCann, 1968; S. Corbett, *The Hairy Horror Trick,* Little, Brown, 1969; Jean Fritz, *George Washington's Breakfast,* Coward-McCann, 1969; Carol Iden, *Sidney's Ghost,* World Publishing, 1969; J. Van der Veer, *To the Rescue,* Harcourt, 1969; Pura Belpré, *Ote,* Pantheon, 1969; P. Showers, *Look at Your Eyes,* A. & C. Black, 1969, Crowell, 1976; E. Titus, *Anatole and the Thirty Thieves,* McGraw-Hill, 1969.

D. Fife, *What's New, Lincoln?,* Coward-McCann, 1970; Roberta Greene, *Two and Me Makes Three,* Coward-McCann, 1970; E. Titus, *Anatole and the Toyshop,* McGraw-Hill, 1970; Judith Viorst, *Try it Again, Sam: Safety When You Walk,* Lothrop, 1970; D. Fife, *What's the Prize, Lin-*

*coln?,* Coward-McCann, 1971; John Knoepfle, *Dogs and Cats and Things Like That* (poems), McGraw-Hill, 1971; S. Corbett, *The Hateful Plateful Trick,* Little, Brown, 1971; E. Titus, *Basil and the Pygmy Cats,* McGraw-Hill, 1971; Beatrice S. DeRegniers, *It Does Not Say Meow and other Animal Riddle Rhymes,* Seabury, 1972; Mary L. Solot, *100 Hamburgers: The Getting Thin Book,* Lothrop, 1972; P. Belpré, *Dance of the Animals: A Puerto Rican Folk Tale,* F. Warne, 1972; Zibby Oneal, *The Improbable Adventures of Marvelous O'Hara Soapstone,* Viking, 1972; S. Corbett, *The Home Run Trick,* Little, Brown, 1973; F. N. Monjo, *Clarence and the Burglar,* Coward-McCann, 1973; Diane Wolkstein, *The Cool Ride in the Sky,* Knopf, 1973; E. Titus, *Anatole in Italy,* McGraw-Hill, 1973; Edna Barth, *Jack-o'-Lantern,* Seabury, 1974; R. W. Armour, *Sea Full of Whales,* McGraw-Hill, 1974; *The History of Mother Twaddle and the Marvelous Achievements of Her Son Jack,* Seabury, 1974; J. Johnston, *Speak Up, Edie!,* Putnam, 1974; S. Corbett, *The Hockey Trick,* Little, Brown, 1974.

Dorothy Van Woerkom, *The Queen Who Couldn't Bake Gingerbread,* Random House, 1975; Mary Q. Steele, *Because of the Sand Witches There,* Greenwillow Books, 1975; D. Fife, *Who Goes There, Lincoln?,* Coward-McCann, 1975; P. Showers, *Follow Your Nose,* Crowell, 1975; E. Titus, *Basil in Mexico,* McGraw-Hill, 1975; Pat D. Tapio, *The Lady Who Saw the Good Side of Everything,* Seabury, 1975; Patricia Lauber, *Clarence and the Burglar,* Worlds Work, 1975; P. Showers, *How Many Teeth?,* Crowell, 1976; S. Corbett, *The Black Mask Trick,* Little, Brown, 1976; Grimm Brothers, *The Table, the Donkey, and the Stick,* McGraw-Hill, 1976; Alice Schertle, *The Gorilla in the Hall,* Lothrop, 1977; Joanna Galdone, *The Tailypo,* Seabury, 1977; Peggy Parish, *Zed and the Monster,* Doubleday, 1979; Richard W. Armour, *Monster of the Deep,* McGraw-Hill, 1979; *Anatole and the Pied Piper,* McGraw-Hill, 1979; Hans C. Andersen, *The Steadfast Tin Soldier,* Seabury, 1979.

**"It's such a lovely day,"** the lady said to her cat one beautiful Spring morning. **"Let's have a picnic by the river."** ■ (From *The Lady Who Saw the Good Side of Everything* by Pat Decker Tapio. Illustrated by Paul Galdone.)

**And lo! as he looks, on the belfry's height
A glimmer, and then a gleam of light.**
■ (From *Paul Revere's Ride* by Henry Wadsworth Longfellow. Illustrated by Paul Galdone.)

*ADAPTATIONS*—Filmstrips; all produced by Weston Woods: "The Little Red Hen," "The House that Jack Built," "The Old Woman and her Pig," "Old Mother Hubbard and her Dog."

*SIDELIGHTS:* "When I was about fourteen my family and I left Budapest. On arrival in New Jersey I was promptly enrolled in high school. The Hungarian language did not prove very useful in the United States and in an effort to get me over the barrier I had to attend three English classes every day in addition to a biology class. When it came to my turn to read from Shakespeare's *Midsummer Night's Dream,* I was highly embarrassed. Not only did I have an accent that amused the whole class, but I also failed to understand most of what I was trying to read. In the biology class, however, I felt more successful; when it was discovered that I was proficient in the drawing of grasshoppers I was soon drawing them for all the other pupils.

"Shortly afterward, we moved to New York City. To help support my family in the struggle to get started, I worked during the day as busboy, electrician's helper on unfinished skyscrapers, fur-dyer, and so on. At night I attended art schools: the Art Student League and the New York School of Industrial Design. Eventually, four years of working in the art department of Doubleday & Company determined my direction. I loved everything in the world of book production, the people and the challenges, and there I had a chance to design my first book jacket. That led into free-lancing.

"I lived in the Greenwich Village section of New York City, and while I free-lanced and built up a busy career in book jacket designing, I kept up my interest in fine arts by drawing and painting and by long sketching vacations in Vermont. I also became increasingly interested in book illustration.

"After four years spent in the U.S. Army Engineer Corps, during which I contributed to *Yank Magazine* in my spare time, I settled down in Rockland County, New York—with

a wife and, eventually, two children and assorted animals—and resumed free-lancing, leaning more and more toward illustrating children's books."

Galdone, who is a painter and sculptor as well as an illustrator, divides his time between his farm in Tunbridge, Vermont and his house and studio on fifteen acres in New City, Rockland County, New York. The house was designed by Galdone, his wife and an architect brother-in-law. "Esie's [his wife, Jannelise] brother designed it while he was in California. He used descriptions of the land area from our letters; he didn't see the house or the land until ten years after he designed it." [Lee Bennett Hopkins, *Books Are by People,* Citation Press, 1969.[1]]

The land surrounding his home provides the author-illustrator with the opportunity to pursue two of his favorite pasttimes—gardening and the outdoors. "One of the most valuable things in life to me is time. Time to work, to live, to be out under the sky, and to be with my family.

"I love the outdoors. I love everything about nature. Look at these trees. Trees give you such permanence."[1]

Galdone has illustrated and written a great many children's books. In 1957 and 1958 he was runner-up for the Caldecott Award for *Anatole* and *Anatole and the Cat* respectively. Today he continues to illustrate and write. "Children's books provide me with much freedom of their naturally whimsical nature."[1]

"I particularly enjoy adapting and making picture books of favorite old tales. I find this most satisfying and I like to fancy myself in such good company as Caldecott, Arthur Rackham, Walter Crane, Doré—real inspirations and a constant challenge. . . ."

The artist's illustrations are primarily done in pen and ink and wash, and have been well-received by both children and book critics alike. "For bright joyous drawings, one has only

**...But by your stump you'll tell your tale.** ■ (From *Dance of the Animals* by Pura Belpré. Illustrated by Paul Galdone.)

to turn to Paul Galdone's work. His retellings of simple animal folk tales are always clear and concise. In *The Monkey and the Crocodile* . . . Galdone astounds the reader with the variety of colorful pictures in which just the two animals appear . . . ," wrote a reviewer for *Book World*.

A *Library Journal* critic, reviewing the illustrator's version of *The Three Little Pigs,* said, ". . . Paul Galdone gives new life to the childhood classic with his colorful and realistic pictures. In each one, he manages to capture the mood of the moment, and, through subtle touches, adds much to the story. . . ."

One of Galdone's most recent works is his retelling of a tale from the Brothers Grimm, *The Table, the Donkey, and the*

*Stick.* Reviewing this picture book for *Horn Book,* a critic noted, "Paul Galdone has wisely chosen a story which is less familiar than most of the others he has retold and illustrated. . . . A minor episode and the irrelevant coda in the original version have been judiciously omitted by the artist whose typically entertaining illustrations—full of verve, exaggerated characterizations, and earthy humor—make a well-balanced picture book."

*HOBBIES AND OTHER INTERESTS:* Hiking, forestry, gardening, painting, and sculpting.

*FOR MORE INFORMATION SEE:* Kunitz and Haycraft, editors, *Junior Book of Authors,* H. W. Wilson, 1934; Bertha Mahoney Miller and others, compilers, *Illustrators of Chil-*

*dren's Books, 1946-1956*, Horn Book, 1958; Lee Kingman and others, compilers, *Illustrators of Children's Books, 1957-1966*, Horn Book, 1968; Lee Bennett Hopkins, *Books Are by People: Interviews with 104 Authors and Illustrators of Books for Young Children*, Citation Press, 1969; *Horn Book*, June, 1966, April and December, 1969, October, 1970, June, 1974, August, 1975, April, 1977; Doris de Montreville and Donna Hill, editors, *Third Book of Junior Authors*, H. W. Wilson, 1972.

# GIEGLING, John A(llan) 1935-

*PERSONAL:* Surname is pronounced Guy-gling; born January 23, 1935, in Sioux Falls, S.D.; son of Ernest and Helen (Freese) Giegling. *Education:* Attended Augustana College, 1953-55; South Dakota State University, B.S., 1960. *Home:* 600 South Kiwanis Ave., Apt. 119, Sioux Falls, S.D. 57104.

*CAREER:* National Audubon Society, teacher at camp for adults in Greenwich, Conn., and librarian at national headquarters, New York, N.Y., 1961-65; *Purple Martin News*, Griggsville, Ill., associate editor, 1971-72; Pettigrew Museum, Sioux Falls, S.D., curator, 1975-76. *Military service:* National Guard, 1955-57. *Member:* National Audubon Society, National Wildlife Society, Society for the Preservation of Birds of Prey, Saskatchewan Natural History Society, South Dakota Ornithologists Union, Sioux Falls Audubon Society (president), Siouxland Creative Writers Club.

**"Some years back, by a small stream, Pierre had constructed a cabin from the hardest most weather-resistant logs he could find." ■** (From *Black Lightning* by John Giegling. Illustrated by John Schoenherr.)

*WRITINGS: Warrior of the Skies*, Doubleday, 1970; *Black Lightning: Three Years in the Life of a Fisher*, Coward, 1975. Contributor of a monthly column to the *Purple Martin News*. Has also contributed to *National Wildlife, Pennsylvania Game News, Colorado Outdoors, Audubon* Magazine, *Sierra Club Bulletin, Twelve/Fifteen, The California Condor* and other magazines.

*WORK IN PROGRESS:* Three nature novels about two species of birds and one species of animal.

*SIDELIGHTS:* "I have always loved the outdoors —especially the birds and animals—since I was a small boy too young to read. I grew up on a farm near Canistota, South Dakota—thirty miles from Sioux Falls. And I was always pestering someone to identify a particular bird—until I was given a field guide to identify them myself. Which I did very well.

"As an adult I have traveled quite a bit and lived in many places—from Anchorage, Alaska to New York City, from California to Illinois. At the present I am finishing up another book. I hope to be able to write more, but so far not too much money has resulted from my efforts. But I have had tremendous support from many people, and will continue with my best efforts. I do want to write."

*HOBBIES AND OTHER INTERESTS:* Hiking, reading, travel, discussions, good plays and movies, music.

# GLAUBER, Uta (Heil) 1936-

*PERSONAL:* Born June 8, 1936, in Pirmasens, Germany; daughter of Paul (a purchasing agent) and Gudula (Schmoll) Heil; married Heinrich Glauber (an electronics engineer), October 6, 1957; children: Vanna, Luca, Mattia. *Education:* Attended Academy of Fine Arts, Berlin, 1950-54. *Politics:* None. *Religion:* Protestant. *Home:* Via Poggio Belvedere, 5, 22030 Lipomo, Como, Italy.

**UTA GLAUBER**

*CAREER:* Free-lance illustrator and graphic artist.

*WRITINGS: Il Lungo viaggio dell'acqua,* Monadori (Milan), 1963; *Abends wenn ich schlafen geh,* Herder (Freiburg), 1965; (illustrator) Gertrud von Walther, *Heile, heile Segen* (children's picture book), Herder, 1967; (illustrator) Gertrud von Walther, *The Four Seasons* (originally written but never published in German), translated by Patricia Crampton, Abelard, 1968; (and illustrator) *How the Willow Wren Became King: Story and Pictures* (juvenile, based on a story by the brothers Grimm), Abelard, 1970; *Petruska,* Pantheon, 1971; *Il Gioco delle Cose,* Bompiani (Milan), 1973; *The Fogs* (picture book based on poetry by Johann Wolfgang von Goethe), Emme Edizioni (Milan), 1978.

**And ever since then, neither he nor his family is allowed to come out during the day.** ■ (From *How the Willow Wren Became King* by Uta Glauber. Illustrated by the author.)

*WORK IN PROGRESS:* Text and illustrations for two children's books; paintings for a one-man show in Milan, Italy, 1972.

*SIDELIGHTS:* "I began painting picture books, at the moment in which, having my own children to bring up, I realised the necessity of the colour's experience in the esthetic education, and that the growth of sensitivity and esthetic receptivity assume a fundamental importance on the psyche of the child.

"I avoid illustrating texts so as not to influence the child's imagination and I inclose the text in the image of an autonomous value. Often I first give birth to a picture and then I seek the text.

"The first children's books I made were exclusively painted, but recently I joined the painted elements with some pencil or quinqina painted traits to better show the structural differences in Nature to the child."

*HOBBIES AND OTHER INTERESTS:* Child psychotherapy in an institution for orphans, painting and design.

## HAAS, Irene 1929-

*PERSONAL:* Born June 5, 1929, in New York City; married Philip Clark (a banker); children: James, Jo Ann. *Education:* Attended Black Mountain College, North Carolina; Pratt Institute, Brooklyn; Art Students League, New York. *Home:* Manhattan, New York.

*CAREER:* Illustrator. Began as a scenic designer for summer stock theater; designed patterns for china, fabrics, and wallpaper; became a free-lance illustrator for magazines, record album covers, posters, and advertisements; through the help of an artist's agent, she began illustrating children's books, 1954. Her works have been exhibited by the American Institute of Graphic Art. *Awards, honors:* Illustrated Beatrice Schenk De Regniers' books, *A Little House of Your Own,* 1955, and *Was It a Good Trade?,* 1956, which were named among the *New York Times* Choice of Best Illustrated Children's Books of the Year; the *Horn Book*'s Honor List for *There Is a Dragon in My Bed,* 1961, *Tatsinda,* 1963, *Emily's Voyage,* 1967; Irma Siminton Black Award and The Owl Prize for *The Maggie B.,* 1975, and 1977, respectively.

**...They were walking up and down excitedly, worrying only about their appearance.** ■ (From *How the Willow Wren Became King* by Uta Glauber. Illustrated by the author.)

*ILLUSTRATOR*—All published by Harcourt, except as noted: Richard Banks, *Mysterious Leaf,* 1954; Beatrice Schenk De Regniers, *Little House of Your Own,* 1955; B. S. De Regniers, *Was It a Good Trade?,* 1956; Paul Kapp, *Cat Came Fiddling,* 1956; B. S. De Regniers, *Something Special,* 1958; Sesyle Joslin, *There Is a Dragon in My Bed,* 1961; S. Joslin, *Dear Dragon, and Other Useful Letter Forms,* 1962; Elizabeth Enright, *Tatsinda,* 1963; E. Enright, *Zeee,* 1965; Emma Smith, *Emily's Voyage,* 1966; Myra Cohn Livingston, *Come Away,* Atheneum, 1974; (and author) *The Maggie B.,* Atheneum, 1975; Ruth Craft, *Carrie Hepple's Garden,* Atheneum, 1979.

*SIDELIGHTS:* Irene Haas spent her childhood in New York, where she was born on June 5, 1929 in an atmosphere where there "... was always plenty of time to think, to be lazy, to dream, and to be alone." In high school she supervised as many art projects as she could.

After studying at Black Mountain College in North Carolina and at Pratt Institute in Brooklyn, New York, Haas attended the Art Students League in New York where she studied painting, etching and lithography. After completing her studies she began her art career as a scenic designer for summer stock theater, and then designed wallpaper and china patterns. "After overcoming a burning ambition to be a scenic designer and finding, after a few summers of stock, that I had neither the muscles, patience nor personality for such an ambitious career, I designed patterns for china and wallpaper, and studied etching and lithography—beautiful media, and a fine school for technique and patience. After that I went, very slowly, with the help of an artist's agent,

**Margaret and James ate the beautiful sea stew and dunked their muffins in the broth, which tasted of all the good things that had cooked in it. For dessert they had the peaches with cinnamon and honey, and glasses of warm goat's milk. ■** (From *The Maggie B.* by Irene Haas. Illustrated by the author.)

**IRENE HAAS**

into the field of magazine and advertising illustration, and this agent was responsible for a very happy meeting with Margaret McElderry at Harcourt, Brace and finding the work I love best.''

In 1954 Haas received her first book commission for illustrating *The Mysterious Leaf* by Richard Banks. The first book was followed by twelve others until 1975 when Haas became the author, as well as the illustrator for *The Maggie B*. ''I don't know if it is true for other illustrators or writers for children, but I honestly believe that my style and taste stem from and is an extension of what I liked as a child. I loved pictures I could 'live' in, literally for hours. They were completely conceived by the artist, full of atmosphere and detail. It was wonderful to discover something new, no matter how minute. Realizing how gratifying these illustrations were—and still are—and how much they enriched my life, it is a great joy to find that I am able to make more of these alive little worlds for children.''

*FOR MORE INFORMATION SEE:* Doris de Montreville, editor, *Third Book of Junior Authors*, H. W. Wilson, 1972.

## HALE, Kathleen 1898-

*PERSONAL:* Born May 24, 1898, in Scotland; daughter of Charles Edward and Ethel Alice Aylmer (Hughes) Hale; married Douglas McClean (a bacteriologist), 1926 (died, 1967); children: two sons. *Education:* Attended Manchester School of Art; Reading University College of Art; Central School of Arts and Crafts, London; East Anglican School of Painting and Drawing. *Home:* Tod House, Forest Hill, Oxford, England.

*CAREER:* Author and illustrator. Worked for the Ministry of Foods, England, 1918; after the war, she held various small jobs such as minding babies, mending, and collecting bad debts for a window cleaner; later began designing book jackets and posters; started writing the ''Orlando'' books for her children. Her works have been exhibited at numerous galleries, including Grosvenor Galleries, Vermont Gallery, and Leicester Galleries. *Member:* Society of Industrial Arts (fellow).

*WRITINGS*—All self-illustrated: *Henrietta: The Faithful Hen*, Transatlantic, 1943, reissued, Allen & Unwin, 1967; *Manda*, J. Murray, 1952, Coward-McCann, 1953; *Henrietta's Magic Egg*, Allen & Unwin, 1973.

''Orlando'' series; self-illustrated: *Orlando (the Marmalade Cat): A Camping Holiday*, Scribner, 1938; *Orlando's Evening Out*, Penguin, 1941; *Orlando's Home Life*, Penguin, 1942; *Orlando (the Marmalade Cat) Buys a Farm*, Transatlantic, 1942; *Orlando (the Marmalade Cat) Becomes a Doctor*, Transatlantic, 1944; *Orlando (the Marmalade Cat): His Silver Wedding*, Transatlantic, 1944; *Orlando's Invisible Pyjamas*, Transatlantic, 1947, new edition, J. Murray, 1964; *Orlando (the Marmalade Cat) Keeps a Dog*, Transatlantic, 1949; *Orlando (the Marmalade Cat): A Trip Abroad*, Country Life, 1949, Transatlantic, 1950; *Orlando the Judge*, J. Murray, 1950; *Orlando's Country Peepshow*, Chatto & Windus, 1950; *Orlando (the Marmalade Cat): A Seaside Holiday*, Country Life, 1952; *Orlando's Zoo*, J. Murray, 1954; *Orlando (the Marmalade Cat): The Frisky Housewife*, Country Life, 1956; *Orlando's Magic Carpet*, J. Murray, 1958; *Orlando (the Marmalade Cat) Buys a Cottage*, Country Life, 1963; *Orlando and the Three Graces*, J. Murray, 1965; *Orlando (the Marmalade Cat) Goes to the Moon*, J. Murray, 1968; *Orlando (the Marmalade Cat) and the Water Cats*, J. Cape, 1972.

Illustrator: Mary Rachel Harrower, *I Don't Mix Much with Fairies*, Eyre & Spottiswode, 1928; M. R. Harrower, *Plain Jane*, Coward-McCann, 1929; Charles Perrault, *Puss in Boots*, Houghton, 1951.

*SIDELIGHTS:* **May 24, 1898.** Born in Scotland. At the age of five Hale's father died and she remembered the unhappiness that followed and caused her to become a ''problem child.'' She recalled that she learned little at school and spent much of her time ''sitting outside the classroom in disgrace. The headmistress was a remarkable woman, and, in spite of having six hundred girls in her care, had time to consider my unworthy case. She decided, since I had a talent for drawing, writing original essays, and French, that I should be allowed to spend my time at these lessons and let the rest go by. She even arranged for me to attend Life classes at the Manchester School of Art which, at my age then, was unheard of. I had a most progressive art mistress at the High School, who directly formed my future, and for whom I have an undying gratitude and affection.'' [*Illustrators of Children's Books, 1946-1956*, Horn Book, 1958.[1]]

After graduation from high school Hale won a scholarship for art at Reading University for two years.

**1917.** Sold her bicycle to pay for her fare to London where she got a job in the Ministry of Foods and was drafted to a market gardener's nursery. ''Though without previous experience I bluffed my way as a 'carter,' and managed to work the old hand plough, with the wise aid of my enormous cart-horse. Though the plough sent me spinning sidewise at each end of the furrow, we did it, Prince and I. Also I had to

(From *Orlando the Judge* by Kathleen Hale. Illustrated by the author.)

drive a huge wagon up to Covent Garden Market, at night, sleeping on vegetables while Prince plodded on his way."[1]

After the war Hale had a variety of jobs such as babysitting, mending and working for an interior decorator until finding employment in her own artistic field. She designed book jackets, posters, illustrated children's stories and continued studying art in London.

**1926.** Married Douglas McClean, a bacteriologist. The couple moved to the country where they had two sons.

**1938.** Illustrated her first book, *Orlando the Marmalade Cat: A Camping Holiday.* "Orlando," a sophisticated cat, caught children's imagination at once and the book sold many thousands of copies. It became the first of a successful series; the last one, *Orlando and the Three Graces,* was published in 1965, almost thirty years after the first famous "Orlando" book. Her books were initially written for her two young sons because she found "too few stories for little children except *Babar the Elephant.*"[1]

**1967.** Husband died.

**1973.** *Henrietta's Magic Egg* was published. Besides writing and illustrating children's books, Hale has exhibited her art in numerous galleries.

Kathleen Hale lives at Forest Hill in Oxford, England.

Hale's works are included in the Kerlan Collection at the University of Minnesota.

*HOBBIES AND OTHER INTERESTS:* Painting.

*FOR MORE INFORMATION SEE:* Bertha Mahony Miller and others, editors, *Illustrators of Children's Books, 1946-1956,* Horn Book, 1958.

## HECHTKOPF, Henryk 1910-

*PERSONAL:* Born April 5, 1910, in Warsaw, Poland; son of Isaac (an official) and Ida (Sister in a Child-house; maiden name Rosenman) Hechtkopf; married Alicia Zielinski. *Education:* Attended Warsaw University, Warsaw, Poland, 1929; Warsaw Art Academy, Warsaw, Poland, 1930; Magister of Warsaw University, Warsaw, Poland, 1933. *Home and office:* 19 Hashmonaim Street, Bat-Yam, Israel 59496.

*CAREER:* Illustrator and painter. Polish Acoustics, Warsaw, Poland, assistant stage manager, 1934-35; Rekino, Warsaw, Poland, graphic designer and illustrator, 1936-39; Central Film Studio, Lodz, Poland, stage manager, 1950-57; free-lance illustrator, 1957—; High School of Arts, Tel-Aviv, Israel, art teacher, 1959-71. Board member of art cooperative, Lodz, Poland, 1946-50. *Exhibitions:* Exhibited in Warsaw, Lodz, Katowitz, Krakow, and Wroclaw, Poland, 1935-57; Tel-Aviv, Israel, 1963; Bat Yam Museum, Bat-Yam, Israel, 1963, 1972; Petah-Tiqua, 1966; Jerusalem, 1972; plus many others. *Member:* Polish Painter Association, Jewish Art Association, Jewish Culture Organization (board member and art section chairman, 1947-51), Painters and Sculpture Association, Film Authors Association. *Awards, honors:* Municipality of Warsaw, prize for young artist, 1925; Municipality of Bat-Yam, Israel, prize for painting, 1965.

**Huge waves crashed onto the deck and tossed the ship high into the air.** ■ (From *Jonah's Journey* by Danah Haiz. Illustrated by H. Hechtkopf.)

*ILLUSTRATOR: Warsaw Getto: Twenty-four Paintings from Warsaw Gettos,* Nevatim (Tel-Aviv), 1960; *My Israel* (juvenile; colored pictures of Israel), Lewin-Epstein (Israel), 1964; D. Cohen, *Thirty-six Hassidic Stories,* Massada Press (Israel), 1964; Raphael Saporta, *A Basket in the Reeds,* Lerner, 1965; Asher Barash (author), Murray Roston (translator), *Golden Treasury of Jewish Tales,* Massada Press, 1965, Dodd, 1966; Levin Kipnis, *Bible Stories* (three books), Samuel Simson, Ltd. (Israel), 1972, 1976, 1979; A. Broides, *Boker-or,* Samuel Simson, Ltd., 1972; Danah Haiz, *Jonah's Journey,* Lerner, 1972; Cecil P. Golann, *Mission on a Mountain: The Story of Abraham and Isaac,* Lerner, 1975; Ruth F. Brin, *The Story of Esther,* Lerner, 1976; Ruth F. Brin, *David and Goliath,* Lerner, 1976; D. Levin, *Taltali,* Bney-Brak (Israel), 1976; T. S. Wilenski, *Fable Books* (sixteen books), Samuel Simson, Ltd., 1976; T. S. Rosenberg, *Yossef Mokir Shabbos,* Bney-Brak, 1977; T. S. Rosenberg, *Hashowas Avaida,* Bney-Brak, 1977.

Has also illustrated *Pictures Tell,* a series of thirteen books by Nitza Naftali, N. Nir, T. S. Wilenski, N. Perski and N. Melumad, Yavneh Publishing House, 1967-79; and a series of Bible Learn Books by V. Avivi, A. Minkovitz and N. Gavrieli, Yavneh Publishing House, 1973-75; plus many other books for children.

*SIDELIGHTS:* ''I feel and think that to work and create for children, to take a part and have influence in the education of children is one of the most important tasks, because the future and image of the world depends on it. I am lucky that I can take my modest part, in that. Each new book I have to illustrate opens, for me, a new source of impressions though I have been employed in this field over thirty years. It happens that my wife will come into my studio and, astonished, ask me why I have a weeping or a laughing face. She doesn't know that I have designed a weeping cat or a laughing elephant.

''I am an active painter, but the true fulfillment of my life I see in my work for children. As far as being influenced by another artist I feel my best teachers are the children. I study their colored designs and their naive, natural color. Feeling and sincerity are the best guide in my search for solutions. The more a mature painter/illustrator has a soul of a child—the more, I think, he is a good illustrator.

''And yet a weighty reason for me personally—as Israelian—to work especially for my Israelian young people, is one million Jewish children were exterminated in the holocaust in the years 1940-45.''

## HOLZ, Loretta (Marie) 1943-

*PERSONAL:* Born June 4, 1943, in Holden, Mass.; daughter of Joseph Siro and Loretta (Crump) Celle; married George Ernest Holz (an electronics engineer and inventor), August 22, 1965; children: G. Andrew, Matthew J. *Education:* Emmanual College, Boston, Mass., B.A., 1965; Rutgers University, M.Ed., 1972. *Home and office:* 97 Grandview Ave., North Plainfield, N.J. 07060.

(From *Mobiles You Can Make* by Loretta Holz. Drawings by the author.)

**HENRYK HECHTKOPF**

**LORETTA HOLZ**

*CAREER:* German teacher in junior high school in Bergen-field, N.J., 1965-66; German and English teacher in Warren, N.J., 1966-69; freelance author, designer, photographer, lecturer and teacher, 1969—. *Member:* International Guild of Craft Journalists, Authors, and Photographers, Embroiderers' Guild of America (Garden State chapter), Society of Craft Designers, Handcraft Guild of Central Jersey.

*WRITINGS: Teach Yourself Stitchery,* Lothrop, 1974; *Mobiles You Can Make,* Lothrop, 1975; *How to Sell Your Art and Crafts,* Scribner, 1977; *Jumping Jacks: Easy to Assemble Full Color Toys that Move,* Dover, 1977; *Make It and Sell It,* Scribner, 1978; *The How-To Book of International Dolls,* Crown, 1979. Regular contributor to *Creative Crafts* and *Profitable Craft Merchandising.*

*SIDELIGHTS:* " Doing crafts and writing about them are my hobbies as well as my job and I enjoy both. I like to create a new design or think of a new way something could be done and then try it. I have had no formal training in art but I enjoy doing original designs and I believe all people can create as long as they give themselves a chance. Through my books I try to encourage readers to try the projects I have designed and then go on to try their own ideas using the techniques they have learned.

"To date most of my articles and books have been mainly about crafts but I hope to branch out to other areas while continuing my interest. . . . I have a great many different interests including gardening, Oriental cooking, puppets, the theater, religion, and computers to name a few. I hope soon to have time to write fiction, perhaps novels for young adults. A shortage of time is my main problem. . . .

"I am an addictive reader . . . of both fiction and non-fiction of many different types."

## HOMZE, Alma C. 1932-

*PERSONAL:* Surname is pronounced Home-ze; born October 28, 1932 in Washington, D.C.; daughter of J. Glenn and Edith (Carland) Cross; married Edward L. Homze (a professor at University of Nebraska), March 21, 1959; children: Eric, Heidi. *Education:* Wilson Teachers College, Washington, D.C., B.S., 1954; Pennsylvania State University, M.Ed., 1957, D.Ed., 1963. *Home:* 3450 Woodshire Pkwy., Lincoln, Neb. 68502 *Office:* Teachers College, University of Nebraska, Lincoln, Neb. 68508.

*CAREER:* Elementary teacher in Washington, D.C., Richmond, Va., Emporia, Kan., and Schweinfurt, Germany; Kansas State Teachers College, Emporia, lecturer in education, 1961-65; University of Nebraska, Lincoln, assistant professor of education, 1965-68, associate professor of education, 1968—. *Member:* National Council of Teachers of English, Childhood Education International, International Reading Association.

*WRITINGS:* (With husband, Edward L. Homze) *Germany: The Divided Nation* (juvenile), Thomas Nelson, 1970; (with husband, Edward L. Homze) *Willy Brandt: A Biography* (juvenile), Thomas Nelson, 1974. Contributor to education journals in the teaching of reading, language arts and children's literature.

*WORK IN PROGRESS:* A young people's book of German legends.

*SIDELIGHTS:* "I lust for travel, for life from a suitcase, for a new place. I have traveled, camped, explored, enjoyed, indeed savored the uniqueness of villages all over the world!"

**Alma C. Homze, with husband.**

# HOUGH, Richard (Alexander) 1922-
## (Bruce Carter)

*PERSONAL:* Born May 15, 1922, in Brighton, Sussex, England; son of George (a banker) and Margaret (Esilman) Hough; married Helen Charlotte Woodyatt (now a writer and illustrator of children's books), July 17, 1943; children: Sarah Hough Garland, Alexandra, Deborah, Hough Moggach (now a novelist), Bryony. *Education:* Attended Frensham Heights, Farnham, England. *Home:* Old Manse, Lower Chedworth, Cheltenham, Glos. GL45 4AP, England. *Agent:* James Brown Associates, 24 West 43rd St., New York, N.Y. 10036.

*CAREER:* John Lane, The Bodley Head Ltd. (publishers), London, England, editor, then manager, 1947-55; Hamish Hamilton Ltd. (publishers), London, editor of children's books, 1955-70. *Military service:* Royal Air Force, pilot, 1941-46.

*WRITINGS: The Fleet That Had to Die,* Viking, 1958; *Admirals in Collision,* Viking, 1959; *The Potemkin Mutiny,* Pantheon, 1960; (editor) *Great Auto Races,* Harper, 1961; *A History of the World's Sports Cars,* Harper, 1961; (with Michael Frostick) *A History of the World's Classic Cars,* Harper, 1963; *Death of the Battleship,* Macmillan, 1963; (editor) *First and Fastest,* Harper, 1963; *Dreadnought: A History of the Modern Battleship,* Macmillan, 1964, 2nd edition (introduction by C. S. Forester), G. Allen, 1968; (with Mi-

More than any of the other birds, they (the mockingbirds) not only accept the arrival of humans but positively welcome them, twit-twitting about you the moment you land, and following you, or walking beside you, on your wanderings. Whenever you look at them they seem to be looking at you with concern and affection. ■ (From *Galapagos: The Enchanted Islands* by Richard Hough. Illustrated by Charlotte Hough.)

chael Frostick) *A History of the World's Racing Cars,* Harper, 1965; (editor) *The Motor Car Lover's Companion,* Harper, 1965; *The Big Battleship,* Harper, 1966; (with L.J.K. Setright) *A History of the World's Motorcycles,* Harper, 1966; *The Great Dreadnought: The Strange Story of H.M.S. Agincourt,* Harper, 1967; *A History of the World's High Performance Cars,* Harper, 1967; *The Long Pursuit,* Harper, 1969; *The Blind Horn's Hate,* Norton, 1971; *Captain Bligh and Mr. Christian,* Dutton, 1973; *The Mountbattens,* Dutton, 1975; *One Boys War,* Heinemann, 1975; *Adieu to My Grand-daughter,* Simon & Schuster, 1976; *The Great Admirals,* Morrow, 1978; *Man-o-War,* Scribner, 1979; *Wings Against the Sky,* Morrow, 1979; *The Last Voyage of Captain Cook,* Morrow, 1979.

Under pseudonym Bruce Carter: *Into A Strange Lost World,* Crowell, 1953; *Speed Six,* Harper, 1956; *Target Island,* Harper, 1957, 2nd edition, Hamish Hamilton, 1967; *The Kidnaping of Kensington,* Harper, 1958; *Four-wheel Drift,* Harper, 1960; *Fast Circuit,* Harper, 1962; *Nuvolari and the Alfa Romeo,* Coward, 1968; *Jimmy Murphy and the White Duesenberg,* Coward, 1968; *The Airfield Man,* Coward, 1966; *Galapagos: The Enchanted Islands,* Addison, 1975; *Buzzbugs,* Warne, 1977.

*WORK IN PROGRESS:* Three adult novels of the R.A.F. in World War II to be published by Morrow; a biography of Admiral Lord Nelson.

**RICHARD HOUGH**

*SIDELIGHTS:* "In my rare moments of retrospection, being a 'workaholic,' it occurs to me that my pleasure and total commitment to writing, whether for children or adults, is founded on the enthusiasms of my childhood and adolescence and young manhood, with all the many varied colours and experiences with which they provided me: a staid, conservative home life with few events of note, during which my imagination may have beaten about ineffectually like a moth against the window pane of a brightly-lit room. My wife and her mother opened the window when I was seventeen, and then the war swept me away, in the midst of which we married. The colours were very vivid and various in those years, 1941-45. And then we had children, three rather quickly and one much later, and it was hard going to pay the bills, until about 1958 when I had my first big seller, and a long *New Yorker* serial which pumped me full of unaccustomed wealth and much needed self-confidence.

"My childhood enthusiasms—flying, maritime history, science fiction, animals and adventure—have touched and often totally dominated the nature of my writing ever since.

"I am humbly grateful that I have seemingly been blessed with the skill to enjoy myself in this way!"

Richard Hough's books are included in the Kerlan Collection at the University of Minnesota.

## ISH-KISHOR, Sulamith   1896-1977

*PERSONAL:* Born in 1896, in London, England; daughter of Ephraim and Fanny Ish-Kishor. *Education:* Attended Hunter College (now of the City University of New York).

*CAREER:* Author. Began writing at the age of five; as an adult, has written articles on music, art, theatre, and personalities. *Awards, honors:* Schwartz Juvenile Award of the Jewish Book Council, 1964, for *A Boy of Old Prague;* runner-up for Newbery Medal, 1970, for *Our Eddie.*

*WRITINGS: The Bible Story,* United Synagogue of America, 1921; *The Heaven on the Sea, and Other Stories* (illustrated by Penina Ish-Kishor), Bloch Publishing, 1924; *Children's Story of the Bible,* Hebrew Publishing, 1930; *Children's History of Israel from the Creation to the Present Time,* Hebrew Publishing, 1933; *Magnificent Hadrian: A Biography of Hadrian, Emperor of Rome* (introduction by Theodore Dreiser), Minton, Balch, 1935; *Jews to Remember* (illustrated by Kyra Markham), Hebrew Publishing, 1941; *American Promise: A History of the Jews in the New World* (illustrated by Grace Hick), Behraman, 1947; *Everyman's History of the Jews,* Fell, 1948; *The Palace of Eagles, and Other Stories* (illustrated by Alice Horodisch), Shoulson Press, 1948; *Friday Night Stories* (adaptation of Louis Ginzberg's *The Legends of the Jews*), Women's League of the United Synagogue of America, 1949.

*A Boy of Old Prague* (ALA Notable Book; illustrated by Ben Shahn), Pantheon, 1963; *The Carpet of Solomon: A Hebrew Legend* (illustrated by Uri Shulevitz), Pantheon, 1966; *Pathways through the Jewish Holidays,* edited by Benjamin Efron, Ktav, 1967; *Our Eddie,* Pantheon, 1969; *Drusilla: A Novel of the Emperor Hadrian* (illustrated by Thomas Morley), Pantheon, 1970; *The Master of Miracle: A New Novel of the Golem* (illustrated by Arnold Lobel), Harper, 1971.

Also contributor to numerous newspapers and periodicals, including *New York Times, New York Herald-Tribune, New Yorker,* and *Menorah Journal.*

*SIDELIGHTS:* Sulamith Ish-Kishor was born in London, England in 1896; the daughter of Ephraim and Fanny Ish-Kishor. She began writing at the early age of five and had had some of her poems published by the time she was ten. When she was an adolescent she moved to the United States where she later attended Hunter College in New York City.

Ish-Kishor wrote articles on music, art, theater and personalities, as well as numerous books with Jewish themes for children. Many of her books were set in the past. Her award winning book, *A Boy of Old Prague,* told of ghetto life in the sixteenth century. *Our Eddie,* a contender for the Newbery Medal in 1970, took place at the turn of the century.

*FOR MORE INFORMATION SEE: Horn Book,* August, 1969, August, 1970, December, 1971.

(Died June 23, 1977)

**SULAMITH ISH-KISHOR**

**A heavy black smoke flashing with red sparks rolled up out of the hole in the earth. The dreadful voice, now ten times louder than before, burst out exultingly, "Free! Free! Merchant, I thank thee! Take this magic carpet. It will transport its owner to any place in the world in the twinkling of an eye."** ■ (From *The Carpet of Solomon* by Sulamith Ish-Kishor. Illustrated by Uri Shulevitz.)

All the day they hunted,
And nothing could they find,

(From *Three Jovial Huntsmen, A Mother Goose Rhyme* adapted by Susan Jeffers. Illustrated by the adapter.)

**SUSAN JEFFERS**

# JEFFERS, Susan

*EDUCATION:* Graduated from Pratt Institute.

*CAREER:* Author and illustrator of books for children. *Awards, honors: Three Jovial Huntsmen* and *Wild Robin* were selected for the American Institute of Graphic Arts Book Show in 1973-74 and 1976 respectively; *Three Jovial Huntsmen* was a runner-up for the Caldecott Medal in 1974, was selected by the Children's Book Showcase in 1974, and given a citation by the Brooklyn Art Books for Children in 1974, 1975, 1976; received the Golden Apple award presented at the Biennale of Illustrators, Bratislava, for *The Three Jovial Huntsmen.*

*WRITINGS*—All self-illustrated: (Reteller) *Three Jovial Huntsmen* (based on Mother Goose's story of the same name), Bradbury Press, 1973; *All the Pretty Horses,* Macmillan, 1974; (reteller) *Wild Robin* (based on a tale in *Little Prudy's Fairy Book* by Sophie May), Dutton, 1976; *If Wishes Were Horses* (based on Mother Goose's story), Dutton, 1979.

Illustrator: Victoria Lincoln, *Everyhow Remarkable,* Crowell-Collier Press, 1967; Lawrence G. Blochman, *Understanding Your Body,* Macmillan, 1968; (with Rosemary Wells) Robert W. Service, *The Shooting of Dan McGrew and the Cremation of Sam McGee,* A. & W. Publications, 1969; (with R. Wells) Charlotte Pomerantz, *Why You Look Like You Whereas I Tend to Look Like Me,* Young Scott Books, 1969; Joseph Jacobs, *The Buried Moon,* Bradbury Press, 1969; Penelope Proddow, *The Spirit of Spring: A Tale of the Greek God Dionysus,* Bradbury Press, 1970; Harriette S. Abels, *The Circus Detectives,* Ginn, 1971; Mary Q.

Steele, *The First of the Penguins,* Macmillan, 1973; Robert Frost, *Stopping By Woods on a Snowy Evening,* Dutton, 1978; Hans Christian Andersen, *Thumbelina,* Dial, 1979.

*SIDELIGHTS:* As a young student, Susan Jeffers' mother encouraged her to pursue an art career. "[My art career] began in a tiny school in Oakland, New Jersey, when I was chosen to paint a history mural with the usual Egyptians harvesting in muddy tempera fields. I suspect that I was selected as much for my ability to keep poster paint from running, as for my drawing talent. Yet, I was on my way. Happily for me I have a very kind mother. She spent hours teaching me how to look at things. Best of all, she gave me a feeling of immense joy in my work."

After graduating from Pratt Institute in 1964 Susan Jeffers worked in the art departments of publishing houses. Then in 1968 she began her first book, *The Buried Moon.* In that same year she opened her own studio with Rosemary Wells. "It was frightening to think of working free lance, but it was the only alternative." [1]

*FOR MORE INFORMATION SEE: Horn Book,* February and April, 1974, February, 1975, April, 1977.

# KJELGAARD, James Arthur   1910-1959 (Jim Kjelgaard)

*PERSONAL:* Surname pronounced *Kel*-guard; born December 5, 1910, in New York City; grew up on a farm in Pennsylvania; died July 12, 1959, in Milwaukee, Wisconsin; son of a physician; married; children: Karen.

*CAREER:* Author of books for young people. Before turning to writing, Kjelgaard held a variety of jobs, including trapper, teamster guide, surveyor's assistant, factory worker, and plumber's apprentice. *Awards, honors:* Western Writers of America Spur Award, 1957, for *Wolf Brother.*

*WRITINGS: Forest Patrol* (illustrated by Tony Palazzo), Holiday House, 1941; *Rebel Siege,* Holiday House, 1943; *Big Red* (illustrations by Bob Kuhn), Holiday House, 1945, reissued, Bantam, 1976 [another edition illustrated by Shannon Sternweis, Junior Deluxe Editions, 1966]; *Buckskin Brigade* (illustrated by Ralph Ray, Jr.), Holiday House, 1947; *Snow Dog* (illustrated by Jacob Landau), Holiday House, 1948, reissued, Grosset, 1961; *Kalak of the Ice* (illustrated by B. Kuhn), Holiday House, 1949; *A Nose for Trouble,* Holiday House, 1949; *Wild Trek,* Holiday House, 1950, reissued, E. M. Hale, 1963; *Chip, the Dam Builder* (illustrated by R. Ray), Holiday House, 1950; *Irish Red, Son of Big Red,* Holiday House, 1951, reissued, Grosset, 1961; *Fire-Hunter* (illustrated by R. Ray), Holiday House, 1951; *The Explorations of Pere Marquette* (illustrated by Stephen J. Voorhies), Random House, 1951; *Trailing Trouble,* Holiday House, 1952; *The Coming of the Mormons* (illustrated by S. J. Voorhies), Random House, 1953; *Outlaw Red, Son of Big Red,* Holiday House, 1953; *The Spell of the White Sturgeon,* Dodd, 1953; *Haunt Fox* (illustrated by Glen Rounds), Holiday House, 1954, reissued, Scholastic Book Services, 1970; *Cracker Barrel Trouble Shooter,* Dodd, 1954.

*Lion Hound* (illustrated by J. Landau), Holiday House, 1955; *The Lost Wagon,* Dodd, 1955; *Desert Dog,* Holiday House, 1956; *Trading Jeff and His Dog,* Dodd, 1956; *Wildlife Cameraman* (illustrated by Sam Savitt), Holiday House, 1957; *Double Challenge,* Dodd, 1957; *We Were There at the Oklahoma Land Run* (illustrated by Chris A. Kenyon, Jr.),

JIM KJELGAARD

Grosset, 1957; *Wolf Brother,* Holiday House, 1957; *Swamp Cat* (illustrated by Edward Shenton), Dodd, 1957; *Rescue Dog of the High Pass* (illustrated by E. Shenton), Dodd, 1958; *The Land Is Bright,* Dodd, 1958; *The Black Fawn,* Dodd, 1958; *The Story of Geronimo* (illustrated by Charles B. Wilson), Grosset, 1958; *Hi Jolly* (illustrated by Kendall Rossi), Dodd, 1959; *Stormy,* Holiday House, 1959; *Ulysses and His Woodland Zoo* (illustrated by K. Rossi), Dodd, 1960; *Boomerang Hunter* (illustrated by W. T. Mars), Holiday House, 1960; *The Duck-Footed Hound* (illustrated by Marc Simont), Crowell, 1960; *Tigre* (illustrated by Everett R. Kinstler), Dodd, 1961; *Hidden Trail,* Holiday House, 1962; *Fawn in the Forest, and Other Wild Animal Stories* (illustrated by S. Savitt), Dodd, 1962; *Furious Moose of the Wilderness* (illustrated by Mort Kuenstler), Dodd, 1965; *Two Dogs and a Horse* (illustrated by S. Savitt), Dodd, 1964; *Dave and His Dog, Mulligan* (illustrated by S. Savitt), Dodd, 1966; *Coyote Song* (illustrated by Robert MacLean), Dodd, 1969.

Editor: *The Wild Horse Roundup* (illustrated by Paul Brown), Dodd, 1957; *Hound Dogs and Others* (illustrated by P. Brown), Dodd, 1958, reprinted, Books for Libraries, 1970.

*ADAPTATIONS*—Movies and filmstrips: "The Explorations of Pere Marquette" (filmstrip; color, with a teaching guide), David J. Goodman, 1957; "Big Red" (motion picture; 89 minutes, sound, color), starring Walter Pidgeon, Walt Disney Productions, 1962; "Big Red" (filmstrip; sound, color, with a teaching guide; adapted from the Walt Disney motion picture), Walt Disney Productions, 1971; "Big Red's New Trainer" (filmstrip; color, with filmstrip facts; adapted from the Walt Disney motion picture), Encyclopaedia Britannica Films, 1962; "Big Red to the Rescue" (filmstrip; color, with filmstrip facts; adapted from the Walt Disney motion picture), Encyclopaedia Britannica Films, 1962.

*SIDELIGHTS:* **December 5, 1910.** Born in New York City, the son of a physician. Kjelgaard's early childhood was spent on a seven hundred and fifty acre farm in the Pennsylvania mountains until it was sold. The family then moved to Galeton, Pennsylvania where Kjelgaard and his brothers spent many hours hunting and fishing—two hobbies that he never outgrew. "Those mountain farms produced more rocks to the acre than anything else. But they provided my brothers and me with plenty of ammunition for fighting the neighboring boys across the creek. One of our jobs was to shoo the cows out of the corn patch, which was more exciting than it sounds. There was always two or three yearling bulls in the dairy herd, and when we wanted to get home quickly, we'd each grab one by the tail. The bulls would light out for the barn, their feet hitting the ground about every two yards, and ours in proportion. But the really entrancing thing was the forest that surrounded us: mountains filled with game, and trout streams loaded with fish." [Jim Kjelgaard, *Big Red,* Holiday House, 1976. [1]]

(From the movie "Big Red," starring Walter Pidgeon. Copyright 1961 by Walt Disney Productions.)

**The big setter paid no heed, but bounded on after the fleeing rabbit. A half jump ahead of the dog, it flashed beneath a rock pile and disappeared.** ■ (From *Big Red* by Jim Kjelgaard. Illustrated by Bob Kuhn.)

"If I had pursued my scholastic duties as diligently as I did deer, trout, grouse, squirrels, etc., I might have had better report cards!'' [Jim Kjelgaard, *The Spell of the White Sturgeon,* Dodd, Mead and Co., 1953. [2]]

**1938.** Decided to pursue a full-time writing career. Kjelgaard held a variety of jobs before becoming a full time writer for young people. At one time or another he had worked as a teamster, laborer, factory worker, plumber's apprentice and surveyor's assistant.

**1941.** Published his first book, *Forest Patrol,* based on the wilderness experiences of himself and his brother, a forest ranger. "Story hunts have led me from the Atlantic to the Pacific and from the Arctic Circle to Mexico City. Stories, like gold, are where you find them. You may discover one three thousand miles from home or, as in *The Spell of the White Sturgeon,* right on your own door step."

**1945.** Published his best-loved book, *Big Red,* a dog story about an Irish Setter. "I've always had at least one dog and sometimes as many as seven dogs at one time. Most of them were valiant dogs. Bud, an Airedale, held a bear at bay alone three times in one year. Any good bear hunter will tell you it takes a pack of dogs to do that. Mac, a little spaniel, would trot through pheasant swamps all day long and never tire. Then there were Colonel, Joe, Pete, and many, many oth-

ers. To do justice to any of my dogs would take much more space than I have in this message to you.

"My present dog is Jerry, another spaniel, who cost me just seventy-five cents. Jerry has a heart as big as the outdoors, where he and I go hunting. He'll swim icebound creeks, hunt all day in rough going, and do anything except quit! Jerry is one of the best dogs I've ever had." [Jim Kjelgaard, "I've Had Many Wonderful Dogs," *Young Wings,* January, 1949.[3]]

**1948.** *Snow Dog,* the tale of a trapper and his half-wild dog was published. "Chiri, in *Snow Dog,* had his start in a dog I saw in the North. As I approached a trapper's isolated cabin, a dog only slightly smaller than a shetland pony bounded out to greet me, as friendly as any month-old puppy, though he could easily have killed a man. He had been born in the wild, his owner said. The dog feared nothing; but once he was forced to run from a wolf pack. I also heard there of a huge black wolf, an outlaw too cunning for the traps set for him, that was killed either by a dog or by another wolf. I found something here and there, and all of it seemed to tie together. When everything was thoroughly mixed, *Snow Dog,* just wrote itself.

"I am now hot on the trail of a new dog hero, a sheepherder. Before writing about him, I hope to spend some time on a sheep ranch." [3]

**The sun had passed its zenith and was starting its dip westward when Kin got home.** ■ (From *Rebel Siege* by Jim Kjelgaard. Illustrated by Charles Banks Wilson.)

**1953.** Of his homelife, he wrote: "I am married to a very beautiful girl and have a teen-age daughter. Both of them order me around in a shameful fashion, but I can still boss the dog! We live in Phoenix, Arizona."[2]

"The nicest part about writing books for . . . young people is meeting [them]. I have met [them] in schools, on playgrounds, and on at least two radio programs devoted exclusively to books for young people. These programs were NBC's 'Carnival of Books,' conducted by Ruth Harshaw, and the Milwaukee Public Library's 'Young Moderns and Authors Talk Books,' conducted by Norma Rathburn, Chief of Children's Work at the library.

"It was a bleak January day when I appeared on Ruth Harshaw's 'Carnival of Books.' I arrived early. In the lobby I saw four solemn-faced young people, each one carrying a copy of the book scheduled for broadcast. All four were trying hard not to look at me. Two librarians—Roberta Forsyth of Chicago and Edith Scholl—brought groups of boys and girls to witness the broadcast. Miss Scholl's group had traveled nearly a hundred miles. They had to get out of bed at three in the morning so that they could arrive on time.

"The first time I met a group of young readers, I rashly promised to answer all their questions. I learned! Now I promise to *try* to answer. The criticisms, I find, are intelligent and constructive. One eleven-year-old took me to task because, in writing about a thunderstorm, I had a peal of thunder followed by a flash of lightning. Everyone knows, of course, that the lightning comes first. One ten-year-old asked me to explain how much venom a rattlesnake injects when it strikes and how much poison is injected."

**July 12, 1959.** Died in Milwaukee, Wisconsin. Prior to his death at the age of forty-eight Kjelgaard had written thirty-nine books for children, several hundred short stories and articles, and had edited two books, *Hound Dogs and Others* and *Wild Horse Roundup.*

*FOR MORE INFORMATION SEE:* Stanley J. Kunitz and Howard Haycraft, editors, *Junior Book of Authors,* second edition revised, H. W. Wilson, 1951; Obituaries—*Publishers Weekly,* August 10, 1959; *Wilson Library Bulletin,* September, 1959.

(Died July 12, 1959)

# KREDEL, Fritz 1900-1973

*PERSONAL:* Born February 8, 1900, in Michelstadt, Odenwald, Germany; emigrated to the United States in 1938, later became a naturalized citizen; son of an army major in the Hessian field artillery; married Anna Epstein, 1926; children: Stephen, Judith Charlotte. *Education:* Studied under Rudolf Koch at Kunstgewerbeschule, Offenbach-am-Main, and under Victor Hammer in Vienna. *Address:* 180 Pinehurst Ave., New York, N.Y. 10033.

*CAREER:* Early jobs included apprentice to a pharmacist and supervisor of a farm; art teacher, Kunstgewerbeschule, Offenbach-am-Main, Germany, 1925-34, Cooper Union Art School, New York, 1940-42; helped to maintain the workshop of Koch in Frankfort-am-Main, 1934-36; artist and illustrator. *Military service:* Served in the German Army during World War I. *Member:* Grolier Club, Maximilian Gesellschaft Club (Hamburg), Verein Deutsche Buchkuenstler Club (Offenbach). *Awards, honors:* Golden Medal for book illustration at the World Exhibition, Paris, France, 1938; Silver Jubilee Citation of the Limited Editions Club, 1954; Goethe Plaquette in Germany, 1960.

*WRITINGS: Das Kleine Buch der Voegel und Nester* (illustrated by the author), Insel-Verlag, 1935; *Odenwaelder Geschichten* (illustrated by the author), Bauersche Giesserei, 1938; *Blutiger Kehraus, 1918,* Hammerpresse, 1948; (with George Salter) *Am Wegesrand,* Goldene Brunnen, 1961.

Illustrator: Rudolf Koch, *Das Schreibbuechlein: Eine Anleitung zum Schreiben,* Baereneiter-Verlag, 1930; Koch, *Das Blumenbuch,* Insel-Verlag, 1930, reissued, 1962; Grimm Brothers, *Fairy Tales,* Limited Editions, 1931; Heinrich Hoffman-Donner, *Slovenly Peter,* Harper, 1935; Benvenuto Cellini, *The Life of Benvenuto Cellini,* Limited Editions,

**FRITZ KREDEL**

**The judge then, pointing to Pinocchio, said to them: "That poor devil has been robbed of four gold pieces; take him up, and put him immediately into prison."** ■ (From *Pinocchio* by C. Collodi. Illustrated by Fritz Kredel.)

"Nay, move thou must, and 'tis better to risk falling now, than fall for certain with another bullet in thee later on." ■ (From *Moonfleet* by J. Mead Falkner. Illustrated by Fritz Kredel.)

1937; *Schnitzelbank,* Press of the Woolly Whale, 1938; Jeanette P. Brown, *Caterpillar, Caterpillar,* Harper, 1939; Charles and Mary Ann Lamb, *Tales from Shakespeare,* Garden City Publishing, 1939; Kay Boyle, *The Youngest Camel,* Little, Brown, 1939; *Glass Flowers from the Ware Collection in the Botanical Museum of Harvard University,* Harcourt, 1940; Justin B. Atkinson, *Cleo for Short,* Howell, Soskin, 1940; Giovanni Boccaccio, *Decameron,* Limited Editions, 1940; Caius Julius Caesar, *Gallic War,* Noble, 1940; Otto Fuhrmann, *Gutenberg and the Strasbourg Document of 1439: An Interpretation,* Press of the Woolly Whale, 1940; Anna Eleanor R. Roosevelt, *Christmas,* Knopf, 1940; Caroline D. P. Snedecker, *White Isle,* Doubleday, 1940; Frederick P. Todd, *Soldiers of the American Army, 1775-1941,* Bittner, 1941, revised edition, H. Regnery, 1954; Constance B. Burnett, *Shoemaker's Son,* Random House, 1941; John Kieran, *Nature Notes,* Doubleday, 1941, reprinted, Books for Libraries, 1969; Creighton Peet, *Defending America,* Harper, 1941; Leslie Weiner, *Alameda,* Harper, 1941; Hans Christian Andersen, *Andersen's Fairy Tales,* Heritage, 1942; Arensa Sondergaard, *My First Geography of the Americas,* Little, Brown, 1942; William M. Thackeray, *The Rose and the Ring,* Limited Editions, 1942; Charles Dickens, *A Christmas Carol,* Peter Pauper Press, 1943; Hertha Pauli, *Silent Night,* Knopf, 1943.

William Shakespeare, *The Comedies of Shakespeare,* A. S. Barnes, 1944; Plato, *The Republic,* Heritage, 1944; Pedro A. de Alarcon, *Three-Cornered Hat,* Bittner, 1944; Daniel Defoe, *Robinson Crusoe,* Doubleday, 1945; Nathan G. Goodman, editor, *Benjamin Franklin Reader,* Crowell,

1945; Carlo Collodi, pseudonym of Carlo Lorenzini, *The Adventures of Pinocchio,* Grosset, 1946; John Ruskin, *King of the Golden River,* World Publishing, 1946; Opal Wheeler, *H.M.S. Pinafore,* Dutton, 1946; Otto Zoff, *Riddles Around the World,* Pantheon, 1946; Edward C. Wagenknecht, editor, *Story of Jesus in the World's Literature,* McClelland, 1946; Lewis Carroll, pseudonym of Charles L. Dodgson, *Alice's Adventures in Wonderland [and] Through the Looking Glass and What Alice Found There,* Random House, 1946; Aesop, *Aesop's Fables,* Grosset, 1947; Dale Eunson, *The Day They Gave Babies Away,* Farrar, Straus, 1947; H. C. Andersen, *Shorter Tales,* Heritage, 1948; Andersen, *Longer Tales,* Heritage, 1948; Robert Fortenbaugh, *Nine Capitals of the United States,* Maple Press, 1948; Jean Hersholt, reteller, *Aladdin and the Wonderful Lamp,* Limited Editions, 1949; H. C. Andersen, *The Complete Andersen,* Limited Editions, 1949; Gwendolyn Bowers, *The Adventures of Philippe: A Story of Old Kebec,* Aladdin, 1949.

*French Wit and Wisdom,* Peter Pauper Press, 1950; Eric Posselt, editor, *The World's Greatest Christmas Stories,* Prentice-Hall, 1950; C. Dickens, *Christmas with Mr. Pickwick,* Peter Pauper Press, 1950; J. Meade Falkner, *Moonfleet,* Little, Brown, 1951; John W. Mackail, *Holy Bible for Young Readers,* Peter Pauper Press, 1951; Robert B. Considine, *Panama Canal,* Random House, 1951; William O. Steele, *Golden Root,* Aladdin, 1951; G. Boccaccio, *The Nymphs of Fiesole,* Editiones Officinae Bodini, 1952; Henry Beston, *Fairy Tales,* Aladdin, 1952; Hieronymus K. F. Munchausen, *Singular Adventures of Baron Munchausen,* Limited Editions, 1952; Jean Krofsky, *Gardener's Cookbook,* Crowell, 1952; Arthur Little, *Christ Unconquered,* Prentice-Hall, 1952; Alfred Noyes, *Daddy Fell into the Pond, and Other Poems,* Sheed, 1952; W. O. Steele, *Over-Mountain Boy,* Aladdin, 1952; Harry J. Owens, *Doctor Faust: A Play Based upon Old German Puppet Versions,* Caxton Club, 1953; Adele G. Nathan, *Seven Brave Companions,* Aladdin, 1953.

Johann D. Wyss, *Swiss Family Robinson,* Doubleday, 1954; (with Warren Chappell) Stephen V. Benét, *John Brown's Body,* Rinehart, 1954; Fulton J. Sheen, *The True Meaning of Christmas,* McGraw, 1955; Bible, *Book of Books,* Kenedy, 1956; Bible, *Book of Life,* Kenedy, 1956; Robert S. Lemmon, *All about Moths and Butterflies,* Random House, 1956; Anthony Trollope, *Warden,* Longmans, Green, 1956; Andrew Lang, translator, *The Song-Story of Aucassin and Nicolette,* Gravesend Press, 1957; Hellmut Lehmann-Haupt, *The Life of the Book,* Abelard-Schuman, 1957; Samuel Epstein and Beryl Williams, *All about the Desert,* Random House, 1957; *Tom Paine: Freedom's Apostle* (ALA Notable Book), Crowell, 1957; Heinrich Heine, *Poems,* Longmans, Green, 1957; *Dolls and Puppets of the Eighteenth Century,* Gravesend Press, 1958; *Mein Lesebuch Fuer das 3 und 4 Schuljahr,* Bayerischer Schulbuch-Verlag, 1958; Shirley Barker, *The Trojan Horse,* Random House, 1959; A. Trollope, *Barchester Towers,* Saunders, 1959.

*A Bibliographical Confession,* Gravesend Press, 1960; Christoph M. Wieland, *Die Wasserkufe, Oder der Einsiedler und die Seneschallin von Aquilegia,* Buettenfabrik Hahnemuehle, 1960; Leonard Wibberley, *The Time of the Lamb,* Washburn, 1961; Jean L. Latham, *The Story of Eli Whitney,* Harper, 1962; Marion Brown and Ruth Crone, *Silent Storm,* Abingdon, 1963; H. Pauli, *Little Town of Bethlehem,* Duell, Sloan, 1963; Jane Austen, *Emma,* Limited Editions, 1964; H. Hoffman-Donner, *Der Struwwelpeter,* S. Mohn, 1965; Louise Bogan and William J. Smith, compilers, *The Golden*

*Journey,* Reilly, 1965; *Der Roman von Tristan und Isolde,* Trajanus-Presse, 1966; Berechiah ben Natronai, *Fables of a Jewish Aesop,* Columbia University Press, 1967; Mac-Edward Leach, compiler, *The Book of Ballads,* Limited Editions, 1967; Belle B. Sideman, compiler, *The World's Best Fairy Tales,* Reader's Digest Association, 1967; Francois M. A. de Voltaire, *Candide; or, The Optimist,* Peter Pauper Press, 1967; Gail Peterson, compiler, *Proverbs to Live By: Truths That Live in Words,* Hallmark Editions, 1968.

Shirley R. Murphy, *Elmo Doolan and the Search for the Golden Mouse,* Viking, 1970; Kenneth S. Goldstein, compiler, *Thrice Told Tales: Folktales from Three Continents,* Hammerhill Paper, 1970; John C. Gardner, editor, *The Complete Works of the Gawain-Poet,* Feffer & Simons, 1970; Charles R. Darwin, *The Descent of Man and Selection in Relation to Sex,* Limited Editions, 1971; Alan Doan, re-teller, *Aesop's Fables,* Hallmark Editions, 1971; Ambrose Bierce, *The Devil's Dictionary,* Limited Editions, 1972.

Also illustrator of editions of *Much Ado About Nothing, The Innocents Abroad,* and *Lives of the Most Eminent Painters,* for the Limited Editions Club.

*SIDELIGHTS:* Fritz Kredel was born on February 8, 1900 in Michelstadt, Odenwald, Germany. When he was four he asked his father to draw him "a locomotive with smoke coming out." When his father complied, he then asked for one without smoke; and to this drawing the young artist carefully added his own smoke spirals. The same year he was overwhelmed when his father donned his distinguished military uniform (he was a soldier in the Hessian field artillery). Kredel could only ask his father: "Why don't you always dress like this? You look so shabby otherwise."

At the age of sixteen he was taken into the German army, but in less than a year the war was over and he was discharged. Thirty years later he wrote a book about his army experiences entitled *Blutiger Kehraus, 1918.* His teenage army service also sharpened his study of military uniforms and of costumes in general.

"After the Real Gymnasium I went to war as *Fahnenjunker* to become an army officer. After the war I was first apprenticed in a pharmacy, and later worked with horses on a farm in Pomerania. Always fond of making drawings and water colors, I went finally to the Art School in Offenbach-am-Main and became a student of Professor Rudolf Koch. In 1924 I went to Italy with Professor Victor Hammer from Vienna. Returning to Offenbach in 1925, I taught art under Koch. Left school in 1934 after Koch's death and went to Frankfort-am-Main to continue with other students the *Werkstatt Rudolf Koch.* In 1936 went to Austria to join my friend, Professor Hammer, again. Came to the United States September, 1938. Have become a citizen and feel just fine over here." [Bertha E. Mahony and others, compilers, *Illustrators of Children's Books: 1744-1945,* Horn Book, 1947. [1]]

Kredel used a variety of styles for the various texts that he illustrated for the Limited Editions Club including: *The Complete Anderson, The Innocents Abroad, Much Ado About Nothing, A Christmas Carol* and others. He also illustrated many of the "All About Series" of juveniles (Random House). His illustrated books steadily won places among the fifty books annually chosen by the American Institute of Graphic Arts.

(From *The Silent Storm* by Marion Marsh Brown and Ruth Crone. Illustrated by Fritz Kredel.)

His hobbies included carving gingerbread moulds, toy soldiers, horses, and artillery pieces. He enjoyed repairing old furniture and restoring old clocks and firearms. One of his favorite hobbies was puppet play—he carved and manipulated his own puppets.

In 1973 a retrospective show of his work over the past fifty years was held at the Grolier Club in New York. At the age of seventy-three he died in New York on June 10 of that same year.

Paul Standard, writing in *Publishers Weekly,* described Fritz Kredel as ". . . an artist so versatile and spirited, with interests so wide, and talents so quicksilvery, as to defy all categories by making them overlap." Standard went on to say that Kredel's diverseness makes him ". . . a Renaissance man among illustrators. His drawings in flowing wash and line, his vigorous woodcuts of botanical and animal subjects, his gift for making historical settings, costumes, landscapes, arms and armor, military uniforms, galloping horses, and heraldic, mechanical and architectural details all become extensions of the person. . . . It is hard to imagine a task of illustration to which Kredel's powers would not happily respond. . . ."

*FOR MORE INFORMATION SEE:* N. Kent, "Fritz Kredel: Master Xylographer," *American Artist,* April, 1946; Bertha E. Mahony and others, compilers, *Illustrators of Children's Books, 1744-1945,* Horn Book, 1947; B. E. Miller and others, compilers, *Illustrators of Children's Books,*

...The six servants took their leave, saying to their former master, "Your wishes are fulfilled, and you no longer require us. We will therefore journey on and seek our fortunes." ■ (From "The Six Servants" in *Grimms' Fairy Tales* by the Brothers Grimm. Illustrated by Fritz Kredel.)

*1946-1956,* Horn Book, 1958; Muriel Fuller, editor, *More Junior Authors,* H. W. Wilson, 1963; Diana Klemin, *The Art of Art for Children's Books,* Clarkson Potter, 1966; Paul Standard, "Kredel: Renaissance Man Among Illustrators," *Publishers Weekly,* September 4, 1967; Lee Kingman and others, compilers, *Illustrators of Children's Books, 1957-1966,* Horn Book, 1968; Diana Klemin, *The Illustrated Book,* Clarkson Potter, 1970; Obituaries—*New York Times,* June 13, 1973; *Publishers Weekly,* June 25, 1973.

(Died June 10, 1973)

## KREMENTZ, Jill 1940-

*PERSONAL:* Born February 19, 1940, in New York, N.Y. *Education:* Attended Master's School; student at Drew University, 1958-59, and Columbia University. *Home:* 228 East 48th St., New York, N.Y. 10017.

*CAREER:* Free-lance photographer. *Harper's Bazaar,* New York, N.Y., secretary, 1959-60; *Glamour,* New York, N.Y., assistant to features editor, 1960-61; *Show,* New York, N.Y., reporter and columnist, 1962-64; *New York*

*Herald Tribune,* New York, N.Y., staff photographer (first woman to hold this position with a New York city newspaper since World War II), 1964-65; *People* magazine, contributing photographer, 1964—; free-lance photographer in Viet Nam, 1965-66; *Status and Diplomat,* New York, N.Y., associate editor with status of staff photographer, 1966-67; *New York* (magazine), New York, N.Y., contributing editor, 1967-68; Time-Life, Inc., New York, N.Y., correspondent, 1969-70. Public relations representative. Indian Industries Fair (New Delhi), 1961. *Exhibitions:* The Delaware Arts Museum, Wilmington, Del.; The Morris Museum, Morristown, N.J.; Madison Art Center, Wisconsin; work is in the permanent collections of The Museum of Modern Art and The Library of Congress. *Awards, honors: A Very Young Dancer* was named to American Institute of Graphic Artists 50 Books of the Year, *School Library Journal* Best Books of the Year, and the *New York Times* Best Seller List of Children's Books, all in 1976; *A Very Young Rider* and *A Very Young Gymnast* were selected by the *School Library Journal* as best books of the year.

*WRITINGS: The Face of South Vietnam* (a book of photographs, with text by Dean Brelis), Houghton, 1968; *Sweet Pea: A Girl Growing Up in the Rural South* (a book of photographs with accompanying text; foreword by Margaret Mead), Harcourt, 1969; *Words and Their Masters* (a book of photographs, with text by Israel Shenker), Doubleday, 1973; *A Very Young Dancer,* Knopf, 1976; *A Very Young Rider,* Knopf, 1977; *A Very Young Gymnast,* Knopf, 1978; *A Very Young Circus Flyer,* Knopf, 1979; *A Very Young Skater,* Knopf, 1979. Contributor to national and international magazines and newspapers, including *Vogue, Newsweek, Esquire, Holiday, Time, Life,* and *New York Times Book Review.*

*SIDELIGHTS:* **February 19, 1940.** Born in New York, Krementz was raised in Morristown, a fashionable New Jersey suburb. "Most of the other girls were dreaming about meeting the perfect guy, having a beautiful wedding and settling down. That was fine but I knew it wasn't for me. My fantasy life always consisted of me having a career, of being financially independent. The career I had in mind definitely had something to do with journalism—but I had never even met a photographer so I didn't think of that possibility." [Jill Krementz, "In Focus," *American Girl,* December, 1976.[1]]

**1959.** After graduation from boarding school and a year as an art major at Drew University left her hometown for New York City where she worked as a secretary and editorial assistant for *Harper's Bazaar.* "I somehow had the idea that once you were 18, you could do anything you wanted. And I had always wanted to come to New York and work for a newspaper or magazine." [Randy Sue Coburn, "Krementz and Her Subjects," *The Washington Star,* July 11, 1976.[2]]

**1960.** Worked as assistant to the features editor for *Glamour* Magazine, saved $1000, and "with a friend, I decided to take a trip around the world. I traded my sewing machine for a simple Kodak, a Brownie. There were three ways to set the lens: portrait, group or scenic." [Lawrence Mahoney, "Jill Krementz . . . Getting the Picture Is Focus of Her Life," *The Miami Herald,* April 4, 1975.[3]]

**1962-1964.** After returning from her world trip, Krementz joined the staff of *Show* in New York as a reporter and columnist. The magazine's art director and photographer, Henry Wolf, taught her how to load and operate her new camera: "I got a Nikon, learned how to work it and began

**JILL KREMENTZ**

spending lunch hours and weekends photographing people on the streets. Then I started getting my pictures published and suddenly it seemed I'd found my career."[1]

**1963.** Sold a set of her pictures to the *Herald Tribune.* "It was November 23, 1963, and Kennedy was dead in Dallas. I could sense that many of my colleagues felt I was being callous but, even though I was as devastated as everyone else, I still felt a great need to record an event I knew was already becoming history. I guess that's when I first realized that more than anything else I wanted to be a journalistic photographer.

"I went to Bloomingdale's and photographed the people staring at stacks of TVs. I called The New York *Times* and they let me photograph the front page coming off the presses. I took pictures in the newsroom and then I followed the papers out into the streets. I took the pictures over to *The Herald Trib.*"

After that, Krementz left *Show* Magazine and associated with the photographers at the *Herald Tribune.* "They were very nice to me. There I learned how to work within a deadline; how to develop film and make prints in 20 minutes; how to work with editors and writers. I spent another year racing around, taking pictures of everything and anything—like fires at four a.m.—and selling them, sometimes, for about $15."[1]

(From *Sweet Pea: A Girl Growing Up in the Rural South* by Jill Krementz. Photos by the author.)

**1964-1965.** After a few months as a free-lancer, she was hired by the *Tribune*. She was the youngest full time photographer ever and the only woman photographer on the newspaper since World War II. "I had a certain aggression. I used to worry about it, but I had a wonderful photographer as a teacher and he let me know that aggression is part of it.

"Ira Rosenberg taught me everything—the meaning of craftsmanship, how to think on my feet and how to go the extra mile for a good picture. More than anything else, he taught me that even if I got a page one picture, that today's paper was already yesterday's and I better concentrate on the next assignment. In short: Be a pro. . . ."[3]

**1965-1966.** Free-lance photographer in Vietnam. "I went to photograph Vietnam behind the lines. Everyday you could open the newspaper and see pictures of soldiers in steel helmets. I was not a combat photographer like Dickey Chapelle (a gung-ho woman parachutist photographer who was killed on patrol). Of course, I saw and photographed soldiers. All I really remember is the mud on their faces and that they all looked very young.

"My photography, generally speaking, is peripheral. I went around often with two young nuns. I didn't talk much, so most people thought I was French, too. I went to hospitals, orphanages, race tracks, NCO clubs, funerals and weddings of the Vietnamese, USO shows, beaches, mess halls, the collecting point for a U.S. graves registration platoon."[3]

**1968.** Published her first book, *The Face of Vietnam*. "I tried not to photograph with any political viewpoint, but when I returned I was very much opposed to what the war was doing to these people. There was little realization that their homes were ancestral shrines. Families who made their living from the sea were moved to inland wastes—there was such little regard to lifestyles." [Philip F. Crosland, "Photographer Brings Personalities to Life," *The Morning News*, Wilmington, Del., September 16, 1975.[4]]

**1969.** *Sweet Pea: A Girl Growing Up in the Rural South* was published. This book was one of Krementz's proudest accomplishments. Sweet Pea was a ten-year-old black girl living with her family in poverty in Alabama. The pictures and text, written in Sweet Pea's words, focused on the girl's joyous moments. "She was more of my fantasy life of childhood, and they say every creative person goes back and digs in their childhood. I'm basically a Pollyanna, Sweet Pea was the most popular girl in her class, and she sang in the choir. I could have only been in a choir where you just had to move your lips."[2]

**1970.** Began photographing authors. Sold her pictures to magazines and newspapers that ran book reviews. Krementz has contributed to such national magazines as: *Vogue, Newsweek, Holiday, Time, Life,* and *New York Times Book Review* and has become one of the most sought-after portrait photographers in New York. "After four or five years as a free-lance photographer, I decided I should specialize. Just as a free-lance writer does. One writer led to another. There was a void. I read a lot, always have. I like writers. A lot of them are my friends. They're warm, kind and interesting people. I've read most of their books, and if I haven't read one, I try to read it before I go to see them. I spent $106 on Henry Miller's books before I went out to Pacific Palisades to photograph him.

"A lot of people think of me as a portrait photographer or portraitist because I photograph so many writers, but I really think of myself more as a documentary photographer because I am basically documenting the lives of all these writers. The portraits are published with reviews and articles about the writers, but my real dream is that all of these photographs will one day be part of a university's archives available to anybody who wants to know how any of these writers lived."[3]

**1976.** *A Very Young Dancer*, a book about a ten-year-old ballet student, published. "When I wasn't at the ballet, I was reading every book I could find, listening to ballets, or watching performances, trying to understand it. My brain just wouldn't let loose of it. I also spent a lot of time sharpening my technique for the dancers, learning how to do things like capture a dancer at the peak of elevation."[2]

Krementz was commissioned to do official portraits for four members of the United States cabinet—Defense Secretary, Harold Brown, Transportation Secretary, Brock Adams, Secretary of State, Cyrus Vance, and Health, Education, and Welfare Secretary, Joseph Califano.

"I spend about a year working on each of [my] books. I'm with the subjects when they win and when they lose—when things go well and when they don't. I think that television too often shows us the end results of success and I am more interested in the process towards that final goal. I think that children need role models and I hope that these books will provide them. When I was a little girl I studied ballet and I think that if I had had a book such as *A Very Young Dancer*, I would have seen deeper and more exciting possibilities. As it was, it seemed that ballet lessons or lessons of any sort, were simply something we should all do after school—either that or go outside and play.

"More and more children are entering the world of performing arts and sports at an early age. I hope that these books will feed their fantasies and give them good goals to dream about.

"I also hope more than anything else that these books will show that the only way you really accomplish anything worthwhile in life is through hard work. It seems to me that this is the most important thing that young people, or anyone for that matter, can *ever* learn."

*HOBBIES AND OTHER INTERESTS:* Reading, tennis.

*FOR MORE INFORMATION SEE: Newsweek,* February 5, 1968, July 31, 1978; *Saturday Review,* February 17, 1968; *Mademoiselle,* March, 1968; *New York Times Book Review,* November 9, 1969; *Boston Sunday Globe,* December 28, 1969; *The Miami Herald,* April 4, 1975; *The Morning News,* Wilmington, Del., September 16, 1975; *The Washington Star,* July 11, 1976; *American Girl,* December, 1976.

# KUBINYI, Laszlo    1937-

*PERSONAL:* Born in 1937. *Education:* Attended Boston Museum School and the Art Students League in New York City. *Residence:* New York, N.Y.

*CAREER:* Traveled throughout the world, particularly the Middle East; played the dumbek (a Middle Eastern drum) in an Armenian orchestra; author and illustrator of children's books.

**This time Shukru was hitting them with bags of black pepper.** ▪ (From *The Cat and the Flying Machine* by Laszlo Kubinyi. Illustrated by the author.)

**LASZLO KUBINYI**

*WRITINGS:* (Self-illustrated) *The Cat and the Flying Machine,* Simon & Schuster, 1970; (self-illustrated) *Zeki and the Talking Cat Shukru,* Simon & Schuster, 1970.

Illustrator: Paul Anderson, *The Fox, The Dog, and the Griffin,* Doubleday, 1966; Christoforo Columbo, *Across the Ocean Sea: A Journal of Columbus's Voyage* (edited by George Sanderlin), Harper, 1966; William C. Harrison, *Dr. William Harvey and the Discovery of Circulation,* Macmillan, 1967; Coralie Howard, *What Do You Want to Know?,* Simon & Schuster, 1968; Kay Hill, *And Tomorrow the Stars: The Story of John Cabot,* Dodd, 1968; Martin Gardner, *Perplexing Puzzles and Tantalizing Teasers,* Simon & Schuster, 1969; Robert Froman, *Science, Art, and Visual Illusions,* Simon & Schuster, 1969; Jeanne B. Hardendorff, *Witches, Wit, and a Werewolf,* Lippincott, 1971; Betty Jean Lifton, *The Silver Crane,* Seabury, 1971; Adrien Stoutenburg, *Haran's Journey,* Dial, 1971; Tony Hillerman, *The Boy Who Made Dragonfly: A Zuni Myth,* Harper, 1972; Maureen Mollie Hunter McIlwraith, *The Haunted Mountain* (ALA Notable Book), Harper, 1972; Morton Friend, *The Vanishing Tungus: The Story of a Remarkable Reindeer People,* Dial, 1972; F. N. Monjo, *Slater's Mill,* Simon & Schuster, 1972; David C. Knight, *Poltergeists: Hauntings and the Haunted,* Lippincott, 1972; Arthur S. Gregor, *Witchcraft & Magic: The Supernatural World,* Scribner, 1972.

Peter Putnam, *Peter the Revolutionary Tsar,* Harper, 1973; Felice Holman, *I Hear You Smiling, and Other Poems,* Scribner, 1973; Maia Wojciechowska, *Winter Tales from Poland,* Doubleday, 1973; Julie Edwards, *The Last of the Really Great Wangdoodles,* Harper, 1974; Natalie Maree Belting, editor, *Our Fathers Had Powerful Songs,* Dutton, 1974; Lloyd Alexander, *The Wizard in the Tree,* Dutton, 1975; Margaret Greaves, *The Dagger and the Bird: A Story of Suspense,* Harper, 1975; Ellen Pugh, *The Adventures of Yoo-Lah-Teen: A Legend of the Salish Coastal Indians,*

Dial, 1975; Miriam Anne Bourne, *Patsy Jefferson's Diary,* Coward, 1976; Martin Gardner, *More Perplexing Puzzles and Tantalizing Teasers,* Archway, 1977; Lloyd Alexander, *The Town Cats and Other Tales,* Dutton, 1977.

*SIDELIGHTS:* Laszlo Kubinyi was born in 1937 and was raised in Ohio and Massachusetts. He studied art at the School of the Museum of Fine Arts in Boston and at the School of Visual Arts and the Art Students League in New York City.

A world traveler, Kubinyi now lives with his wife in New York City.

# LAMB, Charles   1775-1834   (Elia)

*PERSONAL:* Born February 10, 1775, in London, England; died December 27, 1834, in Edmonton, England; buried at Edmonton; son of John Lamb (a lawyer's clerk and confidential attendant); brother of Mary Lamb (the author); children: Emma Isola (adopted). *Education:* Attended Christ's Hospital, 1782-89; classmate of Samuel Taylor Coleridge (the poet). *Home:* Edmonton, England.

*CAREER:* Essayist, critic, and poet. Clerk in the South Sea House, 1789-92; worked in the accountant's office and in the examiner's office of the East India Company, 1792-1825; became mentally deranged and was hospitalized for six weeks, 1795-96.

*WRITINGS*—Essays; all originally published under pseudonym, Elia, and later under the author's real name: *Elia: Essays which Have Appeared under that Signature in the London Magazine,* [London], 1823, later editions published as *The Essays of Elia,* Putnam, 1848, reissued, Dutton, 1976 [other editions illustrated by R. Swain Gifford, James D. Smillie, Charles A. Platt, and F. S. Church, W. Paterson, 1885; C. E. Brock, Dutton, 1929; Gordon Ross, Heritage Press, 1943]; excerpt from *The Essays of Elia* published separately—*A Dissertation upon Roast Pig,* K. Tompkins, 1874, reissued, Pyramid, 1968 [other editions illustrated by L. J. Bridgman, Lothrop, 1888; Wilfred Jones, L. Hart, 1932; Richard Floethe, Peter Pauper Press, 1952]; *The Last Essays of Elia,* [London], 1833, reissued, St. Martin's, 1957 [another edition illustrated by C. E. Brock, Scribner, 1900]; excerpts from *The Last Essays of Elia* published separately—*Detached Thoughts on Books and Reading,* privately printed, 1894; *Old China,* Redcoat Press, 1940; *A Masque of Days,* Cassell, 1901.

Other essays: *Specimens of English Dramatic Poets Who Lived about the Time of Shakespeare,* Longman, 1801, reprinted, Johnson Reprints, 1970; *The Art of the Stage as Set Out in Lamb's Dramatic Essays,* Remington, 1885.

Poems: (With Charles Lloyd) *Blank Verse,* [London], 1798; (with sister, Mary Lamb) *Poetry for Children,* [London], 1809, reprinted, Books for Libraries, 1970; *Album Verses, with a Few Others,* E. Moxon, 1830.

Stories and tales: *A Tale of Rosamund Gray and Old Blind Margaret,* Lee & Hurst, 1798; (with Mary Lamb) *Tales from Shakespeare,* T. Hodgkins, 1807, reissued, Hart, 1976 [other editions illustrated by John Gilbert, Routledge, 1876; Albert Hencke, F. A. Stokes, 1893; Harold Copping, R. Tuck, 1901; Arthur Rackham, Dutton, 1909; M. L. Kirk, F. A. Stokes, 1911; Norman M. Price, Scribner, 1915;

Louis Rhead, Harper, 1918; Elizabeth Shippen Green Elliott, D. McKay, 1922; Maud and Miska Petersham, Macmillan, 1923, reissued, 1956; Frank Godwin, J. C. Winston, 1924; R. Farrington Elwell, Houghton, 1925; Fritz Kredel, Garden City Publishing, 1939; Elinore Blaisdell, Crowell, 1942; John C. Wonsetler, Macmillan, 1950; Leonard Weisgard, Junior Deluxe Editions, 1955; Karel Svolinsky, Golden Pleasure Books, 1962; Richard M. Powers, Macmillan, 1963]; *The Adventures of Ulysses*, [London], 1808 [other editions illustrated by M. H. Squire and E. Mars, R. H. Russell, 1902; Otho Cushing, Ginn, 1917; Doris Pailthorpe and T. H. Robinson, F. A. Stokes, 1926]; (with M. Lamb) *Mrs. Leicester's School; or, The History of Several Young Ladies, Related by Themselves*, M. J. Godwin, 1809 [another edition illustrated by Winifred Green, Dent, 1899]; *The King and Queen of Hearts*, M. J. Godwin, 1809; (with M. Lamb) *Beauty and the Beast*, [London], 1811; *Prince Dorus; or, Flattery Put Out of Countenance*, Field & Tuer, 1889.

Plays: *John Woodvil*, T. Plummer, 1802; *Mr. H.; or, Beware a Bad Name* (two-act), M. Carey, 1802. Also author of *The Wife's Trial; or, The Intruding Widow*, 1828, and *The Pawnbroker's Daughter*, 1830.

Selections: *Some Essays of Elia* (illustrated by C. O. Murray), Appleton, 1886; *Charles Lamb, in Pipefuls* (selected by Walter Lewin), [Liverpool, England], 1890; *Tales from Shakespeare's Tragedies* (edited by William J. Rolfe), Harper, 1891; *Tales from Shakespeare's Comedies* (illustrated by W. J. Rolfe), Harper, 1891; *Lamb's Essays: A Biographical Study* (selected by Elizabeth Deering Hanscom), Lothrop, 1891; *The Best Letters of Charles Lamb* (edited, with an introduction, by Edward G. Johnson), A. C. McClurg, 1892; *Bon-Mots of Charles Lamb and Douglas Jerrold* (edited by Walter Jerrold; illustrated by Aubrey Beardsley), Dent, 1893; *Selections from the Essays of Elia* (edited by Caroline Ladd Crew), Leach, Shewell, 1897; *Selections from His Essays, Letters, and Verse*, Doubleday & McClure, 1899.

*Selected Essays of Charles Lamb* (edited, with an introduction, by Ernest Dressel North), Silver, Burdett, 1901; *Select Essays of Elia* (edited by John F. Genung), American Book Co., 1909; *Miscellaneous Prose* (by Charles and Mary Lamb; edited by E. V. Lucas), Methuen, 1912; *Charles Lamb: Prose and Poetry, with Essays by Hazlitt and De Quincey*, Clarendon Press, 1921; *Lamb's Criticism: A Selection from the Literary Criticism of Charles Lamb* (edited, with an introduction, by E. M. W. Tillyard), Cambridge University Press, 1923, reprinted, Folcroft, 1973; *Lamb* (edited by Bliss Perry), Doubleday, Page, 1922; *Selected Letters of Charles Lamb* (edited by G. T. Clapton), Methuen, 1925; *Miscellaneous Essays and Sketches by Charles Lamb* (illustrated by C. E. Brock), Dutton, 1929; *Charles Lamb in Essays and Letters* (edited by Maurice Graland Fulton), Macmillan, 1930; *Twenty Essays of Elia, Selected for the Light They Shed upon the Life and Personality of Charles Lamb*, Holt, 1932; *Everybody's Lamb, being a Selection from The Essays of Elia, the Letters and the Miscellaneous Prose of Charles Lamb* (edited by A. C. Ward; illustrated by Ernest H. Shepard), Harcourt, 1933; *Select Essays*, Peter Pauper Press, 1934; *The Best of Lamb* (edited by E. V. Lucas), Methuen, 1934, reprinted, 1962; *Essays and Letters* (edited by J. Milton French), Doubleday, Doran, 1937; *Selected Letters* (edited, with an introduction, by T. S. Matthews), Farrar, Straus, 1956; *Favorite Tales from Shakespeare* (edited by Morris Schreiber; illustrated by Donald Lynch), Grosset & Dunlap, 1956; *A*

*Lamb Selection: Letters and Essays* (edited, with an introduction, by F. B. Pinton), St. Martin's, 1965; *Ten Tales from Shakespeare* (illustrated by Janusz Grabianski), F. Watts, 1969; *Romeo and Juliet* (illustrated by Brian Froud), F. Watts, 1971; *A Midsummer Night's Dream* (illustrated by B. Froud), F. Watts, 1972; *The Wit and Wisdom of Charles Lamb* (selected by E. D. North), Folcroft, 1974.

Collections: *The Letters of Charles Lamb* (with a sketch of his life by Thomas Noon Talford), two volumes, E. Moxon, 1837, revised edition, G. Bell, 1886; *The Prose Works of Charles Lamb*, three volumes, E. Moxon, 1838; *The Works of Charles Lamb*, two volumes, Harper, 1838; *The Poetical Works of Charles Lamb*, H. G. Bohn, 1841, Hubbard Brothers, 1873; *Literary Sketches and Letters, being the Final Memorials of Charles Lamb, Never before Published*, D. Appleton, 1848; *Eliana, being the Hitherto Uncollected Writings of Charles Lamb*, W. Veazie, 1864; *The Complete Correspondence and Works of Charles Lamb*, four volumes, 1870; *The Complete Works in Prose and Verse of Charles Lamb* (edited by R. H. Shepherd), Chatto & Windus, 1875; *The Complete Works of Charles Lamb*, W. T. Amies, 1879; *The Dramatic Essays of Charles Lamb*, Dodd, Mead, 1891; *The Life, Letters, and Writings of Charles Lamb*, six volumes (edited and illustrated by Percy Firzgerald), W. W. Gibbings, 1892, reprinted, Books for Libraries, 1971; *Poems, Plays, and Miscellaneous Essays of Charles Lamb*, Macmillan, 1895; *Essays by Charles Lamb*, Maynard, Merrill, 1895; *The Works of Charles and Mary Lamb*, seven volumes (edited by E. V. Lucas), Methuen, 1903-05, reprinted, Scholarly Press, 1971; *The Works of Charles Lamb*, 12 volumes (edited by William Macdonald), Dutton, 1903-16; *The Works of Charles and Mary Lamb* (edited by Thomas Hutchinson), Oxford University Press, 1924; *The Works of Charles Lamb* (edited by T. Hutchinson), Oxford University Press, 1924; *The Collected Essays of Charles Lamb*, two volumes (illustrated by C. E. Brock), Dutton, 1929; *The Complete Works and Letters of Charles Lamb*, Modern Library, 1935, reissued, 1963; *The Letters of Charles Lamb, to which Are Added those of His Sister, Mary Lamb*, three volumes (edited by E. V. Lucas), Dent, 1935, reprinted, AMS Press, 1968; *The Letters of Charles and Mary Ann Lamb*, two volumes (edited by Edwin W. Marrs, Jr.), Cornell University Press, 1975.

*ADAPTATIONS*—Recordings: "Tales from Shakespeare," read by Julie Harris, Caedmon, 1976.

*SIDELIGHTS:* **February 10, 1775.** Born in the Temple, London. Brother of Mary Ann (the author) and John. A taint of mania in his background was to inflict him for a short duration and overshadow his sister's life. Lamb became her voluntary self-sacrificing guardian. "I was born, and passed the first seven years of my life, in the Temple. Its church, its halls, its gardens, its fountain, its river, I had almost said—for in those young years, what was this king of rivers to me but a stream that watered our pleasant places? . . .

"Indeed, it is the most elegant spot in the metropolis. What a transition for a countryman visiting London for the first time—the passing from the crowded Strand or Fleet-street, by unexpected avenues, into its magnificent ample squares, its classic green recesses!

"The same day which gave me to the world, saw London happy in the celebration of her great annual feast. This I cannot help looking upon as a lively omen of the future

CHARLES LAMB

**...Being thus disappointed in his revenge, and despoiled of his riches, he said, "I am ill. Let me go home; send the deed after me, and I will sign over half my riches to my daughter."** ■ (From *Tales from Shakespeare* by Charles and Mary Lamb. Illustrated by Karel Svolinsky.)

great good will which I was destined to bear toward the city.

"I was born . . . in a crowd. This has begot in me an entire affection for that way of life, amounting to an almost insurmountable aversion from solitude and rural scenes. This aversion was never interrupted or suspended, except for a few years in the younger part of my life, during a period in which I had set my affections upon a charming young woman. Every man while the passion is upon him, is for a time at least addicted to groves and meadows and purling streams. During this short period of my existence, I contracted just familiarity enough with rural objects to understand tolerably well ever after the *poets,* when they declaim in such passionate terms in favor of a country life.

"For my own part, now the fit is past, I have no hesitation in declaring, that a mob of happy faces crowding up at the pit door of Drury-lane Theatre, just at the hour of six, gives me ten thousand sincerer pleasures, than I could ever receive from all the flocks of silly sheep that ever whitened the plains of Arcadia or Epsom Downs.

"This passion for crowds is no where feasted so full as in London. The man must have a rare *recipe* for melancholy, who can be dull in Fleet-street. I am naturally inclined to hypochondria, but in London it vanishes, like all other ills. Often, when I have felt a weariness or distaste at home,

have I rushed out into her crowded Strand, and fed my humour, till tears have wetted my cheek for unutterable sympathies with the multitudinous moving picture, which she never fails to present at all hours, like the scenes of a shifting pantomime.

"The very deformities of London, which give distaste to others, from habit do not displease me. The endless succession of shops where *Fancy miscalled Folly* is supplied with perpetual gauds and toys, excite in me no puritanical aversion. I gladly behold every appetite supplied with its proper food. The obliging customer, and the obliged tradesman—things which live by bowing, and things which exist but for homage—do not affect me with disgust; from habit I perceive nothing but urbanity, where other men, more refined, discover meanness: I love the very smoke of London, because it has been the medium most familiar to my vision. I see grand principles of honor at work in the dirty ring which encompasses two combatants with fists, and principles of no less eternal justice in the detection of a pickpocket. The salutary astonishment with which an execution is surveyed, convinces me more forcibly than a hundred volumes of abstract polity, that the universal instinct of man in all ages has leaned to order and good government.

"Thus an art of extracting morality from the commonest incidents of a town life, is attained by the same well-natured alchemy, with which the Foresters of Arden, in a beautiful country,

'Found tongues in trees, books in the running brooks, Sermons in stones, and good in every thing,'

"Where has spleen her food but in London? Humour, Interest, Curiosity, suck at her measureless breasts without a possibility of being satiated. Nursed amid her noise, her crowds, her beloved smoke, what have I been doing all my life, if I have not lent out my heart with usury to such scenes!" [*Everybody's Lamb,* edited by A. C. Ward, Harcourt, 1933.[1]]

"From my childhood I was extremely inquisitive about witches and witch-stories. My maid, and more legendary aunt, supplied me with good store. But I shall mention the accident which directed my curiosity originally into this channel. In my father's book-closet, the *History of the Bible,* by Stackhouse, occupied a distinguished station. The pictures with which it abounds—one of the ark, in particular, and another of Solomon's temple, delineated with all the fidelity of ocular admeasurement, as if the artist had been upon the spot—attracted my childish attention. There was a picture, too, of the Witch raising up Samuel, which I wish that I had never seen. . . . Stackhouse is in two huge tomes—and there was a pleasure in removing folios of that magnitude, which, with infinite straining, was as much as I could manage, from the situation which they occupied upon an upper shelf." [W. Carew Hazlitt, *Mary and Charles Lamb: Poems, Letters and Remains,* Scribner, 1874.[2]]

**1781.** Attended William Bird's School. "Bird wore one of those flowered Indian gowns, formerly in use with schoolmasters; the strange figures upon which we used to interpret into hieroglyphics of pain and suffering. But boyish fears apart—Bird I believe was in the main a humane and judicious master.

"O, how I remember our legs wedged in to those uncomfortable sloping desks, where we sat elbowing each other—and the injunctions to attain a free hand, unattainable in that position; the first copy I wrote after, with its moral lesson 'Art improves Nature'; the still earlier pot-hooks and the hangers some traces of which I fear may yet be apparent in this manuscript; the truant looks side-long to the garden, which seemed a mockery of our imprisonment; the prize for best spelling, which had almost turned my head, and which to this day I cannot reflect upon without a vanity, which I ought to be ashamed of—our little leaden inkstands, not separately subsisting, but sunk into the desks; the bright, punctually-washed morning fingers, darkening gradually with another and another ink-spot: what a world of little associated circumstances, pains and pleasures mingling their quotas of pleasure, arise at the reading of those few simple words—'Mr. William Bird, an eminent Writer and Teacher of languages and mathematics in Fetter Lane, Holborn!' "[1]

**1782.** Entered Christ's Hospital School. His schoolmate, Samuel Coleridge, was to remain a devoted life-long friend. "It is, in a word, an Institution to keep those who have yet held up their heads in the world from sinking; to keep alive the spirit of a decent household, when poverty was in danger of crushing it; to assist those who are the most willing, but not always the most able, to assist themselves; to separate a child from his family for a season, in order to render him back hereafter, with feelings and habits more congenial to it, than he could even have attained by remaining at home in the bosom of it. It is a preserving and renovating principle, an antidote for the *res angusta domi,* when it presses, as it always does, most heavily upon the most ingenuous natures.

"For the Christ's Hospital boy feels that he is no charity-boy; he feels it in the antiquity and regality of the foundation to which he belongs; in the usage which he meets with at school, and the treatment he is accustomed to out of its bounds; in the respect, and even kindness, which his well known garb never fails to procure him in the streets of the metropolis; he feels it in his education, in that measure of classical attainments, which every individual at that school, though not destined to a learned profession, has it in his power to procure, attainments which it would be worse than folly to put it in the reach of the labouring classes to acquire: he feels it in the numberless comforts, and even magnificences, which surround him; in his old and awful cloisters, with their traditions; in his spacious school-rooms, and in the well-ordered, airy, and lofty rooms where he sleeps; in his stately dining-hall, hung round with pictures by Verrio, Lely, and others, one of them surpassing in size and grandeur almost any other in the kingdom; above all, in the very extent and magnitude of the body to which he belongs, and the consequent spirit, the intelligence, and public conscience, which is the result of so many various yet wonderfully combining members. Compared with this last-named advantage, what is the stock of information, (I do not here speak of book-learning, but of that knowledge which boy receives from boy,) the mass of collected opinions, the intelligence in common, among the few and narrow members of an ordinary boarding-school?

"The Christ's Hospital boy is a religious character. His school is eminently a religious foundation; it has its peculiar prayers, its services at set times, its graces, hymns, and anthems, following each other in an almost monastic closeness of succession. This religious character in him is not always untinged with superstition. That is not wonderful, when we consider the thousand tales and traditions which must circulate, with undisturbed credulity, amongst so

**Where is Pease-Blossom?** ▪ (From *Tales from Shakespeare* by Charles and Mary Lamb. Illustrated by Arthur Rackham.)

many boys, that have so few checks to their belief from any intercourse with the world at large; upon whom their equals in age must work so much, their elders so little. With this leaning towards an over-belief in matters of religion, which will soon correct itself when he comes out into society, may be classed a turn for romance above most other boys. This is to be traced in the same manner to their excess of society with each other, and defect of mingling with the world. Hence the peculiar avidity with which such books as the Arabian Nights Entertainments, and others of a still wilder cast, are, or at least were in my time, sought for by the boys. I remember when some half-dozen of them set off from school, without map, card, or compass, on a serious expedition to find out *Philip Quarll's Island.* "[1]

An exasperating stammer kept Lamb from attending a university. "Such a one as myself, who has been *defrauded* in his young years of the sweet food of academic institution.

"Yet can I fancy, wandering 'mid thy towers,
Myself a nursling, Granta, of thy lap;
My brow seems tightening with the Doctor's cap,
And I walk *gownéd;* feel unusual powers."

[Edmund Blunden, *Charles Lamb and His Contemporaries*, Archon Books, 1967.[3]]

**1789.** Clerkship in South-Sea House. "Here are still to be seen stately porticos; imposing staircases; offices roomy as the state apartments in palaces—deserted, or thinly peopled with a few straggling clerks; the still more sacred interiors of court and committee rooms, with venerable faces of beadles, door-keepers—directors seated in form on solemn days (to proclaim a dead dividend,) at long worm-eaten tables, that have been mahogany, with tarnished gilt-leather coverings, supporting massy silver inkstands long since dry;—the oaken wainscots hung with pictures of deceased governors and sub-governors, of Queen Anne, and the two first monarchs of the Brunswick dynasty;—huge charts, which subsequent discoveries have antiquated;—dusty maps of Mexico, dim as dreams,—and soundings of the Bay of Panama!—the long passages hung with buckets, appended, in idle row, to walls, whose substance might defy any, short of the last, conflagration:—with vast ranges of cellarage under all, where dollars and pieces of eight once lay, an 'unsunned heap,' for Mammon to have solaced his solitary heart withal,—long since dissipated, or scattered into air at the blast of the breaking of that famous BUBBLE.—

"The very clerks which I remember in the South-Sea House . . . had an air very different from those in the public offices that I have had to do with since. They partook of the genius of the place!

"They were mostly (for the establishment did not admit of superfluous salaries) bachelors. Generally (for they had not much to do) persons of a curious and speculative turn of mind. Old-fashioned, for a reason mentioned before. Humorists, for they were of all descriptions; and, not having been brought together in early life (which has a tendency to assimilate the members of corporate bodies to each other), but, for the most part, placed in this house in ripe or middle age, they necessarily carried into it their separate habits and oddities, unqualified, if I may so speak, as into a common stock. Hence they formed a sort of Noah's ark. Odd fishes. A lay-monastery. Domestic retainers in a great house, kept more for show than use. Yet pleasant fellows, full of chat—and not a few among them had arrived at considerable proficiency on the German flute."[1]

**1792.** Appointed clerk in the East India House where he was to remain for thirty-three years.

**1795.** Spent six weeks in madhouse at Hoxton.

**1796.** Letter to Coleridge during convalescence. "The six weeks that finished last year & began this your very humble servant spent very agreeably in a mad house at Hoxton—. I am got somewhat rational now, & dont bite any one. But mad I was—& many a vagary my imagination played with me, enough to make a volume if all told—

"Coleridge, it may convince you of my regards for you when I tell you my head ran on you in my madness as much almost as on another Person, who I am inclined to think was the more immediate cause of my temporary frenzy—. The sonnet I send you has small merit as poetry but you will be curious to read it when I tell you it was written in my prison house in one of my lucid Intervals

"to my sister

"If from my lips some angry accents fell,
  Peevish complaint, or harsh reproof unkind,
  Twas but the Error of a sickly mind,
And troubled thoughts, clouding the purer well,
  & waters clear, of Reason: & for me
  Let this my verse the poor atonement be,
My verse, which thou to praise: wast ever inclined
  Too highly, & with a partial eye to see
No Blemish: thou to me didst ever shew
  Fondest affection, & woudst oftimes lend
An ear to the desponding, love sick Lay,
  Weeping my sorrows with me, who repay
But ill the mighty debt, of love I owe,
  Mary, to thee, my sister & my friend—"

[*The Letters of Charles and Mary Ann Lamb*, edited by Edwin W. Marrs, Cornell University Press, 1975.[4]]

**September 22, 1796.** In a fit of madness Mary Ann fatally stabbed her mother and injured her father. "My poor dear dearest sister in a fit of insanity has been the death of her own mother. I was at hand only time enough to snatch the knife out of her grasp. She is at present in a mad house, from whence I fear she must be moved to an hospital. God has preserved to me my senses,—I eat and drink and sleep, and have my judgment I believe very sound. My poor father was slightly wounded, and I am left to take care of him and my aunt . . . mention nothing of poetry. I have destroyed every vestige of past vanities of that kind.

"My poor dear dearest sister, the unhappy & unconscious instrument of the Almighty's judgments to our house, is restored to her senses; to a dreadful sense & recollection of what has past, awful to her mind & impressive (as it must be to the end of life) but temper'd with religious resignation, & the reasonings of a sound judgment, which in this early stage knows how to distinguish between a deed committed in a transient fit of frenzy, & the terrible guilt of a Mother's murther. I have seen her. I found her this morning calm & serene, far very very far from an indecent forgetful serenity; she has a most affectionate & tender concern for what has happened. Indeed from the beginning, frightful & hopeless as her disorder seemed, I had confidence enough in her strength of mind, & religious principle, to look forward to a time when *even she* might recover tranquillity. . . .

"On that first evening my Aunt was laying insensible, to all appearance like one dying,—my father, with his poor forehead plaisterd over from a wound he had received from a daughter dearly loved by him, & who loved him no less dearly,—my mother a dead & murder'd corpse in the next room—yet was I wonderfully supported. I closed not my eyes in sleep that night, but lay without terrors & without despair. I have lost no sleep since. I had been long used not to rest in things of sense, had endeavor after a comprehension of mind, unsatisfied with the 'ignorant present time,' & this kept me up. I had the whole weight of the family thrown on me, for my brother, little disposed (I speak not without tenderness for him) at any time to take care of old age & infirmities had now, with his bad leg, an exemption from such duties, & I was now left alone."[4]

"Since this has happened, [John] has been very kind and brotherly; but I fear for his mind: he has taken his ease in the world, and is not fit himself to struggle with difficulties,

(From *Tales from Shakespeare* by Charles and Mary Lamb. Illustrated by Frank Schoonover.)

**...He presumed in the gentlest manner to take her by the hand, calling it a shrine, which if he profaned by touching it, he was a blushing pilgrim, and would kiss it for atonement.** ■ (From *Tales from Shakespeare* by Charles and Mary Lamb. Illustrated by Maud and Miska Petersham.)

nor has much accustomed himself to throw himself into their way. . . .

"Thank God, I can unconnect myself with him, and shall manage all my father's moneys in future myself, if I take charge of Daddy, which poor John has not even hinted a wish, at any future time even, to share with me."[1]

"Poor Mary, my mother indeed *never understood* her right. She loved her, as she loved us all with a Mother's love, but in opinion, in feeling, & sentiment, & disposition, bore so distant a resemblance to her daughter, that she never understood her right. Never could believe how much *she* loved her—but met her caresses, her protestations of filial affection, too frequently with coldness & repulse,—Still she was a good mother, God forbid I should think of her but *most* respectfully, *most* affectionately. Yet she would always love my brother above Mary, who was not worthy of one tenth of that affection, which Mary had a right to claim. But it is my Sister's gratifying recollection, that every act of duty & of love she could pay, every kindness (& I speak true, when I say to the hurting of her health, & most probably in great part to the derangement of her senses) thro' a long course of infirmities & sickness, she could shew her, she ever did.

"I hope that *I* shall thro' life never have less recollection nor a fainter impression of what has happened than I have now; tis not a light thing, nor meant by the Almighty to be received lightly; I must be serious, circumspect, & deeply religious thro' lif[e;] & by such means may *both* of us escape madness in future if it so pleases the Almighty—"[4]

**February, 1797.** His Aunt Hetty died. "My poor old aunt . . . the kindest, goodest creature to me when I was at school, who used to toddle there to bring me good things, when I, school-boy like, only despised her for it, and used to be ashamed to see her come and sit herself down on the old coal-hole steps as you went into the old Grammar School, and open her apron and bring out her basin with some nice thing she had caused to be saved for me,—the good old creature is now lying on her deathbed. I cannot bear to think on her deplorable state. To the shock she received on that our evil day, from which she never completely recovered, I impute her illness. She says, poor thing, she is glad she is come home to die with me; I was always her favorite." [Anne Gilchrist, *Mary Lamb*, Roberts Brothers, 1883.[5]]

She occupied

> ". . . the same grave-bed
> Where the dead mother lies.
> Oh, my dear mother! oh, thou dear dead saint!
> Where's now that placid face, where oft hath sat
> A mother's smile to think her son should thrive
> In this bad world when she was dead and gone?
> And where a tear hath sat (take shame, O son!)
> When that same child hath proved himself unkind.
> One parent yet is left—a wretched thing,
> A sad survivor of his buried wife,
> A palsy-smitten, childish, old, old man,
> A semblance most forlorn of what he was."[5]

**April, 1797.** "I have taken [Mary] out of her confinement, and taken a room for her at Hackney, and spend my Sundays, holidays, &c., with her. She boards herself. In one little half year's illness, and in such an illness of such a nature and of such consequences! to get her out into the world again, with a prospect of her never being so ill again—this is to be ranked not among the common blessings of Providence. May that merciful God make tender my heart, and make me as thankful, as in my distress I was earnest, in my prayers. Congratulate me on an ever-present and never-alienable friend like her.

"She is quite well,—but must not, I fear, come to live with us yet a good while. In the first place, because at present it would hurt her, & hurt my father, for them to be together: secondly from a regard to the world's good report, for I fear, I fear, tongues will be busy *whenever* that event takes place. Some have hinted, one man has prest it on me, that she should be in perpetual confinement what she hath done to deserve, or the necessity of such an hardship I see not. . . ."[4]

**1799.** Their father died. Charles and Mary Lamb began a life of dual loneliness. "We house together, old bachelor and maid, in a sort of double singleness; with such tolerable comfort, upon the whole, that I, for one, find in myself no sort of disposition to go out upon the mountains, with the rash king's offspring, to bewail my celibacy. We agree pretty well in our tastes and habits—yet so, as 'with a difference.' We are generally in harmony, with occasional bickerings—as it should be among near relations. Our sympathies are rather understood, than expressed; . . .

"We are both great readers in different directions. While I am hanging over (for the thousandth time) some passage in old Burton, or one of his strange contemporaries, she is abstracted in some modern tale, or adventure, whereof our common reading-table is daily fed with assiduously fresh supplies. Narrative teazes me. I have little concern in the progress of events. She must have a story—well, ill, or indifferently told—so there be life stirring in it, and plenty of good or evil accidents. The fluctuations of fortune in fiction—and almost in real life—have ceased to interest, or operate but dully upon me. Out-of-the-way humours and opinions—heads with some diverting twist in them—the oddities of authorship please me most.

"She 'holds Nature more clever.' I can pardon her blindness to the beautiful obliquities of the Religio Medici; but she must apologise to me for certain disrespectful insinuations, which she has been pleased to throw out latterly, touching the intellectuals of a dear favourite of mine, of the last century but one—the thrice noble, chaste, and virtuous,—but again somewhat fantastical, and original-brain'd, generous Margaret Newcastle.

"In a season of distress, she is the truest comforter; but in the teazing accidents, and minor perplexities, which do not call out the *will* to meet them, she sometimes maketh matters worse by an excess of participation. If she does not always divide your trouble, upon the pleasanter occasions of life she is sure always to treble your satisfaction. She is excellent to be at a play with, or upon a visit; but best, when she goes a journey with you."[1]

"—I am afraid we are not placed out of the reach of future interruptions. But I am determined to take what snatches of pleasure, we can, between the acts of our distressful drama . . .—"[4]

**1805.** Mary in asylum for a month. "When she discovers symptoms of approaching illness, it is not easy to say what is best to do. Being by ourselves is bad and going out is bad. I get so irritable and wretched with fear that I constantly hasten on the disorder. You cannot conceive the misery of such a foresight. I am sure that for the week before she left me I was little better than light-headed. I now am calm, but sadly taken down and flat. My waking life has much of the confusion, the trouble and obscure perplexity of an ill dream.

"Meantime she is dead to me, and I miss a prop. All my strength is gone, and I am like a fool, bereft of her coöperation. I dare not think lest I should think wrong, so used am I to look up to her in the least as in the biggest perplexity. To say all that I know of her would be more than I think anybody could believe or even understand; and when I hope to have her well again with me it would be sinning against her feelings to go about to praise her, for I can conceal nothing that I do from her. She is older and wiser and better than I, and all my wretched imperfections I cover to myself by resolutely thinking on her goodness. She would share life and death, Heaven and hell, with me. She lives but for me; and I know I have been wasting and teasing her life for five years past incessantly with my cursed drinking and ways of going on. But even in this upbraiding of myself I am offending against her, for I know that she has clung to me for better for worse; and if the balance has been against her hitherto it was a noble trade. . . ."[5]

**1807.** *Tales From Shakespeare* published jointly by Charles and Mary Lamb. "[Mary] is doing for Godwin's bookseller twenty of Shakespeare's plays, to be made into children's tales. Six are already done her, to wit: *The Tempest, A Winter's Tale, Midsummer Night's Dream, Much Ado*

**I digress into Soho, to explore a bookstall. Methinks I have been thirty years a collector.** ■ (From *Everybody's Lamb,* a collection of letters and essays of Charles Lamb. Edited by A. C. Ward. Illustrated by Ernest H. Shepard.)

*About Nothing, The Two Gentlemen of Verona,* and *Cymbeline.* The *Merchant of Venice* is in forwardness. I have done *Othello* and *Macbeth,* and mean to do all the tragedies. I think it will be popular among the little people besides money. It is to bring in sixty guineas. Mary has done them capitally. . . ."[5]

**1809.** "We are at 34 Southampton Buildings, Chancery Lane, and shall be here till about the end of May; then we remove to No. 4 Inner Temple Lane, where I mean to live and die, for I have such a horror of moving that I would not take a benefice from the king if I was not indulged with non-residence. What a dislocation of comfort is comprised in that word 'moving.' Such a heap of little nasty things, after you think all is got into the cart: old dredging-boxes, worn-out brushes, gallipots, vials, things that it is impossible the most necessitous person can ever want, but which the women who preside on these occasions will not leave behind if it was to save your soul. They'd keep the cart ten minutes to stow in dirty pipes and broken matches, to show their economy. Then you can find nothing you want for many days after you get into your new lodgings. You must comb your hair with your fingers, wash your hands without soap, go about in dirty gaiters. Were I Diogenes I would not move out of a kilderkin into a hogshead, though the first had had nothing but small beer in it, and the second reeked claret."[5]

**1810.** Mary in asylum.

**1815.** Mary in asylum for ten weeks. "She has left me very lonely and very miserable. I stroll about; but there is no rest but at one's own fire-side, and there is no rest for me there now. I look forward to the worse half being past, and keep up as well as I can. She has begun to show some favorable symptoms. The return of her disorder has been frightfully soon this time, with scarce a six-months' interval. I am almost afraid my worry of spirits about the [East India] House was partly the cause of her illness; but one always imputes it to the cause next at hand; more probably it comes from some cause we have no control over or conjecture of. It cuts sad, great slices out of the time, the little time we shall have to live together. I don't know but the recurrence of these illnesses might help me to sustain her death better than if we had no partial separations."[5]

**1821.** Brother John died. "We are pretty well, save colds and rheumatics, and a certain deadness to everything, which I think I may date from poor John's loss . . . and how, when he died, though he had not been dead an hour, it seemed as if he had died a great while ago, such a distance there is betwixt life and death; and how I bore his death, as I thought, pretty well at first, but afterwards it haunted and haunted me; and though I did not cry or take it to heart as some do, and as I think he would have done if I had died, yet I missed him all day long, and knew not till then how much I had loved him. I missed his kindness and I missed his crossness, and wished him to be alive again to be quarreling with him (for we quarreled sometimes), rather than not have him again."[5]

**1822.** Wrote *Confessions of a Drunkard*. "It is to the weak, the nervous; to those who feel the want of some artificial aid to raise their spirits in society to what is no more than the ordinary pitch of all around them without it. This is the secret of our drinking. Such must fly the convivial board in the first instance, if they do not mean to sell themselves for term of life.

". . . If you are gifted with nerves like mine, aspire to any character but that of a wit. When you find a tickling relish upon your tongue disposing you to that sort of conversation, especially if you find a preternatural flow of ideas setting in upon you at the sight of a bottle and fresh glasses, avoid giving way to it as you would fly your greatest destruction. If you cannot crush the power of fancy, or that within you which you mistake for such, divert it, give it some other play. Write an essay, pen a character or description,—but not as I do now, with tears trickling down your cheeks.

"I took my degrees through thin wines, through stronger wine and water, through small punch, to those juggling compositions, which, under the name of mixed liquors, slur a great deal of brandy or other poison under less and less water continually, until they come next to none, and so to none at all. But it is hateful to disclose the secrets of my Tartarus.

"Twelve years ago I was possessed of a healthy frame of mind and body. I was never strong, but I think my constitution (for a weak one) was as happily exempt from the tendency to any malady as it was possible to be. I scarce knew what it was to ail any thing. Now except when I am losing myself in a sea of drink, I am never free from those uneasy sensations in head and stomach, which are so much worse to bear than any definite pains or aches.

"At that time I was seldom in bed after six in the morning, summer and winter. I awoke refreshed, and seldom without some merry thoughts in my head, or some piece of a song to welcome the new-born day. Now, the first feeling which besets me, after stretching out the hours of recumbence to their last possible extent, is a forecast of the wearisome day that lies before me, with a secret wish that I could have lain on still, or never awaked.

"Life itself, my waking life, has much of the confusion, the trouble, and obscure perplexity, of an ill dream. In the daytime I stumble upon dark mountains."[1]

**1825.** Retired from the East India House, he received a pension of two-thirds his salary. "I have a glimpse of freedom, of becoming a gentleman at large, but I am put off from day to day. I have offered my resignation, and it is neither accepted nor rejected. Eight weeks am I kept in this fearful suspense. Guess what an absorbing state I feel it. I am not conscious of the existence of friends present or absent. The East India Directors alone can be that thing to me or not. I have just learned that nothing will be decided this week. Why the next? Why any week? It has fretted me into an itch of the fingers; I rub 'em against paper . . . rather than not allay this scorbuta. . . .

"It is now six and thirty years since I took my seat at the desk in Mincing-lane. Melancholy was the transition at fourteen from the abundant play-time, and the frequently-intervening vacations of school days, to the eight, nine, and sometimes ten hours' a-day attendance at a counting-house. But time partially reconciles us to anything. I gradually became content—doggedly contented, as wild animals in cages.

"It is true I had my Sundays to myself; but Sundays, admirable as the institution of them is for purposes of worship, are for that very reason the very worst adapted for days of unbending and recreation. In particular, there is a gloom for me attendant upon a city Sunday, a weight in the air. I miss the cheerful cries of London, the music, and the ballad-singers—the buzz and stirring murmur of the streets. Those eternal bells depress me. The closed shops repel me. Prints, pictures, all the glittering and endless succession of knacks and gewgaws, and ostentatiously displayed wares of tradesmen, which make a week-day saunter through the less busy parts of the metropolis so delightful—are shut out. No book-stalls deliciously to idle over—No busy faces to recreate the idle man who contemplates them ever passing by—the very face of business a charm by contrast to his temporary relaxation from it. Nothing to be seen but unhappy countenances—or half-happy at best—of emancipated 'prentices and little tradesfolks, with here and there a servant maid that has got leave to go out, who, slaving all the week, with the habit has lost almost the capacity of enjoying a free hour; and livelily expressing the hollowness of a day's pleasuring. The very strollers in the fields on that day look anything but comfortable.

"But besides Sundays I had a day at Easter, and a day at Christmas, with a full week in the summer to go and air myself in my native fields of Hertfordshire. This last was a great indulgence; and the prospect of its recurrence, I believe, alone kept me up through the year, and made my durance tolerable. But when the week came round, did the glittering phantom of the distance keep touch with me? or rather was it not a series of seven uneasy days, spent in restless pursuit of pleasure, and a wearisome anxiety to find out how to make the most of them? Where was the quiet, where the promised rest? Before I had a taste of it, it was vanished. I was at the desk again, counting upon the fifty-one tedious weeks that must intervene before such another snatch would come. Still the prospect of its coming threw something of an illumination upon the darker side of my captivity. Without it, as I have said, I could scarcely have sustained my thraldom.

"I had grown to my desk, as it were; and the wood had entered into my soul."[1]

**July, 1825.** "A pretty severe fit of indisposition which, under the name of a nervous fever, has made a prisoner of me for some weeks past, and is but slowly leaving me, has reduced me to an incapacity of reflecting upon any topic foreign to itself. . . .

"And truly the whole state of sickness is such; for what else is it but a magnificent dream for a man to lie a-bed, and draw daylight curtains about him; and, shutting out the sun, to induce a total oblivion of all the works which are going on under it? To become insensible to all the operations of life, except the beatings of one feeble pulse?

"If there be a regal solitude, it is a sick bed. How the patient lords it there? what caprices he acts without controul! how king-like he sways his pillow—tumbling, and tossing, and shifting, and lowering, and thumping, and flatting, and moulding it, to the ever varying requisitions of his throbbing temples.

"He changes *sides* oftener than a politician. Now he lies full length, then half-length, obliquely, transversely, head and feet quite across the bed; and none accuses him of tergiversation. Within the four curtains he is absolute. They are his Mare Clàusum.

"How sickness enlarges the dimensions of a man's self to himself! he is his own exclusive object. Supreme selfishness is inculcated upon him as his only duty. 'Tis the Two Tables of the Law to him. He has nothing to think of but how to get well. What passes out of doors, or within them, so he hear not the jarring of them, affects him not."[1]

**1829.** "My sister is again taken ill and I am obliged to remove her out of the house for many weeks, I fear, before I can hope to have her again. I have been very desolate indeed. . . . But town, with all my native hankering after it, is not what it was. . . . I was frightfully convinced of this as I passed houses and places—empty caskets now. I have ceased to care almost about anybody. The bodies I cared for are in graves or dispersed. . . . Less than a month I hope will bring home Mary. She is at Fulham, looking better in her health than ever, but sadly rambling, and scarce showing any pleasure in seeing me, or curiosity when I should come again. But the old feelings will come back again, and we shall drown old sorrows over a game of piquet again. But 'tis a tedious cut out of a life of fifty-four to lose twelve or thirteen weeks every year or two. And to make me more alone, our ill-tempered maid is gone, who, with all her airs, was yet a home-piece of furniture, a record of better days. The young thing that has succeeded her is good and attentive, but she is nothing; and I have no one here to talk over old matters with. Scolding and quarreling

have something of familiarity and a community of interest; they imply acquaintance; they are of resentment which is of the family of dearness. Well, I shall write merrier anon. 'Tis the present copy of my countenance I send, and to complain is a little to alleviate. May you enjoy yourself as far as the wicked world will let you, and think that you are not quite alone, as I am."[5]

**1830.** "I have brought my sister to Enfield, being sure she had no hope of recovery in London. Her state of mind is deplorable beyond any example. I almost fear whether she has strength, at her time of life, ever to get out of it. Here she must be nursed and neither see nor hear of anything in the world out of her sick chamber."[5]

**1833.** "Mary is ill again. Her illnesses encroach yearly. The last was three months, followed by two of depression most dreadful. I look back upon her earlier attacks with longing: nice little durations of six weeks or so, followed by complete restoration, shocking as they were then to me. In short, half her life she is dead to me, and the other half is made anxious with fears and lookings forward to the next shock. With such prospects it seemed to me necessary that she should no longer live with me and be fluttered with continual removals; so I am come to live with her. . . ."[5]

**February, 1834.** The last words Lamb wrote about Mary: "I bear my privations very well. I am not in the depths of desolation, as heretofore. . . . It is no new thing for me to be left to my Sister. When she is not violent, her rambling chat is better to me than the sense and sanity of this world. Her heart is obscured, not buried; it breaks out occasionally; and one can discern a strong mind struggling with the billows that have gone over it. I could be no where happier than under the same roof with her. Her memory is unnaturally strong—& from ages past, if we may so call the earliest records of our poor life, she fetches thousands of names and things, that never would have dawned upon me again; & thousands from the ten years she lived before me. What took place from early girlhood to her coming of age principally, lives again (every important thing, and every trifle) in her brain with the vividness of real presence. For two hours incessantly she will pour out without intermission all her past life, forgetting nothing, pouring out name after name to the Waldens! as a dream; sense & nonsense; truths & errors huddled together; a medley between inspiration & possession."[5]

**1834.** Coleridge died. "When I heard of the death of Coleridge, it was without grief. It seemed to me that he long had been on the confines of the next world,—that he had a hunger for eternity. I grieved then that I could not grieve. But since, I feel how great a part he was of me. His great and dear spirit haunts me. I cannot think a thought, I cannot make a criticism on men or books, without an ineffectual turning and reference to him. He was the proof and touchstone of all my cogitations. He was a Grecian (or in the first form) at Christ's Hospital, where I was deputy Grecian; and the same subordination and deference to him I have preserved through a life-long acquaintance.

"He was my fifty years old friend without a dissension. Never saw I his likeness, nor probably the world can see again. I seem to love the house he died at more passionately than when he lived. I love the faithful Gilmans more than while they exercised their virtues towards him living. What was his mansion is consecrated to me a chapel."[4]

**December 27, 1834.** Died in Edmonton.

"I have been laughing, I have been carousing,
Drinking late, sitting late, with my bosom cronies—
All, all are gone, the old familiar faces.

"I loved a love once, fairest among women,
Closed are her doors on me, I must not see her—
All, all are gone, the old familiar faces.

"I have a friend, a kinder friend has no man.
Like an ingrate, I left my friend abruptly;
Left him, to muse on the old familiar faces.

"Ghost-like I paced round the haunts of my childhood.
Earth seem'd a desert I was bound to traverse,
Seeking to find the old familiar faces."[3]

*FOR MORE INFORMATION SEE:* Alexander Ireland, *List of the Writings of William Hazlitt, Leigh Hunt, and Charles Lamb,* J. R. Smith, 1868, reprinted, B. Franklin, 1970; Alfred Ainger, *Charles Lamb,* Macmillan, 1882, reprinted, Scholarly Press, 1901; William Carew Hazlitt, editor, *Lamb and Hazlitt: Further Letters and Records Hitherto Unpublished,* Dodd, Mead, 1899, reprinted, AMS Press, 1973; Bertram Dobell, *Sidelights on Charles Lamb,* Scribner, 1903; E. V. Lucas, *The Life of Charles Lamb,* Methuen, 1905, reprinted, R. West, 1973; Joseph C. Thomson, *Bibliography of the Writings of Charles and Mary Lamb,* J. R. Tutin, 1908, reprinted, Gale, 1971; George Daniel, *Recollections of Charles Lamb,* E. Mathews & Marrot, 1927, reprinted, Folcroft, 1974; Edmund Blunden, *Charles Lamb and His Contemporaries,* Cambridge University Press, 1933, reprinted, Archon, 1967, reprinted, R. West, 1973; A. C. Ward, *Frolic and the Gentle: A Centenary Study of Charles Lamb,* Methuen, 1934, reprinted, Kennikat, 1970; Orlo Williams, *Charles Lamb,* Duckworth, 1934, reprinted, Folcroft, 1973.

Will E. Howe, *Charles Lamb and His Friends,* Bobbs-Merrill, 1944, reprinted, Greenwood Press, 1972; Elizabeth Rider Montgomery, *Story behind Great Stories,* McBride, 1947; Katherine Anthony, *The Lambs: A Study of Pre-Victorian England,* Hammond, 1948, reprinted, Greenwood Press, 1973; John M. Brown, editor, *The Portable Charles Lamb,* Viking, 1949, reprinted, Greenwood Press, 1975; Reginald L. Hine, *Charles Lamb and His Hertfordshire,* Macmillan, 1949, reprinted, Greenwood Press, 1974; J. M. Brown, *Still Seeing Things,* McGraw-Hill, 1950; Walter R. Bett, *Infirmities of Genius,* Philosophical Library, 1952; B. Jessup, "Mind of Elia," *Journal of the History of Ideas,* April, 1954.

George L. Barnett, *Charles Lamb: The Evolution of Elia,* Indiana University Press, 1964, reprinted, Haskell House, 1972; Elizabeth Drew, *Literature of Gossip,* Norton, 1964; (for children) Trudy West, *Young Charles Lamb,* Roy, 1965; (for children) Laura Benét, *Famous English and American Essayists,* Dodd, Mead, 1966; Brian Doyle, editor, *Who's Who of Children's Literature,* Schocken Books, 1968; Wallace Nethery, *Eliana Americana: Charles Lamb in the United States, 1849-1866,* Plantin Press, 1971; Edwin W. Marrs, Jr., editor, *The Letters of Charles and Mary Ann Lamb,* two volumes, Cornell University Press, 1975; Robert Frank, *Don't Call Me Gentle Charles: Discourses on Charles Lamb's Essays of Elia,* Oregon State University Press, 1976.

MARY and CHARLES LAMB

## LAMB, Mary Ann   1764-1847

*PERSONAL:* Born December 3, 1764, in London, England; died May 20, 1847, in St. John's Wood, London, England; daughter of John Lamb (a lawyer's clerk and confidential attendant); sister of Charles Lamb (the author); children: Emma Isola (adopted). *Education:* Attended William Bird's day-school in London.

*CAREER:* Author.

*WRITINGS: Helen* (poem; published with Charles Lamb's *John Woodvil*), T. Plummer, 1802; (with brother, Charles Lamb) *Poetry for Children,* [London], 1809, reprinted, Books for Libraries, 1970; (with C. Lamb) *Tales from Shakespeare,* T. Hodgkins, 1807, reissued, Hart, 1976 [other editions illustrated by John Gilbert, Routledge, 1876; Albert Hencke, F. A. Stokes, 1893; Harold Copping, R. Tuck, 1901; Arthur Rackham, Dutton, 1909; M. L. Kirk, F. A. Stokes, 1911; Norman M. Price, T. C. & E. C. Jack, 1915; Louis Rhead, Harper, 1918; Elizabeth Shippen Green Elliott, D. McKay, 1922; Maud and Miska Petersham,

Macmillan, 1923, reissued, 1956; Frank Godwin, J. C. Winston, 1924; R. Farrington Elwell, Houghton, 1925; Fritz Kredel, Garden City Publishing, 1939; Elinore Blaisdell, T. Y. Crowell, 1942; John C. Wonsetler, Macmillan, 1950; Leonard Weisgard, Junior Deluxe Editions, 1955; Karel Svolinsky, Golden Pleasure Books, 1962; Richard M. Powers, Macmillan, 1963]; (with C. Lamb) *Mrs. Leicester's School; or, The History of Several Young Ladies, Related by Themselves*, M. J. Godwin, 1809 [another edition illustrated by Winifred Green, Dent, 1899]; (with C. Lamb) *Beauty and the Beast*, [London], 1811.

Collections and selections: *Mary and Charles Lamb: Poems, Letters, and Remains, Now First Collected, with Reminiscences and Notes* (edited by W. Carew Hazlitt), Chatto & Windus, 1874; *The Works of Charles and Mary Lamb*, seven volumes (edited by E. V. Lucas), Methuen, 1903-05, reprinted, Scholarly Press, 1971; *The Works of Charles and Mary Lamb* (edited by Thomas Hutchinson), Oxford University Press, 1924; *The Letters of Charles Lamb, to Which Are Added Those of His Sister, Mary Lamb*, three volumes (edited by E. V. Lucas), Dent, 1935, reprinted, AMS Press, 1968; *Ten Tales from Shakespeare* (illustrated by Janusz Grabianski), F. Watts, 1969; *Romeo and Juliet* (illustrated by Brian Froud), F. Watts, 1971; *A Midsummer Night's Dream* (illustrated by B. Froud), F. Watts, 1972; *The Letters of Charles and Mary Lamb*, two volumes (edited by Edwin W. Marrs, Jr.), Cornell University Press, 1975.

*SIDELIGHTS:* **December 3, 1764.** Born in the Crown Office, Inner Temple, London. Mary Lamb was the third of seven children, four of whom died in infancy. One little sister, Elizabeth, lived long enough to mark an impression in Lamb's mind: "The little cap with white satin ribbon grown yellow with long keeping, and a lock of light hair, always brought her pretty, fair face to my view, so that to this day I seem to have a perfect recollection of her features." [Anne Gilchrist, *Mary Lamb*, Roberts Brothers, 1883.[1]]

Lamb's household circle consisted of a mother and father whose faculties and health failed early, a maiden aunt, and a younger brother, Charles, the life-long recipient of Lamb's total love and devotion. John, an older bachelor-brother lived away from home. "... Dear, little, selfish, craving John." [W. Carew Hazlitt, *Mary and Charles Lamb: Poems, Letters and Remains*, Scribner, 1874.[2]]

"My mother was a perfect gentlewoman; my aunty as unlike a gentlewoman as you can possibly imagine a good old woman to be; so that my dear mother ... used to distress and weary her with incessant and unceasing attention and politeness to gain her affection. The old woman could not return this in kind and did not know what to make of it—thought it all deceit, and used to hate my mother with a bitter hatred, which, of course, was soon returned with interest. A little frankness and looking into each other's characters at first would have spared all this, and they would have lived as they died, fond of each other for the last ten years of their lives. When we grew up and harmonized them a little they sincerely loved each other."[1]

Attended William Bird's School. In her reflections of her school master, Mary wrote: "If any of the girls who were my school-fellows should be reading through their aged spectacles tidings from the dead of their youthful friend Starkey, they will feel a pang as I do at having teased his gentle spirit.

"They were big girls, it seems, too old to attend his instructions with the silence necessary; and, however old age and a long state of beggary seems to have reduced his writing faculties to a state of imbecility, in those days his language occasionally rose to the bold and figurative, for, when he was in despair to stop their chattering, his ordinary phrase was, 'Ladies, if you will not hold your peace, not all the powers in heaven can make you.'"[1]

**1775.** Charles born. Lamb became the self-appointed foster-mother of her baby brother, though their mother had not died.

### "NURSING.

"O hush, my little baby brother:
Sleep, my little baby brother;
   Sleep, my love, upon my knee.
What though, dear child, we've lost our mother?
   That can never trouble thee.

"You are but ten weeks old to-morrow;
   What can *you* know of our loss?
The house is full enough of sorrow.
   Little baby, don't be cross.

"Peace! cry not so, my dearest love;
   Hush, my baby-bird, lie still;
He's quiet now, he does not move;
   Fast asleep is little Will.

"My only solace, only joy,
   Since the sad day I lost my mother,
Is nursing her own Willy boy,
   My little orphan brother."[1]

**1785.** "In early life I passed eleven years in the exercise of my needle for a livelihood. . . . Needlework and intellectual improvement are naturally in a state of warfare. Even fancy work, the fairest of the tribe! How delightful the arrangement of her materials! The fixing upon her happiest pattern, how pleasing an anxiety! How cheerful the commencement of the labor she enjoys! But that lady must be a true lover of the art, and so industrious a pursuer of a predetermined purpose, that it were pity her energy should not have been directed to some wiser end, who can affirm she neither feels weariness during the execution of a fancy piece, nor takes more time than she had calculated for the performance.

". . . It would prove an incalculable addition to general happiness and the domestic comfort of both sexes, if needlework were never practiced but for a remuneration in money? As nearly, however, as this desirable thing can be effected, so much more nearly will woman be upon an equality with men as far as respects the mere enjoyment of life. As far as that goes, I believe it is every woman's opinion that the condition of men is far superior to her own.

"'They can do what they like,' we say. Do not these words generally mean they have time to seek out whatever amusements suit their tastes? We dare not tell them we have no time to do this; for if they should ask in what manner we dispose of our time we should blush to enter upon a detail of the minutiae which compose the sum of a woman's daily employment. Nay, many a lady, who allows not herself one-quarter of an hour's positive leisure during her waking hours, considers her own husband as the most industrious of men if he steadily pursue his occupation till the hour of dinner, and will be perpetually lamenting her own idleness.

"*Real business* and *real leisure* make up the portions of men's time,—two sources of happiness which we certainly partake of in a very inferior degree. To the execution of employments in which the faculties of the body or mind are called into busy action there must be a consoling importance attached, which feminine duties (that generic term for all our business) cannot aspire to.

"In the most meritorious discharges of those duties the highest praise we can aim at is to be accounted the helpmate of *man;* who, in return for all he does for us, expects, and justly expects, us to do all in our power to soften and sweeten life.

"In how many ways is a good woman employed in thought or action through the day, that her *good man* may be enabled to feel his leisure hours *real, substantial hollduy,* and perfect respite from the cares of business! Not the least part to be done to accomplish this end is to fit herself to become a conversational companion; that is to say, she has to study and understand the subjects on which he loves to talk. This part of our duty, if strictly performed, will be found by far our hardest part. The disadvantages we labor under from an education differing from a manly one make the hours in which we *sit and do nothing* in men's company too often anything but a relaxation; although as to pleasure and instruction, time so passed may be esteemed more or less delightful.

"To make a man's home so desirable a place as to preclude his having a wish to pass his leisure hours at any fire-side in preference to his own, I should humbly take to be the sum and substance of woman's domestic ambition. . . .

"If a family be so well ordered that the master is never called in to its direction, and yet he perceives comfort and economy well attended to, the mistress of that family (especially if children form a part of it) has, I apprehend, as large a share of womanly employment as ought to satisfy her own sense of duty; even though the needle-book and thread-case were quite laid aside, and she cheerfully contributed her part to the slender gains of the corset-maker, the milliner, the dressmaker, the plain worker, the embroidress and all the numerous classifications of females supporting themselves by needlework, that great staple commodity which is alone appropriated to the self-supporting part of our sex.

"Much has been said and written on the subject of men engrossing to themselves every occupation and calling. After many years of observation and reflection I am obliged to acquiesce in the notion that it cannot well be ordered otherwise.

"If, at the birth of girls, it were possible to foresee in what cases it would be their fortune to pass a single life, we should soon find trades wrested from their present occupiers and transferred to the exclusive possession of our sex. The whole mechanical business of copying writings in the law department, for instance, might very soon be transferred with advantage to the poorer sort of women, who, with very little teaching, would soon beat their rivals of the other sex in facility and neatness. The parents of female children who were known to be destined from their birth to maintain themselves through the whole course of their lives, with like certainty as their sons are, would feel it a duty incumbent on themselves to strengthen the minds and even the bodily constitutions of their girls so circumstanced, by an education which, without affronting the preconceived habits of society, might enable them to follow

some occupation now considered above the capacity, or too robust for the constitution, of our sex. Plenty of resources would then lie open for single women to obtain an independet livelihood, when every parent would be upon the alert to encroach upon some employment now engrossed by men, for such of their daughters as would then be exactly in the same predicament as their sons now are. Who, for instance, would lay by money to set up his sons in trade, give premiums, and in part maintain them through a long apprenticeship; or, which men of moderate incomes frequently do, strain every nerve in order to bring them up to a learned profession; if it were in a very high degree probable that, by the time they were twenty years of age, they would be taken from this trade or profession, and maintained during the remainder of their lives by the *person whom they should marry?* Yet this is precisely the situation in which every parent, whose income does not very much exceed the moderate, is placed with respect to his daughters.

"Even where boys have gone through a laborious education, super-inducing habits of steady attention accompanied with the entire conviction that the business which they learn is to be the source of their future distinction, may it not be affirmed that the persevering industry required to accomplish this desirable end causes many a hard struggle in the minds of young men, even of the most hopeful disposition? What, then, must be the disadvantages under which a very young woman is placed who is required to learn a trade, from which she can never expect to reap any profit, but at the expense of losing that place in society to the possession of which she may reasonably look forward, inasmuch as it is by far the most *common lot,* namely, the condition of a *happy* English wife?

". . . I should be inclined to persuade every female over whom I hope to have any influence to contribute all the assistance in her power to those of her own sex who may need it, in the employments they at present occupy, rather than to force them into situations now filled wholly by men. With the mere exception of the profits which they have a right to derive by their needle, I would take nothing from the industry of man which he already possesses.

"'A penny saved is a penny earned,' is a maxim not true unless the penny be saved in the same time in which it might have been earned. I, who have known what it is to work for *money earned,* have since had much experience in working for *money saved;* and I consider, from the closest calculation I can make, that a *penny saved* in that way bears about a true proportion to a *farthing earned.* I am no advocate for women who do not depend on themselves for subsistence, proposing to themselves to *earn money.* My reasons for thinking it not advisable are too numerous to state—reasons deduced from authentic facts and strict observations on domestic life in its various shades of comfort. But if the females of a family *nominally* supported by the other sex find it necessary to add something to the common stock, why not endeavor to do something by which they may produce money *in its true shape?*

"It would be an excellent plan, attended with very little trouble, to calculate every evening how much money has been saved by needlework *done in the family,* and compare the result with the daily portion of the yearly income. Nor would it be amiss to make a memorandum of the time passed in this way, adding also a guess as to what share it has taken up in the thoughts and conversation. This would be an easy mode of forming a true notion and getting at the exact worth of this species of *home* industry, and perhaps might place it in a different light from any in which it has hitherto been the fashion to consider it.

"Needlework taken up as an amusement may not be altogether unamusing. We are all pretty good judges of what entertains ourselves, but it is not so easy to pronounce upon what may contribute to the entertainment of others. At all events, let us not confuse the motives of economy with those of simple pastime. If *saving* be no object, and long habits have rendered needlework so delightful an avocation that we cannot think of relinquishing it, there are the good old contrivances in which our grand-dames were wont to beguile and lose their time—knitting, knotting, netting, carpet-work, and the like ingenious pursuits—those so often praised but tedious works, which are so long in the operation that purchasing the labor has seldom been thought good economy. Yet by a certain fascination they have been found to chain down the great to a self-imposed slavery, from which they considerately or haughtily excused the needy. These may be esteemed lawful and ladylike amusements. But, if those works more usually denominated useful yield greater satisfaction, it might be a laudable scruple of conscience, and no bad test to herself of her own motive, if a lady who had no absolute need were to give the money so saved to poor needlewomen belonging to those branches of employment from which she has borrowed these shares of pleasurable labor."[1]

**September 22, 1796.** Lamb's sanity collapsed under the demands of years of nightly and daily attendance upon her invalid mother. Worn out by a close application to needlework and strained beyond the utmost of physical endurance, Lamb grasped a knife from the table, injured her father and fatally stabbed her mother.

In asylum in Islington. "My dear mother . . . is always in my poor head and heart.

"I have no bad, terrifying dreams. At midnight, when I happen to awake, the nurse sleeping by the side of me, with the noise of the poor mad people around me, I have no fear. The spirit of my mother seems to descend and smile upon me and bid me live to enjoy the life and reason which the Almighty has given me. I shall see her again in Heaven; she will then understand me better. My grandmother, too, will understand me better, and will then say no more, as she used to do, 'Polly, what are those poor, crazy, moythered brains of yours thinking of always?'

> "Thou and I dear friend,
> "With filial recognition sweet, shall know
> One day the face of our dear mother in Heaven;
> And her remembered looks of love shall greet
> With answering looks of love, her placid smiles
> Meet with a smile as placid, and her hand
> With drops of fondness wet, nor fear repulse."[1]

**1799.** Father died. Charles and Mary Lamb began a life of dual loneliness.

**1805.** In an asylum for a month.

**September, 1805.** "You would laugh, or you would cry, perhaps both, to see us sit together, looking at each other with long rueful faces, and saying, 'How do you do?' and 'How do you do?' and then we fall a-crying, and say we will be better on the morrow. [Charles] says we are like tooth-ach and his friend gum bile—which, though a kind of

(From *Tales of Shakespeare* by Charles and Mary Lamb. Illustrated by Arthur Rackham.)

ease, it but an uneasy kind of ease, a comfort of rather an uncomfortable sort."[2]

**1806.** "I have no power over Charles—he will do—what he will do. But I ought to have some little influence over myself. And therefore I am most manfully resolving to turn over a new leaf with my own mind.

". . . and I know my dismal faces have been almost as great a drawback upon Charles's comfort, as his feverish, teazing ways have been upon mine."[2]

**1807.** Commissioned by Mary Godwin to adapt twenty selections from Shakespeare's plays into short prose stories for children. Mary wrote fourteen comedies and Charles supplied six tragedies. The *Tales from Shakespeare* were well received and have never really been superseded. ". . . We often sit writing on one table (but not on one cushion sitting), like Hermia and Helena in the *Midsummer Night's Dream;* or rather, like an old literary Darby and Joan, I taking snuff and he groaning all the while and saying he can make nothing of it, which he always says till he has finished, and then he finds out he has made something of it.

"I have wished to make these tales easy reading for very young children. To the utmost of my ability I have constantly kept this in my mind; but the subjects of most of them made this a very difficult task. It was no easy matter to give the histories of men and women in terms familiar to the apprehension of a very young mind. For young ladies, too, it has been my intention chiefly to write, because boys are generally permitted the use of their fathers' libraries at a much earlier age than girls are, they frequently having the best scenes of Shakespeare by heart before their sisters are permitted to look into this manly book; and therefore, instead of recommending these tales to the perusal of young gentlemen who can read them so much better in the originals, I must rather beg their kind assistance in explaining to their sisters such parts as are hardest for them to understand; and when they have helped them to get over the difficulties, then perhaps they will read to them—carefully selecting what is proper for a young sister's ear—."[1]

**1809.** *Mrs. Leicester's School* and *Poetry for Children* published jointly. *Poetry for Children,* their last joint effort, was not well received. Few of the poems have survived, though several were written with tenderness, charm, and humor.

**1810.** In asylum.

**1815.** In asylum for ten weeks.

**1817.** "We have left the Temple. . . . Our rooms were dirty and out of repair, and the inconveniences of living in chambers became every year more irksome, and so at last we mustered up resolution enough to leave the good old place that so long had sheltered us, and here we are, living at a brazier's shop, No. 20, in Russell street, Covent Garden, a place all alive with noise and bustle; Drury Lane Theater in sight from our front and Covent Garden from our back windows. The hubbub of the carriages returning from the play does not annoy me in the least; strange that it does not, for it is quite tremendous. I quite enjoy looking out of the window and listening to the calling up of the carriages and the squabbles of the coachmen and link-boys. It is the oddest scene to look down upon. . . . It is well I am in a cheerful place, or I should have many misgivings about leaving the Temple.

"Charles has had all his Hogarths bound in a book; they were sent home yesterday, and now that I have them all together, and perceive the advantage of peeping close at them through my spectacles, I am reconciled to the loss of their hanging round the room, which has been a great mortification to me. In vain I tried to console myself with looking at our new chairs and carpets, for we have got new chairs and carpets covering all over our two sittingrooms; I missed my old friends and could not be comforted. Then I would resolve to learn to look out of the window, a habit I never could attain in my life, and I have given it up as a thing quite impracticable. . . ."[1]

**Spring, 1820.** "Our solitary confinement has answered its purpose even better than I expected. It is so many years since I have been out of town in the spring that I scarcely knew of the existence of such a season. I see every day some new flower peeping out of the ground, and watch its growth; so that I have a sort of intimate friendship with each. I know the effect of every change of weather upon them—have learned all their names, the duration of their lives, and the whole progress of their domestic economy. My landlady, a nice, active old soul that wants but one year

of eighty, and her daughter, a rather aged young gentlewoman, are the only laborers in a pretty large garden; for it is a double house, and two long strips of ground are laid into one, well stored with fruit-trees, which will be in full blossom the week after I am gone, and flowers, as many as can be crammed in, of all sorts and kinds. But flowers are flowers still; and I must confess I would rather live in Russell street all my life, and never set my foot but on London pavement, than be doomed always to enjoy the silent pleasures I now do. We go to bed at ten o'clock. Late hours are life-shortening things, but I would rather run all risks, and sit every night—at some places I could name—wishing in vain at eleven o'clock for the entrance of the supper tray, than be always up and alive at eight o'clock breakfast, as I am here. We have a scheme to reconcile these things. We have an offer of a very low-rented lodging a mile nearer town than this. Our notion is to divide our time in alternate weeks between quiet rest and dear London weariness. We give an answer to-morrow; but what that will be . . . I am unable to say. In the present state of our undecided opinion, a very heavy rain that is now falling may turn the scale. . . . Dear rain, do go away, and let us have a fine, chearful sunset to argue the matter fairly in. My brother walked seventeen miles yesterday before dinner. And, notwithstanding his long walk to and from the office, we walk every evening; but I by no means perform in this way so well as I used to do. A twelve-mile walk, one hot Sunday morning, made my feet blister, and they are hardly well now."[2]

**1827.** In asylum.

**1829.** In asylum.

**1834.** Charles Lamb died.

**May 20, 1847.** Laid to rest at Edmonton in the same grave with her brother, Charles. "Our love for each other has been the torment of our lives. . . ."[2]

*FOR MORE INFORMATION SEE:* Anne B. Gilchrist, *Mary Lamb,* Roberts Brothers, 1883, reprinted, AMS Press, 1972; William C. Hazlitt, *The Lambs: Their Lives, Their Friends, and Their Correspondence,* Scribner, 1897, reprinted, AMS Press, 1973; Helen Ashton and Katharine Davies, *I Had a Sister: A Study of Mary Lamb, Dorothy Wordsworth, Caroline Herschel [and] Cassandra Austen,* L. Dickson, 1937, reprinted, Folcroft, 1974; N. S. Tillett, "Mary Lamb," *South Atlantic Quarterly,* January, 1948; Katharine S. Anthony, *The Lambs: A Study of Pre-Victorian England,* Hammond, 1948, reprinted, Greenwood Press, 1973; John M. Brown, *Still Seeing Things,* McGraw-Hill, 1950; Brian Doyle, editor, *Who's Who of Children's Literature,* Schocken Books, 1968; James S. Cox and S. S. Cox, *Samuel Taylor Coleridge and Mary Lamb: Two Recent Discoveries,* Toucan Press, 1971.

# LAMPLUGH, Lois 1921-

*PERSONAL:* Surname is pronounced Lamploo; born June 9, 1921, in Barnstaple, Devonshire, England; daughter of Aubrey Penfound and Ruth (Lister) Lamplugh; married Lawrence Carlile Davis (now a bursar of a school for maladjusted boys), September 24, 1955; children: Susan Ruth, Hugh Lawrence. *Education:* Educated privately in England. *Home:* Springside, Bydown, Swimbridge, Devon, England. *Agent:* A. P. Watt & Son, 26/28 Bedford Row, London, England.

**Ned paused a moment at the foot of the Forge cottage steps and glanced up at the windows; he hoped his mother would look out. He had no intention of calling to her or taking the dogs indoors; he just hoped she would happen to see him with his charges.** ■ (From *The Sixpenny Runner* by Lois Lamplugh. Illustrated by William Stobbs.)

*CAREER:* Formerly on editorial staff of Jonathan Cape Ltd., London, England; author of books for young people. Served in Auxiliary Territorial Service, World War II. *Member:* P.E.N., West Country Writers' Association.

*WRITINGS*—All juveniles except where indicated: *The Stream Way* (adult), Golden Galley Press, 1948; *The Pigeongram Puzzle,* J. Cape, 1955, Verry, 1960; *Nine Bright Shiners,* J. Cape, 1955; *Vagabonds' Castle,* J. Cape, 1957, Verry, 1965; *Rockets in the Dunes,* J. Cape, 1958; *The Sixpenny Runner,* J. Cape, 1961; *Midsummer Mountains,* Verry, 1961; *The Rifle House Friends,* Deutsch, 1965; *The Linhay on Hunter's Hill,* Deutsch, 1966; *The Fur Princess and the Fur Prince,* Dent, 1969; (with Peter Dickinson) *Mandog,* B.B.C. Publication, 1972; *Sean's Leap,* Deutsch, in press. Author of television documentary, "Coleridge," Harlech Television, 1966. Writer of more than three hundred stories, "Honeyhill," (juvenile; each of five-minute duration), Harlech Television, 1967-69.

*WORK IN PROGRESS:* A children's book with a Cornish village setting.

*SIDELIGHTS:* "It is possible that I became a writer simply because I happened to spend the first eighteen years of my life in or near the village of Georgeham [where] in the 1920's Henry Williamson was living—for part of the time in a cottage he rented from my grandmother. (He wrote most, if not all, of *Tarka the Otter* in that cottage.)"

A country child, Lamplugh still prefers country living, adding "for all that, I wrote my first children's books when I was living and working in London—perhaps a form of escape, since they were set in North Devon." She wrote a great deal of unpublished work, mainly novels and verse, in her teens, and had a book accepted for publication by Faber in 1942. It was an account of her experiences in the Auxiliary Territorial Service and the War Office withheld approval of publication on the grounds that it would discourage recruiting. The manuscript remains unpublished.

"In my teens, in the late thirties, I did not have the opportunity to go to a university, and I still find it slightly surprising to have managed to graduate.

"In 1971, a new venture in education for the mature student, The Open University, was set up at Milton Keynes, Buckinghamshire, England. It has been referred to as 'the University of the second chance.' (Some of its material is now being used in universities in the United States, I understand.) I became a student in 1972 (one works at home, and is in touch with one's tutor by post, telephone, and at occasional tutorials). At the rate of one full credit course a year, I have now graduated as a Bachelor of Arts of the University. The six credits included history, literature, music, educational studies, and social sciences. During these years I have written little; *Sean's Leap* was written during the 'long vacations' between courses—late October to February.

"I am now back in Devon, living within five miles of my birthplace. My children are now, of course, grown: my daughter is nursing and my son is hoping to go to university later this year. I have been doing a certain amount of part-time teaching at the residential school for maladjusted boys at which my husband is bursar: the story of *Sean's Leap* came out of that experience. But writing remains the activity that is most important to me, and I hope to be able to go on producing books—as long as the ideas come!"

*HOBBIES AND OTHER INTERESTS:* Listening to music, especially Italian opera, gardening, reading, walking in the countryside.

# LAZAREVICH, Mila 1942-

*PERSONAL:* Born April 24, 1942, in Philadelphia, Pa.; daughter of Lazar Kosto (a welder) and Olga (Smith) Lazarevich; married Lawrence P. DiFiori (an illustrator), October 14, 1967. *Education:* Philadelphia College of Art, B.A., 1963; University of Pennsylvania, M.A., 1966. *Politics:*

**MILA LAZAREVICH**

(From *Settle Your Fidgets* by Carol Farley. Illustrated by Mila Lazarevich.)

Independent. *Religion:* Eastern Orthodox Christian. *Home and office:* 225 East 63rd St., 9F, New York, N.Y. 10021.

*CAREER:* Illustrator. Hoedt Studios, Philadelphia, Pa., designer, 1963-64; Hussian School of Art, Philadelphia, Pa., art studio teacher, 1964-72; Philadelphia College of Art, Philadelphia, Pa., art history teacher, 1966-70; free-lance illustrator, 1972—. *Exhibitions:* Art Alliance, Philadelphia, Pa.; Fischmann-Wiener Gallery, Philadelphia, Pa.; Commercial Museum, Philadelphia, Pa.; and many group shows from 1963-70. *Member:* Graphic Artists Guild, C. G. Jung Foundation.

*ILLUSTRATOR:* Ann Lawrence, *Tom Ass: Or the Second Gift,* Walck, 1972; William Wise, *Cities Old and New,* Parents' Magazine Press, 1973; William Wise, *Leaders, Laws and Citizens: The Story of Democracy and Government,* Parents' Magazine Press, 1973; Ted Hughes, *Meet My Folks,* Bobbs, 1973; Paul Showers, *The Bird and the Stars,* Doubleday, 1975; Freya Littledale, editor, *Strange Tales from Many Lands,* Doubleday, 1975; Michael Gross, *The Fable of the Fig Tree,* Walck, 1975; Carol Farley, *Loosen Your Ears,* Atheneum, 1977; Carol Farley, *Settle Your Fidgets,* Atheneum, 1977; Anne Snyder, *The Old Man and the Mule,* Holt, 1978.

*SIDELIGHTS:* "I have always loved pictures and was fascinated by them as early as the icons I used to see in church as a child. There was never any doubt in my mind that I wanted to be an artist, but it wasn't until 1972 that I decided to enter the field of children's books.

"After illustrating ten books, I am more impressed by the great power the picture carries especially in influencing young people. I work in various mediums, but essentially in some line technique with tone, color separations or full color."

## LENT, Henry Bolles   1901-1973

*PERSONAL:* Born November 1, 1901, in New Bedford, Mass.; died October 26, 1973; children: Henry, David. *Education:* Attended Yale University; graduated from Hamilton College. *Home:* Woodstock, Vt.

*CAREER:* Author and advertising executive. Worked at various jobs during summer vacations as a college student, including jobs with road construction crews and schooner fishermen; later became associated with a New York advertising agency, serving as a copywriter, supervisor, and later vice-president.

*WRITINGS: Diggers and Builders* (self-illustrated), Macmillan, 1931; *Clear Track Ahead!* (illustrated by Earle Winslow), Macmillan, 1932; *Full Steam Ahead!* (illustrated by E. Winslow), Macmillan, 1933; *The Waldorf-Astoria,* privately printed, 1934; *Grindstone Farm* (illustrated by Wilfrid S. Bronson), Macmillan, 1935; *Tugboat* (illustrated by E. Winslow), Macmillan, 1936; *The Air Pilot* (illustrated by George and Doris Hauman), Macmillan, 1937; *The Bus Driver* (illustrated by E. Winslow), Macmillan, 1937; *The Captain* (illustrated by E. Winslow), Macmillan, 1937; *The Farmer* (illustrated by Berta and Elmer Hader), Macmillan, 1937; *The Storekeeper* (illustrated by G. and D. Hauman), Macmillan, 1937; *The Fire Fighter* (illustrated by E. Winslow), Macmillan, 1939.

*Flight 17* (illustrated by G. and D. Hauman), Macmillan, 1940; *Aviation Cadet: Dick Hilton Wins His Wings at Pensacola,* Macmillan, 1941; *Sixty Acres More or Less: The Diary of a Week-End Vermonter,* Macmillan, 1941; *Air Patrol: Jim Brewster Flies for the U.S. Coast Guard,* Macmillan, 1942; *Bombardier Tom Dixon Wins His Wings with the Bomber Command,* Macmillan, 1943; *PT Boat: Bob Reed Wins His Command at Melville,* Macmillan, 1943; *Seabee: Bill Scott Builds and Fights for the Navy,* Macmillan, 1944; *Straight Down* (illustrated by Adolph Treidler), Macmillan, 1944; *Straight Up* (illustrated by Raymond Lufkin), Macmillan, 1944; *Ahoy, Shipmate! Steve Ellis Joins the Merchant Marine,* Macmillan, 1945; *"This Is You Announcer": Ted Lane Breaks into Radio,* Macmillan, 1945; *Fly It Away!,* Macmillan, 1946; *Eight Hours to Solo,* Macmillan, 1947; *I Work on a Newspaper* (photographs by James B. Walsh), Macmillan, 1948.

*O.K. for Drive-Away: How Automobiles Are Built,* Macmillan, 1951; *From Trees to Paper: The Story of Newsprint,* Macmillan, 1952; *Here Come the Trucks* (illustrated by Renee George), Macmillan, 1954; *The Helicopter Book,* Macmillan, 1956; *Men at Work in New England,* Putnam, 1956, reissued, 1967; *Flight Overseas,* Macmillan, 1957; *Men at Work in the South,* Putnam, 1957, reissued, 1970; *Jet Pilot,* Macmillan, 1958; *Jet Pilot Overseas,* Macmillan, 1959; *Men at Work in the Great Lakes States,* Putnam, 1958, reissued,

**HENRY BOLLES LENT**

1971; *Men at Work on the West Coast,* Putnam, 1959, reissued, 1968.

*Men at Work in the Mid-Atlantic States,* Putnam, 1961, reissued as *Men at Work in the Middle Atlantic States,* 1970; *Man Alive in Outer Space: Our Space Surgeons' Greatest Challenge,* Macmillan, 1961; *Submarine: The Story of Basic Training at the Navy's Famed Submarine School,* Macmillan, 1962; *Your Place in America's Space Program,* Macmillan, 1964; *The Book of Cars: Yesterday, Today, Tomorrow,* Dutton, 1966; *The Peace Corps: Ambassadors of Goodwill,* Westminster Press, 1966; *Agriculture U.S.A.: America's Most Basic Industry,* Dutton, 1968; *The Automobile, U.S.A.: Its Impact on People's Lives and the National Economy,* Dutton, 1968; *What Car Is That?* (illustrated by John Raynes), Dutton, 1969; *Car of the Year, 1895-1970,* Dutton, 1970; *The X Cars: Detroit's One-of-a-Kind Autos,* Putnam, 1971.

*SIDELIGHTS:* Henry Lent's children were very influential in his writing career. Their inquisitive minds led the advertising man to do extensive research, with the result being information books for young people. One of the author's books, *Fly It Away,* was written after a visit to an airplane factory. A critic for *Horn Book* commented, "What are the processes by which a small airplane is prepared for an individual buyer? Mr. Lent answers this question in an instructive volume, interesting to readers of all ages."

Later, Lent himself learned how to fly an airplane along with his younger son, David. Their various experiences became the basis for the book, *Eight Hours to Solo.* A reviewer for *Atlantic* noted, "There is no plot, only straight reporting about the lessons—but it is very superior reporting with natural dialogue and expert characterization."

**The beautiful beast—equipped with side-mounted wire wheels, leather-trimmed seat, power steering, disc brakes, air conditioning and optional hardtop—carried a price tag of $13,000 plus.**
■ (From *The X Cars: Detroit's One-of-a-Kind Autos* by Henry B. Lent.)

Even after his children had grown up, Lent continued to supply information to satisfy the curiosity of youngsters. Out of his interest in aviation, the author soon began to write about space exploration. Lent's *Man Alive in Outer Space* gave an account of the medical aspects of sending a man through space. A *New York Times* critic observed, "The book is thorough, brightly written, and a pleasure to read." A few years later the author wrote *Your Place in America's Space Program,* which emphasized the job possibilities in the astronautical field. "For the young reader headed for a career in this country's space program this book is a must.... It would most certainly show a young aspiring space expert how to set about finding his future niche in astronautics," wrote a reviewer for *Christian Science Monitor.*

Lent's latest works have dealt with the automotive industry. In reviewing the author's book, *The Look of Cars: Yesterday, Today, Tomorrow,* a *Library Journal* critic noted, "The most original sports book of the season and probably the one with the widest possible readership, this is highly recommended for the car buffs as well as all future car owners."

*FOR MORE INFORMATION SEE:* Stanley J. Kunitz, editor, *Junior Book of Authors,* revised edition, H. W. Wilson, 1951.

(Died October 26, 1973)

## LIPPINCOTT, Joseph Wharton    1887-1976

*PERSONAL:* Born February 28, 1887, in Philadelphia, Pa.; son of Joshua Bertram and Joanna (Wharton) Lippincott; grandson of Joshua Ballinger Lippincott, founder of the publishing firm of J. B. Lippincott & Co., and Joseph Wharton, founder of Swarthmore College and University of Pennsylvania's Wharton School of Finance and Commerce; married Elizabeth Schuyler Mills, October, 1913 (died November 20, 1943); married Virginia Jones Mathieson, September 20, 1945; children: (first marriage) Joseph W. Lippincott, Jr. (president and chairman of the board of J. B. Lippincott & Co.), M. Roosevelt, Elizabeth (Mrs. E. Harry Wilkes); stepchildren: Mary Mathieson O'Neill, Joan Mathieson. *Education:* B.S., University of Pennsylvania, 1908. *Politics:* Republican. *Religion:* Society of Friends. *Residence:* "Oak Hill," Bethayres, Pa.

*CAREER:* J. B. Lippincott Publishing Company, Philadelphia, Pa., office boy, 1908, vice-president, 1915-25, president, 1927-48, chairman of the board, 1948-58; author. Founder of the Joseph W. Lippincott Award for outstanding achievement in the field of librarianship, 1936; University of Pennsylvania, associate trustee, chairman of the board of libraries, member of the board of business education; member of board of directors, Free Library of Philadelphia; secretary and member of board of trustees, Moore Institute of

Arts, Science, and Industry. *Military service:* Served with the United States Naval Reserve during the First World War.

*MEMBER:* National Association of Book Publishers (president, 1929), American Booksellers Association, National Geographic Society, American Game Protective Association, Master of Fox Hounds Association of America, Sons of the Revolution, Mayflower Descendants (governor, 1927), Pennsylvania Audubon Society, Philadelphia Academy of Fine Arts, Philadelphia Athaneum, Aquarium Society of Philadelphia, Philadelphia Zoological Society, Franklin Institute, Wilderness Club, Explorers Club, Racket Club, Brook Club, Publishers' Lunch Club, Downtown Club, Zeta Psi, Huntington Valley Country Club.

*WRITINGS: Bun, a Wild Rabbit* (self-illustrated), Penn, 1918, revised edition, illustrated by George F. Mason, Lippincott, 1953; *Red Ben, the Fox of Oak Ridge* (self-illustrated), Penn, 1919, revised edition published as *Little Red, the Fox* (illustrated by G. F. Mason), Lippincott, 1953; *Gray Squirrel* (self-illustrated), Penn, 1921, revised edition, illustrated by G. F. Mason, Lippincott, 1954; *Striped Coat, the Skunk* (self-illustrated), Penn, 1922, revised edition, illustrated by G. F. Mason, Lippincott, 1954; *Persimmon Jim, the 'Possum* (self-illustrated), Penn, 1924, revised edition, illustrated by G. F. Mason, Lippincott, 1955; *Long Horn, Leader of the Deer,* Penn, 1928, revised edition, illustrated by G. F. Mason, Lippincott, 1955; (with G. J. Roberts) *Naturecraft Creatures,* Lippincott, 1933; *The Wolf King* (illustrated by Paul Bransom), Penn, 1933; *The Red Roan*

*Pony* (illustrated by Lynn Bogue Hunt), Penn, 1934, revised edition, illustrated by C. W. Anderson, Lippincott, 1951; *Chisel-Tooth the Beaver* (illustrated by Roland V. Shutts), Penn, 1936; *Animal Neighbors of the Countryside* (illustrated by L. B. Hunt), Lippincott, 1938.

*Wilderness Champion: The Story of a Great Hound* (illustrated by P. Bransom; a Junior Literary Guild selection), Lippincott, 1944, reissued, Grosset, 1970; *Black Wings, the Unbeatable Crow* (illustrated by L. B. Hunt), Lippincott, 1947; *The Wahoo Bobcat* (illustrated by P. Bransom; a Junior Literary Guild selection), Lippincott, 1950; *The Phantom Deer* (illustrated by P. Bransom), Lippincott, 1954; *Old Bill, the Whooping Crane,* Lippincott, 1958; *Coyote, the Wonder Wolf* (illustrated by Ed Dodd), Lippincott, 1964.

Contributor to various periodicals including, *Nature Magazine, Publishers Weekly,* and *Field and Stream.*

*SIDELIGHTS:* Lippincott's father and grandfather were president of the family's publishing firm founded in 1792. Thus, at a very early age he became accustomed to meeting leading writers at the Lippincott family home in Pennsylvania.

At twenty-one, after graduation from the University of Pennsylvania, whose Wharton School his maternal grandfather had founded, Lippincott went to work in the family's publishing business. He began his publishing career by dusting books in the stockroom, but by 1915 he had become a vice-president and, by the age of forty, president of the pub-

**The swamp, never entirely asleep, teemed with life and pleasant sounds as birds and beasts went about their usual pursuits.** ■ (From *The Wahoo Bobcat* by Joseph Wharton Lippincott. Illustrated by Paul Bransom.)

**JOSEPH WHARTON LIPPINCOTT**

lishing firm. The Lippincott company published numerous best sellers while he served as president, including *Kitty Foyle* (1939) by Christopher Morley, *My Friend Flicka* (1941) by Mary O'Hara, and *The Egg and I* (1945) by Betty MacDonald.

Lippincott served as president and later as chairman of the board for over thirty years. He once remarked: "Publishing is terrific! For heaven's sake let everybody in the organization have a good time! Let them in on the profits if you do well!" ["Publisher's Gallery," *Saturday Review,* May 22, 1948.[1]]

As a man with tremendous energy, Lippincott claimed that: "You're either born with a good pituitary gland or you're dead in your tracks."[1]

In 1936 Lippincott founded the Joseph Wharton Lippincott Award for outstanding achievement in librarianship, a profession he considered to be one of the most respectable and one of the most important in our educational system. In 1950 he addressed the A.L.A. Conference: "There is today, and there should be, tremendous interest in librarianship. Nearly eleven thousand new books and new editions were issued by American publishers last year—most of them very good and needed—only a few of them sort of bad. And with this great increase over past years, go smaller homes where there is scarcely room for a family—much less a bookworm—and higher living costs (which leave comparatively less for the purchase of books by the public). If this tendency increases (and I fear it will), the library must and will be the savior of American literature." [Joseph W. Lippincott, "Presentation Address," *Wilson Library Bulletin,* September, 1950.[2]]

Lippincott was interested in different areas of sports, ranging from polo to yacht racing to managing horse shows. He was particularly enthusiastic about exploring nature's untamed environment and its inhabitants. The publisher hunted and fished throughout the United States and was in charge of several big game hunting expeditions in Alaska, Canada, Mexico, Austria, and Bavaria. He collected animals for museums and gained an immeasurable amount of material for his books, articles, and lectures—the latter often being accompanied by his own motion pictures. The publisher-sportsman consequently grew to admire the wild animals he hunted and trapped on his expeditions. His respect for their ability to survive resulted in a number of nature books.

In *Wilderness Champion,* Lippincott unraveled a tale about a dog and his relationship with the domestic life of man and the wild ways of a wolf. "Mr. Lippincott is a knowledgeable sportsman. His style is forthright, unpretentious, but he can make you remember the wilderness and the suspense of the chase, the savagery of titanic battles, almost as clearly as if you had seen them first hand . . . ," observed a critic for the *New York Times.* A reviewer for *Kirkus* wrote, "A rugged and dramatic dog story—good adventure—and sound background of the life in the wilds."

The sportsman wrote about the friendship between a small boy and a wild bobcat in *Wahoo Bobcat.* A *Horn Book* reviewer noted, "Mr. Lippincott has again written a story about animals and people which young readers will like and which has atmosphere, pace, and color." In reviewing the same book, a critic for the *Chicago Sunday Tribune* commented, "Joseph Wharton Lippincott is a naturalist who has known and loved the wilds for half a century. Out of his deep knowledge and understanding he has written this latest tribute to wilderness life. . . . *The Wahoo Bobcat* will delight true nature lovers of any age over 10."

In *Old Bill, the Whooping Crane,* Lippincott incorporated a story about the life-style of a whooping crane with the importance of conservation programs. "An excellent nature portrait. . . . [The author] has drawn an accurate and fascinating picture of the life, habits, and behavior of this wild creature," wrote a reviewer for *Booklist.* A *Horn Book* critic observed, "The absorbing interest of the book . . . lies in the beauty and reality of the settings, whether in the far north or on the Reserve, and in the sense it gives of being eye-witness to the fabulous bird migrations. . . ."

Upon retirement in 1958 as chairman of the board of his publishing company, Lippincott devoted his time to his many hobbies and interests and to his writing. On October 22, 1976 the author of seventeen books for children died at the age of eighty-nine in Huntington Valley, Pennsylvania. "If you waste one minute, it's lost."[1]

*HOBBIES AND OTHER INTERESTS:* Hunting, fishing, polo, horse and yacht racing.

*FOR MORE INFORMATION SEE: Kirkus,* November 15, 1944; *New York Times,* November 26, 1944; *Saturday Review,* May 22, 1948; *Horn Book,* September, 1950; *Chicago Sunday Tribune,* November 12, 1950; *Wilson Library Bulletin,* September, 1950; *Current Biography Yearbook,* 1955; *Booklist,* June 15, 1958; *Horn Book,* August, 1958; Muriel Fuller, editor, *More Junior Authors,* H. W. Wilson, 1963; (obituary) *Publishers Weekly,* November 1, 1976.

(Died October 22, 1976)

*and bubbles,*

(From *Sometimes I Dance Mountains* by Byrd Baylor. Photographs by Bill Sears, drawings by Ken Longtemps.)

# LONGTEMPS, Kenneth 1933-

*PERSONAL:* Born August 9, 1933, in Saranac Lake, N.Y.; son of Kenneth (a civil service employee) and Harriet (Favro; a telephone operator) Longtemps; married Elaine Mendolia (a painter), August 29, 1964; children: Sean Kenneth. *Education:* Rhode Island School of Design, B.F.A., 1959. *Home and office:* 362 Clinton Street, Brooklyn, N.Y. 11231.

*CAREER:* L. W. Frohlich Advertising Agency, New York, N.Y., designer, 1960-61; Home Life Insurance Co., New York, N.Y., art director, 1961-63; Hallmark Gallery, New York, N.Y., exhibition designer, 1963-64; free-lance illustrator, 1964—. *Exhibitions:* Society of Illustrators, "My Show," 1974, annual exhibitions, 1961, 1963, 1965, 1968, 1969, 1971, 1972, 1973. *Military service:* U.S. Air Force, staff sergeant, 1951-55. *Member:* Society of Illustrators. *Awards, honors: The Day It Snowed in Summer* was named one of the best illustrated children's books by *Time* Magazine, 1969; received award of excellence for title spread for *Sound of Sunshine, Sound of Rain,* Society of Illustrators, 1972.

*ILLUSTRATOR:* Marguerite Vance, *A Rainbow for Robin,* Dutton, 1966; Nina Bawden, *The White Horse Gang,* Lippincott, 1966; Dahlov Ipcar, *General Felice,* McGraw, 1967; Madelaine Duke, *The Secret People,* Doubleday, 1968; Suzanne Butler, *Chalet at Saint-Marc,* Little, Brown, 1968; Herbert N. Wong and Matthew F. Vessel, *Our Tree,* Addison-Wesley, 1969; Florence Parry Heide, *The Day It Snowed in Summer,* Funk & Wagnalls, 1969; Barbara S. Hazen, *Danny Dougal: The Wanting Boy,* Lion Press, 1970; Florence Perry Heide, *The Little One,* Lion Press, 1970; Florence Perry Heide, *Sound of Sunshine, Sound of Rain,* Parent's Magazine Press, 1970; Sir Compton MacKenzie, *The Stairs That Kept Going Down,* Doubleday, 1973; Byrd Baylor, *Sometimes I Dance Mountains,* Scribner, 1973; James R. Berry, *Dar Tellum,* School Book Service, 1974; Ann McGovern, adapter, *The Magic Pot,* Macmillan, 1975.

*SIDELIGHTS:* "Motivation—I am that type of person who needs 'something' to illustrate. Only rarely have I sat down to simply do a drawing. My best work comes when I am given an assignment that I must research, think about and in many instances, live with for a period of time. Then the sketches begin, the rough thoughts and shapes (of which 90% usually are discarded), the growing awareness of new thoughts on the work that cause the work to achieve levels I had never considered. The final work, however, is usually very close to the idea I had in mind when I began the sketches; but little discoveries along the creative way have widened the dimensions of the original conception. Hopefully I have given the finished illustration a depth that goes beyond the mere interpretation of a page of text. Picture-making for me is not just the depiction of a scene from the text. The illustration has to make its own statement about the text, and if successful I have added to the book by giving it an imagery that will give the reader a deeper understanding of the story.

"Techniques is a word I shy away from. I have attempted to learn and master many 'techniques' and/or 'materials' simply because they are tools of my craft to give myself a 'vocabulary.' When the work is going in the right direction the method of rendering the finished art comes from the work itself. If one has the 'vocabulary' I mentioned, then the final statement just seems to happen, sometimes with new discoveries in terms of form, color, etc. If one has a thorough understanding of his craft, one is left absolutely free to pursue the creative idea and therein lies personal growth and artistic development. Perhaps this sounds a bit pompous—but, it works for me. . . .

"I was not influenced by one single influence, but by the history of illustration itself; specifically how styles and trends repeat themselves usually through the influence of advertising."

**Whenever he could he dropped in at school and sat in the back of the room. At first the children laughed and laughed. Abe was twenty three.** ■ (From *Barefoot Abe* by Sadyebeth and Anson Lowitz. Illustrated by Anson Lowitz.)

## LOWITZ, Sadyebeth (Heath)   1901-1969

*PERSONAL:* Born December 3, 1901, in Richmond, Mich.; daughter of J. Alexander and Sadie (Allington) Heath; married Anson C. Lowitz (an advertising executive and author), September 12, 1925 (died January 22, 1978); children: Roberta Frances (Mrs. John Ross Hamilton). *Education:* University of Michigan, B.A., 1925; Columbia University, M.A., 1927. *Religion:* Congregationalist. *Residence:* Greenwich, Conn.

*CAREER:* Author of children's books. Dean of Finch Junior College, 1947-48; trustee of Knox School and Greenwich (Conn.) Historical Society; member of board of governors, University of Michigan; president of Round Hill Church Guild, Greenwich.

*WRITINGS*—With husband, Anson C. Lowitz; all "Really Truly Story" juvenile series: *The Pilgrims' Party,* Stein & Day, 1931, revised edition, Lerner, 1967; *General George the Great,* Stein & Day, 1932, revised edition, Lerner, 1967; *The Cruise of Mr. Christopher Columbus,* 1932, revised edition, Lerner, 1967; *The Magic Fountain,* Stein & Day, 1936, revised edition, Lerner, 1967; *Mr. Key's Song,* Stein & Day, 1937, revised edition, Lerner, 1967; *Barefoot Abe,* Stein & Day, 1938, revised edition, Lerner, 1967; *Tom Edison Finds Out,* Stein & Day, 1940, revised edition, Lerner, 1967.

(Died, 1969)

## MacINTYRE, Elisabeth   1916-

*PERSONAL:* Born November 1, 1916, in Sydney, Australia; daughter of Norman John (a grazier) and Laura (Rendall) MacIntyre; married John Eldershaw (an artist), August 21, 1950; children: Jane. *Education:* Attended Sydney Church of England Girls Grammar School; East Sydney Technical College, art student. *Address:* 46 Wigram Rd., Glebe, N.S.W. Australia 2037.

*CAREER:* Lever's Advertising Agency, Lintas, Australia, designer, 1937-42; free-lance artist, 1942—. Writer and illustrator of books for children; cartoonist for magazines and television, including "Ambrose Kangaroo" series carried by Australian Broadcasting Commission and British Broadcasting Corp. *Awards, honors:* "Picture Book of the Year" medal from the Australian Book Council for *Hugh's Zoo,* 1965; literature fellowship from Australian Council, 1973; fellowship from Australia-Japan Foundation, 1977.

*WRITINGS*—Self-illustrated, except as indicated: *Ambrose Kangaroo,* Scribner, 1942; *The Handsome Duckling,* Dawfox, 1942; *The Black Lamb,* Dawfox, 1942; *The Forgetful Elephant,* Dawfox, 1942; *The Willing Donkey,* Dawfox, 1942; *Ambrose Kangaroo Has a Busy Day,* Australian Consolidated Press, 1944; *Susan Who Lives in Australia,* Scribner, 1944; *Katherine,* Harrap, 1946.

*Willie's Woollies: The Story of Australian Wool,* Georgian House, 1951; *Mr. Koala Bear,* Scribner, 1954, new edition, Angus & Robertson, 1966; *Jane Likes Pictures,* Scribner, 1959.

(Illustrator) Ruth Fenner, *The Story House,* Angus & Robertson, 1962; *Hugh's Zoo,* Knopf, 1964; *Ambrose Kangaroo Goes to Town,* Angus & Robertson, 1964; *The Affable, Amiable Bulldozer Man,* Knopf, 1965; *Ninji's Magic,* illustrated by Mamoru Funai, Knopf, 1966.

**ELISABETH MacINTYRE**

*The Purple Mouse,* Nelson, 1975; *It Looks Different When You Get There,* Hodder & Stoughton, 1978; *Ambrose Kangaroo Delivers The Goods,* Angus & Robertson, 1978. Contributor of stories and articles to magazines.

*WORK IN PROGRESS:* Books about Japan.

*SIDELIGHTS:* "Write about myself! *Which* Elisabeth MacIntyre? Looking back over the different sorts of person who have answered to that name, I am amazed to see how one can change so much—and yet still be essentially the same 'me.' It is like looking at a lot of old photographs. Surely I could never have worn those clothes? Done those things? Believed in those issues? Then, taking everything in its right context, one sees how one thing inevitably led to the next—how no step would have been possible without having taken the step before it.

"My Scottish grandfather was one of the earliest pioneers in establishing big cattle stations (ranches to you!) in North Australia. When I was young we lived in the country. I loved it—owned a pony and always had a large assortment of pets. I never walked anywhere it was possible to ride, and at that stage of my life my only ambition was to be something to do with horses—*anything,* as long as it was to do with beautiful well-bred horseflesh. I couldn't imagine any other life being worth living.

"Then—isn't it amazing how we can change! In my late teens we moved to Sydney. It wasn't the same, riding around and around in a park. I sold my darling pony—and have hardly ever been on a horse since.

"It was at about this time that I had to face up to the shattering fact that, as a result of a fall from a horse when I was quite young, I had become deaf. It happened so slowly—I couldn't believe that something like that could happen to *me*.

"Now I firmly believe that everyone has something or other to overcome, and we are all given the strength needed to make something positive from what might seem like a tragedy. (But at the time I wasn't nearly so philosophical!)

"It was hard at the time—very hard. The picture I see of me at that time is like someone lost—bewildered—as if suddenly abandoned on another planet. I trained as a commercial artist, mainly because it seemed the way I could best earn a living. I was not a good student, being more interested in drawing things the way I would like them to be, rather than how they actually were.

"Next picture is of artist and ideas—woman in a large advertising agency. I was fascinated by the visual communication of ideas—but could not make myself believe in the sort of ideas I was supposed to communicate. I have always loved books, and always loved animals. Like other Australian children, most of the books I loved were from England or America. I felt there was a need for Australian children to grow up with books about things they could relate to. So, while the top pages of my layout pads were covered with sketches of radiant girls marrying handsome millionaires simply because they used the right sort of toilet soap—the bottom pages would be alive with drawings of Australian animals having the sort of adventures that would be likely to happen to Australian children.

"Then came the picture of a brisk-looking lady in what looks like a policewoman's uniform. Yes, me again! At the beginning of World War II I joined the Women's Land Army, and was sent to a cold bleak mountainous part of the country to pick apples, pack apples, prune apple trees. The uniform was only for show. Out in the orchards we wore all the woollies possible to squeeze inside large boiler-suits, coats (because it was usually raining or snowing) and gumboots large enough to fit over several pairs of warm socks. I will always remember the historic occasion when, away up on a ladder amongst the topmost branches of an apple tree, someone handed me a letter from Alice Dalgliesh at Scribners, saying they would publish my first book: *Ambrose Kangaroo,* and suggesting that I should do a picture book about what it was like in Australia because so many American children had fathers and brothers in the services stationed in that remote continent 'down under' that nobody seemed to know anything about. It was a mean blustery day, sharp little bullets of sleet stung my face as I trudged down the hillside to the primitive barracks where we were housed; but nothing worried me—my gumboots squelching through mud beat out the rhythm: *This-is-young Susan-who lives-in Australia, with-her-toys and-her-books and-her . . . paraphanalia. . . .*

"Living in a primitive part of the country and working with all sorts of interesting people gave me a love for that sort of thing that has lasted all my life. After leaving the Land Army I wrote and illustrated several books; then for years did what I called 'Documentary Strips' and stories about different Australian ways of life. I married a well-known landscape artist, and for six months of every year we would travel to little-known parts of the country. Where possible, living in a caravan; but away out in the Centre, and up in the North the roads were just good enough to take a truck. Then we camped—'awa-a-ay outback,' each year in a different direction. In mountain ranges around the inland sea of prehistoric

times in the Centre. Tropical jungle in North Queensland and the Barrier Reef. Aboriginal missions and cattle stations in the Northern Territory. Old whaling ports down South. Across the flat emptiness of the Nullabor Plain to Western Australia. . . . You name it, we've been there—the hard way!

"Next picture: devoted mother of longed-for daughter. The next two decades of my life were spent as an ordinary suburban mum who wrote, drew, did television cartoons, and anything else I could sell. I had to—my marriage had broken up and we had to live. I had neither the time nor the peace of mind to do more than three or four books.

"I gave up doing children's books because I couldn't afford to do them. As I see it, unless one's work is a generous overflowing of ideas you are happy to share; a 'harsh voice' takes over, and what you should joyfully give, becomes that that you *have* to sell.

"THEN, in a rather bleak period when I was wondering what to do next, I was awarded a Literature Fellowship by the Australian Government. Marvellous! But by then, books for young people were different; and young people were different. Goals I had had before were no longer relevant. To see things in perspective I went to America. Then to Europe. For three happy years I lived in Italy. From there, saw things on a universal plane. How little we understand each other! Families, friends, peoples, countries, we all go around in glass cases—few people understand more than what they *see*.

"The first book of my new genre was *The Purple Mouse*. About a girl who was deaf—a subject I know a great deal about! In it, I wanted to say something my own life has proved: that in overcoming any big hurdle, one automatically overcomes a lot of minor hurdles, and achieves a state of strength and freedom one would not otherwise have had.

"I write books because they are the only way I can say things I think should be said. To me, there is nothing so fascinating as what really does happen; I like serious things to be lightened with humor, and amusing things taken seriously. I write for young people because they fascinate me—they are so old so young; going into a world so different from what has gone before, and with more 'awful warnings' than precedents as guidelines. Nobody was able to help me when I was young—perhaps that is why I try to write the books I would like to have read a long time ago!

"Or perhaps it is just that I write because of my insatiable curiosity. If somebody is rude to me I want to know why they were rude; to find out more about them, then see how everything is different to what it had seemed—it all makes an interesting story. Or migrants; people from all over the world are changing places as never before. I think we should all know a lot more about each other so as to benefit by all the best that each country has to offer, rather than criticize each other for being different. We have a superficial tourist-level knowledge of other countries and cultures—but know so little about them as *people*.

"Travelling alone, I like to go to other countries and live there. After a month or so, one gets the feeling of the place and the people. Then comes a great longing to express the affinity one feels—the samenesses rather than the differences. (That is another reason why I write for young people; they are growing into a world where international understanding is more important than ever before.)

His tastes are quiet,

his wants are few,

He plays

the

piano . . .

. . . and gardens too.

(From *Mr. Koala Bear* by Elisabeth MacIntyre. Illustrated by the author.)

and his second best pair of trousers.

(From *Ambrose Kangaroo* by Elisabeth MacIntyre. Illustrated by the author.)

"For me, writing is a private and solitary life. I belong to various societies and such—but never go to meetings. I feel that time and energy wasted in mass annoyance with publishers could be better spent in perfecting one's work. But some of my best friends are writers; and it is good to see them sometimes, and be reminded that they, as I do, work *so hard* over each page they write—and, like me, are always miserably aware of the great gap between the actual and the ideal. The one firm guideline I have is from the Bible, '. . . the letter killeth, but the spirit giveth life.' In times of despair—we all have them—I try to remember it is the spirit of the thing I am trying to express, and never mind about the rich, beautiful, prose!

"I am now working on two books about Japan after a wonderful visit to that beautiful country. I'm not sure what I will do next—it will be something interesting!"

*FOR MORE INFORMATION SEE: Young Reader's Review,* March, 1967.

## MACK, Stan(ley)

*EDUCATION:* Attended the Rhode Island School of Design.

*CAREER:* Art director, *New York Times Book Review* and *New York Herald Tribune Book Week;* author and illustrator of children's books. *Awards, honors: One Dancing Drum* was listed among the *New York Times* Choice of Best Illustrated Children's Books of the Year in 1971, and was chosen by the Children's Book Showcase in 1972; *The Preposterous Week* was one of the books chosen as part of the American Institute of Graphic Arts Children's Book Show in 1971-72; Mack has also been honored by the Society of Illustrators and the Art Directors Club.

*WRITINGS*—All self-illustrated: (With Gail Kredenser) *One Dancing Drum,* S. G. Phillips, 1971; *Ten Bears in My Bed: A Goodnight Countdown,* Pantheon, 1974; *The King's Cat Is Coming!,* Pantheon, 1976; *Where's My Cheese?* (a Junior Literary Guild selection), Pantheon, 1977.

Illustrator: Gail Kredenser, *The ABC of Bumptious Beasts: Poems,* Crown, 1966; Edward Lear, *The Story of the Four Little Children Who Went Round the World,* Crown, 1967; James E. Seidelman and Grace Mintoyne, *The 14th Dragon,* Harlin Quist, 1968; Carolyn Wolff, *Three People,* Harlin Quist, 1968; Marguerita Rudolph, *Star Bright,* Lothrop, 1969; Ennis Rees, *Potato Talk,* Pantheon Books, 1969; Robert M. Jones, compiler, *Can Elephants Swim?,* Time-Life Books, 1969; Erich Kaestner, *The Little Man and the Big Thief,* Knopf, 1969; Thomas Roberts, *The Magical Mind*

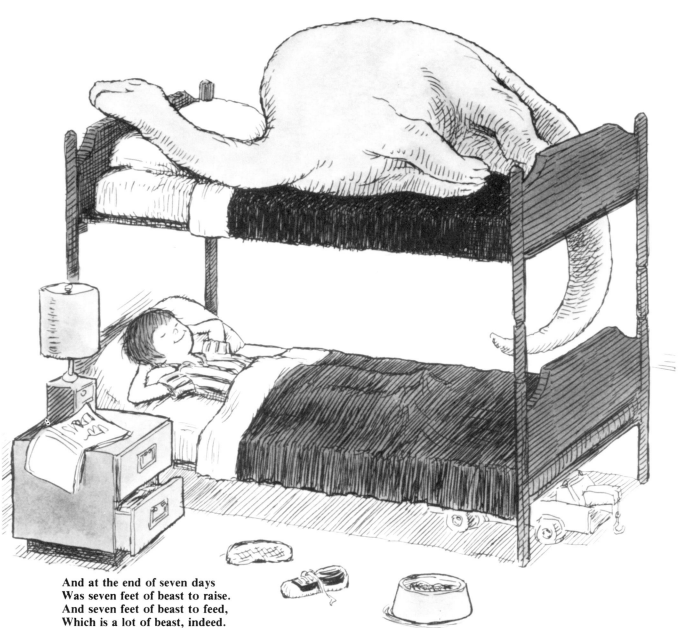

And at the end of seven days
Was seven feet of beast to raise.
And seven feet of beast to feed,
Which is a lot of beast, indeed.
■ (From *Jethro's Difficult Dinosaur* by Arnold Sundgaard. Illustrated by Stan Mack.)

*Adventure of Hannah and Coldy Coldy,* Knopf, 1971; Matt Robinson, *A Lot of Hot Water,* Random House, 1971; George Keenan, *The Preposterous Week,* Dial, 1971; Paula Scher, *The Brownstone,* Pantheon Books, 1973; Arnold Sundgaard, *Jethro's Difficult Dinosaur,* Pantheon, 1977.

*SIDELIGHTS:* Stanley Mack was born in Brooklyn. He spent his childhood in Providence, Rhode Island where he attended public schools, eventually earning his B.F.A. from The Rhode Island School of Design.

Mack has been the art director for the New York *Times* Sunday magazine, the *Times* book review section and the New York *Herald Tribune's Book Week.* He has also contributed art work to numerous magazines including, *Life, Esquire, Holiday* and *Saturday Review.*

Illustrator for many children's books, Mack has also written and illustrated his own books, including *Where's My Cheese?* which was a Literary Guild selection for 1977. He

has been honored by the Society of Illustrators and the Art Directors Club and his work has been exhibited at the Museum of Modern Art in New York City. Besides illustrating books, he has made animated films for the Children's Television Workshop.

*Ten Bears in My Bed* was a feature of the Children's Television Workshop.

## MORDVINOFF, Nicolas    1911-1973 (Nicolas)

*PERSONAL:* Born September 27, 1911, in St. Petersburg (now Leningrad), Russia; came to the United States, 1946, naturalized, 1952; married Barbara Ellis, 1956; children: Michael, Alexandra, Peter. *Education:* Graduated from the University of Paris. *Home:* Hampton, New Jersey.

**"This no ordinary bear," agreed one. "With our own eyes we saw him teaching his brothers the white man's walking war dance."** ■ (From *Alphonse, That Bearded One* by Natalie Savage Carlson. Illustrated by Nicolas.)

*CAREER:* Artist, illustrator, and author. Began drawing at an early age; as a college student, he contributed cartoons and illustrations to French magazines and newspapers; traveled to Tahiti, 1934, where he worked on developing his own artistic style for the next thirteen years; arrived in New York to embark on a career as an illustrator of children's books, 1946. His works have been exhibited as one-man shows at various galleries, including the Luyber Gallery in New York, 1949, Wickersham Gallery, 1970, and Galerie 9 in Paris, 1970; works in public collections can be seen at the New York Public Library and the Metropolitan Museum of Art. *Awards, honors:* Caldecott Medal, 1952, for *Finders Keepers,* and runner up, 1951, for *The Two Reds; New York Herald Tribune* award (shared with author, Natalie S. Carlson), 1954, for *Alphonse, That Bearded One;* listed among the *New York Times* choice of best illustrated books of the year, 1954, for *Circus Ruckus,* 1955, for *Chaga,* and 1958, for *The Magic Feather Duster;* American Institute of Graphic Arts certificate of excellence, 1955-57.

*WRITINGS*—Under pseudonym Nicolas; all self-illustrated; all published by Harcourt, except as noted: (With Will, pseudonym of William Lipkind) *The Two Reds,* 1950; (with Will) *Finders Keepers,* 1951; (with Will) *Even Steven,* 1952; (with Will) *The Christmas Bunny,* 1953; (with Will) *Circus Ruckus,* 1954; *Bear's Land,* Coward, 1955; (with Will) *Chaga,* 1955; (with Will) *Perry the Imp,* 1956; *Coral Island,* Doubleday, 1957; (with Will) *Sleepyhead,* 1957; (with Will) *The Magic Feather Duster,* 1958; (with Will) *Four-Leaf Clover,* 1959; (with Will) *The Little Tiny Rooster,* 1960; (with Will) *Billy the Kid,* 1961; (with Will) *Russet and the Two Reds,* 1962; (with Will) *The Boy and the Forest,* 1964.

Illustrator: William Standish Stone, *Thunder Island,* Knopf, 1942; W. S. Stone, *Pepe Was the Saddest Bird,* Knopf, 1944; W. S. Stone, *Ship of Flame: A Saga of the South Seas,* Knopf, 1945; Caroline Guild, *Rainbow in Tahiti,* Doubleday, 1948; Andre Norton (pseudonym of Alice Mary Norton), *Star Man's Son,* Coward, 1952; William Lipkind, *Boy with a Harpoon,* Harcourt, 1952; Willis Lindquist, *Burma Boy* (ALA Notable Book), Whittlesey House, 1953; W. Lipkind, *Boy of the Islands,* Harcourt, 1954.

Under pseudonym Nicolas: Earl and Marjory Schwalje, *Cezar and the Music Maker,* Knopf, 1951; Marie Halun Bloch, *Big Steve,* Coward, 1952; Rudyard Kipling, *Just So Stories,* Doubleday, 1952; Natalie S. Carlson, *Alphonse, That Bearded One,* Harcourt, 1954; Loren D. Good, *Panchito,* Coward, 1955; William Owen Steele, *Davy Crockett's Earthquake,* Harcourt, 1956; W. O. Steele, *Daniel Boone's Echo,* Harcourt, 1957; N. S. Carlson, *Hortense: The Cow for a Queen,* Harcourt, 1957; Natalie S. Carlson, *Evangeline: Pigeon of Paris,* Harcourt, 1960.

*SIDELIGHTS:* **September 27, 1911.** Born in St. Petersburg (now Leningrad) into an upper-class Russian family—his grandfather was Admiral Alexander Mordvinoff. "From the time I was three I always wanted to draw and paint, and I always drew horses. I love horses." [Lee Bennett Hopkins, *Books Are By People,* Citation Press, 1969.[1]]

**1918.** When the Russian revolution came, fled with his parents to Finland and then to Paris where he grew up. "I was barely seven years old, but I remember traveling in a horse-drawn sleigh."[1]

Mordvinoff attended schools in Paris and studied at the Lycée Jeanson de Sailly and the École des Roches. He was

**NICOLAS MORDVINOFF**

graduated from the University of Paris with a degree in Latin, philosophy, and languages.

**1929.** While still a student, sold cartoons and illustrations to French newspapers and magazines.

**1934.** Freeing himself from the hectic pace of Paris, Mordvinoff fled to the tranquility of the South Pacific. For thirteen years he traveled from island to island painting and developing his own style. "While I was in Tahiti, World War II broke out. I wanted desperately to fight in the war, but I couldn't get into the army. The French wouldn't take me, the Russians wouldn't take me, and neither would the United States. I decided to make my way as close to the fighting as possible, but I never managed to! I got to Mango River, and I stayed there for two years, painting and living among the natives. I was the only white man living on the island. There was a schooner that came twice a year. If you wanted to leave, you had to do it when it came or wait another six months.

"The natives bought my work. They called them photographs. They paid me in pearls. One day the chief of the island, a descendant of South Pacific kings, came to me and asked if I would make a photograph of his wife. I told him I would and asked if I could meet her. 'She's dead,' he replied. However, he did have a poor photograph that had been taken of her by a visitor.

"I did a portrait painting from the photograph and, when it was ready, the chief came to my studio. I put it on the easel. The chief sat down, looked at it, walked up to it, touched it,

**They buried the bone and set off down the road. The first person they met was an apprentice barber. He was just learning how to cut hair and couldn't find anybody to practice on.** ■ (From *Finders Keepers* by Will and Nicolas.)

and said, 'She's alive again!' He pulled out a huge, beautifully colored pearl to pay me for the portrait. It was the biggest pearl I had ever seen." [1]

Returning to Tahiti, he met author William S. Stone who persuaded him to illustrate his book. "I remember once in Tahiti during the last war I had all my etchings seized by the police and almost went to jail myself for reproducing in one of my etchings a backyard wall on which was the inscription, '*Vive de Gaulle.*' Such things generally happen in critical periods. At that time, France was tragically split into two factions: for Marèchal Petain or for General de Gaulle. The Gaullists were very strong in Tahiti. I was as ardently for de Gaulle as any of them. But because the local politicians had no particularly glorious deeds or events to fill up their time, they turned their attention toward my etchings, seeing a lack of respect for the General where I saw only a picture, and if anything else, a tribute to his popularity." [From the Caldecott Award acceptance speech by Nicolas Mordvinoff, *Horn Book,* August, 1952.[2]]

**1942.** Illustrated Stone's book, *Thunder Island.*

**1944.** Illustrated Stone's book, *Pepe Was the Saddest Bird.*

**1945.** Illustrated Stone's book, *Ship of Flame.* The success of the Stone-Mordvinoff collaboration induced him to come to the United States.

**1946.** Arrived in New York City. Rented an apartment in Greenwich Village East, a Bowery area. "This was a terrible experience. I couldn't find a job, and I had no money. For one year I starved.

"I became very ill. One day while I was in bed, I remembered a man I had met in Tahiti who told me to look him up if I ever came to New York. I did. The man invited me to his cottage in Massachusetts. I missed three trains because I was too weak to pack my few things." [1]

Mordvinoff spent the next two years on the small island off the coast of Massachusetts before returning to New York City where he held his first one-man show of his paintings in a 57th Street gallery. "I sold two paintings; one was returned!" [1]

**1950.** *The Two Reds* was published. The book was written with Will Lipkind, an author whose friendship Mordvinoff had accepted. "Will is an anthropologist by profession and a poet by inclination. We talked of doing a book together over a glass of sherry. I saw a red cat on the windowsill and said, 'Let's do a book about that.' Will told me we needed more for a story. Returning from shopping that night, I saw a boy with red hair. So *The Two Reds,* the cat and the boy, became the book.

"Upon publication of the book a nice young man at F.A.O. Schwarz (the toy store on New York's Fifth Avenue) did a

"By my whiskers I smell fish?" And the cat followed his nose. "By my whistle I smell fire." And the boy followed his nose. ▪ (From *The Two Reds* by Will. Illustrated by Nicolas.)

whole window on the book. (The 'nice young man' was Maurice Sendak.) The book was immediately banned in Boston. People claimed it was subversive—especially when the two people who created it had names like Lipkind and Mordvinoff.''[1]

**1951.** Despite the controversy, *The Two Reds* was runner-up for the Caldecott Medal. The team of Will and Nicolas (their pseudonyms) published another dozen books. "A picture book must have complete unity in text and pictures. And I cannot well imagine working in any other way than Will Lipkind and I do. We work in such a close relationship that when a book is finished, it is sometimes hard for us to remember who was responsible for what idea. Story, pictures, design, type and even color are conceived as one whole. It is fascinating to see the book grow from the first miniature dummy, through many phases, to its last run through the printing press, to its binding.... At no time is it a quick or easy process and the work is never in any proportion to the material reward. It is a work of love.''[2]

**1952.** Winner of the Caldecott Medal for his book, done with Will Lipkind, *Finders Keepers.* "I remember some time in February when I had spent the better part of the night working. By early morning I was asleep and having a dream. I was mounting up into a boxing ring. In the opposite corner was a huge, fierce-looking prize-fighter with cauliflower ears and no nose to speak of. The bell rang. I jumped. But it was my doorbell. The mailman was bringing a special delivery letter at seven o'clock in the morning! Being but half awake, I tossed the letter onto my desk and went right back to bed. Then it occurred to me that I might relapse into the same dream. And the last thing I wanted was to see myself con-

fronted again with that ferocious pugilist. 'Might as well take a look at my mail,' I said to myself.

"And there it was, the announcement of the Caldecott Award! You can guess that this woke me up. It was still very early in the morning. But the first thing I did was to call and wake up Margaret McElderry [his editor]. All I said was 'Viva Zapata!' And she knew right away what had happened.''[2]

The award opened new horizons for Mordvinoff in the field of children's literature. "It seems to me that in human nature, fulfillment of a lasting desire very often comes too late or brings some sort of disillusionment. Once, I remember, for a long time I had wanted to own a horse. And at one time, circumstances being favorable, I realized my desire. But who likes to ride alone? I had to have a second horse. Now, when you have two horses, there is always one of the two that has something wrong, a sore of some kind, a lost shoe, a split hoof. I felt obliged to get a third horse. And to take care of three horses and as many saddles, various bridles and harnesses means a full-time job. Therefore, I could not paint or draw any more. It was a great relief when I succeeded in getting rid of them all.

"I had also wanted to have a car. As a result, I spent one entire summer vacation sitting in a smoky garage while mechanics kept on discovering new things to repair. It was the most expensive vacation I ever had!

"Shall I admit now that I hoped some day to win the Caldecott Medal? I did. And I am very happy about it. This time there will be no disillusionment, I am sure. I shall not have to groom the Medal like a horse, and there is no leather harness or bridle attached to it. Neither are there any mechanical parts that will have to be repaired. Instead, it will be a source of pride and continuing pleasure and a constant stimulus to strive for finer picture books."[2]

**1956.** Married Barbara Ellis. The couple had three children, Michael, Alexandra, and Peter.

**1964.** *The Boy and the Forest,* the last book that Mordvinoff and Lipkind collaborated on, was published. Mordvinoff also wrote and illustrated several books himself. "All art forms are subjected to what could be called a *confusion of values.* Book illustrations are no exception. Thus, among some people, there is a tendency to believe that anything destined for children should be sweet and not too unconventionally imaginative or not realistic in the true sense of the word. For example, in illustrations grown-up people should not be shown smoking or mistreating an animal, and they must be more than decently dressed. Why? Just think of the pictures children see in magazines, newspapers, and on the screen today. Of course, there is a great difference between encouraging bad instincts and simply mentioning casual facts of everyday life. Many people smoke, most change their clothes at least once a day. Some occasionally kick a dog. I have seen it done. And most children have—or will, anyway! It is surprising that we have not yet seen candy-covered picture books. But children, like grownups, cannot thrive on candy alone.

"Do not misunderstand me. I am not saying that illustration cannot be at the same time sweet and good, as it can be rough and good. Unfortunately, often it turns out to be sweet and bad or at times rough and bad, as, for instance, in the comic books. Never enough sincere effort is made in between these extremes. Often timid attempts to free or 'modernize' a style result in illustrations with static, lifeless figurines. No wonder they can't smoke."[2]

**1969.** With his wife and three children, lived in an old farmhouse in Hampton, New Jersey. "The children are not too impressed with me. But I'll tell you a story about an incident that happened.... I received a letter from Lynda Bird Johnson on White House stationery. She is very interested in children's books. I showed the letter to Michael [his eldest son]. 'Is this real?' he asked. 'Are you serious?' I explained to him that his father was a famous illustrator. 'Yeah, but that famous?' he puzzled."[1]

By the end of the sixties Mordvinoff had stopped doing children's books and had returned to painting. "I have stopped doing children's books. It was an interlude in my life. I do not want to get stuck doing one thing until the day I die."[1]

**1970.** His works were exhibited in the Wickersham Gallery and Galerie 9 in Paris. His works were also exhibited in public collections at the New York Public Library and at the Metropolitan Museum of Art.

**May 5, 1973.** Committed suicide at his home in Hampton, New Jersey. He was sixty-two years old. "An illustrator is primarily an artist. An artist is a man whose urge for expression makes him unable to find any other purpose in life....

"To please on the surface is no more than to attract attention by a bright display in the window of an empty story. It is a form of treachery. Any form of art to survive has to be lively, sincere, honest and truthful. Art is life and life is no candy."[2]

*FOR MORE INFORMATION SEE:* Henry C. Pitz, "Nicolas Mordvinoff," *Horn Book,* August, 1952; Lee Bennett Hopkins, *Books Are by People,* Citation, 1969; Obituaries: *Publishers Weekly,* May 28, 1973.

(Died May 5, 1973)

## MORRISON, Lucile Phillips    1896-

*PERSONAL:* Born September 8, 1896, in Los Angeles, Calif.; daughter of Lee A. and Catherine (Coffin) Phillips; married Wayland Augustus Morrison, December 27, 1917; children: Wayland Lee, Richard Holt, Lee Allen, Keith Norman, Patricia Lee. *Education:* Vassar College, A.B., 1918, George Pepperdine College, M.A., 1958. *Religion:* Congregationalist. *Home:* 1134 Rancho Rd., Arcadia, Calif. 91006.

*CAREER:* Lee A. Phillips Inc., director, 1930-49, vice-president, 1938-42, president, 1942-49; American Institute of Family Relations, Los Angeles, Calif., intern, 1952-53, associate counselor, 1954-55, counselor, 1955-64, also vice-president of the board of directors until 1964; licensed psychologist; marriage, family, and child counselor; author. Trustee or member of the boards of directors of numerous institutions and organizations, including Scripps College, trustee, 1930-72, honorary trustee, 1972, chairman of the educational policy committee, 1965-70; Duarte (Calif.) Community Service Council, founding member, president, 1946-48, vice-president, 1948-50, health chairman, 1951-54; Claremont University Center, constituent member of the board of fellows, 1967-70, graduate school committee member, 1968-70, member of the advisory board for the Institute of Antiquity and Christianity, Claremont Graduate School, 1968—; California School of Professional Psychology, board of directors, 1972, executive council, 1973, member of the academic commission, 1974.

*MEMBER:* American Association of Humanistic Psychology, American Association of Marriage Counselors, American Psychological Association, Child Study Association of America, Western Psychological Association, California Psychological Association, California State Marriage Counselors Association, New York Academy of Sciences, Academy of Psychologists in Marital Counseling, Academy of Religion and Mental Health, American Association of University Women, Phi Beta Kappa, Delta Kappa Gamma, Psi Chi, D.A.R., Women's University Club (Los Angeles), Southern California Symphony Association, Historical Society of Southern California.

*WRITINGS:* (Editor) *Doll Dreams,* four volumes, privately printed, 1927-32; *Mystery Gate* (illustrated by Winifred Bromhall), F. A. Stokes, 1928; *The Attic-Child* (illustrated by Mable Pyne), F. A. Stokes, 1929; *The Blue Bandits* (illustrated by M. Pyne), F. A. Stokes, 1930; (editor) *An Introduction to the World of Books,* Scripps College, 1934; *The Lost Queen of Egypt,* F. A. Stokes, 1937, reissued, Lippincott, 1965.

Also author with Robert M. Taylor of *Taylor Johnson Temperament Analysis: Research and Development of Test and Manual,* 1963-67.

*SIDELIGHTS:* In *The Lost Queen of Egypt* Morrison wove a tale based on the life of Ankhsenamon, daughter of King Akhenaten and Queen Nefertiti. "Lucile P. Morrison has written a most extraordinary book.... [The] scholarly ab-

**Ankhsenpaaten rejoiced that there were no lessons to mar the freedom of a day which held such promise. Somewhere in the garden Kenofer would be working, and there she was determined to be. ■** (From *Lost Queen of Egypt* by Lucile Morrison. Decorations by Franz Geritz.)

sorption in her sources sometimes overlays the story with detail and makes it move a bit slowly. But it gives us such a book as we never have had before about Egypt . . . ,'' noted a reviewer for *Horn Book*. A critic for the *New York Times* commented, ''One realizes Mrs. Morrison's own pleasure in the task she set herself, a task which was so evidently a labor of love. . . .''

*HOBBIES AND OTHER INTERESTS:* Archaeology and doll collecting.

*FOR MORE INFORMATION SEE: Horn Book*, September, 1937; *New York Times*, November 28, 1937.

# PAPASHVILY, George    1898-1978

*PERSONAL:* Born August 23, 1898, in Kobiantkari, Georgian Soviet Socialist Republic; emigrated to the United States in 1923; naturalized in 1944; son of peasants; married Helen Waite (an author). *Education:* Received no formal schooling, but was trained to make ornamented riding crops and swords. *Address:* R D 4, Quakertown, Penn. 18951.

*CAREER:* Humorist and essayist. During his life, Papashvily held many jobs, including well digger, taxi cab driver, and wild pig hunter in Constantinople (now Istanbul); dishwasher and housepainter, and in a silk mill, garage, and statue factory in New York City; in a glue factory in Pittsburgh, Penn.; in a railroad yard and garage in Ambridge, Penn.; in several automobile factories in Detroit, Mich.; movie extra in Hollywood, Calif.; and farmer in Quakertown, Penn. Beginning in 1943, Papashvily began sculpting and by 1946 was devoting most of his time to this, with exhi-

bitions in numerous museums, including the National Academy, New York City; the National College of Fine Arts, Washington, D.C.; the Boston Museum of Fine Arts, the Pennsylvania Academy of Fine Arts; Allentown Art Museum, Allentown, Penn.; Philadelphia Art Alliance; Lehigh University Art Gallery, Bethlehem, Penn.; Scripp College Art Gallery, Claremont, Calif.; Reading Public Museum and Art Gallery, Reading, Penn.; and the William Penn Memorial Museum, Harrisburg, Penn.

*MILITARY SERVICE:* Served in the Russian Army for six years during World War I, and in the Georgian National Army during the Russian Revolution; in the United States, he was a member of the National Guard. *Member:* Artists Equity Association, Audubon Artists, Philadelphia Art Alliance.

*WRITINGS*—All written with wife, Helen Papashvily: *Anything Can Happen*, Harper, 1945, reissued, 1966; *Yes and No Stories: A Book of Georgian Folk Tales* (illustrated by Simon Lissim), Harper, 1946; *Thanks to Noah* (illustrated by Jack Wilson), Harper, 1951; *Dogs and People* (illustrated by Marguerite Kirmse), Lippincott, 1954; (with the editors of Time-Life Books) *Russian Cooking*, Time-Life Books, 1969; *Home and Home Again*, Harper, 1973.

*ADAPTATIONS:* José Ferrer and Kim Hunter starred in the 1952 Paramount motion picture based on the best seller, *Anything Can Happen.*

*SIDELIGHTS:* **August 23, 1898.** Born in Kobiantkari, Georgia, a village in the U.S.S.R. ''Kobiantkari was a very small

(From the movie "Anything Can Happen," starring Jose Ferrer and Kim Hunter. Copyright 1952 by Paramount Pictures Corporation.)

place; the thirty-eight families who lived there were like a single household, and what happened to one concerned all.

"True, it was a poor village without a post office, a mill, or a store. The church was a small building deep in the woods, where a priest came now and again for services.

"The houses did not set along streets or around a square but were scattered helter-skelter over the mountainside, some a quarter mile apart, others within hailing distance, a few side by side, but all linked together by a narrow track more path than road.

"No one had more than an acre, or at most two, of stony hillside for his own. All the good fields had to be rented from a prince who had lived so long in Moscow that his home and his language were both forgotten, and in fifty years he had never so much as touched his own ground with his own foot. The land meant nothing to him—only the money it would bring. This prince sent his relative, a man named Nestor, 'Cruel Nestor' the village called him, to manage his estate and collect the share of the crop due him for using his land. After that was paid, little was left.

"Of course, Kobiantkari had no hospital, no doctor, no school, no teacher. Worst of all, there was nobody, not one single person in the whole village that knew how to read or write. It made life hard.

"Yet no one in Kobiantkari ever wanted to leave and go to make another life in another place. Although the village might be poor and small, not even a pinpoint on the map, those who lived there thought it the center of the world. They would not have changed their mountainside for Tbilisi or Vladikavkaz, no, not even for St. Petersburg, where the Russian Czar sat on a golden throne in a marble palace and ate meat twice a day.

"For Kobiantkari had meadows blue with primroses, thickets of blackberries, and whole hillsides of wild cornelian cherry trees, bright with golden flowers in the spring, hung with ruby fruit in summer. Through the village ran a stream called *Chwenes Tskale,* 'Our Own,' with water so delicious it was always said you could eat it as well as drink it. Best of all, those who lived in Kobiantkari had each other—neighbors, friends, relatives—to share sorrow and joy.

"My father had golden hands, and he could do anything that came his way—weave willow baskets fine enough to hold flour, make wheels for buffalo carts, braid rope—but there was no one in Kobiantkari rich enough to pay him in cash. For that he had to go to Dushet, a town two miles away. Even there, work was scarce. My father thought himself lucky to be hired one or two days in a week. Whenever he did bring home a day's wages, we counted out the coins on the table after supper—seven, eight, nine, maybe ten showre pieces were the most he could earn, and it took one hundred showre to make one ruble. Some cash, too, we had to spend now and then, one showre for salt, another for tea, half a showre for a spool of thread. Nevertheless, two or three we managed always to save, and my father let me drop them into an earthen jar where we kept the new house money.

"My mother wanted to teach me and my father, too, how to read and write. We had no book, no pencil, and no paper, but my father sanded a straight pine board on both sides, rounding the corners neatly, and for markers he whittled thin sticks to a point and charred one end in the fire.

"'It is as good, it is better than any slate,' my mother said. 'See, I make *a* and after you learn that, I can brush it away—like this—and show you *b*.'

"Almost every night we drew our letters—*a* we learned, and *b,* and then *g,* which in our alphabet comes third.

"'*G* is your letter,' my mother said.

"*G* looked like a fish swimming toward me. I made so many *G*'s I wore out our marking stick, and my father had to cut and char another.

"After *G* came *D* shaped like a flower with a stem and a leaf. *D* was our David's letter. I drew a whole garden of *D*'s on the board.

"At *E* my father, who could shoe a horse, make a barrel, or split a tree in half with one stroke, gave up.

"'There is a time to learn everything,' he said, 'and the time for letters is past. For me. Not for you.'

"I kept on through *i* and *k* and *l,* but there the lessons stopped and so did our happy life." [George and Helen Papashvily, *Home and Home Again,* Harper, 1973.[1]]

**1904.** "When I was six, my mother died. My brother, David, who was not yet two, went to live with our Aunt Salome—*Mamedah,* we called her, which means 'Father's Sister.' She was a widow. In the first summer of her marriage, cholera spread through the village. In those times there were no doctors, at least not for poor people, and many died, among them Mamedah's husband, and after him, his brother and his brother's wife and two of their children. Left only was their baby, Sandro. Mamedah took this nephew for her own son, just as later she took our David.

"All she had was a little vineyard, less than two acres, but by making wine and baking bread for the neighbors, she managed to keep herself and the two boys. Although Sandro was ten or twelve years older than David, he was a kind of extra brother to him and to me, too, when I went sometimes to visit my aunt.

"For after my mother died, I stayed with my father, and he and I lived alone—alone, that is, except for our horse and my dogs, who kept me company when my father went away to work.

"Years afterward, when I had already gone from home, my father married again. My stepmother, Nina, I saw many times, but my father's second family, born after I left Georgia, were all strangers to me. From letters, I knew I had two sisters, Maro and Leila, and two brothers, Alexander and Irvandis."[1]

**1912.** Having received no formal education, Papashvily was apprenticed to a sword maker. "On a cool morning in early September, my few clothes washed and mended and tied in a bundle, my father and I walked to Dushet. The articles were signed with a glass of wine to seal the bargain, and I began my career as a sword maker by sweeping the floor, going for water, cleaning the shoes, washing the dishes, and polishing the copper pots before I went to bed.

"The first weeks I felt as lost as a blind man dropped in a well, for there were no sounds, no scents to give me a clue to life, no cock crow to say day had come, no whiff of smoke from the neighbor's chimney to tell which way the wind stood, no creaking cart to let me know my father was coming home. But slowly I grew used to the stagnant air, the clamor in the streets, the strange faces, and I told myself (sometimes I almost believed it) that this was not too bad a life. Other apprentices on our street had masters who cursed and starved and overworked and often beat them. My sword maker was good-natured even when he was drunk, which was most of the time."[1]

**1914.** When the sword maker died, young Papashvily became apprenticed to a leather worker from the same village of Dushet. "My new master, I discovered in the next few days, was very unlike my old one. He never wasted a minute's time in a *duquani* or sitting around the table. He fed us as cheaply as he could, although I will say for him he ate what he gave us. He was not an easy man to please. The knife must be held just so; the strips cut exactly straight; the awl set plumb for each punch. Back he sent even rough thongs to be trimmed over—two times, five times, but when at last he said, 'Good enough,' it was worth the trouble.

"Altogether I liked it better than the sword maker's. The shop was a busy one. The journeyman named Leo, who had finished his time two years before and now worked for wages, was good-natured and patient and ready to show me what he knew, and as the weeks passed we grew to be good friends.

"As the weeks turned into months, the leather maker gave me finer and finer work to do—braided crop handles became my specialty."[1]

That same year the assassination of Austria's Archduke Ferdinand began World War I and Papashvily enlisted in the Russian Army. "'Why is everybody in such a hurry?' I asked Leo one day.

"'Some kind of an archduke was killed.'

"'Where?'

"'Who knows. Far away someplace.'

"'Why was he killed?'

"'Who knows?'

"'There must have been a reason.'

"'You don't need a reason to kill an archduke.'

"'But what has that to do with all the extra work brought in the shop to be finished at once?'

"'The officers hope to make a war out of the dead archduke.'

**You know, my life is sometimes very dull here. I am alone from dark to dark. Of course, for you it's quite a different thing. You have a chance to see the world. Tell me of your experiences. Tell me of the human beings you shine upon.** ■ (From *Yes and No Stories* by George and Helen Papashvily. Illustrated by Simon Lissim.)

"'Why a war?'

"'Why? To earn promotions, naturally, and medals and estates and prizes.'

"'It doesn't make any sense.'

"'Of course not,' Leo said, 'and in any case it is no business of ours. See—while you are busy asking questions you have cut your strap too short. Start another piece.'''[1]

Papashvily served in the Russian Army during World War I and in the Georgian National Army during the Russian Revolution. "In Persia, in Turkey, and then in the United States, wandering from place to place, living in dark rooms, lost in the crowded streets, working at a hundred jobs, a stranger in a strange land, I cheered myself through the loneliest hours thinking how one day I would go back to Georgia; I would walk up the mountainside where my foot knew every stone; I would see my father's face again; I would eat the bread and drink the wine of home."[1]

**1922.** Emigrated to the United States. Papashvily tells his American story in dialect in *Anything Can Happen:* "The weeks seemed extra long that first half year I was in New York. No holidays, no feast days, no celebrations to break up the time and then when Saturday came around I had only twelve dollars, at most fourteen dollars in my pay envelope.

"The man I met in Central Park on my first day in America gave me a job in his garage like he promised. But after I was there about two months his wife's mother got sick and they closed up and moved to the country. With my poor language, it wasn't easy to find another place.

"I tried silk mill and after that factory where they made statues—ugly ones—from plaster. I stayed there until head artist gave me camel to cast, only looked like a cow, this camel. I was ashamed to make such a monstrosity animal so I

changed shape little bit here and there to give some camel personality to it.

"But when artist saw he got mad and told me how many schools he was in—London, Paris, Dresden—(just my point, no camels living in any of those places, certainly) and I'm fired again.

"Then I went for house painter but somehow the boss and me didn't suit each other. Finally I met a Georgian, there were only two, three of us in New York this time, who worked in a cleaning factory and he took me for his assistant. It was awful place. I dipped the clothes to take away spots. The gas we used came up in my head and through my throat and out my ears. My every piece of meat whole week long was spiced with that gas.

"After this I went in Ambridge [Pennsylvania] and got work in a railroad yard and after that in garage. The months rolled by. I was nearly three years from Tiflis now. Three years. In all that time except for those first few months in New York I never heard one word spoken in my own language—Georgian.

"My days were flat and between the dish and my mouth food turned to sawdust. Even wine lost its pleasure and in my heart lay a cold stone that wouldn't melt. I knew what my sickness was. Loneliness.

"True . . . I had a good job I liked in the Packard factory. And by little by I began to make some American friends, men who worked beside me in the shop and they paid me honor to invite me to their homes. In so many things our ways were different, but I liked them. I liked the habit they had of laughing all the time—even at themselves; and the way they snapped the chains of old ideas and dared to try everything, to live and die by their own experience. For me, it was a new kind of bravery.

"All this was good but it didn't help the gnawing at my heart. In fact the more American friends I made seemed the lonelier I got. I felt like an ax had chopped my life in two and I missed the part that was left in Georgia. I wanted my new friends but I wanted somebody, too, that I could remember home with. Then I could be a whole man again." [George and Helen Papashvily, *Anything Can Happen,* Harper, 1945.[2]]

**1932.** Worked in several automobile factories in Detroit. Papashvily held countless jobs, including dishwashing and taxi cab driving. "It's a heart-tearing sight to watch a person sicken and grow thin but oh so worse to see a city die before your eyes. Yet that's what happened to Detroit the winter of 1932. The city, so bright before and full of living, died.

"First the factories went and then one by one the little shops, where somebody made his few pennies, closed and left the empty windows staring like dead eyes into deserted streets. The new houses and office buildings stood half finished because everywhere the money was running out like blood draining away.

"Came each pay, more and more men found the pink slip that means don't come back again, clipped to their checks. I watched so many, when it was their turn, and saw them pale like men who feel the first chill of typhus. Because it was a kind of typhus, this depression, only the dying was slower.

"And why did all this happen? Nobody knew. A stock market in New York? That's what some people thought. But then like others said, 'How can a stock market thousands of miles away, never saw me, reach out and take away my piece of bread here in Detroit?'

"For my part I didn't know the answer, if there was one. Only it seemed a shame to keep my job longer when men with families needed it, so I quit. With a coupla [sic] hundred dollars more I had saved by this time, I started a wrecking business to buy old cars, scrap them and sell the parts and metal for what I could get."[2]

During the Depression Papashvily left Detroit and moved to Hollywood, California where he became a movie extra. "In Hollywood there wasn't much choice of jobs that time except to be in the movies. So I went in the casting office and the next thing I'm in the movies, too. But always they called me to play Cossacks. No variety.

"One day, I forget if I was turning back the hordes of Genghis Khan that time or was I being mean to the Volga boatmen again, well anyway, I got disgusted. I said to myself: If you wanted to ride a horse all day and wear a *cherkesska* and a fur hat you could have stayed home in Kobiantkari. No, you came in America for something different. Better you look to find that something.

"So I went to San Francisco and I looked for a job there."[2]

For a time, Papashvily ran a lunch business and joined the National Guard. While in California, he met and married Helen Waite. "At last the great day came; the ceremony was over and I'm a married man. And after all the congratulations were said and we got enough good wishes to furnish our life for a century it came time to sit down at the beautiful table where candles shone and roses bloomed and the food—well maybe some of the American guests were little surprised and shocked to see this different kind of wedding refreshment. But no so surprised they couldn't eat with brisk appetite and not so shocked they didn't come back for second, and might as well tell the truth, third and fourth helpings.

"But at last we were on our way. Person can enjoy to have one wedding but for my part I don't think I could ever live through two.

"Even with best advices in the world still it's hard for an American girl to marry with a foreigner and learn different ways, different food, different language.

"But I must say, everything considered, my wife, Helena Gerbertovna, got along pretty well. She learned how to make *ajepsandal,* that's onions fried until they turn to golden rings, then mixed with baked eggplant and tomatoes, and she got to be very good at corn bread. She even picked up a few words in Georgian and she made the acquaintance of my countrymen. Only mostly, with the exception of Dzea Vanno, they were all so long from home they acted more like Americans.

"In fact only once Helena Gerbertovna ever got off on her wrong feets and still when I remember it makes me laugh—but not out loud if Helena Gerbertovna can see me.

"A short time before I married I had good luck with an invention I made. All my life I was making inventions just for

Unless you've loved an animal—given one a corner of your heart to live in, then this book is not for you.
■ (From *Thanks to Noah* by George and Helen Papashvily. Illustrated by Jack Wilson.)

fun. When I was about ten years old I invented a wooden gun with wooden bullets and I shot a rabbit with it. And the only thing about the war I enjoyed was the piles of junk machinery we had, all so badly made that whatever you did to them was an improvement.

"Now I found out that in America they're crazy about any kind of inventions, especially those that work, and they're glad to pay good money for them. The trick is to find a way to make simple something that's hard to do or else figure out a complicated process for easy things so they look more important.

"A short time after we married I was working with duplicating paper. Nothing very interesting but to be near the place it was made we moved to the South, a small town in Virginia. No Greeks or Syrians or Russians in that town. Nobody. I guess I was the only foreigner inside the city limits."[2]

**1935.** Moved to Bucks County, Pennsylvania with his wife. There they established Ertoba Farm. "First thing I found out is that one of the best ways to make money on a farm is by not raising chickens. But it cost me a thousand dollars and took me a year to find this out. A very unsocial animal, chickens, picking each other to death. And stupid besides. Flopping and fluttering, creating commotions, they practically invite foxes and dogs and skunks and weasels to chase them.

"Well after chickens I tried goats. Why people don't try to understand goats? They have silky coats and gentle mouths and the dantiest appetite can be—a special weed here, patch of sweet grass there, few pear tree leaves for appetizer; a crunch of bitter stalk; a snuffle at the clover blossoms—they pick like meadow was a cafeteria counter. Besides they give milk that's all cream. What more could a person want? But you can't get nobody to buy their milk or the good cheese from it neither. All have prejudices. 'Goats smell.' Ridiculous. They don't smell half as much as people.

"So next I tried bees, then corn and after that sheep and grain and pigs and flax. I was working right through the farm bulletins and pretty soon almost nothing be left except Drying Fruit for the Export Market and Raising Peafowl for Pin-Money and Pleasure."[2]

HELEN and GEORGE PAPASHVILY

On their farm George Papashvily discovered from a neighbor what vocation he really wanted to follow. "The sculptor, Aaron Ben Shmuel, lived near our farm and I used to help him move stones. They were wonderful, those stones, but I had no idea I could carve them. We kept boarders then to make a living. Queer people. All wanted to write or paint, or do something, but most of them, instead of doing it, just talked about it.

"I said, 'You fellows can go on and discuss. From now I am going to be sculptor.' So I went out and made me a sheep from a piece of oak.

"After that I started to carve trays and benches from wood. Then, one day, I chiseled myself out of five dollars and bought a piece of stone.

"Although I helped Shmuel move his stones, I was almost never around when he worked on them, so I had no idea how to start. But finally I carved a sheep, and it is right here now, out on the terrace. After that I lost all desire to carve in wood." [From an article entitled "The Sculpture of George Papashvily," Dorothy Grafly, *American Artist*, October, 1955.³]

The artist borrowed the tools for his first stone sculptures from the men who worked in a nearby quarry. During World War II Papashvily worked in a factory, but when the war ended he returned to his farm.

**1944.** Became a United States citizen.

**1945.** *Anything Can Happen*, a book describing Papashvily's experiences as an immigrant and written with his wife, Helen, was published. The book was an international success. "We had a little money then, so I stayed home and worked at my stones. I never knew anything but work, so I just kept on working. When I finished one piece, I started another the next day."³

**1951.** First exhibition at the Allentown Art Museum. Later that year, Papashvily had his first one man gallery show. "I don't make sculpture. I just bring out what I find in the stone. It has been there all along, waiting for someone to see it."³

**1954.** *Dogs and People*, another book written with his wife, was published.

**1973.** The Papashvilys wrote another book which described their return trip to George Papashvily's native Georgia after an absence of more than forty years. *Home and Home Again* was published that year. "When I met and married an American girl, the first promise I made her was that I would take her to Georgia. But there came the Depression and then the war, and in those long years I built a new life. I was an American citizen. I had a home. I had work.... My days were full of the present.

"Time went by. The few letters I received told me little. During the war and for two years afterward I heard nothing at all. When at last word came it was to say my father and my aunt were dead. After that I did not think of Georgia so often. And yet—I did not forget.

"Spring never came to our Pennsylvania hillsides but I remembered the Cornelian cherries would be in golden bloom above Dushet, and when it was harvest time, I always wondered who gathers now the grapes my aunt planted, who sits in the dappled sun beneath her arbor, who drinks the wine? When I dreamed, I dreamed always of Kobiantkari where I was born, a village on the mountainside above a stream that has no name but 'Our Own.'

"How often I thought to return, but somehow it was never possible. Time and money, as everybody knows, seldom keep company and where one is the other is not, and so it was with me. But finally a day came when by chance I had both, and I said to my wife, 'Let us go to Georgia.'

"'When?'

"'As soon as we can pack our suitcases.'"[1]

**March 29, 1978.** Died in Cambria, California five months before his eightieth birthday.

*FOR MORE INFORMATION SEE: New York Times,* December 31, 1944; *Springfield Republican,* December 31, 1944; George and Helen Papashvily, *Anything Can Happen,* Harper, 1945, reissued, 1966; *Saturday Review of Literature,* January 13, 1945; Stanley J. Kunitz, editor, *Twentieth Century Authors,* first supplement, H. W. Wilson, 1955; D. Grafly, "Sculpture of George Papashvily," *American Artist,* October, 1955; G. and H. Papashvily, *Home and Home Again,* Harper, 1973; Obituaries—*New York Times,* March 31, 1978; *Time,* April 10, 1978.

(Died March 29, 1978)

# PAPASHVILY, Helen (Waite) 1906-

*PERSONAL:* Born December 19, 1906, in Stockton, Calif.; daughter of Herbert (a contractor) and Isabella Findlay (Lochead) Waite; married George Papashvily (an author; died, 1978). *Education:* Attended the University of California at Berkeley. *Address:* R D 4, Quakertown, Penn. 18951.

*CAREER:* Author. Has done bibliographical research, collected books for private libraries, and worked in several bookstores, owning and managing the Moby Dick Bookshop, Allentown, Penn., 1939-50.

*WRITINGS: All the Happy Endings: A Study of the Domestic Novel in America, the Women Who Wrote It, the Women Who Read It, in the Nineteenth Century,* Harper, 1956, reprinted, Kennikat, 1972; *Louisa May Alcott* (illustrated by Bea Holmes), Houghton, Mifflin, 1965.

With husband, George Papashvily: *Anything Can Happen,* Harper, 1945, reissued, 1966; *Yes and No Stories: A Book of Georgian Folk Tales* (illustrated by Simon Lissim), Harper,

1946; *Thanks to Noah* (illustrated by Jack Wilson), Harper, 1951; *Dogs and People* (illustrated by Marguerite Kirmse), Lippincott, 1954; (with the editors of Time-Life Books) *Russian Cooking,* Time-Life Books, 1969; *Home and Home Again,* Harper, 1973.

*SIDELIGHTS:* **December 19, 1906.** Born in Stockton, California to Herbert and Isabella Waite. Helen Papashvily was educated at the University of California at Berkeley.

In the early 1930's she met and married George Papashvily, a young immigrant from the Soviet state of Georgia. "Many years ago when we ... announced our decision to marry we were warned separately and privately against such folly.

"Our respective friends, for we had as then no mutual ones, pointed out that we shared very little in common. Our language, our nationality, our religion, our education, our cultural background could scarcely have been more dissimilar.

"According to all the charts and the questionnaires marriage counselors devise, and on the basis of the graphs that can predict happiness statistically, our friends had some justification for their forebodings.

"Perhaps time might have proved them right except that we soon discovered our early life and training had not been so *very* different after all, even though we grew up a world apart.

"For both of us, it seemed, had passed our childhood under the same kind of tutelage, and from earliest infancy each had been protected, disciplined, supervised, companioned, amused and instructed by beloved dogs—Duke, an Irish setter and Laddie, a collie who rest now in the foothills beyond the San Joaquin Valley in California and Basar, Juliko and Murka, golden trackers, buried in a mountain valley on the southern slope of the Caucasus." [George and Helen Papashvily, *Dogs and People,* Lippincott, 1954.[1]]

**1935.** With her husband bought Ertoba Farm in Quakertown, Pennsylvania. "After we married and had our first home, we needed a dog, of course, to share it. That was when we bought Keddana. A little later his mate, another Murka, was a present to us and to Keddana. Although both were German shepherds, they were completely unlike in personality and temperament.

"Keddana (which means 'dove-colored' in Georgian and soon became shortened to Keddy) was well mannered, well bred and good-looking, and since no one had ever challenged it, very sure of his place in the world. While far from stupid, he always gave the impression that it was just slightly bad form to be too bright. We loved him very dearly but privately, to ourselves, we sometimes called him Mr. Smug.

"It has often puzzled us that so many of the people we meet own canine geniuses while our dogs seem to be only fair to muddling middle bracket I Q's, just about able, as the saying goes, to get out of their own way (if not always out of ours).

"The one exception was Murka who, in the opinion of all her friends, and she had scores, was the smartest dog that ever lived. There is no doubt she knew exactly what she wanted and how, with a minimum of effort to achieve her objective. She was shrewd, calculating, competent, almost always right and like many superior beings beautiful, good humored and immovably stubborn as well. She had a highly developed sense of the dramatic, a wide streak of ham and sometimes she laughed although, to tell the truth, we seldom caught the joke.

"It is not always convenient to belong to a dog of this caliber but we would not change a minute of the seventeen joyous years she and Keddana gave us before they left us within the same month.

"We had their children too and grandchildren and great-grandchildren—nearly two hundred puppies that went to delight as many boys and girls and make as many homes happier. Two of Murka's puppies we kept for ourselves. The first was a beautiful silver-gray girl we called Fox. She was wild and shy, happy and sad, given to rushes and retreats.

"Later on we had one of Fox's sisters. We named her Kitri, which in Georgian means 'cucumber,' because she looked as fat and sleek as one. Black and gold, merry and loving, she was a puppy all the fifteen years she lived.

"Now we have Kitri's son, Acavar, with a burnished coat, topaz eyes and golden heart to match. Like every dog we ever owned, he is our favorite."[1]

**1939.** Owned and managed the Moby Dick Bookshop in Allentown, Pa. until 1950. Helen Papashvily worked in several bookstores and has done bibliographical research and collected books for private libraries.

**1945.** First book, *Anything Can Happen*, written with her husband, was published.

**1954.** *Dogs and People*, another book co-authored with her husband, was published. The book was created from the Papashvilys' own love for dogs and their personal experience in dog training and raising. "We did not go into the puppy business with any preconceived plan (hence our stern warnings to others). At first we gave our puppies away but the tried-and-true friends who can be trusted with a 'free' puppy will never, in the widest acquaintance list, equal the production capacity of a good brood matron.

"'All sentimental twaddle,' a real friend of dogs told us when we said it seemed a betrayal of our relationship with our dogs to make a profit on them. 'Dogs should be rare expensive items . . . sold at a premium . . . limited by law to a small number . . . apportioned only to a long waiting list of desirable owners. . . . Then you'd never see a homeless dog kicked and chased from one corner to the other.'

"Our reaction was never quite that violent, but eventually we concluded (and a sad commentary on human nature it is) that most people—not all, but far too many—equate value and price. A dog that costs nothing is worth just exactly that.

"We never wanted our dogs to win prizes or be best of show. And fortunately so, perhaps, for probably to be quite honest they lacked the proper points to acquire such honors. We were satisfied to supply strong, healthy, well-tempered puppies, good specimens of a beautiful breed, at reasonable prices to families that wanted a trustworthy companion. There is room in the world, or should be, for good dogs as well as for outstanding champions."[1]

**1956.** Using her literary background, Papashvily wrote a book about the domestic novel, a literary form hitherto ignored by literary critics. *All the Happy Endings* was published. "I have had a wide correspondence with readers of the domestic novel. . . .

"Throughout the nineteenth century this peculiar literary form, . . . flourished as never before or since. Hundreds of authors turned out thousands of titles that sold millions of copies. Scarcely a literate woman in the United States but read some of these novels—*The Wide, Wide World, Ishmael; or In the Depths, Tempest and Sunshine, Elsie Dinsmore, St. Elmo, Sunnybank*—to name but a few that in time acquired a kind of subclassic status.

"Now these sentimental tales and their authors are almost, if not quite, forgotten by a new generation of readers; accorded only the briefest mention by literary historians, banished from library shelves. Yet such books possess greater value today, perhaps, than when they were written, for in them, as in all popular literature, are mirrored the fears and anxieties and frustrations, the plans and hopes and joys of those who read them so avidly. Their crumbling pages reveal the dream world of women—as it existed in the nineteenth century and lingered on to influence the twentieth.

"The domestic or, according to its critics, the sentimental novel was in general what the terms imply—a tale of contemporary domestic life, ostensibly sentimental in tone and with few exceptions almost always written by women for women. This and a certain similarity in the binding style, 'large, handsome duodecimo, cloth, gilt,' would seem, at first glance, to be all many of the domestic novels had in common.

"Like all who write on popular literature, I owe a great debt to James D. Hart's *The Popular Book*, to Frank Luther Mott's *Golden Multitudes* and most especially to Herbert Ross Brown's *The Sentimental Novel in America 1789-1860*. Only Dr. Brown's encouragement coupled with his assurance that he did not intend to carry his definitive study chronologically farther in a future volume emboldened me to attempt this work." [Helen Papashvily, *All the Happy Endings*, Harper, 1956.[2]]

Helen Papashvily is credited with writing down her husband George's experiences as an immigrant in America, which later developed into their best seller, *Anything Can Happen*. Originally, one sketch appeared in *Common Ground*, and at the suggestion of an editor at Harper, the material was expanded into a book.

She has also written several books of her own. Of *All the Happy Endings*, the *New York Times* wrote, "The author . . . is fortunately more interested in the social aspects of the fiction she describes than in discovering forgotten literary gems, and therein lies the value of her book. She writes with clarity and vigor and she has provided a chart through a sentimental wilderness that few nowadays would have the temerity to enter. It is a book worth the prayerful consideration of all who are concerned with the world of women." Added *Saturday Review:* "Like most theses, Mrs. Papashvily does not tell the whole story of the domestic novel or of the social revolution it helped bring about. She slurs over some of the writers and novels that do not conform to her pattern. But on the whole she has made an important contribution to our understanding of the nineteenth century and its women. Happily she is entertaining to boot." The *Christian Science Monitor* noted that the book, ". . . is endlessly informative, and as accurate as could be expected of a book with so much detail. In the last forty years it has been the fashion to make a jest of those earlier novels, and Mrs. Papashvily cannot quite resist that tone though she gives them a serious sociological purpose. For the most part her tone is crisp, even a little acid about woman's situation in a man's world. Her readers, who recall her writing in *Anything Can Happen,* are prepared for the light touch. . . ."

*FOR MORE INFORMATION SEE:* George and Helen Papashvily, *Anything Can Happen,* Harper, 1945, reissued, 1966; Stanley J. Kunitz, editor, *Twentieth Century Authors,* first supplement, H. W. Wilson, 1955; *New York Times,* October 21, 1956; *Christian Science Monitor,* October 22, 1956; *Saturday Review,* November 10, 1956; G. and H. Papashvily, *Home and Home Again,* Harper, 1973.

# PARADIS, Marjorie (Bartholomew) 1886?-1970

*PERSONAL:* Born about 1886, in Montclair, New Jersey; married Adrian F. Paradis. *Education:* Attended Columbia University.

*CAREER:* Author of children's books. Taught writing courses at the Chautauqua Writers Workshop and the YWCA.

*WRITINGS—*Fiction: *A Dinner of Herbs,* Century, 1928; *The Caddis,* Century, 1929; *The New Freedom: A Comedy in Three Acts* (play), Samuel French, 1931; *It Happened One Day: A Novel,* Harper, 1932; (with Adele Louise De Leeuw) *Golden Shadow,* Macmillan, 1951; *Timmy and the Tiger* (illustrated by Marc Simont), Harper, 1952; *One-Act Plays for All-Girl Casts,* Plays, 1952; *Midge Bennett of Duncan Hall,* Abelard, 1953; *Time Is Now,* Abelard, 1953; (with A. L. De Leeuw) *Dear Stepmother,* Macmillan, 1956; *Maid of Honor,* Dodd, 1959; *Mr. De Luca's Horse* (illustrated by Judith Brown), Atheneum, 1962; *Flash Flood at Hollow Creek* (illustrated by Albert F. Michini), Westminster Press, 1963; *Jeanie* (illustrated by Alex Stein), Westminster Press, 1963; *Too Many Fathers* (illustrated by Charles Geer), Atheneum, 1963.

*ADAPTATIONS—*Movie: "This Side of Heaven", adaptation of *It Happened One Day,* Metro-Goldwyn-Mayer, 1934.

*SIDELIGHTS:* "I was born in Montclair, New Jersey, but I grew up in Brooklyn, New York, and attended Erasmus Hall and, later, Columbia University.

"As a little girl, I was very fearful about my mother. I thought that if I were not along to take care of her when she went out, she would fall over a precipice. Of course that would be a difficult thing to do in Brooklyn, where there are no precipices. Still I worried about her, and that's really why I raised such ructions when she left me home." [From an article entitled "Timmy's Imagination," by Marjorie Paradis, *Young Wings,* August, 1952.[1]]

Besides writing several children's books, she taught courses at the Chautauqua Writers Workshop and the YWCA. She and her husband, Adrian F. Paradis, lived in Brooklyn and Westchester, New York.

In 1952 she wrote a book, *Timmy and the Tiger,* to help children overcome their many and common fears. "My book, *Timmy and the Tiger,* was written for a very special boy, a boy who, like Timmy, has a lot of imagination. Anyone with a real imagination can think of the greatest lot of things to be afraid of. Grown-up people are like that, too. But they don't call it fear; they say it is worry. What difference does the

**MARJORIE PARADIS**

name make? Worry and fear are really one and the same thing.

"Many books have been written to help people get the best of their fears, but those books are mostly for older people. Boys and girls have been overlooked. If they admit that they are afraid of this or that, they are scolded and told not to be cowards. Naturally they hide their fears, and then the fears grow worse, just as potatoes put in a dark closet sprout and spoil.

"So I figured that I might be able to help other boys and girls if I wrote about Timmy and his secret fears, his shame over these fears, and his courage in rising above them." [1]

Paradis collaborated with Adèle de Leeuw on a book, *It Happened One Day,* in 1932 and in 1934 that book was adapted as a Metro-Goldwyn-Mayer movie, "This Side of Heaven." *Too Many Fathers,* a book that combined the imagination of a child with the reality of a situation—one of her favorite themes—was published in 1963.

Throughout many of her writings, Paradis demonstrated a talent for developing characters which were appealing to young readers. The author's book, *Golden Shadow,* was jointly written with Adèle Louise De Leeuw and dealt with the adventures of a young heroine during the post-Civil War years. A reviewer for the *Library Journal* found it "[an] excellent study of family and sibling relationships with an appealing love story. . . ."

*Too Many Fathers* was one of Paradis' more recent books. Like some of the author's previous books, the story combines the imagination of a child with the reality of a situation. A review in *Horn Book* noted, "Liveliness, humor, characters that are both engaging and convincing, and conversation that rings true make this an unusually good story of contemporary young people."

*HOBBIES AND OTHER INTERESTS:* Portrait painting and hooking rugs.

*FOR MORE INFORMATION SEE*—Obituary: *New York Times,* July 8, 1970.

(Died July 2, 1970)

## PARISH, Peggy 1927-

*PERSONAL:* Born in 1927, in Manning, S.C.; daughter of Herman and Cecil (Rogers) Parish. *Education:* University of South Carolina, 1944-48; graduate work at Peabody College, 1950. *Home:* Manning, S.C.

*CAREER:* Author. Teacher, 1948-67, in Texas and New York; part-time instructor in creative dancing, 1948-52; has also worked in advertising. *Member:* Authors' Guild.

*WRITINGS: My Golden Book of Manners* (illustrated by Richard Scarry), Golden Press, 1962; *Good Hunting Little Indian* (illustrated by Leonard Weisgard), Young Scott Books, 1962; *Let's Be Indians* (illustrated by Arnold Lobel), Harper, 1962; *Willy Is My Brother* (illustrated by Shirley Hughes), W. R. Scott, 1963; *Amelia Bedelia* (illustrated by Fritz Siebel), Harper, 1963, reissued, Scholastic Book Services, 1970; *Thank You, Amelia Bedelia* (illustrated by F. Siebel), Harper, 1964; *The Story of Grains: Wheat, Corn, and Rice* (pictures by William Moyers), Grosset & Dunlap, 1965; *Amelia Bedelia and the Surprise Shower* (illustrated by F. Siebel), Harper, 1966; *Key to the Treasure* (illustrated by Paul Frame), Macmillan, 1966, reissued, 1971; *Let's Be Early Settlers with Daniel Boone* (illustrated by A. Lobel), Harper, 1967; *Clues in the Woods* (illustrated by P. Frame), Macmillan, 1968; *Little Indian* (illustrated by John E. John-

**PEGGY PARISH**

son), Simon & Schuster, 1968; *A Beastly Circus* (illustrated by Peter Parnall), Simon & Schuster, 1969; *Jumper Goes to School* (illustrated by Cyndy Szekeres), Simon & Schuster, 1969; *Granny and the Indians* (illustrated by Brinton Turkle), Macmillan, 1969.

*Ootah's Lucky Day* (illustrated by Mamoru Funai), Harper, 1970; *Granny and the Desperadoes* (illustrated by Steven Kellogg), Macmillan, 1970; *Costumes to Make* (illustrated by Lynn Sweat), Macmillan, 1970; *Snapping Turtle's All Wrong Day* (illustrated by J. E. Johnson), Simon & Schuster, 1970; *Sheet Magic: Games, Toys, and Gifts from Old Sheets* (illustrated by L. Sweat), Macmillan, 1971; *Haunted House* (illustrated by P. Frame), Macmillan, 1971; *Come Back, Amelia Bedelia* (illustrated by Wallace Tripp), Harper, 1971; *Granny, the Baby, and the Big Gray Thing* (illustrated by L. Sweat), Macmillan, 1972; *Play Ball, Amelia Bedelia* (illustrated by W. Tripp), Harper, 1972; *Too Many Rabbits* (illustrated by Leonard Kessler), Macmillan, 1974; *Dinosaur Time* (illustrated by A. Lobel), Harper, 1974; *December Decorations: A Holiday How-To Book* (illustrated by Barbara Wolff), Macmillan, 1975; *Pirate Island Adventure* (illustrated by P. Frame), Macmillan, 1975; *Good Work, Amelia Bedelia* (illustrated by L. Sweat), Morrow, 1976; *Let's Celebrate: Holiday Decorations You Can Make* (illustrated by L. Sweat), Morrow, 1976; *Teach Us, Amelia Bedelia* (illustrated by L. Sweat), Morrow, 1977; *Mind Your Manners* (illustrated by Marilyn Hafner), Greenwillow, 1978; *Zed and the Monsters* (illustrated by Paul Galdone), Doubleday, 1979; *Be Ready at Eight* (illustrated by Leonard Kessler), Macmillan, 1979; *Beginning Mobiles* (illustrated by Lynn Sweat), Macmillan, 1979.

*ADAPTATIONS*—Filmstrips: "Amelia Bedelia," "Thank You, Amelia Bedelia," "Come Back, Amelia Bedelia," and "Play Ball, Amelia Bedelia."

*SIDELIGHTS:* Born and raised in Manning, South Carolina, Peggy Parish attended the University of South Carolina where she received a degree in English in 1948. She taught English and creative dancing in the Oklahoma panhandle country and third grade in the Kentucky coal-mining areas before moving to New York City where she taught third grade for many years at the Dalton School.

After teaching, Parish decided to write a book. Although she had never taken a writing course, writing had always been easy for her. At first her manuscripts met with rejection by publishers until she was introduced to some editors who helped her with her first books.

Since 1962 Parish has written over thirty books for children including her popular "Amelia Bedelia" books for primary children. "Sometimes it seems to take forever to plan and write a book. Other times the plot for a book seems to pop out of no place begging to be put down on paper. This is what happened with *Too Many Rabbits.* It required no conscious effort on my part. The words just seemed to flow and I really enjoyed writing it.

"I wish this would happen more often, but it has happened only a couple of times for me. Usually a book takes a lot of thinking, planning, and just hard work in writing and rewriting time and time again before it's ready to be published.

"Children have always been my life, so writing stories for children came naturally. I do have special feelings about writing for children. I don't try to teach anything in my stories—I write just for fun."

**Amelia Bedelia got some scissors. She snipped a little here and a little there. And she changed those towels.** ■ (From *Amelia Bedelia* by Peggy Parish. Illustrated by Fritz Siebel.)

Parish is presently a children's book reviewer on "Carolina Today" television show an NBC affiliate station in Columbia and also runs a children book review service.

*FOR MORE INFORMATION SEE: Horn Book,* December, 1963, December, 1966, August, 1969, October, 1970, December, 1971, August, 1972, August, 1974, August, 1976, April, 1977, June, 1977; Margery Fisher, *Who's Who in Children's Books,* Holt, 1975.

# PETERSHAM, Maud (Fuller) 1890-1971

*PERSONAL:* Born August 5, 1890, in Kingston, New York; daughter of a Baptist minister; married Miska Petersham; children: Miki (a son). *Education:* Graduated from Vassar College; studied art at the New York School of Fine and Applied Art. *Home:* Woodstock, New York.

*CAREER:* Author and illustrator of books for children. *Awards, honors:* Runner-up for the Caldecott Medal, 1942, for *An American ABC;* Caldecott Medal, 1946, for *The Rooster Crows.*

*WRITINGS—*With husband, Miska Petersham: *Miki,* Doubleday, Doran, 1929; *The Ark of Father Noah and Mother Noah,* Doubleday, Doran, 1930; *The Christ Child, as Told by Matthew and Luke,* Doubleday, Doran, 1931; *Auntie and Celia Jane and Miki,* Doubleday, Doran, 1932; *Miki and Mary: Their Search for Treasures,* Viking, 1934; *The Story Book of Things We Use,* J. C. Winston, 1933; *The Story Book of Houses,* J. C. Winston, 1933; *The Story Book of Transportation,* J. C. Winston, 1933; *The Story Book of Food,* J. C. Winston, 1933; *The Story Book of Clothes,* J. C. Winston, 1933; *Get-a-Way and Háry János,* Viking, 1933.

*The Story Book of Wheels, Ships, Trains, Aircraft* (each story also published separately), J. C. Winston, 1935; *The Story Book of Earth's Treasures: Gold, Coal, Oil, Iron and Steel* (each story also published separately), J. C. Winston, 1935; *The Story Book of Foods from the Field: Wheat, Corn, Rice, Sugar* (each story also published separately), J. C. Winston, 1936; *The Story Book of Sugar,* reissued as *Let's Learn about Sugar* (illustrated by James E. Barry), Harvey House, 1969; *Stories from the Old Testament: Joseph, Moses, Ruth, David* (each story also published separately), J. C. Winston, 1938; *The Story Book of Things We Wear,* J. C. Winston, 1939 [each story published separately in 1939 as *The Story Book of Cotton, The Story Book of Wool, The Story Book of Rayon, The Story Book of Silk,* the last reissued as *Let's Learn about Silk* (illustrated by J. E. Barry), Harvey House, 1967].

*An American ABC* (illustrated by the authors), Macmillan, 1941, reissued, 1966; *America's Stamps: The Story of One Hundred Years of U.S. Postage Stamps,* Macmillan, 1947, reissued, 1967; *The Box with Red Wheels,* Macmillan, 1949, reissued, 1973; *The Circus Baby,* Macmillan, 1950, reissued, 1972; *Story of the Presidents of the United States of America,* Macmillan, 1953, reissued, 1966; *Off to Bed: Seven Stories for Wide-Awakes,* Macmillan, 1954; *The Boy Who Had No Heart,* Macmillan, 1955; *The Silver Mace: A Story of Williamsburg,* Macmillan, 1956, reissued, 1961; *The Peppernuts,* Macmillan, 1958; *Shepherd Psalm,* Macmillan, 1962.

*Illustrator—*with husband, Miska Petersham: William Bowen, *Enchanted Forest,* Macmillan, 1920; Carl Sandburg, *Rootabaga Stories,* Harcourt, 1922, reissued, 1974; Charles Lamb, *Tales from Shakespeare,* Macmillan, 1923; C. Sandburg, *Rootabaga Pigeons,* Harcourt, 1923; Sisters of Mercy (St. Xavier College, Chicago), *Marquette Readers,* Macmillan, 1924; Mabel Guinnip La Rue, *In Animal Land,* Macmillan, 1924; Margery Clark, *Poppy Seed Cakes,* Doubleday, 1924; Inez M. Howard, Alice Hawthorne, and Mae Howard, *Language Garden: A Primary Language Book,* Macmillan, 1924; Harriott Fansler and Isidoro Panlasigui, *Philippine National Literature,* Macmillan, 1925; Bessie B. Coleman, W. L. Uhl, and J. F. Hosic, *Pathway to Reading,* Silver, Burdette, 1925; Florence C. Coolidge, *Little Ugly Face, and Other Indian Tales,* Macmillan, 1925; John W. Wayland, *History Stories for Primary Grades,* Macmillan, 1925.

Elizabeth C. Miller, *Children of the Mountain Eagle,* Doubleday, 1927; *Everyday Canadian Primer,* Macmillan, 1928; Marguerite Clement, *Where was Bobby?,* Doubleday, Doran, 1928; Wilhelmina Harper and A. J. Hamilton, compilers, *Pleasant Pathways,* Macmillan, 1928; W. Harper and A. J. Hamilton, compilers, *Winding Roads,* Macmillan, 1928-29; Harper and Hamilton, compilers, *Heights and Highways,* Macmillan, 1929; Harper and Hamilton, compilers, *Far Away Hills,* Macmillan, 1929; E. C. Miller, *Pran of Albania,* Doubleday, Doran, 1929; Miller, *Young Trajan,* Doubleday, 1931; Sydney V. Rowland, W. D. Lewis, and E. J. Marshall, compilers, *Beckoning Road,* J. C. Winston, 1931; S. V. Rowland, W. D. Lewis, and E. J. Marshall, *Rich Cargoes,* J. C. Winston, 1931; Rowland, Lewis, and Marshall, *Wings of Adventure,* J. C. Winston, 1931; Rowland, Lewis, and Marshall, *Treasure Trove,* J. C. Winston, 1931.

Carlo Collodi, pseudonym of Carlo Lorenzini, *Adventures of Pinocchio,* Garden City Publishing, 1932; Johanna Spyri, *Heidi,* Garden City Publishing, 1932; Jean Young Ayer, *Picnic Book,* Macmillan, 1934; Post Wheeler, *Albanian Wonder Tales,* Doubleday, 1936; Marie Barringer, *The Four and Lena,* Doubleday, 1938; Miriam Evangeline Mason, *Susannah, the Pioneer Cow,* Macmillan, 1941; Emilie F. Johnson, *Little Book of Prayers,* Viking, 1941; *Story of Jesus: A Little New Testament,* Macmillan, 1942, reissued, 1967; Ethan A. Cross and Elizabeth Carney, editors, *Literature,* 1943-46; Mother Goose, *The Rooster Crows: A Book of American Rhymes and Jingles,* Macmillan, 1945; Association for Childhood Education, Literature Committee, *Told under the Christmas Tree,* Macmillan, 1948; Elsie S. Eells, *Tales of Enchantment from Spain,* Dodd, 1950; Washington Irving, *Rip Van Winkle [and] The Legend of Sleepy Hollow,* Macmillan, 1951; Benjamin Franklin, *Bird in the Hand,* Macmillan, 1951; Eric P. Kelly, *In Clean Hay,* Macmillan, 1953; M. E. Mason, *Miss Posy Longlegs,* Macmillan, 1955.

*SIDELIGHTS:* **August 5, 1890.** Born in Kingston, New York. The daughter of a Baptist minister, Petersham was raised with her three sisters. "A parsonage with four lively girls was certainly not a dull place. One of the many clergymen who visited our home once said that the only way to sleep in our house was to put a pillow over one's head as well as under! Leaving Kingston we went to live in Sioux Falls, South Dakota, then on to Newburg, New York, and finally to Scranton, Pennsylvania. My sisters and I fidgeted about through long church services and daily morning prayers, but the stories told by visiting missionaries at our table were as exciting as fairy tales to me. We were busy with school and play in winter and spent beautiful summer months with our Quaker grandfather. We were a bit in awe of Grandfather who believed that children should be seen, not heard, and should share in household duties.

**The Children of Williamsburg hurried past the gaol with fear and dread. Outside the gaol stood the pillary and stocks. Those who committed petty crimes were fastened here for all to see. Bolder boys threw sticks or stones at these unhappy culprits. ■** (From *The Silver Mace* by Maud and Miska Petersham. Illustrated by the authors.)

**The mother entered from the stove room with a huge pot of steaming soup and poured it out into wooden bowls before each of the children.** ■ (From *In Clean Hay* by Eric P. Kelly. Illustrated by Maud and Miska Petersham.)

"I loved picture books as a child and was always happy with pencil and paper in my hands." [Lee Bennett Hopkins, *Books Are by People,* Citation Press, 1969.[1]]

Petersham graduated from Vassar College and studied art in New York. Besides studying art, she worked for an advertising agency where she met her future husband, Miska. "After graduating from Vassar, I studied for one easy-going year at the New York School of Fine and Applied Art, living at the Three Arts Club. My first job was in the art department at the International Art Service, an advertising firm. Here I met Miska. After our marriage we started working on our own, free-lancing."[1]

**1920.** Began illustrating books for children when Willy Pogány, a well known illustrator and friend of her husband, gave them a children's book to illustrate that he was too busy to do. "My real art training came from working with Miska. He had graduated from the Budapest Art Academy and received several years of intensive training in different forms of art."[1]

**1929.** *Miki,* her first book written with her husband was published. The book is named after her only son. "At first we illustrated books written by others, but often we found no place in the text that lent itself to illustration, so we decided to plan a book of our own with both pictures and text.... Encouraged by May Massee [our editor], we laid out a dummy for *Miki,* working out the pictures first and then a text, which we thought would have to be rewritten by an author of children's books. We sent the dummy to May, and her answer was, to our surprise, 'We want the book just as it is!'

"Miska and I worked long hours in the studio with everything else neglected or forgotten. Ideas for books were not found by searching for them. They came out of the blue and were connected with life around us, with places we had visited, or what was foremost in our thoughts at the moment. The ideas took shape on scratch paper that was cut and folded to form a small book. Playing with roughs of pictures and text—it seemed easier to think with pictures than with words—the ideas grew to a dummy of the size and format of the book as we wanted it. If we were lucky and the dummy was accepted, the serious work of making finished drawings began. This meant hours of research as we were careful of fine details of costumes and local color where we felt this was important. Also, to cut the printing cost of full-color illustrations, we ourselves made the color separations on glass or acetate, and *this* was tedious work!"[1]

**1931.** *The Christ Child* published. "Miska and I had fun working on books for children for it often meant travel with sketchbook in hand. We wandered about in Palestine for three months before we made the illustrations for our book *The Christ Child.*"[1]

"After three months of travel in Palestine, we settled down to finish up illustrations for the book. We were living in a strange city and we were a little homesick. A baby boy was born in the apartment house where we were staying and we often left our desks and wandered into the garden to watch him sleeping there. Then we would go back to our drawings for *The Christ Child.* It was only when we left that we discovered the baby's name was 'Christian Emmanuel.' And so we dedicated that book to him." [*Caldecott Medal Books: 1938-1957,* edited by Bertha Miller and Elinor Whitney Field, Horn Book, 1957.[2]]

**1946.** Received, with her husband, the Caldecott Award for *The Rooster Crows: A Book of American Rhymes and Jingles.* The book had been designed while her son served in World War II. "Our son, Miki, was a navigator in the air force during the Second World War. After listening to the disturbing 11:00 p.m. news each night, I found that I could put myself to sleep by repeating rhymes and jingles I had known as a child. This led to the idea for the book. Collecting material and making the illustrations for this volume was a protective device for us during the worries of those days. Receiving the Caldecott Award was a happy surprise and very satisfying to us."[1]

**1950.** *Circus Baby* published. According to Petersham, their books were closely intertwined with their lives. "A visit to Sarasota, where the Ringling Brothers Circus made its winter quarters, gave us the idea for *Circus Baby,* and the hunting lodge where we ourselves spent one summer inspired *The Peppernuts.* Our life and work are so closely related that anyone who knows our books knows us."[1]

**1960.** Husband, Miska, died. Petersham sold the house they had built and lived in for forty years and moved to a smaller home, but in the same beloved town of Woodstock, New York where they had settled.

**1969.** In an interview, Petersham described her life. Her son, Miki, was affiliated with the art department at Kent University in Ohio and she had two grandchildren, Mary and Michael, who were college students. "Actually, I have two houses. This is the one where I now live. My other house, although I no longer own it, is perhaps more real to me. It is the house and studio Miska and I built and where we lived and worked some 40 years. It is a rambling house made of stone with hand-hewn beams and casement windows, a happy storybook house standing in a pine grove. I do like the view from this present house, though. I can see the nearby mountain, and over my mountain I see stars with infinity for background, which give me faith and peace.

"From the day the first seed catalog arrives until the first frost, my principal interest is my garden; I take time out for modeling clay, embroidering pictures in yarn, and sitting at my desk playing with ideas for another book for children, which as yet has not worked out to my satisfaction. I am a true branch of my homespun forefathers in many ways but am impractical and easy-going and like certain luxuries. My friends of many years are old, so I suppose I am too—in fact, I have 79 years to account for."[1]

**November 29, 1971.** Died. When asked what makes a good children's book, she replied: "For a children's book, both pictures and text must tell the story with enough drama to hold a child's attention on every page. It should not be a book to be read once and then cast aside; it should be something a child will cherish."[1]

*FOR MORE INFORMATION SEE:* I. S. Green, "Maud and Miska Petersham," *Horn Book,* July, 1946; L. Barksdale, "Petershams—Caldecott Medal Winners for 1946," *Publishers Weekly,* June 22, 1946; Bertha E. Mahony and others, compilers, *Illustrators of Children's Books, 1744-1945,* Horn Book, 1947; Elizabeth Rider Montgomery, *Story behind Modern Books,* Dodd, 1949; Stanley J. Kunitz and Howard Haycraft, editors, *Junior Book of Authors,* second revised edition, H. W. Wilson, 1951; Bertha Miller and Elinor Whitney Field, editors, *Caldecott Medal Books: 1938-1957,* Horn Book, 1957; Bertha E. Mahoney Miller and others, compilers, *Illustrators of Children's Books, 1946-56,* Horn Book, 1958; Lee Bennett Hopkins, *Books Are by People,* Citation Press, 1969; Obituaries— *New York Times,* November 30, 1971; *Washington Post,* December 3, 1971; *Publishers Weekly,* December 13, 1971.

(Died November 29, 1971)

# PETERSHAM, Miska 1888-1960

*PERSONAL:* Given name was Petrezselyem Mikaly; born September 20, 1888, in Toeroekszentmiklos, near Budapest, Hungary; emigrated to the United States, 1912, later became a naturalized citizen; married Maud Fuller; children: Miki (a son). *Education:* Attended art school in Budapest and in London. *Home:* Woodstock, New York.

*CAREER:* Author and illustrator of books for children. *Awards, honors:* Runner-up for the Caldecott Medal, 1942, for *An American ABC;* Caldecott Medal, 1946, for *The Rooster Crows.*

*WRITINGS*—With wife, Maud Petersham: *Miki,* Doubleday, Doran, 1929; *The Ark of Father Noah and Mother Noah,* Doubleday, Doran, 1930; *The Christ Child, as Told by Matthew and Luke,* Doubleday, Doran, 1931; *Auntie and Celia Jane and Miki,* Doubleday, Doran, 1932; *Miki and Mary: Their Search for Treasures,* Viking, 1934; *The Story Book of Things We Use,* J. C. Winston, 1933; *The Story Book of Houses,* J. C. Winston, 1933; *The Story Book of Transportation,* J. C. Winston, 1933; *The Story Book of Food,* J. C. Winston, 1933; *The Story Book of Clothes,* J. C. Winston, 1933; *Get-a-Way and Háry János,* Viking, 1933.

**The animals were very, very sad.**
**They wanted to play with the baby.**
■ (From *The Box With Red Wheels* by Maud and Miska Petersham. Illustrated by the authors.)

*The Story Book of Wheels, Ships, Trains, Aircraft* (each story also published separately), J. C. Winston, 1935; *The Story Book of Earth's Treasures: Gold, Coal, Oil, Iron and Steel* (each story also published separately), J. C. Winston, 1935; *The Story Book of Foods from the Field: Wheat, Corn, Rice, Sugar* (each story also published separately), J. C. Winston, 1936; *The Story Book of Sugar,* reissued as *Let's Learn about Sugar* (illustrated by James E. Barry), Harvey House, 1969; *Stories from the Old Testament: Joseph, Moses, Ruth, David* (each story also published separately), J. C. Winston, 1938; *The Story Book of Things We Wear,* J. C. Winston, 1939 [each story published separately in 1939 as *The Story Book of Cotton, The Story Book of Wool, The Story Book of Rayon, The Story Book of Silk,* the last reissued as *Let's Learn about Silk* (illustrated by J. E. Barry), Harvey House, 1967].

*An American ABC* (illustrated by the authors), Macmillan, 1941, reissued, 1966; *America's Stamps: The Story of One Hundred Years of U.S. Postage Stamps,* Macmillan, 1947, reissued, 1967; *The Box with Red Wheels,* Macmillan, 1949, reissued, 1973; *The Circus Baby,* Macmillan, 1950, reissued, 1972; *Story of the Presidents of the United States of America,* Macmillan, 1953, reissued, 1966; *Off to Bed: Seven Stories for Wide-Awakes,* Macmillan, 1954; *The Boy Who Had No Heart,* Macmillan, 1955; *The Silver Mace: A Story of Williamsburg,* Macmillan, 1956, reissued, 1961; *The Peppernuts,* Macmillan, 1958.

Illustrator—with wife, Maud Petersham: William Bowen, *Enchanted Forest,* Macmillan, 1920; Carl Sandburg, *Rootabaga Stories,* Harcourt, 1922, reissued, 1974; Charles Lamb, *Tales from Shakespeare,* Macmillan, 1923; C. Sandburg, *Rootabaga Pigeons,* Harcourt, 1923; Sisters of Mercy

(From *Tales from Shakespeare* by Charles and Mary Lamb. Illustrated by Maud and Miska Petersham.)

(St. Xavier College, Chicago), *Marquette Readers,* Macmillan, 1924; Mabel Guinnip La Rue, *In Animal Land,* Macmillan, 1924; Margery Clark, *Poppy Seed Cakes,* Doubleday, 1924; Inez M. Howard, Alice Hawthorne, and Mae Howard, *Language Garden: A Primary Language Book,* Macmillan, 1924; Harriott Fansler and Isidoro Panlasigui, *Philippine National Literature,* Macmillan, 1925; Bessie B. Coleman, W. L. Uhl, and J. F. Hosic, *Pathway to Reading,* Silver, Burdette, 1925; Florence C. Coolidge, *Little Ugly Face, and Other Indian Tales,* Macmillan, 1925; John W. Wayland, *History Stories for Primary Grades,* Macmillan, 1925.

Elizabeth C. Miller, *Children of the Mountain Eagle,* Doubleday, 1927; *Everyday Canadian Primer,* Macmillan, 1928; Marguerite Clement, *Where Was Bobby?,* Doubleday, Doran, 1928; Wilhelmina Harper and A. J. Hamilton, compilers, *Pleasant Pathways,* Macmillan, 1928; W. Harper and A. J. Hamilton, compilers, *Winding Roads,* Macmillan, 1928-29; Harper and Hamilton, compilers, *Heights and Highways,* Macmillan, 1929; Harper and Hamilton, compilers, *Far Away Hills,* Macmillan, 1929; E. C. Miller, *Pran of Albania,* Doubleday, Doran, 1929; Miller, *Young Trajan,* Doubleday, 1931; Sydney V. Rowland, W. D. Lewis, and E. J. Marshall, compilers, *Beckoning Road,* J. C. Winston, 1931; S. V. Rowland, W. D. Lewis, and E. J. Marshall, *Rich Cargoes,* J. C. Winston, 1931; Rowland, Lewis, and Marshall, *Wings of Adventure,* J. C. Winston, 1931; Rowland, Lewis, and Marshall, *Treasure Trove,* J. C. Winston, 1931.

Carlo Collodi, pseudonym of Carlo Lorenzini, *Adventures of Pinocchio,* Garden City Publishing, 1932; Johanna Spyri, *Heidi,* Garden City Publishing, 1932; Jean Young Ayer, *Picnic Book,* Macmillan, 1934; Post Wheeler, *Albanian Wonder Tales,* Doubleday, 1936; Marie Barringer, *Four and Lena,* Doubleday, 1938; Miriam Evangeline Mason, *Susan-*

*nah, the Pioneer Cow,* Macmillan, 1941; Emilie F. Johnson, *Little Book of Prayers,* Viking, 1941; *Story of Jesus: A Little New Testament,* Macmillan, 1942, reissued, 1967; Ethan A. Cross and Elizabeth Carney, editors, *Literature,* 1943-46; Mother Goose, *The Rooster Crows: A Book of American Rhymes and Jingles,* Macmillan, 1945; Association for Childhood Education, Literature Committee, *Told under the Christmas Tree,* Macmillan, 1948; Elsie S. Eells, *Tales of Enchantment from Spain,* Dodd, 1950; Washington Irving, *Rip Van Winkle [and] The Legend of Sleepy Hollow,* Macmillan, 1951; Benjamin Franklin, *Bird in the Hand,* Macmillan, 1951; Eric P. Kelly, *In Clean Hay,* Macmillan, 1953; M. E. Mason, *Miss Posy Longlegs,* Macmillan, 1955.

*ADAPTATIONS*—Filmstrip: "The Box with Red Wheels," Threshold Filmstrips, Macmillan, 1974.

*SIDELIGHTS:* **September 20, 1888.** Born in Toeroekszentmiklos, near Budapest, Hungary, Petersham's given name was Petrezselyem Mikaly. When he was seven years old he

**Sometimes on that kind of a January night the stars look like numbers, look like the arithmetic writing of a girl going to school and just beginning arithmetic.**
■ (From *Rootabaga Stories,* Part One, by Carl Sandburg. Illustrated by Maud and Miska Petersham.)

managed to save some money and bought a box of paints. From then on, he dreamed of becoming an artist. As a young man he attended the Art School in Budapest. Although he was very poor, he managed to spend summers in Italy studying painting by going without meals and walking to save on carfare.

**1911.** Studied for a year in London, England. "I left Hungary . . . soon after I finished art school. When I arrived in England, the customs official asked me if I had anything to declare. I answered in French that I was a painter, meaning that no painter would have any luxury articles. The customs man looked at me, marked my strange assortment of luggage 'free' and asked no further questions and I was in England where I had long wanted to be.

"With a name which no Englishman could pronounce, and knowing but a few words of the language, I found myself in a difficult situation. For a time I wandered about with my paintbox and was happy discovering the countryside and watching the people. After the little money I had brought

**MISKA and MAUD PETERSHAM**

with me had vanished, I found earning a living was a tough proposition. A few book covers and a few odd jobs of lettering hardly paid for my scanty and often far-between meals of fish and chips. At rare times only did I have tea with sugar.

"Then a rich friend of mine turned up in London. I knew he must be rich, for although he had left Hungary for America but a few years before, here he was with two months vacation, traveling and visiting back home, and now seeing London. One day he asked me what success I had had in England and I told him that success was not remotely possible. Then he asked why I didn't go to America. I was very much surprised, for I couldn't understand who there could be in America who would appreciate art. I could see no opportunity for an artist in a land inhabited by Indians and cowboys.

"As a boy I had read eagerly stories by Fenimore Cooper and books about America by the German writer with a fanciful mind, Karl May, who, although he had never been in America, outdid any American author with his exciting tales of Indians and palefaces. In Europe we thought him a marvel, as he himself was the hero of all the tales he wrote. My friend then told me that he would pay my passage back to England if in America, within six months, I could not make a living. In five minutes I had made my decision." [Maud and Miska Petersham, "A Short Tale," *Caldecott Medal Books: 1938-1957*, edited by Bertha Mahoney Miller and Elinor Whitney Field, Horn Book, 1957.[1]]

**1912.** Emigrated to the United States. "In a short time I was on a boat coming into New York harbor. No one had told me that I needed money to enter the United States of America and all but a few dollars of the little I had left after paying for my ticket had been spent on the boat. I had had a wonderful trip but had practically no money left. There were three friends with me and we pooled our money. It made about

**At last in the afternoon, the queen of the Cracked Heads came with her cracked head to say good-by to me. She was sitting on a ladder feeding baby clocks to baby alligators....** ■ (From *Rootabaga Stories,* Part Two, by Carl Sandburg. Illustrated by Maud and Miska Petersham.)

For this is the place the nail-eating rats come to from all over the Rootabaga country. Father rats and mother rats send the young rats there to eat nails and get stronger. ■ (From *Rootabaga Stories,* Part Two, by Carl Sandburg. Illustrated by Maud and Miska Petersham.)

seventy-five American dollars which we put in a roll with the larger denominations on the outside carefully held in place with a rubber band. One of my friends, who had been in America before, stood first in line. Supposedly slipping the money back in his pocket after he had shown it to the official, he passed it to me. When called upon, I produced a roll of money, loose and considerable looking, with no rubber band, and this I in turn passed back to the friend following me.

"This little incident over successfully, we felt quite happy but we were not in America yet, as we had to pass the doctor's inspection and that is very frightening to any foreigner, for if the doctor said 'no' we knew there was no chance of entry. But to my surprise the doctor looked at me with a nice big smile on his face and asked if I spoke English and what my profession was. I told him my English was not very good but that I was hoping to improve it in America and was also hoping to make my living with art. Then he patted me on the back and assured me that in America I would have no trouble in earning my living with art, although it might take a little time to get acquainted with the new country. He shook hands and wished me good luck and happy days in America. And that was my entrance into this country.

"This friendly, open country was amazing and unbelievable to me. The language was to my liking. If I could not make myself understood right away, people would listen and help and in many cases 'yes' or 'no' was enough without any frills. My friend was right. In six months I was working. I had an apartment with another friend. I owned a new suit of clothes from Wanamaker's and a pair of American-made shoes that all Europeans longed for, and I had extra money in my pocket for a glass of beer with which I was presented a roast-beef sandwich. I had misjudged America and no doubt about it.

"But it was a little disappointing about the Indians; and then one day I saw them. They were on Madison Avenue—feathers, war paint and all—just as they had been in the stories I had read. I followed them only to find they were part of a circus opening that day at the Hippodrome.

"I knew there were many Hungarians in America, but I was greatly surprised at something that happened. A friend of mine was coming from Europe and I had given him directions in a letter, written in Hungarian, of how to find my apartment if I should miss him at the boat. When he arrived

he decided it was all so simple he would not bother me but would come to the apartment by himself. He took the wrong subway and landed in the Bronx—180th Street, but not the right place. Trying to retrace his steps and start over again he was completely lost. Finally at a subway station which was not busy he approached the ticketchopper, a big colored boy who sat half reclining, reading a newspaper and with his feet comfortably placed on top of the machine. My friend spoke a little English but with a terrific accent. The boy listened, then reached for the letter to see for himself the address for which my friend was asking. He turned the letter over and continued reading to the end, laughing and apparently enjoying. Amazed, my friend asked where he had learned the Hungarian language and the boy answered, 'Why, I come from Pittsburgh.'

"I found here a country that I had dreamed of, but never thought could really exist; I found ideals and principles that I had always believed in. I don't think any American-born can appreciate this country as I do."[1]

Petersham married Maud Fuller, a fellow artist-illustrator. Together they began a long career illustrating and writing children's books. The couple had one son, Miki.

**1942.** Runner-up for the Caldecott Medal for *An American ABC.* "In the books we make I am happy when we can picture some of those wonderful things which American children can claim as their heritage. Working on *An American ABC* book meant a great deal to me aside from the making of the pictures."[1]

**1946.** Winner of the Caldecott Medal for *The Rooster Crows: A Book of American Rhymes and Jingles.* "In *The Rooster Crows* we have tried to put into the hands of children little snatches of story that are rightfully theirs. And now we are working on a book of United States postage stamps, those small squares of paper commemorating events of which American children can be so proud. We are trying to put before the children of this country those things which are theirs for the taking.

". . . We have received the Caldecott Award. We are proud and happy because it comes to us as an assurance that the love, the hard work, and any skill we may possess, which we have put into our work, have been considered worthy. If we have given any child real joy or have made him a little more appreciative of the beautiful in this world, we are satisfied.

"Although dawn is the proper hour for the Cock to crow, with us it is tonight that the 'Rooster is Crowing.'"[1]

**1947.** *America's Stamps: The Story of One Hundred Years of U.S. Postage* was published. Petersham continued to write and illustrate children's books from his home in Woodstock, New York throughout the 50's.

**1958.** Last book, *The Peppernuts,* was published.

**May 15, 1960.** Died.

*FOR MORE INFORMATION SEE:* I. S. Green, "Maud and Miska Petersham," *Horn Book,* July, 1946; L. Barksdale, "Petershams—Caldecott Medal Winners for 1946," *Publishers Weekly,* June 22, 1946; Bertha E. Mahony and others, compilers, *Illustrators of Children's Books, 1744-1945,* Horn Book, 1947; Elizabeth Rider Montgomery, *Story behind Modern Books,* Dodd, 1949; Stanley J. Kunitz and

**The white cloth goes into large presses and comes out at great speed, yard after yard, printed in many different colors all at the same time.** ■ (From *The Story Book of Things We Wear* by Maud and Miska Petersham.)

Howard Haycraft, editors, *Junior Book of Authors,* second revised edition, H. W. Wilson, 1951; Maud and Miska Petersham, "A Short Tale," *Caldecott Medal Books: 1938-1957,* edited by Bertha Mahoney Miller and Elinor Whitney Field, Horn Book, 1957; Bertha E. Mahony Miller and others, compilers, *Illustrators of Children's Books, 1946-56,* Horn Book, 1958; Obituaries—*New York Times,* May 16, 1960; *Publishers Weekly,* May 23, 1960; *Horn Book,* August, 1960; *Library Journal,* September 15, 1960; Lee Bennett Hopkins, *Books Are by People,* Citation, 1969; *Horn Book,* August, 1976.

(Died May 15, 1960)

# POLSENO, Jo

*EDUCATION:* Whitney Art School, A.F.A.; has also studied at the Ecole des Beaux Arts, Marseilles, France.

*CAREER:* Author and illustrator of children's books.

*WRITINGS*—All illustrated by the author: *Secrets of Redding Glen: The Natural History of a Wooded Valley,* Golden Press, 1973; *Secrets of a Cypress Swamp: The Natural History of Okefenokee,* Golden Press, 1976; *This Hawk Belongs to Me,* McKay, 1976.

Walk down Lexington Avenue around five o'clock on any afternoon and listen to the noise—the laughter and the screams from the kids playing in the street. ■ (From *This Hawk Belongs to Me* by Jo Polseno. Illustrated by the author.)

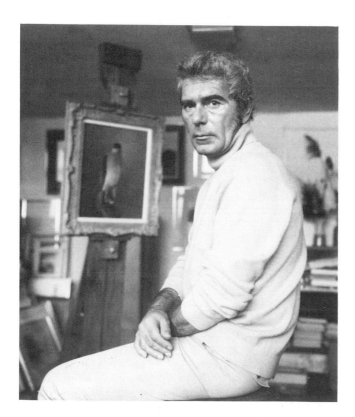

**JO POLSENO**

Illustrator: Cora Cheney, *Plantation Doll,* Holt, 1955; Mrs. Mickey Klar Marks, *Fine Eggs and Fancy Chickens,* Holt, 1956; Lorena A. Hickok, *Story of Helen Keller,* Grosset, 1958; Alf Evers, *Open the Door,* F. Watts, 1960; Elizabeth C. Walton, *Treasure in the Sand,* Lothrop, 1960; Joy Lonergan, *When My Father Was a Little Boy,* F. Watts, 1961; William Wise, *The House with the Red Roof,* Putnam, 1961; Teri Martini, *What a Frog Can Do,* Reilly & Lee, 1962; Mark Twain, pseudonym of Samuel Langhorne Clemens, *The Adventures of Tom Sawyer,* Grosset, 1963; Anita Klever, *Stories Jesus Told,* Rand McNally, 1967; Marian Potter, *Copperfield Summer,* Follett, 1967; Scott Corbett, *Cop's Kid,* Little, Brown, 1968; Elizabeth P. Kerby, *The Conquistadors,* Putnam, 1969; Clyde R. Bulla, *New Boy in Dublin: A Story of Ireland,* Crowell, 1969; Roland Bertol, *Charles Drew,* Crowell, 1970; Berniece Freschet, *The Flight of the Snow Goose,* Crown, 1970; Lucy Salamanca, *Lost in the Everglades,* Golden Press, 1971; Roma Gans, *Bird Talk,* Crowell, 1971; Victoria Cox, *Nature's Flying Janitor,* Golden Press, 1974; Alice Thompson Gilbreath, *Nature's Squirt Guns, Bubble Pipes and Fireworks: Geysers, Hot Springs, and Volcanoes,* McKay, 1977.

SIDELIGHTS: *Secrets of a Cypress Swamp* drew praise from a *Publishers Weekly* reviewer who wrote: "Jo Polseno, a gifted painter, adds to his laurels with this exploration of the flora and fauna of an exotic part of the world. . . . The exquisite paintings make even a swamp rat attractive. . . . Here is a worthy followup to the artist's previous success, 'Secrets of Redding Glen.'" Susan Sprague added in *School Library Journal:* ". . . Polseno sustains a near poetic mood throughout. Lovely to read and look at."

FOR MORE INFORMATION SEE: *Publishers Weekly,* July 19, 1976; *School Library Journal,* November, 1976.

# PRINCE, J(ack) H(arvey)   1908-
## (Don Aquillo; Jon Clinton; Dean Wardell)

*PERSONAL:* Born November 10, 1908, in London, England; son of Thomas Harvey (a grocer and postmaster) and Louisa (Taylor) Harvey. *Education:* Northampton College of Advanced Technology (now City University), F.B.O.A., 1929, F.S.M.C., 1929. *Home:* 1/15 Dudley St., Balgowlah, New South Wales 2093, Australia.

*CAREER:* Involved in private research and optometrical activities until 1940; British Optical Association, lecturer in comparative ocular anatomy, 1935-46; Royal Air Force, research in night vision, 1940-45; lecture tours in Australia, New Zealand, Canada, and England, 1946-52; Ohio State University, Columbus, instructor, 1952-54, assistant professor, 1954-56, associate research professor of ophthalmology, 1956-66; writer and illustrator, 1966—. Scientific adviser to professional organizations in the United States.

*MEMBER:* Fellowship of Australian Writers, Zoological Society (London; fellow), Royal Zoological Society of New South Wales (member of council), Sigma Xi. *Awards, honors:* Research medal from British Optical Association, 1958.

*WRITINGS: Ocular Prosthesis,* E. & S. Livingstone, 1946; *Visual Development,* E. & S. Livingstone, 1949.

*Recent Advances in Ocular Prosthesis,* E. & S. Livingstone, 1950; *Comparative Anatomy of the Eye,* C. C Thomas, 1956.

(With Charles Diesem, Gordon L. Ruskell, and Irma Eglitis) *Anatomy and Histology of the Eye and Orbit in Domestic Animals,* C. C Thomas, 1960; *Visual Acuity and Reading in Relation to Letter and Word Design,* Ohio State University Institute for Research in Vision, 1960; *Comparative Legibility of Highway and Advertising Signs under Dynamic Condi-*

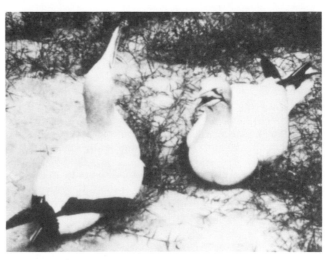

The male gannet points his bill to the sky to tell his mate he is about to take flight. ■ (From *Languages of the Animal World* by J. H. Prince. Photos by J. H. Prince.)

*tions,* Ohio State University Institute for Research in Vision, 1962; (contributor) Arnold Sorsby, editor, *Modern Ophthalmology,* Butterworth & Co., 1962; *Spectral Absorption of the Retina and Choroid from 340 to 1700 Millimicrons,* Ohio State University Institute for Research in Vision, 1962; (editor with others) *The Rabbit in Eye Research,* C. C Thomas, 1964; *Aging and Pathology of the Retina,* C. C Thomas, 1965; *Small Boats,* Angus & Robertson, 1968; *Animals in the Night: Senses in Action after Dark* (juvenile), Angus & Robertson, 1968, Thomas Nelson, 1971; *Better Life after Fifty,* A. H. & A. W. Reed, 1969.

(Contributor) *Duke's Physiology of the Domestic Animals,* Cornell University Press, 1970, revised edition, 1979; *You and Your Eyes,* A. H. & A. W. Reed, 1970; *The Universal Urge,* Thomas Nelson, 1972; *Weather and the Animal World* (juvenile), Thomas Nelson, 1974; *How to Judge People,* Rydge Publications, 1974; *Languages of the Animal World,* Thomas Nelson, 1975; *Diet for Good Health,* Rigby, 1975, revised edition, 1977; *Everyday Health Problems and How to Deal with Them,* Rigby, 1975; *All About Headaches,* Rigby, 1975; *Plants That Eat Animals* (juvenile), Thomas Nelson, 1978; (with Jack Murphy) *The Lady Bowler,* Reed & Rigby, 1978; *How Your Body Works,* Rigby, 1979; *Preventing Strokes,* Rigby, 1979; *Overcoming Sexual Problems,* Rigby, 1979; *Dealing with Tension,* Rigby, 1979; *Developing Your Personality,* Rigby, 1979; *Strokes Can Be Avoided,* Rigby, 1979; (contributor) *Encyclopedia of Australian Fishing,* Bay Books, 1979; *The First 100 Years: A History of the Royal Zoological Society of NSW for Centenary Celebration,* Royal Zoological Society, 1979.

Under pseudonym Don Aquillo: Contributor of numerous articles to *Koolewong.*

Under pseudonym Jon Clinton: *Buying Australian Shares,* A. H. & A. W. Reed, 1968, 3rd edition, 1970; *Investment in Australia, New Zealand, and Asia,* A. H. & A. W. Reed, 1969; *Reducing Your Income Tax,* A. H. & A. W. Reed, 1970, 10th edition, 1979; *Buying New Zealand Shares,* A. H. & A. W. Reed, 1971; *How You Can Save Tax,* Rydge Publications, 1972; *Today's Ways to Minimize Income Tax, Gift Duty, and Death Duties,* Rydge Publications, 1974; *Living and Having More; Dying and Paying Less,* Rydge Publications, 1976, 2nd edition, 1978.

J. H. PRINCE

Under pseudonym Dean Wardell: *Instant Handywoman,* Rigby, 1975, revised edition, 1977; *Furniture Restoration,* Rigby, 1977; *Property Protection,* Rigby, 1979. Contributor of more than three hundred articles on zoology and outdoor sports to magazines. Convener and honorary editor of *Koolewong.*

*WORK IN PROGRESS: How Animals Hunt.*

*SIDELIGHTS:* Prince has traveled all of Canada, U.S.A., New Zealand, and most of Europe and South America.

"I retired early from the Ohio State University to prolong my life, and to do what I'd always wanted to do—write. I can't say that any books express my views exclusively, 'they all deal with facts or established ideas.' All books are illustrated by me.

"I consider my most important work to be *The Rabbit in Eye Research* because of its review in the *New York City Veterinarian* that it would become 'the acknowledged authority in the field.'"

*HOBBIES AND OTHER INTERESTS:* Art, literature, music, politics, walking.

## RANDS, William Brighty   1823-1882 (Matthew Browne, Henry Holbeach, T. Talker)

*PERSONAL:* Born December 24, 1823, in Chelsea, England; died April 23, 1882. *Education:* Had little formal schooling.

*CAREER:* Author of miscellanies and books for children. Held various jobs during his youth, including work in a warehouse, on the stage, and as an attorney's clerk; committee room reporter at the House of Commons until 1875. Worked as a writer and editor on the London *Illustrated Times,* 1855-71; helped to found *The Citizen.* Hymn writer and part-time preacher in a Brixton chapel.

*WRITINGS: The Frost upon the Pane* (a Christmas story), [London], 1854; (author of a biographical sketch) *The Poetical Works of Robert Bloomfield,* Knight & Son, 1855; *Chain of Lilies, and Other Poems,* [London], 1857; (under pseudonym T. Talker) *Tangled Talk: An Essayist's Holiday,* A. Strahan, 1864; *Lilliput Levee* (short poems; illustrated by John Everett Millais and George John Pinwell), [London], 1864, Routledge, 1868; (under pseudonym Henry Holbeach) *Henry Holbeach: Student in Life and Philosophy,* A. Strahan, 1865, [New York], 1866; (under pseudonym Matthew Browne) *Views and Opinions,* A. Strahan, 1866, reissued, Lost Cause Press, 1957; (under pseudonym Matthew Browne) *Chaucer's England,* Hurst & Blackett, 1869, reprinted, AMS Press, 1970.

(Under pseudonym Henry Holbeach) *Shoemakers' Village,* [London], 1871; *Lilliput Revels,* Routledge, 1871 [another edition illustrated by Griselda Wedderburn, J. Lane, 1905]; *Lilliput Lectures* (illustrated by J. E. Millais), [London], 1871; *Lilliput Legends* (illustrated by Millais), [London], 1872; (under pseudonym Matthew Browne, author of introduction) George Eliot (pseudonym of Mary Ann Evans Cross) *Complete Poems,* Estes & Lauriat, 1888; *Lazy Lessons and Essays on Conduct,* J. Bowden, 1897; *Lilliput Lyrics* (illustrated by Charles Robinson; edited by R. Brimley Johnson), J. Lane, 1899; *The Young Norseman* (illus-

trated by Morris M. Williams), D. Nutt, 1907; (under pseudonym Matthew Browne) *Lilliput Land* (excerpts from *Lilliput Levee*), Hodder & Stoughton, 1911; *Miss Hooper's Hoop, and Other Poems* (selections from *Lilliput Revels;* illustrated by Charlotte Hough), Tudor Press, 1949.

Contributor to *Contemporary Review, Saturday Journal, Pall Mall Gazette, The Spectator,* and many juvenile magazines.

*SIDELIGHTS:* "England produced several writers of Nonsense verse whose best works followed the early Lear and *Struwwelpeter* and just preceded 'Lewis Carroll', one or two of whom do not deserve to be forgotten.

"The most famous of these is William Brighty Rands (1823-82), whom Harvey Darton ranks as second only to Lear and Dodgson. Little is known about his life: he was for a time a preacher, though he never took up the ministry, and he was often very hard up and drew his most regular income as official shorthand reporter to the House of Lords. He wrote many books under his own name, no name, and various pseudonyms, but he is remembered only by a sprinkling of poems and short tales, most of which were collected in *Lilliput Levee* (1864) and *Lilliput Lectures* (1871) after many of them had appeared in *Good Words for the Young.*

"One or two of his more serious poems for children survive in anthologies, such as that beginning 'Great, wide, beautiful, wonderful World, With the Wonderful water round you curled', and 'The Pedlar's Caravan', but he is best and most suitably remembered by his fantastic and Nonsense verses and poems, most of which appeared in *Lilliput Levee.*

"Rands was an exceedingly uneven writer and seldom managed to sustain a poem of any length. 'Lilliput Levee' itself is a case in point: though the fun, exuberance and joy of life carry it almost to the end—and the whole outburst of mild mischief and genuine child-thinking hardly suffers at all from the occasional crudities of the verse. But he is at his best with sheer, light-hearted Nonsense:—

> Ba-ba, black wool,
>
> Have you any sheep?
>
> Yes sir, a pack-full,
>
> Creep, mouse, creep!
>
> Four-and-twenty little maids
>
> Hanging out the pie,
>
> Out jumped the honey-pot
>
> Guy-Fawkes, Guy!
>
> Cross-latch, cross-latch,
>
> Sit and spin the fire,
>
> When the pie was opened,
>
> The bird was on the briar!

(From *Lilliput Lyrics* by Henry Holbeach. Illustrated by Charles Robinson.)

"Some of the Nonsense stories in verse are better still: 'Tumble-down Towers', for example. But these have long been out of print and are hard to find." [Roger Lancelyn Green, *Tellers of Tales,* Franklin Watts, 1965]

*FOR MORE INFORMATION SEE:* A. H. Miles, *The Poets and the Poetry of the Nineteenth Century,* Hutchinson, 1891-97.

## REEVES, Joyce 1911-
### (Joyce Gard)

*PERSONAL:* Born in 1911, in London, England. *Education:* Lady Margaret Hall, Oxford, B.A. *Home:* Kent, England.

*CAREER:* Author. Served as an administrative officer, with the Ministry of Economic Warfare, London, and with the Supreme Headquarters of the Allied Expeditionary Force, Frankfurt, 1940-45; studio potter, 1947-56; has also taught school and worked for a literary agent. *Member:* Society of Authors.

*WRITINGS*—all under pseudonym, Joyce Gard: (Adaptor) Jules Verne, *Journey to the Centre of the Earth,* Hutchinson Educational, 1961; *Woorroo* (illustrated by Ronald Benham), Gollancz, 1961; *The Dragon of the Hill,* Gollancz, 1963; *Talargain the Seal's Whelp,* Gollancz, 1964, published in America as *Talargain,* Holt, 1965; *Smudge of the Fells,* Gollancz, 1965, Holt, 1966; *The Snow Firing,* Gollancz, 1967, Holt, 1968; *The Mermaid's Daughter,* Holt, 1969; *Handysides Shall Not Fall,* Kaye & Ward, 1975; *The Hagwaste Donkeys,* Pelham Books, 1976.

Under Joyce Reeves, translator from the French on aspects of contemporary art.

*SIDELIGHTS:* Joyce Gard uses a combination of fact and fiction in her novels, which have been highly praised by numerous book reviewers. "Vivid, excellent writing, the skillful blending of fantasy and history and a plot filled with suspense make this an outstanding work . . . ," commented a *New York Times* critic about the author's novel, *Talargain.* In examining Gard's *Smudge of the Fells,* a *Library Journal* reviewer noted, "The writing is highly skilled, the characters are varied and well defined. The tension created makes this a good suspense story. . . ." Of the author's novel, *The Mermaid's Daughter,* a review in the *Times Literary Supplement* said, "The rich and rapturous telling will undoubtedly thrill the impressionable adolescent girls of sensibility and spirituality. . . ."

*HOBBIES AND OTHER INTERESTS:* Contemporary art, archaeology, listening to music.

*FOR MORE INFORMATION SEE: Horn Book,* April, 1970.

(From *Smudge of the Fells* by Joyce Gard. Jacket design by Alan Cober.)

## RILEY, James Whitcomb    1849-1916
### (Benj. F. Johnson, of Boone)

*PERSONAL:* Born October 7, 1849, in Greenfield, Indiana; died July 22, 1916, in Indianapolis, Indiana; son of Reuben A. (a lawyer) and Elizabeth (Marine) Riley. *Education:* Attended local schools. *Home:* Indianapolis, Indiana.

*CAREER:* Poet. Early jobs included sign painter and wandering musician for a patent-medicine company. Newspaperman, the *Anderson Democrat*, 1877, and the *Indianapolis Journal*, 1877-85. *Member:* American Academy of Arts and Letters. *Awards, honors:* M.A., Yale University, 1902; Litt.D., Wabash College, 1903, and University of Pennsylvania, 1904; LL.D., Indiana University, 1907. Riley's birthday was declared an official holiday in Indiana, 1915; his home on Lockerbie Street in Indianapolis and his birthplace have been made into public memorials.

*WRITINGS*—Poems; all published by Bowen-Merrill, except as noted: (Under pseudonym Benj. F. Johnson, of Boone) *"The Old Swimmin'-Hole"*, *and 'Leven More Poems*, Merrill, Meigs, 1883; *The Boss Girl: A Christmas Story, and Other Sketches*, 1886, reprinted, Books for Libraries, 1971; *Afterwhiles*, 1887; *Old-Fashioned Roses*, 1888; *Pipes O' Pan at Zekesbury*, 1889; (with Edgar Wilson Nye) *Fun, Wit, and Humor*, 1890; *Sketches in Prose, and Occasional Verses*, 1891; *An Old Sweetheart*, 1891, reissued as *An Old Sweetheart of Mine*, 1902; *Neighborly Poems*, 1891; *The Flying Islands of the Night*, 1892 [another edition illustrated by Franklin Booth, Bobbs-Merrill, 1913]; *Green Fields and Running Brooks*, 1893; (with E. W. Nye) *Poems and Yarns*, Neely, 1893; *Poems Here at Home* (illustrated by E. W. Kemble), Century, 1893; *Armazindy*, 1894; *The Days Gone By, and Other Poems*, E. A. Weeks, 1895; *A Tinkle of Bells, and Other Poems*, E. A. Weeks, 1895; *A Child-World*, 1897, reprinted, Books for Libraries, 1972; *Rubaiyat of Doc Sifers* (illustrated by C. M. Relyea), Century, 1897; *Riley Child-Rhymes* (illustrated by Will Vawter), 1899, reprinted, Books for Libraries, 1970; *Riley Love-Lyrics* (illustrated by William B. Dyer), 1899 [another edition illustrated by W. Vawter, Bobbs-Merrill, 1920]; *Home-Folks*, 1900; *Riley Farm-Rhymes* (illustrated by W. Vawter), 1901; *The Book of Joyous Children* (illustrated by W. Vawter), Scribner, 1902, reprinted, Books for Libraries, 1969.

Poems published by Bobbs-Merrill, except as noted: *Out to Old Aunt Mary's*, 1903; *His Pa's Romance* (illustrated by W. Vawter), 1903; *Gems from Riley*, De Wolfe, Fiske, 1904; *A Defective Santa Claus* (illustrated by W. Vawter and C. M. Relyea), 1904; *Riley Songs O' Cheer* (illustrated by W. Vawter), 1905; *The Runaway Boy* (illustrated by Ethel F. Betts), 1906; *Morning*, 1907; *The Raggedy Man* (illustrated by E. F. Betts), 1907; *The Boys of the Old Glee Club*, 1907; *Riley Child Verse* (illustrated by E. F. Betts), 1908; *Home Again with Me* (illustrated by Howard C. Christy), 1908; *Riley Songs of Summer* (illustrated by W. Vawter), 1908; *Old School Day Romances* (illustrated by E. Stetson Crawford), 1909; *Riley Roses* (illustrated by H. C. Christy), 1909; *Riley Songs of Home* (illustrated by W. Vawter), 1910; *A Hoosier Romance, 1868* (illustrated by John W. Adams), Century, 1910; *The Girl I Loved* (illustrated by H. C. Christy), 1910.

*When She Was about Sixteen* (illustrated by H. C. Christy), 1911; *When the Frost Is On the Pumpkin, and Other Poems* (illustrated by W. Vawter), 1911; *A Summer's Day,*

**JAMES WHITCOMB RILEY**

*and Other Poems* (illustrated by W. Vawter), 1911; *Down around the River* (illustrated by W. Vawter), 1911; *The Lockerbie Book* (edited by Hewitt H. Howland), 1911; *Mrs. Miller*, 1912; *All the Year Round* (illustrated by Gustave Baumann), 1912; *The Prayer Perfect, and Other Poems* (illustrated by W. Vawter), 1912; *Knee-Deep in June, and Other Poems* (illustrated by W. Vawter), 1912; *Away*, 1913; *A Song of Long Ago*, 1913; *Her Beautiful Eyes*, 1913; *He and I*, 1913; *Do They Miss Me*, 1913; *When My Dreams Come True*, 1913; *The Riley Baby Book* (illustrated by William Cotton), 1913; *The Rose*, 1913; *Good-Bye, Jim* (illustrated by H. C. Christy), 1913; *When She Comes Home*, 1914; *To My Friend*, 1914; *A Discouraging Model* (illustrated by H. C. Christy), 1914; *Just Be Glad*, 1914; *The Glad Sweet Face of Her*, 1914; *Contentment*, 1914; *The Old Times*, 1915; *Riley Songs of Friendship* (illustrated by Will Vawter), 1915; *The Old Soldier's Story*, 1915; *The Hoosier Book* (edited by H. H. Howland), 1916; *Riley Hoosier Stories* (illustrated by W. Vawter), 1917; *The Name of Old Glory*, 1917; *A Host of Children* (illustrated by E. F. Betts), 1920; *Riley Fairy Tales* (illustrated by W. Vawter), 1923.

Collections and selections: *The Poems and Prose Sketches of James Whitcomb Riley*, 16 volumes, Scribner, 1897-1914; *The Complete Works of James Whitcomb Riley*, six volumes, Bobbs-Merrill, 1913, reprinted, AMS Press, 1974; *James Whitcomb Riley's Complete Works*, 10 volumes, Bobbs-Merrill, 1916; *Letters of James Whitcomb Riley* (edited by William L. Phelps), Bobbs-Merrill, 1930, reprinted,

AMS Press, 1973; *The Best Loved Home Ballads of James Whitcomb Riley,* Blue Ribbon Books, 1931; *Selected Poems* (edited by W. L. Phelps), Bobbs-Merrill, 1931; *The Best Loved Poems of James Whitcomb Riley* (illustrated by E. F. Betts), Blue Ribbon Books, 1932, reissued, Grosset & Dunlap, 1961; *The Best Loved Poems and Ballads of James Whitcomb Riley* (illustrated by E. F. Betts), Blue Ribbon Books, 1934; *The Complete Poetical Works of James Whitcomb Riley,* Bobbs-Merrill, 1937, reissued, Grosset & Dunlap, 1963; *Favorite Poems of James Whitcomb Riley* (edited by W. L. Phelps), Triangle Books, 1938; *Joyful Poems for Children* (illustrated by Sally Tate), Bobbs-Merrill, 1946, reissued, 1960; *The Gobble-Uns 'll Git You Ef You Don't Watch Out!* (illustrated by Joel Schick), Lippincott, 1975.

*ADAPTATIONS*—Movies: "The Old Swimmin' Hole," Charles Ray Film Co., 1921, Arnold Blumberg, 1967; "The Girl I Loved," United Artists, 1923; "An Old Sweetheart of Mine," Metro Pictures, 1923.

*SIDELIGHTS:* **October 7, 1849.** Born in the rural town of Greenfield, Indiana. Father, Reuben Riley, was a lawyer and a member of the state legislature. "The first thing I remember was my father's riding up to the woodhouse door with a deer hanging from the pommel of his saddle; and about the second thing I remember was the bugler who galloped west on the National Road with news of the death of President Taylor.

"Then [as I grew older] was the floodtide of interrogation points. I could ask more questions than grandfather in Paradise could answer in a year." [Marcus Dickey, *The Youth of James Whitcomb Riley,* Bobbs-Merrill, 1919.[1]]

"Before I was old enough to read I remember buying a book at an old auctioneer's shop in Greenfield. I can not imagine what prophetic impulse took possession of me that I denied myself the ginger cakes and candy that usually exhausted my youthful income. The slender little volume must have cost all of twenty-five cents. It was Francis Quarles' *Divine Emblems* (first printed in England in 1635)—a neat little affair about the size of a pocket Testament. I carried it around with me all day long. It gave me delight to touch it.

"'What have you there, my boy?' a passer-by would ask.

"'A book,' I would answer.

"'What kind of a book?'

"'Poetry-book.'

"When asked if I could read poetry, I shook my head and turned away embarrassed—but I held on to my Poetry-book." [Marcus Dickey, *The Maturity of James Whitcomb Riley,* Bobbs-Merrill, 1922.[2]]

**1855.** Educated at various local tuition-supported schools. "My first teacher, Mrs. Frances Neill, was a little, old, rosy, rolly-poly woman—looking as though she might have just come rolling out of a fairy story, so lovable she was and so jolly and so amiable. Her school was kept in a little old one-story dwelling of three rooms, and—like a bracket on the wall—a little porch in the rear, which was part of the playground of her 'scholars,'—for in those days pupils were very affectionately called 'scholars.' Her very youthful school was composed of possibly twelve or fifteen boys and

girls. I remember particularly the lame boy, who always had the first ride in the swing in the locust tree at 'recess.'

"This first teacher was a mother, too, to all her 'scholars.' When drowsy they were often carried to an inner room—a sitting-room—where many times I was taken with a pair of little chaps and laid to slumber on a little made-down pallet on the floor. She would ofttimes take three or four of us together; and I can recall how my playmate and I, having been admonished into silence, grew deeply interested in looking at her husband, a spare old blind man sitting always by the window, which had its shade drawn down. After a while we became accustomed to the idea, and when our awe had subsided we used to sit in a little sewing chair and laugh and talk in whispers and give imitations of the little old man at the window."[1]

Except for this first experience, Riley had little interest in his school days. "Omit the school-room from my history entirely and the record of my career would not be seriously affected.

"My school life was a farce all the way through. My *Second Reader* said: 'Some little boys do not love their books.' I did not love mine. I never heartily learned a school-book lesson in my life. When I did answer a question the answer was whispered in my ear by some one. I copied my blackboard work from the classmate next to me. I could have learned had I tried, but my obstinate nature could not brook the fact that I was sent to school. My nature was full of perversity. I tried McGuffey's *Speller* but the author was so incoherent in his thought I gave up in despair. The book showed haste in preparation and was doubtless an answer to the call of a greedy publisher. I seldom saw the inside of a grammar. . . . Language came to me naturally. When I was a boy, schools were run on the principle that the hardest method of learning was the best. Flogging was still in favor as was also the stupid old system of forcing boys to learn by rote. My father was an old-fashioned man, very strict in his rule over his children. One of his rules applied to certain books they were forbidden to read. Naturally I wanted to read those books. I did not care a rap for the books he and my teachers prescribed. I read the forbidden books, although I had to steal them from the library to do it. That was my introduction to mythology."[1]

Fortunately, one of his last teachers encouraged Riley to read the best literature. "My last teacher, I remember with an affection no less fervent than my first. He was a man of many gifts, a profound lover of literature and a modest producer in story and in song, in history, and even in romance and drama, although his life-effort was given first of all to education. To him I owe possibly the first gratitude of my heart and soul, since, after a brief warfare, upon our first acquaintance as teacher and pupil, he informed me gently but firmly that since I was so persistent in secretly reading novels during school hours he would insist upon his right to choose the novel I should read, whereupon the 'Beadle' and 'Munro' dime novels were discarded for masterpieces of fiction; so that it may be virtually recorded that the first study of literature in a Hoosier country school was (perhaps very consciously) introduced by my first of literary friends and inspirers, Captain Lee O. Harris of Greenfield."[1]

**January, 1870.** Entered Greenfield's first public school, Greenfield Academy. Left at the end of the first term when he received a barely satisfactory report card. "They did not think I would amount to much at home. Being a lawyer my

Granny's come to our house,
   Ho! my lawzy-daisy!
All the children round the place
   Is ist a-runnin' crazy!
■ (From *James Whitcomb Riley's Complete Works* by James Whitcomb Riley. Illustrated by Ethel Franklin Betts.)

**James Whitcomb Riley, from the portrait by John Singer Sargent.**

father believed in facts. He had little use for a boy who could not learn arithmetic. There were others of the same opinion. My schoolmates had an aptitude for figures and stood well in their classes. The result was half the town pitied me. Again and again I was told I would have to be supported by the family.''[1]

**Spring, 1870.** Resolved not to stay on the farm. This decision created tension in Riley's relationship with his father which lasted for several years. ''My father had moved to the edge of town and was tending a garden. He was a good gardener. I was poor. Like Rumty Wilfer, I had never yet obtained the modest object of my ambition, which was to wear a complete new suit of clothes, hat and boots included, at one time. I desired to go into 'society,' and one evening resolved to make the attempt. I stood before the glass, in an old suit and was putting on a paper collar and a butterfly tie. My big toe was coming through my shoe, and to give my white sock the color of the shoe at that point I stained my toe with ink. With his usual contempt for 'fashion,' my father looked at me from the tail of his eye and said with the curl of the lip, 'Well, my son, now that you are ready to go into *society,* we'll go into the *garden* and hoe weeds.' I followed him. After we had hoed a little while, I fell behind and grew melancholy and saucy. 'You don't seem to like *work,*' said my father sarcastically. 'No!' I thundered. Seizing the end of my hoe-handle with both hands, I flung it into a neighbor lot, leaped the fence and walked down-town, leaving my father white with rage. In about an hour I came back. Leaning against the fence, I said, 'Father, I am here, not to hoe weeds, but to tell you I am sorry I spoke to you in anger.' He gazed at me in astonishment. The silence was painful. Then he said in a tone of tenderness I had not heard before, 'My son, come down to the office to-night. I want to talk to you.' At the

office we came to an understanding. He went his way and I went mine.''[1]

**August, 1870.** Riley's mother died. His bereavement strengthened his desire to leave home. ''I was alone . . . till as in a vision I saw my mother smiling back upon me from the blue fields of love—when lo! she was young again. Suddenly I had the assurance that I would meet her somewhere in another world. I was gathering the fruit of what had been so happily impressed on me in childhood. I had seen that the world is a stage. Now I saw that the universe is a stage. Another curtain had been lifted.''[1]

**December, 1870.** ''Something had to be done. I knew it—and my father knew it. So I went over to Rushville to sell Bibles.

''It turned out that citizens of Rushville had all the Bibles they needed; they had not time to read those they had.''[1]

**1871.** Became a house-painter. ''I was not quite so melancholy as Tom Sawyer, but the walls of that house did have

But others said, in a kinder way,
They missed the songs she used to sing—
They missed the smiles that used to play
Over her face, and the laughin' ring
Of her glad voice—that *every* thing
Of her old s'lf seemed dead and gone,
And this was the ghost that they gazed on.

■ (From *A Hoosier Romance* by James Whitcomb Riley. Illustrated by John Wolcott Adams.)

a far-reaching look like a continent, just as the long un-whitewashed fence looked to Tom.''[1]

This endeavor failed, so he established himself in his own shop as a sign-painter. "While waiting for the turn of fortune, I covered all the barns and fences with advertisements. All the while I was nibbling at the rhyme-maker's trade, and this was a source of irritation to my father. The outlook was not encouraging. He thought I should devote my time exclusively to painting.''[1]

**1872.** First opportunity to leave his native town. Joined a traveling patent-medicine show as a sign-painter, minstrel and jingle-writer. Later toured with the Graphic Company, an itinerant group of sign-painters. "I started on my voyage for the Golden Fleece. It was delightful to bowl over the country. My blood ran through me like a gulf-stream. I laughed all the time. Miles and miles of somber landscapes were made bright with merry song and when the sun shone and all the golden summer lay spread out before me, it was glorious. I drifted on through it like a wisp of thistle-down, careless of how, or when, or where the wind should anchor me.''[1]

**Summer, 1874.** While pursuing a youthful ambition to become a public entertainer, made his first solo performance at Monrovia, Indiana. "I picked out a village far from home so that if I failed nobody would hear of it. By the almanac I was twenty-five, but as a booster of entertainments, callow as a celery in a tile. Still sticking to my trade, I was hanging round a paint shop in Mooresville. When

For only, now, at the road's next bend
To the right we could make out the goble-end
Of the fine old Huston homestead—not
Half a mile from the sacred spot
Where dwelt our Saint in her simple cat—
Out to old Aunt Mary's.
■ (From *Out to Old Aunt Mary's* by James Whitcomb Riley. Illustrated by Howard Chandler Christy.)

business was dull I loafed at the photograph gallery and wrote articles for the Mooresville *Herald.* Sometimes the *Herald* was out of space; then I just loafed around the gallery. The elocution bee was buzzing in my bonnet, and having created a furor by reciting to a few friends in a parlor one night, I concluded to cut loose and try it alone. Nobody would know me over there in the cross-roads village, and I fancied that I might make quite a hit as The Greatest Imitator and Caricaturist of the Age. So I rolled up some paint brushes in long sheets of white paper from the *Herald* office, borrowed a hat and a guitar, threw a light overcoat over my arm, and like Obadiah, the son of Abensina, went forward to see the hills rising before me. I remember that my overcoat was rather shabby, but by turning it wrong-side out the lining gave it a tolerable appearance, as it hung on my arm. After walking a short distance, the hack came along, an old covered quail-trap that plied between towns. I gave the driver forty cents and about noon he landed me safely at the little tavern in Monrovia.''[2]

**Winter, 1874.** Became associate editor of the *Greenfield News,* but in a few months the paper changed ownership. "I strangled the little thing. Then I continued to grind out poetry for 'literary departments.' I more than supplied the foreign demand with plenty left over for home use. When I sent an editor a prose sketch he advised me to try poetry. I

**Lawzy! don't I rickallect
That-'air old swing in the lane!**
(From *Child Rhymes* by James Whitcomb Riley.
Illustrated by Will Vawter.)

**His home on Lockerbie Street.** ■ (From *James Whitcomb Riley's Complete Works* by James Whitcomb Riley.)

did so and scribbled away at the rate of 2:40 a ream. Then he advised me to try prose again. This was too much. Pursuing the tenor of my own way, I had my hair cut, painted a sign or two and played the guitar.''[1]

**April, 1875.** ''A Destiny'' published in *Hearth and Home*. Riley was paid eight dollars for this modest beginning. Unfortunately, the magazine folded shortly after the poem was published. ''I have long fondled the actual belief that I am a poet, but it pains me to add that I have latterly received such evidence to the contrary that I have no hope of ever proving it to the world. . . . I am sure that all the poems I have ever written, if bundled together, would not bring as much in market value as a bundle of radishes. In fact, I never succeeded in selling but one poem in my life, and I think there must have been some fatal mistake about that, for the editor when I next wrote, gleefully offering him another effort, wrote me saying he regretted that the sudden suspension of the magazine since the publication of my first poem compelled the return of my second. And I have always thought the death of that hitherto prosperous publication was on my hands.''[2]

**1875.** Entered his father's law office, but stayed only three months. ''It was my father's ambition to make me a lawyer, and I struggled to satisfy his wishes; but bless you, that profession was not my bent. I could not learn the stuff fast enough to forget it. . . . In the dog-days of a summer hot as the hinges of Purgatory, I tucked my 'law poems' up my sleeve, turned my back on the attorney business, and my

face to a future as mysterious and hopeless as a block of mining stock.''[1]

**Summer, 1875.** ''There I was in Greenfield, *blue* as the zenith over my head, no money, no way to leave town except walk, and right out on the National Road the dust was flying and the fates fashioning my way of escape. Down that road came the Wizard Oil Company, a band of musicians and comedians in a traveling chariot drawn by horses that cantered and ran as if they were ballasted with quicksilver. The manager of the company had discharged a man at Knightstown. I took the vacant place, mounted to a seat beside the manager and bowled away to Fortville.''[1]

**September, 1875.** ''I am having first rate times considering the boys I am with. They . . . are hardly my kind, but they are pleasant and agreeable and with Doctor Townsend for sensible talk occasionally, I have really a happy time. We sing along the road when we tire of talking, and when we tire of that and the scenery, we lay ourselves along the seats and dream the happy hours away as blissfully as the time honored baby in the sugar trough. I shall not attempt an explicit description of all that I have passed through, but will give a brief outline.

''We 'struck' Fortville first . . . stayed over night and came near dying of loneliness. There is where I 'squeeled' on street business, that is, that portion of it where I was expected to bruise the bass drum. Well, I have been 'in clover' ever since, and do what I please and when I please. I

**The Old Riley homestead.** ■ (From *James Whitcomb Riley's Complete Works* by James Whitcomb Riley.)

made myself thoroughly solid with 'Doxy' (the playful patronymic I have given the Doctor) by introducing a blackboard system of advertising which promises to be the best card out. I have two boards about three feet by four, which during the street concert, I fasten on the sides of the wagon and letter and illustrate during the performance and through the lecture. There are dozens in the crowd that stay to watch the work going on that otherwise would drift from the fold during the drier portion of the Doctor's harangue. Last night at Winchester I made a decided sensation by making a rebus of the well-known lines from Shakespeare—

> 'Why let pain your pleasures spoil,
> For want of Townsend's Magic Oil?'—

with a life-sized bust of the author.''[1]

**January 10, 1877.** First poem published in the *Indianapolis Journal.* ''Many men live in a community for years and years, carefully concealing the latent poetry in their hearts, and pass for reputable citizens; but it was my fate by an unfortunate current of events very early in my career to be betrayed and branded as a poet.''[1]

**April-August, 1877.** Employed as an assistant editor on the *Anderson Democrat.* Known as the ''Jingling Editor.'' ''There is no cessation of the arduous labors of my position and I am grateful for it, for I think the newspaper school an excellent one and filled with most valuable experience. I am still at the crank, but even with that I have daily acquired some new proficiency. I have written many poems that I

have laid away—the kind I publish are only intended for the casual reader. . . . The better ones I reserve for better distinction.''[1]

**August 2, 1877.** ''Leonairie'' a poem imitating Edgar Allen Poe's style, was featured in the *Kokomo Dispatch* as a newly discovered work of Poe. Riley had devised the scheme to prove his theory that ''. . . all that is required to make a poem successful and popular is to prove its author a genius known to fame.''[1]

''The poem was written . . . in the town of Anderson, Indiana, while I was a very callow writer on the *Democrat,* of that place; and, being rallied to desperation over the weekly appearance of my namby-pamby verses, by the editor of a rival sheet, I devised the Poe-poem fraud simply to prove, if possible, that critics of verse would praise from a notable source what they did not hesitate to condemn from an emanation opposite. By correspondence (still preserved) the friendly editor of a paper (the Kokomo, Indiana, *Dispatch*—still conducted by same Ed.) assisted me in foisting the hoax on the public through his columns—this for reasons obvious; while still further to conceal the real authorship of the poem, as soon as published with its editorial hurrah, I attacked its claimed worth and authenticity in my paper. Then every one who knew me, knew, of course, I didn't write a rhyme of it. And so it went—and went—and kept on going—till at last the necessary exposé. Papers everywhere lit into me—friends read all this, and stood aside—went round the other way. The paper upon which I gained the meager living that was mine excused me—and no other paper wanted such a man—wouldn't even let me print a card of explanation—not for weeks, while I stood outside alone, and walked around the Court-House square at night, and through the drizzle and the rain peered longingly at the dim light in the office where I used to sleep, with a heart as hard and dark and obdurate as the towel in the composing-room.'' [*Letters of James Whitcomb Riley,* edited by William Lyon Phelps, Bobbs-Merrill, 1930.[3]]

**September, 1878.** Regular contributor to the *Kokomo Tribune,* the *Indianapolis Saturday Herald,* and the *Indianapolis Journal.* Continued to entertain the public on the lecture platform. "Everything about me is tangled—tangled—tangled.... The old promises for my brilliant future are still promising—they never let up on that, and I'm still believing as of old that I'm goin' to make it. Though just now I'm considerably muddled with a complication of prospects. Of course I don't want to go on a newspaper if the lecture business *will* pan out, but would like to reserve even that in case the lecture *shouldn't* pan out as I'm hoping.

"My lecture is on poetry and character.... It is in layers ... fruit-caked together with original poems, dialect and otherwise. My idea is to have it less profound than entertaining, but I think I'll have quite a tang of the former element. I do indeed. Tell you what I need: genial companionship, but I'm clear out of gun-shot of it here. It's getting awful. People all stop talking as I pass along the street, and stare at me like a 'sum' in compound interest. Can't get me 'fixed'—nor I them, and it's just naturally bearing down, and shuttin' me up like a Chinese lantern or a concertina—that's better—and squeezin' all the music out o' me. I've been trying to rest, but I don't believe I'm doing it."[3]

**November, 1879.** Began regular employment with the *Indianapolis Journal.* Established permanent residence in that city. "I had a peculiar position. My editor-in-chief was one of the most indulgent men in the world and let me do pretty much as I pleased. I wrote when I felt like it, and when I did not, nothing was said. At first when called on for a certain thing by a certain time I grew apprehensive and nervous but I soon solved the problem. I learned to keep a stack of poems and prose on hand, and when there was a big hole in the paper and they called for 'copy' I gave them all they wanted. Sometimes it would be a book review, again a so-called editorial, and oftener some odds and ends that I had written in spare moments—and once a week perhaps an unsigned skit or a jingle for the old cigar box.

"An advantage, or disadvantage, of the newspaper profession is that its members are compelled to know the shams of the world, the weakness of the community, its vanities and mistakes. All of which flowed through the *Journal* rooms—dull speakers called to have it said in print that they were eloquent—women wanted to shine in the society column—men in the wrong wanted to be reported right—and now and then a crack-brained philosopher came with a story as long as his linen duster—and bores came asking two minutes of time and taking two hours. The world with its excellence and follies flows through the reportorial rooms. Thus, I had a constant and inexhaustible supply of new expressions from all sorts and conditions of men, and new ideas simply or extravagantly told. Many of the phrases picked up in this way were ready for use without polishing, for the speech of the people is usually full of rhythm, if we have the ear to hear it; and it is usually direct. Thus, I was brought into contact with all phases of life. My journalistic work gave me an insight into human nature, which I could have acquired in no other way. It taught me also to try to give the public what it wants."[2]

**January, 1882.** First reading in Boston, "the city of twisting streets.

"Everything is well, and I am going to 'make it'—dead sure! I have been very flatteringly received, and the letters I brought are of much importance. With them yesterday I was piloted around to a wonderful extent—meeting not only notables to whom they were addressed, but 'boosted' on by the recipients till I knew everybody of the ilk—all who were not out of town. The *Transcript* did not need an introduction—remembering me without, and—I am glad to insure you—with some little enthusiasm. I met Oliver Optic yesterday—a very boy-like old man, who already had a ticket to my show. John Boyle O'Reilly was out of town but is back to-morrow. *Positively* assured of an audience of at least two thousand people—the best. Longfellow himself would come, he told me, but that his physicians are just now restricting his gambolings. Dan Macauley and I saw the grand old man yesterday, in spite of the doctors who have tried to shut the world away from him. He was very, very gracious, and complimented me beyond all hope of expression....

"There are many peculiar features about Boston. I have seen Beacon Street, the Old South Church, Boston Common, and the Bridge where Longfellow stood at midnight, when the clocks were giving the thing away, and so forth.

"To begin with, I like Boston ... but New England—? Of course I see it—what I see of it—in the most unlovely season; but it strikes me as the coldest, bleakest, barrenest and most forbidding country on earth. I would not die here for one hundred and fifty dollars a night. I would rather die in mid-ocean, with a bull shark for my burial casket.... Positively I am very homesick, but have only a pull now of a week or so further—then I will shake the everlasting snows from my feet, and get back to Indiana like a four-time winner.

"Every day and night, while in the city here, is crowded full of rare delights; but that only serves to heighten the lonesome, cheerless, dreary, weary experiences in the country. And, talk of the country! I tell you there is a country town here every mile-post and each one of them, to me, more desolate and uninviting than the last."[2]

**July, 1883.** First poetry book, *The Old Swimmin' Hole and 'Leven More Poems* published. "[I] set the little skiff afloat on the waves of public life with trepidation. I had no way of knowing its fate. Making a book, is the most ticklish, unsafe and hazardous of all professions. I was reminded of the preface in *Tales of the Ocean,* the old book which fed my hunger for stories in childhood. Its author laid no claim to literary excellence, and was prepared for rough handling from the critics; but he claimed to know 'every rope in the ship,' to be familiar with nautical life, just as I claimed to know the things in Hoosier life, of which my old farmer had been singing. When my book began to sell from the *Journal* counting-rooms, I knew that its sails were spread, like those for the old *Ocean Tales,* and that its streamers were gaily flying, but whether it would meet with prosperous breezes or have to struggle with adverse gales and perhaps founder in stormy seas, yet remained concealed in the womb of time."[2]

Onc't they was a little boy
wouldn't say his prayers—

(From *The Gobble-Uns'll Git You Ef You Don't Watch Out,* based on James Whitcomb Riley's
"Little Orphant Annie." Illustrated by Joel Schick.)

**April, 1885.** While ill, Riley wrote a friend a self-description and career evaluation. The poet was thirty-six. "I am lying flat o' my gifted back and writing with my toes. I have seen better days. Guess I'm goin' to have another bile,—there's a red streak coiled around my leg now like a boa-constrictor and great grief! how 'turts! If you never visited Mount Vesuvius during business hours, come and see my bile when it erupts. . . .

"I am a blonde of fair complexion, with an almost ungovernable trend for brunettes. Five feet six in height—though last state fair I was considerably higher than that—in fact I was many times taken for old High Lonesome, as I went about my daily walk. Used to make lots of money but never had any on hand. It all evaporated in some mysterious way. My standard weight is a hundred and thirty-five, and when I am placed in solitary confinement for life I will eat onions passionately, bird-seed I never touch. I whet my twitter exclusively on fish-bone. My father is a lawyer, and lured me into his office once for a three-months sentence. But I made good my escape, and under cover of the kindly night, I fled up the Pike with a patent-medicine concert-wagon, and had a good time for two or three of the happiest years of my life. Next I struck a country paper and tried to edit, but the proprietor he wanted to do that, and wouldn't let me, and in about a year I quit tryin' and let him have his own way, and now it's the hardest thing in the world for me to acknowledge that he is still an editor and a most successful one. Later I went back home to Greenfield, Ind., near Indianapolis,—east, and engaged in almost everything but work and so became quite prominent. Noted factions and public bodies began to regard me attentively, and no grand jury was complete without my presence! I wasn't, howev-er, considered wholly lost till I began to publish poetry brazenly affixing my own name to it. But I couldn't get any money for it, although stranger editors wrote me letters of praise regarding it. Then I sent a little of the best of it to two or three real poets East, and they commended it, and I showed their letters, and have been paid ever since. Still I am not rich. A skating-rink proprietor who yearns to be a poet should be regarded with suspicion.

". . . Mainly . . . the foregoing truthfully outlines my brief career. But I've been blue over being 'downed' again by the blasted lameness, and I'm trying to keep cheerful."[3]

**December, 1885.** First prose book *The Boss Girl,* published. "It is better than I dared to hope, however hard I set my teeth and wished and wished and wished. The last sketch is my pet—'The Spider'. . . .

"The book is clean out of print—a week ago. Next edition delayed by paper—'ad-dam it! and had it been ready would have been exhausted too. Too bad!'"[2]

**March, 1886.** Began a series of readings with Bill Nye. Authors' readings were the rage and the Nye-Riley combination became quite popular. "Nye is simply superb on the stage—and no newspaper report can half-way reproduce either the curious charm of his drollery—his improvisations—inspirations and so forth. At times his auditors are hysterical with delight. . . . Newspapers all sent reporters, quite an audience in themselves, as they sat in betabled phalanx in the orchestra-pen, and laughed and whooped and yelled and cried, wholly oblivious of their duty half the time. . . . With Nye for company the trials of travel are

**We find his glad heart owning still
The freshness of his youth.**

■ (From *James Whitcomb Riley's Complete Works* by James Whitcomb Riley. Illustrated by Howard Chandler Christy.)

lessened till now I am almost content with what seems my principal mission here on earth, i.e., to spread over and run all around it like a ringworm.''[2]

**November, 1887.** Invited to read at Chickering Hall, New York. This success marked national acceptance for Riley. ''Off at next gasp for New York and Bill Nye. As yet I am not at liberty to state my mission, but in confidence you must know that I go there to read with American Authors. Is not that a great big and all-swelled-up honor for the little bench-leg poet out of this blessed Hoosier Nazareth? Only think of it!—introduced by James Russell Lowell to thousands of the crowned heads of the strictly élite literary eye-and-ear auditors of that Athens! Oh, heavens!—I feel indeed that I am a poor sewing girl.''[2]

**Fall, 1887.** *Afterwhiles* published. ''I have been at work on a book; if it proves successful I shall be the happiest little man in the world—for I have been long under the harrow. A beautiful book in press, dedicated to my mother, 160 pages of *puore* [sic] poetry. . . . Up and at it as fast as a Mussulman's screech and new rhymes can wobble into

ranks. Am writing better stuff than ever, with my best book now in hands of publishers. Thousands of 'em sold and the money purt-nigh right in my pocket—and out again. We call the volume *Afterwhiles*.''[2]

**January, 1890.** The Riley-Nye partnership dissolved at Louisville, Kentucky. Nye remained a close friend of Riley. ''Nye has the heart of a woman and the tenderness of a child. Always in good humor, never finicky, I could not imagine a more charming traveling companion. We were constantly playing practical jokes on each other or indulging in some mischievous banter before the audience. On one occasion, coming before the footlights for a word of general introduction, Mr. Nye said, 'Ladies and gentlemen, the entertainment to-night is of a dual nature. Mr. Riley and I will speak alternately. First I come out and talk until I get tired, then Mr. Riley comes out and talks until *you* get tired!' Thus the sallies and kickshaws bubbled merrily on, every night something new to spring on the audience. Besides I learned to know in Bill Nye a man blessed with as noble and heroic a heart as ever beat. But the making of trains, which were all in conspiracy to outwit me, schedule or no schedule, and the rush and tyrannical pressure of inviolable engagements, some hundred to a season and from Boston to the Rocky Mountains, were a distress to my soul. Imagine yourself on a crowded day-long excursion; imagine that you had to ride all the way on the platform of the car; then imagine that you had to ride all the way back on the same platform; and lastly, try to imagine how you would feel if you did that every day of your life—and you will then get a glimmer—a faint glimmer—of how one feels after traveling about on a reading or lecturing tour.''[2]

**Spring, 1890.** At forty, took an active part in the publication of his books. ''There seems to be so much of the lottery principle in [book publication]. What I confidently think will take well with the public does not take, and what I fear will not go, goes. And so it is, as I learn from all available experiences of literary friends. At best the monetary success is unworthy recompense for all the trials and anxieties one must endure. For fifteen years I have been striving to attain an audience for my verse, and long ago would have given up in sheer despair but that I had a more practical calling [income from the *Journal* and the platform] by which I could put bread in my mouth, and also pie. The majority of mankind is more in sympathy with dimes than rhymes. A poet must, therefore, equip himself, someway, with *means,* that's all! Longfellow did it by teaching; Bryant by newspaper work; Stoddard, the same; and so on with the whole-kit-and-bilin' of the twittering brotherhood that 'get there' as well as versify. Singing *alone* will not pay except in the rarest instances.''[2]

**October, 1890.** *Rhymes of Childhood* published. ''Am just now going to press with a Holiday book, entitled *Rhymes of Childhood*—nearly a hundred poems, dialect and serious equally. In it the enthusiastic writer goes scampering barefoot from page to page, with no more sense of dignity than socks, and the like wholesome rapture in heels and heart. I think of what a child Lincoln must have been, and the same child-heart at home within his breast when death came by. It is all in the line of *Fact*—that's the stuff that makes good fiction, romance, and poetry. I digress to say this, but I glory in the crime.''[2]

**Summer, 1891.** Visited England and Scotland. ''My first trip abroad taught me that the United States is a fine country in which to live. I saw a great many Americans in

London, who, ashamed of their country, mingled with the British and attempted to disguise their nationality. Many of them succeeded, much to the gratification of all true Americans. I was told on my return that I had criticized my native land. I had not. If all Americans liked me half as well as I like them I would be indeed a proud and grateful man."[2]

**1893.** Having led a Bohemian life, Riley established permanent residence at 528 Lockerbie Street, Indianapolis. "Think of it. I never owned a desk in my life and don't know what it is to own a library. Where do I write? Everywhere—sometimes on the kitchen table in my sister's house, then in the parlor and again on the printer's case—just where the fancy seizes me. Queer how and where authors write. Andrew Lang wrote best in a rose garden—Tolstoi sat on a bed and put his inkstand on a pillow—Dumas used an ebony desk—the lid to Mary Anderson's table was mother-of-pearl. None of your luxuries for the little bench-leg poet. Give him a bleak room, the more uncomfortable the better. . . . Chance first led me into Lockerbie Street. Chance has brought me many gifts. Chance has signally contributed to my salvation."[2]

**1896.** *Child-World* published. "Another book—which same headstrong thing has insisted upon rhyming, chiming and subliming itself to the other side of 200 pages. And here, seeing it at last in type, I'm wondering, thus belatedly, who else'll want to wade so vast a width of all unbroken verse."[2]

**October, 1896.** Reading tour of the Southwest. Although Riley was a veteran traveler, he never overcame his fear of trains and traveling alone. "Nine times out of ten, when I travel with a trunk, the thing is lost. Recently, I discovered that my friends who have 'gone beyond the line' are having fun with me at my expense. Since crossing the divide Nye has been steering me into wrong trains and smiling about it. So I burden myself no more with heavy baggage. If I travel with a trunk I am haunted with the fear that it will be lost. I go about the country with a grip, and I keep a tenacious hold on it all day, but I never feel quite safe about it at night. If there is ever a horrible railway accident and among the debris is discovered a valise with an arm attached to it, they may bury it without further identification as the fragments of the Hoosier Poet."[2]

**1897.** Maintained that his poetry was essentially visionary. "Everything I write seems to me as if I had simply found it and no right to it . . . and I don't think I have. It is exactly on the principle of the dreams I have had—dreams that were mine undeniably, but I in no wise responsible for their mental construction—therefore with no right to claim any of their excellence in that particular, an excellence sometimes extraordinary. In dreams I have built pages and pages of marvelous verse that floated before the mental vision as smooth and pure and lucid as the clearest print—verse that charmed the author at times with excellently molded sentences of purest poetry, that he dwelt upon and extolled and read again and again. All that is the dream's composition and the poet did not write a line of it and can not claim it. . . . That is my theory, and I am only proud because I have found the poem."[2]

**1902.** Received an honorary M.A. from Yale University. He remarked: "I just wanted to get behind the door and hide myself."[2]

(From *James Whitcomb Riley's Complete Works* by James Whitcomb Riley. Illustrated by Howard Chandler Christy.)

**1903.** Last successful reading tour. "A long experience has taught me not to be ambitious to instruct anybody from the footlights. An audience does not want that, but it does want to be cheerfully entertained. It never tires of simple, wholesome, happy themes. Give it what it desires—here is the secret, if there is any secret in it. Make things as entertaining to the audience as to yourself. An audience is cosmopolitan in character, a neighborly gathering, all on a level. The rich are there, and they are interested in the poor, since they came originally from the ranks of those who walk by the wayside. They know as I know that the crude man is generally moral, for Nature has just let go his hand. She's just been leading him through the dead leaves and the daisies. When I deal with such a man in my readings, I give him credit for every virtue; but what he does and the way he does it is *his* way, not mine. It is my office to interpret him.

"I talk of the dear old times when there were no social distinctions, of pioneer homes and towns, where there was a warm welcome for all, just as if all were blood brothers as Kipling says. I muse or romp happily amid the scenes of my childhood and the paradise is promptly recognized and appreciated by my audience. The difficult thing, the delicate office, is to know what to choose, and when to stop."[2]

**February, 1904.** Given an honorary Degree of Letters from the University of Pennsylvania.

**1906.** Trip to Mexico City. "I can not say whether I shall write a poem on this tropic land. I never can tell in advance about what my poetry is to be. I wait for the spirit to move me."[2]

**JAMES WHITCOMB RILEY**

**1908.** Elected to the National Institute of Arts and Letters. "If I am not misinformed it is the aim of the National Institute to stimulate devotion to high ideals in all the arts, and to extend practical encouragement to beginners of promise. And with these purposes I deeply and sincerely sympathize. The West, as a contributor to the various branches of American art, has risen almost under my own eye. No one more keenly appreciates the high value of the service that may be rendered by the Institute and Academy than I do."[3]

**October 7, 1910.** "Riley Day" observed in the Indiana school system. Addressed a letter to the children of his home city. "You are conspirators—every one of you, that's what you are; you have conspired to inform the general public of my birthday, and I am already so old that I want to forget all about it. But I will be magnanimous and forgive you, for I know that your intent is really friendly, and to have such friends as you are makes me—don't care how old I am! In fact it makes me glad and happy that I feel as absolutely young and spry as a very schoolboy—even as one of you—and so to all intents I am.

"Therefore let me be with you throughout the long, lovely day, and share your mingled joys and blessings with your parents and your teachers, and in the words of little Tim Cratchit: 'God bless us, every one.'"[3]

**1911.** Suffered a paralytic stroke. "I have finished my work; my end has come . . . [I have been] through gathering years, tried and vexed with one infirmity after another, till it seems at last I've acquired the whole measly assortment, from vanishing teeth, wired eyesight and thick hearing, to bone-erysipelas of my very soul!—Not one of the

long calamitous list but drills away at me, night and day, till, like the desperate Dutchman, I feel liable at any minute to '*jump der dock off!*' But I try not to complain—however poorly I succeed."[3]

**1915.** National Commissioner of Education directed "Riley Day" to be observed in all schools throughout the country.

**July 22, 1916.** Died at Lockerbie Street, Indianapolis in his sleep. ". . . My steps are turning gladly toward the light, and it seems to me sometimes I almost see God's face."[1]

"Everybody's learning all the time. Never any venture of my life was any more than a trial at some attainment—an experiment—not a forecast certainty of accomplishment. The fact is, keeps me duly humble, and ought to. Whatever good is wrought is not our doing  it is *through* us, not *of* us. And that is what God wants to beat in us, and when we just won't have it so, why, then He lets loose of us that we may see, and the whole united populace as well, that here is another weighed-and-found-wanting candidate for enduring glory."[2]

*FOR MORE INFORMATION SEE:* Edgar W. Nye, *A Guest at the Ludlow,* Bowen-Merrill, 1897, reprinted, Gregg, 1969; John A. Howland, *James Whitcomb Riley in Prose and Picture,* Handy & Higgins, 1903, reprinted, R. West, 1973; Albert J. Beveridge, "James Whitcomb Riley—Poet of the People," in his *Meaning of the Times, and Other Speeches,* Bobbs-Merrill, 1908; Michael Monahan, "Our Best Loved Poet (Riley)," in his *New Adventures,* Doran, 1917; Robert C. Holliday, "Hoosier Highlights," in his *Broome Street Straws,* Doran, 1919; Marcus Dickey, *The Youth of James Whitcomb Riley,* Bobbs-Merrill, 1919, reprinted, R. West, 1973; Meredith Nicholson, "James Whitcomb Riley," in her *Man in the Street: Papers on American Topics,* Scribner, 1921; Marcus Dickey, *The Maturity of James Whitcomb Riley,* Bobbs-Merrill, 1922; Bliss Carman, *James Whitcomb Riley,* Heartman, 1925, reprinted, R. West, 1973; E. L. Masters, "James Whitcomb Riley," in *Essays of Today,* edited by Odell Shepard and Robert Hillyer, Appleton-Century, 1928.

William L. Phelps, editor, *Letters of James Whitcomb Riley,* Bobbs-Merrill, 1930, reprinted, AMS Press, 1973; Anthony Russo and Dorothy A. Russo, *A Bibliography of James Whitcomb Riley,* Indiana Historical Society, 1944, reprinted, Haskell House, 1972; John B. Martin, *Indiana,* Knopf, 1947; G. Van Riper, "James Whitcomb Riley Centennial Year Celebrated in Indiana," *Publishers Weekly,* November 26, 1949; Minnie B. Mitchell, *James Whitcomb Riley as I Knew Him: Real Incidents in the Early Life of America's Beloved Poet,* Old Swimmin' Hole Press, 1949; Richard E. Banta, compiler, *Indiana Authors and Their Books, 1816-1916,* Wabash College Press, 1949; Harriet L. Fitzhugh and P. K. Fitzhugh, *Concise Biographical Dictionary of Famous Men and Women,* revised and enlarged edition, Grosset & Dunlap, 1949; George A. Phelps, *Holidays and Philosophical Biographies,* House-Warven, 1951; Jeannette Nolan and others, *Poet of the People: An Evaluation of James Whitcomb Riley,* Indiana University Press, 1951; Richard Crowder, *Those Innocent Years: The Legacy and Inheritance of a Hero of the Victorian Era, James Whitcomb Riley,* Bobbs-Merrill, 1957; Peter Revell, *James Whitcomb Riley,* Twayne, 1970.

For children: Ward Griffith, *Fifty Famous Americans,* Whitman, 1946; Laura Benét, *Famous American Poets,*

Dodd, Mead, 1950; David E. Scherman and Rosemarie Redlich, *America: The Land and Its Writers*, Dodd, Mead, 1956; Minnie B. Mitchell, *James Whitcomb Riley: Hoosier Boy*, Bobbs-Merrill, 1962; L. Benét, *Famous Poets for Young People*, Dodd, Mead, 1964; Everett S. Allen, *Famous American Humorous Poets*, Dodd, Mead, 1968; L. Edmond Leipold, *Famous American Poets*, Denison, 1969; L. E. Leipold, *Heroes of a Different Kind*, Denison, 1973; L. E. Leipold, *Great American Poets*, Denison, 1973.

# ROBINSON, Charles   1870-1937

*PERSONAL:* Born October 22, 1870, in Islington, London, England; died March 13, 1937; son of Thomas (an artist and engraver) and Eliza Ann (Heath) Robinson; brother of artists Thomas Heath and William Heath Robinson; married Edith Mary Favatt, 1897; children: two sons, four daughters. *Education:* Admitted to Royal Academy Schools, also attended Highbury School of Art, West London School of Art, and Heatherleys. *Home:* Maple Tree Cottage, Botley, Chesham, Buckinghamshire, England.

*CAREER:* Artist and illustrator. Apprenticed to Waterlow & Sons, Ltd. as a lithographic artist. His works were exhibited at Royal Academy, Royal Institute of Painters in Watercolours, and in Liverpool and Bristol, England. *Member:* Savage Club, Sketch Club (London; life honorary member and past president).

*ILLUSTRATOR:* Aesop, *Aesop's Fables*, Dent, 1895; Robert Louis Stevenson, *A Child's Garden of Verses*, Scribner, 1895; Henry D. Lowry, *Make Believe*, John Lane, 1896; Gabriel Setoun (pseudonym of Thomas N. Hepburn) *The Child World*, John Lane, 1896; Eugene Field, *Lullaby-Land* (edited by Kenneth Grahame), John Lane, 1898; Barrington MacGregor, *King Longbeard; or, Annals of the Golden Dreamland*, John Lane, 1898; William B. Rands, *Lilliput Lyrics* (edited by R. Brimley Johnson), John Lane, 1898; (with brothers, Thomas and William Heath Robinson) Hans Christian Andersen, *Fairy Tales from Hans Christian Andersen*, Dent, 1899; William E. Cule, *Child Voices*, A. Melrose, 1899; Charles Perrault, *Tales of Passed Time*, Dent, 1899; George Sand (pseudonym of Amantine Aurore Lucile Dupin) *The Master Mosaic-Workers* (translation from the French by C. C. Johnson), Dent, 1899.

*The True Annals of Fairy-Land*, three volumes, Dent, 1900-02; John J. Bell, *Jack of All Trades*, John Lane, 1900; Percy Dearmer, *The Little Lives of the Saints*, Wells, Gardner, 1900; Friedrich H. C. De La Motte Fouque, *Sintram and His Companions* [and] *Aslauga's Knight*, Dent, 1900; Norman Garstin, *The Suitors of Aprille*, John Lane, 1900; Homer, *The Adventures of Odysseus* (retold in English by F. S. Marvin, R. J. G. Mayor and F. M. Stawell), Dent, 1900; Henry De Vere Stackpoole, *Pierrette*, John Lane, 1900; Clare Bridgman, *A Book of Days for Little Ones*, Dutton, 1901; C. Bridgman, *The Bairn's Coronation Book*, Dent, 1902; C. Bridgman, *The Shopping Day*, Dutton, 1902; John Henry Burn, editor, *The Mother's Book of Song*, Wells, Gardner, 1902; Douglas W. Jerrold, *Fireside Saints*, Blackie & Son, 1904.

*A Bookful of Fun*, T. Sealy Clark, 1905; I. Henry Wallis, *The Cloud Kingdom*, John Lane, 1905; Evelyn Sharp, *The Child's Christmas*, Blackie & Son, 1906; Katharine Tynan, *A Little Book of Courtesies*, Dent, 1906; Lewis Carroll (pseudonym of Charles Lutwidge Dodgson), *Alice's Adventures in Wonderland*, Cassell, 1907; E. Sharp, *The Story of*

(From *The Happy Prince* by Oscar Wilde. Illustrated by Charles Robinson.)

the Weathercock, Blackie & Son, 1907; Evelyn Martinengo-Cesaresco, *The Fairies' Fountain, and Other Stories*, Arnold Fairbairns, 1908; *The True Annals of Fairyland in the Reign of King Cole*, two volumes, Dent, 1909.

Ruth Arkwright, *Brownkins, and Other Fancies*, Wells, Gardner, 1910; Jacob and Wilhelm Grimm, *Grimm's Fairy Tales* (translation from the German by L. L. Weedon), Dutton, 1910; Jessie Pope, *Babes and Birds*, Blackie & Son, 1910; Netta Syrett, *The Vanishing Princess*, David Nutt, 1910; Frances E. H. Burnett, *The Secret Garden*, Heinemann, 1911; Alice Talwin Morris, *My Book about the Empire*, Blackie & Son, 1911; J. Pope, *The Baby Scouts*, Blackie & Son, 1911; Percy Bysshe Shelley, *The Sensitive Plant*, Heinemann, 1911.

(With others) William Blake, *Songs of Innocence*, Dutton, 1912; Anatole France (pseudonym of Jacques Anatole Thibault), *Bee, the Princess of the Dwarfs* (retold in English by Peter Wright), Dutton, 1912; Handasyde (pseudonym of Emily H. Buchanan), *The Four Gardens*, Heinemann, 1912; A. T. Morris, *More about the Empire*, Blackie & Son, 1912; J. Pope, *Babes and Beasts*, Blackie & Son, 1912; Harold Fielding, *Margaret's Book*, Hutchinson, 1913; W. J. Minnion, *Topsy Turvy*, The Connoisseur, 1913; C. Perrault, *Fairy Tales* (edited by Frederick C. Tilney), Dutton, 1913; Ernest T. Thurston, *The Open Window*, Chapman & Hall, 1913; Oscar Wilde, *The Happy Prince, and Other Tales*, Duckworth, 1913, reissued, Citadel, 1946; Agnes and Egerton Castle, *Our Sentimental Garden*, Heinemann, 1914; Washington Irving, *Rip Van Winkle*, F. A. Stokes, 1914; A. T. Morris, *A Child's Book of Empire*, Blackie & Son, 1914.

**Then the angel plucks a handful of flowers which they carry with them up to God, there to bloom more brightly than ever upon earth.** ■ (From "The Angel" in *Fairy Tales from Hans Christian Andersen,* translated by Mrs. E. Lucas. Illustrated by Charles Robinson.)

(From *The Secret Garden* by Frances Hodgson Burnett. Illustrated by Charles Robinson.)

Robert Herrick, *Robert Herrick* (poems), Wells, Gardner, 1915; William Shakespeare, *The Songs and Sonnets of William Shakespeare*, Duckworth, 1915; E. Sharp, *What Happened at Christmas*, Blackie & Son, 1915; Alice Margaret Stevenson, *Bridget's Fairies: A Masque of Education*, R.T.S., 1919; Grace Rhys, *The Children's Garland of Verses*, Dent, 1921; John G. Stevenson, *Father Time Stories* [London], 1921; Brenda Girvin and Monica Cosens, *Wee-Men*, Hutchinson, 1923; A. A. Milne, *Once on a Time* [London], 1925; Winifred Radcliffe, *The Saint's Garden*, S.P.C.K., 1927; *Mother Goose Nursery Rhymes*, Collins, 1928.

All written by Walter Copeland Jerrold: (Under pseudonym Walter Copeland) *The Farm Book*, Dutton, 1901; (under pseudonym W. Copeland) *The Book of the Zoo*, Dent, 1902; *Nonsense! Nonsense!*, Blackie & Son, 1902; (editor) *The Reign of King Oberon*, Dent, 1902; (editor) *The Big Book of Nursery Rhymes*, Blackie & Son, 1903; (under pseudonym W. Copeland) *The Black Cat Book*, Blackie & Son, 1905; (under pseudonym W. Copeland) *Picture Books for Children*, Blackie & Son, 1905-08; (under pseudonym W. Copeland) *Babes and Blossoms*, Blackie & Son, 1908; (editor) *The Big Book of Fairy Tales*, Blackie & Son, 1911; (editor) *The Big Book of Fables*, Blackie & Son, 1912.

*SIDELIGHTS:* **October 22, 1870.** Born in the borough of Islington, London; the second child in a family of four brothers and two sisters, son of Thomas Robinson, an artist and engraver, and Eliza Ann (Heath) Robinson. Unlike his artist brothers, Thomas and William, Charles was not christened with his mother's maiden name (Heath), but was named after his father's brother and companion, Charles. W. Heath Robinson recalled two incidents from their childhood together. "Although at the time [our] holidays seemed to be full of excitement, in retrospect they seem to have followed a tranquil course. However, one . . . incident . . . stuck in my memory. No one, with the exception of Jonah, has been swallowed by a whale and lived to talk about it. My brother Charles was nearly swallowed by a whale, and talked very much about it afterwards. He was justly proud of this distinction, and we, while affecting to make light of the matter, secretly envied him. But we shared a kind of reflected glory. An old whale, apparently dead, was washed up on the sands. There was great excitement, and people crowded to see it. One of the boatmen, in playful mood, lifted Charles from the ground and seated him on the monster's head. To everyone's surprise it was found to be alive, but this last indignity was too much for it. The whale gave a monstrous gasp, and a final heave shook its whole body as it expired. Charles was sent sprawling on the sands. As he stoutly maintained, no one could doubt the intention of the whale to end its ill-spent life by making a meal of him." [W. Heath Robinson, *My Line of Life*, Blackie & Son, Ltd., 1938.[1]]

**1882.** Received secondary education at the Old Islington High School. Student, for a brief period, at the Highbury School of Art.

**1885.** Signed apprenticeship indentures with the printers, Waterlow & Son. While apprenticing to George Sidney Waterlow, Robinson attended art schools as an evening student, among them West London School of Art and Heatherleys.

His brother, W. Heath Robinson, recollected: "Charles at the beginning of his artistic career was not quite so fortunately placed as Tom and I. Instead of becoming a whole-time student at the school of art he was apprenticed to a lithographer, and only attended the class in the evening. In the long run this handicap, if such it was, does not seem to have affected his work. Whether he would have benefited by a more academic training it would be difficult to say. Perhaps it would have checked his delightful freedom and his most original fancy."[1]

**July, 1892.** Admitted to the Royal Academy, but was soon forced to resign for financial reasons.

**Mid 1890's.** Did architectural drawings and newspaper advertisements. Also worked for the Society for Promoting Christian Knowledge. Drew illustrations for the children's magazines of Marcus Ward, Cassell, and others.

Worked at his father's studio—two rooms atop Number One, Danes Inn. W. Heath Robinson, who also worked at this studio, wrote: "I worked in my father's studio at Danes Inn in the Strand. This was, for my father, conveniently near to the editorial offices of the *Penny Illustrated Paper*. Danes Inn was a dreary place after Hampstead Heath. It was as cold as stone, of which material the two tall rows of houses which composed it were mainly built. They were separated by a courtyard paved also with stone.

"My father occupied a suite of two rooms at the top of No. 1. It was approached by a very wide circular stairway with an iron railing to deter anyone so disposed from throwing themselves on to the pavement below. A stall smell of old dinners pervaded the place and belied the otherwise prison-like character of the building. The depressed spirit was not greatly refreshed on entering my father's door. The front room in which we worked overlooked the courtyard, and the air was dry and smelt of dust. The walls were hung with one or two old charts, and I can remember an ancient macabre print representing, in allegorical form, the Spirit of 'Gout' gnawing the foot of some victim of this complaint. The dried body of some poor puss of long ago was suspended near the fireplace and grinned with fiendish glee at an old blunderbuss on the wall. This was rather gruesome and the less understandable because the Robinsons were always fond of their cats. In retrospect, a long procession of them passes before me. Boss, Nelson, Wolsey, Peter, Barty, George Barker, Sheringham, Fred and Saturday Morning—the last, an immense veteran of thirteen years, who still survives and dreams away his declining years by the fireside. Here he waits resignedly for his passing to some feline paradise where he will join all the old Robinson cats. Was this poor blackened mummy all that remained of some long since deceased Robinson pet? On the mantleshelf was one of my father's ship models, now a wreck in a sea of dust; a sad reminder of the days when my father wished to be a sailor."[1]

**1895.** Made his very first sale to Wells, Gardner, Darton & Co.—an illustration of one of his father's nonsense rhymes.

Hired by the Bodley Head publishing firm to illustrate Robert Louis Stevenson's *A Child's Garden of Verses*, a success which launched his career. One critic observed: ". . . He has depicted childhood in all its remoteness from the grown-up land, in its heroic and fantastic imaginings, in its long thoughts and its short sight . . . Poet and artist meet and part in an interesting fashion. And it is not merely as a book of graceful pictures that this one which Mr. Robinson has done so much to make beautiful will be treasured. It is Stevenson's exquisite *Child's Garden* with still more childhood put into it." [Leo de Freitas, *Charles Robinson*, St. Martins Press, 1976.[2]]

He said, "I am surprised, I expect it's a party; it's lucky I woke."■ (From *Margaret's Book* by H. Fielding Hall. Illustrated by Charles Robinson.)

**Away she danced, and away she had to dance, right away into the Dark Forest.** ■ (From "The Red Shoes" in *Fairy Tales from Hans Christian Andersen,* translated by Mrs. E. Lucas. Illustrated by Charles Robinson.)

W. Heath Robinson wrote: "I envied the success my brothers had gained. Charles had become famous with his illustrations to *A Child's Garden of Verses*.... This was followed by the illustration of other books of a similar character written by H. D. Lowry, Gabriel Setoun, I. Henry Wallis and Walter Gerald."[1]

**1896.** His Christmas cards were bound in a booklet with a text written by himself entitled *Christmas Dreams,* under the *nom de plume,* Awfly Weirdly.

Won the Metropolitan Sketch Clubs' Competition. The First Prize of figures and The First Prize for design. In an article on this prize-winning work, an art critic wrote: "The individuality of these drawings promises a good deal, and if Mr. Robinson, who seems so far to have escaped the influence of three of his contemporaries to quite a remarkable degree, and to be neither Charles Ricketts, R. Anning Bell nor Aubrey Beardsley, but himself, will go on in the same path, one may expect a personal style of that will take a far higher place than the exercises in the style of the three clever designers whose name I have quoted."[2]

**April, 1897.** Married Edith Mary Favatt. Took their first home in West End Lane. W. Heath Robinson recalled: "Charles's wedding soon followed his early prosperity.... He was one of those happy and gifted people who inevitably attract many friends. He became the centre of an admiring group of artists, authors, and even publishers. Many of these attended the feast; John Lane, H. D. Lowry, Walter Gerald, Evelyn Sharp and the Rev. Percy Dearmer were among the many guests. The last named conducted the ceremony at the church. It could not be called a society wedding, but it was a great marriage feast for all that. It took place on a sunny day in April when the almond blossom was out and thoughts of weddings and betrothals were in the air. Even the older guests were inspired by this genial influence, by the lovely spring afternoon, the light dresses, the smiling faces, the flowers and the champagne. They laughingly recalled their own wedding days and long years of happiness since.

"The next morning, festivities were continued on a modified scale, but at last they gradually died down, and the full realization dawned upon us that Charles was married. This event marked an important stage in the history of the Robinson family. It was the first wedding in the younger generation."[1]

**1899.** Illustrated along with his brothers, William and Thomas, *Fairy Tales from Hans Christian Andersen.* The brothers had acquired the nickname, "The Three Musketeers."

**1902.** A member and later President of the Highgate 30 Club, which was "founded . . . for the discussion of papers, debate, and social intercourse."

Began his closest friendship with Walter C. Jerrold after publication of *Nonsense! Nonsense!.* The two of them collaborated on over twenty books.

**1903-1912.** Designed many richly illustrated Christmas gift books—*The Big Book of Fairy Tales, The Big Book of Nursery Rhymes* and *The Big Book of Fables.*

He was dedicated to the concept of "the book beautiful," a theory which held that a book's text, layout, illustrations, and cover should constitute an integrated whole.

**1907.** Upset his publisher when he depicted Alice in *Alice's Adventures in Wonderland* with short hair.

**1911.** For his work on *The Secret Garden,* by Francis Hodgson Burnett, he employed his eldest child, Bay Robinson, as a model.

**1914.** Enrolled as a member of the Volunteer Training Corps during World War I and reached rank of second lieutenant. He executed hand-drawn route maps and illustrated military instruction books.

**1920's.** After the war, with the return of regular commissions from such illustrated periodicals as *Graphic, Pan* and *Queen,* family moved to a cottage in Botley, Buckinghamshire.

**1925.** A. A. Milne's *Once On a Time* published and included what many critics believed to be Robinson's very finest black and white illustrations.

**1926-1927.** President of the London Sketch Club. As W. Heath Robinson described the organization: "It consisted of a group of artists, who met every Friday evening in the winter season and made sketches. After this a hot meal of a very substantial quality was provided followed by music and various entertainments.... There were many members who have since become famous. These included Frank Reynolds, H. M. Bateman, Dudley Hardy, De la Bere, Edmund Dulac, Sheringham, John Hassall, Lawson Wood, Bert Thomas and Ernest Moore. A few of the members were painters, but they were mostly magazine and book illustrators, poster artists, cartoonists and humorous artists. There were also many lay members, amongst whom were representatives of other professions. They used to assemble after the work was done on Friday evening, and many of them being professional entertainers, made valuable contributions to the evening's programme. For the artists, these meetings provided opportunities not always to be found in their everyday work. Undeterred by the opinion of anyone other than our fellow-artists, we gave a free rein to our fancies and imagination. Since those early days, they have had many distinguished members, amongst whom may be numbered the Great George Parlby, my brother Charles, Albert Toft, Alfred Leete, Fred Taylor, Barribal and Tom Downey."[1]

**1929.** His closest friend, Walter C. Jerrold, died.

Robinson sent a portrait of W. C. Jerrold to the man's daughter, Hebe. "So, my dear child, I hope you feel that it is a good portrait. I know it is a good painting, and I hope you will accept it as a token of lasting memory of the best man I have ever known. Your affectionate, but down trodden uncle, Charles Robinson."[2]

**March 13, 1937.** Died. His death profoundly affected his surviving artist-brothers. W. Heath Robinson wrote: ". . . My brother Charles died. It was unbelievable. He was always so alive with an irrepressible vitality, it seemed impossible it could cease. His life had been one of work and some hardship. It had been a brave and successful struggle to be an artist and at the same time to bring up a large family. Yet there was always something of youth and of being on holiday about Charles. I went into his studio a few days before he died. Besides unfinished pictures, there was the incompleted model of a Spanish galleon. It was already taking shape. Painted here and there with brilliant colour it gave promise of the proud and beautiful thing it was to have been. Although unfinished, it was a triumph of the spirit over the years and the many vicissitudes of life that had at last laid him low.

"This was at an age when most men retire, but artists seldom retire. Younger men with new ideas and newer ways of looking at things may overtake them and push them aside, but like Charles they go down fighting. I am sure that Tom, the eldest of the three Musketeers, has not given up hope of painting the greatest masterpiece of his life.

"Charles inherited his love for making ships from my father, whom he resembled in other ways. He was more concerned with his painting and his ship models than with theories about art. He was an artist first of all and last of all. He had that magic assistance so often given to genius. If he wanted to build a ship, the materials somehow rose to his hands. As with his painting, it was all so easy and instinctive with him."[1]

*FOR MORE INFORMATION SEE:* W. Heath Robinson, *My Line of Life,* Blackie & Son, 1938; Brian Doyle, editor, *Who's Who of Children's Literature,* Schocken, 1968; Leo de Freitas, *Charles Robinson,* St. Martins Press, 1976.

# ROBINSON, T(homas) H(eath)  1869-1950

*PERSONAL:* Born June 19, 1869, in Islington, London, England; died in 1950; son of Thomas (an artist and engraver) and Eliza Ann (Heath) Robinson; brother of artists Charles and William Heath Robinson. *Education:* Studied at Cook's Art School and Westminster Art School, London, England.

*CAREER:* Artist and illustrator.

*ILLUSTRATOR:* Frank Rinder, reteller, *Old-World Japan: Legends of the Land of the Gods,* G. Allen, 1895; Elizabeth C. Gaskell, *Cranford,* Macmillan, 1896; Paulina Elizabeth Ottilia Louisa (Queen Consort of Charles I, King of Roumania) and Alma Strettell Harrison, *Legends from River and Mountain,* Dodd, 1896; William M. Thackeray, *The History of Henry Esmond,* G. Allen, 1896; Nathaniel Hawthorne, *The Scarlet Letter,* Bliss & Sands, 1897; (with Emily J. Harding) John Milton, *Milton's Hymn on the Morning of Christ's Nativity,* G. Allen, 1897; Laurence Sterne, *A Sentimental Journey,* Bliss & Sands, 1897; William Canton, *A Child's Book of Saints,* Dent, 1898; *Fairy Tales from the Arabian Nights,* Dent, 1899; (with brothers Charles and William Heath Robinson) Hans Christian Andersen, *Fairy Tales from Hans Christian Andersen* (translated by Mrs. E. Lucas), Dent, 1899; Bernard Minssen, editor, *A Book of French Song for the Young,* Dent, 1899.

Wilhelm Hauff, *Lichtenstein* (adapted by L. L. Weedon), E. Nister, 1900; Jane Porter, *The Scottish Chiefs,* Dent, 1900; Grace Aguilar, *The Vale of Cedars, and Other Tales,* Dent, 1902; Paul Creswick, *Robin Hood and His Adventures,* Dutton, 1902; Katharine F. Boult, reteller, *Heroes of the Norselands,* Dent, 1903; Thomas Hughes, *Tom Brown's School Days,* Dent, 1903; Charles Kingsley, *The Heroes,* E. Nister, 1903; Elizabeth T. Meade Smith, *Stories from the Old Old Bible,* George Newnes, 1903; George Eliot (pseudonym of Marian Evans Cross), *The Mill on the Floss,* Blackie & Son, 1904; Edmund Spenser, *Una and the Red Cross Knight, and Other Tales from Spenser's Faery Queen* (edited by Naomi G. Royde-Smith), Dutton, 1905; Margaret Duncan Kelly, *The Story of Sir Walter Raleigh,* T. C. & E. C. Jack, 1906; Omar Khayyam, *Rubaiyat of Omar Khayyam* (translated by Edward FitzGerald), Dutton, 1907; Margaret Duncan Coxhead, *Mexico,* T. C. & E. C. Jack, 1909.

*Tales and Talks form History,* Blackie & Son, 1911; S. B. Macy, *The Master Builders,* Longmans, Green, 1911; Fraekni Fridthjofr, *The Song of Frithiof* (retold by G. C. Allen), H. Frowde, 1912; S. B. Macy, *The Book of the Kingdom,* Longmans, Green, 1912; Johann David Wyss, *Swiss Family Robinson,* George H. Doran, 1913; (with Frank O. Salisbury) George Robinson Lees, *The Life of Christ,* S. W. Partridge, 1920; Arthur Guy Terry, *Tales from Far and Near,* Row, Peterson, 1926; Bible, *The Child's Bible* (edited by John Stirling), Cassell, 1928, reissued as *The Story Bible,* 1930; Arthur Lincoln Haydon, *The Book of Robin Hood,* Warne, 1931; Lawrence Wilson, *Story of Cortes,* Dutton, 1933; Margaret Gibbs, *Saints Beyond the White Cliffs,* Hollis & Carter, 1947, reprinted, Books for Libraries, 1971.

Also illustrator for several boys' magazines, including *Chums.*

*SIDELIGHTS:* **June 19, 1869.** Born in Islington, North London, the eldest of the three artistic Robinson brothers. His youngest brother, W. Heath Robinson recalled: "My brother Tom was a great reader and, as the eldest son, had read more than any of us. His advice, therefore, was considered valuable. Nevertheless, some caution had to be used in accepting this, as very naturally he could not always resist the temptation to advise the purchase of a book which he particularly wanted to read. Choosing a birthday book required care, and it would sometimes be necessary to go into town to get it. The local shops had only a limited selection.

"On one birthday I remember searching through Holywell Street, known as Booksellers' Row, with Tom, and with the money for my present held tightly in my pocket. The Row was a delightful place in which to rummage for books. Its narrow way permitted little more than pedestrian traffic, and this was of the quietest character. There was no hurry; it appeared to be always afternoon, or at the earliest the luncheon hour. All of its frequenters seemed to have plenty of leisure. A smell of old books and stale houses pervaded the Row. There was not much ventilation or light, as the upper stories of some of the shops overhung the way beneath and approached closely to one another across the street.

"Most of the shops were devoted to the sale of books both old and new, and others to the sale of things you could not buy elsewhere in London. The old books were displayed in wooden trough-like boxes outside the shops. It was always exciting to hunt through these, though as a rule they only contained technical works, books of sermons and statistics, and such dry provender. There was always a chance of finding something of value, dropped in by accident, perhaps.

"Tom officiously advised examining these very completely but I wanted a brand-new book, with illustrations if possible, for my birthday present. As usual, Tom won the argument, and I had for my present an old and tattered copy of a romance called *The Castle of Ehrenstein.* Tom assured me that I should never regret the purchase and undertook to read it for me first. I did not quite see the point of this, but his good intentions were apparent. There was another advantage afforded by the transaction, one which I probably should not have had in buying a new book. There was some change left over from my shilling, which we were able to spend on some fruit in Clare Market nearby. Tom was right. I never regretted the choice we had made. It was the cause of one of the most exciting adventures of my boyhood.

"Some days after, when Tom had read the book and I was about to begin the first chapter, he approached me furtively,

**Thus, then, drawn along by the tortoise, we proceeded with a hazardous rapidity.** ■ (From *The Swiss Family Robinson* by Johann David Wyss. Illustrated by T. H. Robinson.)

first looking back over his shoulder to see that no one else was within hearing.

"'Don't be frightened,' he whispered mysteriously into my ear. 'I have an awful secret to tell you. Nobody else knows about it, and I can only tell you if you promise faithfully not to reveal it to a soul.'

"I was deeply impressed, and promised on my oath not to say a word to anybody about it.

"'I've made a terrific discovery,' he told me. 'This house is built on an old castle which is haunted. I've already explored the banqueting hall, old dungeons and torture chambers. The chains are still hanging on the walls, so there is no doubt what the chambers were used for.'

"I was thrilled.

"'If you can get into the castle, couldn't you take me with you?' I asked.

"'Yes,' he replied. 'I want to show you all these wonderful things; but there is one condition I am forced to make. You must be blindfolded.'

"'But what's the good of my going with you, if I can't see anything?' I complained.

"'Oh, you needn't bother your head about that,' he answered. 'I'll explain everything as we go along. Then you won't need to see them.'

"I had to be content with this, and an appointment was made for the following evening in the passage by the kitchen. This, he told me, was not far from the entrance to the castle he had discovered. He said that he could not say more. When the time came for the adventure I was a little afraid, but kept the appointment punctually. Tom was already there, and fortunately no one else except Boss, the black cat, who seemed to sense the mystery in the air. A handkerchief was tied over my eyes, and various passes were solemnly made in front of me to test the effectiveness of the binding. When all was ready I was turned round so many times that I did not know in which direction I was facing.

"My heart was beating loudly as we started off. After passing along a gallery (as Tom called it), we stopped.

"'I now press a secret spring,' my guide announced, 'and in the wall a stone rolls slowly back, revealing the entrance to the castle. Through the ages this has sunk so low that we must enter upon our hands and knees.'

"I negotiated this quite successfully without bumping my head.

"'We are now in the main corridor that leads to the banqueting hall,' said Tom in a subdued voice.

"The corridor proved to be very crooked, and frequently turned back on itself. I questioned Tom about this peculiarity, and he replied, after advising me to talk as quietly as possible, that the twists in the passage were contrived by the old baron who owned the castle long ago, in order to baffle any enemy who might have gained an entrance to the stronghold. I could quite see the wisdom of this. Though not an enemy, I was certainly baffled.

"Presently a door was opened.

"'We are now in the banqueting hall,' Tom said. 'On the right you see the dais—at least you would see it if you weren't blindfolded. Down the center of the hall is a long oaken table at which the serfs had their meals. A rusted dagger can still be seen on a table beneath the musician's gallery.'

"We retraced our steps along the crooked passage and came to stairs.

"'These,' said Tom, 'lead to the turret, and to the chamber in which the princess was imprisoned and died from starvation. Her ghost still comes forth to haunt the castle.'

"'Must we explore the turret?' I asked nervously, but Tom assured me encouragingly: 'No harm can touch you, so long as I am near.'

"We mounted the stairs and found ourselves at the door of the princess's chamber. I fancied I heard my mother's voice in conversation behind the door, but Tom hurried me away.

"'The ghost is about to haunt the castle,' he told me, 'and it would be fatal if she saw us.' We hurried down the stairs.

"'Now,' said Tom, 'I will take you to the deepest dungeons.'

"He led me down and down until at the bottom of the last flight of stairs we entered a small chamber, which, even through the handkerchief, smelt cold and damp.

"'This is the deepest dungeon of all,' I was informed. 'You will notice the bones crunching beneath your feet.'

"They felt rather like coals, but as I was blindfolded and my brother was not, he must have been right. Leaving the dungeon, we now proceeded along another winding passage. This seemed interminable, but at last we came to a sudden halt. Tom muttered an oath.

"'Odds bodikins!' he said. 'We can go no farther. The gallery is blocked by a huge carved-oak chest, with a human skull on top of it.'

"This was alarming, and I clutched his arm.

"'No harm is done,' he comforted me, 'but this is a sign that our time is up and we must return.'

"We hurried along a seemingly endless series of passages, until at last we crawled through the secret doorway. Tom untied the handkerchief, and I found myself outside the kitchen door."[W. Heath Robinson, *My Line of Life*, Blackie & Son, Ltd., 1938.[1]]

W. Heath Robinson also remembered: "One night I was sleeping with my brother Tom, when we were disturbed by the stealthy opening of the bedroom door. What time it was, there was no means of telling, but it felt like the middle of the night, and as if all in the house, except ourselves and our mysterious visitor, were long since fast asleep. We could see nothing, but presently we heard shuffling footsteps approaching the bed. My brother and I held one another and were too terrified to do more than gasp, 'who's that?' The only reply was an inarticulate growl. After creeping slowly round the bed, the footsteps returned towards the door. We heard them pass out, and the door close.

**He met an old witch on the road, she was so ugly, her lower lip hung right down on to her chin.**
■ (From "The Tinder Box" in *Fairy Tales from Hans Christian Andersen*, translated by Mrs. E. Lucas. Illustrated by T. H. Robinson.)

**The naughty boy! to shoot the old poet who had been so kind to him, and given him the warm wine and the best apple.** ■ (From "The Naughty Boy" in *Fairy Tales from Hans Christian Andersen,* translated by Mrs. E. Lucas. Illustrated by T. H. Robinson.)

"With the morning our courage returned, but when we talked over our experience with my father no solution of the mystery could be found. Almost without intending to do so, we allowed the incident to develop in our minds. I was surprised to learn that Tom had seen a lantern standing outside the door, with a fierce dog beside it. No doubt, too, our visitor was a tall, dark man with a black visor hiding his face. The more we thought of the affair, the more these details increased, until finally we were proud to be the possessor of such an experience, and of the part we had played."[1]

**1881.** Educated at Islington High School as well as the Islington School of Art.

Later Tom Robinson studied at Cook's Art School and Westminster Art School, both in London. "At art school, I studied under Solomon J. Solomon, R.A., and Professor Fred Browne, but I can only ascribe my enthusiasm for art to hereditary sources and family surroundings. My grandfather was a wood engraver, my father and uncle were artists well known in their time. It was natural that my two brothers, Charles and W. Heath Robinson, and myself should have had every encouragement and complete understanding of our desires. More information about my two brothers and myself may be had from my brother, W. Heath Robinson's autobiography, *My Line of Life*." [*Illustrators of Children's Books, 1744-1945*, compiled by Bertha E. Mahony, and others, Horn Book, 1947.[2]]

**1895.** Published his first illustrations in Frank Rinder's *Old-World Japan: Legends of the Land of the Gods*.

W. Heath Robinson, the youngest artist-brother, wrote: "Charles's apprenticeship had now for some time come to an end. Tom and he were following what was almost a tradition in the family Robinson. They were making drawings, and selling them too, for reproduction in books and magazines. This was in the days when Aubrey Beardsley, who exercised an influence over all of us, was in his prime; when Sims had begun to harrow us with his weird conceptions, and when Charles illustrated that delightful edition of *A Child's Garden of Verses* by Robert Louis Stevenson.

"My brother, Tom [received a commission] to illustrate that famous series of articles on London by George R. Sims to be published in the *Strand Magazine*. These two innocents used to wander all over the town in search of subjects for ar-

**The populace stormed the Tuileries, even women and children fought among the combatants....** ■ (From "What the Moon Saw" in *Fairy Tales from Hans Christian Andersen*, translated by Mrs. E. Lucas. Illustrated by T.H. Robinson.)

**There now commenced a siege of Uterysdale which lasted several weeks.** ■ (From *The Book of Robin Hood* by A. L. Haydon. Illustrated by T. H. Robinson.)

ticles and illustrations. Opium Dens, Thieves' Kitchens and other picturesque hells were visited, but the wanderers came through unscathed."[1]

**1896.** Drew what many consider his best work for William Makepeace Thackeray's *The History of Henry Esmond*.

**1900.** Married. W. Heath Robinson wrote: "Charles was already married, and Tom, after all, submitted to the yoke before me. He married a daughter of the late John Francis Barnett, the composer of a cantata based on *The Ancient Mariner*, 'Paradise and the Peri,' and many other pieces well known in his day and often played at the present time."[1]

**1901.** Illustrated Elizabeth C. Gaskell's *Cranford*, a work which led to many subsequent commissions. W. Heath Robinson noted: "Tom had illustrated among other books *The Sentimental Journey* and *Cranford*, both published by Bliss, Sands & Co. in the years 1897 and 1901 respectively. I do not think these classics have ever been more beautifully illustrated. He was influenced not so much by the decorative line work of the British School as by the earlier illustrators, and even more by that great Spanish artist and master of line, Vierge."[1]

**1920's** and **1930's**. Worked for numerous boys' magazines, among them *Chums* for which he illustrated many of the school stories of Gunby Hadath, Hylton Cleaver and St. John Pearce.

**1950.** Died. Although not as decorative as his brothers, Charles and William, Thomas Heath Robinson's strength lay in his down-to-earth approach to illustration. The man took great pains to ensure accuracy in matters of dress, place, and historical detail.

*FOR MORE INFORMATION SEE*: William Heath Robinson, *My Line of Life*, Blackie & Son, 1938; Bertha E. Mahony, and others, *Illustrators of Children's Books, 1744-1945*, Horn Book, 1947; Brian Doyle, editor, *Who's Who of Children's Literature*, Schocken, 1968.

## ROBINSON, W(illiam) Heath 1872-1944

*PERSONAL:* Born May 31, 1872, in Hornsey, North London, England; died September 13, 1944; son of Thomas (an artist and engraver) and Eliza Ann (Heath) Robinson; brother of artists Thomas Heath and Charles Robinson; married Josephine Latey; children: one daughter, four sons. *Education:* Attended schools in London; studied art at the Islington Art School and Royal Academy Schools. *Home:* London, England.

*CAREER:* Artist, cartoonist, and illustrator of children's books; also designed scenery for stage productions. *Member:* Savage Club, London Sketch Club.

*WRITINGS*—All illustrated by the author: *Humours of Golf*, Dodd, Mead, 1923; (for children) *Bill the Minder*, Doubleday, Doran, 1924; (for children) *Adventures of Uncle Lubin*, F. A. Stokes, 1925; *Book of Goblins: A Collection of Folklore and Fairy Tales*, Hutchinson, 1934; *Absurdities: A Book of Collected Drawings*, Hutchinson, 1934; *Railway Ribaldry: Railway Humour*, Great Western, 1935; (with Kenneth R. G. Browne) *How to Live in a Flat*, Hutchinson, 1936; (with K.R.G. Browne) *How to Make a Garden Grow*, Hutchinson, 1938; *My Line of Life* (autobiography), Blackie, 1938, reprinted, E. B. Publishing, 1974; (with K.R.G. Browne) *How to Be a Motorist*, Hutchinson, 1939; (with K.R.G. Browne) *How to Be a Perfect Husband*, Hutchinson, 1939; *Let's Laugh! A Book of Humorous Inventions*, Hutchinson, 1939; (with Cecil Hunt) *How to Make the Best of Things*, Hutchinson, 1940; (with C. Hunt) *How to Build a New World*, Hutchinson, 1941; *Heath Robinson at War* (humorous drawings), Methuen, 1942; (with C. Hunt) *How to Run a Communal Home*, Hutchinson, 1943.

Illustrator: William W. D. Rouse, *The Giant Crab, and Other Tales from Old India*, D. Nutt, 1897, reprinted, Minerva Press, 1975; Hans Christian Andersen, *Danish Fairy Tales and Legends*, Bliss, Sands, 1897; John Bunyan, *Pilgrim's Progress*, Bliss, Sands, 1897; Miguel de Cervantes Saavedra, *The Life and Exploits of the Ingenious Gentleman Don Quixote de la Mancha*, Bliss, Sands, 1897, another edition, Dent, 1902; William Crooke, *The Talking Thrush, and Other Tales from India*, Dent, 1899, another edition, Dutton, 1938; (with others) Arabian Nights, *Arabian Nights' Entertainments*, G. Newnes, 1899; (with brothers Thomas H. and Charles Robinson) H. C. Andersen, *Fairy Tales from Hans Christian Andersen*, Dent, 1899.

Edgar A. Poe, *The Poems of Edgar Allan Poe*, G. Bell, 1900; Charles and Mary Ann Lamb, *Tales from Shakespeare*, Sands, 1902; Johan H. E. Schuck, *Medieval Stories*, Sands, 1902; Arabian Nights, *The Child's Arabian Nights*,

G. Richards, 1903; Roland Carse, *The Monarchs of Merry England: James I to Edward VII*, T. F. Unwin, 1908; William Shakespeare, *Shakespeare's Comedy of Twelfth Night*, Hodder, Stoughton, 1908; Rudyard Kipling, *A Song of the English*, Hodder, Stoughton, 1909; R. Kipling, *Collected Verse*, Doubleday, Page, 1910; H. C. Andersen, *Hans Andersen's Fairy Tales*, Constable, 1913, Doubleday, Doran, 1924; W. Shakespeare, *Shakespeare's Comedy of a Midsummer-Night's Dream*, Constable, 1914; Charles Kingsley, *Water-Babies*, Constable, 1915; Walter de la Mare, *Peacock Pie*, Constable, 1916.

Charles Perrault, *Old Time Stories*, Constable, 1921; Francois Rabelais, *The Works of Mr. Francis Rabelais*, privately printed, 1921; Elsie S. Munro, *Topsy-Turvy Tales*, J. Lane, 1923; Norman Hunter, *The Incredible Adventures of Professor Branestawn*, J. Lane, reprinted, Bodley Head, 1965; Richard F. Patterson, *Mein Rant*, Blackie, 1940; Geoffrey Chaucer, *Historias de Chaucer*, [Lisbon], 1940; Liliane M. C. Clopet, *Once Upon a Time*, F. Muller, 1944; C. Perrault, *Perrault's Complete Fairy Tales*, Dodd, Mead, 1971.

Contributor of drawings to various periodicals, including *Little Folks, The Sketch, The Bystander, The Graphic, Illustrated Sporting and Dramatic News, London Opinion, Strand Magazine,* and *Puck.*

*SIDELIGHTS:* **May 31, 1872.** Born in Hornsey Rise, North London. Son of Thomas Robinson, an engraver and artist, and Eliza Ann Heath. "I was born ... in the suburb of Hornsey Rise in the North of London. Although this was not within the sound of Bow Bells, except perhaps on a very quiet day, I am not far wrong in calling myself a Cockney. My father, who was also born in North London, but nearer to the sound of Bow Bells, was one of a family of artists and craftsmen. Some of these, though unknown to the present generation, did excellent work according to the standards of their day.

"My grandfather, Thomas Robinson, the patriarch of the family, started life as a bookbinder in his native town of Newcastle-on-Tyne. In this capacity he bound books for Thomas Bewick, the wood engraver. It is pleasing to think that he may have bound some of those precious first editions of the works of the famous artist and craftsman. He also bound books for George Stephenson, the father of the locomotive, and knew him personally. Eventually, precisely when I do not know, he came up to London to seek his fortune, and travelled from Newcastle in a collier, probably working his passage.

"In London he abandoned bookbinding and became a wood engraver. He engraved drawings by Sir John Gilbert, Du Maurier, Charles Green, Fred Walker and other famous artists, for such journals as *The London Journal* and *Good Words.*

"My father worked hard to provide for our little community, which consisted of nine souls, six of whom were children. These included the three musketeers, Tom, the eldest and, in virtue of his years and dominating personality, the leader of the gang; Charles, who had a technique all his own in dealing with our daily problems; and William, about whom all this fuss is being made. Then there were my two sisters, Mary and Florence, and my youngest brother, George, a mere baby, who was regarded with amused tolerance by his elder and more knowing brothers. The family circle was enlarged about this time by the addition of my mother's sister and youngest brother, protégés of my parents. It is true that

**The wrecks dissolve above us,**
**their dust drops down from afar—**
**Down to the dark, to the utter dark,**
**where the blind white sea-snakes are.**

■ (From *Song of the English* by Rudyard Kipling. Illustrated by W. Heath Robinson.)

we had a general servant, a kitchen maid, a nurse, a house-maid and a cook; but as all these retainers were united in one person, our household was not greatly increased thereby.

"My own generation lived at least in reasonable comfort, though not luxuriously. I suspect, however, that we were always living to the top of my father's income. In spite of the precariousness of this, the family budget was so nicely balanced that the younger members never realized how close to the door was the wolf. Fortune was kind, and no calamities overtook us, other than those which in the ordinary course of nature overtake the families of Smith, Brown, Jones and Robinson alike.

"There were no photographs to help the illustrator in those days. He had to depend for his material on sketches made by the special correspondent of the newspaper, or on written descriptions. These, however, were very accurate. A portrait drawn by my father from such a description led to the arrest of a famous criminal, Lefroy, the murderer. With what awe we used to examine, with our hands held well behind us, those strange chart-like sketches, covered with written notes and explanations. Perhaps it was a bird's-eye view of a British square, showing the spot where the Arabs broke through, where the stand was made. All this was actually drawn and recorded on the spot." [W. Heath Robinson, *My Line of Life,* Blackie & Son, Ltd., 1938.[1]]

"We always watched keenly the development of my father's drawings, and our interest in the news of the day was thus kept continually alive. Sometimes we made drawings of the same events at his side. We knew all about the campaigns in Afghanistan and the Zulu wars. I could draw a passable Zulu, with feathered head-dress, long oval shield and assegai, at an early age. We were deeply stirred by the news of Isandhlwana and of Rorke's Drift, and were grieved at the death of the Prince Imperial. We had, I am afraid, a secret sympathy with that dethroned monarch, Cetewayo. Then there was the bad news of Majuba Hill. How we wished we could do something about it! We carefully followed in imagination the Khartoum relief expedition as it progressed stage by stage up the Nile. Finally the news that Khartoum was recaptured and Gordon avenged allowed us to breathe again."[Langston Day, *The Life and Art of W. Heath Robinson,* Herbert Joseph Ltd., 1947.[2]]

"How shall I describe a good mother? Perhaps in depicting our household, its contentment, the fortitude with which its troubles were borne, and the smooth running of the wheels of our daily life in spite of the occasional roughness of the road, I shall best describe the mother of our family. Quiet in the background, directing, organizing, placating, she was responsible for all of these.

"My father's income was mainly derived from his illustrations in the *Penny Illustrated Paper,* the P.I.P., as it was generally called. This was a weekly paper and certainly the pioneer of the Sunday illustrated papers of to-day. My father's contribution . . . was usually the frontpage illustration and that on a double inside page. He was responsible for these features for a great number of years. His work had great journalistic value, and a large public looked for it every week. His subjects included battles, crimes, society functions, earthquakes, and storms and wrecks at sea. These last inspired him most. He was still the boy who wanted to be a sailor. He was extremely conscientious in the attention he paid to correctness of detail, and his drawings were full of animation. How vigorously his British soldier, with one hand grasping the colours of his regiment, hewed his way

through the enemy! How criminal was his criminal fleeing from justice; how tragic the scene of the crime, with the little cross to mark where the body was found! What elemental upheavals were his storms!

"The bounds of my daily life as a child, although embracing the whole of my visible world, were confined within narrow limits. Saturday provided almost the only opportunity for exploring these. On that day there was no school, but a welcome lull in the daily routine of the week. Anything might happen on Saturday; it was a day of adventure, an unknown quantity in time. Eagerly anticipated, it so impressed itself on my mind that to this day the close of the week brings something of that old thrill of expectation.

"All the other days led up to this, and each was characterized by its nearness to or distance from the end of the week. They had their own individual characteristics too. Monday is still associated in my mind with all that is humdrum and according to routine. I was oppressed by a reaction from the freedom of the week-end. It was a dreary day as a rule. I believe that if weather reports were carefully examined it would be found that Monday was more often rainy than fine.

"On Tuesdays, the weather seems to have cleared, since, as I remember, it was often windy and bright. This was fortunate, as Tuesday was washing day, and the linen was drying in the sun and wind on the clothes line in the back garden. This was washing day also for most of the houses in the road. Nearly all the gardens were alive and glorious with flapping banners. Neighbours' pants and petticoats flouted one another unabashed across the garden walls. But it was a muddling sort of day for all that, and the steam from the wash-house seemed to penetrate the lower rooms. All the household linen was washed at home and dried in the garden, and those responsible for these activities let themselves go and made a day of it.

"There was not much time to spare for children on washing day. We were always in the way, and the back garden was unplayable because of the clothes props and the wind-blown sheets and under-garments. However, there was one consolation for us; although it was invariably late in coming to the table, we had Irish stew for the midday meal. Perhaps this was a concession to the taste of our Irish washerwoman. Maybe this was her best defence against the ravages to the constitution caused by continually bending over a steaming tub, in a welter of soap suds.

"Wednesday and Thursday were just ordinary days, though Thursday was already receiving the glow of the approaching end of the week. After school on Friday, the eve of the great day, we were once more free. Friday night was bath night, and in a tub before the bright kitchen fire we were bathed one by one. Stimulated by this operation, and by a hard rubdown with a warm, sweet-smelling towel, our imaginations glowed with thoughts of what we should do to-morrow. Afterwards, as we supped from our basins of hot soup, we planned great doings, greater than we were likely to achieve. Then, in the snug warmth of our beds, we dreamt of their accomplishment.

"Saturday held many delightful possibilities, but the most thrilling of all was a walk along the Great North Road. This was to us a road of enchantment, and the main road of England. It led directly to High Barnet, St. Albans and to York, and finally by roundabout ways to Scotland. These enchanted places could be reached by simply walking straight along the road that passed near our home, if only

Puck.　　On the ground
　　　　Sleep sound:
　　　　I'll apply
　　　　To you eye,
　　Gentle lover, remedy.
■ (From *A Midsummer Nights Dream* by William Shakespeare. Illustrated by W. Heath Robinson.)

you were able to keep going long enough. Better still, with Dick Turpin's Black Bess to carry you, the journey to York could be made in one night. English history had marched up and down this road. It had been trodden by armies, rebels, knights, highway robbers; by such well-known travellers as Dick Whittington, Dick Turpin, and not so long before by Oliver Twist and the Artful Dodger. Two or three more young adventurers would now be added to the list.

"On fine summer mornings the pleasant sport of butterfly catching, or rather trying to catch them, led us through many country lanes. After climbing Muswell Hill, past tall trees and gardens, we wandered along Colney Hatch Lane, a fa-

vourite haunt of whole families of butterflies. Merely regarded as sport, I do not remember that our butterfly catching was remarkable. The butterflies of North London were so swift on the wing. Seeming to enjoy the antics we performed with our nets in our endeavours to catch them, they sported with us rather than we with them. They have all flown long since, and together with the hedges, trees and flower-strewn verges of the lane, are no more.

". . . Our mother, who took charge of our religious welfare, only insisted that we should attend one service every Sunday. With the physical happiness of so many to care for, she had no time for religious controversy. Chapel and church were alike to her. That they were places of worship was all that mattered.

"Sunday dinner was my mother's crowning feat of the week. In the morning the kitchen was the centre of intense activity. The sirloin of beef would be turning before the fire, suspended from a meat jack. This was a cylindrical brass instrument, fastened to the shelf above the fireplace. Being operated by clockwork, it had to be wound up now and again. The whole of the cooking operations were hidden from view by a zinc-lined cupboard called a meat screen. This was open to the fire at the back, and had shelves upon which the plates and dishes were kept hot. These shelves could be reached through a door in the front of the screen. The potatoes were roasting beneath the joint, and both had to be continually basted with the gravy. There was an oven too, in which a great fruit pie was baking. The work was strenuous, and as the jack ticked regularly in the warm air of the kitchen, the smell of cooking stole gradually through the house, foretelling the delights in store for us.

"The stout and ale were supplied from a public house nearby. Without claiming to be superior, we were a little above fetching this ourselves in jugs, as some of the neighbours were not ashamed of doing. Instead, the potman brought it to our door in foaming cans, with a rich smell of fermentation. The empty cans were hung upon the area railings to be taken away by the potman. In the evening, my brothers and I went unwillingly to church.

"Although not haunted by ghosts, and quite an ordinary dwelling house of the period, our home, in some unaccountable way, lent itself to . . . hauntings of the imagination. It was a tall, three-storied, stuccoed house with a basement. The room in which we had our meals and mostly lived was a small parlour on the basement floor in the front of the house. It was a rather dark room, although the basement was only a little below the street level. Behind it were the kitchen and scullery, opening on to the back garden. The lower part of the house was lit by gas—a poor light in those days, and the rest of the house by oil lamps and candles; so that after dark no part of the house was free from the mystery of flickering shadows which electric light has stolen from us.

"The narrow passage on the ground floor was, of course, called the Hall. At night it was lit by a gas lamp in an ornamental globe. It was approached by a flight of stone steps leading up to the front door. This floor was only used on Sundays and on ceremonial occasions, and for parties. It was rather grand. Here were the two most important rooms in the house, in which you had to be careful of the furniture and which you only entered attired in your best clothes. These rooms were collectively known as the drawing-room, and were separated by folding doors. We were upon our dignity on the ground floor.

"Our bedroom was at the top of the house, and dark and narrow was the staircase up which you hurried at night, candlestick in hand. We slept two in a bed. If we were unable to go to sleep at once, we would hear the noises of the house in the basement far below, a door shutting, or a clatter of plates as supper was prepared for our parents. Then there would be silence, and we would drop off to sleep one by one.

"It happened that on each side of our house, which was one of a row of similar houses, there dwelt a sea captain. Each of these captains had one or more sons, by whom we were proud to be befriended. We all had swings in our gardens, but we, being only the sons of an artist, had the smallest

swing of the three. We admitted that this was quite right; the sons of a sailor would naturally want to swing higher. But we could not help being a little envious of the possessor of one of the swings. It was painted green, and had a gilded weather-cock erected above it. Our friends were a little older than we, and had a greater knowledge of the mysteries of life. This they willingly imparted to us in serious talks across the garden wall on summer evenings, in exchange for our milder experiences. Their patronage was welcome to us.

"In the days of which I now write, school does not seem to have played the all-important part in a boy's daily life that it does to-day. This can, at least, be said of the children of parents with small incomes. We were sent of necessity to the best day-school in the neighbourhood, provided that the fees were not too high, and that the school was near enough for the children to walk to and fro twice a day. For the rest, we were left very much to ourselves.

"As day-scholars, we spent a large part of our time at home, or with home as the centre of our activities. This freedom was allowed us, not from any lack of interest on the part of our parents, but from a faith in the instinct of children for finding the best way to occupy their time. No doubt this confidence was not always justified, but on the whole it was not misplaced. While every help and encouragement was given, the initiative was always left with us. Without attempting to dogmatize about education, I feel that I owe much to my home life, and little to school. We had to provide our own amusements, and to make many of the things we played with; to the humours of which I was not blind and to which I still respond.

"We had to be creative, and to use our imaginations continually and at every turn, to make our crude efforts seem real to us. We had no mechanical models of steamships or trains. I think I may attribute the seeds of inspiration for the humorous drawings which I have since attempted to these early efforts to make things out of homely materials originally intended for some wholly different purpose. In such circumstances drawing became a necessity, and a normal means of expression. My father consistently encouraged it. Our slate stories were an outcome of this. They were told by means of a drawing on a slate, the different stages of the story being presented by gradually modifying the picture, with the aid of sponge and slate pencil. Sometimes they were tales of adventure, of shipwreck, of pirates, of castaways on a desert island and the shifts they were put to. Perhaps the subject would be of a different kind; some great engineering feat, such as building a bridge between two mountains. The bridge would in all likelihood cross a foaming torrent, with full-rigged treasure ships riding on the water. It might be the digging of a coal-mine in the bowels of the earth. They were moving pictures in more than one sense.

"Another outlet for any creative skill we possessed was provided by our model theatres. At first we depended upon the materials supplied by the shops, such as those published by Pollock and Remington. A wider field was found for our imaginations when we made our own stage. This was larger and permitted much more ambitious effects than were to be obtained in the ordinary stages bought at shops. The standardized materials we formerly relied upon were of no use to us now. We had to write our own plays, and design our own characters and scenes to fit the new theatre. Our pantomime would take weeks to prepare. There was the lighting with little candles to be arranged. There were trap-doors for the sudden appearance and disappearance of demons and fairies, and many other striking effects. They all had to be tested and rehearsed many times. Our first night was a great occasion, and if our audience was not quite so enthusiastic as we had hoped, we certainly enjoyed it ourselves. We were in the privileged position; we were behind the scenes. The mysteries to be unfolded were no mysteries to us.

"No doubt there were many children in those days, and perhaps there are many to-day, who have found and still find amusements in this way. Let us hope so, as it would be difficult to exaggerate the value of the mental exercise involved, or the stimulant provided in this way for a healthy imagination. I must acknowledge the great part they played in my education.

"Romance and mystery flourished in this atmosphere. . . .

"An ever-extending scope for imagination was revealed in the books I now began to read. Discarding nursery tales and fairy stories such as those of the Grimms, Hans Andersen and others, I now began to read boys' books; *Robinson Crusoe,* and tales by such writers as Captain Marryat, Harrison Ainsworth, Fenimore Cooper, Lord Lytton, G.P.R. James and even Sir Walter Scott. I call them 'boys' books,' though I doubt whether any of these authors professed to write for boys. These were sold in coloured paper covers for the price of fourpence halfpenny. Books would be given to us for birthday presents, after a diplomatic hint as to the one we wanted. Sometimes the money was given to us to make the purchase ourselves."

**1878.** "An epoch-marking day at this early stage of my career was when, amidst the congratulations of the family and their smiles of encouragement, I came down to breakfast in my first pair of breeches. The next in importance was certainly the day when I started my school education. This day marked the beginning of a new stage. Life was about to begin in earnest.

"The school was on the opposite side of the road, and I was escorted on this first occasion, in a state of trepidation, by an old family nurse. She had been with our family at the time of my birth, and in virtue of her long service and care of me, when I was so little able to care for myself, she exercised a sort of proprietary right over my person. At my christening she strongly objected that not enough water had been used; some other quite ordinary children, christened at the same time, being treated more liberally in this respect. For this reason, perhaps, she henceforth devoted her life to making up for this rather feeble beginning to my spiritual career.

"'Miss Mole's' was the name of the Dame school to which I was taken. The staff consisted of Miss Mole and her mother. These ladies divided their time between housekeeping duties, the education of a few young children of the neighbourhood, and the care of Mr. Mole, Miss Mole's brother. He was a smart young man with a dignified manner. He was only to be seen occasionally. We sometimes used to arrive in the morning as he was about to leave for the city, Miss Mole seeing him off, brushing his coat and putting on a few finishing touches. He was too manly to take notice of us, and we, regarding him with awe, wondered what he did in the city. No doubt something very important; for he was always arrayed in top-hat and frock-coat, and wore light kid gloves.

"One of my earliest memories is of Mrs. Mole, a bent old lady in a white cap and dark apron. Her old knotted fingers and crinkled nails pointed out the letters in Mavor's Spelling Book. She would read to us the stories of Jane Bond, who had a kind face, and of many another juvenile heroine or

(From "The Goblin City" in *The Giant Crab and Other Tales,* retold by W.H.D. Rouse. Illustrated by W. Heath Robinson.)

hero. The system at Miss Mole's was in no way irksome and we had enough time left over from our tasks to amuse ourselves by drawing on our slates."

**1881.** Attended grammar school in London. "The education I received . . . although on the whole of a meagre character, had some advantages. I certainly managed to learn to read and write, which, after all, are accomplishments worth having. I also learnt some very elementary arithmetic, a little history and geography. My head was never worried with foreign or dead languages, which perhaps was good for it at that time of mental confusion. The teachers, with one exception did not inspire me with a wish to learn; no doubt I appeared very dull, and it is possible that I did not inspire them with any wish to teach.

"The exception was a mistress, who, I believe, had a genius for teaching. She certainly had the advantage of teaching me a subject which I had never approached before, and of beginning at its most elementary stage. But so truly did she lay the foundations that little difficulty was felt in the further development of the subject. Every step forward was made from a well-secured position, and the new position was consolidated. Beyond this, she had the art of inspiring interest in the subject she taught, and a friendly personality that made it a pleasure to satisfy her. The subject, strangely enough, was electricity and magnetism. The interest aroused by this teacher's methods gave me the first real satisfaction I derived from my school education.

"I sometimes flatter myself with the thought that having made so promising a beginning I might in the end have become a great scientist. Unfortunately, or fortunately for the world of science, I left the school before these studies had advanced beyond the rudimentary stage, and they were never resumed.

"There were little or no classical studies, but many branches of science were taught; physiology, chemistry, electricity and magnetism. We had an impressive array of apparatus, such as retorts, Leyden jars, batteries, magnets and electrical machines of various kinds. Interesting and odoriferous experiments were carried out. The headmaster was greatly interested in all these subjects, and I can remember a lecture of his in which he prophesied that some day telegrams would be sent without wire. . . .

"One of our masters was a very old gentleman, who delighted in propounding to the boys his own theory of the evolution of man. 'It is all nonsense,' he said, 'to imagine that man was descended from the apes. Of course not; he was descended from the bear.' I do not think we were very interested in any case, but he proceeded to prove his theory by comparative anatomy. We did not understand his arguments, but were quite prepared to take his word for it. He was a kind, but obstinate and fussy old man. Quite innocent of any intention to commit an injustice, he would often, through shortsightedness, punish the wrong boy, and no one could persuade him of his error. However, he was very popular. I can remember that when at last he announced his retirement into private life, we all subscribed and presented him with a gold watch. It bore a suitable inscription, expressing our appreciation of his long and unwarying services. The ceremony was an affecting one and took place before the assembled school. After a short and complimentary speech by the headmaster, each one of us shook hands with our departing friend. We were naturally somewhat taken aback at the beginning of the next term to find him back in his place again, as fussy and busy as ever. When at last he did leave, nobody suggested that he should be given another gold watch.

"It was so often my misfortune to miss the beginning and foundation of the subjects I was taught at school, or not to have them deeply impressed upon me before passing on. Whether this was only my own particular misfortune I have no means of telling, but in my case it resulted in mental confusion and lack of interest. Like most children of my age, I was eager and curious, and waiting to be interested; but I must confess that my schools rarely supplied this want. On fitting occasions I received physical punishment, and very likely deserved it, though I never admitted it at the time. But I was never cruelly punished. The harm that may result from a want of system in teaching is of a more subtle kind. In this way many hours of the most sensitive and impressionable time of a child's life may be squandered and worried away. Education at that time, however, was not regarded scientifically, and my conscientious, if misguided, teachers had more excuse for their failures than the teachers of to-day."

**1884.** "When I was about twelve years old, I was sent to the Islington High School, whither my brother Tom and Charles had preceded me. This school was founded in 1830, and was then known as the Proprietary School of Islington. To quote the rules, the object of the school was 'to provide a course of Education for Youth, to comprise Classical Learning, the Modern Languages, Mathematics and such other branches of Useful Knowledge as may be advantageously introduced; together with religious and moral instruction, in conformity with the doctrines and discipline of the Church of England.' It was more expensive than the school which I had left and had some pretensions to being a public school. Most of the masters had university degrees, and wore caps and gowns when teaching. This impressed me very much at first.

"The object in sending us to this school was to add a final polish to our education and give it a more classical tone than could be acquired at our former school. I cannot say that in my case this end was attained. Tom and Charles did well enough, and when I arrived had already distinguished themselves. Whether I started in the middle of a term and could not make up for the time thus lost, I cannot remember. My fate still pursuing me, I rarely seemed to start at the beginning of my subjects or, if I did, to be well grounded in them. Much of the time I spent at this school was in this manner thrown away.

"Perhaps, after all this time, I am inclined in my mind to exaggerate my failure. I find in a report of this period that I was not merely good, but V. Good, in Geography and History; Fair in Reading, and that I showed Good Ability and Progress in Free-Hand drawing."[1]

Vacations consisted of trips to the seaside.

**1887.** Went to Islington Art School, a preparatory school for the Royal Academy. "Greater enthusiasm than that of the young art student of my student days, it would be difficult to find. His pathetic devotion to his varying ideals and his soaring ambitions are among the finest things I have known. Yet in retrospect, there is something sad in the thought that so many have dropped out or for some reason or other abandoned their ideals, some for lack of means to continue their studies, others because a more remunerative prospect has opened before them and others again because they have found the limits of their abilities.

"I was about fifteen years of age when my parents realized that I should not benefit by staying longer at school, and so I left and joined this gallant band. My father and I had no hesitation in selecting the path I should follow. Not that I had excelled in drawing to any remarkable degree, but that I showed far greater liking for this than for any other pursuit. I did not want to be anything else than an artist. I was a little contemptuous of those of my acquaintance who started life under the restraints of an office. At the same time deep, down in my heart, I secretly envied them the amount of pocketmoney they always seemed to possess, and all they could do with it. We made the best of our position, however, and gloried in our comparative poverty and freedom.

"First of all I went to an art school in Islington where I met one or two other art students with the same hopeful outlook on life. We worked hard intermittently and talked a lot about art. The vexed questions that cause so much controversy today amongst art critics we answered long ago, to our satisfaction at least. Frankly, there was no limit to my ambition. Not that I told myself I should rival Velasquez or Rembrandt, but there was at that stage of my artistic career a pleasing indefiniteness as to my future development. To me as yet anything seemed possible. I flattered myself with the possibilities rather than the probabilities of what was waiting for me in the future.

"My ideas of an artist's life were taken from the lives of the great masters which I loved to read. It was only a matter of choosing whether I should paint frescoes in cathedrals and monasteries, or whether I should wander all over the world

(From "The Snow Queen: A Tale in Seven Stories" in *Fairy Tales from Hans Christian Andersen*, translated by Mrs. E. Lucas. Illustrated by W. Heath Robinson.)

painting mountain scenery or old cities, and, on an occasional visit to my own country, the woods and fields of England. This last seemed to me the ideal life.

"Tom and Charles were following the same profession. At a solemn meeting we decided on the various rôles we should play in the world of art, thus avoiding overlapping and competition. Tom, as a kind of artistic cock of the walk, took upon himself the rôle of Michael Angelo. Charles and I had to be content with those of Raphael and Titian respectively. After a while, with the full approval of the committee of three, I altered my rôle to that of a follower of Claude and Turner.

"This amicable arrangement did not prevent us interchanging our rôles at times. I can remember about this time, knocking off a few sketches of a heroic character. ''The Triumph of Order over Chaos' was a pet theme of mine, also 'Creation' or 'The Last Judgment' were subjects that never daunted me. Tom likewise at times did not disdain a landscape and Charles would adopt either of our rôles when required. In this way he discovered a versatility that never left him, bringing fresh surprises to us almost to the end of his life.

"It was a little difficult to descend from these ambitious flights to the comparative drudgery of drawing a vase, a cube, and a cone arranged on a board, or the plaster cast of a piece of ornament from the Ghiberti Gates at Florence. We lived in a world of plaster of Paris. The studio was crowded with plaster casts of the Discobolus, busts of Roman emperors and empresses, the Venus de Medici, the head and shoulders of the Hermes of Praxiteles and fragments of many other well-known examples of the plastic arts. The walls were hung with casts of hands and feet of famous statues and with architectural fragments. We became so accustomed to drawing fragments, that we were inclined to prefer figures in a state of mutilation to the common-place examples with a normal number of limbs. The plaster often became chipped and being unwashable it had to be painted periodically. In this way much of the modelling in course of time became smoothed out.

"We tackled this unpromising material with a zeal which, at this distance of time, I cannot help admiring, though I may regret that so much youthful enthusiasm should have been expended in this manner. Doubtless we derived some good from this method of teaching, but we had little else for years when so much of a more life-like interest was awaiting our study. Fortunately we had opportunities to cultivate our imagination. A great incentive to this was the monthly Sketch Club.''[1]

**1890-1892.** Attended, intermittently, the schools of the Royal Academy. He dismissed having to draw from the classical antiquities in the British Museum as ''a dreadful practice.'' [A. E. Johnson, *W. Heath Robinson*, Adams & Charles Black, 1913.[3]]

"I had now been drawing antiques for the last five or six years, and found to my dismay that I was to continue to do so. I do not question the value that drawing from the antique may have for the art student, but too much time was given to working up the modelling with delicate chalk stipples, a tedious and laborious process. One young lady so excelled in this that her drawing of Hercules struggling with the Hydra rivalled the finest crochet work. However, these studies were, to my great joy, varied with painting and drawing from life. My attendance at the schools was never very regular,

and I had few opportunities of entering into the social life of the students or making new friendships. Amongst those of my contemporaries, who in varying degrees have since become famous were Charles Sims, Derwent Wood and Montford, the sculptors, G. E. Stampa and Lewis Baumer, both regular contributors to *Punch,* Byam Shaw, Frank O. Salisbury and Harold Speed. Of these several have passed away.

"The necessity to earn my living was now becoming more and more urgent, and my all too brief academic career came to an end.''[1]

**Early 1890's.** "I was still leading an untrammelled existence and was jealous of the least infringement on my liberty. I was faithful as far as possible to my ideal of an artist's life. I can justly say that I was not mercenary and was innocent of any desire to become wealthy. If riches came my way with no effort on my part to obtain them, that was another matter. No doubt as an artist I should know the right way to use them. It was the peculiar privilege of an artist to have a clearer insight into the real value of such dross, and many other things too, so I held. I now felt that to preserve my valued freedom and spirit of independence I could not for much longer be wholly dependent upon my parents. They had ungrudgingly supported me as long as their slender means warranted them to do so. Although anxious for me to earn my living, they were even prepared to strain further their resources on my behalf. They were not much more worldly and provident than I proved to be. I now determined, if it were possible, to make this sacrifice unnecessary. Tom and Charles were both earning their living and this made my position more difficult to endure.

"The problem now confronting me was complicated by the number of ways by which it seemed possible to solve it. It was only on closer examination and after many tentative experiments that the difficulties they nearly all presented were evident to me. Portrait painting promised a lucrative living, but so few people wanted their portraits painted, at any rate by me. Church decoration would have been congenial work, but nearly all the churches were decorated. Those who commissioned work for the decoration of theatres or houses or for the illustration of books and magazines were as unresponsive to my overtures as the buyers of subject pictures or landscapes. I was equally unsuccessful in convincing scene painters of the value of the help I could give them. At last I realized that I should have to take one of these branches of my profession and heroically persevere with it in spite of every discouragement and temptation to turn aside.

"For the immediate purpose I had in view, it must be admitted my final choice was not a wise one. Even before the day when Tom, Charles and I had undertaken our different rôles in art, I had a love for the life of a landscape painter or such as I fondly imagined it to be. It still possessed me and I resolved to gain my independence by success in this congenial occupation. My idea of the life of a landscape painter was to live in the open air and in lonely communion with nature. To be hardened to all weathers, heat, cold and all climates. To be equally at home in raging storms and under the dazzling sun of the desert. To be unfettered by the restraints and conventions of life in town. This was the way to live. The where might be anywhere. Sometimes, perhaps, in the Swiss Alps or the Himalayan Mountains and Tibet. At other times my wanderings might take me to Greece, to Rome or to Egypt and back again to the Norfolk Broads. Greenland would surely be visited, and hence some dashing sketching expedition to the polar regions was not without the bounds of the landscape painter's wide possibilities. All these and many other wonderful places would be taken in my stride.

"I was an incorrigible day-dreamer, and in my foolish infatuation, I pictured myself tramping the country roads without a care and returning from some painting expedition in the Austrian Alps or by the Bay of Baiae. My clothes were worn almost to rags, but by Turner and by Constable, what did that matter to one who despised the vanity of the neatly clothed townsman and held as naught his approval! My face was a rich brown by exposure to the weather and my hair was blowing in the wind. Upon my back was strapped my paintbox, some few superb works of art, destined for the National Gallery via the Royal Academy, and my scanty baggage. With what admiration and envy was I greeted on my return by those few intellectuals who—and so on.

"As a matter of fact it did not quite work out like this. I found that my daydreams were apt to lead me on in this manner and leave me in the end, as La Belle Dame sans Merci left that other wretched wight—on the cold hillside. Greece, Rome and the Himalayas were a long way off, so I wisely decided to begin on some place nearer home. These more remote fields could be attacked at a later time. The scene I selected for my operations was the wide neighbourhood of Hampstead Heath, Parliament Hill Fields and Highgate Ponds, which had the advantage of being within walking distance of my home.

"We now lived in Stroud Green, a suburb in the North of London, which covered the once green hill we knew as the Hog's Back. Our house was still farther from the original starting-point of the Heath Robinsons. This outward trend had begun before we were born.

"My Hampstead Heath period, though productive of much happiness and good health to me, did not bring me appreciably nearer to the end I had in view. I seemed as far from earning my living at the end of my Hampstead summer as at the beginning. I took some paintings to a dealer. I think his shop was in the Balls Pond Road. He was quite a pleasant man. He greeted me warmly and examined my work very critically and silently. So long did he remain gazing through half-closed eyes and with his head on one side, that my hopes began to rise. Surely, thought I, if my work was of no interest at all to him he would have known this at once. At length, he began to rub his chin thoughtfully and shake his head slowly.

"'How long have you been painting?' he asked.

"'About four or five years,' I replied.

"'Have you ever sold a painting before?' he queried.

"'No,' was my brief answer.

"He then asked: 'Have you got to depend upon your own earnings for a living?'

"I explained to him that this was certainly how I was placed.

"'Well in that case I should try something else,' he said kindly. He then helped me to tie up my canvases again, and shaking hands, bade me good-bye in a very friendly manner."[1]

**1894.** Went to work in his father's studio in Dane's Inn off the Strand.

**Mid 1890's.** Sold a picture to the firm of Cassell. Had several drawings published in the journal, *Good Words*. "The narrow pass of Paternoster Row and its immediate neighbourhood were now invaded. Hodder & Stoughton, the Religious Tract Society, Warne's, Cassell's, and Partridge's were all subjected in turn to a kind of artistic barrage.

"Partridge's, amongst their other publishing activities, dealt in the sale of clichés, that is of blocks reproducing drawings that had already been published, a kind of second-hand transactions. I was once asked to convert a print from one of these, a diagrammatic reproduction of some fishes from a book on natural history, to an illustration for a fairy story. I had to paint over the indication numbers and draw in a baby seated comfortably among the fishes. The fishes were all very stiff and in profile, but the result was considered satisfactory. It certainly appeared to be economical for I suppose they only had to pay for the baby, the price for which was not high although the baby was a fat one. The fishes, if they had to be paid for at all, they could have had at second-hand rates. These and other publishing houses put up a good defence, but at last a breach was made. To my great joy I sold a drawing to Cassell's for *Little Folks*. Other triumphs soon rewarded my persistency. Work began to come to me instead of my having to hunt for it. It was a satisfaction to be sought for, but I regretted those long tramps and the sense of adventure that accompanied them, the hope with which I set out in the morning and the joy when success rewarded me.

"I was soon to make some illustrations for *Good Words*. Very immature they were, as I am sure [the editor] realized; nevertheless, I received generous encouragement which I gratefully remember."[1]

(From *The Water Babies* by Charles Kingsley. Illustrated by W. Heath Robinson.)

Took his first studio in Howland Street. A few months later, he moved to a studio in Gower Street. "It now became necessary for me to take a farther step in my great adventure and to find a studio of my own. My old friend and artist comrade P. J. Billinghurst was in the same position, and we resolved to take a studio together. We discovered one which seemed to meet our requirements both as to rent and accommodation, in Howland Street, a turning off the Tottenham Court Road. Our landlady was Madame Schmidt, a stout red-faced lady who was partly Nordic and partly Hebrew. There were many other tenants in the house evidently of the same strain. Besides ourselves, the only one of the community who was of British stock was Murdoch, a Scottish artist, who lived in a cavelike studio deep down in the basement of the house. He started life as a hosier in some obscure town or village in Scotland. He felt the call and, with a truly heroic courage, threw away the means of a livelihood and came to London to paint pictures. How he subsisted I could never discover, but I believe that Mme. Schmidt was good to him. He lived entirely for his work, which, as I remember it, was sometimes obscurely allegorical and rather wild. His gestures were slow and gentle and his eyes were alight with enthusiasm. One felt that he ought to have been a genius—perhaps he was.

"Our own studio was a small square room like a box with a top light. It was constructed of match-boarding and had no side windows. It was built over a stable, but how a stable could be in such a position was a mystery to us. There was no possible entrance to it, that we could discover, in the neighbourhood. Nevertheless a stable was undoubtedly there. We could hear the horses stamping below. We should not have objected to this very much had the stable been clean, but unfortunately this was not the case. Now and again an overpowering smell of stale stable would steal through the planks of the floor and pervade the room. To-day I wonder, when I remember how long we endured this, yet we worked hard for some months in our little box which we had furnished as neatly as our means would allow."[1]

**1897.** Received a commission to illustrate a series of Indian tales, *The Giant Crab,* collected by Dr. W.H.D. Rouse —Robinson's first success. "On my way I had a slight skirmish with the publishing house of David Nutt in the 'Strand.' Some time after they were to publish one of the first books I ever illustrated. This was *The Giant Crab* written by W.H.D. Rouse. It was a collection of stories for children based on Indian folklore. They were so naïvely and humorously written, I have seldom had a subject to illustrate that made a stronger appeal to me. As with most of the books I illustrated in these early days, I would like to illustrate them all over again."[1]

Dr. Rouse liked his work. In 1941 Heath wrote to him: "I remember how encouraged I was by your appreciation of my illustrations in the book, and in those days encouragement was specially valuable to me. I remember, too, how much I enjoyed the work. The stories seemed to suit me exactly, as they would now. I often wish I had to illustrate them all over again, but this time with bright colours. They gave me such free play for using that fancy I love to exercise as few other subjects have done."[2]

Commissioned by the publishers Bliss, Sands to illustrated *Don Quixote, Pilgrim's Progress* and *Danish Fairy Tales and Legends* by Hans Christian Andersen. "It is not often that opportunities occur for illustrating the same work twice, though I have been fortunate enough to illustrate one three times. This was *Hans Andersen's Fairy Stories.* The first

time was for a cheap reprint published in the year 1897. As may be expected the work for this was very crude. The second time was for an edition published by J. M. Dent in the year 1902. This was illustrated by Tom, Charles, and myself in collaboration. The last time I illustrated these stories was for an edition published by Constable in the year 1913. As far as my drawings were concerned, this was certainly the best and was, I hope, enhanced by the many colour illustrations. These three books show well what development I had made as a book illustrator in that period."[1]

**1899.** Worked in the company of Tom and Charles Robinson as well as other artists in studios in New Court, Carey Street.

On submitting sketches to editors: "It's not a bad plan when you've hatched out some ideas that you think are really good, to put in one or two duds for throw-outs. The unfortunate thing is, of course, they choose the duds!"[2]

Illustrated another Hans Christian Andersen volume, this time in collaboration with his brothers. Illustrated *The Talking Thrush* by Dr. Rouse and executed 130 drawings for *The Arabian Nights.* "I now illustrated *The Talking Thrush* by W. H. D. Rouse, and made many drawings for a popular edition of *The Arabian Nights* published in serial form by Constable. This was followed by my illustrations for an edition of *Don Quixote* especially adapted for young people, and then by my contributions for the Hans Andersen to which Tom and Charles also contributed. Both of these works were published by J. M. Dent. . . . This work of mine though still at times immature, began to show a diversion from the work I did under the influence of Beardsley and the other illustrators of his time. The illustration of Don Quixote, for whom I had and still have a great love, demanded a different treatment, a treatment which came more and more natural to me. It found its greatest opportunities in *The Works of Rabelais* which I was now to illustrate. I like to think that this change in my work accompanied a change in my outlook on life. At the least it was more personal and derived its inspiration, not so much from the work of other artists, as from the subject I was illustrating."[1]

**1900.** Drew macabre illustrations for a volume by Edgar Allan Poe. ". . . I illustrated the poems of Edgar Allan Poe for the Endymion series of Poets published by George Bell & Sons. This was the most serious task of the kind that I had as yet undertaken and the first in which there was not some element of humour. In looking to-day at the work of these early years, I must admit that much of it was immature, and over ambitious. I often overestimated my abilities. For this reason every drawing was a fresh adventure into new countries in which I found some advantage for myself and openings for further adventures. Although confined within such narrow limits, where there were no dragons to slay nor barren wildernesses or mountains to cross, it was for me a life of joyful enterprise."[1]

**1902.** Assignments that year included another volume of *Don Quixote, Medieval Stories* by Professor Schück and *Monarchs of Merry England* by Roland Carse.

Wrote and illustrated his first book, *Uncle Lubin,* a whimsical fantasy for children. (Published again in 1925 as *Adventures of Uncle Lubin.*) "At this period I became conscious that I was being haunted by a strange little genius. He was not altogether unfamiliar to me. I fancy that he had haunted me almost unrecognized for many years. Now for some inscrutable reason he made himself more and more evident.

(From *The Incredible Adventure of Professor Branestawm* by Norman Hunter. Illustrated by W. Heath Robinson.)

Where he came from I cannot tell. At some time in his existence he must have wandered long in Alice's Wonderland. The only book he seems to have read was Gilbert's *Bab Ballads,* but even these he did not read as we read them; he took them quite seriously as we do 'Shakespeare' and *Smiles' Self Help* and *Eric, or Little by Little.* He was sincerity itself, and he had the simplicity of a child combined with the wisdom of old father William. No mortal could compare with him for ingenuity and inventiveness. He could do wonderful things with a piece of knotted string. There was one thing he lacked and that was a sense of humour; perhaps this was not a loss, for strangely enough it made him all the more humorous."[1]

"It seemed wrong, however, to laugh at one so earnest, so guileless and free from cynicism, but at times he was irresistible. Fortunately he was far too busy to care whether I laughed or not. My Good Genius in many ways, he introduced me to new friends and revived old friendships that were almost forgotten. He tempted me along a path which ran quite independently of that followed by my more serious work. He first came to life as Uncle Lubin."[2]

"It is interesting to notice the success with which writers such as W. S. Gilbert, Rudyard Kipling and many others, have illustrated their own works; some with little or no training in drawing. the lack of this, instead of being a hindrance, seems even to have imparted to their illustrations an unsophisticated charm that would otherwise have been wanting. Not often have artists written to their drawings so successfully. I do not, of course, refer to those geniuses who are, at the same time, both artists and authors. There is something amusing in the thought of an artist writing a book, an author making a drawing, or, say, a flautist painting a picture. In such changes of rôle we are too intrigued to be critical. We take a kindly view, and make allowances for weaknesses, due to the use of a foreign medium, which elsewhere we should not pass over so lightly.

"Unfortunately, Uncle Lubin was not a best-seller, but I have reason to believe that he endeared himself to those children in whose library he was placed. In the few copies of the original edition that I have seen in late years, the line drawings have often been coloured by some childish hand. Though the colours are gaudy, I flatter myself that this was a sign of loving appreciation. I have often been asked by parents, who in their own childhood have lived with Uncle Lubin, where they could buy a copy of his 'Adventures' for their children. Children's books receive so much wear and tear that they rarely survive one generation. Having some knowledge of the use of string, I have been able to keep my copy intact. I have even heard of a hand-basket being used to contain the dismembered pages of an old and well-worn copy."[1]

Did humorous advertising for the firms Lamson Paragon as well as Connolly Brothers, makers of leather goods. "My good genius, now in the guise of Uncle Lubin, not content with furthering my professional aims, began to interest himself in my private life and decided it was time I married. My future wife and I had already decided this for ourselves, having been engaged to be married for some little while, but unfortunately we could not afford to do so. This was no obstacle to Uncle Lubin, who, in an underhand way, brought about the possibility of a fulfilment of our wishes. I received a mysterious letter from one who signed himself Chas. Ed. Potter of Toronto. He informed me that he had been reading *The Adventures of Uncle Lubin,* which had convinced him that I was the artist to illustrate some advertisements he was writing. He further asked me to make an appointment with

him at an hotel, the name of which I had never heard before. I believe it was called 'Tranter's Hotel.'

"I had so often heard of the nefarious dealings of unscrupulous tricksters from the other side of the Atlantic, that I felt this was a case for using caution. I made an appointment and duly called at the hotel. I found it to be a very homely and old-fashioned house tucked away in some quiet square near to St. Paul's Cathedral. I was shown into his room, a snug little bed-sitting-room, and introduced myself to Chas. Ed. Potter. I cannot remember what I expected to see, but he was not at all of the gangster type; on the contrary he was the most amiable little man, who beamed at me in a friendly way through a pair of gold-rimmed glasses. I could easily imagine that Uncle Lubin and he got on very well together. Nevertheless I remained on my guard; for you never know what wiles may be practised to take advantage of an innocent artist.

"While agreeing to do the drawings, I did so only on condition that I received cash payment for each one as it was delivered. Cash in those days meant solid gold. In effect, I was to deliver a drawing with one hand while he was to pay into the other its worth in gold. Chas. Ed. Potter appeared to see nothing unusual in these stipulations and readily agreed to them, though I fancy a twinkle of amusement escaped through the gold-rimmed glasses.

"Every two or three days for the next few weeks I called at the hotel with my drawings. One of us seated on a chair and the other on the bed, we then discussed and planned the next set. I was soon ashamed of my suspicions and my stipulations lost all meaning. It was, however, so satisfactory to return from my visits with a little pile of gold in my pocket, that I could not remove the conditions I had imposed.

"So at last we were able to be married. I have to thank Uncle Lubin not only for his help in this important event in my life, but for a great friendship which began in a little bed-sitting-room in Tranter's Hotel by St. Paul's Cathedral many years ago.

"The advertisements were for the Lamson Paragon Supply Co. Ltd., with whom I now entered into a long and happy association. Chas. Ed. Potter returned to Toronto, where he is now engaged in overseas trade promotion and many other activities, in which good will is the inspiration. Later J. M. Evans, now the Managing Director of Lamson Paragon, came to me with an introduction from him. Advertising, I am told, is a serious science, and I have no doubt it is, but to me as an illustrator it has always been great fun. Perhaps at times I saw too much fun in it and needed a restraining hand."[1]

**1903.** Illustrated *The Works of Mr. Francis Rabelais.* "One of the first to whom Uncle Lubin introduced me was that enterprising publisher Grant Richards. . . . It was through this introduction too, that I was commissioned to illustrate *The Works of Rabelais* also published by Grant Richards about two years later. It is a testimony to the publisher's enterprise, at any rate, that he should commission the author of 'Uncle Lubin' to illustrate 'Rabelais.'"[1]

Married Josephine Latey. "Our wedding took place . . . after a long engagement. I was very busy at the time, and had much work to finish on the day before. In spite of the many willing friends, I did not finish work until the small hours. On my wedding morn, I was up betimes, as most bridegrooms are. After a quick breakfast I hurried down to

Seven Sisters Road and bought the ring and my rather thin trousseau. Having suitably arrayed my person, I went to the church with my brother George, who supported me as Best Man.

"Our wedding needs little description. It was much as other weddings. The bridegroom was punctual, and waiting patiently at the altar rails. He was trying to appear not at all embarrassed, or concerned at the delay of the bride. This, he was encouragingly assured, was not unusual with brides on these occasions. In the quiet expectancy of the church he dared not look round. When at length a stir at the entrance and a rustling of dresses among the congregation announced the bride's arrival, he pretended that it was a matter of no great moment. Unfortunately my preparations had been so harried that I had not the time to study and memorize the service. However, in spite of one or two errors, which threatened the solemnity of the ceremony, we were duly married."[1]

Their first home was a furnished flat in the Holloway Road, at the top of a tall building, served by no lifts and next door to the Holloway Empire. Although cheerful, this had its disadvantages. Heath wrote: "Our evenings were enlivened by occasional bursts of applause which we could hear through the wall separating us from the theatre. When we were entertaining and conversing with friends, the applause would sometimes occur at inopportune moments and make an expected commentary on our conversation."[2]

**1908.** Illustrated an edition of Shakespeare's *Twelfth Night.* "In the first decade of the century, there began to appear that de luxe series of books to which Arthur Rackham and Edmund Dulac made such fine contributions. The appearance of these books was partly due to the development of the three-colour process of reproductions. Unfortunately, this method could only be used on a certain kind of paper that was impossible for the rest of the book. Consequently the colour pictures had to be stuck in, making the book a scrapbook. This was not true book-making, but they were nevertheless handsome volumes.

"I was commissioned by Hodder & Stoughton to illustrate *Twelfth Night* to be published in this form. The work was a joy to me from beginning to end; my drawings were designed to give a free illustration of the drama. I am afraid that at times I have not resisted its many temptations to make a picture irrespective of its value as an illustration. But on the whole I tried to preserve the atmosphere of the play as I felt it. The philosophic clown appealed to me all through the work and I endeavoured to insinuate something of his philosophy into the drawings. The art of the book illustrator, as I understood it, did not consist solely in literally illustrating the incidents. His relationship to the work he was treating was much the same as that freer one adopted by a musical composer towards his subject. This play, and the fact that the illustrations were to be in colour, gave me such opportunities as I had not enjoyed before."[1]

Drew the illustrations for Rudyard Kipling's *A Song of the English.* "The next important task I undertook, was the illustration of an edition of Rudyard Kipling's *A Song of the English* to be published by Hodder & Stoughton. . . . It became necessary for me to meet the author and discuss the proposed book with him. For this purpose, I travelled down to Burwash where he lived at that time. This was an excursion I shall always remember. I was met at Heathfield and journeyed thence in a motor-car. There were few cars on the road in those days and this in itself was a joyful experience

as we drove through the pleasant Sussex lanes. Bateman's, the house at Burwash, where Rudyard Kipling lived, was a fine old building with stone mullioned windows. It was in the midst of wind-blown Sussex country. There was a faint smell of the sea in the air wafted across the few miles of country from the shore where the Coast wise lights of England watch the ships of England go. It was a fitting setting in which to find the author of *A Song of the English.*

"He met and entertained me with a quiet affability, which speedily removed the shyness I felt at first in his presence. Before long I was quite at home with him. His own knowledge of illustration gave him an appreciation of the artist's point of view. While making suggestions, he realized that the illustrator must have as free a hand as possible. His sympathetic understanding of my part in the undertaking made me feel that I was consulting with a brother artist. I spent a happy and for me a helpful day. It was a great inspiration for the work I had in hand to be in such close association with the author's interesting personality. I am always glad to remember that he was satisfied with my illustrations to his book. This was followed by another Kipling volume, *Collected Verse,* which was published by Doubleday Page & Co. of New York. This had a wider range of subject than *A Song of the English* and was consequently more difficult to illustrate. The Canadian National Gallery bought one of the originals, entitled 'The Three Decker.' This was a great encouragement to me."[1]

(From "Alone" in *Poems of Edgar Allen Poe* by Edgar Allen Poe. Illustrated by W. Heath Robinson.)

**1909.** Relocated with his family outside of London in Hatch End, Pinner. "We had now been married about four years, and with our two children, Joan and Oliver, found that we had outgrown our quarters. We were rather tired, too, of a flat life in Holloway. Greatly daring, we emigrated to Hatch End, Pinner, in still rural Middlesex. It was an adventure we never regretted. We rented a house where I could work at home. It was amongst a little group of similar villas, surrounded on nearly every side by open country. The garden was a piece of old pasture land, and, as we found, grew beautiful flowers. Most of our neighbours, as amateur gardeners, vied with one another, and we joined in the contest with zest, if not with much success."[1]

**1911.** Organized "The Frothfinders Federation," dedicated to country strolls and communal singing. "Don Quixote attracted me as do all wanderers, from Herodotus to George Borrow. I do not include in these, those great men who travel to the ends of the earth and benefit mankind by their scientific discoveries, but those who wander along the country roads seeking other things. Don Quixote was the Prince of these. Such were Christian in *The Pilgrim's Progress,* St. Francis d'Assisi and many another pilgrim. It was this love of mine that made 'Uncle Lubin' and 'The King of Troy' wander along their narrower roads. It was this love, too, that makes me enjoy so much a day's walk in the country. There must be no certain goal but that sense of mild adventure to be found on an unknown road. Yes, there was more than a trace of vagrancy in the Heath Robinsons.

"All the Robinsons—Tom, Charles, George and Will—were of course members. We used to meet at an appointed place near Pinner, early on Saturday afternoon. We would then take a long walk, which we planned to end at some hostelry, usually the Crown at Stanmore. As all the world of those days knew, this house was kept by Mr. and Mrs. Marsh. I suppose that Mr. Marsh would be called a good example of the typical English landlord, a fact of which he seemed well aware. Anyhow, like that rather mythical figure, he was tall, stout, somewhat red in the face, and in manner bluff and hearty. Certainly we were entertained generously, and our sharpened appetites appeased. Everything was on a lavish scale, from the roast beef to the beer. After the meal, we roused Stanmore with our songs and choruses. We would then return to Pinner, still joyfully singing along the country lanes.

"There must be something of the pagan in me, for whom these choruses had an almost religious sublimity. I do not think there is anything which so closely unites a group of people as a chorus. Especially is this so when it is inspired by good ale, beef, vegetables and friendship. For a few minutes you are completely at one with each other. The chorus ends and you are individuals again. But perhaps . . . I am a sentimental man."[1]

**1912.** Created a celebrated backcloth (backdrop used as scenery) for a London stage production, *Kill that Fly.* "An interesting instance of reproducing my lighter work in model form occurred about this time. I designed a scene in a Revue at the old Alhambra Theatre of Variety entitled *Kill that Fly.* It was composed and arranged by the late George Grossmith, junior, in collaboration with André Charlot. The scene was called 'Epsom Ups and Downs' as imagined by Mr. Ascot Heath Robinson. The back cloth consisted of a picture of a Heath Robinson racecourse. This wound in extravagant serpentine curves over the ups and downs. The foreground was occupied by a model of my well-known Starting Machine. This worked quite successfully and proved that it

was possible by mechanical means to start all of the horses at one time. I am not a racing man, but I can well understand that this is necessary in horseraces.

"Amongst the crowd Mr. Ascot Heath Robinson meandered gracefully, a not very sportsmanlike but still an interesting and picturesque figure. Not being an actor, I could not appear in person on the stage, and the part was cleverly played by Mr. René Koval, an actor practised in such impersonations. Great pains were taken that the resemblance should be as close as possible. We would stand side by side, while my counterpart was made up to resemble me. So exact was the resemblance, that I trembled to think of the great confidence I was reposing in my double. The criminal possibilities were obvious, but my trust was never abused."[1]

Joined the London Sketch Club. "At this time, I became a member of the London Sketch Club. It consisted of a group of artists, who met every Friday evening in the winter season and made sketches. After this a hot meal of a very substantial quality was provided followed by music and various entertainments."

The expression "Heath Robinson contraption" had passed into the British vernacular. This was due to the many humorous Heath Robinson drawings which depicted complex and outlandish machines meant to do prosaic tasks (in the manner of the American Rube Goldberg's drawings). "Whatever success these drawings may have had was not only due to the fantastic machinery and devices, and to the absurd situations, but to the style in which they were drawn. This was designed to imply that the artist had complete belief in what he was drawing. He was seeing no joke in the matter, in fact he was part of the joke. For this purpose, a rather severe style was used, in which everything was laboriously and clearly defined. There could be no doubt, mystery, or mere suggestion about something in which you implicitly believed, and of this belief it was necessary to persuade the spectator. At the slightest hint that the artist was amused, the delicate fabric of humour would fade away. I do not pretend that this end was always achieved, but I was so far successful as to be frequently identified personally with my drawings.

"I was imagined by some people to be a kind of ingenious mad-hatter, wandering around absent-mindedly, with my pockets full of knotted string, nails and pegs of wood, ready to invent anything at a moment's notice. I was once interviewed by a hopeful young journalist. When he entered the house, he glanced suspiciously at the lock on the front door, expecting, I suppose, to find some ingenious device for opening and shutting it. His eyes wandered inquiringly round the hall, and I think he was disappointed that here were no pullies and mechanical devices for doing things. Seated in my studio he took out his notebook and opened fire.

"'Now Mr. Robinson, where do you get your ideas? Do you dream of them or what?'

"These are always difficult questions to answer so I mumbled a non-committal reply.

"'Of course you were trained as an engineer?' he queried with his head on one side.

"I could only answer 'No.'

"He seemed a little incredulous of this.

(From *Bill the Minder* by W. Heath Robinson. Illustrated by the author.)

"'All your inventions would work, you know,' he said with an encouraging smile. I was doubtful of this, but I grinned as though I thought it quite likely.

"My drawings were frequently carried out as life-size models. A flying ship from one of my drawings was seen at a water carnival on Lake Saranac. The report does not say that it acutally flew, but, as my guiding spirit would say, 'It ought to have done so.' One gratifying sign of the appreciation of my drawings was the number of suggestions I received from all over the world. It was good to feel that I had so many friends, for friends indeed they were; few things unite people so intimately as a kindred sense of humour."[1]

". . . Earnest men were like children out of school. Nothing pleased them more than to see that which held them so tyrannically treated with levity. These were the type of men to which I had to appeal. They were men with great knowledge of machines and whose lives were devoted to them. . . . There must always be this cooperation between the jester and his audience."[2]

**1913.** ". . . I illustrated *Hans Andersen's Fairy Stories* for the third time. It is interesting to bear in mind that a great number of our fairy stories are derived from European folklore. In their original forms, they were not intended for children. Some of them were very terrifying. The Grimms used them freely, removing from them as much as possible, though not always successfully, their frightening characteristics.

"Hans Andersen and Perrault do not appear to have relied upon these sources nearly as much, if at all. Most of Hans Andersen's stories at any rate seem to have originated in his own mind, and have no suggestion of the macabre. It is this happier tone which I have tried to reproduce in my drawings. There are, however, certain traditions in connexion with the illustration of fairy stories, which cannot be ignored. Gnomes and fairies, at least in all European countries, have a family resemblance. An artist cannot invent an entirely new kind of gnome. Perhaps it is this that has convinced many children both young and old that fairies really exist.

"The illustration of classics is much governed by tradition. Sometimes this has been created in recent years. Sir John Tenniel created traditional forms for Alice, the Mad Hatter and the Duchess. To every dweller in Wonderland he gave a shape that the illustrator may not depart from. Dickens illustrations also depend to a certain extent upon his early illustrators, such as Phiz, for their types. It is true that these have developed and grown to a ripe growth in the drawings of later artists such as Fred Barnard, but their figures as we see them have evolved from the types set by the early interpreters of Charles Dickens. They have become like Micawber, Pecksniff, Falstaff and Alice, more and more real and recognizable as the immortal companions of mankind. Shakespeare had to wait centuries for a satisfactory illustrator, but Sir John Gilbert's Falstaff makes him visible to us for all time.

"Even Sir John Gilbert's accepted version of Falstaff is said to be not entirely his own creation but the portrait of a well-known actor of the past. He no doubt, adopted traditions that may have been handed down from the day of Shakespeare, gradually taking more and more definite form. It seems that an artist only plays a part in his creations. He focuses and passes on what was already in the universal heart of the race. Mankind and Michael Angelo painted 'The Last Judgment.'

"Every new book to be illustrated brought with it its own problems. The Kipling books, Hans Andersen and *Twelfth Night* had to be considered from widely different points of view. The last was seen through a golden haze of Elizabethan romance; the Kipling subjects in the colder and whiter light of modern times."[1]

**1914.** Illustrated an edition of Shakespeare's *A Midsummer Night's Dream*.

**1915-1918.** During the war years, he satirized the German army and gave moral support to the resistance with his fanciful drawings.

**1917.** Commissioned by an American syndicate to do a series of drawings on the American Expeditionary Force and consequently visited the front in France. "To-day it is difficult to imagine how we felt about the war. . . . Peace in Europe had appeared to be so deeply rooted, it seemed an impossibility that British soldiers should fight on European soil. Not since the Crimea had we sent an expeditionary force to the continent, and to France not since the days of Napoleon. At first we were filled with a wild excitement at the prospect of we knew not what experiences. There was a sense of adventure abroad, even for those who were not going to fight. But underneath all of this was an anger as well as dread which everyone personally felt.

"Early in August the war had not seriously broken the routine of our lives. We went to our work, and took our summer holidays as usual. We had planned to have this annual recreation at Seaford. I can remember the delay of our private bus filled with children and luggage on its way to Victoria. The roads were rendered nearly impassable by the troops, cavalry and infantry, and by the crowds of people to see them off; all were in the gayest spirits. It was the departure of the first expeditionary force to France. It was at Seaford we began to understand, though only imperfectly as yet, what war would mean for us. It was here we began slowly to realize the fate of the gallant force that left for France when we were setting out on our holiday. The necessity for more and more soldiers was being proclaimed in the newspapers, and recruiting was proceeding apace at Seaford as at every other town and village in the country. Then there were fears of an invasion, and a powerful light from Newhaven Harbour searched the seas every night, while barbed wire began to appear on the cliffs and downs.

"On returning to town and work. I found that already a change was taking place. Publishers were beginning to restrict their enterprise within narrower channels, and these were all connected with the war. There was now no demand for purely artistic productions, for new editions of Shakespeare or other classics, unless they bore some connexion with the all-absorbing topic. Even humour was now taking only one direction. At first I found this difficult to follow and was faced with the possibility of no work. The Moratorium, which was proclaimed by the Government at this time, promised to make things easier for us. However, it was not long before we discovered that this device had two faces, one of which smiled kindly on us while the other frowned. As the war developed, I at last found an opening for my humorous work. The much-advertised frightfulness and efficiency of the German army, and its many terrifying inventions, gave me one of the best opportunities I ever enjoyed.

"I was now engaged upon a series of drawings mostly published by *The Sketch* and *The Bystander*. These continued until the end of the war. It is interesting to note that the humorous artist's idea of the German soldier at this early stage in the hostilities was mainly derived from old news pictures of the Franco-Prussian War. It was only later that we abandoned these anachronisms. Besides many instances of 'Breaches of the Hague Conventions' by the enemy, these drawings contained suggestions to our War Office of methods and inventions to combat those that were directed against us. Although I cannot truthfully state that they were ever acted upon, they were at least received gratefully by the men in the trenches.

"For the greater part of the war period we lived at Pinner, though we had now moved nearer to the village. It was here that we had our first experience of raids by aeroplanes, as distinguished from Zeps. In June, 1917, fifteen aeroplanes raided London, killing thirty-one people, ten of whom were children. Sixty-seven people were injured. We could see these raids in the distance from Pinner. But the moonlight raids which soon followed were more visible because of the searchlights and shrapnel.'''

**1919.** The Robinsons relocated farther out in the country, at Cranleigh, in Surrey. A devoted family man, he was now the father of four sons and one daughter. "... We came to Cranleigh to banish 'Frightfulness' in all its forms from our minds and to lead peaceful country lives. We forgot that we were not country people. But this did not matter very much; we were not out of place. Few of our neighbours could truthfully be called country people. They were mostly retired men and their families—superannuated members of the various services with comfortable pensions, business men and professional men. There were a few artists to leaven the community, which conscientiously we tried to do. Lawson Wood, the well-known humorist, lived at Cranleigh when I first went there. He had a passion for conversions. I do not use this word in a religious sense. He delighted to transform old cottages or farmhouses into beautiful dwellings with lovely gardens.

"The country has a growing attraction for us all, particularly for those of us who have been bred in cities. First of all, we are compelled to form our ideas of what it is like from books and pictures, and I think we are even influenced by the films. A convention grows up in our minds. At holiday time we gaily venture into the country, hoping to see our ideas realized. The country people, at reasonable rates, are only too ready to help us in this.

"One advantage that an artist has over others lies in the fact that he does not belong to any particular class. Class distinctions do not exist for him to the same extent as they do for other people. One day he may be entertained by the squire, and the next evening may find him hob-nobbing in the village inn with the squire's footman. Mind, I do not say that I did this sort of thing, but there was nothing to prevent me. For the artist in a country village, where such distinctions are apt to be rigorously observed, these privileges are more particularly necessary. His right to them was generally admitted and his social vagaries smiled upon by all."[1]

Robinson had developed an early and abiding love for what he called "the ordinary people."[2]

He affectionately referred to housepainters as "brothers of the brush."[2] "... These people ['the common people'] are partners in the work of the greatest artists who have lived to proclaim the eternal beauty of the normal life of man.

"Even the humourous artist's part in this is not negligible. His humour may be merely refreshing and lighthearted jollity, without which the world would be a sadder place to live in. It may be bitter and contemptuous, or even patronizingly generous, but it can be human and full of charity. This last kind of humour may raise a laugh at the ordinary man, at his foibles and difficulties, but it is a brother's laugh in which he could join. Behind it all is a deep understanding of the vital part he plays and his courage in playing it."[1]

**1921.** Illustrated Perrault's *Old Time Stories*, his first non-satirical project in some time.

**April, 1923.** Began radio broadcasting. One such program had Robinson instructing his listeners on how to fill in a grid they had before them, square by square, and in so doing, create an illustration of their own. On other programs, he gave wild descriptions of the devices which supposedly surrounded him at the studio.

**1924** Authored and illustrated the children's book, *Bill the Minder,* about a boot cleaner who displayed a great talent for minding unruly children. "... I wrote and illustrated *Bill the Minder,* a more ambitious undertaking than *The Adventures of Uncle Lubin*. It was composed for older children than the readers of the earlier work, yet it was inspired by the same spirit. It was concerned first of all with Bill, a minder of children, the Virtuous Boadicea, one of his young charges, and the King of Troy. The last was not of the house of Priam, but a member of a later and hitherto unknown dynasty. He had lost his throne through the machinations of some evilly disposed ministers. Bill, Boadicea, and the other children of Crispin, the mushroom gatherer, formed the nucleus of an army which undertook to restore the good old monarch to his throne. The army set out on its journey, meeting with strange adventures, and, as it progressed, its numbers were increased by many strange and interesting people it met by the way. These included 'The Sicilian Charwoman,' 'The Ancient Mariner,' 'The Lost Grocer,' 'The Respectable Gentleman,' 'The Real Soldier,' and 'The Mixed Triplets.' Each had a story to tell to beguile the way, and all contributed finally to the restoration of the old king to his throne.

"Children ... played a great part in our lives.... Perhaps it was this that induced me to write and illustrate *Bill the Minder,* upon which I was at work during this time. With [my children's] many cousins, who often visited them, we seemed to be always surrounded by children, and occupied by the problems they present. In the love and wonder they inspired there was a fullness of life that is beyond my power to describe. But their mother's devotion, and complete absorption in her task of controlling this lovely and unruly vitality, was most wonderful of all."[1]

Interviewed by the press on writing and illustrating for children, he was asked whether he found that children have the same sense of humour as grown-up people. He replied: "It is somewhat difficult to say. My experience taken generally is that humour as understood by grown-ups is of later growth, but that to broad humour, such as the humour of a chair being pulled away from someone about to sit down, they are very sensitive. The very smart child, the child who gives a quick answer back, is more inclined to be witty than to be humorous. But children are intensely sensitive to the grotesque, and one must remember this so that one may interest and amuse without frightening them. I don't think children's

**Uncle Lubin was able to start on his voyage.** ■ (From *The Adventures of Uncle Lubin* by W. Heath Robinson. Illustrated by the author.)

books ought to be made deliberately childish; and in writing or illustrating children's stories one should remember that children are always trying to live up to you, and they resent your trying to live down to them. Their world, limited at first and gradually growing wider, is a very serious thing to them, and their questions go to prove this. One of the best children's books, I think, that ever was written is *Struwwelpeter;* it appeals to all children because it takes their world seriously."[2]

**1930.** "... I was engaged upon the designs for the decoration of the Knickerbocker Bar and the Children's Room in the *Empress of Britain.* My designs were painted on large wooden panels in my studio at Highgate. They were then removed to the shipbuilding yards of Messrs. John Brown, near Glasgow, to be fitted into the places allotted to them. I spent three or four days at Clydebank to put the finishing touches to my work. These days were made very interesting for me by the strenuous activities connected with shipbuilding which were continually going on around me. I saw the *Queen Mary* in the early stages of her construction, a long low skeleton lying by the side of one of the banks."[1]

**1934.** A special "Heath Robinson house" was exhibited which featured working replicas of his many wild gadgets. "'The Gadgets' was a marvel of electrical engineering. It presented problems never found before by an electrical engineer and probably no engineer will be faced with them again. My designs were made without thought of the difficulties involved in realizing them. I did not trouble my head about the matter, and let myself go; yet they were nearly all successfully carried out. Messrs. Venreco Ltd., were responsible for this and for the happy interpretation of the many sketches and designs I made for the house, the figures, the costumes and the innumerable other details of the show.

Rarely can a comic artist gauge the effect of his work upon the public. He may see it reproduced in the magazine, but can have little idea of the way in which it is received. He works blindly and thus a great stimulus is missed. This could not be said of my work on 'The Gadgets.' I had enough of this stimulus in watching the amusement of the crowds of visitors; though I did overhear one earnest visitor condemning it as impracticable."[1]

**1935.** Prepared a book, *Railway Ribaldry,* to celebrate the centenary of the Great Western Railway. "... The Great Western Railway celebrated its centenary. In their anxiety that the celebrations should really celebrate, the directors, the heads of the publicity department, the stationmasters, engine-drivers, ticket collectors and all engaged in the working of the railway, naturally turned to me. I joyfully collaborated with a series of drawings published under the title *Railway Ribaldry.*

"In a foreword to this work from which I quote, they state:

"'The Great Western Railway celebrates its one hundredth birthday this year, but unlike other Centenarians such as trees and turtles, grows more youthful after a century of existence.'

"But surely they are too modest and the implied apology was unnecessary? Their mature wisdom wanted no further proof than their selection of one so well equipped for the work, one who had a knowledge of engineering and also of celebrating. The preparation of these drawings necessitated an intensive study of the history of 'The Great Western Railway.' Besides this, the History of Railway Engineering throughout the country from the days of 'Puffing Billy' to the 'Cheltenham Flier' had to be exhaustively considered."[1]

**1936.** "In the year that followed, the collaboration between Kenneth R. G. Browne and myself began. Our first book *How to Live in a Flat* was followed a year later by *The Perfect Husband,* and we are now preparing an important work on Gardening, entitled *How to make a Garden Grow.* This collaboration seems to have solved a difficulty that I have often found with my lighter drawings. They rarely lend themselves to illustration in the ordinary sense of that term. It is the equal partnership in our mutual productions which is so satisfactory, at least to me. Instead of the finished story being handed to the artist to illustrate, we start level. Before we begin our different parts, we discuss the matter between us. In this way each is able to help the other. A consistency between the writer's and the artist's work is secured which cannot easily be obtained in any other way. My partner in these undertakings has a delightful sense of humour. It is great fun devising with him these little plots to make our readers laugh at themselves and one another.

"Kenneth R. G. Browne is the son of the late Gordon Browne, whose excellent work as a book illustrator and magazine illustrator are well known to those of my own generation and of the next generation too. He was the son of Hablot K. Browne, more popularly known as 'Phiz,' to whom we are indebted for some of the types by which we recognize the characters created by Charles Dickens.

"Such an arrangement as that existing between Kenneth R. G. Browne and myself is only possible with lighter publications. Authors of more serious subjects naturally have their own ideas as to the illustration of their works. The artist must be subject to the writer. He may not have too free a hand and perhaps trump the author's tricks.

"But occasions sometimes arise when the illustrator's tendency to enlarge on his subject is excusable and even necessary. He may have to make more illustrations than the subject, taken literally, affords. He may not, as the composer of anthems is at liberty to do, repeat the same phrase over and over again. He may not make more than one illustration to the same passage. In these cases a certain elasticity in his consideration of the story is useful. He is compelled to take the slightest excuse for an illustration. I knew an artist who boasted that he once illustrated the word 'The.'"[1]

**1939.** World War II began. Writing to a friend in Canada in the forties, he said: "All the younger men and women are now being called up for war service of some kind and the veterans are taking their places in civilian life, so perhaps when I write to you next I shall be a butcher, or perhaps a house agent, unless I am fortunate enough to be made the manager of a public house. . . .

"We have one small joint of meat a week, but my wife has a genius for coaxing it through the seven days, assisted by vegetables. On Monday we have it warmed up, on Tuesday it is stewed, on Wednesday curried, on Thursday minced, and it finally fades away on Friday and Saturday in nourishing soups. . . .

"Here am I leading very nearly a blameless life and there are many in the same position. Smoking less than usual and perhaps not at all before long. Alcoholic indulgences reduced to a minimum. Never out late at night—it is not worth it in the blackout—and rising with the lark in the summertime when we alter our clocks. In fact, we lead lives of great temperance and restraint without credit for our self-denial."[2]

**1940.** After the death of K. R. G. Browne, began a series of "How to . . ." books in collaboration with Cecil Hunt—*How to Make the Best of Things, How to Build a New World, How to Run a Communal Home.*

**December, 1940.** ". . . I am holding the fort here not as a Home Guard, an A.R.P. Warden, an Auxiliary Fireman, or a Fifth Columnist, but as a little of all of them except the last. Quite unofficially I am told that my aim with the stirrup-pump could not be excelled even by William Tell. Fortunately as yet I have not been compelled to give any public demonstration. The technique of my blacking out is much admired in the neighbourhood and is the despair of Hitler."[2]

"It all depends upon what 'old age' means. If it means *sans* everything—in spite of the assistance of ear specialists, eye specialists, dentists, doctors, and other specialists, to check the inevitable progress—then all I would ask is a seat in the sun outside some country inn. That and a pipe and what contemplation I should be capable of. But I should much prefer to go on as I am, only more so."[2]

**August, 1944.** ". . . I have to go into [the] hospital for an operation, after which I shall need some time to recuperate, so that you see I shall not be able to undertake anything for some little time. Moreover, I have many arrears of work to make up before I undertake anything new."[2]

**September 13, 1944.** Died in Cranleigh in Surrey. "In the light of the lives of Lawrence of Arabia, of Marco Polo, of Sinbad or Robinson Crusoe it must be confessed that my life appears to have been uneventful. But in its narrower sphere it has not been without variety and adventure. I have had hills of difficulty to surmount, though never a view of Mount Everest. Although I have not trodden the Sahara desert, I have had barren places to cross as arid to me. In a low-lying country a haystack may appear as high as a mountain."[1]

"Each of us is given a bag of treasures, and it is up to us to make the best of it. If we don't, we have only ourselves to blame."[2]

*FOR MORE INFORMATION SEE:* William Heath Robinson, *My Line of Life* (autobiography), Blackie, 1938, reprinted, E. B. Publishing, 1974; Langston Day, *The Life and Art of W. Heath Robinson,* M. Joseph, 1947, reprinted, British Book Center, 1977; Brian Doyle, editor, *Who's Who of Children's Literature,* Schocken Books, 1968; John N. C. Lewis, *Heath Robinson: Artist and Comic Genius,* Barnes & Noble, 1973; (obituary) *Current Biography,* 1944.

## ROSS, Tony 1938-

*PERSONAL:* Born August 10, 1938, in London, England; son of Eric Turle Lee (a magician) and Effie Ross; married Carole Jean D'Arcy (divorced); children: Philippa, George, Alexandra. *Education:* Liverpool College of Art, diplomas, 1960, 1961. *Politics:* None. *Religion:* Methodist. *Home:* 5 Timber St., Macclesfield, Cheshire, England.

*CAREER:* Smith Kline & French Laboratories, graphic designer, 1962-64; Brunnings Advertising, art director, 1964-65; Manchester Polytechnic, Manchester, England, lecturer, 1965, senior lecturer in illustration, 1971-72. Consultant in graphic design. *Member:* Society of Industrial Artists and Designers.

*WRITINGS*—All self-illustrated juveniles: *Tales from Mr. Toffy's Circus,* six volumes, W. J. Thurman, 1973; (editor) *Goldilocks and the Three Bears,* Andersen, 1976; *Hugo and the Man Who Stole Colors,* Follett, 1977, published in England as *Hugo and the Man Who Stole Colours,* Andersen, 1977; (editor) *The Pied Piper of Hamelin,* Andersen, 1977; *Hugo and the Wicked Winter,* Sidgwick & Jackson, 1977; *Norman and Flop Meet the Toy Bandit,* W. J. Thurman, 1977; (editor) *Little Red Riding Hood,* Andersen, 1978; *Hugo and Oddsock,* Andersen, 1978; *The Greedy Little Cobbler,* Andersen, 1979; (editor) *Mother Goose,* Andersen, 1979.

Illustrator: Iris Grender, *Did I Ever Tell You . . . ,* Hutchinson, 1977. Contributor of cartoons to magazines, including *Punch* and *Town.*

*WORK IN PROGRESS:* (Self-illustrated) *Two Monkey Tales* for Longmans (London); (with Jon Talbot) *The Most Unusual Computer* for Kaye and Ward; (self-illustrated) *Jack and the Beanstalk;* (self-illustrated) *Dear Mole.*

*SIDELIGHTS:* "As a small child in England during the war, I learned respect for children's things. Toys and books were scarce, therefore treasured. Christmas was the time for new books, and unwittingly, on the living room rug, I met Beatrix Potter, E. H. Shepard, Arthur Rackham, Edward Ardizzone, and surprisingly enough, Gustave Doré. Once I was given my grandfather's copy of *Don Quixote* illustrated by Doré. I do not remember liking the stern engravings, although I was impressed by them, and for the first time, I became aware of the illustrator's craft. I was eight years old.

"My training as an etcher, and my liking of graphic, rather than fine, artists, gave me a love of black line on white paper.

(From *Hugo and the Man Who Stole Colours* by Tony Ross. Illustrated by the author.)

My colours tend to be transparent inks and watercolours, laid lightly, not obscuring the line. To me, a children's illustrator is a creator of worlds for kids, and so I prefer to write my own texts. I like telling stories, I like to see children laugh, I like to draw.''

*HOBBIES AND OTHER INTERESTS:* Sailing small boats, cats, the monarchy, collecting toy soldiers, lamb cutlets.

*FOR MORE INFORMATION SEE: Graphis 177.*

## RUHEN, Olaf   1911-

*PERSONAL:* Born August 24, 1911, in Dunedin, New Zealand; son of Carl and Margaret (Johnson) Ruhen; married Claire Strickland, December, 1936; married Madeleine Elizabeth Thompson, March 21, 1959; children: Carl Anthony. *Education:* Otago Boys High School, Dunedin, N.Z., student, 1925-28. *Home:* 9 Cross St., Mosman, Sydney, N.S.W., Australia. *Agent:* John Cushman, 25 West 3rd St., New York, N.Y. 10036.

*CAREER:* Farming and deep-sea fishing, 1928-37; *Evening Star Co.,* Dunedin, N.Z., journalist, 1938-41, 1945-47; *Consolidated Press,* Sydney, Australia, journalist, 1947-49, 1949-53; *Sydney Morning Herald,* journalist, 1953-56; freelance writer, 1956—. University of Adelaide, first director of school of creative writing. *Military service:* Royal New Zealand Air Force, bomber pilot, 1941-45, became flying officer; still in Reserve. *Member:* International P.E.N. (vice-president, Sydney branch, 1960-61), Australian Society of Authors (founding member), Fellowship of Australian Writers. *Awards, honors:* Winner of the Qantas short story award, 1976.

*WRITINGS: Land of Dahori,* Lippincott, 1957; *Naked under Capricorn,* Lippincott, 1957; *White Man's Shoes,* Macdonald, 1960; *Tangaroa's Goldchild,* Little, 1962; *Mountains in the Clouds,* Rigby, 1963; *The Flockmaster,* Macdonald, 1963; *Minerva Reef,* Angus & Robertson, 1963; *Lively Ghosts,* Hodder & Stoughton, 1964; *The Broken Wing,* Hodder & Stoughton, 1965; *Writing,* Cheshire, 1965; *Harpoon in My Hand,* Angus & Robertson, 1966; *Corcoran's the Name* (Child Study Association book list), Angus & Robertson, 1966, Farrar, Straus, 1968; *Sydney Rocks,* Rigby, 1966; (with Maurice Shadbolt) *Isles of the South Pacific,* National Geographic Society, 1968; *Australian Fisheries,* Doubleday, 1968; *Scan the Dark Coast,* Hodder & Stoughton, 1969; *Port Macquarie Sketchbook,* Rigby, 1970; *Parramatta Sketchbook,* Rigby, 1971; *Historic Buildings of Sydney,* Rigby, 1972; *This Changing Land,* Angus & Robertson, 1972; *Southern Highlands Sketchbook,* Rigby, 1974; *Balmain Sketchbook,* Rigby, 1975; *Port of Melbourne 1835-76,* Cassell, 1976; *The Day of the Diprotodon,* Hodder & Stoughton, 1976; *Bound for Botany Bay,* Hamlyn, 1976; (with W. Hudson Shaw) *Lawrence Hargrave,* Cassell, 1977; *The Tongans,* Pacific Publications, 1978; *Sydney Harbour,* Collins, 1978. Contributor to *Encyclopedia Britannica, Saturday Evening Post, Reader's Digest,* other international and most Australian periodicals, forty-three short story anthologies and has had several hundred short stories published.

*WORK IN PROGRESS: The Jealous Gods of Captain Bully Hayes; The Captain Cook Tradition; Bullock Teams: A History of New South Wales.*

*SIDELIGHTS:* "My birthplace, Dunedin, in New Zealand, was a university town and boasted some poets, some writers on learned subjects, and even a couple of novelists. But

**OLAF RUHEN**

The country was bone dry this year. There was water in our creek--it never ran dry. But it was the smallest trickle now, just a sliver of wet slime joining the pools. In the pasture, the grass was a straw white and straw dry. Among the trees the undergrowth, high as a man on a horse, crackled and broke when you rode through it. ■ (From *Corcoran's the Name* by Olaf Ruhen. Jacket illustrated by Jennifer Tuckwell.)

when I was a child, no one, it seemed to me, wrote about the world I knew. My reading was all of alien worlds, entrancing but quite remote. I read a lot and spent much time alone on a wild shore to which the winds and seas drove up from the Antarctic, for a long illness had kept me in bed a year and semi-convalescent much longer. When at last I read in some light fiction a description of the coast I knew very well, I found much in the print that I did not recognize. When I checked, though, I found it existed all right; my understanding and my knowledge of my own country was much enlarged through the recorded experience of others.

"I left school at a time of economic depression when the only opportunities for work were in the fields, in the bush, on the mountains, and best of all, at sea. But I found the hard slogging work enjoyable as long as I tried to do it better than my companions, or faster, or with more of a finish. I spent about ten years of my life this way and did not think of writing though I had done well at it at school and had filled in some sick-bed time this way. When I wrecked my small seagoing schooner I wrote articles and stories primarily to make some spare-time money.

"At this stage it seemed very important to me that readers should share my high opinion of other members of the fishing fleet, of their sea-boats capable of coping with the gales of the 'Roaring Forties' where our work lay, and of the freedom and joy of the life as well as its hazards. That was where involvement began. It developed until it became of great importance to me that others should know my world as I knew it, as it came to me through my eyes, ears and nose; that they should know the pleasures of touch and taste as I knew them, and come to understand the philosophy that developed for me from these sensations of my world. For everyone's world is different.

"All this newfound enthusiasm brought me into the profession of journalism through the good offices of an editor who liked my work and thought that this was where my life should lie. But I had been in it hardly long enough to learn the basic skills when the Second World War thrust me into another kind of life, in the air. I found that navigating the atmosphere, while not quite comparable to the pleasures of being at home on the oceans, had its own pleasures and presented challenges that induced a good many of us to look very closely at human life and the purposes of human ability. It also took me to new countries, introducing me to the Northern Hemisphere. And it thrust me into the companionship of different kinds of people. Since most of those with whom I served in aircrew were at least ten years younger than I, I became attuned to changing forms, changing worlds, changing life-styles over a much longer period of development than most.

"When the war finished I went to Australia, a country new to me. Since I wrote about adventure, editors began to send me where adventure might be found. And now a different factor began to show its influence.

"Of the stories that had awakened my imagination in childhood, those that I liked best were Polynesian—Maori folk tales. During the period of my childhood illness, a brother of mine was a doctor in the Friendly Islands, the islands of Tonga. In the places where I later worked I tended to choose Maoris as companions. I was enamoured of the South Seas and the splendid people who had opened them up, thousands of years before Europeans had felt at home on the oceans.

"So I directed my travels, when I could, towards the South Sea, the South Pacific Ocean and discovered a new admiration for those other Oceanic people, the Melanesians. I am at home on islands, and I have been lucky in my travels. In New Guinea, for example, I was attached to an expedition that made the first contact with the wild members of three previously unknown tribes. I have sailed with Polynesian captains in waters not very well known. With Tongans, who hunt the whale for the meat their coral islands do not provide, I've gone in open boats, to use the weapons we made ourselves, to bring in the fifty-ton quarry, hunting without explosives and navigating without instruments.

"Perhaps a deciding factor in such expeditions is an intense curiosity about the human past. We cannot tell where man is going until we compare his present location with where he has been, and by looking at the primitive, as it still exists, we can make an estimate of how man has developed. Perhaps I am searching too deeply for my motives: what I have gained most from a life of writing is the friendship of men and women I admire, whether they live in grass huts or in penthouses in the high-rise buildings. It is a privilege and a joy to be a writer."

# SAMUELS, Gertrude

*PERSONAL:* Daughter of Sam and Sarah Samuels; children: Paul. *Education:* Attended George Washington University.

*CAREER:* Staff member of *New York Post, Newsweek,* and *Time* prior to 1943; *New York Times,* New York, N.Y., staff writer for Sunday department, 1943-75, staff writer and photographer, 1947-75. Special United Nations observer for United Nations Children's Fund in eight European countries, 1948. War correspondent in Korea, 1952. *Member:* Authors Guild, Dramatists Guild, American Newspaper Guild, Writers Guild of America, Actors Studio, Playwrights Unit (New York). *Awards, honors:* Front Page Awards of American Newspaper Guild for articles on Little

**GERTRUDE SAMUELS**

Rock crisis and drug addiction; George Polk Award of Long Island University for articles on school desegregation; citation from Overseas Press Club for international reporting; various photography awards.

*WRITINGS: Report on Israel,* Herzl Press, 1960; *B-G, Fighter of Goliaths: The Story of David Ben-Gurion,* photos by Samuels, Crowell, 1961; *The People vs. Baby: A Documentary Novel,* Doubleday, 1965; *The Secret of Gonen,* photos by Samuels, Avon, 1969; *Run, Shelley, Run!* (ALA Notable Book), Crowell, 1974; *Mottele: A Partisan Odyssey,* Harper, 1976; *Adam's Daughter,* Crowell, 1977; *Of David and Eva, A Love Story,* New American Library, 1978. Author of several plays, including "The Corrupters," 1969. "The Plant That Talked Back" and "Judah The Maccabee and Me," the latter two produced in New York at Lambs Club Theatre, January 26, 1970, "The Assignment," produced in England, 1974, broadcast over Radio Oslo (Norway), 1976. *New York Times* articles anthologized in school texts and other books; "The Corrupters," included in *The Best Short Plays, 1969,* edited by Stanley Richards, Chilton, 1969. Contributor of articles and pictures to *Nation, National Geographic, Saturday Evening Post, Harper's, Look, Redbook,* and *The Nation. Run, Shelly, Run!,* produced as a teleplay for NBC television.

*SIDELIGHTS:* Gertrude Samuels was born in Manchester, England, went to school there, and later attended George Washington University in Washington, D.C. From there, she went to work at the *New York Post,* moved on to *Time* and *Newsweek,* and for over twenty years was the only staff writer for *The New York Times* Sunday Magazine. As writer, foreign correspondent, and photographer for *The Times,* she traveled throughout the States, Europe, the Middle East, and the Far East to cover human interest stories ranging over a wide variety of subjects, from education, Indian affairs, juvenile justice, and prisons, to the Korean War, Vietnam, and the emergence of the new State of Israel. She covered the plight of refugees, was a former consultant to

UNICEF, and has had a dual involvement with Israel: with the victims of the Holocaust, and with the late David Ben-Gurion.

Recently Samuels left *The Times* to devote herself full time to her writing and photography.

*FOR MORE INFORMATION SEE: U.S. Camera,* January, 1961; *New York Times Book Review,* May 7, 1967; *Variety,* February 14, 1970.

## SAWYER, Ruth    1880-1970

*PERSONAL:* Born August 5, 1880, in Boston, Massachusetts; died June 3, 1970; daughter of Francis Milton (an importer) and Ethelinda J. (Smith) Sawyer; married Albert C. Durand, M.D., June 4, 1911; children: David, Margaret (Mrs. Robert McCloskey). *Education:* Columbia University, B.S., 1904. *Religion:* Unitarian. *Home:* Gull Rock, Hancock, Maine.

*CAREER:* Short story writer and author of books for children. New York *Sun,* feature writer; was sent to Ireland, 1905, 1907, where she began collecting folk tales. Began storytelling professionally for the New York Lecture Bureau, 1908, and started the first storytelling program for children at the New York Public Library. *Awards, honors:* Newbery Medal, 1937, for *Roller Skates;* Regina Medal, 1965; Laura Ingalls Wilder Medal, 1965; Caldecott Medal, 1945, for *The Christmas Anna Angel* (illustrated by Kate Seredy), and 1954, *Journey Cake, Ho!* (illustrated by Robert McCloskey).

*WRITINGS: The Primrose Ring,* Harper, 1915; *Seven Miles to Arden,* Harper, 1916; *A Child's Yearbook* (illustrated by the author), Harper, 1917; *Herself, Himself, and Myself,* Harper, 1917; *Doctor Danny* (illustrated by J. Scott Williams), Harper, 1918; *Leerie* (illustrated by Clinton Balmer), Harper, 1920; *The Silver Sixpence* (illustrated by James H. Crank), Harper, 1921; *Gladiola Murphy,* Harper, 1923; *The Tale of the Enchanted Bunnies,* Harper, 1923; *Four Ducks on a Pond,* Harper, 1928; *Folkhouse: The Autobiography of a Home* (illustrated by Allan McNab), D. Appleton, 1932; *Tono Antonio* (illustrated by F. Luis Mora), Viking Press, 1934; *The Luck of the Road,* Appleton-Century, 1934.

*Picture Tales from Spain* (illustrated by Carlos Sanchez), F. A. Stokes, 1936; *Gallant: The Story of Storm Veblen* (published serially as *Hillmen's Gold*), Appleton-Century, 1936; *Roller Skates* (illustrated by Valenti Angelo), Viking Press, 1936, reissued, Dell, 1966; *The Year of Jubilo* (illustrated by Edward Shenton), Viking Press, 1940, reissued, 1970; *The Least One* (illustrated by Leo Politi), Viking Press, 1941; *The Way of the Storyteller,* Macmillan, 1942, reissued, Viking Press, 1965; *Old Con and Patrick* (illustrated by Cathal O'Toole), Viking Press, 1946; *The Little Red Horse* (illustrated by Jay Hyde Barnum), Viking Press, 1950; (contributor) "Crippled: An Appeal to Motorists," in *Challenge of Ideas: An Essay Reader,* edited by John Gehlmann, Odyssey, 1950; *Journey Cake, Ho!* (illustrated by Robert McCloskey), Viking Press, 1953, reissued, 1970; *A Cottage for Betsy* (illustrated by Vera Bock), Harper, 1954; *The Enchanted Schoolhouse* (illustrated by Hugh Tory), Viking Press, 1956; (contributor) "On Reading the Bible Aloud," in *A Horn Book Sampler of Children's Books and Reading,* edited by Norma R. Fryatt, Horn Book, 1959; *How to Tell a Story,* F. E. Compton, 1962; *Daddles: The Story of a Plain Hound-Dog* (illustrated by Robert Frankenberg), Little, Brown, 1964; *My Spain: A Storyteller's Year of Collecting,* Viking Press, 1967.

**RUTH SAWYER**

Christmas stories: *This Way to Christmas,* Harper, 1916, revised, 1970 [another edition illustrated by Maginal Wright Barney, Harper, 1924]; *The Long Christmas* (illustrated by V. Angelo), Viking Press, 1941, reissued, 1966; *The Christmas Anna Angel* (illustrated by Kate Seredy), Viking Press, 1944; *This is the Christmas: A Serbian Folk Tale,* Horn Book, 1945; *Maggie Rose: Her Birthday Christmas* (illustrated by Maurice Sendak), Harper, 1952; *The Year of the Christmas Dragon* (illustrated by Hugh Tory), Viking Press, 1960; *Joy to the World: Christmas Legends* (illustrated by Trina S. Hyman), Little, Brown, 1966.

Contributor of over 200 articles, stories, poems, and serials to periodicals, including *Atlantic Monthly* and *Outlook.*

*ADAPTATIONS:* "The Primrose Ring" (motion picture), Lasky Feature Play Co., 1917; Margaret D. Williams, *Christmas Apple* (two-scene play; adaptation of a story in *This Way to Christmas*), Samuel French, 1939; "Journey Cake, Ho!" (filmstrip; color, with sound and picture-cued text booklet), Weston Woods Studios, 1967.

*SIDELIGHTS:* **August 5, 1880.** Born in Boston, Massachusetts, the last of five children—all the rest were boys. Her father was an importer. The family lived in New York City. "One has to be born; I was in Boston. My father was Francis Milton Sawyer, my mother Ethelinda J. Smith, of old Lexington stock.''

As a child she had an Irish nurse, Johanna, who was a wonderful storyteller and an inspiration to her. ''Fortunately for [me] there were no psychologists or psychoanalysts in [my] day. But there was a beloved nurse, Johanna. [My] family was a busy family, and a methodical one withal, and [I] was brought up on bells and whistles and family prayers. From the time that [I] was a very young child [I] began to grow a keen, steadfast, and never-diminishing sense of rebellion. [I] hated to be regulated by bells and whistles; hated that schedule that was pinned above [my] bed which told [me] as soon as [I] was able to read what [I] was supposed to be doing every hour in the day.

''Although William Butler Yeats had not then written his *Land of Heart's Desire,* I think [I] must have stood often, as did the little newly-married bride, made desperate by the too-often nagging of a workaday mother-in-law, crying with her from that threshold where the fairy primroses had been scattered:

''Come fairies, take me out of this dull house.
Let me have all the freedom I have lost,
Work when I will, idle when I will.
Fairies, come take me out of this dull world.
For I would ride with you upon the wind,
Run on the top of the dishevelled tide,
And dance upon the mountain like a flame.

''Luckily for [me], Johanna provided fairies for [me]; and [my] family provided books. And whatever freedom came down through those first ten years came through these mediums of books and fairies.'' [From an acceptance paper by Ruth Sawyer, *Newbery Medal Books: 1922-1955,* edited by Bertha Mahoney Miller and Elinor Whitney Field, Horn Book Inc., 1955.[2]]

**1904.** Received her B.S. degree from Columbia University. ''[I] went to private school in New York City—Annie C. Brackett's; then to Packer Institute, Brooklyn and the Garland Kindergarten Training School in Boston; and then to Cuba to help organize kindergartens. [I] finished with a scholarship at Columbia University—degree B.S. in Education.''[1] Following her degree, Sawyer became a feature writer for the New York *Sun.*

**1905-1907.** Sent to Ireland where she began collecting folk tales for a series of articles on Irish folklore, festivals and Irish cottage industries. Much later she recounted these folk tales in her books.

**1908.** Began story telling for the New York Lecture Bureau and started the first story telling program for children at the New York Public Library.

**1910.** At the invitation of Anne Carroll Moore, told her Christmas story, which she had found in Ireland, *The Voyage of the Wee Red Cap,* for the first time to a group of Irish American children at the New York Public Library. ''I shall always remember the faces of the American-born Irish boys who came over from a nearby parochial school. I shall always remember Miss Moore's lighting of candles; and the Christmas wishes that came out of that first library story hour. Those candles have never gone out for me; they still burn and always will.''[2]

The following year *The Voyage of the Wee Red Cap* was published in *Outlook* Magazine with other of her Irish tales.

**1911.** Married a physician, Albert C. Durand and had two children; a son and a daughter. The family lived in Ithaca, New York, overlooking Lake Cayuga. Her daughter (Mrs. Margaret Durand McCloskey) recalled her life with her mother: ''Family life in an upstate New York town was peaceful and full of the small excitements of childhood. . . . My father was an enthusiastic fisherman; so was Mother, due to her early Maine upbringing with four brothers. During a Maine summer, a special treat for all of us was to hire a boat at Lincolnville Beach and row out with the coming tide to the ledge off Frohock Point or maybe to Haddock Ledge. We caught flounder and cunner and tommy cod, though I don't remember any haddock. . . . When we had to sell the house in Maine, we spent several summers in the Adirondacks and turned from saltwater to freshwater fishing. . . .

''Water is Mother's favorite element, whether she fishes it or sails it. For several summers we had a boat named *Mr. Gilligan* on Cayuga Lake, and Mother became an expert captain, nosing the cruiser in and out of the slip and running her down the lake to picnic or just to cool off with a swim.

''The name Ruth Sawyer is associated with Christmas, and Christmases were truly festive, but just as vivid in my memory is Fourth of July. We were among the lucky generations of children who still celebrated the Fourth in the grand tradition, compared with which today's holiday is an anemic affair indeed. For our family, the ritual did not vary much from year to year. Before breakfast, we children shot off the small firecrackers, one-inchers, in one glorious crackle, or whirled around on our heels, crunching those poppy things that stuttered and banged with a satisfying but not frightening sound. After breakfast, more small crackers and some big enough to toss a can a foot or more with a lovely muffled roar. It was just enough time for Mother to make a picnic lunch for the major wild-strawberry expedition of the year. These were outings we viewed with mixed emotions, as we were itching to get back to the firecrackers; but then if we didn't pick our quota of berries, we couldn't expect any of the celestial shortcake for supper or the jam, which never lasted long enough, anyway. (I can't remember if my brother ever malingered to the extent that, according to Mother, one uncle did. He had filled a basket with grass and sprinkled it over with berries, blue in that case, and lazed away the rest of the afternoon.)

''Then we came home to more and larger crackers and supper, with the shortcake every bit as heavenly as we had remembered, and afterwards, the gathering of the neighbors. As our house was higher on the Heights than most of the others, it was the perfect spot for rockets. There were sparklers for the little ones, Roman candles for the older children, and Catherine wheels. Squibs sound too English, but I am sure there were other things besides rockets. They were set off by grownups only, but those marvelous arching explosions so enchanted us that even the most recalcitrant child would shut up, and the evening ended in brilliant faraway bursts over the lake—and silence.

''Soon after the Fourth, the summer meant Maine and Maine meant blueberries as well as fishing. I hope that the bulldozing and blacktopping of our countryside will somehow be curbed so that our space-exploring descendants may still, if they choose, explore the delights of berry picking. Mother was, and is, a berry picker par excellence, and blueberries are her favorites. She did wonderful things with rasp-

**They lived in a log cabin, t'other side of Tip Top Mountain.** ■ (From *Journey Cake, Ho!* by Ruth Sawyer. Illustrated by Robert McCloskey.)

berries, strawberries, blackberries, and cranberries, but somehow the smell of the sunny blueberry pastures stayed in the muffins and the pancakes and the pies.

"No memory of childhood can be complete, in our house at least, without recalling the animals who shared it with us. A Maltese cat named Jock was the first, and no other cat ever filled his boots, because in our heart he was the perfect cat. Although other dogs came and went, the perfect dog was a Border collie (named Laddie, naturally) who wandered in off the street and decided to stay.

"Mother had a lovely garden with tulips in May that were her pride. Every year she fought a battle with the rabbits, but the discovery of a nest of motherless ones in the cold frame

. . . made her forget her animosities, and we raised six on a medicine dropper. The next spring they returned in force and bit the tulip of the hand that fed them." [From an article entitled, "Our Fair Lady," by Margaret Durand McCloskey, *Horn Book,* October, 1965.[3]]

**1936.** *Picture Tales from Spain,* a collection of Spanish tales which she had heard when she visited that country, were published.

**1937.** Received the Newbery Award for her book, *Roller Skates.* In her acceptance speech she defined her belief in a child's freedom: "If there be any point to *Roller Skates*—which I very much doubt—it lies in the urge of free-

Jeremy was one of her special summer friends. He was a year older than Maggie Rose and came to visit his grandmother every year---last of June through Labor Day. ■ (From *Maggie Rose--Her Birthday Christmas* by Ruth Sawyer. Illustrated by Maurice Sendak.)

dom for a child. There are always among us children who are not, to use the present-day phrase, well adjusted.

"There is, of course, this matter of being afraid to give freedom to young children. I believe they have that within themselves which makes it possible for them to meet the world and life, and interpret it more nearly aright than can we. They carry with them that inheritance of faith and imagination undimmed; and that tremendous surging desire to know, to see, to feel and to do, which is rarely betrayed. In our desire as adults to lay hold of a child's life, to grip it, mold it to our own values, we do unwittingly a great harm. We confront children with our own fears, our own lack of faith; to safeguard them we attempt to thrust between them and life those many false illusions which we have picked up in our own twisting, turning way. Children make a far more advantageous highroad. A free child is a happy child; and there is nothing more lovely; even a disagreeable child ceases to be disagreeable and is liked. . . ."[2]

**1954.** Received the Caldecott Medal for *Journey Cake, Ho!* "Where did *Journey Cake, Ho!* have its start? It began a hundred years ago in the mountains of Kentucky, North Carolina, and Tennessee. The people told the story. They sang it. They laughed over it. But the story I have written is different from any of the versions I have heard, but the bare bones are the same. And I like it.

"When I wrote the story, I was hoping Robert McCloskey [my son-in-law] would like the story and find Johnny the sort of boy he wanted to make pictures of. He did." [From an article entitled, "I Hope You Like It," by Ruth Sawyer, *Young Wings,* December, 1953.[4]]

**1965.** Received the Laura Ingalls Wilder Award for her substantial and lasting contribution to children's literature. In her acceptance speech she said: "It is a most happy coincidence that I am receiving the Laura Ingalls Wilder Award in Detroit. Some thirty years ago, I met Mrs. Wilder here. We both had come to speak and to autograph our books at one of the many book fairs that were springing up like alfalfa all over the country.

"It so happened that our books had grown from childhoods that held deep significance for us. Between our turns, we visited together. I found Laura Ingalls Wilder a most modest person. She spoke her pleasure that the children of that time enjoyed the childhood of the small Laura, and she expressed her eager hopes that the children of the future might still enjoy her books. I think she had no realization that she had

**"This is the beginning of our holiday ride!"** shouted **Miklos, climbing into the sleigh between his father and Anna.** ■ (From *The Christmas Anna Angel* by Ruth Sawyer. Illustrated by Kate Seredy.)

written pure Americana for those children.'' [From Ruth Sawyer's acceptance speech in *Horn Book,* October, 1965.[5]]

**June 3, 1970.** Died. Sawyer lived in Hancock, Maine with her husband prior to her death.

*FOR MORE INFORMATION SEE:* Stanley J. Kunitz and Howard Haycraft, editors, *Junior Book of Authors,* second revised edition, Wilson, 1951; Ruth Sawyer, ''I Hope You Like It,'' *Young Wings,* December, 1953; J. Overton, ''Ruth Sawyer,'' in *Newbery Medal Books, 1922-1955,* edited by Bertha E. Miller and E. W. Field, Horn Book, 1955; R. H. Viguers, ''For Ruth Sawyer,'' *Horn Book,* December, 1961; *Horn Book,* April, 1964, April, 1965; Virginia Haviland, *Ruth Sawyer,* Walck, 1965; ''Regina Medal Winner, Ruth Sawyer Durand,'' *Catholic Library World,* January, 1965; E. M. Jewett, ''Ruth Sawyer Durand,'' *Catholic Library World,* February, 1965; Margaret McCloskey, ''Our Fair Lady,'' *Horn Book,* October, 1965; Obituaries—*New York Times,* June 6, 1970; *Horn Book,* August, 1970.

# SEARIGHT, Mary W(illiams)  1918-

*PERSONAL:* Surname is pronounced Sea-right; born January 4, 1918, in Cordell, Okla.; daughter of John Quitman (a rigger) and Grace (Giles) Williams; married Harold Newton Mock, December 15, 1946 (deceased); married Paul James Searight (owner of an office supply store), June 13, 1953; children: (first marriage) Gregory Newton; (second marriage) Sara Ann. *Education:* St. Francis Hospital School of Nursing, San Francisco, Calif., Diploma, 1940; University of California, San Francisco, B.S. (with honors), 1960, M.S., 1961; University of California, Berkeley, extension courses, 1961-65. *Home:* Lumberjack Close, The Sea Ranch, Calif. 95445.

*CAREER:* Nurse at Tulare County Hospital, Tulare, Calif., 1940-42, at Kaiser Shipbuilding Co., Richmond, Calif., 1942-45, at Puunene Plantation Hospital, Puunene, Maui, Hawaii, 1945-46; Fairmont (Alameda County) Hospital, San Leandro, Calif., head nurse and out-patient clinic supervisor, 1948-50; U.S. Veterans Administration Hospital, Fresno, Calif., staff nurse and evening supervisor, 1950-52; nurse in ophthalmologist's office, Berkeley, Calif., 1952-54; Contra Costa Health Department, Pleasant Hill, Calif., clinic nurse, 1954-55; Concord Community Hospital, Concord, Calif., part-time staff nurse, 1955-61; Merritt College, Oakland, Calif., instructor in nursing, 1962-66; University of California, School of Nursing, San Francisco, lecturer and project director, 1966-68; director of nursing workshops and consultant, 1967—. University of Minnesota, visiting summer lecturer, 1970, 1971. Sonoma County Comprehensive Health Planning, member of executive committee, coordinating committee, and board of directors, 1970-72. Sonoma State College, professor of nursing, 1971—, department of nursing, chair, 1971-77. *Member:* American Nurses' Association, American Association of University Women, California Nurses' Association, California Teachers' Association, American Association of University Professors, American Association of Colleges of Nursing, Sigma Theta Tau.

*WRITINGS: Your Career in Nursing* (juvenile), Messner, 1970, reissued, 1977; (editor) *The Second Step: Baccalaureate Education for Registered Nurses,* Davis, 1976. Writer of reports on nursing education; contributor to nursing journals.

**MARY W. SEARIGHT**

*WORK IN PROGRESS:* Papers and monographs related to nursing education.

*SIDELIGHTS:* ''As a small child, I wanted to be a nurse. Pets, friends, and my younger brother were my patients. As there had been no nurses in our family, my parents wondered at my interests, but neither they nor I made any serious effort to further it as I grew older. During the Depression, the idea of attending a college or school of nursing was so remote it was not even considered. In high school I took commercial courses; graduating in 1935 when jobs of any kind were very scarce, I felt fortunate to find one as a housekeeper.

''One day the woman for whom I worked asked what I planned to make of my life. I told her that I had wanted to become a nurse. Her reply was, 'Why don't you?' That was the spark of encouragement I needed. She helped me explore schools of nursing while continuing to work and save my money. Within two years I was ready to enter the Saint Francis Hospital School of Nursing in San Francisco where I completed the three year diploma program, graduating in 1940. This was a big milestone for me. I had no thought then that I would eventually continue my education, obtain baccalaureate and graduate degrees in nursing, become a nurse educator and administrator, and write a book.

''*Your Career in Nursing* was written because I believe that many students select nursing as their goal without a clear idea about the nature of the educational programs and the options open to them.

''My particular interest during the past eight years has been the development of collegiate programs planned especially for registered nurses who seek a Bachelor of Science degree in nursing. My most recent publication, *The Second Step: Baccalaureate Education for Registered Nurses,* speaks to that topic, describing the pioneering program developed at Sonoma State College in California while I was chairperson of the Department of Nursing. I believe nurses can and will assume increasing responsibility for health care and that baccalaureate, masters, and doctoral preparation for nurses will increase dramatically.

"At the present time the majority of nurses do not hold academic degrees. More avenues must be found to provide career mobility. Toward this end, I am involved in directing research and program planning to serve the educational needs of registered nurses."

*HOBBIES AND OTHER INTERESTS:* Home decorating, gourmet cooking, gardening.

## SEIXAS, Judith S. 1922-

*PERSONAL:* Born August 7, 1922, in New York, N.Y.; daughter of Irving Abraham (a stockbroker) and Edythe (Carr) Sartorius; married Frank A. Seixas (a physician), September 29, 1946; children: Peter, Abigail Seixas Horowitz, Noah. *Education:* Carleton College, B.A., 1944; Columbia University, M.A., 1945; Rutgers School of Alcohol Studies, certificate, 1969. *Home and office:* 2 Summit Dr., Hastings-on-Hudson, N.Y. 10706.

*CAREER:* Hunter Model School, New York, N.Y., member of psychological testing staff, 1946; Children's Court, White Plains, N.Y., psychologist, 1947; National Opinion Research Center, researcher, 1967; Westchester Council on Alcoholism, Westchester County, N.Y., counselor and director of educational services, 1969-75; Alcoholism Ser-

**But a drink of alcohol is different. It has lots of calories, so it is fattening.** ■ (From *Alcohol--What It Is, What It Does* by Judith S. Seixas. Illustrated by Tom Huffman.)

**JUDITH SEIXAS**

vices (consulting and educational firm), Hastings-on-Hudson, N.Y., director, 1975—; *Reader's Digest,* Pleasantville, N.Y., counselor in employee alcoholism program, 1976-79. Faculty member, San Diego Summer School of Alcohol Studies, 1972. American Field Service, member of Americans Abroad committee, 1960-72, president, 1962. *Member:* International Council on Alcoholism, National Council on Alcoholism, Alcohol and Drugs Problems of North America, American Orthopsychiatric Association, New York State Federation of Professional Health Educators.

*WRITINGS: Alcohol—What It Is, What It Does* (for young people), Greenwillow, 1977; (contributor) Nada J. Estes and M. Edith Heinemann, editors, *Alcoholism: Development, Consequences, and Interventions,* Mosby, 1977; *Living with a Parent who Drinks Too Much,* Greenwillow, 1979.

*SIDELIGHTS:* "My work is basically with alcoholics and their families: counseling, treatment, and referral. I have lived in Hastings for twenty-eight years and feel very involved with this community and, of late, with teen-age drinking problems."

**MEYER SELTZER**

## SELTZER, Meyer 1932-

*PERSONAL:* Born April 28, 1932, in Chicago, Ill.; son of Sam (a physician) and Bella (Eisenberg) Seltzer; married Deanna Taxman (a librarian and teacher), August 14, 1960; children: Elisa, Margo. *Education:* Roosevelt University, B.A., 1954; School of the Art Institute of Chicago, B.F.A., 1962. *Home and office:* 744 W. Buckingham Place, Chicago, Ill. 60657.

*CAREER:* Devenny-Wood Ltd., Chicago, Ill., apprentice in a photo and art studio, 1962-65; Don Levy Design, Chicago, Ill., designer, 1965; Scott, Foresman and Co., Glenview, Ill., art director, 1965-77; free-lance designer and illustrator, 1977—. Board of Directors, Belmont Harbor Neighbors, 1970-76. *Military service:* U.S. Coast Guard Reserve, active duty, 1954-58, reserve duty, 1958—. *Member:* Society of Typographic Arts, Artists Guild of Chicago, Reserve Officers Association. *Awards, honors:* Chicago Graphics, 1966, 1967, 1969; Communigraphics, 1971; Chicago 4, 1971, 1973; Creativity, 1971; The One Show, 1974; Illustration/Chicago (three awards), 1974; Sixth Biennial of Graphic Arts of Brno (Czechoslovakia), 1974; Exphotage I and III; International Poster Annual, Volume 15.

*ILLUSTRATOR:* Edna W. Chandler, *Will You Carry Me,* A. Whitman, 1965. Has also illustrated book covers, textbooks, posters and has done magazine illustration.

*SIDELIGHTS:* "I did *Will You Carry Me* just before I went to work for Scott, Foresman. During the twelve years I

worked for Scott, Foresman, I did primarily advertising design, but also photography, illustration (both for elementary, high school and college texts and for advertising) book design and poster design. I won quite a few awards and found it very rewarding.

"Time came for me to leave Scott, Foresman and I took my family to Israel for three weeks (where I shot a story for one of Scott, Foresman's primary social studies books on Kibbutz).

"Came back to Chicago and before I could get quite organized, I was snowed under with work.

"I work primarily with ink and Dr. Martin's colors ... sometimes drawing over with tempera or pencil or magic marker, simple color stuff, sometimes pencil, sometimes pen/ink. Would like to explore other media, but volume of work and short deadlines have kept me hopping.

"In the beginning, I used to despair that my drawing was not as good as it should be. Now I'm only unhappy about 90% of the time—when I think my work is not as good as I could have made it with: a little more time, more inspiration, better luck, time to start over, and less pressure from other jobs.

"I enjoy graphic design, children's illustration (for whatever use—advertising, trade book, poster, mural or textbook.)

"I feel blessed that I can make a living at something that is so much fun."

**The driver laughed.**
**"I have too many coconuts now," he said.**
**"Where do you want to go!"**
■ (From *Will You Carry Me?* by Edna Walker Chandler. Illustrated by Meyer Seltzer.)

dry, loose sand
poor traction

damp, packed sand
good traction

wet, loose sand
poor traction

**"If you walk on loose, dry beach sand, traction is difficult. If you walk where the beach sand is moisturized by waves, traction is better. Underwater the sand becomes loose again, and traction is poor again."** ■ (From *Tractors* by Herbert S. Zim and James R. Skelly. Illustrated by Lee J. Ames.)

# SKELLY, James R(ichard)   1927-

*PERSONAL:* Born May 23, 1927, in Evansville, Ind.; son of Kenneth (a manufacturer) and Lydia (Scheips) Skelly. *Education:* Attended Ohio State University, 1947-48; Case Western Reserve University, B.A., 1955. *Politics:* Conservative. *Religion:* Conservative. *Home and office address:* P.O. Box 23734, Fort Lauderdale, Fla. 33307.

*CAREER:* Cleveland Aquarium, Cleveland, Ohio, curator, 1953-55; Cleveland Museum of Natural History, Cleveland, staff biologist, 1955-56, registrar, 1956-60; Holy Cross Hospital, Fort Lauderdale, Fla., chemist, 1963-66; Artists and Writers Press (a former subsidiary of Golden Press), assistant editor, 1966-68; free-lance writer, 1968—. Part-time chemist with Laboratory for Research in Ophthalmology, Case Western Reserve University Medical School, 1956-61. *Military service:* U.S. Merchant Marine, 1944-46. U.S. Army, 1949-52. *Member:* Writers Guild.

*WRITINGS*—All with Herbert Spencer Zim; all juveniles; all published by Morrow: *Machine Tools*, 1969; *Hoists, Cranes, and Derricks*, 1969; *Trucks*, 1970; *Cargo Ships*, 1970; *Telephone Systems*, 1971; *Tractors*, 1972; *Metric Measure*, 1974; *Pipes and Plumbing Systems*, 1974; *Eating Places*, 1975.

*WORK IN PROGRESS:* "I rarely talk about the things I'm working on, and this is not one of those rare occasions. I find you expend your talent when you do that, and you should receive something when you tell what you're discovering or have discovered in the past. It's all an author has to sell."

*SIDELIGHTS:* "After the first blushes of being published, I think the main motivation to writing is the intense interest in an idea that doesn't seem to have been expressed as well as I can do it. Of course, one must also keep an eye on the market, unless one is very well-heeled."

*HOBBIES AND OTHER INTERESTS:* Fishing, sailing, and writing novels ("but publishers reject them.").

# STADTLER, Bea   1921-

*PERSONAL:* Born June 26, 1921, in Cleveland, Ohio; daughter of David and Minnie (Gorelick) Horwitz; married Oscar Stadtler (a dentist), January 31, 1945; children: Dona (Mrs. Howard Rosenblatt), Sander, Miriam. *Education:* Attended Case Western Reserve University, 1953-62; Cleveland College of Jewish Studies, B.J.S., 1970. *Religion:* Jewish. *Home:* 24355 Tunbridge Lane, Beachwood, Ohio 44122. *Office:* 26500 Shaker Blvd., Beachwood, Ohio 44122.

*CAREER:* Teacher of Judaic studies in religious school in Cleveland, Ohio, 1950-55; Temple Beth Sholom, Cleveland, Ohio, supervisor, 1955-60; Cleveland College of Jewish Studies, Cleveland, Ohio, registrar, 1959—. Member of the Executive Committee of the National Council for Jewish Education; member of board of directors of Ethnic Heritage Committee, 1976—. *Member:* Society of Israel Philatelists, Pioneer Women (president, 1955-57). *Awards, honors:* Charles and Bertie Schwartz prize from the National Jewish Welfare Board, for *The Holocaust*, 1975.

*WRITINGS: Once Upon a Jewish Holiday* (Hebrew readiness text for second grade), KTAV, 1965; *Once Upon a Jewish Holiday Workbook*, KTAV, 1965; *The Adventures of Gluckel of Hameln* (juvenile), United Synagogue Book Ser-

**BEA STADTLER**

vice, 1967; *The Story of Dona Gracia Mendes* (juvenile), United Synagogue Book Service, 1969; *Jews in the Land of the Free and the Land of the Brave* (seventh grade text), Temple, 1970; *Personalities of the American Jewish Labor Movement* (young adult), Education Department, Workmen's Circle, 1972; *Lessons from Our Living Past* (third grade text), Behrman House, 1972; *Hatzala Mishchakim* (title means "Rescue from the Sky"; juvenile and adult), Jewish Agency, 1972; *The Holocaust: A History of Courage and Resistance* (juvenile), Behrman House, 1973, revised edition, 1974. *Teaching the Holocaust to Children*, Second Jewish Catalog, 1977.

Scripts: "Aliya," commissioned by the Jewish Community Center, presented for the entire Jewish community, 1965; "Faces of Resistance," commissioned by the Jewish Community Center and other affiliated organizations, presented for the Jewish community of Cleveland, 1970; "Israel a Land of Many Colors," commissioned by the Jewish Community Center, Jewish Welfare Federation and the Educational Directors Council, in honor of the twenty-fifth anniversary of Israel, presented for the entire community, 1973.

Filmstrip: "The Adventures of Debbie and Danny Dollar," commissioned by the Jewish Community Federation. Filmstrip was written, directed and produced by the author.

Slide lecture: "Israel, Where It All Comes Together," commissioned by the Jewish Community Federation, for presentation in secular high schools, 1973; "The History of Zionism through Israel's Postage Stamps," 1978.

Author of column "For the Young Reader," in *The Cleveland Jewish News, Boston Jewish Advocate, Philadelphia Jewish Exponent, Pittsburgh Jewish Chronicle, Kansas City Jewish Chronicle, Baltimore Jewish Times, The York Jewish Journal,* and others, 1963—. Assistant editor of *Israel Philatelist.* Contributor of several articles, stories and poems to *World Over, More World Over Stories, Fun-in-Learning About Passover, Fun-in-Learning About Chanukah, Kadima, Jerusalem Post, Jewish Spectator, Jerusalem, Lamish-*

*pacha,* and many other magazines and books. Author of *Solomon The King,* libretto for a rock opera, 1976.

*WORK IN PROGRESS:* A juvenile book on Zionism; a horse story; research on Hassidic legend; a juvenile biography on Enzo Sereni entitled *Rescue From The Sky;* a juvenile book on the holocaust; a picture book story entitled *A Fish Story.*

*SIDELIGHTS:* "I lost my father when I was quite young and had always been a rather lonely child. My brothers were ten and eight and a half years older than I and so I turned to reading. I probably borrowed more books from the local public library than any other kid in the neighborhood. Although I liked sports very much and excelled in most of them, I had few friends because they just chummed together and went to each other's houses—I was alone and on the outskirts of the neighborhood in which I went to school.

"Perhaps that early reading, which pattern continued and still does, was the prelude to my writing. I have written poetry as long as I can remember and friends still get angry when they get a 'store-bought' card from me—they want a Bea Stadtler original. But writing stories for children began about the time I had my own daughter and could start telling her stories. Besides *Alice in Wonderland* and the *Pied Piper,* I began making up my own. Later I began publishing them. I had a writing class with a wonderful teacher, Eleanore Leuser from whom I learned a great deal. But writing is a cross between a chore and a delight. When I write a biography every detail must be meticulously researched or I am not satisfied. And if I should get a letter that something is incorrect I agonize over it until I check it out—but usually I am correct.

"After the research comes the piecing together and having the character emerge as someone we can identify with in this day and age. I once began a book about Hillel who lived about thirty years before Jesus. It was very interesting to me that I could almost put him into the same milieu as Watergate which was going on at the time I was writing this chapter. Unfortunately the publisher decided not to continue publishing biographies.

"Sometimes a story comes about from children I teach or speak to; sometimes it comes about from something I read or something that happened to an idea and suddenly the typewriter is going off on its own, merrily banging its keys, as though possessed by fingers other than mine. I love to write and entertain children with stories—now I have my grandchildren to tell stories to."

## STOBBS, William 1914-

*PERSONAL:* Born June 27, 1914, in South Shields, England; *Education:* Attended the King Edward VI School of Art, 1933-38; Durham University, B.A., 1938, M.A., 1945.

*CAREER:* London School of Printing and Graphic Arts, London, Eng., head of the design department, 1948-58; Maidstone College of Art, Kent, Eng., principal, 1958—; artist and illustrator of Children's books. *Member:* Society of Industrial Artists. *Awards, honors:* Kate Greenaway Medal, 1958, for *Kashtanka* and *A Bundle of Ballads.* The Horn Book's Honor List for *Greyling: A Picture Story From the Island of Sheltand.*

*WRITINGS*—All self-illustrated picture books: (Reteller) *The Story of the Three Bears,* McGraw, 1965; (reteller) *The Story of the Three Little Pigs,* McGraw, 1965; *The Golden Goose,* Bodley Head, 1966, McGraw, 1967; (with Amabel Williams-Ellis) *Life in England,* Blackie, 1968; *Henny Penny,* Bodley Head, 1968, Follett, 1970; (with A. Williams-Ellis) *Georgian England,* Blackie, 1969; *A Mini Called Zak,* Bodley Head, 1973; *A Is an Apple Pie,* Bodley Head, 1974; *A Rolls Called ARK,* Bodley Head, 1974; (reteller) *Puss in Boots,* McGraw, 1975; *The Derby Ram,* McGraw, 1975; *Old Mother Wiggle Waggle,* Bodley Head, 1975; *Johnny Cake,* Viking, 1975; (reteller) *The Country Mouse and the Town Mouse,* Pelham Books, 1976; *A Car Called Beetle,* Bodley Head, 1976; *A Gaping Wide-Mouthed Frog,* M. Joseph, 1977.

Illustrator: Ronald Syme, *Hakluyt's Sea Stories,* Heinemann, 1948; David W. MacArthur, *Traders North,* Collins, 1951, Knopf, 1952; R. Syme, *Balboa: Finder of the Pacific,* W. Morrow, 1952; Syme, *Champlain of the St. Lawrence,* W. Morrow, 1952; Syme, *Columbus: Finder of the New World,* W. Morrow, 1952; Syme, *I, Gordon of Khartoum,* Burke, 1953; Syme, *La Salle of the Mississippi,* W. Morrow, 1953; Syme, *Magellan: First around the World,* W. Morrow, 1953; Syme, *John Smith of Virginia,* W. Morrow, 1954; Syme, *Gipsy Michael,* Hodder, Stoughton, 1954; Ronald Welch, *Knight Crusader,* Oxford University Press, 1954; Syme, *They Came to an Island,* Hodder, Stoughton, 1955; Syme, *Henry Hudson,* W. Morrow, 1955 (published in England as *Hudson of the Bay,* Hodder, Stoughton, 1955); Lois Lamplugh, *Nine Bright Shiners,* J. Cape, 1955; Syme, *Ice Fighter,* Hodder, Stoughton, 1956; Syme, *Isle of Revolt,* Hodder, Stoughton, 1956; Tyler Whittle, *Runners of Orford,* J. Cape, 1956; R. L. Delderfield, *Adventure of Ben Gunn,* Hodder, Stoughton, 1956; Elizabeth Grove, *Wintercut,* Verry, 1957; Mary E. Patchett, *Caribbean Adventures,* Lutterworth Press, 1957; Syme, *De Soto: Finder of the Mississippi,* W. Morrow, 1957; Syme, *Cartier: Finder of the St. Lawrence,* W. Morrow, 1958; Syme, *Forest Fighters,* Hodder, Stoughton, 1958; David S. Daniell, pseudonym of Albert S. Daniell, *Hunt Royal,* Verry, 1958; Syme, *The Man Who Discovered the Amazon,* W. Morrow, 1958 (published in England as *River of No Return,* Hodder, Stoughton, 1958); Syme, *The Spaniards Came at Dawn,* Hodder, Stoughton, 1959; Syme, *Vasco Da Gama: Sailor toward the Sunrise,* W. Morrow, 1959; Syme, *On Foot to the Arctic: The Story of Samuel Hearne,* W. Morrow, 1959 (published in England as *Trail to the North,* Hodder, Stoughton, 1959); Ruth Manning-Sanders, compiler, *A Bundle of Ballads,* Oxford University Press, 1959, Lippincott, 1961; D. S. Daniell, *Mission for Oliver,* Verry, 1959; Anton Chekov, *Kashtanka,* Oxford University Press, 1959, Walck, 1961; Daniell, *The Boy They Made King,* J. Cape, 1959.

Frederick Grice, *Aidan and the Strollers,* J. Cape, 1960; Hilda Lewis, *Here Comes Harry,* Oxford University Press, 1960, Criterion, 1961; R. Welch, *Escape from France,* Oxford University Press, 1960, Criterion, 1961; Syme, *Buccaneer Explorer,* Hodder, Stoughton, 1960; L. Lamplugh, *Pigeongram Puzzle,* Verry, 1960; Syme, *Captain Cook: Pacific Explorer,* W. Morrow, 1960; Lamplugh, *Midsummer Mountains,* Verry, 1961; Madeleine Polland, *Boern the Proud,* Constable, 1961, Holt, 1962; Henry Treece, *The Golden One,* Bodley Head, 1961, Criterion, 1962; Daniell, *Battles and Battlefields,* B. T. Batsford, 1961; William Mayne, *Summer Visitors,* Oxford University Press, 1961; Welch, *For the King,* Oxford University Press, 1961; Syme, *First Man to Cross America: The Story of Cabeza de Vaca,*

(From *A Gaping Wide-Mouthed Waddling Frog* by William Stobbs. Illustrated by the author.)

W. Morrow, 1961; Syme, *Francis Drake: Sailor of the Unknown Seas,* W. Morrow, 1961; Joan E. Cass, *The Cat Show,* Abelard-Schuman, 1962; J. Cass, *The Cat Thief,* Abelard-Schuman, 1962; Syme, *Walter Raleigh,* W. Morrow, 1962; Welch, *Mohawk Valley,* Oxford University Press, 1962; M. Polland, *The White Twilight,* Constable, 1962; Ronald D. Storer, reteller, *King Arthur and His Knights,* Oxford University Press, 1962; Ian Serraillier, *Gorgon's Head: The Story of Perseus,* Walck, 1962; Anita Hewett, *The Little White Hen,* Oxford University Press, 1962, McGraw, 1963; R. Manning-Sanders, *The Smugglers,* Oxford University Press, 1962.

I. Serraillier, *Way of Danger: The Story of Theseus,* Walck, 1963; Rene Guillot, *Rex and Mistigri,* Bodley Head, 1963; Syme, *Francisco Pizarro: Finder of Peru,* W. Morrow, 1963; Polland, *The Queen's Blessing,* Constable Young Books, 1963; R. J. Unstead, *Royal Adventurers,* Odhams Press, 1963; Daniell, *Polly and Oliver Pursued,* Verry, 1964; Syme, *Alexander Mackenzie: Canadian Explorer,* W. Morrow, 1964; Syme, *Invaders and Invasions,* Batsford, 1964, Norton, 1965; Serraillier, *Clashing Rocks: The Story of Jason,* Walck, 1964; Syme, *Francisco Coronado and the Seven Cities of Gold,* W. Morrow, 1965; Syme, *Sir Henry Morgan, Buccaneer,* W. Morrow, 1965; Syme, *John Smith of Virginia,* University of London Press, 1965; Jean MacGibbon, *A Special Providence,* Coward-McCann, 1965; Lamplugh, *Vagabond's Castle,* Verry, 1965; *Jack and the Beanstalk,* Delacorte Press, 1966; Audrey E. Lindop, *The Adventures of the Wuffle,* Methuen, 1966, McGraw, 1968; Syme, *William Penn: Founder of Pennsylvania,* W. Morrow, 1966; Syme, *Quesada of Colombia,* W. Morrow, 1966; A. Williams-Ellis, *Round the World Fairy Tales,* F. Warne,

1966; Williams-Ellis, *Old World and New World Fairy Tales,* F. Warne, 1966; Cass, *The Canal Trip,* Abelard-Schuman, 1966; Serraillier, *Fall from the Sky,* Walck, 1966.

*Monkeys and Magicians,* Blackie, 1967; H. Treece, *Westward to Vinland,* S. G. Phillips, 1967; Syme, *Garibaldi: The Man Who Made a Nation,* W. Morrow, 1968; Mollie Clarke, *The Three Brothers,* Follett, 1967; Unstead, *Some Kings and Queens,* Follett, 1967; Unstead, *Royal Adventurers,* Follett, 1967; Geoffrey Trease, *White Nights of St. Petersburg,* Vanguard, 1968; Peter C. Asbjoernsen, *The Three Billy Goats Gruff,* McGraw, 1968; Syme, *Captain John Paul Jones,* W. Morrow, 1968; Williams-Ellis, *Early and Medieval Times,* Blackie, 1968; Jane H. Yolen, *Greyling,* World Publishing, 1968; Williams-Ellis, *Tudor England,* Blackie, 1968; Syme, *Bolivar: The Liberator,* W. Morrow, 1968; Cass, *The Cats Go to Market,* Abelard-Schuman, 1969; Syme, *Amerigo Vespucci: Scientist and Sailor,* W. Morrow, 1969; Naomi Mitchison, *African Heroes,* Farrar, Straus, 1969; Syme, *Frontenac of New France,* W. Morrow, 1969.

Brothers Grimm, *Rumpelstiltskin,* Bodley Head, 1970; Joseph Jacobs, *The Magpie's Nest,* Follett, 1970; George MacDonald, *The Princess and the Goblin [and] The Princess and the Curdie,* American Education Publications, 1970; Syme, *Vancouver: Explorer of the Pacific Coast,* W. Morrow, 1970; Syme, *Benedict Arnold: Traitor of the Revolution,* W. Morrow, 1970; Cass, *The Cats' Adventure with Car Thieves,* Abelard-Schuman, 1971; J. Jacobs, *The Crock of Gold,* Follett, 1971; Manning-Sanders, *Gianni and the Ogre,* Dutton, 1971; Syme, *Zapata: Mexican Rebel,* W. Morrow, 1971; Syme, *Toussaint: The Black Liberator,* W. Morrow, 1971; Rex Warner, *Athens at War,* Dutton, 1971;

Compton Mackenzie, *Theseus,* Aldus Books, 1972; Elizabeth Poston, compiler, *The Baby's Song Book,* Crowell, 1972; C. Mackenzie, *Jason,* Aldus Books, 1972; Mackenzie, *Achilles,* Aldus Books, 1972; William Cole, compiler, *Poems from Ireland,* Crowell, 1972; Syme, *John Cabot and His Son, Sebastian,* W. Morrow, 1972.

Charles Perrault, *The Little Red Riding Hood,* Walck, 1973; Syme, *Verrazano: Explorer of the Atlantic Coast,* W. Morrow, 1973; Syme, *Marquette and Joliet: Voyagers on the Mississippi,* W. Morrow, 1974; Williams-Ellis, *Fairy Tales from Here and There,* British Book Center, 1977; Williams-Ellis, *Fairy Tales from Everywhere,* British Book Center, 1977; Williams-Ellis, *Fairy Tales from East and West,* British Book Center, 1977; Williams-Ellis, *Fairy Tales from Near and Far,* British Book Center, 1977.

*SIDELIGHTS:* William Stobbs was born in South Shields, County Durham, England on June 27, 1914. He was educated at Durham University where he received his M.A. degree. Subsequently, Stobbs studied at the King Edward VI School of Art before he became an art teacher, artist and illustrator. He feels that his extensive training in art history has influenced the traditional form of his drawings. Renaissance and Chinese drawings have been other influences as well as such artists as Picasso, Rembrandt, and Caravaggio. From 1950 to 1958, Stobbs was head of the design department at the London School of Printing and Graphic Arts.

In the early 1950's Stobbs first gained prominence for his book illustrations. In 1954 he illustrated the Carnegie Award winning book, *Knight Crusader* by Ronald Welch.

Stobbs became principal of Maidstone College of Art in Kent, England in 1958 and has held that position for several years. The Stobbs family has lived in Kent for many years.

By 1959 he was awarded the Kate Greenaway Medal for his illustrations to two books: Checkov's *Kashtanka* and Ruth Manning-Sanders' compilation, *A Bundle of Ballads.* He continued to illustrate many books in the 1960's and 1970's and also produced some excellent picture books.

Stobbs feels that an illustration should enhance the printed word and not be merely a repetition of facts into drawings. His illustrations, for the most part historical or maritime in theme, are strong and vigorous, and male images are characteristically square, tough, wood-hewn figures.

*FOR MORE INFORMATION SEE:* Bertha M. Miller and others, compilers, *Illustrators of Children's Books, 1946-1956,* Horn Book, 1958; John Ryder, *Artists of a Certain Line,* Bodley Head, 1960; M. S. Crouch, "Kate Greenaway Medal Goes to William Stobbs," *Library Association Record,* May, 1960; Brian Doyle, editor, *Who's Who of Children's Literature,* Schocken Books, 1968; Lee Kingman and others, compilers, *Illustrators of Children's Books, 1957-1966,* Horn Book, 1968; Doris de Montreville and Donna Hill, editors, *The Third Book of Junior Authors,* H. W. Wilson, 1972.

## TARKINGTON, (Newton) Booth    1869-1946

*PERSONAL:* Born July 29, 1869, in Indianapolis, Indiana; died May 19, 1946, in Indianapolis; son of John Stevenson (a lawyer) and Elizabeth (Booth) Tarkington; married Laurel Louisa Fletcher, June 18, 1902 (divorced, 1911); married Susannah Robinson, 1912; children: (first marriage) one

**Booth Tarkington, age three.**

daughter (deceased). *Education:* Attended Purdue University and Princeton University. *Home:* Indianapolis, Indiana, and Kennebunkport, Maine.

*CAREER:* Novelist, playwright, illustrator, and author of books for young boys. Served in the Indiana House of Representatives, 1902-03. *Member:* American Academy of Arts and Letters, Ivy Club, Nassau Club (Princeton), Players Club, Century Club (New York), and University Club (Indianapolis). *Awards, honors:* Pulitzer Prizes for fiction for *The Magnificent Ambersons,* 1919, and *Alice Adams,* 1922; Gold Medal of the National Institute of Arts and Letters, 1933; Roosevelt Distinguished Service Medal, 1942; Howells Medal of the American Academy of Arts and Letters, 1945; M.A., Princeton University, 1899; Litt.D., from Princeton University, 1918, De Pauw University, 1923, and Columbia University, 1924; L.H.D., Purdue University, 1939.

*WRITINGS*—Novels and short stories: *The Gentleman from Indiana,* Doubleday & McClure, 1899, reprinted, Scholarly Press, 1971; *Monsieur Beaucaire* (illustrated by C. D. Williams), McClure, Phillips, 1900, reissued, Heritage Press, 1961; *The Two Vanrevels* (illustrated by Henry Hutt), McClure, Phillips, 1902; *Cherry,* Harper, 1903; *In the Arena: Stories of Political Life* (illustrated by A. I. Keller, Power O'Malley, and J. J. Gould), McClure, Phillips, 1905, reissued, Mss Information, 1972; *The Conquest of Canaan* (illustrated by Lucius W. Hitchcock), Harper, 1905, reissued, Literature House, 1970; *The Beautiful Lady,* McClure, Phillips, 1905; *His Own People* (illustrated by Lawrence Mazzanovich and F. R. Gruger), Doubleday, Page, 1907; *The Guest of Quesnay* (illustrated by W. J. Duncan), McClure, 1908; *Beasley's Christmas Party* (illustrated by Ruth S. Clemens), Harper, 1909.

*Beauty and the Jacobin: An Interlude of the French Revolution* (illustrated by C. D. Williams), Harper, 1912; *The Flirt* (illustrated by Clarence F. Underwood), Doubleday, Page, 1913; *The Turmoil* (illustrated by C. E. Chambers), Harper, 1915; *The Magnificent Ambersons*, (illustrated by Arthur W. Brown), Doubleday, Page, 1918, reissued, Avon, 1973; *Harlequin and Columbine, and Other Stories*, Doubleday, Page, 1918; *Ramsey Milholland* (illustrated by Gordon Grant), Doubleday, Page, 1919; *Alice Adams* (illustrated by A. W. Brown), Doubleday, Page, 1921, reissued, Grosset & Dunlap, 1961; *Gentle Julia* (illustrated by C. Allan Gilbert and Worth Brehm), Doubleday, Page, 1922; *The Fascinating Stranger, and Other Stories*, Doubleday, Page, 1923; *The Midlander*, Doubleday, Page, 1924; *Women*, Doubleday, Page, 1925, reprinted, Books for Libraries, 1971; *The Plutocrat*, Doubleday, Page, 1927; *Growth*, Doubleday, Page, 1927; *Claire Ambler*, Doubleday, Doran, 1928; *Young Mrs. Greeley*, Doubleday, Doran, 1929.

*Mirthful Haven*, Doubleday, Doran, 1930; *Wanton Mally* (illustrated by Joseph Simont), Doubleday, Doran, 1932; *Mary's Neck*, Doubleday, Doran, 1932; *Presenting Lily Mars*, Doubleday, Doran, 1933; *Little Orvie* (illustrated by George Brehm), Doubleday, Doran, 1934; *Mr. White, The Red Barn, Hell,* [and] *Bridewater* (novelettes), Doubleday, Doran, 1935; *The Lorenzo Bunch*, Doubleday, Doran, 1936; *Rumbin Galleries* (illustrated by Ritchie Cooper), Doubleday, Doran, 1937; *The Heritage of Hatcher Ide*, Doubleday, Doran, 1941; *The Fighting Littles*, Doubleday, Doran, 1941; *Kate Fennigate*, Doubleday, Doran, 1943; *Image of Josephine*, Doubleday, Doran, 1945; *Three Selected Short Novels*, Doubleday, 1947 (contains *Walterson, Uncertain Molly Collicut,* and *Rennie Peddigoe*); *The Show Piece* (unfinished novel; with an introduction by Susannah Tarkington), Doubleday, 1947.

For children and young adults: *Penrod* (illustrated by G. Grant), Doubleday, Page, 1914, reprinted, Grosset & Dunlap, 1970; *Penrod and Sam* (illustrated by W. Brehm), Doubleday, Page, 1916; *Seventeen*, Grosset & Dunlap, 1916, reprinted, 1970 [other editions illustrated by A. W. Brown, Grosset & Dunlap, 1918; Edwin Tunis, Harper, 1932]; *Penrod Jashber* (illustrated by G. Grant), Doubleday, Doran, 1929.

Plays: (With Harry Leon Wilson) *The Man from Home*, [New York], 1907; (with Julian L. Street) *The Ohio Lady* (four-act comedy), Ebert Press, 1916, later published as *The Country Cousin*, Samuel French, 1921; *Clarence* (four-act comedy), Samuel French, 1919; (with H. L. Wilson) *The Gibson Upright*, Doubleday, Page, 1919; *The Ghost Story* (one-act), S. Kidd, 1922; *Intimate Strangers* (three-act comedy), Samuel French, 1922; *The Wren* (three-act comedy), Samuel French, 1922; *The Trysting Place* (one-act), S. Kidd, 1923; (with H. L. Wilson) *Tweedles: A Comedy*, Samuel French, 1924; *Bimbo: A Pirate*, D. Appleton, 1926; *Station YYYY*, D. Appleton, 1927; *The Travelers*, D. Appleton, 1927; (with H. L. Wilson) *How's Your Health?* (three-act comedy), Samuel French, 1930; *The Help Each Other Club*, D. Appleton, 1934; *Mister Antonio* (four-act), Samuel French, 1935; *Lady Hamilton and Her Nelson*, House of Books, 1945.

Also author of the following plays: (With H. L. Wilson) "The Guardian," 1907; (with Wilson) "Cameo Kirby," 1907; (with Wilson) "Your Humble Servant," 1908; "Springtime," 1908; "Foreign Exchange," 1909; "If I Had Money," 1909; "The Man on Horseback," 1911; (with Wilson) "Up from Nowhere," 1919; "Poldekin," 1920; "Rose Briar," 1922; "Magnolia," 1923; "Colonel Satan," 1930; "Maud and Cousin Bill" (radio play), 1932-33; "Aromatic Aaron Burr," 1938.

Other: (Illustrator) James Whitcomb Riley, *The Boss Girl*, Bowen-Merrill, 1886; *Looking Forward, and Others* (essays), Doubleday, Page, 1926, reprinted, Books for Libraries, 1969; (illustrator) Kenneth Roberts, *Antiquamania*, Doubleday, Doran, 1928; *The World Does Move* (semi-autobiographical), Doubleday, Doran, 1928, reprinted, Greenwood Press, 1976; *Some Old Portraits: A Book about Art and Human Beings*, Doubleday, Doran, 1939, reprinted, Books for Libraries, 1969; (contributor) "Hamlin Garland," in *Commemorative Tributes to Gillette and Howard and Others*, The Academy, 1940; (contributor) "Albert Jeremiah Beveridge," in *Commemorative Tributes of the Academy, 1905-41*, The Academy, 1942; (contributor) "Lew Wallace, 1827-1905," in *There Were Giants in the Land*, Rinehart, 1942; *Your Amiable Uncle: Letters to His Nephews* (self-illustrated), Bobbs-Merrill, 1949.

Collections and selections: *The Works of Booth Tarkington*, 14 volumes, Doubleday, Page, 1918-19; *Strack Selections from Booth Tarkington's Stories* (arranged by Lilian Holmes Strack), W. H. Baker, 1926; *Penrod: His Complete Story* (a collection of all the "Penrod" stories; illustrated by G. Grant), Doubleday, Doran, 1931; *On Plays, Playwrights, and Playgoers: Selections from the Letters of Booth Tarkington to George S. Tyler and John Peter Toohey, 1918-1925* (edited by Alan S. Downer), Princeton University Library, 1959.

**BOOTH TARKINGTON**

(From the movie "Penrod and Sam." Copyright 1931 by First National Pictures.)

(From the movie "Alice Adams," starring Katherine Hepburn and Fred MacMurray. Copyright 1935 by RKO Radio Pictures, Inc.)

(From the movie "Gentle Julia," starring Jane Withers. Copyright 1936 by Twentieth Century-Fox.)

(From the movie "Seventeen," starring Jackie Cooper and Betty Field. Copyright 1939 by Paramount Pictures.)

*ADAPTATIONS*—Movies: "Cameo Kirby," Lasky Feature Play, 1914, Fox Film Corp., starring Alan Hale, 1923, Fox Film Corp., 1929; "Cherry," Vitagraph, 1914; "The Two Vanrevels," Thomas A. Edison, 1914; "Sophia's Imaginary Visitors," adaptation of *Beasley's Christmas Party*, Thomas A. Edison, 1914; "The Man from Home," Lasky Feature Play, 1914, Famous Players-Lasky Corp., 1922; "The Gentleman from Indiana," J. C. Ivers, 1915; "The Turmoil," Columbia Pictures, 1916, Universal Pictures, 1924; "The Flirt," Bluebird Photoplays, 1916, Universal Pictures, 1922; "Seventeen," Famous Players Film Co., 1916, Paramount Pictures, starring Jackie Cooper, 1940; "The Country Cousin," Selznick Pictures, 1919; "The Adventures and Emotions of Edgar Pomeroy," (series of 12 films), Goldwyn Pictures, 1920-21; "The Conquest of Canaan," Famous Players-Lasky Corp., 1921; "Penrod," Marshall Neilan Productions, 1922; "Boy of Mine," Associated First National Pictures, 1923.

"Penrod and Sam," Associated First National Pictures, 1923, First National Pictures, starring Zasu Pitts, 1931, Warner Brothers, starring Spring Byington, 1937; "Gentle Julia," Fox Film Corp., 1923, Twentieth Century-Fox, starring Jane Withers, 1936; "Monsieur Beaucaire," starring Rudolph Valentino and Bebe Daniels, Famous Players-Lasky Corp., 1924, Paramount Pictures, starring Bob Hope and Joan Caulfield, 1946; "The Fighting Coward," Famous Players-Lasky Corp., 1924; "Pampered Youth," adaptation of *The Magnificent Ambersons*, Vitagraph, 1925; "River of Romance," adaptation of "Magnolia," Paramount Famous Lasky Corp., 1929; "Geraldine," Pathe Exchange, 1929; "Mister Antonio," Tiffany-Stahl Productions, 1929.

"Monte Carlo," adaptation of *Monsieur Beaucaire*, starring Jeanette MacDonald, Jack Buchanan and Zasu Pitts, Paramount Publix, 1930; "Father's Son," adaptation of *Old Fathers and Young Sons*, First National Pictures, 1931, Warner Brothers, 1941; "Bad Sister," starring Bette Davis and Conrad Nagel, Universal Pictures, 1931; "Business and Pleasure," adaptation of *The Plutocrat*, starring Will Rogers, Fox Film, 1931; "Alice Adams," starring Katherine Hepburn and Fred MacMurray, RKO-Radio Pictures, 1935, Teaching Film Custodians (excerpts from the RKO-Radio Picture movie; "Dance Sequence," 15 minutes, black and white; "Money Sequence," 15 minutes, black and white), 1946; "Mississippi," adaptation of "Magnolia," starring Bing Crosby, W. C. Fields, and Joan Bennett, Paramount Pictures, 1935.

"Clarence," starring Roscoe Karns, Paramount Pictures, 1937; "Penrod's Double Trouble," Warner Brothers, 1938; "Penrod and His Twin Brother," starring Spring Byington, Warner Brothers, 1938; "Little Orvie," RKO Radio Pictures, 1940; "The Magnificent Ambersons," starring Joseph Cotton, Anne Baxter, and Agnes Moorehead, RKO Radio Pictures, 1942; "Presenting Lily Mars," starring Judy Garland and Van Heflin, Metro-Goldwyn-Mayer, 1943; "On Moonlight Bay," based on the "Penrod" stories, Warner Brothers, 1951; "By the Light of the Silvery Moon," adaptation of *Penrod*, starring Doris Day, Gordon MacRae, and Rosemary DeCamp, Warner Brothers, 1953.

Plays: Ethel Hale Freeman, *Monsieur Beaucaire*, W. H. Baker, 1916; Hugh S. Stange, Stannard Mears, and Stuart Walker, *Booth Tarkington's Seventeen*, Samuel French, 1924.

*SIDELIGHTS:* **July 29, 1869.** "Counting by realistic time, astronomical time, I was born a very short while ago—less than a few minutes ago—and yet my mother's father, Beebe Booth, who lived until I was a grown man, did some soldiering in the War of 1812. In his infancy, if he'd happened to be in France instead of Connecticut, he could have seen Marie Antoinette and Robespierre; and when Wellington died both of my grandfathers were past middle age. When I was born, in a small but active Indianapolis, there was no German Empire, Napoleon Bonaparte's nephew was Emperor of the French, Queen Victoria had more than thirty years to reign over Britain, there weren't any telephones or electric lights in the world; and our Union's supreme war hero, General Grant, was President of the United States.

"This is the long and the short of it; but just after my birth I was so busy getting used to having a body that for a while I wasn't aware of even General Grant. I didn't at once perceive that I'd come among beings of my own kind; I saw people as assistants only; though later, when I was a full year old, I took their principal function to be that of applause.

"I'm explaining that at the age of one year I was a celebrity and regarded myself as such. Babies are like anybody else; they accept the wildest and most ill-founded adulation as deserved tribute; naturally, their self-conceit is egregious. Their minds are already busy, and though they can't use distinct words as symbols of their thoughts, they draw conclusions. Long before they can add two to two they can put two and two together.

"I was seldom approached without a kind of servility and professions of utter admiration. For almost half of my life I'd been entreated daily, and sometimes hourly, to enchant audiences with repetitions of the vocal performances that had made me famous. The outcries evoked by my talent were so inevitable that sometimes, bored, I declined to give a show. One year old, I knew as well as did the boastfulest of my kinsfolk that I was the star of the age because I'd begun to talk when I was only seven months old.

"Having thus begun, at seven months, by calling the dog, I talked on, never saying a thing that wasn't quotable. Behind the Infant Prodigy there still remain in memory—for background of my second year—a few faint pictures like pale old water colors: that pleasant bit of Meridian Street—sunshine on green lawns—our ample brick house and its brick stable in the shade of trees illimitably high; two lovely big ladies dancing about me in ballooning white dresses and indistinguishable from adults, though they were my sister Hautie and a friend of hers, both twelve years old.

"How far back into childhood can we remember? I remember the first snow of my second winter, when probably I hadn't reached the age of eighteen months; I remember how that snow disappointed me. I know it was the first snow of the winter because I'd been looking forward to it. . . .

"A novelist must make the exercising of his memory—as well as other self-searchings—a constant practice, or he will not understand and make real the creatures he puts into his books; but if other people did the inward delving that he professionally does, they would no doubt turn up as much from their own obscured infancies. My earliest recollection isn't here recorded as a feat; it leads to a suggestion." [Booth Tarkington, "As I Seem to Me," *Saturday Evening Post*, July 5, 1941.[1]]

**1872.** Spent a year in California, visiting his famous Uncle Newton, governor of the state. "Uncle Newton made much

(From the movie "On Moonlight Bay," based on the "Penrod" stories, starring Doris Day and Gordon MacRae. Copyright 1951 by Warner Bros.)

**Signori:**
You wouldn't expect to see anything like this, allowed to run loose, anywhere would you? But it does, here on Capri; it has passed us several times, briskly, at dusk. We thought, of course, it was a hermit, a holy man, but it wasn't. It is a German painter, who lives in a handsome villa and has a large, somewhat Mormon, family and number of disciples. They practice what is called "the return to nature," that is, they wear few clothes and live on fruit and cabbage and they sell pictures—oddly enough this madman paints very well. The English colony here (who are "a trifle skeptical") think the cult is just for advertisement. ■ (From *Your Amiable Uncle* by Booth Tarkington. Illustrated by the author.)

of me; so did the circle of gay early Californians surrounding him. Toys almost glutted me; I heard tales loudly told of me, saw groups of expectant faces about me awaiting the delights of my wisdom; and bearded men, as well as hourglass-shaped ladies, professed themselves ravished by photographs of me in kilts and velvet jacket. The flatteries I received might easily have convinced me that I was a philosopher, or a wit, or a great beauty. They did. I thought I was all three.

"Much was made, too, of some imagined companions of mine, a family I'd found in the air. Where I got the name of these ghostly people, the 'Hunchbergs,' and the name of their dog, 'Simpledoria,' nobody knew, nor did I; but Mr. and Mrs. Hunchberg, and their son and daughter, almost grown up, and Simpledoria, appear to have had reality for me. I talked with them at great length, when actual people were present as well as when I was alone. I quoted the Hunchbergs incessantly, played with Simpledoria on the carpet, spoke to him from my bed at night. Uncle Newton gave a dinner for the Hunchbergs, with chairs placed for the

four of them and a plate on the floor for Simpledoria. Through me, the translator as it were, my uncle talked seriously with Mr. Hunchberg, had cigars passed to him and was regretful that he didn't smoke. To my three-year-old eyes those empty chairs weren't vacant; I saw the dear Hunchbergs there, and my uncle understood because in his own childhood he'd had an unseen companion—a boy braver and more dashing than himself and known to him as 'Bill Hammersly.'

"... Someone offered me a glass of champagne. I drank it, and seemed to perceive that in affording me this pleasure life was promising to consist entirely of exaltation. In fact, it's all too significant that even so early I took to champagne, asked for more, got it, and became uninterruptedly talkative. The hardy forty-niners about me made merry, I may be said to have been plied with wine, and it was afterward hushedly related that I astonished the pliers by a precocious talent for absorption. Thus, in one particular line of accomplishment, I am now probably without a living colleague. I doubt that any other inhabitant of the year 1941 has the right, so to put it, of recording that he got howling drunk in the state of California in 1872."[1]

**1873.** Returned to Indianapolis where his family suffered financial reversals. "We didn't return to our fine brick house on Meridian Street; it was lost to us—taken away by the panic. My father, whose commencement address at college had made him secretary to the governor of Indiana, was a 'rising young lawyer,' when, unfortunately, he accepted a judgeship. Though for the rest of his long life his fellow citizens never spoke to him or of him except as Judge Tarkington, in our Hoosier way, the title was inadequate compensation for the clients he lost through his term on the bench. When he returned to the bar he'd begun to get some of them back; but the Panic of '73 banished legal fees to the realm of illusion.

"Suddenly we were poor, lived in a small wooden house; then moved to a side street, where we occupied only a lower floor, with another depleted lawyer and his family over our heads. We still owned our two loved horses, Gray and Fly—my father could never bear to sell a horse—but they were economically in the country, at pasture, and we were no longer carriage folk. . . .

"Possibly I shouldn't remember that disaster at all if we hadn't lost our house and the sunny green yard where I'd played. No recollections of protests or wailings from my father, my plucky mother and my sparklingly pretty fifteen-year-old sister recall it to me; their endurance of the change hadn't a flinch, though the blows must have been heavy and many for all three of them. About me there seemed always [to be] the sound of laughter, and my father's indomitable gaiety kept my world in place, made living in it an experience safely all of gusto and merriment.

"It was at this period, when I was four and five and six, that my complacent view of myself began to be damaged. Explanation mayn't be needed that the shocking vanity of children shocks nobody; mine was inside me and I have been told that I was regarded as a rather solemn little boy, quiet and given to ruminations. Nevertheless, my life, so far, had brought me no cause to look upon myself as imperfect in any detail. My conduct was sometimes directed, but never criticized, and I hadn't yet begun to wonder what sort of person I was—or what sort of looking person I was. A complete content with myself and a subservient world prevailed. . . ."[1]

**1876.** Celebrated returned prosperity, remained an amiable child. "Even when they threw stones at my dog I couldn't fight for him; could only crouch over him, receiving helplessly the missiles upon my own body." [James Woodress, *Booth Tarkington: Gentleman from Indiana,* Lippincott, 1955.[2]]

"We moved into a commodious house in the new North Side, had a yard and big trees again, had a cook again, had a horse and vehicles. . . .

"I hadn't yet been sent to school, and couldn't write; but for a year or two I'd been able to read, though I've no recollection of learning this art. The only child in the house, and enticed by suggestive talk in the small family circle, I'd rather prematurely read *Uncle Tom's Cabin, Don Quixote, Robinson Crusoe* and *The Old Curiosity Shop;* and my first literary attempt was made at about this time. As I couldn't write, my indulgent sister, chivalrously concealing her amusement, became my amanuensis. I dictated to her the opening of a story, and, though the manuscript disappeared, I remember that it concerned a full-grown young man who rode forth from a castle on a bright morning and would have had a startling adventure if I'd been able to construct one for him. I seem to have encountered the obstacle of complete vacuity after the first paragraph or two; nevertheless, I had great praise for the effort, as well as for the now modernistic drawings and water colors that I produced on rainy days."[1]

**1885.** Fascinated by Shakespeare, wrote a fourteen-act melodrama about Jesse James. "It was in Richard the Third that I saw myself as most powerful; and, having learned the part, I became more than ever studious of my dressing-table mirror. Wearing eyebrows and sneering moustachios of burnt cork, and a costume of my own long winter underwear shadowed by an evening cloak of my mother's, I twisted one shoulder higher than the other, and put my sprouting features through gymnastics, muttering malignantly. . . .

"Before long, however, we realized that Shakespeare employed too many dramatis personae for a company still consisting wholly of nucleus; so we decided that I'd better . . . write a play. . . .

"I began the play at once in a school copybook; and few playwrights, I think, have ever been more illimitably copious. At every opportunity, morning, noon or night, dialogue and 'stage business' flowed illegibly in a penmanship notorious in our high school as its worst. I filled copybook after copybook with what I know not, except that any end to it appeared more and more utterly impossible. . . ." [Booth Tarkington, "As I Seem to Me," *Saturday Evening Post,* August 16, 1941.[3]]

**1887.** After a nine week truancy from high school, entered Phillips Exeter Academy in New Hampshire. "Neither then nor afterward did [my parents] either reproach or question me, and I wonder now what they thought I'd been doing with all that vacant time. They didn't ask for an explanation; they couldn't—not any more than I could offer one. For a while, a week or so, they were more silent with me than usual, and then tried to be as before, gay and sympathetically interested when I hesitantly chattered. There was no suggestion that I should return to high school; it was arranged for me to study drawing, working from plaster casts, and to take vocal lessons to steady my uncertain voice. In the autumn I was sent to a New England prep school to prepare for college—Princeton, my mother hoped.

**Drawing in a letter to his father, 1899.**

"At this school, so far from home, I was at first in a condition that I recognized as bewilderment. New England itself, and New England professors, and boys who seemed a new species to me—they were from everywhere over the country except Indianapolis—all, for a time, confused me. Then, after a groping month, I thought that I had the hang of things, I became easy and confident, and thenceforth lived in bewilderment without knowing that I did.

"Sometimes, in retrospect, I glanced toward the dull old days at home and had pangs of compassion for my formerly untraveled self. Good heavens! Back there in Indianapolis I hadn't even known how to dress!

"The caped ulster and concomitants were but items. Utterly too-too in fashionableness, I parted my hair in the middle, with 'bangs,' wore sashes instead of waistcoats—sashes of black or green watered silk with long, dangling fringed ends—and these fantasies, popular among the knowing young, weren't harmonious with my physical style. This was, to put it simply, large-nosed, stooping, and still glunky and twitchy. Thinnest of the thin, I had habitually what's known as a hacking cough and was generally expected by my classmates to finish erelong in a consumption accelerated by nonintermittent smoking."[3]

**1889.** Returned to Indiana, attended business college and art school. Considered himself a "man," but felt that he was treated like a boy. "I smoke at home now all the time.

Mother . . . only says 'Booth, how can you?!?!' about three times an hour now—it used to be seventy-eight.

"Try as hard as I may to suit people, they laugh as I pass. Damn this town. . . . I'm going to emigrate to Africa and wear a coral necklace.''[2]

**1890.** Attended Purdue University.

**1891-1893.** Enrolled at Princeton University, where he distinguished himself in dramatic and literary pursuits. "Easy-going as Princeton life then was, the days were crowded, and so were the nights of writing and drawing for the undergraduate periodicals. My oil lamp burned often enough until dawn and I'd still be loath to stop, though I knew how inconsiderately my roommate would drag me by the ankles out of bed to hustle me, when he could, to my morning place in the chapel choir." [Booth Tarkington, "As I Seem to Me," *Saturday Evening Post,* August 23, 1941.[4]]

He revealed the secret of his success at college. "Between two and five A.M. every night take unlimited Beer, Bananas, Cheese Sandwiches, Chocolate Creams and Cake, Lemon Ice and a Welsh Rarebit. Don't go to bed too early. This is the secret of my constitution.''[2]

"Princeton seniors were inwardly solemn when they took the steps of Old North to sing through the twilights of their last days in college. None, I think, was sadder than I; for I knew that I was coming to the end of two years not an instant of which I would have changed, and that I was to part with friends not a day of whose merry and kind companionship I could bear to spare from the rest of my life.

"My mother and sister came from home for class day; and then, when the hard hour of farewells was over, we went to spend the summer on Narragansett Bay. Whole afternoons I sat alone upon salty rocks, staring at the meaningless water; and I was heavy with dismay because almost suddenly the best of life—thus I bereavedly thought of Princeton—lay behind me.''[4]

**1893-1898.** Painful period of literary apprenticeship back home in Indiana. "Ostensibly I was a somewhat elaborately educated young man who'd soon be on the job, profitably making a place for himself in his own world. This of course was correct expectation, and I'd surely be thought rather disgraceful if I didn't fulfill it. The community didn't lean to gentlemen of leisure—especially not to young gentlemen of leisure. For that matter, neither did I; but unfortunately, I couldn't do anything except write and draw—or amateur-act a little and amateur-sing a little—and Indianapolis didn't much believe that a living could be made out of drawing or writing. Again, neither did I—not out of such drawing and writing as mine.

"I wasn't ambitious. That is, I had no ambition to be anything or to be known as anything. I didn't yearn to be a novelist or a playwright or a distinguished illustrator. On the other hand, I did wish to do something. Having found that I couldn't paint, I mightily yearned to draw good pictures. Therefore I began to draw pictures in earnest—and almost at the same time I began to write a novel. This seems inconsistent and a little odd. I had no conscious wish to write a novel; I didn't deliberately, so to say, begin one or feel anything like the interest in writing that I did in drawing, and yet I began to write a novel. Perhaps it's nearer the truth to say that it began to write itself. It went on writing itself—I had no control of it—and, after wandering whither it would for

several months, it banged its head into a stone wall at the end of a blind alley and seemed to die there. As it appeared to be through with itself, I thought I was through with it, and without regret put the self-willed scribblings away.

"Most of my work was done at night. My mother lamented, but indulged me, and she and my father understood one unreasonable reason why scratching paper till after daylight was more than ever congenial to me. Already I'd begun to appear to be a loafer, and even this reputation was rather better, I thought, than letting it become known that I usually spent fourteen hours of the twenty-four trying to draw and trying to write. In seeming, the night was a cloak; if one had to do foolish things, 't were better they were done after dark.

". . . I sent many too laborious pen-and-ink sketches to *Life,* that fine satiric weekly then to America what *Punch* was to Britain; but they all came back—hurried back, it seemed to me. I worked at short stories, too, many kinds of short stories and all laborious, like my drawings. I set them into various periods, trying to flavor different styles with phrasings suitable to the times and places and the types of people I used. The stories were of seventeenth and eighteenth century England, of eighteenth-century America, of Indiana in the early nineteenth century, of California in '49, of France under Robespierre. The splendid magazines of the 90's, the *Century, Harper's, McClure's* and *Scribner's,* rejected all of these manuscripts so rapidly that sometimes I thought my poor things must have been stopped and returned from Philadelphia; they didn't seem to have had time to get all the way to New York and back.

"I strained and fought with writing, striving to accomplish styles and to chime style with subject; and all the while, though I knew that I worked at drawing because I liked to draw, I hadn't the least idea why I worked twice as hard at writing. My manuscripts pleased me no better than they did the magazines, but I couldn't see just what was wrong with them, nor, naturally, could the editors spare time to tell me. Printed rejection slips clarify only one point.

"For a young man in the middle twenties, my lifelong earnings were unimposing. At ten, I had earned half of fifteen cents for shoveling snow—seven cents plus my share of a one-cent stick of candy halved with the other shoveler. When I was thirteen, my Grandfather Booth had given me a dollar to draw a charcoal portrait of him that hurt his feelings; and at Princeton I'd had fifteen dollars for a Lit. prize story and twenty-five for the words of a prize song. Now, out of a clear sky, *Life* accepted a drawing of mine, a burlesque of Aubrey Beardsley, with accompanying text satirizing a semiprose style of Oscar Wilde's. The check from *Life* was twenty dollars, on one bright flash bringing my total earnings up to sixty-one dollars and seven and a half cents—not counting my share of Punch-and-Judy takings in Marshall, Illinois, or my receipts from the play of Jesse James in our stable, sums later not precisely calculable. I wasn't vitally concerned with money-making, it's true; yet it can't be denied that the amount of one's earnings usually bears some relation to the measure of his usefulness to society. Since my whole previous life had shown only a trifle over forty-one dollars' worth of usefulness, the twenty-dollar boost was inspiriting.

"Squandering ink like water, I flooded the mails with drawings and bits of writing for *Life,* which seemed to have forgotten overnight that I'd successfully established myself as a contributor. Something more than thirty offerings, I think, brought rejection slips before my flush of hope subsided.

**Portrait of Tarkington by James Montgomery Flagg. (Courtesy of the Indianapolis Museum of Art, purchased with funds from the Penrod Society and the Martha Delzell Memorial Fund.)**

". . . As I review those years it seems to me that my family were heroic about me; their embarrassment must have been severe. A white-haired, greatly successful citizen spoke to me one evening on the country-club veranda: 'Booth, I asked your father what you're doing. He says you're still trying to be one of these damn literary fellers.'

"I mumbled, and he looked at me pityingly; but I knew that his pity was for my father.

"One day as I sat facing the fact that I'd been working for four years with blank results, I remembered the novel I'd begun when I came home after Princeton, and abruptly I saw why it had jammed itself into a blind alley. I got the manuscript out, began it again, found that I had some control over the story, and, though I was without any hope that it would ever see print—I couldn't imagine anything of mine doing that—I worked month after month after month upon it."[4]

**1895.** Journeyed to New York City. "The thin young man who had come East to seek his fortune stood upon the steamer's forward deck with the sea breeze blowing upon his eager face and hastening the combustion of the Sweet Ca-

poral cigarette he had just lighted at the spark of its predecessor. Before him the immense castellated sky line that amazed the world swam to meet him as the steamer rushed toward it over the flat water; and, stirred by the wonder of this great sight, he exultantly whispered to himself, 'New York! New York! New York!'

"But to the thin young man upon the ferryboat's forward deck, New York now meant something special that had not concerned him during his school and college adventurings there. Somewhere in the great hazy buildings north of Cortlandt Street there were fateful thresholds inaccessible to him; yet he must try to cross them, for they led to formidable desks where sat men of unlimited power dealing out destiny as cooly as a whist player deals cards. The thin young man's future was somewhere obscurely shuffled into the pile of destinies at the disposal of these potentates—they were managers who produced plays, editors who produced magazines, and publishers who produced books; and in the young man's trunk there were the manuscripts of two plays, of an unfinished novel, and of a now-forgotten number of short stories. The arrival in New York of that Cortlandt Street ferryboat, moreover, took place upon the bright morning of an autumn day a little more than thirty years ago; and the thin young man's name coincided with my own.

(From the movie "Little Orvie," starring Johnny Sheffield. Copyright 1940 by RKO Radio Pictures, Inc.)

(From the movie "Presenting Lily Mars," starring Judy Garland. Copyright 1943 by Loew's, Inc.)

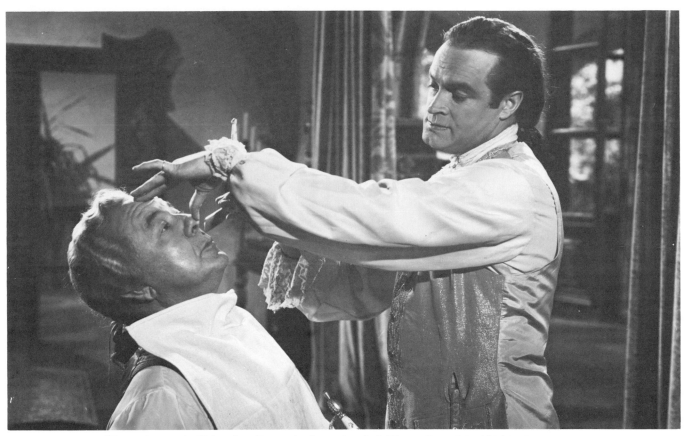

(From the movie "Monsieur Beaucaire," starring Bob Hope. Copyright 1946 by Paramount Pictures Corp.)

(From the movie "By the Light of the Silvery Moon," based on the "Penrod" stories, starring Doris Day and Gordon MacRae. Copyright 1953 by Warner Bros.)

**Maurice Levy appeared, escorting Marjorie Jones, and paid coin for two admissions.** ■ (From *Penrod* by Booth Tarkington. Illustrated by Gordon Grant.)

"Five years of printed rejection slips had not prepared one to receive even an encouraging handmade letter of rejection from an editor, much less a letter of acceptance. Such a letter must be read several times to make certain that the reader's eye is not deceived, and then at intervals to be sure that his memory has not been tricky. But no; all these readings having confirmed the accuracy of the first, it became clear that the thin young man, however embarrassing he might be in his new capacity, was definitely no longer a loafer.

"On my arrival in New York the great publisher said, 'Just condense your novel to one half its present length then we'll have space for it as a serial in the magazine.'

"It seemed to me that he might as well have asked me to condense the Brooklyn Bridge to half its length; yet Mr. McClure had every appearance of believing that such things could be done; that they were done every day, in fact; and that, as a matter of course, I knew how to do them.

"I didn't. I hadn't the remotest idea of what should be done to that ponderous bundle of manuscript to reduce it to half its weight. Nevertheless, I carried it to a lodging on Madison Avenue—for the comrades of the brownstone-front top floor were now dispersed to follow their achieved profes-

sions—and there I nervously began the amputations. At first they were a little dismaying, but before long the surgery became interestingly vindictive. 'Out you come!' seemed to be the very pleasantest thing one could say to a chapter; and so emaciated grew what remained of the manuscript that the new serial began to be known in the magazine office as The Cablegram.'' [Booth Tarkington, *The World Does Move*, Doubleday, Doran, 1928.[5]]

**1896.** Returned to his Indiana home. "New York, however, was not my destination, being but a way station on this decisive journey to the verdant plain that had for me the persistent claim of native soil calling always, however faintly, to its wandering sons, 'Come home!' A stranger, looking forth from his sleeping-car after a night of curving among the hills, might wonder why anybody should come home to this level monotony of landscape and the reiterating shabby back ends of wood and brick country towns, all alike.''[5]

**1899.** Gave up poetry to concentrate on his novel, *The Gentleman from Indiana.*

> "When a fellow's not a poet
> It is better he should know it
>    And be still.
> Peg may spread his wings and fly it
> I should be too wise to try it.—
> But I will.''[2]

The novel was published. A triumphant Tarkington became the toast of New York: "I need the immense stimulus of the

**"And you come to tell me that?"** ■ (From *The Turmoil* by Booth Tarkington. Illustrated by C. E. Chambers.)

Tarkington about the time *Alice Adams* was published, 1921.

life here . . . at home *I* give the stimulus to people; I suggest things—I tell people things . . . here I get something from everyone I meet. . . . You'll have to accept this as the fact—I am very much wiser than when I came, three weeks ago—my mind has opened a great deal, enlarged to new perceptions, in so many and so subtle ways that I can't go into it here for lack of time and space—'twould be like trying to say what the world is like.''[2]

**1900.** Briefly engaged to Helen Pitkin, whom he had met years before. "I was fifteen—and she had the goldest hair and the scarletest stockings! She was the first girl I ever took to the theater—ever bought flowers for. . . . She was still there in '99 [1900 actually]—I went back to see! And one of the Beauties of the Southland—and literary!''[2]

**June 18, 1902.** Tired of being merely a guest at weddings, he became a bridegroom himself, marrying Louisa Fletcher. "I have tipped a bishop with infinite grace. I have toasted brides more prettily than you could dream; I have ushered with notable éclat and put the cooks of distant relatives in the pew reserved for the groom's mother oftener than any man you know. And I have the weddingest clothes you ever see!''[2]

**1902.** Saying "I would as soon be sent to jail as to have to make a speech,''[1] Tarkington campaigned for and won a seat in the Indiana House of Representatives. ''. . . I am no public speaker as you know. The issue of this campaign is to get out the vote. I met a Big Four [New York Central] man today on the street, and I asked him to be sure and vote, and he wanted to know when the election day was. He didn't know there was going to be an election. There are too many that are that way. There are a good many business men who will have more time to vote next time if they don't know when to vote this time. There is the high price of beef, and I have wondered how high it would be under a democratic rule. The great issue is to get out the vote. Vote early but not often. The indifferent voter is a worthless sort of cuss. He is not a very good man. You have got to make him vote. If you get enough of them the result will be the same.''[2]

**1903.** Illness forced resignation from political life. ''. . . In the early spring, I was stricken with typhoid fever which harried me until the summer; and, to soften the noises that came into the open windows of the sick-room, the street was covered with fine sand to the depth of two or three inches for the distance of half a block. In the daytime no automobile would enter the sanded area; but sometimes, after dark, one that had not wandered into that shrouded street before would come chugging and snorting into the sand and be caught there like a fly in soft glue. Then there would be blasphemous metallic roarings, accompanied by simple human cursings, for half an hour perhaps.''[5]

Vacationed in Europe, accompanied by his father, his mother and his wife; experienced an ''adventure'' in Capri. ''For five days the gale has raged—and the island has sprung a leak and is sinking. We have waisted away for lack of food and none of us weighs over 200. Worst of all, Vesuvius is throwing up and erupting and going-on. The sea is *'rolling mountains-high';* we are so weakened by the lack of cigarettes that we have no strength to man-the-pumps. All communication with the mainland is cut off—there is nobody here except Germans and Italians. In addition to the *horrors-of-the-tempest,* Papa John has a boil.

''We have had no water for a long time. It is true there is a little wine left, but only two or three hundred barrels. At the last moment, when the last drop has been drunk and the last chicken eaten (with salad) I shall *'enclose-this-MS.-in-a-copper-cillinder'* and *cast-it-into-the sea,* hoping that it may *come-to-your-hand.* I haven't any copper-cillinder convenient, but no doubt I shall discover one *when-the-time-comes.*

''Later.

''*We-are-growing-very-weak.* Nana exceedingly despondent but still taking a little nourishment at regular intervals; that is: at the table d'hôtel. If it gets any worse we shall have to be *lashed-to-the-mast*—hope we won't quarrel as to who gets the softest side of it.

''Later.

''The leak is gaining. The island makes scarcely any progress. Can't keep her head up to the wind.

''Later still.

''Wonder why we came here. Papa John's boil getting bigger. A slight gleam of hope—if it keeps on enlarging at its present rate, we may be able to cross to the mainland on it.

''Midnight.

''Nothing to live on until breakfast but a dozen chicken sandwiches and a bottle of wine. Hardly think we'll survive. The wind is rising, *howls-dismally-among-the-riggings;* hope no *Pirates* will take advantage of our *dismantled-condition!* What if the *Jolly-Roger* should heave-in-sight on our *Lee-Bow? All-would-be-over!* We have eaten the sandwiches and are reduced to living on shellfish and mollusks, crustaceans culled from the rocks, blue points and broiled lobster, etc! Oh heavens, if it should come to horseflesh! There are only donkeys and we *might* be reduced to Michelangelo. I do not like to think of eating Michelangelo. I think he would have a right to feel hurt with us. But we may be able to sustain-ourselves-for-a-few hours on Nana's furs. They weren't 'cured' so awful well.'' [Booth Tarkington, *Your Amiable Uncle,* Bobbs-Merrill, 1949.[6]]

Eventually, the Tarkingtons were ''saved'' and fell in love with Capri. ''Capri is the true fairy isle. The little town in the lap of the cliffs is set for comic opera—the piazza is the smallest public square you ever heard of; it has its old cathedral and tower, just the same.''[6]

**1904.** Returned to New York, became regular contributor to leading literary magazines.

**1905.** Returned to Capri, determined to devote himself to playwriting; was less than prosperous in his literary endeavors.

**February 4, 1906.** Daughter, Laurel, born.

**1907-1910.** Gained success as a playwright, working with his collaborator, Harry Wilson.

**November 13, 1911.** A lack of creative output and a bout with alcoholism erupted in marital difficulties and resulted in divorce. ''Tarkington charged with cruelty. . . . This will end my book-writing for a while, nobody would buy a book by a wife-strangler. . . . When Louisa told me she wished to change husbands, I agreed, but I thought the divorce 'charges' could be kept quiet. . . . She has been too much coddled. She loves excitement & war (with everything on her side). . . . I can help her no more—my presence had got to be a reproach to her . . . and she hated it. . . . Louisa is, and always will be, dear to me, of course—and whatever she may do to me, so will I not do to her.

''The differences between us are of temperament and habit, and, after nine years of effort, it is apparent to both of us that we cannot reconcile our views of life.''[2]

**January 16, 1912.** Decided to stop drinking and devote himself totally to a literary career. ''Now I'm in condition as I was ten years ago, but with a very piquant realization of wasted time. . . . I want to make up for that time and have the energy to do it, & the 'stuff' stored. I don't want to lose any *more* time.

''[A writer must] go into training in the abstemious sense . . . give up gayeties and much enjoyable company, just as an athlete does. You have to make your mind do its calisthenics. Solitude is almost the whole of that prescription.''[2]

**November 6, 1912.** Married Susannah Robinson.

**1913.** *Penrod* stories became instant success. ''Penrod has been a success because it has kept to *true* boy and avoided book-and-stage boy. . . .

''*One* main thing is to keep out . . . hand-me down boy humor. 'Boy-writers' depend on 'Gee, fellers' and 'Say, kids' and 'kid nicknames'—if you'll note I have utterly avoided this stock stuff . . . even though most boys actually do say 'kids' & 'Gee.'

''I began to see that, just as in his embryo man reproduces the history of his development upward from the mire into man, so does he in his childhood and his boyhood and his youth reproduce the onward history of his race, from the most ancient man to the most modern.''[2]

''Boys are likely to comprehend one another's fundamental characters with a simple clarity—character being more naïvely exposed at that period than later—and adult men who have been 'boys together' have a basic knowledge of one another, no matter how they change. After I had grown to manhood, myself, I found that whenever I met a stranger I had an inclination to seek beneath his adult lineaments for the face he'd had when he was a boy. When I can see the boy's face beneath the man's I'm fairly sure that I know

(From the stage production of "Clarence," starring Glenn Hunter and Helen Hayes. Copyright 1919 by Samuel French.)

**Penrod felt desperate. He had come, that morning, to overwhelm Marjorie, to leave her almost prostrate with admiration and conceivably, weeping with anxiety over the dangerous life his position in the world compelled him to lead. Here was a collapse indeed.** ■ (From *Penrod Jashber* by Booth Tarkington. Illustrated by Gordon Grant.)

what sort of person he really is." [Booth Tarkington, "As I Seem to Me," *Saturday Evening Post*, July 12, 1941.[7]]

**1917.** Served war effort, acting as propagandist. "I wish they'd find me good enough for something besides writing, [but] it's all I can do.

"I have a feeling of shame . . . that I'm not carrying a gun . . . EVERYTHING'S been said and said . . . I want my limber joints and good wind and dependable heart of twenty years ago . . . I don't want to argue . . . I want to call 'em bastards and move toward the brick pile."[2]

**1919.** Awarded Pulitzer Prize for *Magnificent Ambersons*.

**1921.** Awarded second Pulitzer for *Alice Adams*.

**1927.** Diminishing eyesight ended theatrical attendance. "I'm more afraid of using up my eyes & right hand than the supplies of the mystic workman under the outer layers. I don't force that chap. . . . But when I *let* him be one, he's a Simon Legree driving *me*. . . . He *always* wants to go on: *wants* to use my strength to the last thimble of it."[2]

**1923.** Mourned deaths of his father and daughter. Returned to writing in order to assuage his bereavement. "I don't doubt [father] worried unhappily over me at times; but only two or three times, after I was 15, did he ever so much as advise, and then he did it indirectly, gently and by mere suggestion. Seems to me he was right and wise.

"I had one last night with [Laurel] soon after she came. Somehow I knew it was the last, because the shadow had *appeared*—I never knew so strange a communion as that. We talked here in my workroom far into the night. She talked brilliantly, profoundly—it was a search for the meaning of life and death and God—she had always seemed a child, but that night she was a beautiful, brilliant, haggard woman."[2]

The Tarkingtons worked to restore Laurel's will to live. However, when Laurel contracted pneumonia, there was no resistance to fight it. "Yesterday afternoon, about five o'-clock, Laurel had them call me in—and said 'Goodnight'—

"It is over.

"Oh, such a brave and bright and gentle spirit!

"You see the *instrument* of the spirit had become maimed; the spirit could not endure to remain in the instrument after that.

"But all day yesterday, which she begged us to let be '*her* day,' her mind was clear again: she was Laurel.

"Old friend, you must not grieve for her or for me. This was best. She came back to us for a day, and then went on. I think she went *somewhere* and that a day will come when I shall find her and she'll know all I've wanted so long to be to her."[2]

**1928.** Underwent five eye operations.

**August 25, 1930.** Suffered detached retina, went completely blind. "Mrs. Tarkington does so many things to make my work possible that I'm not able to list them. About all I do for myself is to shave—but she changes the razor blades."[2]

**January, 1931.** Sight restored.

**1934.** Returned to children's stories, writing for *Saturday Evening Post*. Tarkington wanted to "analyze . . . the age of seven and its adjacencies, reaching out, too, for some slight exhibition of the relationship between a child of that age and his parents, and also striving to know something of his viewpoint concerning his contemporaries, household pets, worldly distinctions and importances."[2]

**May 19, 1946.** Died following an illness of two months. "Life is only an episode in our passage from infinity to infinity [and] there is no death, only change."[2]

*FOR MORE INFORMATION SEE:* Frederic T. Cooper, "Newton Booth Tarkington," in his *Some American Story Tellers,* Holt, 1911; Robert C. Holliday, "Tarkingtonapolis—From Mule-Car to Flivver," in his *Broome Street Straws,* Doran, 1919; Blanche Colton Williams, "Booth Tarkington," in her *Our Short Story Writers,* Dodd, 1922; Carl C. Van Doren, *Contemporary American Novelists, 1900-1920,* Macmillan, 1922; Charles C. Baldwin, "Booth Tarkington," in his *Men Who Make Our Novels,* Dodd,

**Drawing of Tarkington, age 70. Photo by S. J. Woolf.**

1924; C. C. Van Doren, "Tradition and Transition," in his *American Novel, 1789-1939,* revised and enlarged edition, Macmillan, 1940; Richard Elwell Banta, compiler, *Indiana Authors and Their Books, 1816-1916,* Wabash College Press, 1949; Booth Tarkington, *Your Amiable Uncle: Letters to His Nephews,* Bobbs-Merrill, 1949; Dorothy Ritter Russo and Thelma L. Sullivan, *Bibliography of Booth Tarkington,* Indiana Historical Society, 1949.

Van Wyck Brooks, "Looking Westward," in his *Confident Years, 1885-1915,* Dutton, 1952; E. C. Wagenknecht, "Booth Tarkington, Success," in his *Cavalcade of the American Novel: From the Birth of the Nation to the Middle of the Twentieth Century,* Holt, 1952; John Cournos and H. S. N. K. Cournos, *Famous Modern American Novelists,* Dodd, 1952; James Leslie Woodress, *Booth Tarkington: Gentleman from Indiana,* Lippincott, 1955; J. L. Woodress, "Booth Tarkington's Political Career," *American Literature,* May, 1954; Loring Holmes Dodd, *Celebrities at Our Hearthside,* Dresser, 1959; Laura Benét, *Famous American Humorists,* Dodd, 1959; Winfield Townley Scott, *Exiles and Fabrications,* Doubleday, 1961; W. E. Wilson, "Titan and Gentleman," *Antioch Review,* Spring, 1963; Brian Doyle, editor, *Who's Who of Children's Literature,* Schocken Books, 1968.

Obituaries: *New York Times,* May 20, 1946; *Newsweek,* May 27, 1946; *Time,* May 27, 1946; *Art Digest,* June, 1946; *Current Biography,* June, 1946; *Publishers Weekly,* June 1, 1946; *Saturday Review of Literature,* June 1, 1946; *New Yorker,* June 1, 1946; *Wilson Library Bulletin,* September, 1946; *Current Biography Yearbook,* 1946.

## THOMPSON, David H(ugh)   1941-

*PERSONAL:* Born in New Haven, Conn.; son of Kenneth (a research pharmacist) and Helen Thompson; married Mary Berliner; children: Christopher, Loren. *Education:* Stanford University, A.B. (honors), 1963; University of Wisconsin, Madison, Ph.D., 1974. *Home:* 7105 Hickory Rd. West Bend, Wis. 53095.

*CAREER:* Worked as photographer, 1970-74; University of Wisconsin, Washington County Center, West Bend, assistant professor of biology, 1974-78, environmental consultant, 1978—. Part-time research biologist at Waterways Experiment Station for U.S. Army Corps of Engineers, 1977-78; investigator for project funded by National Audubon Society; teacher of workshops on bird identification and conductor of field studies on birds. Member of conservation committee of Colonial Waterbird Group, 1977—.

*WRITINGS: The Penguin: Its Life Cycle* (self-photographed), Sterling, 1974; (contributor) Bruce Parker, editor, *Terrestrial Biology,* American Geophysical Union, 1978. Contributor of photographs to books, including *The Marvels of Animal Behavior* and *Animal Behavior.*

*SIDELIGHTS:* "I got started in photography when my father gave me a camera to take to Antarctica. The camera became my principal form of recreation and I quickly taught myself how to use it. I specialize in taking good photographs which illustrate some biological concept and which have a scientifically accurate caption."

*HOBBIES AND OTHER INTERESTS:* Piloting.

## TREDEZ, Alain   1926-
## (Alain Trez)

*PERSONAL:* Born February 2, 1926, in Berck-sur-Mer, Pas-de-Calais, France; son of teachers; married Denise Laugier (a children's author), 1950; children: Isabelle, Corinne, Florence. *Education:* Attended the University of Paris and Ecole des Sciences Politiques. *Residence:* Paris, France.

*CAREER: Dominique* (children's magazine), Paris, France, co-editor with wife, 1952—; author and illustrator of books for children, 1958—. *Military service:* Served in the 25th Airborne Division of the French Army as a paratrooper, 1949-50. *Awards, honors: Sophie* received an honorable mention in the *New York Herald Tribune* Children's Book Festival, 1964.

*WRITINGS*—Under pseudonym Alain Trez: *La Preuve,* Denoel, 1965; *L'Amour de A à Z,* A. Michel, 1969.

All under pseudonym Alain Trez, with wife Denise Trez, pseudonym of Denise Tredez; all illustrated by A. Trez: *Circus in the Jungle,* World Publishing, 1958; *Fifi,* World Publishing, 1959; *The Butterfly Chase,* World Publishing, 1960; *Le Petit Chien,* World Publishing, 1961, translation by Douglas McKee and Donine Mouche published as *The Little Dog,* Faber, 1962; *The Magic Paintbox,* World Publishing, 1962; *The Little Knight's Dragon,* World Publishing, 1963; *Sophie* (translation from the French by D. McKee), World Publishing, 1964; *Sophie Runs Away* (translation from the French by McKee), Faber, 1965; *The Royal Hiccups* (translation from the French by McKee), Viking, 1965; *Le Vilain Chat,* World Publishing, 1965, translation by McKee

**They took all the good bones away from him and left him nothing but soup.**

(From *Le Petit Chien* by Denise and Alain Trez. Illustrated by Alain Trez.)

published as *The Mischievous Cat*, Faber, 1966; *Rabbit Country* (translation from the French by McKee), Viking, 1966; *Good Night, Veronica* (translation from the French by McKee), Viking, 1968; *The Three Little Mermaids*, World Publishing, 1969; *Maila and the Flying Carpet* (translation from the French by McKee), Viking, 1970; *The Smallest Pirate* (translation from the French by McKee), Viking, 1970; *Pourquoi Pas?*, L'Ecole des Loisirs, 1971; *The Three Little Mermaids*, Faber, 1977.

*SIDELIGHTS:* As the seventh of eight children, Tredez was born to two schoolteachers in Northern France. His parents had encouraged him to study art but he decided to study law with the notion of entering the diplomatic service. Tredez attended the Ecole des Sciences Politiques in Paris.

It was his army service (1949-1950) that brought him into the art field. According to Tredez, he spent half of his service in the French Army doodling in the brig because, as he explained, he was "undisciplined."

In 1950 he married a children's author, Denise Laugier. Shortly after their marriage the couple was asked to create a children's magazine. Their first book, published in 1958, was created for their daughter Isabelle. The following year another book was created for daughter Corinne. In 1961 when their third daughter, Florence, was born the couple created a children's book for her as well. Together they have produced at least a book a year from 1958 to 1971. Tredez and his family reside in Paris.

Besides illustrating, Tredez's art career has included cartooning, advertising and serious painting. In 1968 the artist had his first major exhibition shown in Paris.

Tredez enjoys creating books for children with his wife. After working out a story line together, she writes the text while he does the illustrations. *Circus in the Jungle* was their first such effort, and a *New York Times* critic noted, "Such an extravaganza could be merely silly, but French cartoonist Alain Trez and his wife deftly shape it into a brief, smartly paced, surprising romp into fantasy." Added *Booklist:* "Not a distinguished picture book, but a diverting one with its childlike imaginings, breezy action, and gaily colored, amusing pictures."

*Fifi* was described by the *Chicago Sunday Tribune* as, "Impish, implausible adventure, told with delightful dead pan...." *Kirkus* observed: "The unabashed manner in which the text and cartoon-like illustrations flirt with nonsense give rise to a humor which is most refreshing." A *Christian Science Monitor* critic made the following comments on *The Butterfly Chase:* "The Trez team pay a delightful tongue-in-cheek tribute to the perseverance of a French butterfly hunter with his honor at stake.... The illustrations, like the text, are bizarre and winsome." Noted the *Chicago Sunday Tribune:* "The authors show an uncanny knack of proceeding from the logical to the illogical to the utterly absurd, all with aplomb and delightful deadpan. Their drawings add to the delight of a captivating book."

Of *The Royal Hiccups*, a *Book Week* reviewer commented: "Stories [by the Trezes] are above all, animated: a lot happens, the pace never drags—one might even say it is melodramatic—and the gay, airy cartoon art by Monsieur Trez deftly complements the brisk narrative.... That the story's revolution is not really satisfactory is small price to pay for the splendidly decorative art. Each drawing is edged like a

rug to give it an oriental tone, and no opportunity is lost to embellish the scene in eye-filling detail."

*FOR MORE INFORMATION SEE: Booklist,* November 15, 1958; *New York Times,* January 18, 1959; *Kirkus,* August 1, 1959; *Chicago Sunday Tribune,* November 1, 1959 and November 6, 1960; *Christian Science Monitor,* November 3, 1960; *Book Week,* September 12, 1965; Lee Kingman and others, compilers, *Illustrators of Children's Books, 1957-1966,* Horn Book, 1968; Doris de Montreville and Donna Hill, editors, *Third Book of Junior Authors,* H. W. Wilson, 1972.

# TREMAIN, Ruthven 1922-

*PERSONAL:* Born June 13, 1922, in New York, N.Y.; daughter of Edwin Ruthven (a sales manager) and Emily (a registered nurse; maiden name, Ninde) Tremain. *Education:* Wellesley College, B.A., 1943. *Politics:* Republican. *Religion:* Episcopal. *Home and office:* 44 West Tenth St., New York, N.Y. 10011.

*CAREER:* Wesleyan University, Middletown, Conn., teaching fellow in physics, 1943-45; *Time* magazine, New York, N.Y., researcher, 1946-49; free-lance artist, soap and package designer, 1950-67; writer and illustrator of children's books, 1962—.

*WRITINGS*—All self-illustrated: (With Joel Rothman) *Secrets With Ciphers and Codes,* Macmillan, 1969; *Summer Diary,* Macmillan, 1970; *My Friends,* Macmillan, 1971; *Fooling Around With Words,* Greenwillow, 1976; *Teapot, Switcheroo, and Other Silly Games,* Greenwillow, 1979. Also creator of *1964 Chin Up Calendar,* Macmillan, 1963; *1964, 1966-1977 Calendar for Children,* Macmillan, 1963, 1965-1976; *1978 Calendar for Children,* Doubleday, 1977; *1979 Calendar for Children,* Doubleday, 1978.

*SIDELIGHTS:* "I simply like to read and write and draw. I enjoy trying to present material to kids in an interesting and entertaining way. My favorite non-working activities are talking to friends, reading, gambling (stock market, poker, backgammon, blackjack), and traveling, especially to casinos."

**RUTHVEN TREMAIN**

# WHAT?

"Oh, for crying out loud!"

(From *Fooling Around With Words* by Ruthven Tremain. Illustrated by the author.)

Tremain's book *Fooling Around With Words* is a collection of puzzles and word and picture games for children. It has been praised by the University of Chicago's Center for Children's Books as "one of the better collections of word games for this reading level" because "almost every entry can teach a child, painlessly, something about the language."

*FOR MORE INFORMATION SEE: Bulletin of the Center for Children's Books,* University of Chicago, January, 1977.

## ULM, Robert   1934-1977

*PERSONAL:* Born April 30, 1934, in Chicago, Ill.; son of Fred (a hotel receptionist) and Anna (Herbst) Ulm; married Helen Hansen (a fashion artist), January 1, 1967 (died March 10, 1969). *Education:* Illinois Institute of Technology, B.S.; also studied at Art Institute of Chicago, and School of Visual Arts. *Politics:* Democrat. *Religion:* Protestant. *Home and office:* 2138 West Roscoe St., Chicago, Ill. 60618.

*CAREER:* Consolidated Book Publishers, Chicago, Ill., illustrator, 1960-61; Sherry Studios, New York, N.Y., illustrator, 1962-70; free-lance illustrator in New York City, 1970-73, and Chicago, 1973—. *Military service:* U.S. Navy, radio technician; served in Pacific theater.

*ILLUSTRATOR:* All children's books published by Children's Press: Susan and John Lee, *Events of the Revolution: The Road to Lexington and Concord,* 1975; S. and J. Lee,

*Events of the Revolution: The Battle for Quebec,* 1975; S. and J. Lee, *Cities of the Revolution: Boston,* 1976; Dennis Fradin, *Illinois in Words and Pictures,* 1976; Dennis Fradin, *Virginia in Words and Pictures,* 1976; Dennis Fradin, *California in Words and Pictures,* 1977; Dennis Fradin, *Ohio in Words and Pictures,* 1977; Dennis Fradin, *Alaska in Words and Pictures,* 1977; Dennis Fradin, *South Carolina in Words and Pictures,* 1977; Dennis Fradin, *Wisconsin in Words and Pictures,* 1977. Contributor to *World Book Encyclopedia.* Contributor to magazines, including *Highlights for Children, Our Wonderful World,* and *Childcraft.*

*SIDELIGHTS:* "I work in all media except etching. In engineering I built television tuners and in art I am still trying to build pictures. LeRoy Neiman was my teacher and friend. His exciting color technique influenced all his students."

*HOBBIES AND OTHER INTERESTS:* Bicycling (all over the Midwest).

(Died October 17, 1977)

**Farmers fed him and let him sleep in their barns. They asked where he was going. He told them he was joining Washington. Some of the families were loyal to King George. But even they would feed a hungry boy.** ■ (From *Battle for Quebec* by Susan and John Lee. Illustrated by Robert Ulm.)

**ROBERT ULM**

# VAETH, J(oseph) Gordon 1921-

*PERSONAL:* Born February 12, 1921, in New York, N.Y.; son of Joseph Anthony (an educator) and Sara (Billard) Vaeth; married Joanne Corell, December 30, 1950; children: Gordon Corell. *Education:* New York University, A.B., 1941. *Religion:* Episcopalian. *Home:* 3000 Tennyson St. N.W., Washington, D.C. 20015.

*CAREER:* U.S. Naval Training Device Center, Port Washington, Long Island, N.Y., head of new weapons and systems division, 1955-58; Department of Defense, Man-In-Space Advanced Research Projects Agency, technical staff member, 1958-60; in electronics industry, 1960-62; National Oceanic and Atmospheric Administration, National Environmental Satellite Service, Washington, D.C., director of systems engineering, 1962—. St. Luke's Church, Sea Cliff, Long Island, N.Y. vestryman, 1955-57. *Military service:* U.S. Naval Reserve, active duty with Navy Lighter-Than-Air commands, 1942-46; now lieutenant, U.S. Naval Reserve (retired). *Member:* American Institute of Aeronautics and Astronautics (associate fellow), British Interplanetary Society, U.S. Naval Institute, Army and Navy Club (Washington, D.C.), Phi Beta Kappa.

*WRITINGS: 200 Miles Up,* Ronald, 1951, revised edition, 1955; *Graf Zeppelin,* Harper, 1958; *To the Ends of the Earth,* Harper, 1962; *Weather Eyes in the Sky,* Ronald, 1965; *Langley: Man of Science and Flight,* Ronald, 1966; *The Man Who Founded Georgia: The Story of James Edward Oglethorpe,* Macmillan, 1968. Contributor of articles to *This Week, Look, New York Times Magazine,* and *Encyclopaedia Britannica,* and to professional and technical journals.

*SIDELIGHTS:* "The subjects I like to write about are people. People who are not well known but who deserve to be remembered for what they stood for or what they achieved.

"Hugo Eckener, commander of the dirigible *Graf Zeppelin,* was the most successful airshipman of all time and the reason lay in the strength of character and inner greatness of the man himself. Roald Amundsen is famous, of course, for having discovered the South Pole. Not so well remembered is that he voluntarily came out of retirement and sacrificed his life trying to find and save another man. Samuel P. Langley should be thought of in much better terms than simply 'the man who tried to invent the airplane and failed.' One of our country's greatest astronomers and experts on the sun, he pioneered the modern science of astrophysics. As for James Edward Oglethorpe, it was he who established the colony of Georgia and, by his qualities of perseverance and leadership, enabled it to survive and develop.

"These personalities had qualities that can serve as inspirations and examples for all of us—which is why I find writing about them so satisfying."

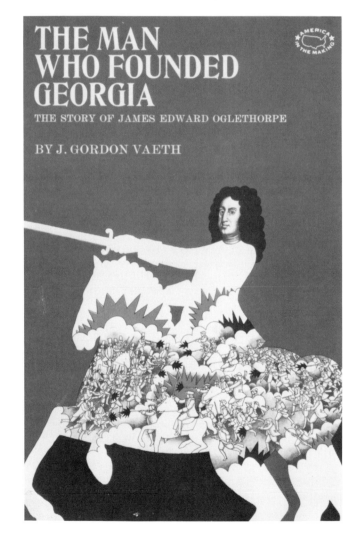

**Military action was in his blood and soldiering was an important part of his heritage. The Oglethorpes could trace their family history through six hundred years. It was a history of service and devoted loyalty to the Crown. ▪** (From *The Man Who Founded Georgia* by J. Gordon Vaeth. Jacket design by Roger Hane.)

J. GORDON VAETH

# VANDENBURG, Mary Lou    1943-

*PERSONAL:* Born December 18, 1943, in Passaic, N.J.; daughter of Nicholas (an industrial electrician) and Louise (a bookkeeper; maiden name, Rosiello) Yacono; married James Joseph Vandenburg, Jr. (a pharmacist), July 2, 1966; children: James Joseph III. *Education:* William Paterson College of New Jersey, B.A. (magna cum laude), 1965; graduate study at New School for Social Research, 1976-77. *Politics:* "Radical for Capitalism." *Religion:* Atheist. *Home:* 125 Sixth Ave., Apt. 5, Clifton, N.J. 07011.

*CAREER:* Elementary school teacher in Clifton, N.J., 1965-66, and Glen Rock, N.J., 1966-67; tutor, 1968-75; Hawthorne Public Schools, Hawthorne, N.J., teacher, 1975—. Lecturer on child development, 1969—; volunteer worker with children, including the handicapped. *Member:* Kappa Delta Pi. *Awards, honors:* Honor certificate from Freedoms Foundation, 1972, for essay "Fostering Patriotism in the Home."

*WRITINGS: Help!: Emergencies That Could Happen to You and How to Handle Them* (juvenile), Lerner, 1975. Contributor to *Massachusetts Teacher* and *Integrity*.

*WORK IN PROGRESS: Fostering Child Development,* with accompanying children's series; *Forbidden Fruit.*

*SIDELIGHTS:* "As a youngster and young adult I was fascinated with nature, human beings, and the creations of man, particularly works of art which integrated truth and beauty. Most inspiring were those art works that concretely displayed the greatness possible to man.

"I have always been involved in a dedicated search to discover the truth and to use these ideas to enlighten myself, enrich my life and to explore my potential. Writing, lecturing, and teaching were the end products of my attempts to utilize my knowledge and experiences concretely.

"During my work as a teacher, I found parents lacked the skills and understandings necessary to foster their child's development. In 1968, I began to lecture to parents groups on aspects of child development. Recently I compiled these lectures into a book entitled *Fostering Child Development*—to present these principles to any adult interested in helping children.

"While doing volunteer work in Ica, Peru, I met a fellow American who was stranded three days in the Andes. Realizing how important it is to train children for any emergencies they might encounter, I wrote the book *Help!,* for my son and other children, so they could learn to develop self-reliance early in their lives.

"My most enjoyable project so far was writing *Forbidden Fruit*—a fiction story that draws upon my personal experiences and struggles to become enlightened. It is set in the contemporary American battlefield of mysticism versus rationality. The characters and events show these two alternatives, the ultimate consequences of each course of life, and the role of art to enlighten any person determined to discover and utilize the truth to develop personal greatness. This book is a tribute to all those creators who have lived and selected the course of rational self-development, for in that process and as a result of their lives, their innovative creations, and their individual greatness, they have also enlightened the minds and elevated the lives of others.

*HOBBIES AND OTHER INTERESTS:* Tae Kwon Do (first degree black belt), participated in local theater productions.

**Learning how to react in emergency situations should not be put off because you think that an adult *might* be present and *might* know what to do if an emergency were to occur. Nor should learning be put off by using the excuse that most people seldom find themselves in emergency situations.** ■ (From *Help!* by Mary Lou Vandenburg. Illustrated by R.L. Markham.)

**JEAN WEBSTER**

# WEBSTER, Alice (Jane Chandler) 1876-1916
## (Jean Webster)

*PERSONAL:* Born July 24, 1876, in Fredonia, New York; died June 11, 1916; daughter of Charles Luther (a publisher) and Annie Clemens (Moffett) Webster; cousin of writer and humorist, Mark Twain (pseudonym of Samuel L. Clemens); married Glenn Ford McKinney, September 7, 1915; children: one daughter. *Education:* Vassar College, B.A., 1901.

*CAREER:* Author. Began writing stories as a college student for the *Vassar Miscellany;* became interested in the handicapped and underprivileged after visiting institutions for the destitute and delinquent.

*WRITINGS*—All published by Century, except as noted: *When Patty Went to College* (illustrated by C. D. Williams), 1903; *The Wheat Princess,* 1905; *Jerry Junior* (illustrated by Orson Lowell), 1907; *The Four-Pools Mystery,* 1908; *Much Ado about Peter* (illustrated by Charlotte Harding and Harry Linnell), Doubleday, Page, 1909; *Just Patty* (illustrated by C. M. Relyea), 1911; *Daddy-Long-Legs* (self-illustrated), 1912, reissued, Grosset, 1969 [another edition illustrated by Edward Ardizzone, Brockhampton Press, 1966, Meredith Press, 1967]; *Daddy-Long-Legs* (four-act play, based on her novel; first produced in New York at the Gaiety Theater, September 28, 1914), Samuel

French, 1922; *Dear Enemy* (self-illustrated), 1915, reissued, Tuttle, 1975.

Also contributor of short stories to newspapers and magazines.

*ADAPTATIONS*—Movies: ''Daddy-Long-Legs,'' First National Exhibitors Circuit, starring Mary Pickford, 1919, Fox Film Corp., starring Janet Gaynor and Warner Baxter, 1931, Twentieth Century-Fox, starring Leslie Caron and Fred Astaire, 1955.

Plays: Eric Maschwitz, *Love from Judy* (musical play; adaptation of *Daddy-Long-Legs;* lyrics by Hugh Martin and Jack Gray; first produced on the West End at Saville Theatre, September 25, 1952), E. Littler, 1952.

*SIDELIGHTS:* **July 24, 1876.** Born Alice Jane Chandler Webster in Fredonia, N.Y., the first child of Charles Luther Webster and Annie (Moffett) Webster. She was named Jane for Mark Twain's mother, and was his grandniece.

After attending the public schools at Fredonia, she prepared at the Lady Jane Grey School, Binghamton, N.Y., for Vassar, which gave her a B.A. degree in 1901. Webster was contributor to a Poughkeepsie, N.Y., newspaper and wrote stories for the *Vassar Miscellany.*

Majoring in English and economics, she had occasion to visit institutions for the destitute and delinquent, which

(From *Dear Enemy* by Jean Webster. Illustrated by the author.)

(From the movie "Daddy Long Legs," starring Fred Astaire and Leslie Caron. Copyright 1955 by Twentieth Century-Fox.)

gave her a firm conviction that there was no reason why underprivileged children could not succeed in life, a thesis she developed with humor and modern spirit in *Daddy-Long-Legs*.

**1912.** *Daddy-Long-Legs*, published. The humorous story tells how a young orphan girl found romance. As a best-seller, it has never been out of print since.

**1915.** Married Glenn Ford McKinney. They had an apartment in New York City overlooking Central Park, and an estate at Tyringham, Mass., in the Berkshire Hills. Here they raised ducks and pheasants.

**June 11, 1916.** Died in a hospital soon after the birth of their daughter; she was not yet forty. A room in the Girls' Service League and a bed at the county branch of the New York Orthopedic Hospital, near White Plains, N.Y., were endowed in her memory.

*FOR MORE INFORMATION SEE:* Stanley J. Kunitz, editor, *Twentieth Century Authors*, H. W. Wilson, 1942.

# WEBSTER, James 1925-

*PERSONAL:* Born March 8, 1925, in New Barhet, Hertfordshire, England; son of James Joscelyn (a bank manager) and May (an organist; Spearman) Webster; married Mary Barbara Windeatt (an artist) in 1950; children: Adrian William, Martin Guy. *Education:* Attended St. Luke's College, Exeter, 1947-49, and Central School of Speech, London, 1949-50; University of London, F.L.C.M., 1955, L.R.A.M., 1956. *Politics:* "Very liberal views." *Religion:* "Very liberal views." *Home:* Westward Ho!, St. Ouen, Jersey C.I, United Kingdom.

*CAREER:* Newton Park College of Education, Bath, England, lecturer in education, 1959-61; Redland College of Education, Bristol, England, senior lecturer in education, 1961-63; University of Bristol, Bristol, England, visiting lecturer in Remedial Linguistics, 1963-77. *Military service:* Royal Air Force, navigator, 1943-47. *Awards, honors:* Guinness trophy for gliding, 1964, 1965, 1966. Evening World trophy in gliding for height gain, 1968, 1977, 1978; unofficial world speed record for sailplanes (500 kph).

*WRITINGS: Practical Reading: Some New Remedial Techniques*, Evans Brothers, 1964; *The Four Aces*, Jonathan Cape, 1965; *The Red Robber of Larado*, Pitman, 1966; *The Ladybird Book of Tricks and Games and Others*, Wills & Hepborough, 1966; *Rescue Stories*, Ginn, 1967; *More Rescue Stories*, Ginn, 1967; *Rescue Adventures*, Ginn, 1967; *Shorty the Hero*, Ginn, 1967; *Shorty and Tom Rabbit*, Ginn, 1967; *Shorty and the Bank Robbers*, Ginn, 1967; *Sally the*

*Seagull*, Ginn, 1967; *Martin the Mouse*, Ginn, 1967; *Brown Beauty*, Ginn, 1967; *Patrick the Parrot*, Ginn, 1967; *Hoppy the Second*, Ginn, 1967; *Snowball*, Ginn, 1967; *Shorty Again*, Ginn, 1967; *Firewater*, Ginn, 1967; *Trouble the Fox*, Ginn, 1967; *Adventure in Jersey*, Ginn, 1967; *Adventure Underground*, Ginn, 1967; *Adventure on the Road*, Ginn, 1967; *Adventure in Scotland*, Ginn, 1967; *City Adventure*, Ginn, 1967; *Reading Failure, with Particular Reference to Rescue Reading*, Ginn, 1967, revised edition, 1971.

*First Helpings*, Thomas Nelson, 1970; *Help Stories*, Thomas Nelson, 1970; *Help Yourself Stories*, Thomas Nelson, 1970; *Ghosts!*, Thomas Nelson, 1974; *The Spy!*, Thomas Nelson, 1974; *The Red Sweater*, Thomas Nelson, 1974; *Lads and Ladders*, Thomas Nelson, 1974; *Dream Holiday*, Thomas Nelson, 1974; *When the Glass Went Down*, Thomas Nelson, 1974; *The Night I Felt a Ghost*, Thomas Nelson, 1974; *The Night I Heard a Noise*, Thomas Nelson, 1974; *The Day I was Buried Alive*, Thomas Nelson, 1974; *The Day We Saved the Flats*, Thomas Nelson, 1974; *Water*, Wills & Hepborough, 1974; *Man in the Air*, Wills & Hepborough, 1974; *The Night I had a Pain*, Thomas Nelson, 1974; *The Day We Found Fang Island*, Thomas Nelson, 1974; *Ghost Train*, Thomas Nelson, 1975; *Razor Rock*, Thomas Nelson, 1975; *The Man in the Black Jacket*, Thomas Nelson, 1975; *Witches' Wood*, Thomas Nelson, 1975; *The Kite Bike*, Thomas Nelson, 1975; *Tall Boy*, Thomas Nelson, 1975; *The Webster Test for Dyslexic*, Ginn, 1972.

*Help for Reluctant Readers*, Thomas Nelson, 1975; *Ladybird Leaders*, Wills & Hepborough, 1975; *Man and His Car*, Wills & Hepborough, 1975; *Man on the Sea*, Wills & Hepborough, 1975; *Roads*, Wills & Hepborough, 1976; *Homes*, Wills & Hepborough, 1976; *Fire*, Wills & Hepborough, 1976; *Rewards*, Arnold, 1976; *Steve Meets Chunky*, Arnold, 1976; *A Chunky Jacket*, Arnold, 1976; *Chunky at School*, Arnold, 1976; *Smoky*, Arnold, 1976; *Chunky Tries Flying*, Arnold, 1976; *Chunky at the Circus*, Arnold, 1976; *The Big Man*, Arnold, 1976; *The Big Man Again*, Arnold, 1976; *Webster's English Work Books*, Thomas Nelson, 1976; *Under the Ground*, Wills & Hepborough, 1977; *The Secret Room*, Arnold, 1978; *A Lucky Day at the Secret Room*, Arnold, 1978; *Buried Treasure at the Secret Room*, Arnold, 1978; *Trouble at the Secret Room*, Arnold, 1978; *Bomber Pilot*, Macmillan, 1979; *Spitfire Pilot*, Macmillan, 1979; *Airline Pilot*, Macmillan, 1979; *Air Taxi Pilot*, Macmillan, 1979. Author of material for British Broadcasting Corporation and Independent Television (ITV).

*WORK IN PROGRESS:* "Young Shorty Stories," twenty-four volumes; "Echoes," series of twelve early reading books and twelve work books; *Glider Pilot; Space Pilot; Chopper Pilot.*

*SIDELIGHTS:* "My writing stems not so much from creative urge, although I am never free from the disease, as from an obsessive desire to slay the dragon of illiteracy. Much of my work arose from my residential reading clinic for dyslexics (the first in Britain) and is based on I.C.G. (Informant Contextual Guessing) . . . ."

*HOBBIES AND OTHER INTERESTS:* Gliding, sportscars, surfing.

*FOR MORE INFORMATION SEE: Psychology*, August, 1965; *Cape Herald*, February 25, 1972; *Remedial Education*, Vol. 12, N. 1, 1977.

## WILLARD, Barbara (Mary)　1909-

*PERSONAL:* Born in 1909, in Hove, Sussex, England; daughter of an actor. *Education:* Attended the Convent of La Sainte Union, Southampton. *Home:* Forest Edge, Nutley, Uckfield, Sussex, England.

*CAREER:* Actress since age eleven; author of adult novels and children's books. Has also written film scripts for British and American film companies in London. *Member:* Society of Authors. *Awards, honors:* Guardian Award for Children's Fiction, 1974, for *The Iron Lily.*

*WRITINGS:* (With Elizabeth H. Devas) *Love in Ambush*, G. Howe, 1930; *Ballerina*, G. Howe, 1932; *Candle Flame*, G. Howe, 1932; *Name of Gentleman*, G. Howe, 1933; *Joy Befall Thee*, G. Howe, 1934; *As Far as in Me Lies*, T. Nelson, 1936; *Set Piece*, T. Nelson, 1938; *Personal Effects*, Macmillan, 1939; *The Dogs Do Bark*, Macmillan, 1948; *Portrait of Philip*, Macmillan, 1950; *Brother Ass and Brother Lion* (play; based on the story *St. Jerome, the Lion and the Donkey* by Helen J. Waddell), J. G. Miller, 1951; *Proposed and Seconded*, Macmillan, 1951; *Celia Scarfe*, Appleton-Century, 1951; *Echo Answers*, Macmillan, 1952; *One of the Twelve* (one-act play), Samuel French, 1954; *He Fought for His Queen: The Story of Sir Philip Sidney*, Warne, 1954; *The Snail and the Pennithornes* (illustrated by Geoffrey Fletcher), Epworth, 1957; *Winter in Disguise*, M. Joseph, 1958; *The House with Roots* (illustrated by Robert Hodgson), Constable, 1959, Watts, 1960; *Son of Charlemagne* (illustrated by Emil Weiss), Doubleday, 1959.

*The Dippers and Jo* (illustrated by Jean Harper), Hamish Hamilton, 1960; *Eight for a Secret* (illustrated by Lewis Hart), Constable, 1960, Watts, 1961; *The Penny Pony* (illustrated by Juliette Palmer), Hamish Hamilton, 1961, Penguin, 1967; *The Summer with Spike* (illustrated by Anne Linton),

**JAMES WEBSTER**

**BARBARA WILLARD**

Constable, 1961, Watts, 1962; *If All the Swords in England* (illustrated by Robert M. Sax), Doubleday, 1961; *Stop the Train!* (illustrated by J. Harper), Hamish Hamilton, 1961; *Hetty* (illustrated by Pamela Mara), Constable, 1962, Harcourt, 1963; *Duck on a Pond* (illustrated by Mary Rose Hardy), Watts, 1962; *The Battle of Wednesday Week* (illustrated by Douglas Hall), Constable Young Books, 1963, published in America as *Storm from the West,* Harcourt, 1964; *The Suddenly Gang* (illustrated by Lynette Hemmant), Hamish Hamilton, 1963; *Augustine Came to Kent* (illustrated by Hans Guggenheim), Doubleday, 1963; *The Dippers and the High-Flying Kite* (illustrated by Maureen Eckersley), Hamish Hamilton, 1963; *Three and One to Carry* (illustrated by D. Hall), Constable Young Books, 1964, Harcourt, 1965; *A Dog and a Half* (illustrated by Jane Paton), Hamish Hamilton, 1964, T. Nelson, 1971; *The Pram Race* (illustrated by Constance Marshall), Hamish Hamilton, 1964.

*The Wild Idea* (illustrated by Douglas Bissett), Hamish Hamilton, 1965; *Sussex,* Batsford, 1965, Hastings House, 1966; *Charity at Home* (illustrated by D. Hall), Constable Young Books, 1965, Harcourt, 1966; *Surprise Island* (illustrated by J. Paton), Hamish Hamilton, 1966, Meredith Press, 1969; *The Richleighs of Tantamount* (illustrated by C. Walter Hodges), Constable, 1966, Harcourt, 1967; *Flight to the Forest* (illustrated by Gareth Floyd), Doubleday, 1967 (published in England as *The Grove of Green Holly,* Constable, 1967, reissued, Penguin, 1976); *To London! To London!* (illustrated by Antony Maitland), Weybright & Talley, 1968; *The Family Tower,* Harcourt, 1968; (with Frances Howell) *Junior Motorist: The Driver's Apprentice* (illustrated by Ionicus), Collins, 1969; *The Toppling Towers,* Harcourt, 1969; *The Pocket Mouse* (illustrated by Mary Russon), Knopf, 1969; (compiler) *Hullabaloo! About Naughty Boys and Girls* (illustrated by Fritz Wegner), 1969.

*The Reindeer Slippers* (illustrated by Tessa Jordan), Hamish Hamilton, 1970; *Chichester & Lewes* (illustrated by Graham Humphreys), Longman Young Books, 1970; *Priscilla Pentecost* (illustrated by Doreen Roberts), Hamish Hamilton, 1970; (compiler) *"I—": An Anthology of Diarists* (illustrated by John Sergeant), Chatto, 1972; *Jubilee!* (illustrated by Hilary Abrahams), Heinemann, 1973; (compiler) *Happy Families* (illustrated by Krystyna Turska), Macmillan, 1974; (editor) *Field and Forest* (illustrated by Faith Jaques), Penguin, 1975; (author of English text) Bunshu Iguchi, *Convent Cat,* Hamish Hamilton, 1975, McGraw, 1976; *The Giant's Feast,* Hamish Hamilton, 1975, Addison, 1976; *Bridesmaid* (illustrated by J. Paton), Hamish Hamilton, 1976; *The Miller's Boy* (illustrated by G. Floyd), Dutton, 1976.

Historical sequence in the "Mantlemass" Series: *The Lark and the Laurel,* Harcourt, 1970; *The Sprig of Broom* (illustrated by Paul Shardlow), Longman Young Books, 1971, Dutton, 1972; *A Cold Wind Blowing,* Longman Young Books, 1972, Dutton, 1973; *The Iron Lily* (ALA Notable Book), Longman Young Books, 1973, Dutton, 1974; *Harrow and Harvest,* Penguin, 1974; *The Eldest Son,* Kestrel, 1977.

*WORK IN PROGRESS:* A seventh book in the "Mantlemass" sequence, *A Flight of Swans.*

*SIDELIGHTS:* Born in Hove, Sussex, England in 1909, Barbara Willard was raised as an only child in a theatrical family. Her father was an actor and at the age of eleven Willard played the part of a boy in Shakespeare's *MacBeth* when her father was acting at Stratford-on-Avon. "Mine was a small family. I was an only child until I was twelve years old, and then I had a brother. He wasn't very much good to me because he was so much younger. . . .

"I was brought up in the theater—that is to say, my father was an actor, and I was on the stage for a time, and my brother and my cousins, all these people were connected with the theater. . . ." [Cornelia Jones and Olivia R. Way, *British Children's Authors,* American Library Association, 1976.[1]]

Besides being a child actress, Willard began writing stories when she was very young. "It seems as though I've always been interested in writing. I suppose I was about seven when I started being interested in writing and reading."[1]

After completion of her formal schooling, Willard went into the theater, but eventually turned to her other love—writing. Her first books were adult novels and to supplement her income she wrote scripts for films in the story departments of various companies and wrote reviews, articles and short stories for various magazines.

It wasn't until 1958 that one of her adult novels led her into the field of children's literature. "Then I wrote a novel called *A Winter in Disguise.* It was about children. Somehow I realized that the best sort of children's book would be just that—a novel about children—but doing things that any child could do, not finding buried treasure or spy-catching or any of those rather worn-out things. *The House with Roots* was the first book I wrote of this kind. It went quite well, so I wrote some more.

". . . Although I wrote a number of grown-up novels, I always wanted to write for children. I made many attempts but I always failed. Then quite suddenly (I don't know what it was), I somehow just hit something, and it all started. This was very exciting. Of course, at the beginning so many ideas come you hardly know which one to choose. It's a very thrilling moment. So far, since I've been writing for young readers, I think I've always been at least one step behind an idea. I can say this, that I've been writing for many years, but of all my writing years, the ones I've most enjoyed are the ones spent writing for young people."[1]

In 1966 she wrote *The Richleighs of Tantamount,* a story which almost wrote itself. This type of easy writing is rare according to the author. "Now, *The Richleighs of Tantamount* was one of those stories that happened absolutely bang. It wasn't only that when I woke up in the morning I didn't know anything about it, but I didn't even know anything about it until lunchtime! I went to London, and it just happened that I was in conversation with somebody who put some tiny little word (and I can't tell you now what it was) into my mind, and I thought I would like to write a story about a family who had everything, and whether it was worthwhile having everything. By the time I came home, as I was driving home in my motorcar about four hours later, I knew everything that happened in that book and also what it was called. That never happened to me before."[1]

The following year *The Grove of Green Holly* (published in the United States as *Flight to the Forest*) was written. "I

**He would surely make for the coast; but there were other shores than the Sussex shore above which the three stood listening intently in the sunshine. ■** (From *Flight to the Forest* by Barbara Willard. Illustrated by Gareth Floyd.)

very much wanted to write a story that had something to do with acting. I wanted also to know what had become of the players in that time in English history when Oliver Cromwell was ruling, and when everybody was very stern and puritanical, and they shut down all the theaters because they were considered to be not at all proper. So, I put all these ideas together, and they turned into the story *The Grove of Green Holly.*

"I gathered background information for it in the way one always gathers background information—out of books written by other people. Everything that's ever happened in the world, really, can be found in some book or other. When I start researching a subject or a period, one book leads to another. The author of one book almost always alludes to others. So you gradually trace your way from title to title, making copious notes on the way, until you have a clear picture of that period. At least, this is what I do."[1]

In 1968 Willard wrote *The Family Tower* and the following year the sequel to it, *The Toppling Towers.* Many of her books, like these two, were written about large families since this type of writing seems to fulfill her desire to be part of a large family. Her only brother was twelve years her junior. "I enjoy writing about families and family relationships because it was a thing I wanted very much when I was young. . . .

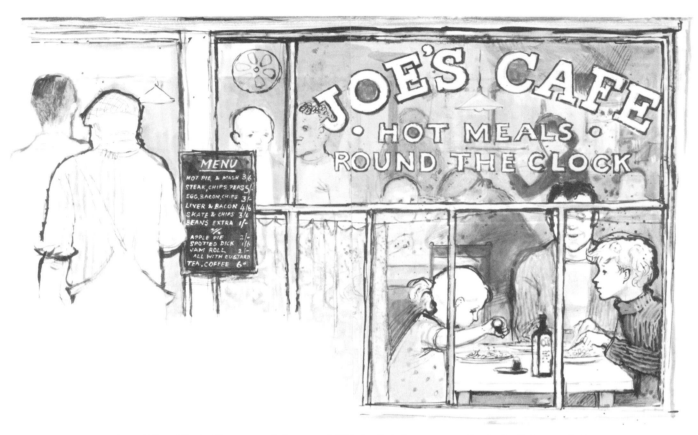

**At midday, Uncle George took Peter and Elizabeth to have a meal in Joe's Cafe round the corner. It was hot and noisy and cheerful. Joe was a friend of Uncle George's and Peter and Elizabeth found themselves with more chips and baked beans than they could eat.** ■ (From *To London! To London!* by Barbara Willard. Illustrated by Antony Maitland.)

"I wrote *The Family Tower* and *The Toppling Towers* because I wanted an enormous family story. I wanted a long book about a very big family, and how, living always in one place because their family work was there, they relied on one another. There were lots of cousins and aunts and uncles. Unfortunately my publisher over here thought that the book as I wanted to write it would be too long, and would be too expensive to produce, and that none of you would buy it. So I wrote it in two parts. *The Family Tower* is the first one. *The Toppling Towers* is the second book, but it isn't strictly speaking a sequel. It's a continuation of the first book. So long as you read the first book you know exactly where you are. People coming into the second book without having read the first may wonder who all the characters are. The thing to do is to read *The Family Tower* first."[1]

During the last two decades Willard has been writing mainly for children who are her favorite audience. "Most children's writers write a lot of books, and there are many reasons for this, some of them merely practical. But one good reason is the pure pleasure of finding an uncynical audience. Stern, uncompromising, but never weary. It is a wonderful appetite to feed, that lovely maw, enticingly open. No wonder children's books proliferate and reviewers grow a bit tetchy at times. Anyway, it is suspect to be prolific, in spite of the fact that great fiction writers of the past had an enormous output.

"Or perhaps it is just that fiction itself has become faintly suspect, its old respectability swallowed in the rather awful earnestness of our fact-worshipping times. And writers may be found who apologize for a mere story, and sometimes consciences are eased because the story is a problem story appropriate to the day—it will teach—help—promote understanding . . . Why not? Many a child will be helped by finding his worries rationally discussed in a fictional setting. In the same way he may be led by a story with a period setting towards a serious interest in history. Perhaps this may be called an approach—that without any ambition to *teach* young readers about themselves as they were however—many years ago, I should like to believe that this kind of story is capable of warming up history; putting the expression, in fact, into so many bald, unthinking statements that make no more impact than some common catchphrase: The Norsemen harried the coast, burning and pillaging . . . Many thousand died of the plague in that week alone . . . Unnumbered dead littered the field. . . .

"I have always written—we all say that; but it is mostly the case, for the bug prefers tender flesh—but never, since the first ecstasies, with as much pleasure and satisfaction as I experience today. And . . . I have written an awful lot by now." [Barbara Willard, *The Thorny Paradise,* edited by Edward Blishen, Penguin, 1975.[2]]

Barbara Willard lives today in Sussex, England with her many cats and dogs. She remains passionately interested in the theatre besides being a prolific children's author.

In a writing career that has already spanned four decades, Barbara Willard's books are many. A *New York Times* review of a 1950's book, *Celia Scarfe,* included, "Miss Willard handles the somewhat contrived theme expertly. There is no bathos, and the emotions ring true, even when they are muted in the traditional British fashion. . . ." The *San Francisco Chronicle* added, "Miss Willard expects little of her novel that she is not capable of giving to it. Her characters are dove-colored but handled with honesty and understanding. The intentions of her story are modest but fulfilled with discernment and restraint."

"Superbly depicted emotional scenes," was how *Horn Book* described *Storm from the West.* "The relationships, childish misunderstandings and worries, are drawn authentically as are the Scottish setting and its people. Moments of Anglo-American fencing add amusement, too, to what could well be the author's most enjoyed story." Commented the London *Times Literary Supplement:* "The restrictions of time—the choice of the holiday adventure form—the necessity for a quick and happy solution—all these keep the book to a merely efficient level, lively, not memorable."

In reviewing *Three and One to Carry*, a *Book Week* critic observed, "A well-paced story with natural characters, sprightly style and a plot which hinges believably on a lost document in the ancient village church. The bond of family affections is skillfully underplayed with an astringent touch of realism. Miss Willard's opening chapter is a model of how to establish characters, delineate a situation and get a story under way." *Horn Book* noted: "The major strengths of the story are in the family relationships and the reality of the characters. Although real drama, inherent in *Storm from the West*, is absent here, children who expect a good family story from the author will not be disappointed."

*Horn Book's* comments on *The Sprig of Broom* included, "In addition to the tantalizing mystery, the book presents history, romance, and a masterful re-creation of life lived long ago. The characters are real and solid, and the story can be read for the engrossing plot and rich background. The author has shown great skill in revealing gradually the information that leads to the solution of the mystery." Observed the London *Times Literary Supplement:* "If the mystery provides the motive force of the story, the main interest lies in the everyday life of a forest community surviving, for the most part undisturbed, away from the affairs of the world. Medley and his wilful, high-spirited love are attractively drawn, but the author's real hero is the forest itself, its changing seasons and moods evoked unobtrusively but always with understanding affection."

*A Cold Wind Blowing* is one of Barbara Willard's most recent efforts. The London *Times Literary Supplement* review included, "It was Rumer Godden who advised those who read and review children's books to treat them like Persian carpets; design, she said, and colour are important—but what really counts is the perfection of the stitching, for if the stitching is less than perfect, the carpet will soon disintegrate. Barbara Willard is one of the few craftsmen writing for young people today whose stitching can be examined under a magnifying glass and found flawless. . . . [Her] chronicle grows in stature with every book." Observed *New Statesman:* "Miss Willard's achievement is the mysterious one of giving her narrative the feel of its period; the language, without being archaic is somehow all of a piece with the story. She's marvellous on the curious wedding of weather and event, on the growth and decline of human passions; and there are big scenes, of a quality that won't easily be forgotten. . . ."

*HOBBIES AND OTHER INTERESTS:* Gardening, cooking, and driving.

*FOR MORE INFORMATION SEE: New York Times*, June 24, 1951; *San Francisco Chronicle*, July 1, 1951; *Times Literary Supplement*, November 28, 1963, October 22, 1971, December 8, 1972; *Horn Book*, December, 1963, December, 1964, October, 1965, December, 1966, October, 1967, June, 1970, August, 1971, August, 1972, February, 1973, June, 1973, February, 1975, February, 1976, April, 1976, April, 1977; *Book Week*, October 31, 1965; *Authors' Choice*, Crowell, 1971; *New Statesman*, November 10, 1972; *The Thorny Paradise*, edited by Edward Blishen, Penguin, 1975; *Children's Literary Review*, Volume 2, Gale, 1976; Cornelia Jones and Olivia R. Way, *British Children's Authors*, American Library Association, 1976.

## WITT, Shirley Hill 1934-
## (Katherine Thundercloud)

*PERSONAL:* Born April 17, 1934, in Whittier, Calif.; daughter of Melvin Ward and Cordelia (Bertiome) Hill; children: Randall Jacobs Witt, Hilary Witt. *Education:* University of Michigan, B.A., 1965, M.A., 1966; University of New Mexico, Ph.D., 1969. *Politics:* Independent. *Religion:* Iroquois Longhouse. *Home:* 1020 15th St., Denver, Colo. 80202. *Agent:* Elizabeth McKee, Harold Matson Co., Inc., 22 East 40th St., New York, N.Y. 10016. *Office:* U.S. Commission on Civil Rights, Suite 1700, 1405 Curtis, Executive Tower, Denver, Colo. 80202.

*CAREER:* University of North Carolina, Chapel Hill, visiting assistant professor of anthropology, 1970-72; Colorado College, Colorado Springs, associate professor of anthropology, 1972-76; U.S. Commission on Civil Rights, Denver, Colo., director of Mountain States Regional Office, 1975—. A founder, vice-president, National Indian Youth Council, 1961-64; member of board of directors of Highlander Center, 1968-70; member of Colorado Springs Human Relations Commission, 1972-75; member of steering committee of National Women's Political Caucus, 1972-74; member of college committee of Colorado Commission on the Status of Women, 1973-75; member of Indian Rights Committee, American Civil Liberties Union, 1975—; member of Federal Women's Program Committee, Denver Federal Executive Board, 1976—; commissioner of City and County of Denver Commission on Civil Rights, 1976-78; president of Rocky Mountain Chapter National Association of Human Rights Workers, 1976—; consultant to U.S. Commission on Civil Rights, American Indian Task Force, Office of Civil Rights, Department of Health, Education and Welfare, and Task Force for Spanish-Speaking Education; observer, NGO Conference on the Discrimination against the Indigenes of the Americas, Geneva, Switzerland, 1977; panel of human rights experts, U.S. Commission on UNESCO, 1978.

*MEMBER:* American Anthropological Association (fellow), American Association for the Advancement of Science, American Association of Physical Anthropologists, American Civil Liberties Union, National Association of Human Rights Workers (vice-president of Colorado chapter, 1973-75); Association of Women in Science. *Awards, honors:* Anisfield-Wolf Award for Race Relations, 1968, for *The American Indian Today;* certificate of appreciation, The City of Colorado Springs for service as a member of the Human Relations Commission, 1972-74.

*WRITINGS: The Saginaw Band of Chippewa Indians,* U.S. Government Printing Office, 1967; (contributor) Stuart Levine and Nancy O. Lurie, editors, *The American Indian*

**SHIRLEY HILL WITT**

*Today,* Everett-Edwards, 1968; *The Tuscaroras,* Crowell, 1972; (editor with Stan Steiner) *The Way: An Anthology of American Indian Life and Literature,* Knopf, 1972.

Author and consultant of scripts for "Silent Heritage: The American Indian," an eleven-part series for University of Michigan Television Center, produced by National Educational Television, 1966-67. Contributor to *Civil Rights Digest, Midcontinent American Studies Journal, Inquiry,* and *Akwesasne Notes;* contributor to newspapers, under pseudonym Katherine Thundercloud.

*WORK IN PROGRESS:* Editing *Costa Rica: Studies in Nutrition and Human Biology;* writing articles to be included in *The Encyclopedia of the American Indians.*

*SIDELIGHTS:* Shirley Hill Witt is a member of the Akwesasne Mohawk Nation, Wolf Clan. She has done research among American Indians, Chicanos, and people living in Appalachia; she has also studied people in Costa Rica and Canada. She writes: "The path of my life has taken me through human situations which have left me with an undeniable need to participate in matters concerning civil—human—rights. This is seen in my writings. . . ."

## WRIGGINS, Sally Hovey    1922-

*PERSONAL:* Surname sounds like Riggins; born May 6, 1922 in Seattle, Wash.; daughter of Winthrop Tewskbury (an investment banker) and Hazel (Norris) Hovey; married W.

Howard Wriggins (diplomat), December 22, 1947; children: Diana (Mrs. Ed. Cundy), Christopher, Jennifer. *Education:* Reed College, B.A., 1944; Haverford College, M.A., 1946. *Politics:* Democrat. *Religion:* Quaker. *Home:* 94 Horton Place, Colombo Sri Lanka, Ceylon. *Agent:* Marilyn Marlow, 575 Madison Avenue, New York, N.Y. 10022. *Office:* C/o Department of State, Colombo Sri Lanka, Washington, D.C. 20520.

*CAREER:* Writer of children's books. United Nations Reliefs Rehabilitation Association, research assistant, 1946-47. Founding committee and first president of Asia-American Forum, Washington, D.C.; Sandy Spring Friends School, Sandy Spring, Md., founding committee; Sidwell Friends School, Washington, D.C.,honorary board member; International Schools Services, New York, N.Y., board member; Quaker United Nations Program, New York, N.Y., committee member. *Member:* Society of Women Geographers, Society of Children's Book Authors, Bank Street Writers Workshop, Cosmopolitan Club.

*WRITINGS:* (Retold) *White Monkey King: A Chinese Fable,* Pantheon, 1977. Work has appeared in *Friends Journal;* prepared exhibition on the "Background and Many Lives of Monkeys" shown at New York, Boston, and Philadelphia Public Libraries.

*WORK IN PROGRESS: Monkey King Goes West,* a sequel to *White Monkey King;* an article on Hsüan-Tsang.

*SIDELIGHTS:* "I have three children variously born in Switzerland, America and Sri Lanka or Ceylon. In addition to several years residence in Europe and Sri Lanka, I traveled with my husband and two older children on an eight month trip around the world. More recently, I spent a year at Oxford with my husband and I traveled to both Alaska and Africa in 1976. Last year I was lucky enough to visit Mainland China.

**SALLY HOVEY WRIGGINS**

**Monkey put his feet together, drew a deep breath, made a mighty leap into the air, and landed about a mile away in a dark-leafed persimmon tree. ■** (From *White Monkey King*, retold by Sally Hovey Wriggins. Illustrated by Ronni Solbert.)

"I began writing for children because we always seemed to be traveling or living abroad and I needed the continuity which writing brings. I love tales of exploration in general and I fell in love with the *Monkey* legends in particular. They are a comic cosmic mixture; both irreverent and serious at the same time as well as being a journey of exploration! This Chinese classic has a lengthy history so that it is akin to dipping into King Arthur legends and history, only since it relates to China, it is even vaster in scope.

"In a nutshell, in the year 629 A.D., a Chinese monk made a journey to India traveling 10,000 miles over terrible deserts and three of the highest mountain ranges in the world. He went in search of Buddhist scriptures and returned after sixteen years of travel to modern-day Sian in China. He left in secret, but the Emperor of China honored him on his return by building the Wild Goose Pagoda for him. This last year I visited this much-restored pagoda and saw a rubbing of Hsuän-Tsang's tombstone.

"This holy man became a religious hero in China and a cycle of legends grew up around him growing over a period of 1,000 years. In the sixteenth century, a great novel, *Journey to the West* (commonly known as *Monkey*) was written, inspired by the monk. Oddly enough, the hero is not the holy monk, but a lively monkey who is very naughty and yet who

redeems himself by taking care of the monk on his journey to the West. *Monkey* is still known and popular in present day China and I gave several copies of *White Monkey King* to Chinese schools when I was there. I have written a sequel, *Monkey King Goes West,* and intend to start on a third book, tentatively entitled, *The Return of Monkey,* all of them retelling different parts of the epic Chinese folk novel.''

## WYETH, N(ewell) C(onvers)    1882-1945

*PERSONAL:* Born October 22, 1882, in Needham, Massachusetts; died October 19, 1945, in Chadds Ford, Pennsylvania; son of Andrew Newell and Henriette (Zirngiebel) Wyeth; married Carolyn Brenneman Bockius, April 16, 1906; children: Henriette Zirngiebel (Mrs. Peter Hurd), Carolyn Brenneman, Nathaniel Convers, Ann (Mrs. John McCoy), Andrew (the painter; father of James Wyeth, the painter). *Education:* Attended Massachusetts Normal Art School and Eric Pape's Art School; studied with C. W. Reed and Howard Pyle. *Politics:* Republican. *Religion:* Unitarian. *Home:* Chadds Ford, Pennsylvania.

*CAREER:* Painter and illustrator. Employed for a while, in the western United States, as a government mail rider. *Awards, honors:* Beck Prize of the Pennsylvania Academy of Fine Arts, 1910; gold medal from the San Francisco Exposition, 1915; Fourth Clarke prize for painting of the Corcoran Art Gallery, Washington, D.C., 1932.

*ILLUSTRATOR:* Robert Louis Stevenson, *Treasure Island,* Scribner, 1911; James Baldwin, *Sampo,* Scribner, 1912; R. L. Stevenson, *Kidnapped,* Scribner, 1913; Stevenson, *Black Arrow,* Scribner, 1916; Sir Thomas Malory, *Boy's King Arthur,* (edited by Sidney Lanier), Scribner, 1917; Paul Creswick, *Robin Hood,* D. McKay, 1917; Jules Verne, *Mysterious Island,* Scribner, 1918; James Fenimore Cooper, *Last of the Mohicans,* Scribner, 1919, reissued, 1972; Daniel Defoe, *Robinson Crusoe,* Cosmopolitan, 1920; Jane Porter, *Scottish Chiefs,* Scribner, 1921; Washington Irving, *Rip Van Winkle,* D. McKay, 1921; Sir Arthur Conan Doyle, *White Company,* Cosmopolitan, 1922; Thomas Bulfinch, *Legends of Charlemagne,* Cosmopolitan, 1924; R. L. Stevenson, *David Balfour,* Scribner, 1924, reprinted, 1961; J. F. Cooper, *The Deerslayer,* Scribner, 1925; Francis Parkman, *Oregon Trail,* Little Brown, 1925; Henry Wadsworth Longfellow, *Courtship of Miles Standish,* Houghton, 1926; J. Verne, *Michael Strogoff; or, The Courier of the Czar,* Scribner, 1927; Charles Kingsley, *Westward Ho!,* Scribner, 1929; H. W. Longfellow, *Son of Hiawatha,* Houghton, 1929; Homer, *The Odyssey,* Houghton, 1929.

Philip A. Rollins, *Jinglebob,* Scribner, 1930; Elizabeth Willis, *Lesby,* Scribner, 1931; Samuel P. Cadman, *Parables of Jesus,* D. McKay, 1931; John Fox, *Little Shepherd of Kingdom Come,* Scribner, 1931; (with Peter Hurd) Mary Mapes Dodge, *Hans Brinker,* Garden City Publishing, 1932; Harvey Allen, *Anthony Adverse,* Farrar, Straus, 1934; Henry D. Thoreau, *Men of Concord,* Houghton, 1936; Kenneth L. Roberts, *Trending to Maine,* Little, Brown, 1938; (with son, Andrew Wyeth) Allen French, *Red Keep,* Houghton, 1938; Marjorie K. Rawlings, *The Yearling,* Scribner, 1939, reissued, 1968; Helen M. Jackson, *Ramona,* Little, Brown, 1939; Edna Johnson and C. E. Scott, compilers, *Anthology of Children's Literature,* Houghton, 1940, reissued, 1960; Charles B. Nordhoff and

**N.C.Wyeth as a young man.**

J. N. Hall, *Bounty Trilogy,* Little, Brown, 1940; James Boyd, *Drums,* Scribner, 1947.

Editor: *Marauders of the Sea* (illustrated by P. Hurd), Putnam, 1935; *Great Stories of the Sea and Ships* (illustrated by Hurd), D. McKay, 1940, reprinted, 1977.

Contributor of writings and drawings to *Scribner's Magazine.*

*SIDELIGHTS:* **October 22, 1882.** Born in Needham, Massachusetts, the eldest of four sons, Wyeth's father came from an old New England family. His mother was the daughter of a Swiss florist. Wyeth spent his early childhood on a farm situated on the banks of the Charles River. "... I can see the dear old Charles silently moving by, screened by the alders, and flecked with myriad crumbs of sunshine. The lone elm is slightly waving back and forth, back and forth. The lay of the land across the river, the dark sentinel cedars along the 'New Road,' the glimpse of Burgesses' black and white chimneys—and the rumble of a team over the 'iron bridge,' and under the bridge the river weeds moving, beckoning—beckoning to me ..." [N. C. Wyeth, *The Wyeths,* edited by Betsy James Wyeth, Gambit, 1971.[1]]

"New England was where I was born, raised and educated ... My ancestor, Nicholas Wyeth, came from Wales to Massachusetts in 1647. The spirit of early days on the Massachusetts coast was an oft-discussed subject in my home.

"I was born in Needham, not far from the town of Plymouth, to which I made many pilgrimages during my boyhood, spending thrilling days in and around that historic territory." [Douglas Allen and Douglas Allen, Jr., *N. C. Wyeth,* Bonanza Books, 1972.[2]]

"My brothers and I were brought up on a farm, and from the time I could walk I was conscripted into doing every conceivable chore that there was to do about the place. This early training gave me a vivid appreciation of the part the body plays in action. ...."[1]

"... It's a strange thing, but I seemed to lack all that imaginative stuff that most kids have. I was quiet and my mother said I was observant, but I saw things as they were, and not as the fairy tales paint them."[2]

**1899.** Left Needham High School after two years and graduated from the Mechanic Art High School in Boston. His education continued at the Massachusetts Normal Arts School. Richard Andrew, an instructor, recognized his ability and encouraged him to choose the career of an illustrator. "I rose to his advice like a trout to a straw."[2]

**1901.** Studied at the Eric Pape School of Art in Boston.

**1902.** Studied with the illustrator, Charles H. Davis, in Mystic, Conn. Some twenty years later, Wyeth criticized this training. "To destroy individuality seems to be the main function of the illustrating classroom today. To turn the embryo mind face to face with technical methods, style, and the restrictions of publishing processes which all figure

**Wyeth in Colorado, October, 1904.**

**Chadds Ford, 1903.**

so prominently in composition, before he is able to feel the divine urge which comes only from a sound initiation into nature's truths is, to my mind, the principal reason why such a tragic percentage of art students fail.

"I know from experience what it means to answer that premature call for pictures. The second week I spent in an art school I was requested to do this as part of the routine, and how I suffered for that entire year. I noted that cleverness was rewarded, stunty and affected methods got the applause, so naturally I concluded that my salvation lay in my ability to develop a new 'stunt.'"[2]

**1902.** Studied with Charles W. Reed. Here he heard about the highly selective Howard Pyle School in Delaware.

**October 18, 1902.** Left home for an interview with Howard Pyle in Wilmington, Delaware. Wyeth was accepted as a probationary pupil. "My most vivid recollection of Howard Pyle was gained during the first five minutes I knew him. He stood with his back to the blazing and crackling logs in his studio fireplace, his legs spaced apart, his arms akimbo. His towering figure seemed to lift to greater heights with the swiftly ascending smoke and sparks from the hearth behind him.

"I was young, ambitious and impressionable. For years, it seemed, I had dreamed of this meeting. Success in winning this master's interest and sympathy to the cause of my own artistic advancement seemed so much to ask, so remote, such a vain hope. But here I was at last, seated before him in the very room in which were born so many of the pictures I had breathlessly admired from boyhood. Paintings and drawings that had long since become a living and indispensable part of my own life.

"And as Howard Pyle stood there, talking gently but with unmistakable emphasis, his large and genial countenance hypnotized me. My rapid reflections were swept beyond the actual man. It was bewildering. I heard every modulation of his voice and I took note of his every word. Occasionally I would answer a question. I remember all this clearly.

"I had come to him, as many had before me, for his help and guidance, and his first words to me will forever ring in my ears as an unceasing appeal to my conscience: 'My boy, you have come here for help. Then you must live your best and work hard!' His broad, kindly face looked solemn as he spoke these words, and from that moment I knew that he

**The Carpetbaggers.** ■ (From *The Pike County Ballads* by John Hay. Illustrated by N.C. Wyeth.)

meant infinitely more to me than a mere teacher of illustration."[2]

**October 27, 1902.** "I've got a perfect little room. The room is $2 a week. As to the studio, for light it's one of the best in town (an old photographer's studio) 50' X 30". The fellow is a typical Yankee named Hoyt. He's from Vermont. Perfect Habits. Shrewd and as economical as possible.

"I had to get an easel of course and Pyle could get a $25 one for $12.60. Hoyt says Don't ye dew it! Make it. He made a slendid [sic] one for himself, lumber (hard pine), iron fixings and all cost four dollars or a little less. Now it's quite a piece of mechanism and needs a cabinetmaker's skill to make one so I bought his for five dollars and he's making himself a new one. . . . The rent for that fine studio is $4 a month. Note (models only 20¢ an hour).

". . . Mr. Pyle [is] stern but open hearted. Just think, he built an $8,000 studio just for the 'boys' as he called them. He says, 'I do this for them because it continually opens up new things to me. Besides it keeps me down to simple drawing which is at the bottom of any body's 'success.'

"He said he was very sorry that I did not come earlier for my work was very practical and looked promising (I have faint prospects of working for *Sat. Eve. Post* already). . . ."[1]

**November, 1902.** "Mr. Pyle lives at Chadds Ford until the middle of November and then moves to Wilmington for the winter, so now we have to come down here Sat. night to the composition lectures. It's almost fifteen miles from W. but only 10¢ carfare (steam).

"The country is elegant, very hilly, almost mountains, and very picturesque. The houses are made out of either stone or brick, and not a stone wall is to be seen.

"The house the boys have is a large brick mansion on top of a hill surrounded with large trees (which are still green), at one time Gen. Greene's headquarters. It's massive, each room having a huge fireplace, the windows being high with heavy paneling. The walls are hung with about 4 or $5,000 worth of Mr. Pyle's originals. He let them have them as long as they wished.

"They have a large orchard of fine eating apples of all sorts, grapes and peaches galore. They also have a large icehouse well filled. They get all this for $100 a year. We arrived here about 6 o'clock last evening. The house was lighted up by a couple of fellows who are still working down here, and every fireplace had a roaring fire in it which was certainly cheerful.

"After partaking of a lunch put up by Mrs. Simpers (our grubber) we straggled along toward Mr. Pyle's house about a mile distant. Reaching the house we walked around the spacious porch (an old colonial mansion, at one time Washington's headquarters, it's situated on the Brandywine River). We saw through the high windows a sight which impressed me much. There was Mr. Pyle reading, his face of great character intently bent on a book, and flocked around the rest of the table were five of his children reading or drawing and on one side Mrs. Pyle with the youngest child in her lap and at her feet a cat and dog lay asleep. Mr. Pyle has never been away from Mrs. Pyle one night since their marriage except once and that was two weeks ago.

**Old Pew.** ■ (From *Treasure Island* by Robert Louis Stevenson. Illustrated by N.C. Wyeth.)

"The composition lecture lasted two hours and it opened my eyes more than any talk I ever heard. It makes Pape look shallow. I could not help to tell you what he said. As to my composition (which was a load of hay stuck in the marsh, the horses urged by the men, one of the men at the wheel, the horses pulling to their utmost), Pyle, I am glad to say, mentioned the fact that the action was good. He told me the first thing where I had trouble, and what I had in mind to do but did not hold to my first idea. He seems to read one's mind. After the lecture we were invited to play ping-pong and in a short time we trudged home."[1]

**January 8, 1903.** Submitted an illustration to the Curtis Publishing Company, which appeared in the February edition of *The Saturday Evening Post*. ". . . The *Post* went wild over my cover and gave me $60 for it."[2]

**February, 1903.** Accepted as a member of the school after four months probation at the Howard Pyle School. "I was asked to Mr. Pyle's house yesterday as he wished to see me, and as near as I can remember this is what he said: 'Wyeth, I've been watching your work very closely and I see you have a great deal of talent but what you need is knowledge, that is, you have not had a good training and thereby no foundation. The man that you have studied with has filled you with ideas and put the right spirit into your work, but he himself, I can see, has had no training. Now, I'll give you the chance, seeing that you are determined and I know will make good use of your time, to enter my school and study with me for one year. I feel that I can teach you a great deal in that time and am positive that it will be of *great* value to you. But meanwhile you will have to drop all other outside work for publishers and devote your entire

**Wyeth with the completed illustration for "The Rakish Brigantine."**

attention to what I think is your most important work in preparation for your future art. Now consult your people and tell them as near as you can what I said. I want you to start Monday morning and from then on you are a member of the Pyle school.' "[1]

**March 16, 1903.** "Mr. Pyle has given me an ideal subject to work on; the subject is 'Indian Summer.' It's a hard one as I'm not aesthetic enough to tackle a poetic subject. But that's what I lack, Mr. P. claims, as he thinks my work too brutal and also that I'm not 'subtle' in my work—that is, for instance, if I'm drawing a man and a horse falling off a cliff, I'd have him on the way down into the deep chasm, man and horse in the air, or something to that effect; now he says to have the horse still on the cliff but make the horse look as if he was going to fall and that will make the observer say, 'Oh! I wish that man would hurry and jump off!' or, 'Why don't that horse jump to one side!' etc. See! he wants me to leave more to the imagination. On the whole I think I am getting along pretty well, but Oh! My! what a pile to learn! . . ." [1]

**May, 1903.** After seven months with Pyle, Wyeth was discouraged. "Oh! I'm having a struggle with my art. There is a great deal more to it than one thinks. In the class we are having facial construction which is terrible hard. I have great trouble in keeping or getting originality into my work. Last night in the composition class Mr. P. said that my work was fanciful and not based on real fact as I usually take Western or Canadian subjects.

"People can talk about art being a 'dead cinch' but they are mightily mistaken. Its grind, grind, grind all the time, from early until late." [1]

**June, 1903.** "I know I will paint something that will tell someday. Just give me time. I've fully decided what I will do. Not altogether Western life, but true, solid American subjects—nothing foreign about them. I have no enthusiasm to see Europe except perhaps the homes of my people and a mere curiosity to see the country, but nothing deeper.

"We had a big argument the other night in which I took up 'That we should work for the benefit of American Art and that there are just as great subjects here to paint.'

"My work lately to a certain degree has gone to pieces. I'm having difficulty technically and also with my color. But I can see myself that I have gone ahead and more so lately in the thinking part of it, which, after all, is the 'big thing.' Mr. P. prophesied that such would happen but in due season I would pick up and be so much the better for it. . . ." [1]

**1903.** Summer school at Chadds Ford with Howard Pyle. ". . . [F]or all days but Sat. and Sun. we get up from 6 to 6:15, breakfast at 6:30, 'Slick up' room and write letters and do odd jobs until 7:30, walk to studio (Old Grist Mill) about 1 m. distant, start work from model 8:00 and work until 12. Home to dinner and spend rest of the day on landscape, supper at 5:30 to 6, go swimming, play ball till dark and from then on *read or write*. Bed 10:30. Sat. we spend as we wish; I usually work on landscape. Sundays—Comp. class 9-11, home to dinner, fool around until 3:00 and thence up to Mr. Pyle's and play tennis, ping-pong, sing or anything we care to. Mr. P. joining in all the sports."[1]

**1904.** Received a commission for Charles Scribner's Sons which inaugurated his career as a book illustrator. "Wednesday I was in New York. My Russian 'sketch' was satisfactory and [I] was told to go on with it, but besides I got a book to illustrate (three illustrations) from Scribner's so will be busy for quite a spell. The illustration I am now at work on is a football picture, 'Hurdling the Line.' I have a boat race to make also and the third one I haven't decided on my subject."[1]

**August, 1904.** Graduated from the Howard Pyle School of Art.

**September 9, 1904.** "Mr. Pyle thinks it an excellent plan for me to go West for a month, so I immediately wrote to the Smithsonian in regards to the ceremonies carried on by the Utes of Utah. I have planned to go in October, which is a likely month for Indian Festivities."[1]

**September 29, 1904.** First trip West. The material Wyeth gathered from his Western trip was in demand for years. "Here I am in the *great West*, and I'll tell you it *is* the great West. After fifty-four hours of riding I reached Denver Tuesday night about 8:30. The ride as soon as I struck Nebraska was most interesting, but from New York to Iowa was simply terrible. Nothing but low flat prairie land full of bogs and sunken streams, dirty nasty little towns surrounded by poor farms of no importance and between these settlements nothing but grass and sky.

"But gradually I caught glimpses here and there of the life of which I have dreamed. First I saw the adobe shack or mud hut made of sods; these are scattered on the limitless plains, thirty and forty miles apart; sometimes around these dwellings would be a woman in a sun-bonnet watching the train pass, or a pony standing by the door patiently awaiting its rider, but usually these places were lifeless.—For a whole day we rode through the plains at the rate of sixty miles an hour, so you can imagine how much of this country I saw.

"Once looking ahead from the car window I made out a cloud of white alkali dust; of course I thought it some windstorm or possibly a stampede of cattle, but soon a black speck appeared and upon coming nearer it proved to be an old stage coming across country. It set me wild! The old driver up in the box with his high sombrero, a long bullwhip in his hand, blue shirt and vest, white kerchief around his neck, high-topped boots and all literally covered with this white dust. These things continually appeared, thus keeping me in a frenzy of excited expectation. . . . I leave Friday night for the plains. I go to a place called Deer Trail in the train and there get a horse and ride forty-five miles to the Hash Knife ranch where I expect to actually take part in the roundup, which happens in a few days.

"Up to date I have spent only about seven dollars since I left New York and that for grub and traveling necessities. But today I blow in my largest expense and that is for my

**She makes a grand light (The Burning of the Bounty).**
■ (From *The Bounty Trilogy* by Charles Nordhoff and James Norman Hall. Illustrated by N.C. Wyeth.)

outfit: saddle, bridle, pair of blankets, boots, spurs, breeches, chaps, slicker (rubber coat) and saddle blanket. This will reach up about $55. I have an experienced cowpuncher who has offered to pick me out a good saddle, which is a very serious and important acquisition.

"You have no idea of the wonderful hospitality of these western people—an easterner can't understand it until he has really experienced it, and I am experiencing it in its best form.

"I am gratified to think that my conceptions of the West were about right. In fact I feel perfectly at home here. All but with the cowpunchers; they are very quiet and reticent, but after a time when [they] find who you are and what purposes you are in their country for, they are sociable and willing to impart all the information they can."[1]

**October 19, 1904.** "Well here I am in *Denver*, back from the 'Roundup.' I have spent the wildest and most strenuous three weeks in my life. Everything happened that could happen, plenty to satisfy the most imaginative. The 'horse pitching' and 'bucking' was bounteous. This was because the horse herd consisted mostly of colts—something unusual. The spills and mishaps were numerous and fierce and one very dramatic thing happened which I shall make use of and that was the death of one of the cowboys. He was thrown and kicked to pieces. . . .

**Pen and ink drawings. ■** (From *Susanna and Sue* by Kate Douglas Wiggin. Illustrated by N.C. Wyeth.)

"For nine days I was in the saddle from 5:30 in the morning until dark, with a half hour taken out for noon 'chuck.' It is a steady strain on a fellow's physical endurance and not only that, but it keeps his nerve and grit in constant use to their limit. Nevertheless it's a grand training, well worth all the privations and hardships. I only wish I had such a training when I was younger. I find that I have the physical end of it, but my nerve and grit foil me at certain times. I've done things these last few weeks that I'd never dreamed I could have accomplished, but when the example is set by twenty or thirty reckless, half-wild men the same spirit is bound to catch all.

"I was never as well in body and mind as I am at present and I feel just like work. I have enjoyed a big room in one of Denver's buildings for a studio in which I am going to live and paint for a month or so. I have subjects enough to paint and they might keep me busy for some time."[1]

**December 14, 1904.** Homeward bound. "December fourteenth!—that glorious day!—What a pleasure it was to turn my face homeward, to follow once more and for the last time the winding trail that disappeared in the blinding rays of the *eastern sun*. What unbounded joy it was to know that in a comparatively short time I would be with my people again in my own dear home.

"Instantaneously I felt reluctant to leave those brutal and rugged mountains, the dry, scorching plains, to abandon for good that long dim trail that lay over the sandy desert like some big lazy snake asleep in the sun.

"How I hated to leave those Indians and how I shall miss the many long silent evenings spent with them in their 'hogans,' seated around a flaring pile of crackling piñon listening to the low plaintive moan of the wind as it swirled down the canyon.

"The life is wonderful, strange—the fascination of it clutches me like some unseen animal—it seems to whisper, 'Come back, you belong here, this is your real home.'"[1]

**1906.** Made his second and last trip West. When asked why he went West, Wyeth responded: "Every man, whether he is an artist or not, has what is commonly called a soul. Sooner or later he yearns to express his soul in some way. He may start out in search of the unusual, the novel or the bizarre, and if he is an artist, he may find certain satisfaction in the theatrical—the great western plains, for instance, where you see a speck on the horizon, and have to travel all day to reach it or you see a mountain that looks a few hours journey off, and you ride three days to get to it. You may have the greatest sympathy for the people you meet, for the picturesqueness of their life and their traditions and clothing—but the time comes when his soul gets restless, and he finds that he has been enjoying a show in which he really has no fundamental part.

"He finds that in order to express himself fully, he has got to come back to the soil he was born on, no matter where it is—it may be the glorious White Mountains of New Hampshire, or the woods of Needham—the call is imperative, he has got to answer it. There is something in his bones that comes right out of the soil he grew up on—something that gives him a power and contract communion with life which no other place gives him."[2]

**April 16, 1906.** Married Carolyn Bockius. ". . . I am in love with Miss Bockius, but I pride myself with a level head. I am no fool. Do you think for a minute I would do anything rash? What can you expect? Here I am down here, I am twenty-two years old. I am working just as hard as God will allow me, I do *no* running 'round as do some—my

**The Vedette. ■** (From *The Long Roll* by Mary Johnston. Illustrated by N.C. Wyeth.)

**I stood like one thunderstruck.** ■ (From *Robinson Crusoe* by Daniel DeFoe. Illustrated by N.C. Wyeth.)

**Robin Hood and the Men of the Greenwood.** ■ (From *Robin Hood* by Paul Creswick. Illustrated by N.C. Wyeth.)

mind is well centered on my work and plenty of that to do. Here is a young lady of great sensibility—of inspiring thought, one strongly appreciative of art, of nature and in many ways of my mind. She has taken a sincere interest in me and my work and it helps me to accomplish what I hope to do. . . . I shall stand by this girl my life throughout, and nobody can ever stop me. . . .

"After April 16th I'll have a home, a home located in the heart of my working atmosphere, a place to retreat, a place that is my own, one of rest, cheer and contentment."[1]

**Spring, 1906.** Career as an illustrator became well established. ". . . Mr. Pyle blew in like a whirlwind last Satur-

day and presented me with the leading article for *Mc-Clure's* for the coming months, or rather the months following August. The subject for the first installment is 'A Montana Hold-up.' I have already started it and it's most surely the strongest thing I ever did of its kind. . . .

"Then Mr. Pyle telegraphed for me from New York and I had to leave immediately. That broke into the 'spell' of the pictures terribly. But I went and met S. S. McClure and received an order for an 'Indian Cover.' 'An Indian playing on a reed, and in a canoe at moonrise,' to represent Indian summer, you know.

"My heavens, things are coming in so fast I don't know

which way to turn. Every chance seems better than the one preceding it. . . .

"By Jove! I'm beginning to believe that illustrating is as hard as any other work with the exception of, perhaps, shorter hours. I've stuck to it pretty steadily outside my western trips and I'm starting to feel it. . . .

"Mr. Pyle has made me a pretty fine offer which I will accept (in writing) this afternoon. The agreement is that I shall devote thirty weeks of my time out of one year to *McClure's* for $4,000 starting no later than July 15th. And furthermore they do not prohibit me from working for other magazines (a restriction that I fought against). You see this gives me a good living and also gives me time to paint, which I most certainly will do. . . ."[1]

**November, 1906.** ". . . Monday I went to New York with a picture for *Century* magazine which was very successful. I landed a big commission from *Scribner's,* one with *Century* and one with *McClure's.* They all want sets of pictures like the Roundup set only different subjects of course. When I returned I found a request for covers for *Ladies' Home Journal*—a firm offer to illustrate a Western story (book) from Chicago publishers, and a reserved order from the Cream of Wheat people for an advertising picture of Western life. I am at work on a big picture for the academy exhibition which is already *sold* to Mr. Krebs. I expect to get about $350 for it besides reproduction rights from *Scribner's.*

"'Fishing for Sturgeon' is the subject. . . ."[1]

**Melissa.** ■ (From *The Little Shepherd of Kingdom Come* by John Fox, Jr. Illustrated by N.C. Wyeth.)

**Captain Nemo.** ■ (From *The Mysterious Island* by Jules Verne. Illustrated by N.C. Wyeth.)

**December 16, 1906.** First child, Carolyn, died in infancy. "We lost our baby Friday morning about eight o'clock. It all transpired like one beautiful dream—but now that it is all over we must think and act philosophically—and we have.

"Dear Carolyn bears up wonderfully and from the minute her heart was almost broken she steadily acquired her normal control and now she seems to bathe in one perfect halo of beautiful thoughts and of wonderful inspirations. The sacrifice has been tremendous, but how it has lifted us and too, how much nearer together it has brought us. . . . How much akin to the beautiful is sorrow.

"I buried the little girl today in Mt. Lebanon cemetery [a little country cemetery beside an Old Quaker Meeting House in Rockland on the Brandywine near Chadds Ford], a beautiful secluded spot, one where Carol and I had often stopped to read the quaint inscriptions there and to walk through the quaint walks of boxwood."[1]

**June, 1907.** Began to feel a desire to do more serious painting than his successful illustrations allowed him to do. ". . . It has been *absolutely* evident to me the past six months of the uselessness of clinging to illustration and hoping to make it a *great* art. 'It is a stepping stone to painting,' so says Mr. Pyle—but I am convinced that it is a stepping stone backwards as well, which will in time leave you in that most unsatisfactory position of 'a good illustrator, but he has *done* his best work.'

"Now I'll tell you why. To begin with, an illustration must be made practical, not only in its dramatic statement, but it must be a thing that will adapt itself to the engravers' and

**Interior view of studio Wyeth built after illustrating *Treasure Island*, completed at the end of 1911.**

printers' limitations. This fact alone *kills* that underlying inspiration to create a thought. Instead of expressing that inner feeling you express the outward thought or imitation of that feeling, because a feeling is told by subtleties and an engraver cannot handle such delicate matter.

". . . To confirm that which I believe I *should* do have been many letters and words from different people in regards to the *Outing* pictures. I have not only heard from individual people, but three of the biggest magazines have sent congratulations, *Scribner's, McClure's* and *Collier's.* That is saying a good deal because the magazines as a rule vie with each other and show so much professional jealousy that they usually say *very* little.

"In every case have they mentioned the *poetry* that I succeeded in getting into the pictures and *not* the effect or action—I consider that a big victory! . . .

"Sometimes I believe I do not fit this life, this busy, bustling life. It does not allow me time to think, to expand, to grow naturally, slowly, healthfully. At times I feel as though I would walk over one of these hills into a secluded valley and lie down, and there remain to grow slowly, oh, so slowly!

"To come in contact with men who talk money, who want to buy me by piecemeal, and in searching for the best they get the worst, because they push and prod, they are disrespectful. They consider you a cog in their clattering machinery, and they drop a dirty check into your bearings that you will run the faster."[1]

**October 21, 1907.** Henriette Zirngiebel born. ". . . The event of my *25th* birthday is now indelibly stamped upon my memory and if all promises hold true to their being, I shall always have a *personal* reminder of the occasion.

"Everything happened and came off so beautifully! The day of the 21st Carolyn showed some signs that afterward proved to be symptoms—not that there was any pain, for there wasn't, only an unusual heaviness, and not at all until 11 o'clock did labor start—and it was all over at 12:45. Absolutely no unnecessary pain and as normal a birth as could possibly happen. . . ."[1]

**1908.** Moved from Wilmington to Chadds Ford, Pennsylvania. "I seem to be drawing closer and closer to the quiet 'domestic' farm life, so to speak. That which embodies poetry and rest. I'm just beginning to love the farm and *home* life of the country.

"The spirit of wandering and adventure is mainly a desire of the past.

"Another thing! I don't believe any man who ever painted a great big picture did so by wandering from one place to another searching for interesting material. By the gods! there's almost an inexhaustible supply of subjects right around my back door, meager as it is.

"I have come to the *full* conclusion that a man can only paint that which he knows even more than intimately, he has got to know it spiritually. And to do that he has got to live around it, in it, and be a *part* of it!

"I feel so moved sometimes toward nature that I could almost throw myself face down into a ploughed furrow—*ploughed* furrow understand! I love it so. The conventional humdrum life is so shallow and meaningless—it seems no more than existing! . . . "[1]

**October 26, 1909.** Daughter, Carolyn, born.

**1911.** Illustrated Robert Louis Stevenson's *Treasure Island,* beginning a thirty year commission for Scribner's Illustrated Classics. Apart from the books published by Scribner's, Wyeth illustrated a number of other books, for adults as well as children. ". . . Work abounds! and it is coming easily too. Have just completed an 'allegory' of summer and have started one of autumn. Both farm subjects. The Houghton Mifflin Co. sent a letter brimming with praise for the *War Time Lovers*—so that is done. With numerous ideas of my own, several definite commissions for sporting subjects, and *Treasure Island,* my summer is enshrouded in hidden pleasures (and no less, hidden struggles too, I suppose). But damn it! I believe I look forward to fights now—it adds zest; it's like putting sand on the track!

"Furthermore, I am feeling like a *man* now! I have bought the most glorious sight in this township for a home! No buildings, but a stunning location, exceptional water, the most enchanting, purliest, and most musical rock-bound brook flowing through it you can imagine—a handsome grove of black walnut trees, a wood lot (around the brook) of oak and beech, a hill looming up back of the 'house sight,' crowned on one side by a glorious ledge and nut trees, and a surrounding field of eight acres of the very best land, besides the section chosen for our house of four acres, and the lower field (clear and tillable) of six acres—eighteen in all.

"I paid $2,000 for it—and to have the deed in my hands gives me a new reason for living! . . .

"Thus culminates a deal I tried to put through a year ago. I'm totally satisfied that this is the little corner of the world wherein I shall work out my destiny. Later on, if the success of my work justifies it, I look forward to a summer cottage in New England—but here, I must acknowledge my soul comes nearer to the surface than any place I know. . . . "[1]

**July, 1911.** ". . . *Treasure Island* completed! I write that as though I were glad.—In one way I am—to know that I pulled through the entire set of seventeen canvases (almost as tall as I am) without one break in my enthusiasm and spirit. The result is I've turned out a set of pictures, without doubt far better in every quality than anything I ever did. Scribner's have expressed their delight over them by wire and letter several times. All this gives the right to feel jubilant and with no little satisfaction from the illustrating viewpoint.

"On the other hand, it was with regret that I packed the last canvas in the big box tonight. I so thoroughly enjoyed the work; I was for some reason able, throughout the series, to keep my pictures fresh and brilliant and striking in their variety of composition and color, dramatic incident and emotional quality. These features are what appealed to Scribner's, and which will, I am convinced, appeal to the public.

". . . Chas. Scribner said that he never in his experience with illustrators for fifty years knew of anyone who could catch the spirit of a theme and push it through with such vim and consistent strength as I can. A rather modest remark for me to pass on—however I am pleased that a man of his experience can say that of me. It bodes well for the future. . . . "[1]

**October 24, 1911.** First son, Nathaniel Convers Wyeth, born. "The little *tout* upstairs is a corker! There was a time (but now it is past) that I wondered just what N. C. stood for. I was inclined to believe (until Oct. 24th) it meant *Never Could.* . . . "[1]

**May, 1913.** First public exhibition of his work at the Pennsylvania Academy of Fine Arts. "It was 'varnishing day' at the Academy—a traditional term adapted, I believe, from the old custom in European galleries, to allow the *exhibitors* to view their works lining the walls, and to retouch or varnish out points that may need it. At one time, I believe, this was considered quite an event, but not now in these days of *clamor* and *rush,* when the *soul* of the artist is forgotten, and *subtleties* take a 'back seat,' in place of which is commercialism and ambition, to strike the clarion sound rather than the low throbbing sound of hidden mysteries. However, I must frankly state, if immodestly, that I was keyed to the highest pitch of eager anticipation: first, to see my own pictures on the wall, and secondly, to see what *others* had to say. I am confident that my eagerness to see *my own* was not the eagerness of one *ambitious* (this feeling I am inwardly proud of), but rather to study it from a fresh viewpoint and to note its carrying powers (technical and poetic) amid all the conflicting surroundings. As I said, my anticipation was intense.

"I went into the galleries wildly anxious to discover my canvases. I swept through the entire building without a discovery.—I grew feverishly anxious that by some mistake they were left out, or that I had been misinformed! Finally, I calmed myself enough to sensibly resort to a catalogue (which had not occurred to me before), and in it I found my name with only one canvas credited to me. For the instant I felt a keen disappointment, but with calm thinking threw it off and went to the gallery where it was hung. The poor thing was stuck on the top row (*skied* is the term) and looked as weak and flat as a pancake. It is needless to say that I was disappointed—in *myself.* The course of my mind at this juncture I cannot possibly put into words—a confusion of blasted hopes, disappointment, *encouragement* and determination may perhaps suggest slightly how I felt. However, I soon calmed myself.

"After reasonable consideration of 'the first-born' I proceeded through the exhibiton, which I enjoyed fully—(a salient proof of my equanimity).

**N.C. Wyeth, 1916.**

"(Of course I can't honestly say that my mind is entirely free of 'personal ambition'—it is *in* me, only I believe I have that tendency in subjugation. You know, *Emerson* even writes somewhere that he dared not trust himself with Fielding because he—Emerson—was not pure enough to interpret his writings.)

"This lengthy 'treatise,' this introspective analysis may make you ask, 'What's it all about?' Well, to speak frankly, *I don't know*. I of course realize that the experience marks an important moment in my life—superficially that it is my first attempt to exhibit, as a *painter,* and then in the deepest sense, the impressions made upon me will in some way affect my work hereafter.

"As to *this* day of peace and rest, I can speak more simply and to the point. I feel that a certain contentment has come over me, a feeling that another *hunk* of that weakness in my character has been laid aside for good—to *show* what I can do. (If I ever exhibit again, in a public exhibition, it will be because something I have is peculiarly adaptive or that 'bread and butter' bids me do it.) Furthermore, in placing even this plaintive weak whisper in the company of 300 other expressions, my eyes seemed to become suddenly *cleansed,* as it were, so that now I come back filled with a clearer vision of my *purpose* in art (not of my art and manner of expression understand, but a clarified understanding that I am placed here in this world to interpret what I see, *for* myself, and *not* for that public that *demands certain things*).

"The occasion has helped me to understand and appreciate more clearly how fortunate I am to be able to illustrate; in other words, to have a *practical* streak, that I can go through life, giving necessary comfort to those dependent upon me and to develop myself under normal conditions, which, made proper use of, should give me health and longevity, incidentally, *red* blood and *a* clear brain.'"[1]

**1913.** Illustrated *Kidnapped* by Robert Louis Stevenson. "My last group of *Kidnapped* created considerable enthusi-

asm, and if I am to judge by the demonstration, were better liked than the earlier ones. I am pleased, for it proved my power to sustain interest and enthusiasm, and perhaps to create an even stronger impetus for the last spring! I am gratified that I 'wound up strong.'"[1]

**March 16, 1915.** Daughter, Ann, born. "At 2:25 *Ann* was splitting the air with her cry!

"Carol kept saying she was afraid it was all a dream. But it's not—about as healthy a little chunk of humanity as you ever saw.

"The children are *wild!* and when we went for the mail this morning, they hailed all the town's folk as they passed and told them the news. The whole village was in a broad grin.'"[1]

**July 13, 1917.** Son, Andrew, born. Before Andrew was a year old, Wyeth recognized the possibility of artistic talent, which later made his son so famous. ". . . The new baby, Andrew, looks almost identically like Ann as I remember her the first day. So you can judge that in stature he is not unlike his grandfather for whom he is named. I think he will be dark; he has the wide eyes, short straight nose and square shoulders (with a goodly chest) which coincide with our sturdy dad. Won't it be strange if he resembles his granddad as nearly as Henriette does her grandmother! . . .

"Andrew is pegging along again nearer the way he should. I think he's the most sensitive and spiritual little body I ever saw. Henriette said last night, as she was looking into his face, 'He looks as though he were going to be a great composer or artist.' That's just it; even as young as he is the power of reflection in his eyes is astonishing.'"[1]

**1919.** Illustrated a book a year, producing some 3,000 illustrations. "The juvenile book field has opened very wide for me, offering splendid opportunities from half a dozen directions, so attractive, in fact, that I am unable to further refuse such tempting propositions. Result: I have con-

**Andy and N.C. Wyeth on Cannibal shore.**

**Self-portrait, 1918.**

tracted to do *Robinson Crusoe*—*twenty* pictures, with originals back, $1,000 down when first three drawings are delivered, and 25¢ royalty on every book after the $1,000 has been worked off at the same rate. This book is for the Cosmopolitan Book Corporation, who are going to advertise it lavishly, devoting editorial space, personal interview articles (with me) and newspaper full-pages all over the country. With no advertising to speak of, Scribner's have sold (advance sale) nearly 10,000 copies of *The Last of the Mohicans*—the Book Corporation claim that they will easily *double* this at least, which will mean $3,000 extra, besides the advance payment. And I get the originals back! An item of great importance which Scribner's would never agree to. They have made a mistake, for with originals back, as I have vainly requested in each contract, I think I would have stuck by them.

"And then *Rip Van Winkle* for McKay in 1921, with *originals back*—price to be paid outright not decided upon yet.

"I seem to be talking a lot about *remuneration,* but the trouble is I haven't thought of it enough before. After all is settled I shall think of it no more. *Westward Ho!* (Kingsley), which was practically agreed upon at Scribner's as my next book, I have read and have already schemed my layout. Scribner's have withheld their contract for so long,

and now with this last *bomb* of mine I don't know whether I'm to do it or not. It's a wonderful story, almost the richest in interest and color I ever read."[1]

**December, 1919.** "My *Miles Standish* cover is done, and I'm highly pleased with it! *Westward Ho!* cover is drawn in and ready for color and looks very promising indeed.

"I feel that this work is all going to come along with real swing and gusto. I want to make Houghton Mifflin the best Xmas books they ever had!"[1]

**1923-25.** "Starting with Carol's illness in 1923 we have passed through a succession of intense worries: the greatest of these (the pressing weight of which is upon us now) is the slow passing of my Mother, who is bearing up heroically under the doom of a fatal cancer. It is just a year to the week that the knowledge of her affliction has been known to us, and in that year we passed through with her what must be worse than death—a complete nervous collapse which rendered her completely helpless both in mind and body. For a time we looked for the end almost daily, when, to the astonishment of all the doctors, my mother made an emphatic turn for the better and on April 1st was able to return home from the sanitorium completely re-

(Cover illustration from *Ladies' Home Journal,* March, 1922.)

stored in her mind and miraculously resigned to meet the inevitable.

"Her physical strength was naturally considerably reduced, but she embraced the few months of grace with a demonstrative thankfulness and enthusiasm which has impressed me as a miracle might do. To take part, as I have, every

two weeks, in the resurrected life of my mother and father—and they with supreme composure facing what so surely lies ahead of them is the most awe-inspiring, the most moving experience I ever had!

"But yesterday a letter from my dad tells of an obvious failing, and I shall leave here Wednesday with two of the

**"The Giant," 1923. The children (from left) are William Clothier Engle (in whose memory the mural was painted), Henriette Wyeth, Ann Wyeth, Andrew Wyeth, Nathaniel Wyeth, Carolyn Wyeth.** ■ (Courtesy of and reprints available from Westtown School, Westtown, Pa.)

**And Lawless, keeping half a step in front of his companion. . . studied out their path.** ■ (From
*The Black Arrow* by Robert Louis Stevenson. Illustrated by N.C. Wyeth.)

**But whaur Tam hung there was neathing but the craig, and the sea belaw, and the solans skirling and flying.** ■ (From *David Balfour* by Robert Louis Stevenson. Illustrated by N.C. Wyeth.)

children whom my mother has not seen lately, to visit her.

"In September last, in the midst of the most depressing period of my mother's illness, little Ann was suddenly operated on for appendicitis. Her rugged health pulled her through peritonitis, but not after a torturing struggle of nearly seven weeks. . . .

"Of course my work had to go on, not only on account of promises and contracts, but for relaxation.

"I have almost a feeling of irreverence when I say that my work, in spite of all, has advanced, and that the future is offering singular opportunities if I can but rise to them.

"The two years represent much work accomplished; a little of it augurs well, some of it resulting indifferently taught me a great deal, and the balance pretty much a failure.

"Besides the usual amount of illustration, I have painted eight large panels averaging 15 X 20 feet and one of them 15 X 30. Five of these are in the First National Bank in Boston—those three others in the Roosevelt Hotel, New York. They have brought me, besides much helpful criticism, an embarrassment of opportunities which I have had to turn aside ruthlessly. I am, so far, rather pleased with my courage to preserve my time and not submit to overwhelming commissions.

"The apotheosis of Franklin for the Franklin Bank, 42nd St., New York will occupy me the coming year, starting Sept. 15th."[1]

**August 11, 1925.** Mother died. ". . . When I walked into the parlor that Thursday morning and looked upon her powerful face, at last calm and serene, I resolved in words, . . . to carry on for her sake into a more important field, an approach nearer to the great possibilities which she . . . gave to me.

"I feel that I have taken the first definite step."[1]

**End of the 1920's.** Became more involved in what Wyeth considered "serious" painting. "I am becoming more encouraged and have sufficient reason to believe that in time I will emerge into the painter's field. I am looking forward to this with all my heart. I am not covetous of gallery honors in this new and superior department of art. It is wholly a desire for more personal and therefore more powerful expression that I seek.

". . . As one self-evident measurement of values, let me say this: that illustration has existed from the beginning of the history of art; in fact, early painting amounted to illustration and nothing more—these early examples remain with us today as a matter of historic interest and not artistic. But since the development of the painter's art into the higher forms of expression, as in Michelangelo, the result [is] of one fundamental trait—an uncontrollable desire to express one's personal feelings toward life. This constant 'welling up' within one can no more be ignored nor suppressed than the feelings of hunger or thirst.

"I suppose the bottommost mistake of all is the prevailing attitude that art is a form of entertainment—a passing diversion."[1]

**February, 1939.** Visited Florida to gather material for illustrating Marjorie Kinnan Rawling's, *The Yearling*.

"'Marge,' as everyone around here calls Mrs. Rawlings, is not especially interesting nor prepossessing in appearance. She's a bit younger than we expected, and although weather-beaten and tough-fibered looking, she looks not very happy, pretty nervous and at loose ends. It may be it is because she's divorced. But she has given heartily of her time and interest and has put me in contact with just the types of backwoods people I wanted to see, and the experience has been quite thrilling. . . .

"Yesterday evening Leonard, the guide, a youngish chap that Canny Boone would have surely selected as a buddy, took me about forty miles into the wilderness to see some captive bears (belonging to Frank Buck, a young fellow was in charge), so saw all I needed to help me in the picturization of old Slewfoot. They all know *The Yearling* and are extremely fond of it, and so many places and things are named after the features in the book. So in this case they had 'Old Slewfoot' in captivity. He's blind and about twenty-four years old, but is large, weighing about 400 lbs., and according to the keeper, 'as gentle as a kitten.' He is kept in a circular corral about thirty yards across and very high, with the few tall yellow pines standing in the enclosure covered part way up with sheet zinc. This was to prevent a large panther, who occupied the same space, from climbing the trees and making a desperate leap to freedom.

"We went to the door of the corral, scratched the bear's head through the wire, then I was invited to come inside to take my photographs. As I walked in, assured in the meantime that the panther was shut in his house cage with the sliding door, the huge old bear caught the scent of a stranger and by means of his keen smell followed directly after me. Well, it may have been perfectly safe and all that, but it was a queer feeling, and the keeper must have felt a little dubious about the bear's action because he headed him off gently with a small stick tapping him on the snout. In the meantime I was quickly snapping some photos. Suddenly old Slewfoot made the quickest pass with that great paw of his you can imagine, and caught the top of the keeper's leather riding-boot and ripped it to his instep, belching a growl and showing his teeth with all the approved fixings. Leonard was in there too and grinned broadly to see me step slowly but steadily toward the door—but I noticed he followed me. The young keeper's nerve was fine though, for he cracked down on the bear's nose with his stick and in five minutes had him sitting dog fashion and scratching his head with his fingers.

"As if this weren't enough excitement for the time—we stood by the closed door, discussing the incident, when we were astonished to observe the panther walk out from behind some scrub growth at the other side of the corral! He'd been lying there all the time! The glances that passed between my bear hunter and the keeper were significant enough. In fact, the keeper asked me not to mention the incident to anyone in Ocala or Silver Springs as he might lose his job.

"I feel ready to tackle *The Yearling* in pictures, and wish I were home and at it now."[1]

**1939.** Son, Andrew, was becoming successful as an artist. Wyeth encouraged all of his children in their endeavors. Henriette and Carolyn were artists, his daughter, Ann, was a composer, and his son, Nathaniel, was an engineer. "The habit of self-conscious picture-building is one phase I have consciously in my teaching tried to avoid. From the time

[Andy] started regular study in the studio at the age of thirteen, I have endeavored to make every phase of academic procedure exciting: from his first studies in perspective, the application of it to cubes, spheres and pyramids, through cast-drawing and still-life painting, and finally figure study and landscape. All this was strictly *objective* teaching—purely representational study, free as possible of mannerisms or stunts. The exciting memories of this succession of his studies are very much alive in my mind, and I am especially happy to say that he can still turn to a pure and simple academic problem with great intrinsic and sustained enthusiasm. This faculty, if kept alive, will, for all his life, be the source of progressive artistic development and unfolding.

"From this long training and contact with factual things, he has not only learned to draw them as they *are,* but has learned to love them for their spiritual values. The factual knowledge of the shape and proportion of a jug has unlocked a fascination for that object, which reveals to him the shape of its insides as well as the phenomena of its hollowness, its weight, its pressure on the ground, its smell, its displacement of air.

"To my mind the aliveness of all our senses at every moment will produce virile expression in art. So you see the training, as he received it, was exciting. The shift from Andy's academic period into creative painting was hardly a shift at all; it was a natural and almost imperceptible transition.

"No one knows more precisely than I do that Andy has only scratched the surface and great problems lie before him. He knows that too, down to the bottom of his feet!

"Andy eats, dreams and sleeps with a deep faith that watercolor has infinite possibilities of power and beauty which have never been touched. He has an unmovable right to this belief, and his search to prove this truth will be, of course, a long, arduous one. The road he travels will doubtlessly be cluttered with variable results.

"Andy's roots are in the ground. I feel exceptionally secure in his emotional potentiality—the quality which gives art its only valid reason to exist.

"As long as I live or just as long as my influence lasts, I will encourage anything the boy wants to do, in any way he wants to do it, providing it promises to forge a link toward greater knowledge and greater power.

"His spirit runs too high to miss doing something every once in awhile in the nature of a fulfillment of a good picture, but these must come like words underscored in a letter, only occasionally."[1]

**1941.** Elected to the National Academy. "This has been, I believe, the busiest winter I have ever put in. Just what the expended effort will represent in accrued knowledge and painting progress is impossible for me to even speculate upon. My main enthusiasms are, as always, it seems, in the *next* thing to be tried, or in some less tangible dream in the future.

"Both Andy and I have submitted panels to the Corcoran (no word yet of our luck). I have two shows of illustrations opening today—twenty in Philadelphia and fifteen in Clearwater, Florida.

"Several possibilities to dispose of the *Children's Anthology* pictures, also *The Yearling* set, are in the wind, but expect nothing to come of it.

"The *nobility* of an artist's personal effort which is springing from the discipline of truth, the richness of understanding, and unmistakably reaching toward the stars, seems only to affect the majority of current commentators—first with suspicion, and thence with boredom.

"Doubtless there are many discriminating people who love the painter's art, who do not recognize or are not bothered by press and art magazine reviews; yet I cannot but think that a sufficient weight of professional opinion, based upon broader understanding, sounder knowledge, and greater vision, with intent to seek out *potentialities* amongst the works of contemporaries, rather than the clever accomplishments of the moment, could not only be a stimulation to the artists themselves but would clarify, for a badly befuddled public, a very muddy situation."[1]

**1943.** Wyeth turned to serious painting, but continued to do commissioned work as well. "Only out of truth can be born a valid personal expression. All the 'natural' talents of youth cannot take the place of *disciplined training*. Beethoven was a prodigy as a boy pianist, but witness the infinite and painstaking training which followed his initial flowering. Without this exhaustive discipline we would never have had the Beethoven of the nine symphonies.

"The theory that a successful and productive artist makes an extraordinary good teacher is entirely wrong. I realize that this point of view contradicts what we used to believe at Home was the truth. I have learned, through hard experience, to know better.

"The obscure and *academic* teachers have always, as the history of art proves, been the important ones. These teachers teach only of the literal truth and do not try to inoculate personal and pet theories into their students, for the simple reason that they *haven't* any.

"Personally, I am spending the remainder of my life in an effort to undo what Reed and Howard Pyle infected me with. (I do not say this with malice for they were extremely generous men.) What I got from both of them, especially Pyle, enabled me to win a living and some fame (neither of which interests me very much now) but denied me the opportunity to release my own personality.

"You might say that my own boy Andy's success and promise is a contradiction of what I have just said. But that would be entirely *wrong* for I never, for a *moment,* attempted to step out of the field of strict academic training in all the years I disciplined him in cast drawing, life and landscape. Of course he profited, I like to think, from the constant influence around him of the best music, the best prints, the best books, in the field of emotional expression, *plus* the sound living of a normal life of duties and experience within the home here in Chadds Ford.

"Art schools, where they dispense *sound* training, are hard to find these days—this is a dreadful thought to contemplate. It's like saying that there are no true teachers of the pianoforte or of the exacting knowledge required for musical composition. What would happen to music if this were so!"[1]

**Wyeth, 1944. Photo by William E. Phelps.**

**1945.** Received an honorary degree from Bowdoin College. "... I know from my own experience that when I create with any degree of strength and beauty I have had no thought of consequences. Anyone who creates for *effect*—to score a hit—does not know what he is missing!

"This period of unprecedented distractions and overstimulation constitutes a fierce antagonist to the accomplishments of the spirit. Whatever is worth discovery in one's heart and mind can only rise to the surface among quiet conditions, in which one thought grows beside another and one has time to compare and reflect. Periods of bleak thinking and austere feeling, that kind that cuts to the bone, are imperative. Experiences which so often masquerade for cultural influences are so often merely cozy and sociable. ...

"... Truly magnanimous people have no vanity, no jealousy; they have no reserves and they feed on the true and solid wherever they find it. What is more, they find it everywhere.

"There is little doubt that the modern mind is opposed to the romantic mind. The modern mind is mainly content to ask and seek causes and consequences—whereas the romantic mind seeks the *significance* of things. The romantic

mind must be restored to its necessary place of leadership. If things have no *significance* things are hollow!

"The greats in all the arts have been primarily romanticists and realists (the two cannot be separated). They interpreted life as they saw it, but, 'through every line's being' soaked in the consciousness of an object, one is bound to feel, beside life as it is, the life that ought to be, and it is *that* that captivates us! All great painting is something that enriches and enhances life, something that makes it higher, wider, and deeper.

"'A great painter is a great man painting.'

"Sound feeling can only exist in a man who is living on all sides the life that is natural to man. Only through this experience can he sense his times and avoid that ever-lurking pitfall of egocentricism. Someone, uncommonly wise, said, 'Nothing is so poor and melancholy as art that is interested in itself and not its subject.'

"To live, to keep one's eyes wide open in wonder, to be surprised by things!

"Here's a quote which I think will interest you—'Great painting like Bach's music, in texture closely woven, subdued like the early Gobelin tapestries, no emphasis, no climaxes, no beginnings or endings, merely resumptions and transitions, a design so sustained that there is no effort in starting and every casual statement is equally great.'

"But of course such depth presupposes another mode of feeling. One has to be a Bach before one can paint in his power and richness. Depth of style can only spring from a deepening of our emotional life. *That* is what we really demand and look for!"[1]

**October 19, 1945.** Three days before his 63rd birthday, Wyeth and his grandson were killed when his car was struck by a train near his home in Chadds Ford. ". . . As I grow older, each season as it progresses becomes more beautiful than anything I ever saw, and then as it merges into the following one my emotions and loves seem to run still higher until at times I feel as though my sense of appreciation *must* break. . . ."[1]

*FOR MORE INFORMATION SEE:* Ernest W. Watson, *Forty Illustrators and How They Work,* Watson-Guptill, 1946; Dudley Lunt, "N. C. Wyeth, 1882-1945," *Horn Book,* September, 1946; (for children) Stanley J. Kunitz and Howard Haycraft, editors, *Junior Book of Authors,* second edition revised, 1951; "Stouthearted Heroes of a Beloved Painter," *Life,* December 9, 1957; Loring Holmes Dodd, *Generation of Illustrators and Etchers,* Chapman & Grimes, 1960; Henry C. Pitz, "N. C. Wyeth," *American Heritage,* October, 1965; Stimson Wyeth, "My Brother, N. C. Wyeth," *Horn Book,* February, 1969; Betsy James Wyeth, editor, *The Wyeths: The Letters of N. C. Wyeth, 1901-1945,* Gambit, 1971; Douglas Allen and Douglas Allen, Jr., *N. C. Wyeth: The Collected Paintings, Illustrations, and Murals,* Crown, 1972.

# YONGE, Charlotte Mary   1823-1901

*PERSONAL:* Surname pronounced Young; born August 11, 1823, in Otterbourne, Hampshire, England; died March 24, 1901, in Elderfield, England; daughter of William Crawley (a retired army officer) and Frances Mary (Bargus) Yonge. *Education:* Educated at home by her father. *Home:* Otterbourne, England.

*CAREER:* Novelist and author of books for children. Editor of the *Monthly Packet,* a periodical for young people, 1851-90, as well as *Monthly Paper of Sunday Teaching,* 1860-75, and *Mothers in Council,* 1890. Taught in the village Sunday School, 1830-1901, and also in the village school.

*WRITINGS*—Fiction: *Abbey Church; or, Self-Control and Self-Conceit,* J. Burns, 1844, reissued, Garland, 1975; *Scenes and Characters; or, Eighteen Months at Beechcroft,* Mozley, 1847 [another edition illustrated by W. J. Hennessy, Macmillan, 1886]; *Langley School,* Mozley, 1850; *Henrietta's Wish; or, Domineering,* Masters, 1850, G. Munro, 1885; *Kenneth; or, The Rearguard of the Grand Army,* J. W. Parker, 1850; *The Two Guardians; or, Home in This World,* Masters, 1852; *The Heir of Redclyffe,* J. W. Parker, 1853, Appleton, 1861, reprinted Scholarly Press, 1971 [another edition illustrated by Kate Greenaway, Macmillan, 1891]; *The Herb of the Field,* Mozley, 1853, Macmillan, 1887; *The Little Duke; or, Richard the Fearless,* J. W. Parker, 1854, also published as *Richard the Fearless; or, The Little Duke,* Appleton, 1856 [other editions illustrated by Dora Curtis,

Dutton, 1910; Beatrice Stevens, Duffield, 1923; Marguerite De Angeli, Macmillan, 1927; George Lawson, Saafield Publishing, 1932; Dorothy Bayley, Appleton-Century, 1936; Federico Castellon, Macmillan, 1954; Tom O'Sullivan, Junior Deluxe Editions, 1955]; *The Castle Builders; or, The Deferred Confirmation,* [New York], 1854, reissued, Garland, 1975; *Heartsease; or, The Brother's Wife,* J. W. Parker, 1854, Appleton, 1861 [another edition illustrated by K. Greenaway, Macmillan, 1902].

*The Lances of Lynwood,* J. W. Parker, 1855, Appleton, 1856 [another edition illustrated by M. De Angeli, Macmillan, 1929]; *The History of Sir Thomas Thumb,* [London], 1855; *Leonard the Lion-Heart,* Mozley, 1856; *The Daisy Chain; or, Aspirations: A Family Chronicle,* J. W. Parker, 1856, Appleton, 1875 [another edition illustrated by J. Priestman Atkinson, Macmillan, 1881]; *Dynevor Terrace; or, The Clue of Life,* Appleton, 1857; *The Christmas Mummers,* Mozley, 1858; *The Strayed Falcon,* [London], 1860; *The Mice at Play,* [London], 1860; *Hopes and Fears; or, Scenes from the Life of a Spinster,* J. W. Parker, 1860, Appleton, 1861; *The Pigeon Pie,* Mozley, 1860, Roberts Brothers, 1869; *The Young Stepmother,* [London], 1861; *The Stokesley Secret,* Derby, 1861, Appleton, 1862; *The Wars of Wapsburgh,* [London], 1862; *Countess Kate,* Mozley, 1862 [another edition illustrated by Gwen Raverat, Random House, 1960]; *Sea Spleenwort, and Other Stories,* Groombridge, 1863; *The Apple of Discord* (play), Groombridge, 1864; *The Trial: More Links of the Daisy Chain,* Appleton, 1864 [another edition illustrated by J. P. Atkinson, Macmillan, 1902].

*The Prince and the Page: A Tale of the Crusade,* Macmillan, 1865 [another edition illustrated by M. De Angeli, Macmillan, 1925]; *The Clever Woman of the Family,* Appleton, 1865, reissued, Garland, 1975; *The Dove in the Eagle's Nest,* Appleton, 1866 [other editions illustrated by W. J. Hennessy, Macmillan, 1901; B. Stevens, Duffield, 1924; M. De Angeli, Macmillan, 1926]; *The Six Cushions,* Mozley, 1867; *The Danvers Papers: An Invention,* Macmillan, 1867; *New Ground (Kaffirland),* Mozley, 1868; *The Chaplet of Pearls; or, The White and Black Ribaumont,* Macmillan, 1868, Appleton, 1869 [other editions illustrated by W. J. Hennessy, Macmillan, 1903; Hazel Ives, L. C. Page, 1926]; *Friarswood Post Office,* Mozley, 1869; *The Caged Lion,* Macmillan, 1870, G. Munro, 1886; *Little Lucy's Wonderful Globe* (illustrated by L. Froelich), Macmillan, 1871 [another edition illustrated by Ann M. Peck, Harper, 1927]; *Journal of Lacy Beatrix Graham, Sister of the Marquis of Montrose,* Bell & Daldy, 1871; *P's and Q's; or, The Question of Putting Upon,* [London], 1872; *The Pillars of the House; or, Under Wode, under Rode,* Macmillan, 1873 ]another edition illustrated by Herbert Gandy, Macmillan, 1901]; *Lady Hester; or, Ursula's Narrative,* Macmillan, 1874.

*My Young Alcides: A Faded Photograph,* Macmillan, 1875; *The Three Brides,* Macmillan, 1876, G. Munro, 1884; *The Disturbing Element,* M. Ward, 1878; *Magnum Bonum; or, Mother Carey's Brood,* Macmillan, 1879, reissued, Garland, 1975; *Burnt Out: A Story for Mothers' Meetings,* W. Smith, 1879-80; *Love and Life: An Old Story in Eighteenth Century Costume,* Harper, 1880; *Cheap Jack,* W. Smith, 1880; *Bye-Words: A Collection of Tales, New and Old,* Macmillan, 1880; *Aunt Charlotte's Picture-Books,* R. Worthington, 1881; *Aunt Charlotte's Nursery-Book,* R. Worthington, 1881; *Aunt Charlotte's Golden Gift,* R. Worthington, 1881; *Lads and Lasses of Langley,* W. Smith, 1881-82; *Talks about the Laws We Live Under; or, At Langley Night-School,* W. Smith, 1882; *Edina's Trousseau,* G. Munro, 1882; *Langley Little Ones,* W. Smith, 1882; *Pickle and His Page-Boy; or,*

*Unlooked For*, W. Smith, 1882; *Sowing and Sewing: A Sexagesima Story*, W. Smith, 1882; *Given to Hospitality*, W. Smith, 1882; *Wolf*, W. Smith, 1882; *Frank's Debt*, W. Smith, 1882; *Unknown to History: A Story of the Captivity of Mary of Scotland* (illustrated by J. W. Hennessy), Harper, 1882, reprinted, Tom Stacey Reprints, 1972 [another edition illustrated by Clara M. Burd, Harper, 1927]; *Langley Adventures*, W. Smith, 1883, Dutton, 1884; *Stray Pearls: Memoirs of Margaret de Ribaumont, Viscountess of Bellaise*, Harper, 1883; (with others) *The Miz-Maze; or, The Winkworth Puzzle: A Story in Letters*, Macmillan, 1883; *The Armourer's Prentices*, G. Munro, 1884.

*Nuttie's Father*, G. Munro, 1885; *The Two Sides of the Shield*, G. Munro, 1885; *Pixie Lawn*, Skeffington, 1885; *Little Rickburners*, Skeffington, 1886; (with J. B. Gould) *Just One More Tale*, Skeffington, 1886; *A Modern Telemachus*, Harper, 1886; *Chantry House*, G. Munro, 1886; *Under the Storm; or, Steadfast's Charge*, G. Munro, 1887; *Beechcroft at Rockstone*, Macmillan, 1888, G. Munro, 1889; *Our New Mistress; or, Change at Brookfield Earl*, G. Munro, 1888; *Nurse's Memories*, Eyre & Spottiswoode, 1888; (with others) *Astray: A Tale of a Country Town*, Hatchards, 1888; *Neighbour's Fare*, Skeffington, 1889; *A Reputed Changeling; or, Three Seventh Years Two Centuries Ago*, Macmillan, 1889; *The Cunning Woman's Grandson: A Tale of Cheddar a Hundred Years Ago*, National Society, 1889; *More Bye-Words*, Macmillan, 1890; *Two Penniless Princesses*, Macmillan, 1891 [another edition illustrated by Stafford C. Good, Macmillan, 1931]; *Old Times at Otterbourne*, Warren, 1891; *The Constable's Tower; or, The Times of Magna Charta*, T. Whittaker, 1891; *That Stick*, Macmillan, 1892; *An Old Woman's Outlook in a Hampshire Village*, Macmillan,

**Charlotte Yonge and her mother, photographed by Lewis Carroll.**

1892; (with Christabel R. Coleridge) *Strolling Players: A Harmony of Contrasts*, Macmillan, 1893; *The Girl's Little Book*, Skeffington, 1893; *The Treasures in the Marshes* (illustrated by W. S. Stacey), T. Whittaker, 1893; *Grisly Grisell; or, The Laidly Lady of Whitburn: A Tale of the Wars of the Roses*, Macmillan, 1893; *The Rubies of St. Lo*, Macmillan, 1894; *The Cook and the Captive; or, Attalus the Hostage* (illustrated by W. S. Stacey), T. Whittaker, 1894.

*The Long Vacation*, Macmillan, 1895; *The Carbonels* (illustrated by W. S. Stacey), T. Whittaker, 1895; *The Release; or, Caroline's French Kindred*, Macmillan, 1896; *The Wardship of Steepcoombe* (illustrated by W. S. Stacey), T. Whittaker, 1896; *Founded on Paper; or, Uphill and Downhill between the Two Jubilees* (illustrated by W. S. Stacey), T. Whittaker, 1897; *The Pilgrimage of Ben Beriah*, Macmillan, 1897; *The Patriots of Palestine: A Story of the Maccabees* (illustrated by W. S. Stacey), T. Whittaker, 1898; *The Herd Boy and His Hermit* (illustrated by W. S. Stacey), T. Whittaker, 1899; *Modern Broods; or, Developments Unlooked For*, Macmillan, 1900.

Histories: *The Kings of England: A History for Young Children*, Mozley, 1848; *Landmarks of History: Ancient History from the Earliest Times to the Mahometan Conquest*, Mozley, 1852; *Landmarks of History: Middle Ages from the Reign of Charlemagne to That of Charles V*, Mozley, 1853; *Landmarks of History: Modern History from the Reformation to the Fall of Napoleon*, Mozley, 1857; *History of Christian Names*, J. W. Parker, 1863, reprinted, Gale, 1966; *Cameos from English History, from Rollo to Edward II*, Macmillan, 1868; *The Pupils of St. John the Divine*, Macmillan, 1868; *A Book of Worthies*, Macmillan, 1869; *A Parallel History of France and England, consisting of Outlines and Dates*, Macmillan, 1871; *History of France*, [London], 1872,

**Charlotte Mary Yonge, age 20.**

**Elderfield, Otterbourne**

Holt, 1879; *Aunt Charlotte's Stories of English History for the Little Ones*, M. Ward, 1873, published in America as *Young Folks' History of England*, Estes & Lauriat, 1879.

*Aunt Charlotte's Stories of Bible History for the Little Ones*, M. Ward, 1875, published in America as *Young Folks' Bible History*, Lothrop, 1881; *Aunt Charlotte's Stories of Greek History for the Little Ones*, M. Ward, 1876, published in America as *Young Folks' History of Greece*, Lothrop, 1878; *Eighteen Centuries of Beginnings of Church History*, Mozley, 1876-79; *Aunt Charlotte's Stories of German History for the Little Ones*, M. Ward, 1877, published in America as *Young Folks' History of Germany*, Lothrop, 1878; *Aunt Charlotte's Stories of Roman History for the Little Ones*, M. Ward, 1877, published in America as *Young Folks' History of Rome*, Lothrop, 1879; *The Story of the Christians and Moors of Spain*, Macmillan, 1878; *Aunt Charlotte's Stories of French History for the Little Ones*, M. Ward, circa 1879, published in America as *Young Folks' History of France*, Estes & Lauriat, 1879; *A Pictorial History of the World's Great Nations, from the Earliest Dates to the Present Time*, S. Hess, 1882; *Landmarks of Recent History*, W. Smith, 1883; *English Church History*, National Society, 1883; (with H. Hastings Weld) *Aunt Charlotte's Stories of American History*, Appleton, 1883; *The Victorian Half-Century: A Jubilee Book*, Macmillan, 1887; *Deacon's Book of Dates: A Manual of the World's Chief Historical Landmarks*, C. W. Deacon, 1888; *John Keble's Parishes: A History of Hursley and Otterbourne*, Macmillan, 1898.

Other non-fiction: *The Instructive Picture-Book; or, Lessons from the Vegetable World*, [Edinburgh], 1857; *Conversations on the Catechism*, Mozley, 1859-62; *A Book of Golden Deeds of All Times and All Lands*, Macmillan, 1864, Sever & Francis, 1866 [another edition illustrated by Clara M. Burd, Macmillan, 1927]; *Keynotes of the First Lessons for Every Day in the Year*, Society for Promoting Christian Knowledge, 1869; *The Seal; or, Inward Spiritual Grace of Confirmation*, [London], 1869; *Scripture Readings for Schools, with Comments*, Macmillan, 1871; *Musings over the "Christian Year" and "Lyra Innocentium,"* Appleton, 1871; *Pioneers and Founders; or, Recent Workers in the Mission Field*, Macmillan, 1871; *Questions on the Prayer-Book*, [London], 1872; *In Memoriam, Bishop Patteson*, [London], 1872; *Questions on the Colleges*, Mozley, 1874; *Questions on the Epistles*, Mozley, 1874; *Life of John Coleridge Patteson, Missionary Bishop of the Melanesian Islands*, Macmillan, 1874.

*Questions on the Gospels*, Mozley, 1875; *Memoir of G. C. Harris*, Macmillan, 1875; *Womankind*, Macmillan, 1877; *Verses on the Gospels*, W. Smith, 1880; *How to Teach the New Testament*, National Society, 1881; *Aunt Charlotte's Evenings at Home with the Poets*, M. Ward, 1881; *Practical Work in Sunday Schools*, National Society, 1881; *Questions on the Psalms*, Hurst, 1881; *English History-Reading Books, Adapted to the Requirements of the New Code*, National Society, 1881-85; *A Key to the Waverley Novels*, Ginn, Heath, 1885; *Teachings on the Catechism for the Little Ones*, W. Smith, 1886; *What Books to Lend and What to Give*, National Society, 1887; *Practical Work in Schools*, E. L. Kellogg, 1888; *Preparation of Prayer-Book Lessons*, W. Smith, 1888; *Hannah More*, Roberts Brothers, 1888, reprinted, Folcroft, 1976; *The Parents Power: Address to the Conference of the Mothers' Union*, Warren, 1889; *Life of H. R. H., the Prince Consort*, W. H. Allen, 1890; *The Slaves of*

*Sabinus, Jew, and Gentile*, National Society, 1890; *Westminster Historical Reading Books*, National Society, 1891; *The Cross Roads; or, A Choice in Life*, National Society, 1892; *The Story of Easter*, M. Ward, 1894; *Gold Dust*, W. B. Conkey, 1900, reissued, Keats, 1973; *The Making of a Missionary; or, Day Dreams in Earnest: A Story of Mission Work in China*, T. Whittaker, 1900; *Reasons Why I Am a Catholic and Not a Roman Catholic*, Wells, Gardner, 1901.

Editor: *Biographies of Good Women*, two series, Mozley, 1862-65; (with E. M. Sewell) *Historical Selections: A Series of Readings on English and European History*, Macmillan, 1868-70; *A Storehouse of Stories*, Macmillan, 1870; E. Van Bruyssel, *The Population of an Old Pear Tree; or, Stories of Insect Life* (translation from the French), Macmillan, 1871; (and translator) Albert de Boys, *Catharine of Aragon and the Sources of the English Reformation*, Hurst, 1881, reprinted, B. Franklin, 1969; *Historical Ballads*, National Society, 1882; (and translator) H. de Witt, *Behind the Hedges*, Masters, 1882; (and translator) *Sparks of Light*, Master, 1882; (and translator) H. d'Ideville, *Memoirs of Marshall Bugeaud*, Hurst, 1884; *Higher Reading-Book for School, Colleges, and General Use*, National Society, 1885.

**When the clause, in the Litany, for all prisoners and captives brought to her the thrill that she had only to look up to see the fulfilment of many and many a prayer....** ■ (From *The Trial: More Links of the Daisy Chain* by Charlotte M. Yonge. Illustrated by J. Priestman Atkinson.)

**She lifted from her cot her little one.** ■ (From *The Heir of Redclyffe* by Charlotte M. Yonge. Illustrated by Kate Greenaway.)

Collections: *Novels and Tales*, 16 volumes, Macmillan, 1879-80.

*ADAPTATIONS*—Plays: Joan Brampton, *Bride Unknown* (three-act; adaptation of *Unknown to History*), H.F.W. Deane, 1953.

*SIDELIGHTS:* **August 11, 1823.** Born in Otterbourne, Hampshire, England. Her father, William Crawley was a retired army officer and her mother was Frances Mary (Bargas) Yonge. Yonge's forefathers were cultivated and good squires who were sound churchmen. Her father gave up his army profession in order to marry her mother and after their marriage he settled down on the estate of his mother-in-law. Less than a year after their marriage, Yonge was born. "I was born at Otterbourne on the 11th of August 1823, and my christening was somewhat hurried to let my father return to my grandfather, who was ill. My sponsors were my eldest uncle, Duke Yonge, my father's favourite sister, Charlotte (Mrs. George Crawley), and my mother's friend, Mrs. Vernon Harcourt.

"I come now to what I can myself remember, either fully, or with such additions that I cannot distinguish recollection from tradition. Let me first describe the place.

"Otterbourne lies about four miles to the south-west of Winchester on what used to be the main road from London to

"No; only I saw that you stayed here all alone," she said, clasping her hands. ■ (From *The Dove in the Eagles Nest* by Charlotte M. Yonge.)

Southampton. It is a long straggling parish, about 3½ miles in length from north-east to south-east, and in most places not more than half or three-quarters of a mile in width.

"The river Itchen bounds it on the east, and most likely the chief population lay near it, for the old church and the two principal farms were close to the river, one being called the Manor Farm and possessing an old house encircled on all sides by a moat, besides possessing a curious picture painted on a panel above the chimney-piece, representing apparently a battle between Turks and Austrians.

"My grandmother's house was in the midst of the village—as a lady said contemptuously, 'just opposite the Green Man,' not that it was the Green Man, but the White Horse.

"A quarter of a mile of lane led to the church, which stood beside the 'Otter.' The large churchyard was belted round with fine elms, and formed a mound on which stood the small old Hampshire Church. It had probably once been a fabric of some beauty, for the doorway had a good Early English border, and there were traces of foliage in some fragments of the heads of the windows.

"In this church, service was once on Sunday, alternately morning and afternoon. The bells were set going when the clergyman was seen at the turn of the lane. My father, when newly arrived, asked what time it would be, and was an-

swered, 'At half-past ten or eleven, sir, or else at no time at all.' This did not mean that there would be none, but that it would be at no regular marked hour. There had been no resident clergyman for many years past.

"[My father] was a remarkably handsome man, nearly six feet high, and very strong, with dark keen eyes, with the most wonderful power both for sweetness and for sternness that I ever knew. Watt's line 'He keeps me by His eye' is almost explained to me by the power those eyes had over me. I loved their approval and their look of affection, and dreaded their displeasure more than anything else. . . .

"He was grave, and external observers feared him, and thought him stern, but oh, how tender he could be, how deeply and keenly he felt!

"His great characteristic was thoroughness. He could not bear to do anything, or see anything done by halves. Whatever he took in hand, he carried out to the utmost and was undaunted in the pursuit, whether it was the building of a church, the fortification of Portsmouth, or the lining of a work-box, or the teaching his little girl to write. All alike he did with all his might; and when busy in really important works, he would still give his whole attention for the time being to the smallest feminine commissions at the county town.

"A religious man from his youth up according to the old orthodoxy, he was always under strong self-discipline, far sterner to himself than to others, giving up indulgences and pleasures without a word, and sacrificing his own comfort and enjoyment continually, as I now see, though I little guessed it then. An eager sportsman and fisherman, he dropped both shooting and fishing except on his holidays in Devonshire, because he thought they wasted time, and he wished not to awaken the passion for them in his son. The yearly visits to Devon, the delight of his heart, were sacrificed while the church building absorbed his spare means; he gave up snuff (which was to men then what smoking is now), because he thought it a selfish indulgence; he was most abstemious, drinking only water in hopes of averting hereditary gout; and busy and hardworked as he came to be, he never had a sitting-room to himself, while his dressing-room was as severely confined to the absolute necessaries of life as a Spartan could wish. Withal he was a great buyer of books and fancier of bindings, collected engravings, and had earlier in life bought a few valuable pictures, which at this time were still in the keeping of his mother at Plymouth, partly because he would not strip her of them, and partly because Mrs. Bargus [his mother-in-law], who had had a narrower education, would have thought them an extravagant purchase; and out of the same consideration for her, he kept out of sight his later acquisition of *La Musée Napoleonne,* four huge volumes of engravings from the Louvre of the First Empire.

"Always kind and considerate and forbearing to the weak, he got on perfectly well with grandmamma, who was always mistress of the house. When I first remember him, the real work of his life had not been found, and he was employing himself as his active mind could best find occupation—carpentering, gardening, and getting the little bit of farm into order; also acting as parish doctor, for before the new poor law, medical advice as almost inaccessible to the poor. There was supposed to be a parish doctor, but as he had no pay he never attended to any one even seriously ill, and for slight ailments there was no one. So with knowledge refreshed by his brother James, and the family medical instinct, also with Buchan's *Domestic Medicine* and a Pharmacopœia, he and my mother doctored the parish, ay, and their children's little maladies, quite successfully.

"My mother was—as I always remember her, for she altered little—a small woman, with very small delicate hands and feet, and fine-grained skin, but a want of clearness of complexion, soft but scanty brown hair, dark blue eyes, a very perfectly made mouth, an aquiline nose, and a contour of face resembling both those of Princess Charlotte and of the Queen [Victoria]. She never had good health, and was capable of little exertion in the way of walking, though her mind and energies were most active, and she could not bear to be a minute idle, knitting almost as quickly and unconsciously as she breathed, reading while she worked, and always earnest in some pursuit. She was always nervous, timid, and easily frightened, and though she controlled herself, excitement told in after illness. Her tears were near the surface, and so were her smiles. She was full of playfulness and mirth, but most eager and enthusiastic, yet always within due bounds; she studied and thought a good deal, and was an ever ready assistant in all my father's plans, comprehending rapidly, delighted to work with and for him, and in fact a perfect companion and helpmeet [helpmate] to him. She used to say how much happier her married life was than her childhood had ever been, and I fancy she was much younger at thirty than she had been at fifteen.

"These were the immediate surroundings which I first recollect. I do not recollect so far back as some people do. I have a hazy remembrance of a green spelling-book, and the room where I read a bit of it to some unaccustomed person. It must have been while I was very young, for I could read to myself at four years old, and I perfectly recollect the pleasure of finding I could do so, kneeling by a chair on which was spread a beautiful quarto edition of *Robinson Crusoe*, whose pictures I was looking at while grandmamma read the newspaper aloud to my mother. I know the page, in the midst of the shipwreck narrative, where to my joy I found myself making out the sense." [Christable Coleridge, *Charlotte Mary Yonge*, Macmillan, 1903.[1]]

**1827.** Yonge was educated at home by her father and mother. Her mother ran a Sunday school in the village. By the time she was six, her mother was giving her lessons in reading, spelling, poetry, geography, arithmetic, grammar, history and cathechism—writing was deferred from a theory that it would cramp her small hand. "Young parents of much ability and strong sense of duty were sure to read and think much of the education of an only child, as I was for so long. The Edgeworth system (as I now know) chiefly influenced them, though modified by religion and good sense. It was not spoiling. There was nothing to make me think myself important; I was repressed when I was troublesome, made to be obedient or to suffer for it, and was allowed few mere indulgences in eating and drinking, and no holidays. And yet I say it deliberately, that except for my occasional longings for a sister, no one ever had a happier or more joyous childhood than mine. I have since had reason to know that I was a very pretty and clever child, or at any rate that my mother thought me so, but I really never knew whether I was not ugly. I know I thought myself so, and I was haunted occasionally by doubts whether I were not deficient, till I was nearly grown up.

"My nursery would frighten a modern mother. It was like a little passage room, at the back of the house, with a birch-tree just before the window, a wooden crib for me, and a turn-up press bed for my nurse; and it also answered the

There was, indeed, a wretched shepherd and his wife, who trembled and looked dismayed when they found that one of the Albricartes still lived; but I could get nothing from them. ■ (From *The Lances of Lynwood* by Charlotte M. Yonge.)

purpose of work-room for the maids. But I did not live much in it. I was one of the family breakfast party, and dined at luncheon so early that I cannot remember when I began, and never ate in the nursery except my supper. Breakfast and supper were alike dry bread and milk. I so much disliked the hot bowl of boiled milk and cubes of bread that I was allowed to have mine separately, but butter was thought unwholesome, and I believe it would have been so, for I never have been able to eat it regularly. As to eggs, ham, jam, and all the rest, no one dreamt of giving them to children. Indeed my mother made a great point of never letting me think that it was any hardship to see other people eating of what I did not partake, and I have been grateful for the habits she gave me ever since.

"My great world was indoors with my dolls, who were my children and my sisters; out of doors with an imaginary family of ten boys and eleven girls who lived in an arbour. The two ungratified wishes of those days were for a large wax doll, and a china doll's service. I was seriously told the cost, and that it was not right to spend so much money on a toy when so many were in need of food and clothes.

"It was absolutely true that my father and mother had very little ready money, and that they did spend as much as they possibly could on the many needs of the poor. No doubt this gave the lesson reality, for it has always served me as a warning against selfish personal expenditure.

**They threw pebbles and bits of mortar down that they might hear them fall, and tried which could stand nearest to the edge of the battlement without being giddy.** ■ (From *The Little Duke: Richard the Fearless* by Charlotte M. Yonge. Illustrated by Jennifer Miles.)

"My only real trouble was terrors just like what other solitary or imaginative children have—horrors of darkness, fancies of wolves, one more gratuitous alarm recurring every night of being smothered like the Princes in the Tower, or blown up with gunpowder. In the daylight I knew it was nonsense, I would have spoken of it to no one, but the fears at night always came back.

"Otherwise I can hardly date my earlier recollections. Mine was too happy and too uneventful a childhood to have many epochs, and it has only one sharp line of era in it, namely, my brother's birth when I was six and a half. I can remember best by what happened before, and what happened after."[1]

**1830.** "On the 31st of January 1830 came the greatest event of my life: my only brother was born. He came with rather short notice, and I remember the being left in the dark in my crib and the puzzled day that ensued. I believe my mother would not have me know the fact till she could see me herself, and soon after breakfast my father took me out to walk across the down to Twyford. There was a deep snow, I had not been properly equipped to encounter it, and though he carried me part of the way I arrived with bitterly cold hands, and when brought to the fire first knew the sensation of aching with cold.

"When I came home . . . I was allowed to hear of my brother, and to see him. I wished him to be called Alexander Xenophon, but was not allowed to hear his name till his christening, when it proved to be Julian Bargus. . . .

"The regular lesson life soon began again, the chief novelty being that my father undertook to teach me to write, thinking that a free hand would be of great service in drawing. . . . He was the most exact of teachers, and required immense attention and accuracy. . . . Being an innate sloven and full of lazy inaccuracy I provoked him often, and often was sternly spo-

ken to, and cried heartily, but I had a Jack-in-the-box temper, was up again in a moment, and always loved and never feared my work with him. So we rubbed on with increasing comfort in working together, well deserved by his wonderful patience and perserverance."[1]

**Summer, 1830.** Yonge turned seven in August. "That summer was further diversified by the measles. My father had no confidence in the . . . apothecaries, and doctored us through it himself alone—yes, and nursed too. I remember his sleeping on the floor in my little room and rising up to give me draughts. He was the best nurse I ever came under, with his tenderness and strength. He read me the *Pilgrim's Progress* out of Southey's edition when I was recovering, and on many Sundays—and how I loved it.

"Then grandmamma brought me . . . a doll of a sort then new with leathern bodies and papier-maché heads. It was the largest and best doll I had ever had, and as I lay in bed with my hand over my treasure, my mother made it clothes. I can recall the pattern of those frocks now. 'Anna' was more the doll of my heart than any other. . . .

"My home life had all this time had much less to mark it than the Devon visits [where her cousins lived]. I remember little but great regularity in lessons. The house was added to enough to provide a schoolroom, where my mother taught me from ten till one, and my brother for part of the time. Afternoon lessons there were none, and I was out of doors, either in the garden with my mother, or the nurse and Julian, or taking walks with these last; playing at ball on the attic stairs on wet days, loving my dolls and the dogs, and being very happy on the whole, though with a dull yearning at times for something to look forward to.

"I read a great many little books over and over again, and tried to garden, but was never tidy or persevering enough to succeed, and, as Julian grew older, we used to play on sandheaps, scrape chalk and brick dust for magnesia and rhubarb, and call ourselves Dr. C. and Dr. J.

"Mamma took me to her Sunday School. The children used to take places, and after three Sundays went into the first class. I began in the second and soon got into the first, where was one companion of my subsequent life, Harriet Spratt. Very unlike the attainments of their grandchildren of the present day [1896] were those of the big girls with whom I found myself, for at seven years old, in six weeks I took the head of the class for knowing 'Who were they of the Circumcision?' I kept my place for three Sundays and then was made a teacher. [She was a teacher for seventy-one years.] It was mistake, for I had not moral balance enough to be impartial, and I must have been terribly ignorant."[1]

**1834.** At the age of eleven, had her first experience with death when her older cousin died. ". . . James, then eighteen, suffered from headache and nosebleeding. He was sent out to Otterbourne for rest and change of air, and for a week was our playfellow as usual. We loved him very much, and it was held as remarkable that Julian, learning Watts's hymn on dress, saying

This is the raiment Angels wear,

paused and observed, 'I think James has that clothing.'

"Indeed he had, and well it was. In a week other symptoms came on that caused his father to be summoned. The next night he was unconscious, and never was fully himself again.

He died on the Sunday. . . . They buried him in our church-yard.

"To me the time was a dull dreary dream. I thought of it with much awe, but I was a frivolous creature of untamed spirits, and I was in much disgrace for being unfeeling. I could not cry, and I was ready for any distraction. It was a great satisfaction to run down the kitchen garden, and recollect the cats must be fed whatever happened! Yet I think I carried something away. Reverence for James I know I did. . . ."[1]

**1835.** "I have no very distinctive recollection of 1835, except that when Julian was five, and I [twelve] we began Latin; my father teaching us, and I, who of course went on the fastest, having to help him to learn. I think too that it was then that my father took my arithmetic in hand. He used to call me at six or half-past, and I worked with him for an hour before breakfast. It was in a degree like the writing lessons. He required a diligence and accuracy that were utterly alien to me. He thundered at me so that nobody could bear to hear it, and often reduced me to tears, but his approbation was so delightful that it was a delicious stimulus, and I must have won it oftener than it used to seem to me, for at the end of the first winter, my watch, the watch of my life, was given me as a reward, to my great surprise. I believe, in spite of all breezes over my innate slovenliness, it would have broken our hearts to leave off working together. And we went on till I was some years past twenty, and had worked up to point of such Greek, Euclid, and Algebra as had furnished forth the Etonian and soldier of sixteen, till his eyes were troubled by Homer and Algebra, and his time too fully occupied. Of course the serious breezes had long been over, and the study together had become very great pleasure. He did hear me read French for a little while, but a capital French master came into the neighbourhood.

"People used to tell us then, as we say to children now, that we had too many books to care for them, but I am sure we did heartily care for our favourites, Scott above all. I think I was allowed a chapter a day of the Waverley novels, provided I first read twenty pages of Goldsmith's *Rome* or some equally solid book.

"As to new books, in those days circulating libraries consisted generally of third-rate novels, very dirty, very smoky, and with remarks plentifully pencilled on the margins. It was thought foolish and below par to subscribe to them, and book-clubs were formed in which each family might either ask for or order a book, which was covered with white cartridge paper with the list of subscribers pasted on one side. After going the round of the society, the books were disposed of either at half price or by auction, any book that no one would bid for being necessarily purchased by its orderer. Thus every one was responsible to all the rest, and though people grumbled sometimes, the plan prevented an immense amount of mischievous reading. People mostly dined at 5.30 or 6, and in the long evening that ensued the books from the club used to be read aloud to the assembled family, and the effect was a guiding power on the parents' part, and a community of interest in the subject before them that scarcely exists now."[1]

**1836.** Yonge looked upon this year as the "finishing era of childhood." In this year, a Mr. Keble, who became a life-long friend, was instituted to the Vicarage and a new church was built. "Already it had become plain that the parish had outgrown as well as grown away from the old church. The first idea had been to raise £300 to enlarge it, and the pro-

**They threw pebbles and bits of mortar down that they might hear them fall, and tried which could stand nearest to the edge of the battlement without being giddy.** ■ (From *The Little Duke* by Charlotte M. Yonge. Illustrated by Michael Godfrey.)

posal had been made, but . . . we were advised to wait for the new incumbent, and he was Mr. Keble! And thus came in the chief spiritual influence of my life! He resided at Hursley, to which this parish was then joined, and he retained Mr. Bigg-Wither as his curate. The church-building plan was taken up at once, and it was decided to have a fresh site more in the centre of the parish. In 1836 church-building was a far less familiar idea than now. . . . What is now done by ready tradesmen had all to be devised, contrived, and executed originally. There were numerous mistakes and failures from these ignorances, but at last a church was produced much in advance of many in reverence and beauty.

"This was to us a time of making friendships. The Kebles had come to Hursley Vicarage, and as this parish was then joined to Hursley, our intercourse was double close, over church-building matters, parish affairs, and one especial blessing of my life, that Mr. Keble prepared me for Confirmation, when I was fifteen. It was done by working through the Catechism and the Communion service, with the last comparing old liturgies, and going into the meaning. It was a great happiness, and opened my mind to Church doctrine, but I well remember the warning at the end against taking these things up in a merely poetical tone for their beauty. He did not call it aesthetically, for he did not love long words.

"The fatherly kindness and the delightful sympathy I received then never failed, through all the years of happy intercourse between our two houses. My master he was in every way, and there was no one like Mrs. Keble for bright tender kindness."[1]

**1838.** At the age of fifteen, Yonge was confirmed into the Church—for the fervent Christian and dedicated Sunday school teacher, this was a highlight in her life. On September 25th, she wrote her cousin, Anne Yonge: "The confirmation is to be next Monday. . . . I went to Hursley yesterday for the last time before it, and Mr. Keble gave me my ticket."[1]

"And is this the son of my brave and noble friend, Duke William? Ah! I should have known it from his likeness. ■ (From *The Little Duke: Richard the Fearless* by Charlotte Yonge.)

**1844.** First book, *Abbey Church*, was published. Before her book was published, there was a family council held as to whether she should be allowed to publish or not. In consenting, it was agreed that Yonge would not accept any money for herself, but that it would be given to charity. When asked what she would have done if her family had forbidden her to publish, she replied, "Oh, I *must* have written; but I should never have published—at least not for many years."[1]

**1853.** *Heir of Redclyffe* published. The book's success made Yonge's name popular. The author had worked on the novel for several years prior to its publication. The book had actually been finished in 1851, but had to first run the gauntlet of her family's approval. The proceeds from the sale of the book were given to the Melanesian Mission. The popularity of the book led Yonge to an intimate intercourse with her beloved pastor and friend, Mr. Keble. "I should like you to know the comfort and peace I had in the little study at H[ursley] V[icarage] yesterday. It is too precious to have him to bring all one's fears of vainglory, etc., to, and hear him say, 'Yes, my dear, I have been thinking a great deal about you

now,' and when he said a successful book might be the trial of one's life—it was so exactly what was nice, not telling one not to enjoy the praise, and like to hear it talked about, but that way of at once soothing and guarding, and his telling me to think of the pleasure it was to my father and mother. . . . I wish I could give you the effect of the peacefulness and subduing happiness of it, especially when I asked for the blessing, and he said, 'you shall have it, such as it is,' and then he took the words he never used with me before, 'prosper Thou her handiwork,' which seemed to seal a daily prayer, and make all bearable and not vain. The going back and chattering in the drawing-room did not hurt that twilight time; and then came a moonlight drive home . . . and then came home prayers—and the first was the collect 'knowest our necessities before we ask'—'and wont to give more, etc.'—It did so seem to fit—that opportunity of pouring out to Mr. K[eble], and being set at rest as to how to look at it coming just when it did—and the peace went on into this morning's church-time. . . ."[1]

**February 26, 1854.** Father died. Yonge and her mother settled down together. "My trouble has come; [my father] had a second attack and died at six to-night. . . . I dread what it will be; I don't think we half believe it yet."[1]

**1856.** *The Daisy Chain* published. Yonge wrote and published an average of three books a year from 1850 to 1900. By

"I hit him, I hit him! 'Tis a stag of ten branches, and I hit him." ■ (From *The Little Duke* by Charlotte M. Yonge. Illustrated by George Lawson.)

1867 she wrote of her success: "We had a wonderful visit yesterday from an utterly unknown little American girl of fourteen or fifteen, who bobbed into the room, rushed up to me, shook hands, ''Miss Yonge, I've come to thank you for your books, I'm an American.' Papa and mamma were, it appears, seeing the church, and were going round by Hursley back to Winchester. It was odd to be thanked by a little bolt upright mite, as if in the name of all the American Republic, for writing for the Church!

"The good *Daisy Chain* has paid £114 this year to the Melanesian Mission."[1]

**September, 1858.** Brother, Julian, married. The young couple came home to Otterbourne House. "I think we must have made a very pretty procession; Julian went into church first with Mrs. Walter and James, and then when the Colonel brought Frances, we six bridesmaids lined the pretty lychgate, all hung with festoons of flowers, and closed in behind her. . . . Julian looked very nice and well, and one longs for their coming home. . . ."[1]

**1862.** Moved with her mother to Elderfield, the name given to a cottage, not far from the Otterbourne House where her brother and sister-in-law lived with their young and growing family. Began work on her book, *History of Christian Names,* which required more research than anything she had written before.

**September 28, 1868.** Mother died after an illness which required constant nursing care from Yonge. "Things have gone on well and quietly; I only wonder what I am that I seem to have no breakdown in me, but cannot help feeling for ever that the 'Ephphatha is sung' when I think of the frowning look with which she would try to make us understand her, and that struggle to say words of praise, 'glorify' so often coming. You cannot think how her work, the illuminated 'Holy, Holy, Holy,' and the 'We look not at the things that are seen but at the things that are not seen,' shone out at that Communion in the morning. It is so very gentle and as she wished, and I really did miss her much more four months ago, when the real response failed me, and I saw her in the state I knew she hoped not to be in, than now that the habit of leaning on her has been so long broken. It is as if the threefold cord of my life had had one strand snapped suddenly fourteen years ago, but slowly, gently untwisted now. It was comfortable that no one touched her who did not love her. No stranger meddled; Hicks made the coffin, and those who carried her were our own people, three the same as carried papa, and two of their sons, one other labourer of Julian's. Frances [her sister-in-law] made a lovely cross of white camellias and roses, and two wreaths. Frances spent most of the day up here, so very sweet and sisterly, and comforted to have won her love these last years."[1]

**1869.** Only trip abroad. "I have been seeing Paris; I found my preconceived notions upset, I admired Notre Dame a great deal more than I expected, the solemnity of the five aisles is so great, and the Ste. Chapelle disappointed me—I think it has never been reconsecrated since Marat had his orgies there, and though it is splendidly repainted there is no altar, and it is only used for Gape Seed. The grand St. Michael at the Louvre, and Marie Antoinette's cell at the Conciergerie were the two things that I cared for most. So much of the old is taken away that there are few really historical bits, even the place where the Swiss Guard fought is gone, though at Versailles we did see Marie Antoinette's balcony, and the door Madame Anguier defended. Versailles op-

pressed me like a great terrible tragedy, between the guilt there and the doom upon it."[1]

**September, 1869.** Arrived home. Was greeted with the shocking and sad news of her beloved cousin Anne's death. "I am so much knocked up to-day, having before not quite recovered the effects of hot journeys and strange food. . . .

". . . I seem to have seen Newton Church more than our own all this time; this is a Sunday I have so often been there, and the hymns are her [Anne] choosing and the same. And her hand was the first on our harmonium, and her voice the first in the new beginning of our choir. And now, oh! surely she is among those that follow the Lamb withersoever He goeth. It is all so like—

> "Comes rushing o'er a sudden thought
> Of her who led the strain,
> How oft such music home she brought.

"But it is a blessed thing for the rest of our lives that it is in our times of praise that we shall meet her above all.

"I believe it was a more than commonly close link that united our dear Anne and me, though I always knew that as one of several sisters she never could need me as much as I needed her, and I was wont to turn to the knowledge of her feeling and opinion many a time when nothing passed between us, being sure that one day I should be with her and talk, after the time began when writing letters was an effort to her. How much the recollection of those ways and thoughts of hers should be with me, and guide me still, having lived with them for more than half a life-time, and written to one another ever since babyhood. The last I had from her was a note before I went away. . . . I am quite well again . . . it was only Sunday and Monday that I was out of order. It is always being brought before me that there are sorrows far more dreadful."[1]

**September, 1873.** Miss Gertrude Walter, Yonge's sister-in-law's youngest sister, moved in with Yonge at Elderfield. Their relationship was a close one—Miss Walter served as her confidant and literary critic until her death in 1897.

At fifty, Yonge was an attractive, humble person. One of her associates described her during these middle years. "Nothing was more marked in her characteristics than her humility and indifference to public opinion. There was a special time in Miss Yonge's life when she became eminently handsome. It was when her hair assumed a lovely grey tinge, and she sometimes allowed herself to be clad in becoming garments. I have seen her look splendid, and people exclaimed at her beauty, while on the other hand her ordinary costume in daily life in the village and in the garden was absolutely regardless of the canons of taste. She evidently spent but little on dress.

"She was kind and polite enough to receive the compliments of her admirers with a little jerk of her head and a slight smile, but the moment it was possible within the limits of propriety she turned herself away and spoke to some one else."[1]

**1881.** Began the series of stories which reproduced the old characters of her earlier books: *Two Sides of a Shield, Beechcroft at Rockstone, Strolling Players, The Long Vacation, Modern Broods.*

CHARLOTTE MARY YONGE

**1885.** Brother, Julian, sold Otterbourne House. The loss of her childhood home was keenly felt.

**1887.** Began to write a story a year for the National Society which was suitable for the higher elementary grades.

**1890.** Became editor of *Mothers in Council.* The woman who approached her with the request for editorship recalled: "This proposition was made in fear and trembling, for I dreaded a refusal, knowing the value of her name and editorship, but the response was immediate and gratifying. She accepted the office of editor to this new venture without any hesitation, and with confidence in its success. From that date until the time when her work on earth was ended, she gave unfailing thought and care to this publication, and through it we became fast friends. The ice was broken, and I was allowed to know something of her noble and unselfish life.

"I felt astonished that amid the ceaseless work she was ever carrying on, literary, domestic, parochial, social, philanthropic, ecclesiastical and devotional, she was able to find time for the constant correspondence and extra business of this new periodical. She had a great faith in our cause. It appealed strongly to her, and she was eager to do all in her power to awaken attention to the importance of its three objects. The Bishop and I had then come to live in the Close, at Winchester, and she was settled in the village of Otterbourne, in her old-fashioned, dearly-loved home of Elderfield about four miles from Winchester, across the beautiful rolling downs. How many a time have I driven over there unexpectedly at all hours of the day to see her, and consult and discuss various points concerning the *Mothers in Council.*"[1]

**1892.** Brother, Julian, died.

**August 13, 1893.** For her seventieth birthday she was presented a volume containing the signatures of the subscribers to the *Monthly Packet,* the magazine she had worked on from 1851 to 1890, when she retired. In 1890 she had written of her retirement: "The *Monthly Packet* has turned me out except as a contributor. It has been going down, *Newbery* and *Atalanta* supplant it, and the old friends are nearly all gone, and the young ones call it goody-goody. So the old coachman who has driven it for forty years is called on to retire! They are very civil about it, and want me to be called Consulting Editor, but that is nonsense, for they don't consult me."[1]

**1897.** Beloved companion, Gertrude Walter, died. "I have had a sorrowful year in the death of the invalid friend who lived with me, and was my memory, and since that my relations have given me a good deal of variety, hardly favourable to work!—"[1]

**1899.** Honored at the presentation of a scholarship in her name for the Winchester High School for Girls. "... I little knew beforehand all they were going to make of it. About 1800 was collected for the scholarship, and this was presented, with a beautifully illuminated address, by the Bishop in the High School, making a wonderful speech about having read the *Little Duke* when he was a small boy, and all that had turned up about the usefullness of the books. Also they gave me a basket of flowers—daisies, heartsease and the like, with violet ribbons to represent the violet, as of course there were none to be had, and ropes of daisy chain hung all about. Afterwards the girls made some very pretty tableaux from the stories, the *Little Duke,* the *Caged Lion,* and the *Chaplet of Pearls,* and had a daisy-chain dance in thin white frocks. It really was as pretty a sight as ever was; the pity was that I had none of my own people with me. ..."[1]

**Spring, 1900.** Became ill, but recovered and continued to write and teach at Sunday school.

**March 24, 1901.** Died at Elderfield, England. "I do think that a woman produces more effect by what she *is* than by a thousand talks and arguments."[1]

*FOR MORE INFORMATION SEE:* Christabel Coleridge, *Charlotte Mary Yonge: Her Life and Letters,* Macmillan, 1903, reprinted, Gale, 1969; Ethel Romanes, *Charlotte Mary Yonge: An Appreciation,* A. R. Mowbray, 1908; Joseph E. Baker, "Charlotte Mary Yonge, and the Novel of Domestic Manners," in his *The Novel and the Oxford Movement,* Russell, 1932, reissued, 1965; Dorothea Blagg, "Charlotte Mary Yonge and Her Novels," in Muriel A. Masefield, *Women Novelists from Fanny Burney to George Eliot,* Nicholson, 1934; Georgina Battiscomb, *Charlotte M. Yonge,* Constable, 1943; Margaret L. Mare and Alicia C. Percival, *Victorian Best Seller: The World of Charlotte M. Yonge,* Harrap, 1948, reprinted, Kennikat, 1970; G. Battiscombe and Marghanita Laski, editors, *Chaplet for Charlotte Yonge,* Cresset Press, 1965; Roger L. Green, *Tellers of Tales,* rewritten and enlarged edition, F. Watts, 1965; Brian Doyle, editor, *Who's Who of Children's Literature,* Schocken Books, 1968.

# CUMULATIVE INDEX TO
# ILLUSTRATIONS AND AUTHORS

## ILLUSTRATIONS INDEX

(In the following index, the number of the volume in which an illustrator's work appears is given *before* the colon, and the page on which it appears is given *after* the colon. For example, a drawing by Adams, Adrienne appears in Volume 2 on page 6, another drawing by her appears in Volume 3 on page 80, another drawing in Volume 8 on page 1, and another drawing in Volume 15 on page 107.)

Illustrations Index

Illustrations Index

Illustrations Index

Maik, Henri, 9: 102
Maitland, Antony, 1: 100, 176;
    8: 41; 17: 246
Malvern, Corrine, 2: 13
Mangurian, David, 14: 133
Manning, Samuel F., 5: 75
Maraja, 15: 86
Marchiori, Carlos, 14: 60
Marino, Dorothy, 6: 37; 14: 135
Markham, R. L., 17: 240
Mars, W. T., 1: 161; 3: 115;
    4: 208, 225; 5: 92, 105, 186;
    8: 214; 9: 12; 13: 121
Marsh, Christine, 3: 164
Marsh, Reginald, 17: 5
Marshall, James, 6: 160
Martin, Rene, 7: 144
Martin, Stefan, 8: 68
Martinez, John, 6: 113
Mason, George F., 14: 139
Massie, Diane Redfield, 16: 194
Matsubara, Naoko, 12: 121
Matsuda, Shizu, 13: 167
Matthews, F. Leslie, 4: 216
Matthieu, Joseph, 14: 33
Matulay, Laszlo, 5: 18
Matus, Greta, 12: 142
Mawicke, Tran, 9: 137; 15: 191
Maxwell, John Alan, 1: 148
Mayan, Earl, 7: 193
Mayer, Mercer, 11: 192; 16: 195-196
Mayhew, Richard, 3: 106
Mays, Victor, 5: 127; 8: 45, 153;
    14: 245
McCann, Gerald, 3: 50; 4: 94; 7: 54
McClary, Nelson, 1: 111
McClintock, Theodore, 14: 141
McCloskey, Robert, 1: 184-185;
    2: 186-187; 17: 209
McClung, Robert, 2: 189
McCrady, Lady, 16: 198
McCrea, James, 3: 122
McCrea, Ruth, 3: 122
McCully, Emily, 2: 89;
    4: 120-121, 146, 197; 5: 2, 129;
    7: 191; 11: 122; 15: 210
McCurdy, Michael, 13: 153
McDermott, Beverly Brodsky,
    11: 180
McDermott, Gerald, 16: 201
McDonald, Jill, 13: 155
McDonald, Ralph J., 5: 123, 195
McDonough, Don, 10: 163
McFall, Christie, 12: 144
McGee, Barbara, 6: 165
McKay, Donald, 2: 118
McKee, David, 10: 48
McKie, Roy, 7: 44
McLachlan, Edward, 5: 89
McNaught, Harry, 12: 80
McPhail, David, 14: 105
McVay, Tracy, 11: 68
Melo, John, 16: 285
Meng, Heinz, 13: 158
Merrill, Frank T., 16: 147
Merryweather, Jack, 10: 179

Meyer, Renate, 6: 170
Meyers, Bob, 11: 136
Micale, Albert, 2: 65
Middleton-Sandford, Betty, 2: 125
Mikolaycak, Charles, 9: 144;
    12: 101; 13: 212
Miles, Jennifer, 17: 278
Milhous, Katherine, 15: 193; 17: 51
Miller, Don, 15: 195; 16: 71
Miller, Jane, 15: 196
Miller, Marcia, 13: 233
Miller, Marilyn, 1: 87
Miller, Shane, 5: 140
Mizumura, Kazue, 10: 143
Mochi, Ugo, 8: 122
Mohr, Nicholasa, 8: 139
Montresor, Beni, 2: 91; 3: 138
Moon, Eliza, 14: 40
Mordvinoff, Nicolas, 15: 179
Morrow, Gray, 2: 64; 5: 200;
    10: 103, 114; 14: 175
Morton, Marian, 3: 185
Moss, Donald, 11: 184
Mozley, Charles, 9: 87
Mugnaini, Joseph, 11: 35
Mullins, Edward S., 10: 101
Munari, Bruno, 15: 200
Munowitz, Ken, 14: 148
Munson, Russell, 13: 9
Murphy, Bill, 5: 138
Mutchler, Dwight, 1: 25
Myers, Bernice, 9: 147
Myers, Lou, 11: 2

Nakatani, Chiyoko, 12: 124
Nason, Thomas W., 14: 68
Navarra, Celeste Scala, 8: 142
Naylor, Penelope, 10: 104
Neebe, William, 7: 93
Needler, Jerry, 12: 93
Negri, Rocco, 3: 213; 5: 67;
    6: 91, 108; 12: 159
Ness, Evaline, 1: 164-165; 2: 39;
    3: 8; 10: 147; 12: 53
Neville, Vera, 2: 182
Newberry, Clare Turlay, 1: 170
Newfeld, Frank, 14: 121
Nicholson, William, 15: 33-34;
    16: 48
Nickless, Will, 16: 139
Nicolas, 17: 130, 132-133
Niebrugge, Jane, 6: 118
Nielsen, Jon, 6: 100
Nielsen, Kay, 15: 7;
    16: 211-213, 215, 217
Ninon, 1: 5
Nixon, K., 14: 152
Noonan, Julia, 4: 163; 7: 207
Nordenskjold, Birgitta, 2: 208
Norman, Michael, 12: 117
Nussbaumer, Paul, 16: 219

Oakley, Graham, 8: 112
Obligado, Lilian, 2: 28, 66-67;
    6: 30; 14: 179; 15: 103

Obrant, Susan, 11: 186
Oechsli, Kelly, 5: 144-145; 7: 115;
    8: 83, 183; 13: 117
Ohlsson, Ib, 4: 152; 7: 57; 10: 20;
    11: 90
Olschewski, Alfred, 7: 172
Olsen, Ib Spang, 6: 178-179
Olugebefola, Ademola, 15: 205
O'Neil, Dan IV, 7: 176
Ono, Chiyo, 7: 97
Orbaan, Albert, 2: 31; 5: 65, 171;
    9: 8; 14: 241
Ormsby, Virginia H., 11: 187
Orozco, José Clemente, 9: 177
Osmond, Edward, 10: 111
O'Sullivan, Tom, 3: 176; 4: 55
Oughton, Taylor, 5: 23
Overlie, George, 11: 156
Owens, Carl, 2: 35
Owens, Gail, 10: 170; 12: 157
Oxenbury, Helen, 3: 150-151

Padgett, Jim, 12: 165
Page, Homer, 14: 145
Pak, 12: 76
Palazzo, Tony, 3: 152-153
Palladini, David, 4: 113
Palmer, Heidi, 15: 207
Palmer, Juliette, 6: 89; 15: 208
Palmer, Lemuel, 17: 25, 29
Panesis, Nicholas, 3: 127
Papas, William, 11: 223
Papish, Robin Lloyd, 10: 80
Parker, Lewis, 2: 179
Parker, Nancy Winslow, 10: 113
Parker, Robert, 4: 161; 5: 74; 9: 136
Parker, Robert Andrew, 11: 81
Parnall, Peter, 5: 137; 16: 221
Parrish, Maxfield,
    14: 160, 161, 164, 165; 16: 109
Parry, Marion, 13: 176
Pascal, David, 14: 174
Pasquier, J. A., 16: 91
Paterson, Diane, 13: 116
Paterson, Helen, 16: 93
Paton, Jane, 15: 271
Payne, Joan Balfour, 1: 118
Payson, Dale, 7: 34; 9: 151
Peat, Fern B., 16: 115
Pederson, Sharleen, 12: 92
Peet, Bill, 2: 203
Peltier, Leslie C., 13: 178
Pendle, Alexy, 7: 159; 13: 34
Peppe, Rodney, 4: 164-165
Perl, Susan, 2: 98; 4: 231;
    5: 44-45, 118; 6: 199; 8: 137;
    12: 88
Pesek, Ludek, 15: 237
Petersham, Maud, 17: 108, 147-153
Petersham, Miska, 17: 108, 147-153
Peterson, R. F., 7: 101
Peterson, Russell, 7: 130
Petie, Haris, 2: 3; 10: 41, 118;
    11: 227; 12: 70
Peyton, K. M., 15: 212

Illustrations Index

Illustrations Index

# AUTHOR INDEX

(In the following index, the number of the volume in which an author's sketch appears is given *before* the colon, and the page on which it appears is given *after* the colon. For example, the sketch of Aardema, Verna, appears in Volume 4 on page 1). This index includes references to *Yesterday's Authors of Books for Children*.

Author Index

Author Index

Author Index

Author Index

Author Index

Author Index

Author Index

Author Index

Author Index

Author Index

Author Index

Author Index

Author Index

Author Index

Author Index

Author Index

Author Index

Author Index

Author Index

**Author Index**

Author Index